Brain, Mind, and Behavior

Floyd E. Bloom is chairman of the Department of Neuropharmacology at the Scripps Research Institute in La Jolla, California. He received his medical education at Washington University in St. Louis and held posts at Yale University and The National Institute of Mental Health before moving to California. He is a member of the National Academy of Sciences and a past president of the Society for Neuroscience. He was Editor-in-Chief of *Science* from 1995 until 2000.

Charles A. Nelson, Ph.D., Distinguished McKnight University Professor of Child Psychology, Neuroscience, and Pediatrics at the University of Minnesota, is a leading develop al cognitive neuroscientist. Dr. Nelson c Arthur Foundation/McDonnell Foundation research n e and brain development.

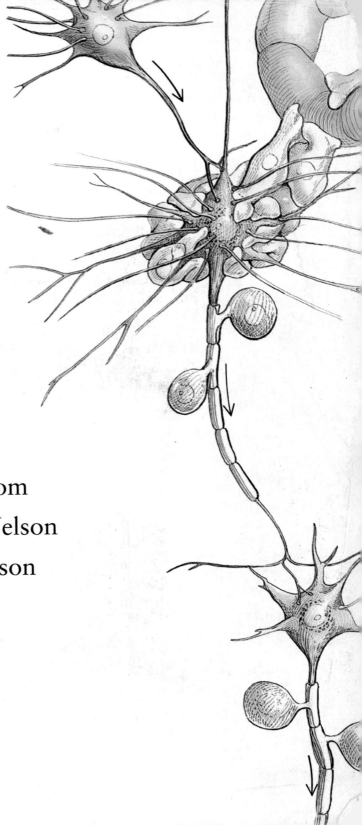

BRAIN, MIND, AND BEHAVIOR

THIRD EDITION

Floyd E. Bloom

Charles A. Nelson

Arlyne Lazerson

An Annenberg/CPB Project

WORTH PUBLISHERS

Major funding for the *Brain, Mind, and Behavior* telecourse and for the television series, *The Brain,* was provided by the Annenberg/CPB Project. Additional series funding is provided by the National Institute of Neurological and Communicative Disorders and Stroke, the National Institute of Mental Health, and the National Institute on Aging.

SPONSORING EDITOR: Jessica Bayne

SENIOR MARKETING MANAGER: Renee Ortbals

DEVELOPMENT EDITOR: Moira Lerner Nelson

PROJECT EDITOR: Christopher Miragliotta, Vivien Weiss

COVER AND TEXT DESIGN: Victoria Tomaselli

ILLUSTRATION COORDINATOR: Bill Page

ILLUSTRATIONS: Fine Line, Carol Donner, Joyce Powzyk, Sally Black

PHOTO RESEARCHER: Jennifer MacMillan

PRODUCTION COORDINATOR: Susan Wein

NEW MEDIA AND SUPPLEMENTS EDITOR: Graig Donini

COMPOSITION: Black Dot Graphics

MANUFACTURING: RR Donnelley & Sons Company

Library of Congress Cataloging-in-Publication Data

Bloom, Floyd E.
  Brain, mind, and behavior/Floyd E. Bloom, Charles A. Nelson.—3rd ed.
    p. ; cm.
  Accompanied by electronic and print supplements for teachers and students. Includes bibliographical references and index.
  ISBN 0-7167-2389-1
  1. Neuropsychology. 2. Brain. 3. Intellect. I. Nelson, Charles A. (Charles Alexander) II. Annenberg/CPB Project. III. Title
  [DNLM: 1. Mental Processes—physiology. 2. Behavior—physiology. 3. Brain. 4. Nervous System Physiology. 5. Psychophysiology. WL 103 B655b 2001]
  QP360 .B585 2001
  612.8'2—dc21

00-042248

Printed in the United States of America

First printing, 2000

CONTENTS

CHAPTER THREE

Life-Span Development
of the Brain   59

CHAPTER FOUR

Sensing   97

CHAPTER EIGHT

Emotions: The Highs and Lows of the Brain 239

CHAPTER NINE

The Human Memory System 275

PREFACE

Since the second edition of this book appeared, enormous amounts of new information have increased our knowledge about the detailed workings of the brain. These advances have occurred at every level of resolution at which scientists are studying the brain, from the molecular realm to the ways in which the brain's circuits accomplish the regulation of thoughts, emotions, and memory. Even so, much remains to be learned as we move toward understanding what is perhaps the most complicated living organ and toward relating the brain's functioning to human thinking, feeling, and behavior. The goal of *Brain, Mind, and Behavior* is to make this ever-growing and exciting body of knowledge about the brain accessible to the interested student who may have little or no background in either biology or psychology.

For the third edition, we have thoroughly revised the text to reflect these new discoveries and some of the concepts by which scientists are weaving these facts into testable theory. As with the second edition, we have expanded the detailed discussions to make the book more useful to students and teachers. Every chapter has been extensively revised. A goal of this edition was not only to include new facts but to emphasize the developmental and neuropsychological aspects of brain functions. This goal was realized through the recruitment of a new co-author, Professor Charles A. Nelson of the University of Minnesota.

In the course of our revisions, we have added two new chapters. A new chapter specifically devoted to the motor control systems resulted from our updating and recasting of the organization of the major sensory systems. In addition, we now explore memory and learning at two levels—first at the level of the neuropsychological operations (Chapter 9) and then in terms of the detailed animal models of learning and memory (Chapter 10).

Other topics that now receive more extended treatment include the nature of chemical neurotransmission and the ways in which drugs are used to treat some brain diseases (Chapter 12). Moreover, we have refined the coverage of prenatal brain and behavioral development (Chapter 3) and given greater attention to the human brain diseases that are currently under intense scientific investigation (Chapter 12). In these instances, attempts have been made to demonstrate how the accelerated accumulation of insight into these medical problems is a result of two major strategic advances. The first is the onslaught of new information about genes that can transmit vulnerability to a brain disease; the second is the ability to apply methods by which the function and metabolic activity of discrete brain regions can be monitored without physical intrusion into the subject's brain as he or she engages in mental activity. Each chapter ends with a summary of its main points and a reminder of the key terms that have been presented, as well as a list of recent articles, reports, and books, annotated to help those students who may wish to read about these subjects in greater depth.

The orientation of the third edition of *Brain, Mind, and Behavior* is as strongly biological as were the two preceding editions.

When we describe behaviors and psychological phenomena, our aim is always to show how those behaviors and phenomena are related to the brain's cellular structure, chemical signals, and operations. The basic tenet of this new edition remains the same: everything that "the mind" does will *ultimately* be explainable in terms of the interactions among the brain's components.

To introduce students to the inner workings of the brain in relation to behavior, we begin in Chapter 1 with the basics of overall brain organization, using everyday language and a purposefully simplified scheme. The second chapter presents a more detailed description of the brain's components; it explains the processes of neural transmission and describes the basic neurotransmitters. The third chapter, extensively revised, describes the key events in neural development from the embryonic unfoldings to the changes seen in old age, taking the perspective that the brain develops and adapts continuously until senescence destroys its capacity to do so.

The next chapters examine how the brain enables the body to sense the world (Chapter 4) and move through it (Chapter 5), exploring the diseases that can impair these essential functions. We examine the basic modules for specific aspects of sensory processing and for the generation and regulation of specific movements. Chapter 6 explores how the brain autonomously coordinates the control of the major organ systems to maintain the appropriate conditions for optimal physical and mental performance, such that the required adaptations are continuously monitored by the brain without their rising to the level of conscious awareness. We then turn our attention to the processes underlying the brain's behavioral responsibilities. In Chapter 7, we explore the mechanisms by which the brain is able to sense the timing of the day's passage and to synchronize body events with the demands of the environment, ranging from waking and sleeping, to eating and drinking, to the coordination of reproductive behaviors with the appropriate seasons for raising the newborn. The brain's varying levels of activity are not merely fluctuations but, in fact, rhythmic variations that coordinate the body with the world around it.

The interacting brain systems where these coordinating events take place are part of larger systems that attach emotional weight to the sensing of specific environmental events (Chapter 8). These emotional highs and lows help determine which of many possible responses will be evoked by a given signal. Our focus throughout these discussions is on the underlying biological base of complex behavioral phenomena; in essence, we demystify some of the mysteries of the brain. It is in this spirit that the most complex issues of brain function—learning and memory—are considered in Chapters 9 and 10. The student is offered new information about the human brain that has emerged from studies of animal nervous systems and from the use of powerful new methods of investigating the brains of human subjects.

In Chapter 11, we take up the most complex action of human brain function, consciousness—perhaps the one major brain capacity that has so far yielded minimally to the reductionist strategies that led to the advances described in the earlier chapters. Finally, Chapter 12 revisits the interplay between clinical sciences and basic research. It explores the contributions of biological understanding to our knowledge of the brain and behavior by comparing neurological and behavioral disorders at the level of biologically verifiable changes and presenting the means by which they result in the signs and symptoms of the diseases.

Supplements

The first edition of *Brain, Mind, and Behavior* was part of a multimedia teaching package built on *The Brain,* the Public Broadcasting System's eight-part television series produced by WNET in New York. This series remains available on cassette and is regularly broadcast on selected stations by the Adult Learning Service of PBS. A second such series, *The Mind,* began airing in the fall of 1988 and is often shown along with *The Brain.* Both series include excellent examples of many of the human problems defined in the textbook.

In addition to these videos, the third edition of *Brain, Mind, and Behavior* is accompanied by a host of electronic and print supplements for both teachers and students. We are pleased that this edition is accompanied by a spectacular CD-ROM, *Fundamentals of*

Human Neuroscience, produced by the Open University of Israel and prepared by Yehuda Shavit, Hebrew University of Jerusalem, and Uri Hasson, Weizmann Institute in Israel. This CD-ROM comprises five modules on research methods, neural communication, vision, movement, and the central nervous system and includes rotating three-dimensional models of the human brain and eye, more than 25 video clips, animations of key physiological processes, and interactive examples of the new neuroimaging technologies.

A new *Study Guide* by Joyce Norman, California State University at Chico, ensures student understanding of the textbook through five levels of review and study, including labeling exercises of important physiological and neurological structures and practice test items. The *Instructor's Manual* has been revised by Nim Tottenham, University of Minnesota, and Ian Harrington, University of Toledo, and includes updated media and classroom resources. The *Test Bank* has been expanded and includes illustration labeling items. A computerized test bank is also available on a dual-platform CD-ROM with on-line testing options.

The book companion World Wide Web site can be found at www.worthpublishers.com/bloom and contains key-term flashcards, practice tests, labeling exercises, simulations and demonstrations, World Wide Web links, and updated information on the latest advances in the study of the brain. Instructors can also find selected illustrations from the textbook and other helpful on-line teaching resources.

Acknowledgements

The authors of the textbook were aided enormously in their efforts to simplify the presentation of this often complex subject matter by the informative medical illustrations created especially for this book by the noted *Scientific American* illustrator Carol Donner, by the new illustrations created for the third edition by Joyce Powzyk, and by the sketches, charts, and graphs rendered by artist Sally Black.

There are many to whom the authors owe their gratitude—for direct assistance or for directing our efforts toward improving the text. Kevin Morrin gave cheerful and timely assistance in library research and wrote much of the glossary. The following teachers who used the first edition gave us the benefit of their experience in reviews that helped shape our visions: Alan Auerbach, Wilfrid Laurier University; Donald P. Cain, University of Western Ontario; Edith E. Cracchiolo, Cerritos College; Linda K. Davis, Mt. Hood Community College; David R. Hertzler, State University of New York at Oswego; Alan Kim Johnson, University of Iowa; Augustus R. Lumia, Skidmore College; William M. Miley, Richard Stockton State College; Maribel Montgomery, Linn-Benton Community College; W. Ronald Salafia, Fairfield University; Michael Sloane, University of Alabama at Birmingham; and Lilburn E. Wesche, Seattle Pacific University.

We are also grateful for the assistance of the instructors whose comments helped guide our work on this edition, including: John P. Bruno, Ohio State University; Marvin Gordon-Lickey, University of Oregon; Henry Heffner, University of Toledo; John G. Hildebrand, University of Arizona; Wendy L. Hill, Lafayette College; Joyce Norman, California State University at Chico; Antonio Nunez, Michigan State University; Linda Rinaman, University of Pittsburgh; Patricia Sifter, DePaul University; Ronald Sketon, University of Victoria; Jeffrey Stern, University of Michigan at Dearborn; Timothy J. Teylor, Northeastern Ohio Universities College of Medicine; and Burton A. Weiss, Rutgers University.

In addition, we would like to thank our spouses, families, and colleagues for bearing with us through this revision process. We also thank Chris Stevens for undertaking numerous mechanical revisions.

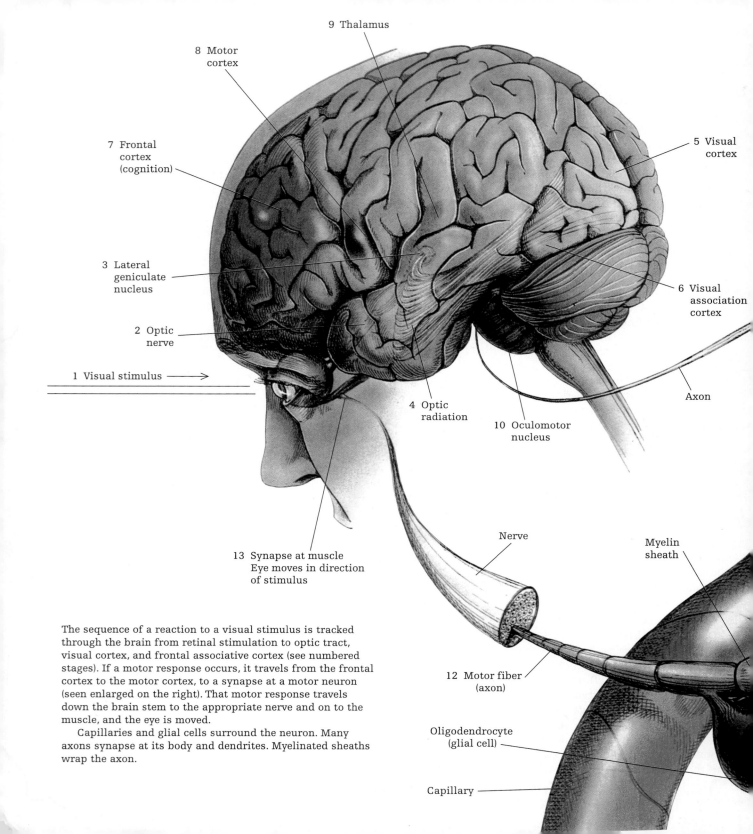

9 Thalamus

8 Motor cortex

7 Frontal cortex (cognition)

5 Visual cortex

3 Lateral geniculate nucleus

6 Visual association cortex

2 Optic nerve

1 Visual stimulus ⟶

4 Optic radiation

10 Oculomotor nucleus

Axon

13 Synapse at muscle Eye moves in direction of stimulus

Nerve

Myelin sheath

The sequence of a reaction to a visual stimulus is tracked through the brain from retinal stimulation to optic tract, visual cortex, and frontal associative cortex (see numbered stages). If a motor response occurs, it travels from the frontal cortex to the motor cortex, to a synapse at a motor neuron (seen enlarged on the right). That motor response travels down the brain stem to the appropriate nerve and on to the muscle, and the eye is moved.

Capillaries and glial cells surround the neuron. Many axons synapse at its body and dendrites. Myelinated sheaths wrap the axon.

12 Motor fiber (axon)

Oligodendrocyte (glial cell)

Capillary

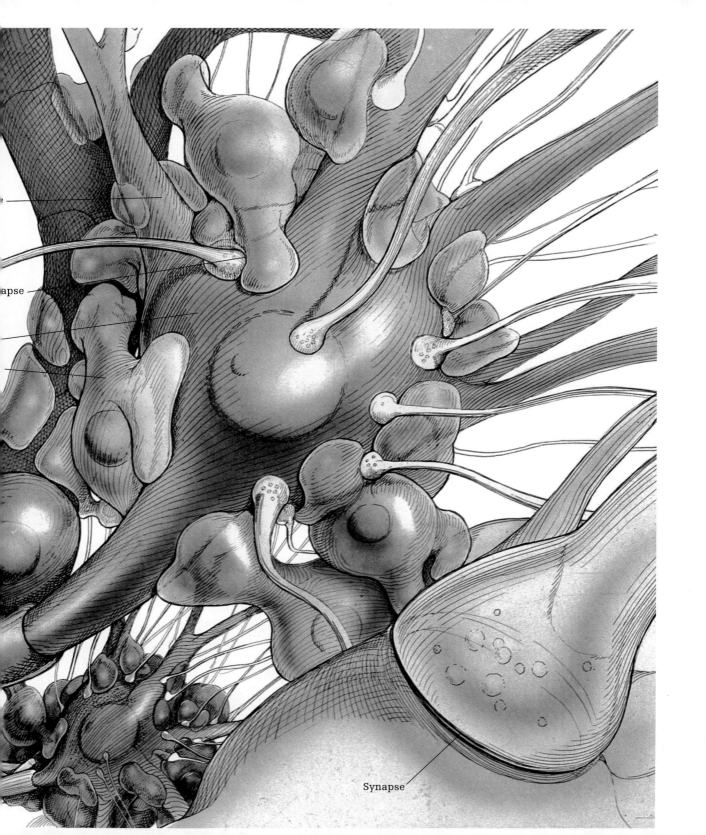

Synapse

Synapse

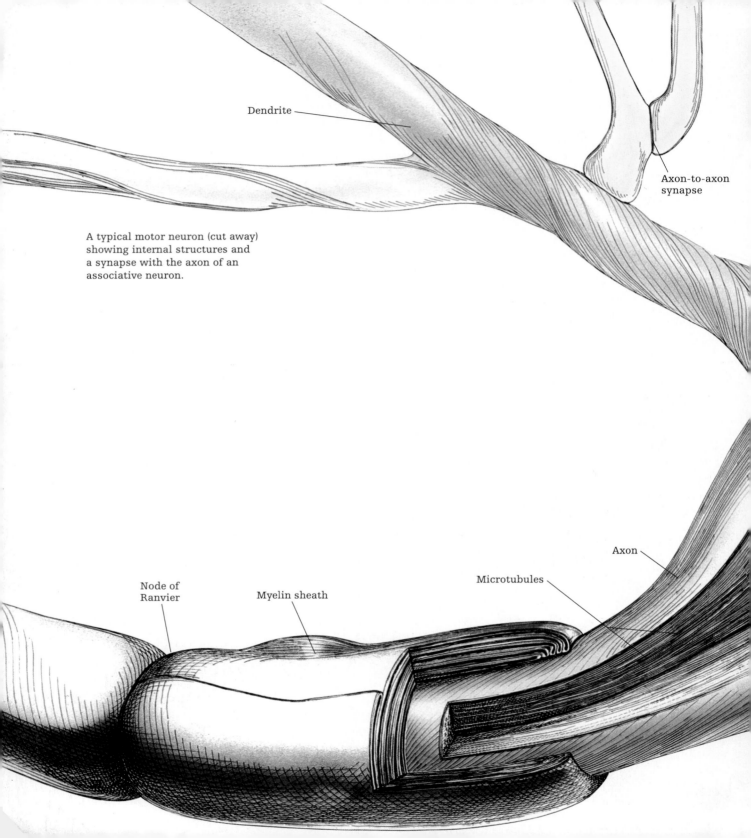

Dendrite

Axon-to-axon
synapse

A typical motor neuron (cut away)
showing internal structures and
a synapse with the axon of an
associative neuron.

Axon

Node of
Ranvier

Myelin sheath

Microtubules

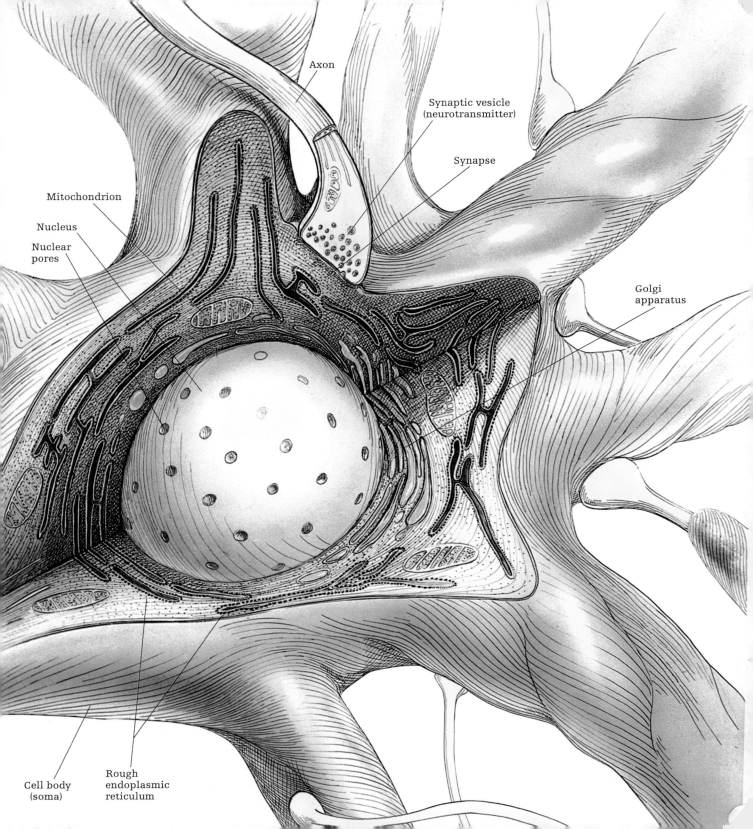

Axon

Synaptic vesicle
(neurotransmitter)

Synapse

Mitochondrion

Nucleus

Nuclear
pores

Golgi
apparatus

Cell body
(soma)

Rough
endoplasmic
reticulum

Brain, Mind, and Behavior

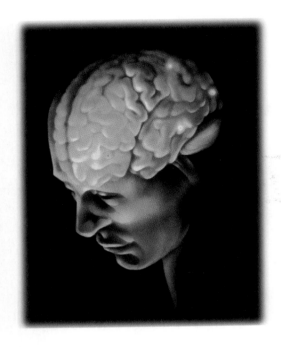

CHAPTER ONE

Introduction to the Nervous System

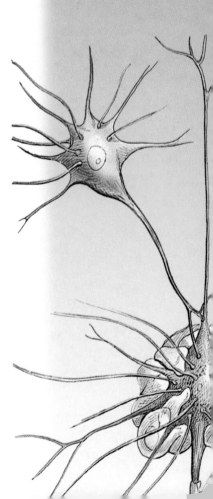

Why Study the Brain?

Our primary focus is the brain: how the brain functions when we see or learn or speak and how it malfunctions to produce mental disorders. Most scientists with that focus would answer the question "Why study the brain?" by saying, simply, that it offers the best chance of discovering why and how you act and react the way that you do and why other human beings do what they do. Perhaps this is also your reason for studying the brain. The human brain, however, may be the most complex living structure in the universe. Consider that your brain is packed with billions of nerve cells and that each cell communicates, on average, with 10,000 others, making up miles and miles of living wires. The nerve cells communicate with each other by means of a multitude of different chemical signals, of which only 40 or so have been identified, although their total number is likely to be far greater.

Not only is the brain structurally and chemically complex, but the entire structure grows, repairs itself, and constantly adapts to the demands of the individual and the environment under the direction of an enormous array of brain-specific genes that scientists are just beginning to inventory and explore.

Nevertheless, for the past half-century, research on the organization and operation of the brain has progressed at an accelerating pace. Scientists from many disciplines have been participating (see box on pages 10 and 11). Gradually, these scientists arrived at a common set of concepts concerning the brain's basic chemical composition, cellular structure, and functional abilities. These common concepts provide them with a common language and, as a result, they benefit from each other's discoveries. All brain researchers, no matter what their discipline or point of view, are now called "neuroscientists."

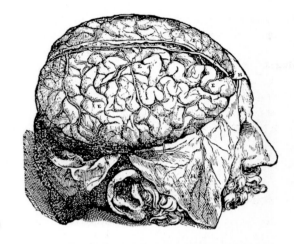

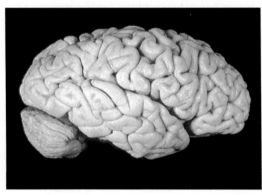

Two images of the brain. *Above:* Andreas Vesalius revolutionized anatomy with the 1543 publication of *De Humani Corporis Fabrica,* which was illustrated by artists of Titian's studio working from the dissected heads of decapitated criminals. *Below:* Photograph of a human brain (side view) removed in an autopsy.

The newest experimental techniques and advances in the understanding of brain structure and function are enabling neuroscientists to study the brain's operations with a precision that was not previously possible. Investigations of memory were originally limited to testing people or laboratory animals to see what they could remember after various learning tasks. Today, investigators can examine specific changes in the activity of specific brain cells as the events of "remembering" take place. Scientists studying the mysterious state of sleep now know which brain structures and transmitters work together in inducing sleep. Recent work is also revealing how the chemistry of pain is transmitted or inhibited.

Brain, Mind, and Behavior

The new techniques and approaches that allow direct study of brain mechanisms also shed new light on the underpinnings of mind and behavior. During the first half of the twentieth century, before it was possible to know much about the brain besides its gross anatomy, many scientists studied how humans and animals behaved as the only precisely measurable aspect of their mental activity, which was otherwise unobservable. In fact, the theory based on this approach is called "behaviorism." Beginning about 1910, behaviorism remained the predominant theoretical approach in psychology (literally the study of the mind) until the 1950s and 1960s. Behaviorists assumed that no one could know what happened inside an organism while it learned or slept or felt pain, so they concentrated instead on administering precisely measured stimuli and recording the organism's observable behavior in response. The organism's interior was considered a "black box"—and what happened in there was considered unknowable.

Now that the brain's workings are open to examination, the term "behavior" takes on new meanings. For example, electrodes precisely implanted to monitor single nerve cells in a monkey's brain show that certain cells are active before the monkey reaches for an object in a learning experiment. Thus, besides observing the monkey's behavior in choosing the correct object, we can now see which specific part of its brain is active during the process of deciding which behavior to perform. In other words, we can see the "behaviors" of the brain itself.

Historically, investigations of the mind were separated from studies of the physical brain and how it generated behavior. The predominant approach was the introspective method, which ignored both the actual behaviors and the physiological operations behind them and instead tried to find scientific techniques for analyzing the contents of consciousness, or mind. "Mind" was an abstract concept that included the conscious awareness of reason and emotion, as well as ones's personality, self-identity, or, depending on one's beliefs, the "soul." Even some contemporary observers believe that the mind exists independently, unconnected to the physical entity of the brain. Others, including the authors of this text, believe that any complete account of mental function must be based on the scientific examination of brain chemistry, structure, and physiology.

what is the mind?

Brain and Mind: A Basic Premise

The lessons of this book are founded on a single basic premise: All the normal functions of the healthy brain and the disorders of the diseased brain, no matter how complex, are ultimately explainable in terms of the basic structural components of the brain and their function.

Everything that the brain does, when it works properly and when it does not, rests on the events taking place in specific, definable locations. However, many of these events are extremely complicated, and often scientists do not know exactly which parts of the brain are most critical or what those parts do. Yet, compared with the almost total ignorance of these processes that persisted well into the twentieth century, we now have a considerable amount of information. We have pieced together a general picture of how the brain is organized and how it functions, a set of concepts that can be considered to form the principles of neuroscience. The exciting brain research going on today no doubt will extend these principles so that the more complex acts of the brain will be understood.

Before we look at these principles, however, we need to consider a controversial concept buried within our basic premise. What does the phrase "everything that the brain does" mean? It certainly means moving, sensing, eating, drinking, breathing, talking, and sleeping. But does it include mental acts—thoughts and dreams, musings and insights, hopes and aspirations?

This book takes the view that "the mind" results when many key cells of the brain work together, just as "digestion" results when the cells of the intestinal tract work together. You may disagree with this view, but that should not stop you from being curious. When a scientist confronts a "fact" that does not "feel right," a typical response is, "Well, I'll wait and see what the next experiments (or interpretations) show." If you disagree with the statement "The mind is the product of the brain's activity," consider the facts that follow in subsequent chapters and then see what you think.

What Does the Brain Do?

Stop for a moment and make a list of all the actions that your brain is engaged in right now. Certainly the action most prominent in your mind is reading. This act can be broken down into several complex subordinate acts: seeing the symbols on the page, assembling the symbols into words, connecting the words with meanings, and then integrating the meanings to form thoughts. While you focus on this book, you are more or less blocking out background sounds—the whispers of those around you, footsteps, the sounds of cars going by, the ticking of the clock. Without thinking about it, you simply suppress those noises while you concentrate on something else. You are also suppressing a lot of information coming into the brain through other sensory channels—where your arms and legs are and whatever position you have just shifted to without thinking; the location of things in the room; the time of day; the location where you are now relative to where you live. Your brain constantly monitors all this information, updating it as the sun comes out or goes behind the clouds, waiting for you to turn your attention to something new.

Has your list been exhausted? In fact, we have only begun. Your brain is performing countless actions even farther out of reach of your active awareness. It is controlling your breathing to maintain just the right amount of oxygen in your bloodstream, as well as adjusting your blood pressure to keep that fresh, oxygenated blood going to your head. It is monitoring and regulating almost all the other internal conditions of your body, such as the nutrient content in your bloodstream, which provides one of the signals to eat again; your body temperature; the amount of water that your body needs to stay in chemical balance; and the hormonal control of your beard growth or lack thereof. The brain works actively at these duties and others and still maintains energy for emergency tasks. If a fire were to break out, for example, your brain would direct you to jump up, grab the baby or the dog, run to the door (whose location has just reentered your active awareness), and escape, all while it adjusts your blood pressure and blood oxygen to appropriate levels. All these brain activities, which are summarized in Table 1.1, fall into general categories: *interacting* with the world around us (seeing, listening, feeling, tasting, smelling, and speaking to others), *moving* the body through the world while internally *regulating* blood pressure and content, *reproducing*, and *adapting* to the world around us through our physical acts and our invisible mental acts, such as *remembering*, *learning*, and *analyzing*.

Sensation

The major means by which we sense the world are *vision* (seeing), *audition* (listening), *gustation* (tasting), *olfaction* (smelling), and *somatic sensation* (feeling touch). Each of these senses collects and channels information through specific organs and segments of the nervous system.

One other kind of sensing almost never appears in such lists, partly because its organ is hidden from view, but largely because it seldom malfunctions. Deep within the bony

structure at the side of the skull and beneath the ears lies a complex sensory organ called the vestibular apparatus. This structure provides us with the sense of balance that we use to monitor the movements of our heads and bodies and to orient ourselves in space. The nerve bundles bringing auditory and gravitational information into the brain travel along similar pathways from the inner ear (see Figure 1.1 on the following page).

Motion

The body engages in two different types of movement: voluntary motions—those that you can control when you want to—and involuntary motions—those that you cannot control (see Figure 1.2 on page 7). Voluntary movements are those that result when you purposely move your limbs, make a face, or wiggle your tongue. Involuntary movements are generally restricted to muscles deep within the body, such as the heart and muscles of the intestinal tract. Both kinds of movements are controlled by the nervous system. You can glimpse an example of involuntary

TABLE 1.1 Some activities controlled by the brain

Interactions with the environment	Actions controlling the body	Mental activities		
Seeing	Breathing	Learning	Creating	Concentrating
Listening	Regulating blood pressure and heat	Remembering	Analyzing	Ignoring
Feeling		Writing	Deciding	Feeling
Smelling	Regulating body positions	Drawing	Calculating	Sleeping
Tasting	Regulating locomotion (e.g., moving)	Reading	Imagining	Dreaming
Balancing	Regulating reflexes (e.g., blinking)			
	Eating and drinking			
Speaking	Regulating hormones			

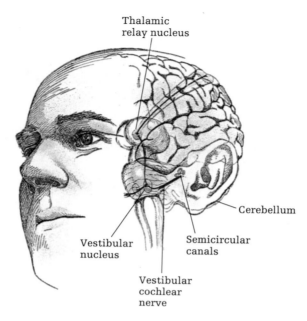

Thalamic
relay nucleus

Cerebellum

Vestibular
nucleus

Semicircular
canals

Vestibular
cochlear
nerve

Figure 1.1 The brain parts important for the sense of balance. The fluid-filled semicircular canals sense the head's rotation and relay that information to the vestibular nuclei in the medulla, to the cerebellum, to the thalamus, and to the somatosensory cortex.

muscle action if you go into a dimly lit room, look at your pupils in the mirror, and suddenly turn on the light. Your pupil contracts almost instantly—and involuntarily—to protect the light-sensing cells of your retina by reducing the amount of incoming light. The goose bumps that you get when you are chilled or thrilled also are involuntary movements: the nerves activate small muscles attached to the hairs on your skin and make them literally "stand on end."

Internal Regulation

The precise regulation of your internal organs depends on the active surveillance of the nervous system. Only occasionally do these organs intrude upon your thinking, such as when your stomach gurgles loudly while the class is silently at work—but you cannot do much to control them directly unless you can have something to eat. When you are aware of being too warm or too cold, you can respond behaviorally by changing your clothes, your locale, or your level of physical activity—but your internal body temperature would likely remain stable regardless of what you did unless you were in extreme situations. As long as you stay in the same general time zone, your brain can even plan for necessary changes in your internal environment in advance, coordinating your kidneys and intestines to the timing of your daily routine of going to work, eating, and sleeping.

Much of the information relayed between the brain and the internal organs is carried by hormones. Hormones are chemicals that are manufactured by organs or glands and secreted into the bloodstream. The brain has special receptor cells for interpreting the messages carried by these chemicals. The brain also manufactures certain hormones, which are released into the bloodstream and activate or regulate certain processes.

Reproduction

The brain coordinates the proper hormonal regulation of the testicles in preparing sperm, the ovaries in preparing ova, and the uterus lining in preparing for implantation of the fertilized egg. The brain monitors the testicles or ovaries by means of a complex set of internal sensing systems. It also issues commands to the reproductive system by means of hormones secreted from the pituitary gland, appended directly to the base of the brain. Small structural differences exist between male and female brains in those

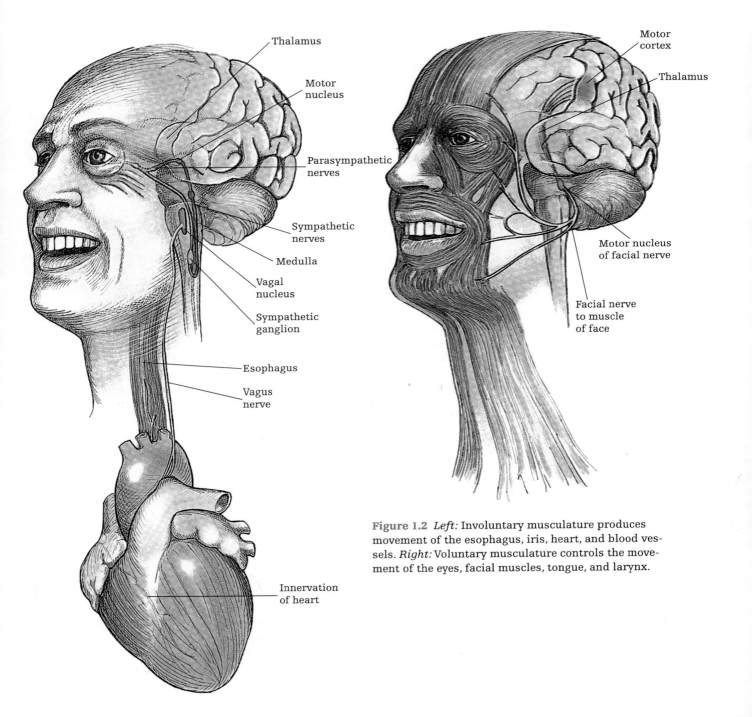

Thalamus

Motor
nucleus

Parasympathetic
nerves

Sympathetic
nerves

Medulla

Vagal
nucleus

Sympathetic
ganglion

Esophagus

Vagus
nerve

Innervation
of heart

Motor
cortex

Thalamus

Motor nucleus
of facial nerve

Facial nerve
to muscle
of face

Figure 1.2 *Left:* Involuntary musculature produces movement of the esophagus, iris, heart, and blood vessels. *Right:* Voluntary musculature controls the movement of the eyes, facial muscles, tongue, and larynx.

parts concerned with reproduction long before the brain urges the body to develop outwardly visible masculine or feminine characteristics.

Adaptation

The world around us is constantly changing, and to survive we must accommodate to new conditions. Our brains act as our agents in such adaptive responses. We adapt to new problems by remembering how we solved similar ones before and by either defending against them or retreating from them. Sometimes we adapt without even thinking: nevertheless, the brain is directing the responses. Our built-in sensing systems implicitly remind us to eat when hungry, drink when thirsty, and sleep when tired, all simple nonthinking adaptations. When an adaptive response leads to a long-lasting change in behavior, we speak of that change as "learning" (see Chapters 7 and 8). As the number of our successful adaptations increases, we enlarge our repertoire of behaviors. With practice and with successful learning of the better solution to a particular condition, many of the responses that we need (such as coming in out of the rain or fastening our seat belts before we drive) become almost unconscious.

Unfortunately, human beings have a tendency to respond to their surroundings in ways that are not good for them, such as habitual overeating or using recreational drugs. Likewise, some mental disorders are characterized by maladaptive behaviors. For example, people with phobias, or irrational fears of particular things or events, may resort to certain problematic behaviors to alleviate their anxiety. People who develop a morbid fear of germs or infection are the classic example. They may wash their hands a hundred times a day, wasting many of their waking hours and damaging their skin.

What Is a Brain?

As already mentioned, the brain is responsible for sensation, motion, internal regulation, reproduction, and adaptation. If you have ever taken biology, you will recognize these activities as the definitive characteristics common to all animals. Even single-cell organisms, such as bacteria, can sense, move, regulate their internal nutritional and respiratory systems, reproduce, and adapt to changes in their environments. Every cell in our bodies, in fact, can respond to some kinds of stimuli in its immediate environment and to some degree regulate its internal environment. Many of our cells can also move independently (white blood cells, for example, chase and capture invading bacteria) and reproduce (such as the cells of our skin). If we left out motion, the list would apply to all plants as well as animals.

If all creatures big and small, with and without a brain, do the same basic things, what is the brain for? Let us say that the brain is an organ specialized to help individual creatures carry out major acts of living. How well an individual can succeed in its environment depends on the complexity and capacity of its brain as well as the demands of the environment. Bacteria move toward light and sense the presence of nutrients, but multicelled organisms can do much more. Multicelled organisms contain different groups of cells that allow them not only to detect changes in the environment, but to adapt to them in more complex ways. These additional capacities give them many advantages in gaining access to nutrients or fleeing from predators. A shark cannot do arithmetic, but it can sense small changes in the electric charge in the ocean that would escape the notice of sophisticated electronic gear. Such special sensing abilities allow the shark to escape, for example, human predators or to sense fresh blood in the water and rush in for the meal. Animals with complex brains can not only remember more experiences, but also solve more complex problems and devise tools with which to make their particular environments more to their liking.

By comparing the structure and function of the human brain with those of other animals, we can begin to ask what is unique about our brain. We can neither fly like an eagle or see as well nor climb mountains that would be a morning romp for a mountain lion, but we are more skilled than other animals at observing, analyzing, and solving complex problems. We can invent and construct airplanes that fly us higher and farther than an eagle, and we can record the construction plans so that later generations can build the planes and even improve their design. We owe many of these abilities to our uniquely strong capacity of language. The human brain's capacity for language eventually led to writing. Once human beings were able to record their thoughts, many did so at length, for the enlightenment of their contemporaries and to communicate with future generations. Because some of the early writing has been preserved, we are able to gain a historical perspective on what our ancestors thought about the brain.

Historical Views of Brain, Mind, and Behavior

The ancient Greeks produced some of the earliest written records of humans thinking about the ability to think. Heraclitus, a Greek philosopher of the sixth century B.C., referred to the mind as an enormous space whose boundaries could never be reached, even by traveling along every path. Speculation about the nature of mental activity is probably as ancient as thinking itself, but agreement about the source of mental activi-

ty is a relatively recent accomplishment. In the fourth century B.C., Aristotle wrote that the brain was bloodless and that the heart was not only the source of nervous control, but also the seat of the soul. (Aristotle is revered today more for his invention of a systematic style of thinking than for his neuroanatomical insights.) The early dissectors of animal brains in the second century A.D. recognized the brain as the center of the system of nerves that caused the body to sense and move, but they took great care to assure the authorities that these functions had nothing to do with thinking and the soul. For the next thousand or more years, those who

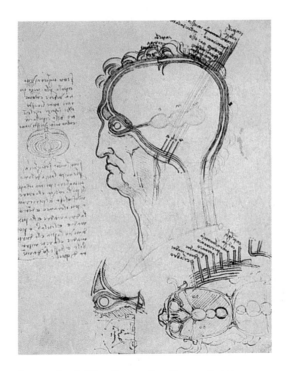

Leonardo da Vinci's passion for anatomy extended to dissection. In this sketch and others, he followed the medieval convention of spherical ventricles, the foremost of which he called the "common sense cell," where the soul was thought to reside.

The name for the general field of research that provides the data on which most of this book is based is *neuroscience,* the science of the nervous system. The general purpose of this field of research is to link the biological and chemical properties of the brain and its component cells to behavior.

Many specialists work within the general field of neuroscience, using a wide range of methods to examine different aspects of brain structure and function. We should at the outset distinguish two categories of research. In *experimental neuroscience,* the scientist perturbs the nervous system of an organism to yield measurable, predictable, and eventually explicable changes. In *clinical neuroscience,* a medical physician or other professional observes a change produced by life events (for example, developmental, infectious, or traumatic events) and tries to understand the effect of the change on brain function.

Throughout history, clinical scientists have identified specific accidents and diseases in their patients that have revealed previously unsuspected aspects of the normal structure, function, and chemistry of the brain. Many fields of medicine are concerned with aspects of bodily function that are ultimately regulated and monitored by the brain. However, the branches of medicine most closely tied to the study of the brain are neurosurgery (a surgical speciality dealing with the brain), psychiatry (the study of behavioral, emotional, and mental diseases), and neuropsychology (the study of the nervous system in relation to normal and abnormal behavior).

Clinical neuroscientists study the brain first by talking to their patients and then testing the operations of the patients' special systems of sensing, moving, and remembering. They can also assess mental function by evaluating the performance of more abstract talents such as solving mathematical problems or drawing. A critical feature of these evaluations is the attempt to link disorders to specific structures of the brain revealed by conventional x rays or by the newer so-called neuroimaging methods (discussed on page 334 in Chapter 11).

The experimental neurosciences have traditionally been divided into the following major disciplines:

Anatomists seek to describe the organization of the elements of the brain. These scientists study the brain's shape and form by gross inspection, or by slicing it into very thin sections and examining the sections under a microscope. Using special dyes, they can discriminate one kind of nerve cell from another. Other types of dyes injected into the brain help to reveal the connections between cells in different places. Still other stains detect the particular chemical that individual neurons use to transmit their intercellular messages.

Physiologists attempt to understand how the brain functions by documenting the patterns of activity of the brain cells. In some cases, signal detectors (electrodes) are placed on the surface of the scalp to record the activity of millions of cells at a time, as in the electroencephalogram (EEG; see Chapter 11). In other cases, very thin electrodes are placed directly within the substances of the brain to record the activity of just one cell at a time. By determining how the single cells or groups of cells alter their activities when the brain is performing a specific task, such as processing light signals that enter through the eyes, the physiologist seeks to determine how neurons work together to achieve the complex behaviors of our brains.

Biochemists investigate the chemical properties of the cells of the brain. When very little was known of how the brain worked, biochemists determined how much of the brain was made of fat, protein, and various sugars. Later they focused on identifying specific proteins and other molecules that act as signals between cells or that amplify the effects of these signals. As more and more distinct chemicals were discovered, the biochemists sought to link changes in them to brain development, to aging, or to specific diseases. For example, patients with Parkinson's disease experience increasing difficulty initiating or terminating voluntary movements and their hands tremble prominently at rest. Only in the 1950s and 1960s was it recognized that their brains lacked normal amounts of a brain chemical called dopamine. By understanding the enzymes that dopamine-containing neurons use to make dopamine, biochemists could developed drugs to replace the missing chemical and help reverse, at least temporarily, the symptoms of the disease. Today, much molecular neurochemistry focuses on discovering the genes used by brain cells.

Psychologists seek to understand the behavioral operations of the brain. Some psychologists analyze the behavior of normal people and define the rules by which they sense, discriminate, store, and recall specific information. Others analyze the behavior of experimental animals under the controlled environment of the laboratory (such as pushing a lever when a red light is on to get a food pellet).

Although we have described the four major disciplines within the neurosciences as though they were separate, much of the work going on now is actually *interdisciplinary*. In this form of research, a given brain system, such as the visual system, or a complex structure, such as the cerebellum, is studied in relation to its function, chemistry, cellular organization, and behavioral operations. Such studies can be undertaken either by a single scientist trained in all those research skills or by teams of specialists who work together. Interdisciplinary neuroscientists might also seek to determine which brain structures and chemicals are critical for the performance of a particular kind of task and analyze how the brain changes when an animal undertakes that task.

Frequently, scientists who study the brain take their cues for future studies from clinical observation. For example, why does one person who has had a stroke become depressed, yet another does not? Why does a person who has had a series of epileptic attacks suddenly start to lose the ability to remember anything new? Other times, knowledge gained from research on experimental animals—such as the discovery of a new chemical signal, or an unexpected connection between parts of the brain—is applied to chemical or brain-function tests on people. Although much has been learned about the brain, there is still much, much more to understand, and much of what we need to know is not yet clear. New methods for studying the brains of healthy and diseased people will be required.

examined the brain took the same precautions. The church, after all, retained authority over human consciousness, or "soul," and the soul, wherever it lay, was not subject to direct investigation.

Analysis by Analogy

Historians of science have observed that thinkers in the past tried to explain how the brain and mind worked by using analogies to the physical world in which they lived. This striking observation was stated more poetically by the philosopher Julian Jaynes (1976): ". . . the metaphors of mind are the world it perceives." The Greek physician Galen, living in the second century A.D., was one of the first to dissect the brains of

The four humors. *Counterclockwise from upper left:* Too much black bile keeps a melancholic man in bed; yellow bile drives the choleric husband to wife-beating; phlegm makes a reluctant mistress; the high-blooded lover plays the lute for his lady.

humans and other animals. The major technological achievements in his day were aqueducts and sewer systems that relied on the principles of fluid mechanics. It is hardly accidental, then, that Galen believed the important parts of the brain to lie not in the brain's substance but in its fluid-filled cavities. Today these cavities are known as the cerebroventricular system, and the fluid that is made there is called cerebrospinal fluid. Galen, however, believed that all physical functions and states of health and ill-health depended on the distribution of four body fluids, or "humors": blood, phlegm (mucus), black bile, and choler (yellow bile). Each humor had a special function: blood carried the animal's vital living spirit; phlegm caused sluggishness; black bile was responsible for melancholy; and yellow bile aroused the temper. So deeply were Galen's views ingrained in Western thought that the role of humors in brain and other organ functions remained largely unquestioned for nearly 1500 years.

By the eighteenth century, more rigorous-minded observers had begun to attack the natural phenomena of the world "scientifically." The undocumented and hypothetical constructs of the past were replaced by the conviction that everything could be explained in terms of mechanics. It was now a world of machines. The brain machinery of the sensing organs for vision and hearing was the first to be revealed. In the early seventeenth century, the German astronomer Johannes Kepler argued that the eye operated essentially like an ordinary optical instrument, by projecting the image of what was being seen onto the special sensory nerves of the retina, the light-detecting tissue at the back of the eye. Some 75 years later, the description of the mechanisms of the inner ear by the English anatomist Thomas Willis led to the recognition that hearing was based on the transformation of sound through the air by the activation of special receptors of the cochlea, a coiled tube of tissue within the inner ear.

These mechanistic discoveries gave rise to a split in thinking about body and mind, which some scholars believe has caused problems ever since. Philosopher and mathematician René Descartes is often cited as the father of this body–mind dualism. Questions of biological science—that is, of what could be "known" about human beings and other animals—could apply only to those structures that they have in common. The processes of perceiving and examining the images received by these structures belonged to a different and separate "mental" world reserved only for humans. Although this permitted a mathematically accurate portrayal of the transformation of optical and auditory images, it did not answer the deeper questions of how the sensations received were synthesized into meaningful images of the world.

In the sixteenth and seventeenth centuries, scientific advances gave rise to accurate descriptions (but not explanations) of electricity. And, as seventeenth-century explorers spread out throughout the world, a more complete notion of the surface of the earth was acquired. The principles of both electricity and geography were eventually applied to concepts of how the brain worked. However, change was slow. When the properties of the nervous system ceased to be regarded as a flow of humors, this explanation was at first replaced by the theories of the "ballonists," who considered the nerves to be hollow tubes through which a flow of gases excited the muscles. Scientists tested this idea by dissecting animals under water. When no gases were observed to bubble up during muscle contractions, the theory went flat.

Although electricity was known at this time, its powers had yet to be applied to

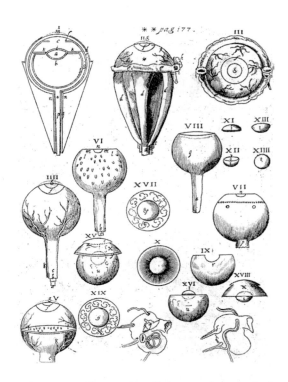

Johannes Kepler protrayed the eye as an optical instrument rather than a divine mystery. This view of body parts as being like other machines was the breakthrough that allowed scientific research to begin.

practical uses. Mid-seventeenth-century industry was instead powered by windmills, flowing rivers, and waterfalls. Thus scientists reasoned that something had to flow from the nerves to cause muscles to contract, and concocted a "vital fluid" theory to replace the gas theory. According to the new theory, an "essence" of the hollow nerves flowed into the muscle, mixed with its fluids, and caused explosive contractions. This "fluid" hypothesis was one of the first to be issued by the newly formed Royal Society of England, about 1661.

The vital-fluid concept eventually gave way to the view, proposed by the physicist

Isaac Newton near the beginning of the eighteenth century, that activity was transmitted by a vibrating "aetherial Medium," which had all the properties later found to belong to biological electricity. Even with the primitive instruments of the eighteenth and nineteenth centuries, it was rather easy to show that both nerves and muscles were electrically excitable. However, the possibility that the nerves and muscles worked by actually generating animal electricity themselves was not immediately recognized. The Italian scientist Luigi Galvani offered that hypothesis near the end of the eighteenth century, and the German biologist Emil du Bois-Reymond reexamined it early in the next century. Du

Bois-Reymond was the first scientist to attempt an explanation of all functions of the brain on chemical and physical grounds. He and his coworkers were the first to measure in a convincing way the electrical properties of living, active nerves and muscles.

Analysis by Observation and Experimentation

In the nineteenth century, medical investigators provided the next level of understanding about the brain. Taking advantage of opportunities provided by the unfortunate victims of the expanding technology of war, medical observers made note of the exact locations of destruc-

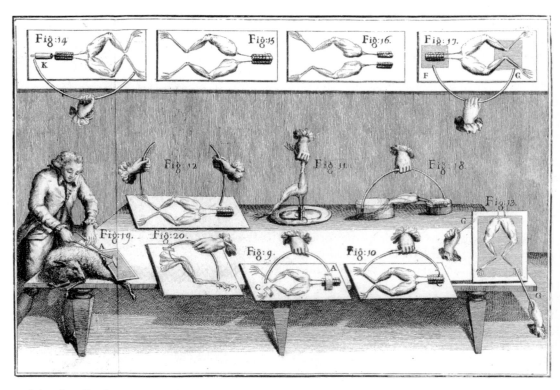

Luigi Galvani's electricity-producing machine one day accidentally sparked a twitch in the leg of a freshly dissected frog. The general observation that electrical stimuli can cause muscles to contract set off the search for "animal electricity."

tive injuries, or lesions, in the brains of soldiers with nonfatal head injuries and related these lesions to their consequent disabilities. Clinical observations connecting specific neurologic or mental problems to specific areas of damage to the brain continue to serve as a major source of information today. The "lesion approach" was also applied experimentally to the brains of animals to locate the brain parts responsible for gross functions, such as response to touch or movement of the limbs.

The Austrian anatomist Franz Joseph Gall carried the concept of localized sensory and motor regions in the brain one step further. Perhaps borrowing an idea from geography, Gall proposed that all human mental faculties—from such well-accepted abilities as speech and movement to the more subtle skills of dexterity, wit, and veneration of the deity—could be located by charting the bulges in the skull that were thought to correspond to bulges in the responsible brain surface below. This transient practice, known as phrenology, soon fell out of favor. A corresponding strategy in animal brain research, however, was more useful. Its proponents believed they could determine the action for which a brain region was responsible by seeing what happened when the region was electrically stimulated. By the end of the nineteenth century, research techniques employing lesions and stimulation had enabled scientists to assign functions to large segments of the brain.

As physical scientists began to explore beneath the surface of the earth and examine in detail the structural and chemical properties of the soil, brain scientists in the late nineteenth and early twentieth centuries began similar "geological" examinations of what lay below the surface features of the brain. Lesions and stimulation experiments had shown that the outer layers of the brain were essential for the highest forms of consciousness and sensory responsiveness. By geological analogy, the layers beneath were assumed to represent structures that were laid down earlier in evolution, the most primitive being the deep structures of the midbrain and hindbrain. When these regions were destroyed, animals could not survive.

Further insight came from detailed analyses of brain structure. Some large cells could even be seen with the aid of primitive microscopes. Although microscopes were available earlier, the complex and compact cellular structure of the brain was not easily examined. Advances were achieved by early microscopists, such as the English anatomist Augustus von Waller, who in the mid-nineteenth century discovered a chemical method that would detect strands of dying nerves (so-called Wallerian degeneration). When the branches of dying neurons took on this stain, they could determine that the long fibers of the nerves outside the brain and spinal cord were extensions of the cells inside the brain and spinal cord. More stains were needed to highlight single cells selectively.

Soon thereafter, by the 1880s, the Italian Camillo Golgi and the Spaniard Santiago Ramón y Cajal were applying improved staining methods intensively. Now the detailed structures of the brain could be resolved into two main classes of cells: the nerve cells, or *neurons*, and the cells that appeared to act like glue between the nerve cells and are called *neuroglia* or sometimes just *glia* (which means "glue"). Microscopic analysis of the brain and its parts then became a third critical "instrument" in the researcher's tool box. However, even though they were using the same staining methods, Cajal and Golgi disagreed bitterly over what they thought they saw in the microscopes. Golgi believed that the brain was composed of large multinucleated cells that formed a complex net, or *syncytium*, whereas Cajal believed that the brain was composed of individual

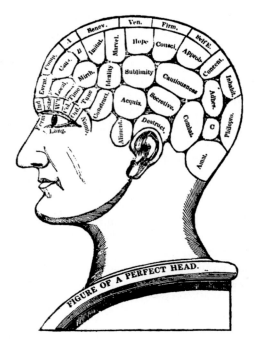

Palpation of bumps on the head became the rage after the introduction of phrenology in 1790. Everyone wanted his or her head read—except, perhaps, those with bumps around the ears, which stood for combativeness, destructiveness, secretiveness, acquisitiveness, and a devotion to food.

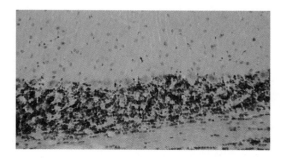

Layering of the cerebellum. At this very low power of magnification, the nerve-cell nuclei appear as deep purplish blue spots. Three basic cellular layers are visible because of the density at which the neurons are packed.

nerve cells that were linked together by their long and tortuous extensions.

The eventual argument went to Cajal. Recognition that the tissue of the brain was composed of individual cells connected by their extensions led to the question of how those cells worked together to perform the functioning of the brain. For decades, arguments raged about whether the process of transmission between neurons was electrical or chemical. By the mid-1920s, however, most scientists were willing to accept the view that is current today; that is, muscles are activated and heartbeat and other peripheral organs are regulated by the passage of chemical signals arising in the nerves. However, as will be described in Chapter 2, biological electricity is an essential process in the spread of excitability within cells, activating chemical messages when it reaches the junctions between neurons.

This chemical-transmission hypothesis was clearly proved in the experiments of the English pharmacologist Sir Henry Dale and the Austrian biologist Otto Loewi. Their discoveries led directly to the use of a fourth investigative strategy, the application of plant extracts and synthetic chemicals directly to the muscles to compare their effects with the effects actually produced by the nerve. Although chemical transmission was considered a necessary and sufficient explanation of the responses to nerve signals in the limbs and viscera, its central role in the links between the neurons of the brain and elsewhere took much longer to demonstrate.

A Contemporary Analogy

The complexity of the brain—even the brains of small animals—that has gradually been revealed by hard-won discoveries staggers the imagination. The history of brain science was surely not completely written in the twentieth century. When this history is complete, the working analogy for the living brain might be the computer, but as will be noted in later chapters it is, at present, a relatively poor and superficial comparison.

Nevertheless, analogies often help scientists to model brain experiments according to some other grand design already recognized in nature—either as we find it, as we see and observe it, or as we imagine it to be. But no model, no matter how closely it simulates the operations of the brain, will be completely acceptable until it can predict features of the brain's operation that are not now readily apparent. The objective of brain scientists is not to develop a model or a machine that can merely simulate or explain some of what we already know the brain can do. Rather, the successful model will explain what the brain does and how.

The Scientific Method

A true experimental science of the brain (or any other object of interest) requires a method that allows for the establishment of certain facts and then uses those facts to ask questions aimed at achieving a fundamental understanding of the brain. The scientific method was developed for just such a purpose. It consists of three separate components: (1) *observation,* the accurate recording of the methods of study, the experimental conditions under which the observations were made, and the results of the experiment; (2) *interpretation,* reasoning about the results to generate hypotheses that can be used to frame future experiments, and (3) *verification,* the repetition of the study by others, using the same conditions, to confirm or refute the results.

The process of working from observations, to formulating an integrative hypothesis, and to evaluating the hypothesis experimentally is known as *inductive reasoning.* Scientists who believe they work in this way

argue that they have no fixed ideas at the start of their investigations but simply allow nature to reveal itself through their painstaking observations. A contrasting strategy, attributed to Aristotle, is deductive reasoning, in which one starts with a global hypothesis and then formulates experiments to test its truth.

Most scientists probably use both strategies. It is virtually impossible not to have some preexisting impressions, or intuitions, before an investigation begins, and it is equally impossible to make observations or conduct an experiment without having these ideas somewhere in the background. Indeed, unless you have some idea of what you are looking for, you probably cannot recognize it when you see it. When data are presented according to the rules of science, it becomes possible, however, for one scientist to question another's interpretation, as was the case between Cajal and Golgi. An outsider without the discoverer's biases (perhaps with significant biases of his or her own) can, and often does, come up with another explanation of the discoverer's results. The practice of science, then, depends on scientists having the opportunity to look at each other's observations and devise new experiments that will confirm their accuracy or suggest another explanation.

The following chapters describe and discuss the results of scientific studies of the brain and other elements of the nervous system. (The box on pages 10 and 11 describes some of the neuroscientist's general methods.) However, before we can make sense of their discoveries, we need to know, in broad outline, the elements of the nervous system and the basic organization of the brain.

The Organization of the Nervous System

To describe "brain" properly, we must understand its relation to the central and

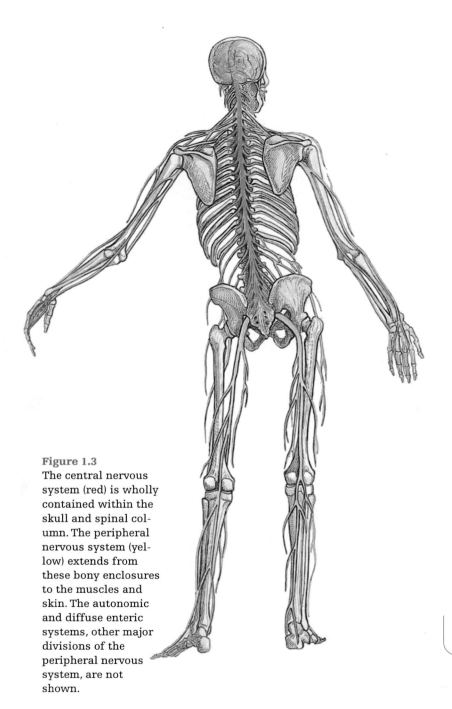

Figure 1.3
The central nervous system (red) is wholly contained within the skull and spinal column. The peripheral nervous system (yellow) extends from these bony enclosures to the muscles and skin. The autonomic and diffuse enteric systems, other major divisions of the peripheral nervous system, are not shown.

peripheral nervous systems. The human nervous system consists of the brain and spinal cord (central nervous system) and all the neural tracts that run from the spinal cord out to muscles, organs, glands, and other tissues (peripheral nervous system). The *central nervous system* (CNS) includes all the parts of the nervous system that lie within the bones of the skull and spine (see Figure 1.3). The brain is that part of the CNS enclosed within the bones of the skull. The other major component of the CNS is the spinal cord.

Nerves extend into and out of the CNS, and when these nerves are beyond the bony protective shelter of the skull and spine, they are considered to be parts of the *peripheral nervous system* (PNS; see Figure 1.3). One division of the PNS, the somatic nervous system (which means "to the body"), consists of the nerves that carry information from the skin, muscles, bones, and joints to the spinal cord and from the spinal cord to the muscles. Some parts of the PNS, however, have only remote connections to the central nervous system and work with only limited supervision. These nerves are a division of the PNS called the *autonomic nervous system* (ANS), a set of structures that are largely responsible for regulating the body's internal environment: the heart, lungs, blood vessels, and other internal organs. In addition, the digestive tract has its own internal autonomous nervous system, the *diffuse enteric nervous system,* which some neuroscientists now consider to be a third division of the PNS. These divisions and functions are described in Chapter 6.

The Organization of the Brain: An Overview

We offer in this chapter only the most basic introduction to the brain's organization. The details are presented in later chapters in the context of specific aspects of the brain's operation. Figure 1.4 and Table 1.2 identify the major anatomical regions of the brain and their subdivisions. These regions can be distinguished during the early stages of embryonic development (described in Chapter 3).

As seen from the format of Table 1.2, the anatomical organization of the brain is largely hierarchical. For example, the forebrain is composed of the diencephalon and the telencephalon; and the diencephalon, in turn, is composed of the thalamus and the hypothalamus. These large divisions and subdivisions are just the beginning of the hierarchy. The hypothalamus, for example, is composed of a number of densely packed groups of nerve cells, that usually function as a collective entity. Each group of tightly clustered cells is termed a nucleus and is visually distinct from the surrounding matter. (Because each nerve cell, like virtually all

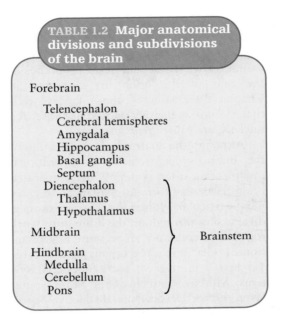

TABLE 1.2 Major anatomical divisions and subdivisions of the brain

Forebrain

    Telencephalon
        Cerebral hemispheres
        Amygdala
        Hippocampus
        Basal ganglia
        Septum
    Diencephalon
        Thalamus
        Hypothalamus

Midbrain

Hindbrain
    Medulla
    Cerebellum
    Pons

} Brainstem

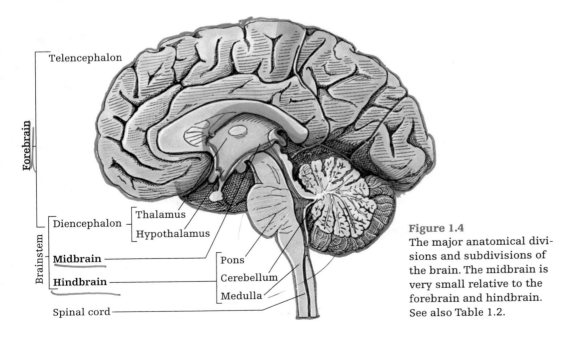

Telencephalon

Forebrain

Diencephalon — Thalamus / Hypothalamus

Brainstem

Midbrain

Hindbrain — Pons / Cerebellum / Medulla

Spinal cord

Figure 1.4
The major anatomical divisions and subdivisions of the brain. The midbrain is very small relative to the forebrain and hindbrain. See also Table 1.2.

other cells in the body, also has its own nucleus, this unfortunate dual use of the word "nucleus" could be confusing to the casual reader. These and other properties of the cells of the brain are discussed in Chapter 2.) Distinct groups of nerve cells that are not as densely packed as those in a nucleus, are called *fields* or *areas*.

Although the anatomical organization of the brain is hierarchical, its operational organization often is not. Widely separated brain parts may form an "alliance" to carry out particular functions. For example, diverse sites throughout the brain must work together to construct an accurate interpretation of what our sense organs detect. Table 1.3 lists a number of such functional systems. Moreover, much of the brain's outer layer, the cortex, develops distinctive operational units both in a horizontal and vertical direction. These horizontal layers and vertical columns, forming a sort of warp and woof pattern like a woven cloth, perform specific functions that will be discussed in appropriate chapters.

We started this chapter by claiming that the brain is the most complex living structure in the universe. You may, by now, have begun to agree. It is, however, as fascinating as it is complex. For this introduction, we will examine only the main structures listed in Table 1.2.

The Forebrain and Its Parts

As just noted, the forebrain structures, the *telencephalon* and the *diencephalon*, are generally credited with performance of the "highest" intellectual functions: thinking, planning, and problem solving.

The telencephalon When you first look at a brain, the most prominent structures are the two large, paired, left and right hemispheres

TABLE 1.3 Some functional brain systems	
System	Function

Sensory
  Receptors in skin, muscle
  Relay nuclei in spinal cord, thalamus
  Cortical areas
	Specific sensing operations
	  Vision
	  Hearing
	  Olfaction
	  Taste
	  Somatic sensation

Motor
  Muscle and spinal motor neurons
  Cerebellum, basal ganglis
  Motor cortex, thalamus, and cortex
	Specific motion components
	  Reflexes
	  Movement-pattern initiation and control
	  Complex movement of joints

Internal regulatory Hypothalamic nuclei and pituitary	Reproduction Appetite Salt and water balance
Behavioral state Medulla, pons, midbrain, and cortex	Sleeping, walking, attention

of the *cerebral cortex,* the brain's outermost layer (see Figure 1.5). The cortex of each hemisphere is subdivided into four sections, or *lobes,* by deep grooves that are called *sulci.* The lobes are named for their locations (see Figure 1.6 on the following page). The occipital lobe is responsible for vision; the temporal lobe for hearing and, in humans, speech as well as some memory and emotional functions; the parietal lobe for sensory responses; and the frontal lobe for motor control and coordination of the functions of the other cortical areas (that is, so-called executive functions, such as planning for tomorrow and next year).

Under the cortex lie the smaller regions of the telencephalon (see Figure 1.7 on pages 24 and 25): the *amygdala,* or amygdaloid complex (named for its nutlike shape; "amygdala" means "almond"), the hippocampus (shaped like a sea horse, which is what "hippocampus" means), the basal ganglia, and the septum (septum means "wall," which the septum forms between two of the brain's fluid-filled cavities, or ventricles). (See Figure 1.7.)

The amygdala, hippocampus, basal ganglia, and septum function together to help regulate emotion, memory, and certain aspects of movement. Together, they are sometimes called *the limbic system* because they are located around the limn or edge of the center of the brain

The diencephalon The subdivisions of the diencephalon are the thalamus and hypothalamus (see Figure 1.4). Both of these structures contain well-defined areas, fields, and nuclei. In the thalamus, these locations serve as relay stations for almost all the information coming into and out of the forebrain. In the hypothalamus are the relay stations for the internal regulatory systems, monitoring information from the autonomic nervous sys-

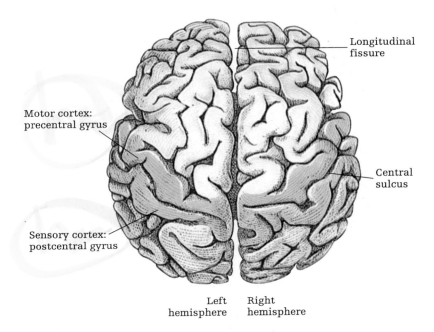

Figure 1.5 The hemispheres of the human cereberal cortex as viewed from above.

tem and commanding the body through those nerves and the hormones of the pituitary.

The Midbrain and Its Parts

The midbrain, named strictly for its location in the middle, is the smallest of the major brain divisions and has the most difficult boundaries to recognize when examining the brain. Some scientists believe that the hierarchy presented in Table 1.2 should be revised to denote the midbrain's small size and relative lack of distinctive features, but other scientists—purists, perhaps—refuse to consider annexing it to some nearby structure. Thus, it remains on its own, situated between the pons and the

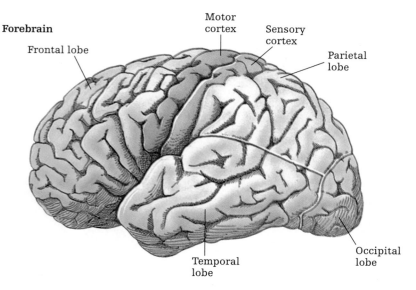

Forebrain

Frontal lobe

Motor cortex

Sensory cortex

Parietal lobe

Occipital lobe

Temporal lobe

Figure 1.6 One hemisphere of the cerebral cortex, showing the location of the four lobes into which it is divided. The divide between the motor cortex and the sensory cortex, the central sulcus, marks the boundary between the frontal and parietal lobes.

diencephalon (see Figure 1.4). On its upper surface are two pairs of small hills (colliculi), collections of cells that relay specific sensory information from sense organs to the brain. The two closest to the pons—the inferior colliculi—relay auditory information; and the two closest to the thalamus—the superior colliculi—relay visual information.

The Hindbrain and Its Parts

The major parts of the hindbrain are the *pons* (bridge), the *medulla oblongata* (often simply called the medulla), and the *cerebellum* (see Figure 1.4, purple area). The structures within the pons, medulla, and cerebellum generally interact with telencephalon structures by relays through the midbrain and the diencephalon, with some exceptions. The fields and nuclei of the pons and medulla, which control respiration and heart rhythms, are critical to

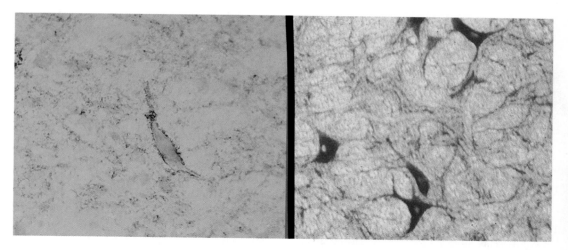

Large neurons in a part of the brainstem called the reticular formation, seen through a light microscope. In left micrograph, a large cell is outlined by almost continuous synaptic terminals at its surface. In right micrograph, several large neurons and their major dendrites appear, but the small axons, glia, dendrites, and synapses in the spaces between the cells cannot be seen.

survival. The cerebellum stores the basic repertoire of learned motor responses. Because the cerebellum is attached to the roof of the hindbrain, it is thought to receive and modify information related to body and limb position before that information makes its way to the thalamus and cortex. The hindbrain, midbrain, and diencephalon together are also called the brainstem. This "stem" contains almost all of the connections between the cerebral cortex and the spinal cord.

Two Basic Concepts of Neuroscience

We end this chapter by summarizing the main principles learned from neuroscience research in the past half-century, which constitute the foundation for the detailed discussions of the remainder of the book.

1. *The nervous system extends to and controls all parts of the body.* The nervous system is the organ of the body responsible for (a) sensing and reacting to the world around us; (b) coordinating the vital functions of all the other organs, eating, drinking, breathing, moving, and reproducing; and (c) storing, organizing, and retrieving past experiences.

2. *The separate functions of the nervous system are carried out by subsystems organized according to area of responsibility.* Each function of the brain—sensing, moving, and all of the regulatory activities—is a responsibility of a separate subsystem. The connections between the parts of the subsystems are specific and critical, and the resulting communication is most easily understood in terms

of a hierarchy. That is, as information is processed through the hierarchy, it travels from "lower" levels, such as structures in the peripheral nervous system and spinal cord, to "higher" levels, such as those in the cerebral cortex. The operations performed on each level can be identified because we know that the activity of one level causes activity in the next level and because some of the actual connections within certain subsystems have been located, but our current knowledge is inadequate to explain these operations in any detail.

The Journey Begins

We are about to begin an intellectual journey through the brain, an exploration of the basis for mind and behavior. At the journey's end, we will have seen that there is strong evidence for a biological basis for how we sense, think about, and react to the world around us. We will examine the basis for the different forms of memory and how the cells of our brains work together to achieve them. And, we will see that serious neurological and psychiatric diseases once attributed to possession by evil spirits are beginning to be characterized by specific scientific hypotheses. Now let us begin our exciting journey into the brain, mind, and behavior.

Key Terms

brain	spinal cord
mind	thalamus
sensation	hypothalamus

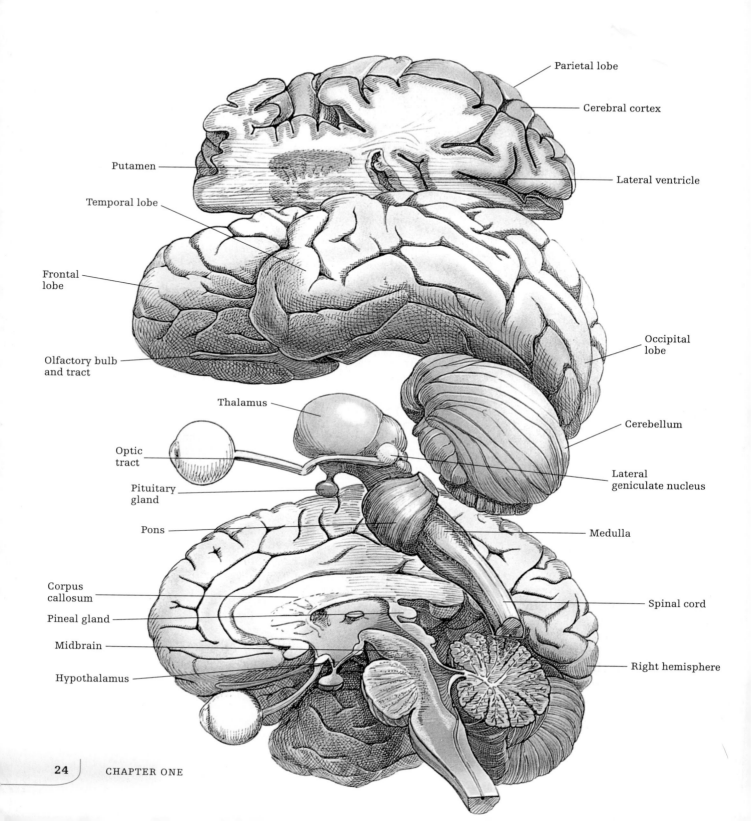

Parietal lobe

Cerebral cortex

Putamen

Lateral ventricle

Temporal lobe

Frontal
lobe

Occipital
lobe

Olfactory bulb
and tract

Thalamus

Cerebellum

Optic
tract

Lateral
geniculate nucleus

Pituitary
gland

Pons

Medulla

Corpus
callosum

Spinal cord

Pineal gland

Midbrain

Right hemisphere

Hypothalamus

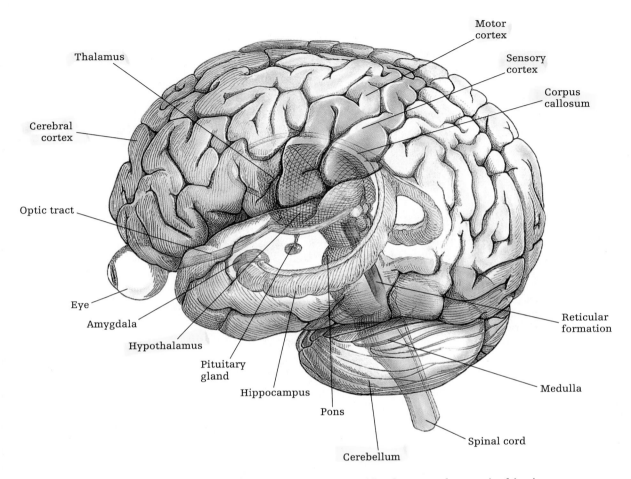

Thalamus

Motor cortex

Sensory cortex

Corpus callosum

Cerebral cortex

Optic tract

Eye

Amygdala

Hypothalamus

Pituitary gland

Hippocampus

Pons

Cerebellum

Reticular formation

Medulla

Spinal cord

Figure 1.7 *Facing page:* The major areas, regions, and some specific places can be seen in this view of a sliced and separated human brain. The left and right cerebral hemispheres and the entire set of structures lying along the midline have been bisected. The internal parts of the left hemibrain are shown as they would appear if dissected free. The eye and optic nerve are shown connected to the hypothalamic mass, from the lower surface of which the pituitary emerges. The pons, medulla, and spinal cord extend from its hind surface. The left side of the cerebellum appears below the left hemisphere, exposing the olfactory bulb. The upper half of the left cerebral hemisphere is also bisected, revealing parts of the basal ganglia (putamen) and a part of the left lateral ventricle. *This page:* The brain assembled, showing major structures active in sensing and internal regulation, as well as those in the limbic areas and brain stem.

motion   cerebellum
adaptation   pons
forebrain   medulla
midbrain   brain stem
hindbrain

Further Reading

Adelman, G., and Smith, B., Eds. 1999. *Encyclopedia of Neuroscience,* 3d ed. Elsevier, New York. An extensive and recently updated series of definitions, short essays, and thought pieces about the brains of organisms, simple and complex; available as a CD-ROM.

Frackowiak, R. S. J. 1997. *Human Brain Function.* Academic Press, San Diego. An excellent overview of the application of non-invasive imaging methods to inquire into the relations between specific brain regions and subsystems with brain activities.

Gazzaniga, M. S., et al. 1999. *The New Cognitive Neurosciences,* 2d ed. MIT Press, Cambridge, MA. A comprehensive book dealing with higher brain functions and their cellular, molecular, and systems operations.

Kandel, E R., Schwartz, J. H., and Jessell, T. M. 2000. *Principles of Neural Science,* 4th ed. Elsevier, New York. The latest edition of the first comprehensive textbook in the neurosciences, emphasizing the needs of medical students.

Shepherd, G. M. 1998. *The Synaptic Organization of the Brain,* 4th ed. Oxford University Press, New York. A masterful depiction of the details of cellular systems at the synaptic level of resolution, written simply enough for the entry-level student to follow.

Worden, F. G., Swazey, J. P., and Adelman, G., Eds. 1975. *The Neurosciences: Paths of Discovery.* MIT Press, Cambridge, MA. Recounts some of the seminal developments in the neurosciences in the twentieth century as they are recalled by the pioneers.

Zigmond, M. J., Bloom, F. E., Landis, S. C., Roberts, J. L., and Squire, L. R. 1998. *Fundamental Neuroscience.* Academic Press, San Diego. A comprehensive textbook written for the entry-level student of the brain sciences, with highly informative schematic depictions of current understanding.

Interactive Resources

The CD-ROM that accompanies this book offers various ways to visualize the material covered in this chapter. Its "Central Nervous System" module includes rotatable, three-dimensional views of several sections of the brain, the spinal cord, and various subcortical structures. In addition, its "Research Methods" module includes various CAT and MRI images of the brain, including a video clip of a coronal MRI scan.

To continue your study online, visit our Web site at www.worthpublishers.com/bloom. Click on "Chapter 1" for resources including practice quizzes, flash cards, simulations, links to related Web sites, and updates on new research.

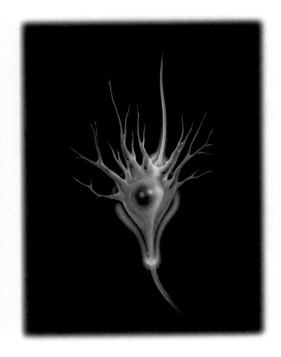

CHAPTER TWO

The Cellular and Chemical Machinery of the Brain

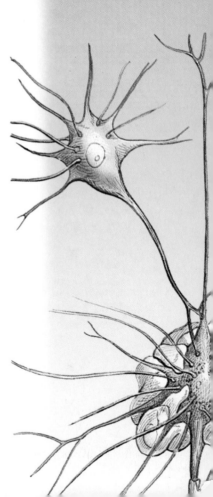

In the preceding chapter, we looked at the sequence of models that people have used over the centuries in attempting to understand and describe the workings of the human brain. It was proposed that the contemporary analogy for the brain's workings may be the computer. At first glance, computers and brains seem to have much in common—both have many very small components, both perform complicated feats that appear to require reasoning, and neither seems to have any moving parts. Just like us, the computer takes in information, processes it in some way, and serves it up in new forms.

Some computers appear to be more powerful than the human brain. A computer that handles very complicated mathematical problems and performs all the detailed calculations in the correct order can work on them all night without getting tired. When done, such a computer might inform us, for example, exactly what time a space shuttle will reenter the earth's atmosphere and, almost to the second, what time it will land back on earth. This computer, however, cannot protect itself against a power blackout, or laugh at a joke, or compose a poem about something it feels. Moreover, a computer's means of operating is extremely rigid, partly because it does not form the same kinds of memory associations that human beings do. If you need a screwdriver for a task and none is at hand, you will think of using a knife, a nail file, a comb, a letter opener, a spoon handle, a coin edge, and so on. These are creative association processes. It has so far proved to be almost impossible to design a computer program that employs ingenuity and imagination, yet humans can employ such reasoning even though we do not understand how we can form such nonsequential, nonlogical—but nevertheless useful—associations. So, like the earlier models for the brain's workings mentioned in Chapter 1, the computer analogy also has its shortcomings.

Perhaps the most telling argument against the computer–brain analogy is the fact that our brain sits atop and constantly interacts with a body—flesh and bone, guts and glands, eyes, ears, and nose. This body changes throughout the life span and even differs from moment to moment (see Chapter 3). Our brain and body create a history together. An odor experienced in childhood and suddenly reexperienced in middle age can cause our brain to call up a flood of memories—details of the place where the experience occurred, such as the quality of sunlight, the colors of a patterned carpet, the arrangement of furniture (see Chapter 9). We might recall how our skin felt against the fabric covering a chair that we were sitting on at the time. We usually remember the other people there, the quality of the emotional interaction taking place, and, most important, how we felt at that moment, whether our emotion was contentment or fear or anger.

Computers can have no such emotional history. If we are to accept the computer model of the brain's workings, it must be in

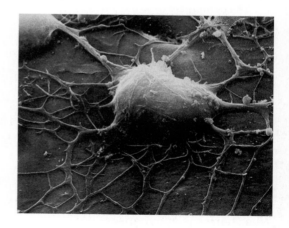

A human nerve cell. The axons that branch out of the cell carry electrical impulses to dendrites, which release chemical messengers to other cells (see Figure 2.4 on page 37 for details of neurotransmitter release).

a very limited way—perhaps at the level of logical reasoning, which is only a small part of what the human brain does.

To know how the brain works—and to understand the ways in which it surpasses the capacities of the most sophisticated of today's supercomputers—we must first gain an understanding of the different cells composing its intricate, dense web of tissue. Because certain of these cells generate chemical and electrical signals, we are able to think and feel and to recall how we thought and felt. These cells are the neurons.

Neurons

Unlike the cells of the liver, kidney, or other organs, individual nerve cells, or *neurons,* do not perform local functions in isolated units. The billions of neurons in the human nervous system "work" by receiving messages from and sending messages to other nerve cells. Sending cells and receiving cells are linked to each other in pathways called *circuits.* In this neuroscience sense, a circuit is composed of connected neurons in a precise, directionally oriented pathway over which the signals travel to link neuron A to neuron B. Neuronal circuits are roughly like the electrical circuits that link the appliances in your home to a central circuit box where the power company brings in the electricity. (See Figure 2.1 for an overview of a simple circuit whose components are considered elsewhere in this chapter.) Neuronal circuits differ from electrical circuits in that the former, usually, are one-way paths (from neuron A to neuron B), whereas, as you may know, the electricity in your house travels both into and out of the appliances that it powers. (Sometimes, neurons, too, connect to each other in such reciprocal circuits—from A to B and from B to A.) In general, a given neuron is connected to a

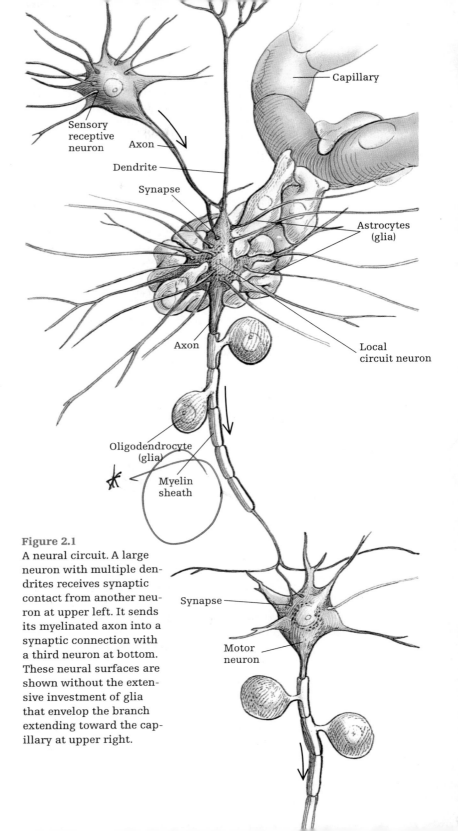

Figure 2.1
A neural circuit. A large neuron with multiple dendrites receives synaptic contact from another neuron at upper left. It sends its myelinated axon into a synaptic connection with a third neuron at bottom. These neural surfaces are shown without the extensive investment of glia that envelop the branch extending toward the capillary at upper right.

Capillary

Sensory receptive neuron

Axon

Dendrite

Synapse

Astrocytes (glia)

Axon

Local circuit neuron

Oligodendrocyte (glia)

Myelin sheath

Synapse

Motor neuron

rather limited number of other neurons from which it receives or to which it transmits information. However, in some cases, an individual neuron may transmit messages to as many as 10,000 other neurons. There are basically just a few patterns of neuronal circuits, with many minor variations (see Figure 2.2 for two of the three most prominent patterns). We will explore all these basic patterns later in the chapter.

The actual linking sites, the specific communication points on the surfaces of nerve cells, are called *synapses* (see Figure 2.1; also see Figure 2.4 on page 37), and the process of information transfer at such sites is called *synaptic transmission*. When neurons communicate through synaptic transmission, the sending cell secretes a chemical, called a *neurotransmitter*, which carries the message from the sending cell to the receiving cell. The chemical signal passes across the small space (about 20 nanometers, or 20 billionths of a meter) that separates even the most closely connected cells in the brain. This small space is often called the *synaptic gap*.

After looking at some of the cellular features of neurons, we will consider the transmission of neural messages further.

What Neurons Have in Common with Other Cells

Neurons have certain features in common with virtually every other cell in the human body. These common features are the plasma membrane; the cytoplasm and organelles within the neurons, glia, and other brain cells that conduct the processes that keep the

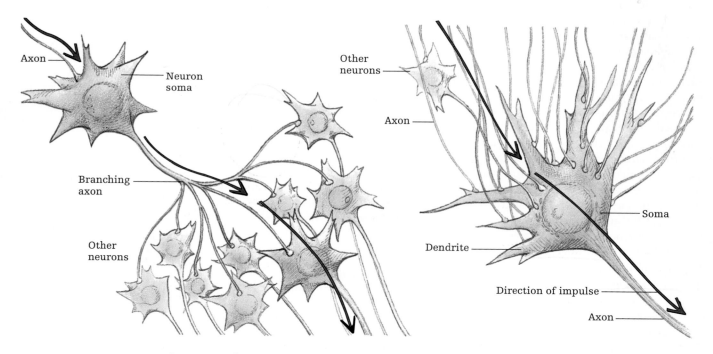

Figure 2.2 Schematic drawings of two of the most common types of neural circuitry. *Left:* A divergent circuit where one neuron, through branchings of its axon, sends its signal to many other neurons. *Right:* A convergent circuit, where one target neuron receives signals from many different neruons.

cell alive; and the cell's nucleus, where the genetic information is stored and consulted.

The Plasma Membrane Like all other cells, neurons have an external wall, or *plasma membrane*. This membrane surrounds the cell and forms a boundary between its interior and the external environment. When a neuron interacts with other neurons or senses changes in the local environment, it does so by means of the array of molecular machinery embedded in the plasma membrane.

The Cytoplasm and Organelles All the material enclosed by the plasma membrane is referred to as the *cytoplasm*. Within the cytoplasm are the *cytoplasmic organelles* (literally, little organs) that cells need to maintain themselves and do their work (see Figure 2.3 on the following page). The organelles include the mitochondria, microtubules, ribosomes, and endoplasmic reticulum. The *mitochondria* provide energy for the cell by converting sugar and oxygen into special energy-providing molecules. *Microtubules* are fine "struts" that help maintain the cell's structure.

The network of internal membrane channels by which the cell distributes the products that it needs to function is called the *endoplasmic reticulum*. Many cells, including neurons, produce some substances to be used within the cell and other substances to be exported for use outside the cell. The products to be secreted to the outside are manufactured by organelles called *ribosomes* that are attached to one kind of endoplasmic reticulum. Because it is studded with these ribosomes, this type of membrane channel is called the *rough endoplasmic reticulum*. The vast amounts of rough endoplasmic reticulum contained in the cytoplasm of neurons mark them as cells that are very active in making products for outside secretion (namely, neurotransmitters).

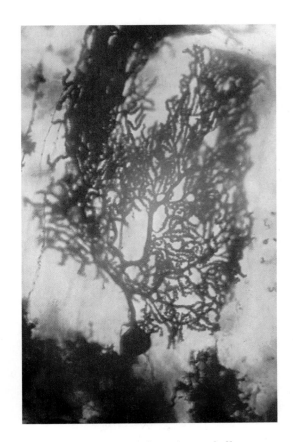

A Golgi-stained neuron from the cerebellar cortex of an adult rat. Subsequent to chemical exposure, this large Purkinje neuron has become totally impregnated with silver, giving it a near-black image that makes it stand out from the unstained cells around it. The elaborate dendritic system arising from the cell body is clearly seen.

Organelles composed of *smooth endoplasmic reticulum* package the products for outside secretion; these membrane-covered packets (generally called vesicles or "little bladders" in other parts of the body) are subsequently shipped to the surface of the cell (typically a glandular cell, such as the adrenal or the thyroid) at the point where the secretion takes place. In neurons, these packets are commonly called *synaptic*

Figure 2.3
The internal structure of a typical neuron. The microtubules provide structural rigidity as well as mechanisms for transport of materials synthesized in the cell body and destined for use in the synaptic zone at bottom. Within the synaptic terminal, synaptic vesicles storing the transmitter, along with vesicles that fulfill other functions in transmitter release and conservation, also appear. On the surface of the postsynaptic dendrite, the presumed location of the receptors for the transmitter are seen. (Figure 2.4 shows more detail.)

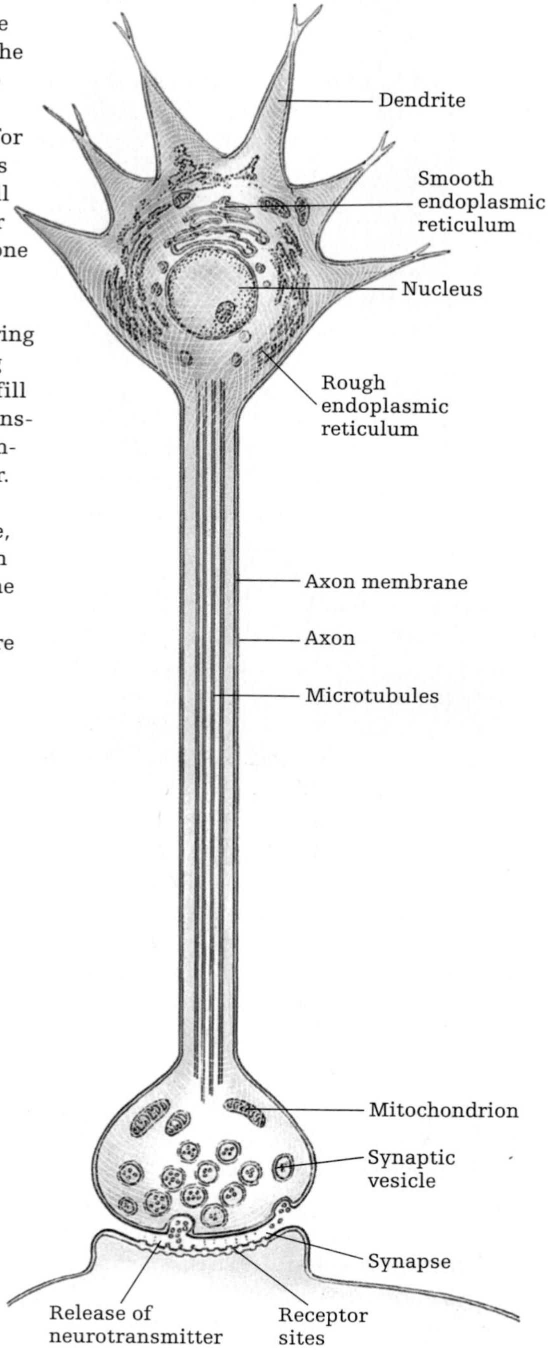

Dendrite

Smooth endoplasmic reticulum

Nucleus

Rough endoplasmic reticulum

Axon membrane

Axon

Microtubules

Mitochondrion

Synaptic vesicle

Synapse

Release of neurotransmitter

Receptor sites

vesicles. A specialized component of the smooth endoplasmic reticulum is called the *Golgi apparatus,* after the Italian Camillo Golgi, who first developed a method for staining this internal structure so that it could be studied under a microscope. It is prominent in all cells specialized for secretory activity.

Products for the cell's own use are synthesized in the numerous ribosomes that exist free within the cytoplasm, unattached to the endoplasmic reticulum.

The Nucleus At the center of the main body of the neuron is the cell's *nucleus.* Here, neurons, like all other nucleated cells, have their genetic information, coded within the chemical structures of genes. The genes carry the instructions that direct the fully developed cell in the making of products that establish the specific shape, chemistry, and function of the cell. Investigators are working to determine how genes are turned on and off at the correct times within each cell. Because mature neurons (unlike almost all the other cells of the body) are unable to divide to form new cells, the genetically specified instructions within any neuron must establish how it will maintain and modify the cell's function throughout its lifetime.

The Unique Features of Neurons

Most cells of the body look, more or less, like smooth spheres, cubes, or flat plates. In contrast, neurons have highly irregular shapes, with one or a few or many protrusions extending from their surfaces. These protruding structures—the axon and dendrites—are the living "wires" by which neurons are linked into neuronal circuits (see Figure 2.1).

The structure of individual neurons was first revealed when his rival, the Spanish microscopist Santiago Ramón y Cajal, insightfully applied another staining method developed by Golgi. This particular Golgi stain uses metallic silver, which binds to the microtubules; it gives stained cells a black color when light is shone through a thin section of the brain under a microscope (see figure on page 31). Before Ramón y Cajal's work proved otherwise, some observers, including Golgi himself, thought the brain was composed of giant multinucleated nets, in which the pool of cytoplasm was common and continuous. Using Golgi's staining method, even with the rather primitive microscopes of the day, Ramón y Cajal was able to establish the basic features of the cellular organization of the brain and to show that the complex structure of the brain is built from individual cells and their connections.

Axons and Dendrites Each nerve cell has one main protruding element called the *axon,* by means of which it sends information to the other neurons in its circuit. Some neurons communicate with more than one target cell, by means of an axon that branches many times to connect with each of the recipients. The branches are called *collateral axons.* Although a neuron may have many collateral axons, only one axon extends from the cell body. Oftentimes, one branch of the axon will loop back to establish circuits with neurons close to the neuron of origin. These special loops are called *recurrent collaterals.*

The other protruding elements of a neuron are called *dendrites,* from the Greek root *dendron,* or "tree," because their shape resembles the branching of a leafless tree. The dendrites protrude from the cell body, or *soma,* and both the dendrites and soma constitute the receiving zone for messages from other cells. The actual mechanisms for message reception lie on the outer surface of the plasma membrane covering the dendrites and soma. Here, incoming axons from other neurons make their synapses, establishing the links of multiple complete neuronal circuits (see Figure 2.1).

Neuronal Organelles The arrangement of organelles within the neuron differs from the relatively random arrangements in other cells: specific locations within the neuron contain different sets of organelles and different molecular products. Rough endoplasmic reticulum and free ribosomes are found only in the cytoplasm of the soma and dendrites, not in the axon. Because axons lack ribosomes and rough endoplasmic reticulum, they must rely on the soma for the manufacture of proteins needed for their function. Compartmentalization of organelles is much less pronounced in the neurons of invertebrate animals, where one generic neuronal extension may serve as both an axon and a dendrite.

Axons, on the other hand, contain the *synaptic vesicles,* not found in dendrites or the soma. The synaptic vesicles store the neurotransmitter molecules that the neuron secretes. Each vesicle is thought to contain thousands of the transmitter molecules (see Figure 2.3).

Both axons and dendrites contain large numbers of microtubules, functioning not only as structural reinforcement for helping the neuron maintain its shape, but also as avenues of transport along which substances may travel from the soma to the axon or dendrites and vice versa. For example, the molecules that are produced by the rough endoplasmic reticulum and packaged on the Golgi apparatus are transported by the microtubules to the ends of the axon. Such transport mechanisms are extremely important in cells whose axons may be hundreds of times as long as the cell body.

The Classification of Neurons

Because neurons come in such a variety of shapes and sizes, the early microscopists

Camillo Golgi (1844–1926). This photograph was taken in the early 1880s, when Golgi was a professor at the University of Padua. In 1906, Golgi and Ramón y Cajal shared the Nobel Prize in physiology and medicine.

Santiago Ramón y Cajal (1852–1934). A poet and artist as well as a histologist of enormous creativity, Ramón y Cajal taught chiefly at the University of Madrid. He made this self-portrait in the 1920s.

used these characteristics, along with a cell's location, to identify and name many types of neurons. But succeeding generations of scientists have used other criteria in typing them. As a result, the same neuron can be labeled in different ways, depending on the context of discussion. This can be confusing, but it is not very different from the way in which we identify ourselves or the people that we know. At various times we may refer to the same young woman as a student, a daughter, a sister, a redhead, a swimmer, a sweetheart, or a member of the Smith family. Neurons, too, have as many labels as they have properties and roles.

One way that scientists classify a neuron is by its task, or function. For example, nerve cells linked into circuits that help us sense the external world or monitor events within our bodies are described as *sensory* neurons. Neurons linked in circuits that produce movement of the body by causing muscles to contract are called *motor* neurons. The same neurons also have other defining features that are used to name them in other contexts. Biochemical features (Which neurotransmitter does a cell use at its synapses?) and morphological features (Is it large or small? Does it have a specific shape?) are two examples of such features.

The hierarchical position of the neuron in the chain of command that makes up the series of circuits in which it functions is another important criterion for classifying neurons. Neurons that are lowest in a hierarchy (closest to the event being sensed or the muscle being activated) are called *primary* or *level-1* sensory or motor neurons. Next in the chain come the *secondary,* or *level-2,* relay neurons ("relay" because they do not initiate signals but pass them along); then the *tertiary,* or *level-3,* relay neurons; and so on. We will employ these concepts when we consider the sensory and motor systems later.

An individual neuron, then, may be referred to by its discoverer (see the Purkinje neuron in Figure 2.2), its shape (such as a pyramidal cell), its specialized function (a sensory cell), its sequential location and function in a circuit (a level-2 relay neuron), or the neurotransmitter that it employs. This practice should give you no great trouble in the discussions that follow, especially now that you are aware of it. The most important point to remember is that, whatever their names may be, virtually all neurons do their work in the same way.

The Regulation of Neuronal Activity

Neurons do their main work, to receive and transmit impulses, by means of electrochemical energy. This energy is generated by the flow of charged chemical particles, or *ions,* through the neuron's membrane.

Readers who do not have a strong background in physics or chemistry might, at this point, want to read the accompanying box, "Some Basic Chemistry: What Is an Ion?" Those who feel ready to forge ahead will have an opportunity to test their chemical recall as we examine the process by which neurons can become active.

The Neuron at Rest

In the fluid that surrounds all cells of the body, positive and negative ions are distributed evenly in equal amounts, neutralizing each other's charges. The ions of sodium, potassium, calcium, and magnesium all have a positive charge; the ions of chloride, phosphate (a combination of phosphorus and oxygen), and certain more complex acids made by cells of carbon and oxygen all have

Some Basic Chemistry: What Is an Ion?

Atoms are composed of *protons* (positively charged particles), *neutrons* (particles with no charge), and *electrons* (negatively charged particles). The atom's *nucleus,* made up of protons and neutrons, is surrounded by electron clouds in specified energy paths, or *shells. Elements* are simple substances composed of identical atoms. Each element has a different characteristic number of protons in the nuclei of its atoms, identical with the number of electrons surrounding the nucleus, so that the atoms are electrically neutral.

Electrons are always arranged so that the shell closest to the nucleus contains 2 electrons; when there are more, the succeeding outer shells can each have only a specified number of electrons. The outermost shell contains the number of electrons left over after the inner shells have been filled. For sodium, which has 11 protons and 11 electrons, the outermost shell contains only 1 electron. Such atoms are highly reactive. Likewise, atoms in which only 1 electron is missing from an otherwise full outer shell also are highly reactive. Chlorine,

for example, containing 17 protons and 17 electrons, is missing just 1 electron from its outermost shell. The reactivity occurs because an atom with just 1 electron in its outer shell is eager to give it up, and an atom missing just 1 electron in its outer shell is eager to acquire one from another atom.

Sodium and chlorine combine to become sodium chloride (table salt). When they do so, the single electron in sodium's outer shell is given up to chlorine's outer shell. Both atoms then become *ions:* the sodium ion is positively charged, because it now contains 1 more proton than the number of electrons; the chlorine ion (called *chloride*) is negatively charged, because it now has 1 more electron than the number of protons. When sodium chloride is mixed in water and dissolves, the ions can separate (dissociate) and exist independently as charged particles while in solution. Many of the body's chemicals also exist in the body's fluids as ions. These positively and negatively charged particles play a major role in the conduction of neural impulses.

a negative charge. Ions of elements such as iron, copper, zinc, and sulfur also are present, though in much lower concentrations (and so are called "trace elements").

Most of the body's proteins are found within cells, including neurons, and are usually found in the form of ions that have a negative charge. As a result, the inside of the neuron (and other cells) is negatively charged, or *negatively polarized,* with respect to the outside. The relative deficiency of positively charged particles inside the cell

means that there is a strong electrical force trying to pull positively charged ions into the cell. However, the plasma membrane does not grant all of the outside substances equal access to the inside; so, in most cells and in inactive neurons, the negative polarity is maintained.

The plasma membrane's selectivity is possible because of the openings, or *channels,* along its length that are specialized to allow the passage of specific substances; there are channels for potassium, channels for sodium, and so forth. Most of these channels are normally closed unless they get a signal to open, so normally nothing passes through. Such channels are said to be "gated." At resting conditions, the gates for some ions, such as potassium, allow more flow through their channels than others, such as sodium, which can enter the cell only during periods of neuronal excitation (see Figure 2.4). Some channels have no gates and permit—from low to modest ion movements at all times.

Another biological mechanism that helps maintain the neuron's inner/outer polarity is the action of efficient ion pumps in the plasma membrane, which are powered by energy supplied by the mitochondria. These pumps exchange extracellular potassium ions for intracellular sodium ions. Although this exchange is electrically neutral, exchanging a positive ion for a positive ion, it does help in removing the excess sodium ions that enter during periods of excitation. Because the inside of the cell is relatively rich in potassium compared with the extracellular fluid and because potassium can move across the membrane much more readily than sodium, the net result is that more potassium tends to flow out spontaneously than can enter. This diffusion of potassium also helps keep the inside of the cell in a net negative state.

In sum, a neuron "at rest" exhibits a voltage difference across the membrane, the inside being negative relative to the outside. This voltage difference amounts to nearly a tenth of a volt, or about 5 percent as much electrical energy as that of a regular flashlight battery—a considerable amount of energy for such a tiny entity. This electrical state of the unstimulated neuron is often called its *resting potential*. The nonneuronal cells of the body are also negatively polarized, but often not so steeply as the neurons.

The Nerve Impulse

A neuron is stimulated to fire—to conduct an impulse—by receiving certain chemical signals at excitatory synapses (see Figures 2.4 and 2.5 on the following two pages). The immediate effect of such signals is to alter the electrical state inside the cell near the active synapse, making the area a bit more positive than it is in the normal resting state. This small shift toward the positive triggers the gates on sodium channels to open, and often on channels that admit calcium as well. The sodium and calcium ions outside an open channel rush in, pulled by the negative electrical force that still exists inside the neuron (even though it is more positive than it was, it remains negative relative to the outside).

The rush of sodium and other positive ions (calcium and potassium) into the cell during this excitation is so successful that the inside of the neuron near the channel becomes positively charged for a very brief time. This positive state causes the adjacent sodium channels to open, which causes the process to repeat over and over down to the end of the axon. Each such reversal of the neuron's interior electrical state from negative to positive is called an *action potential* or *depolarization*. The only other cells of the body that can undergo depolarizations are glandular cells, which can be triggered to secrete.

An action potential lasts less than 1/1000 of a second. It is so brief because the excitation response is self-correcting. During the increased inward flow of sodium and calcium ions, there is also an outward flow of potassium ions and a rapid automatic closing of the sodium and calcium channels in that vicinity. All three events help to restore the resting potential. Throughout the cycle of activity, the ion pumps also work continuously to maintain the low internal concentration of sodium.

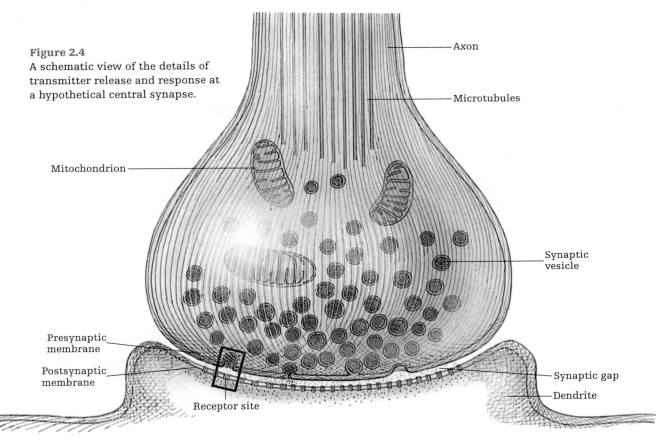

Figure 2.4
A schematic view of the details of transmitter release and response at a hypothetical central synapse.

Axon

Microtubules

Mitochondrion

Synaptic vesicle

Presynaptic membrane

Postsynaptic membrane

Receptor site

Synaptic gap

Dendrite

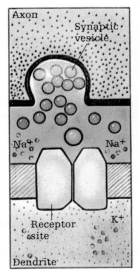

Synaptic vesicle releases neurotransmitter.

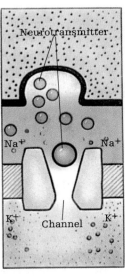

Neurotransmitter on receptor site. Channel opens.

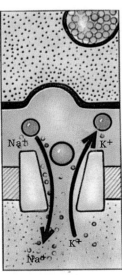

The flow of sodium ions (Na^+) and potassium ions (K^+)

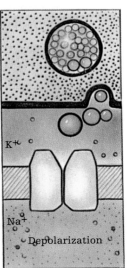

Reuptake of neurotransmitter by presynaptic neuron.

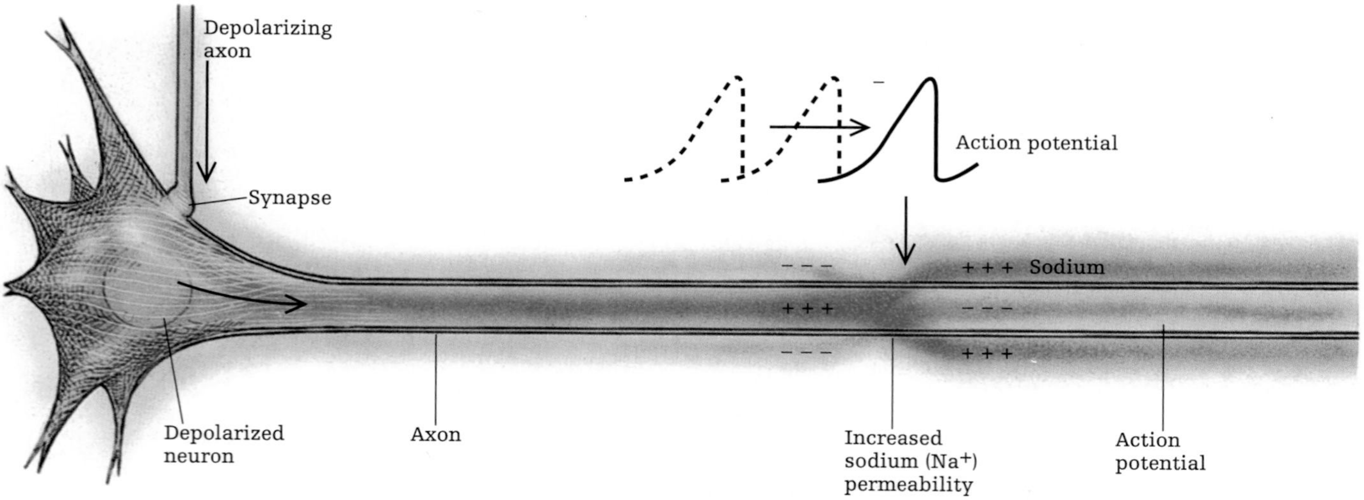

Figure 2.5 When a neuron is activated by an incoming excitatory synaptic connection, the wave of depolarization temporarily reverses the internal negativity of the resting potential. As the wave of depolarization moves down the axon, progressive segments of the axon also undergo this transient reversal. The action potential can be recorded as the positively charged sodium ions (Na^+) flow from the extracellular fluid into the excited, depolarized surfaces of the neuronal membrane.

The succession of action potentials down the axon ensures that the signal maintains its strength the whole way, no matter how long an axon is. When an action potential reaches the synaptic terminals of the axon, it triggers the release of a chemical neurotransmitter, which crosses the synapse and binds to the receptors of its target neuron where, if the signal is excitatory, the process begins again.

The Inhibition of Nerve Impulses

Whereas some neurotransmitters signal neurons to fire, others signal them to hold their fire—that is, to inhibit their firing (see Figure 2.6). The chemical signal passed at inhibitory synapses acts by making the voltage inside the neuron even more negative than it is during its resting state. A common way to accomplish this increased negativity is by triggering the membrane to open, briefly, some channels that allow the inflow of chloride ions. Because these ions have negative charges, they make the inside of the neuron even more negative relative to the outside, so the neuron cannot fire in spite of concurrent ongoing activity at nearby excitatory synapses. Whether a synapse is excitatory or inhibitory depends on the transmitter that the synapse uses and on the nature of the receptor on the receiving cells. A given synapse will be either excitatory or inhibitory in this sense.

How Neurons Communicate

When people speak to one another, they use words to convey the basic content of their communication, adding subtle emphasis and additional meaning by tone of voice, facial expression, and hand and body movements. When nerve cells communicate, their specific chemical messengers, the *synaptic neurotransmitters,* act as the basic conveyors of content. (A given neuron uses the same transmitters for all of its synapses.)

Whereas verbal communication—conversation—is usually a two-way interaction, information at synapses is transmitted in one direction only—from the axon terminals of the sending neuron across the synapse to the receptive surfaces of the receiving neuron. To understand this transmission, which is perhaps the most important of all the steps considered so far, we need to take a closer look at the many events that take place in the synapse and at the kinds of signals that different synapses can generate.

What Happens at Synapses

The neuron sending a message across a synapse is called the *presynaptic* neuron, and the message's recipient is the *postsynaptic* neuron. When the action potential has flowed down the neuron to the end of the axon, the presynaptic neuron releases its neurotransmitter into the synaptic gap. The neurotransmitter has been stored in the synaptic vesicles, and these vesicles find their way to the outer membrane of the axon terminal, fuse with it momentarily, and open, releasing their transmitter molecules into the synapse (see Figure 2.4).

The transmitter molecules diffuse across the gap and encounter receptors to which they can bind on the postsynaptic membrane. Evidently, the transmitter molecules have shapes that lock onto the shapes of the special receptor protein molecules embedded in the postsynaptic membrane, much as pieces of a jigsaw puzzle fit together.

More transmitter molecules may be released than the number of binding sites

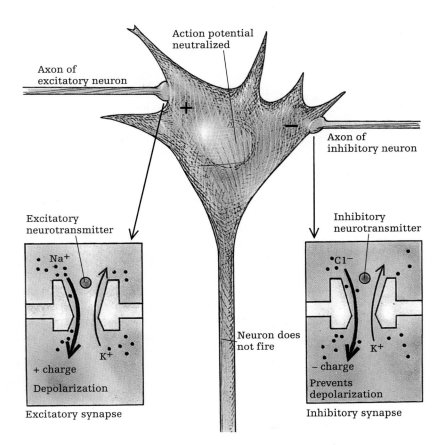

Figure 2.6 The contrasting effects of excitatory *(left)* and inhibitory *(right)* transmitters can be illustrated by the different combinations of ion channels that each type of transmitter influences (Na^+, sodium ions; K^+, potassium ions).

available. This excess transmitter is removed immediately. Sometimes it is destroyed by a special enzyme released from the membrane of the postsynaptic neuron. Sometimes the presynaptic neuron will, thriftily, draw the excess back into its cytoplasm and repackage it into synaptic vesicles. The process, seen in Figure 2.4, is called *reuptake.*

The amount of transmitter released, however, is monitored by the presynaptic neuron. At its synaptic terminals, a neuron also has receptors for its own neurotransmitter, called *autoreceptors,* to provide feedback about the amount of transmitter in the synapse. With this information, the neuron can regulate its production and release of the transmitter. Under periods of extreme activity, the information may go all the way back to the nucleus and activate the genes needed to make the enzymes that will make the transmitter.

Generally speaking, there are only two functional categories of synaptic messages: (1) *excitatory* (depolarizing), in which one cell incites another to act, and (2) *inhibitory,* in which the recipient cell is prevented from firing. Some nerve cells are kept generally silent under a steady barrage of inhibitory commands except when the occasional excitatory transmission stimulates them to become active. For example, the nerve cells in your spinal cord that spur your muscles into activity in order for you to walk or dance are generally silent until excited by impulses from the cells of the motor cortex. Other nerve cells receive constant spontaneous excitatory commands that keep them active without the brain's conscious involvement. For example, the nerve cells that move your chest and diaphragm in the act of breathing respond to other nerve cells "higher" in the chain of command that are activated by the levels of oxygen and carbon dioxide in your blood.

To Fire or Not to Fire

A postsynaptic neuron receiving an excitatory chemical message from another neuron might or might not fire in response to the message. (The same is true for inhibitory messages, but, for ease of discussion here, we will use only excitatory commands as our example.) The incoming signals must reach a certain threshold of strength before the post-synaptic neuron is triggered to fire. One factor in determining the threshold for firing is the amount of neurotransmitter released onto the receiving neuron. A single release from a presynaptic neuron may not be enough to change the receiving cell's resting potential to an action potential.

Often, a summation of many impulses is required to produce the necessary change in potential. This summation can occur in two ways. First, a sending neuron can fire a number of times in rapid succession, so transmitter accumulates in the gap faster than the mechanisms for removing it can work. Second, because a neuron usually receives synapses from many neurons, it may pass the threshold for firing when a number of these other cells fire simultaneously; their combined convergent action then produces enough of a signal to depolarize the postsynaptic neuron.

Conditional Messages

Current knowledge suggests that the major interactions within the circuits of the brain are largely explainable by these "excite" or "inhibit" types of synaptic transmitter messages. However, more complex modifying messages also come into play, and they are important because they enhance or diminish the intensity with which a recipient cell responds to other messages from different sending cells.

We will not consider these mechanisms in detail here but will merely describe such modifying transmitter messages as being *conditional.* By conditional, we mean that recipient cells respond to them only under certain conditions—that is, when these transmitters arrive at their receptors simultaneously with other major excitatory or inhibitory signals coming from other circuits. In a musical analogy, the foot pedals on a piano can be considered conditional in that, to have any effect, their action must coexist with another action. The mere pressing of a foot pedal without striking a note has no value. It modifies the sound of a note only when that note is struck.

Many of the neuronal circuits that are subject to conditional messengers are those whose neurotransmitters seem to be affected in pharmacological treatments for depression, schizophrenia, and certain other brain diseases (a topic that is discussed at more length in Chapter 12). In anticipation of that discussion, we may note that the drugs appear to achieve their beneficial effects in one of two ways. One way is to enhance the potency of the natural transmitter by (1) simulating its ability to activate its receptors, (2) causing more of it to be released at its synapses, or (3) prolonging the actions of the transmitter after its release (for example, by blocking reuptake or slowing the natural destruction of the transmitter). The second way is to reduce the effectiveness of the transmitter at its receptor by antagonizing its ability to bind there; such drugs are called *antagonists*.

The Modifiability of Neuronal Function

So far we have seen that a neuron must successfully meet certain basic requirements to function properly as a member of a specific circuit. It must make the transmitter substance(s) needed to pass along neuronal messages. It must possess the surface receptors suitable to receive incoming transmitter signals. It must have adequate supplies of energy for transporting excess ions back across the membrane. Neurons with long branching axons to support must also transport enzymes, transmitters, and other molecules from the synthesis sites in the central cytoplasm to the distant dendritic and axonal

spots where they are needed. Generally, the rate at which a neuron performs its functions depends on the mass of its dendritic and axonal systems and its overall rate of metabolic activity. (Metabolism is the term for the series of chemical reactions by which the cell extracts energy from nutrients to fuel its enzymes and pumps.)

On the other hand, the cell's metabolic activity varies in response to the demands of interneuronal traffic. The nerve cell can increase its capacity to synthesize and transport specific molecules during periods of high neuronal activity (see Figure 2.7 on the following page). Likewise, a neuron can turn down its level of function when it is underutilized, as might occur with certain disease conditions. This ability to modify fundamental intracellular processes gives the neuron the flexibility to manage its responsibilities at widely different activity levels. However, as a disease state takes hold, the neurons require external help to adapt in full.

Synaptic Transmitters

The general categories and characteristics of the major neurotransmitters are important to know not only because of their vital functions in the normal working brain, but also because their absence or excess may play a major role in brain disease and behavioral disorders. As we have already observed, the brain's reaction to many drugs can be traced to the synaptic transmission process. Some of these drugs can be used to treat a diseased nervous system, although they may wreak havoc on an otherwise normal nervous system.

All known synaptic neurotransmitters in the human nervous system produce one or another of the firing conditions described in the preceding sections: their signal either

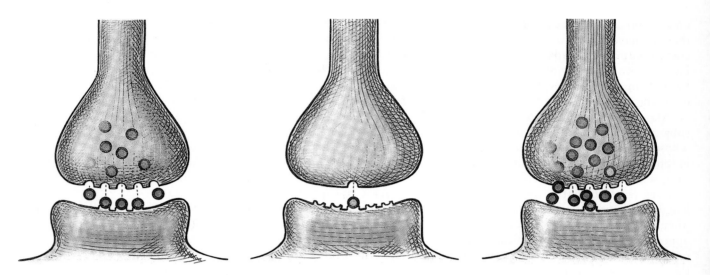

Figure 2.7 Schematic illustration of the adaptive regulatory processes that are used to maintain normal synaptic transmission despite changes, induced by drugs or possibly by disease, in the amounts of transmitter available for release or response. *Left:* The normal condition. *Center:* Transmitter synthesis or storage is deficient, and the postsynaptic cell increases the number of receptors. *Right:* Transmitter content and release are enhanced, and the postsynaptic cell decreases the number and effectiveness of its receptors.

(1) excites receiving cells, causing them to fire, or (2) inhibits them from firing or (3) modifies the excitability of the receiving cell. The major transmitters introduced here are grouped on the basis of the chemical structure of their molecules. Their normal roles in the brain and their influence on behavior will be described at greater length in subsequent chapters.

Amino Acid Transmitters

The simplest transmitters in regard to chemical structure are the amino acids that act as transmitters (see Figure 2.8). The amino acids are the building blocks of proteins, but, as we will see, they have other uses in neurons. The main amino acids that have been identified as neurotransmitters are *glu-*

tamate and *aspartate,* which act as excitatory signals, and *glycine* and *gamma-aminobutyric acid* (commonly called GABA), which act as inhibitory transmitters. These simple amino acid transmitters probably account for the vast majority of transmission signals in the brain. Drugs that are able to produce convulsions, such as strychnine, act by inhibiting neurons' responses to glycine or GABA. That is, the drug blocks the receptors for glycine or GABA and thus prevents the target cells from recognizing the inhibitory messages, allowing concurrent excitations to overwhelm the brain.

Monoamine Transmitters

The monoamine transmitters are slightly more complicated chemically than the amino

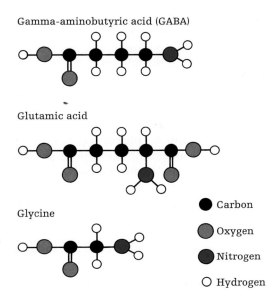

Figure 2.8 The molecular composition of some amino acid transmitters.

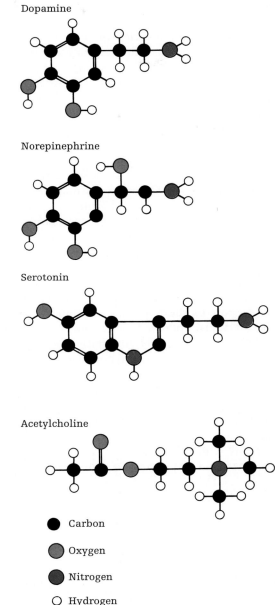

acid transmitters (see Figure 2.9). Their name, monoamine, is based on their chemical structure, in which there is one nitrogen-containing amine group (typically, –NH$_2$). Neurons themselves synthesize these monoamines from amino acids by using enzymes present only in these neurons to make the modifications. Monoamine signals are used much less commonly in the brain than amino acid signals, with perhaps 1 monoamine-using synapse for every 1000 amino acid–mediated synapses. Still, these signals are vital to human neurological well-being. The major monoamine transmitters are dopamine, norepinephrine, epinephrine, and serotonin. The transmitter acetylcholine also is included in this category, although it has a slightly different form of amine. A related molecule, histamine, has similar behavior but possesses two amine groups (making it a diamine).

Figure 2.9 The molecular composition of some monoamine transmitters. Neurons themselves manufacture these transmitters from amino acids.

Acetylcholine *Acetylcholine* is the transmitter that signals your muscles to contract, both the skeletal muscles that allow you to move and the smooth muscles that control some of your hollow organs, such as your stomach. Acetylcholine is historically important because it was the first chemical transmitter to be identified, in 1921. Credit goes to the Austrian scientist Otto Loewi, who with other scientists discovered acetylcholine's ability to perfectly imitate the action of the nerves that can cause the heartbeat to slow down. *Curare,* a poison used by South American hunters and sometimes used during surgical procedures, produces paralysis by preventing acetylcholine from exciting the muscles.

In the brain, there are two large clusters of neurons that use acetylcholine as their transmitter. One cluster is located in the upper part of the midbrain and innervates the thalamus, brain stem, and some parts of the hypothalamus. The other large cluster is located in the anterior hypothalamus and within the ventral septum and provides the cholinergic innervation of the cortex, the hippocampus, and the olfactory bulbs. Acetylcholine neurons of this forebrain cluster are among the neurons to die in the brains of patients with Alzheimer's disease, a disease characterized by progressive deterioration of cognitive functions such as recent memory, directions, and faces (see Chapter 12).

Dopamine, Norepinephrine, and Epinephrine *Dopamine, norepinephrine,* and *epinephrine* are all synthesized from the amino acid tyrosine. Because of the similarity of their chemical structures, with two hydroxyl groups on a benzene ring, they are often referred to collectively as the *catecholamines.*

Each of these transmitters is found in distinct groups of neurons that in the case of dopamine and norepinephrine are limited to a small number of users and pathways. Neurons containing dopamine, for example, are found in dense clusters concentrated in certain regions of the midbrain (the substantia nigra and ventral tegmentum). Likewise, many of the norepinephrine-containing cells in the brain are concentrated in a pair of small clusters (called the locus coeruleus) in the pons. In contrast, the clusters of neurons containing epinephrine are more loosely scattered throughout the medulla. Norepinephrine and epinephrine are also found in cells of the adrenal glands and in the nerves of the sympathetic division of the autonomic nervous system.

Dopamine-mediated circuits are thought to play a role in regulating emotional responses. Other dopamine-mediated circuits are necessary for the control of complex movements. (The brains of people with Parkinson's disease, whose victims suffer from muscle tremors and rigidity and have great difficulty in moving, contain almost no dopamine.) Norepinephrine seems to be necessary for emotional arousal, for attributing a rewarding value to a stimulus, and for regulation of sleep and mood. The quality of the actions of both these transmitters on their synaptic partners suggests that they produce conditional or modulating effects, enhancing the activities of other transmitter messages arriving at the same postsynaptic neurons. The stimulant drugs *cocaine* and *amphetamine* produce their excitant actions on the brain by releasing norepinephrine and dopamine from their synaptic vesicle storage points. Some antidepressant drugs and many blood pressure–regulating drugs act at receptors for norepinephrine and dopamine. Not much is known about the role of epinephrine as a transmitter in the brain, but its location suggests that it may play a part in the way in which the brain helps to regulate blood pressure.

Serotonin Neurons using serotonin as a transmitter are found only in the brain, most of them in a concentrated cluster of cells (called the raphe nuclei) in the pons. This transmitter is thought to function in temperature regulation, sensory perception, and the onset of sleep. The serotonin receptors are the sites at which the hallucinogenic drug LSD acts, as do certain antidepressant drugs. Some of the drugs most commonly used to treat severe depression act at serotonin or norepinephrine synapses to prevent the normal reuptake of these transmitters into the terminals that secreted them.

Peptides and Other Potential Transmitters

Peptides are chains of two or more amino acids linked in a special head-to-foot arrangement like the cars of a train (see Figure 2.10 on the following page). The possibility, and then the proof, that some peptides act as neurotransmitters has attracted considerable interest from researchers in the past 30 years. Recently, neuropharmacologists have been attempting to devise new medications to enhance or antagonize the actions of peptides in neurological disorders. Rapid advances in the understanding of gene structure and gene expression, as well as in the ability to determine the composition of peptides from exceedingly small samples and then to synthesize antagonists for the peptides' receptors, have sped this work along.

Peptide-mediated signals are not exclusive to nerve cells. For example, peptide hormones are secreted by the cells of the pituitary as well as other endocrine glands (see Chapter 6) and within the immune system. In fact, their role as neurotransmitters has been intensively debated. Part of this debate centers on the fact that, though peptides appear to be quite potent, they are present in very low concentrations in the nervous system compared with the amino acid and monoamine neurotransmitters. Another issue is that the peptide-producing neurons have in almost all cases been found to produce an amino acid or monoamine transmitter as well, and, as stated earlier, neurons have generally been thought to utilize only one transmitter. If the peptide does function as a second signal, however, perhaps its purpose is to modulate the effectiveness of the amino acid or monoamine produced by the same neuron. Many scientists take the view that peptides represent a very primitive form of interneuronal signaling.

As more and more peptides are identified within the nervous system and from other tissues, their internal structural similarities (that is, similarities in the order of the amino acids in parts of the peptides' sequences) allow scientists to group them into families of peptides. The family groupings allow useful comparisons. They indicate that certain sequences of amino acids have been highly "conserved" in the course of evolution (that is, they have remained unchanged in spite of other evolutionary changes over long periods of time), presumably because they provide unambiguous signals between secreting and responding cells. There are five major peptide families: (1) oxytocin and vasopressin; (2) the tachykinins; (3) the glucagon-related peptides (such as vasoactive intestinal polypeptide in the brain and glucagon in the pancreas); (4) pancreatic polypeptide-related peptides (with neuropeptide Y the most prominent of all neuropeptides in the brain); and (5) the opioid peptides. Three of these peptide families have been so extensively studied that they merit slightly more detailed descriptions.

Vasopressin and Oxytocin The first well-studied neuropeptides were *vasopressin* and *oxytocin*, two closely related nonapeptides

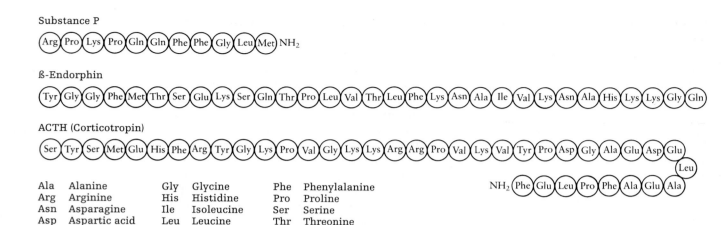

Substance P
Arg–Pro–Lys–Pro–Gln–Gln–Phe–Phe–Gly–Leu–Met NH₂

ß-Endorphin
Tyr–Gly–Gly–Phe–Met–Thr–Ser–Glu–Lys–Ser–Gln–Thr–Pro–Leu–Val–Thr–Leu–Phe–Lys–Asn–Ala–Ile–Val–Lys–Asn–Ala–His–Lys–Lys–Gly–Gln

ACTH (Corticotropin)
Ser–Tyr–Ser–Met–Glu–His–Phe–Arg–Tyr–Gly–Lys–Pro–Val–Gly–Lys–Lys–Arg–Arg–Pro–Val–Lys–Val–Tyr–Pro–Asp–Gly–Ala–Glu–Asp–Glu–Leu
NH₂–Phe–Glu–Leu–Pro–Phe–Ala–Glu–Ala

Ala	Alanine	Gly	Glycine	Phe	Phenylalanine
Arg	Arginine	His	Histidine	Pro	Proline
Asn	Asparagine	Ile	Isoleucine	Ser	Serine
Asp	Aspartic acid	Leu	Leucine	Thr	Threonine
Gln	Glutamine	Lys	Lysine	Tyr	Tyrosine
Glu	Glutamic acid	Met	Methionine	Val	Valine

Figure 2.10 Some common peptides known to act as transmitters. Note the trainlike composition of amino acids linked in a head-to-foot arangement.

(that is, peptides with nine amino acids), each having seven identical amino acids in the same exact order. Both peptides are synthesized in separated clusters of large neurons in the hypothalamus. The axons of these neurons form the neural lobe of the pituitary, also called the *neurohypophysis* or the posterior pituitary. The significance of this structure is the ability of its neurons to directly release their peptides into the bloodstream. In the kidney, vasopressin (also known as *antidiuretic hormone*) facilitates water retention. Vasopressin can also act synergistically with corticotropin-releasing hormone to release the anterior pituitary hormone that controls the stress response (see Chapter 6). Oxytocin stimulates uterine muscle contraction at the end of pregnancy and triggers the milk-ejection reflex when mothers suckle their newborns.

The Tachykinin Peptides In 1931, the Swedish neurochemists Ulf von Euler and John Gaddum discovered an unexpected bioactive substance in extracts of brain and intestine; they named it *substance P* because of its "pressor" (vasoconstrictive) actions. Only after another 40 years were chemical methods developed capable of demonstrating that substance P was an 11 amino acid peptide. Substance P is present in small neuron systems in many parts of the CNS, especially sensory neurons projecting into the spinal cord from the dorsal root ganglia, and has been proposed as the transmitter for nerve fibers bringing sensory information on painful stimuli into the spinal cord (afferent sensory fibers). Brain regions rich in substance P include the midbrain, basal ganglia, hypothalamus, and cerebral cortex. In the human neurologic disease known as Huntington's disease, characterized by severe movement disorders and psychological changes, substance P levels in the substantia nigra are considerably reduced. Recently, novel drugs that can antagonize the effects of substance P have been reported to act as antidepressants. Substance P is now recognized to be a member of a larger family of structurally similar peptides called the *tachykinin* (fast-acting) *peptides*. The peptides in this family (see Figure 2.11) have many common amino acid sequences.

Opioid Peptides As the techniques for collecting and analyzing pure samples of biological substances became increasingly refined, intensive research in the late 1970s quickly led to the purification, isolation, amino acid sequencing, and synthetic replication of not just one but nearly a half-dozen peptides that deserved the term endogenous morphine, or *endorphin*. These peptides are considered a family because they all contain at least one repeat of one or another of two key pentapeptide (five amino acids) sequences: tyrosine-glycine-glycine-phenylalanine-methionine (Met^5-enkephalin) or tyrosine-glycine-glycine-phenylalanine-leucine (Leu^5-enkephalin). Subsequent research has established that there are at least three major genes and three quite dissimilar groups of neurons using these opioid peptides; for example, Met^5-enkephalin and Leu^5-enkephalin are expressed in quite distinct populations of central and autonomic neurons and are much more numerous than those of the other two opioid peptide genes [known to the experts as the *pro-opiomelanocortin* (or *POMC*) gene and the *prodynorphin* gene]. Neurons containing different opioid peptides have been found to be interconnected in some cases (for example, enkephalin-containing neurons project from the entorhinal cortex to the molecular layer of the dentate gyrus of the hippocampus, and dynorphin-containing neurons project from the dentate gyrus to hippocampal pyramidal cells). Neuroscientists are interested in these opioid peptides primarily because they are potential sources of insight in understanding opiate addiction and in developing nonaddictive pain medications.

Other Neurotransmitters The amino acid monoamine and peptide transmitters may not be the only kinds of molecules able to transmit information from one neuron to another. However, the other potential neurotransmitters remain much more controversial. Some evidence supports the existence of very short distance signals mediated by enzymatically formed gases such as nitric oxide, carbon monoxide, and hydrogen sulfide. There is also evidence that fatty acids with a special nitrogen-containing appendix (compounds called *anandamides*) may be among the still-unidentified transmitters whose receptors provide the sites where marijuana produces its effects.

The Tachykinin Peptide Family

Substance P	R	P	K	P	Q	Q	F	F	G	L	M'
Kassinin	D	V	P	K	S	D	Q	F	V	G	L	M'
Neurokinin A		H	K	T	D	S	F	V	G	L	M'
Eledoisin	pE	P	S	K	D	A	F	I	G	L	M'
Neurokinin B		D	M	H	D	F	F	V	G	L	M'

Figure 2.11 A family of neuropeptides shares many amino acids at exactly the same relative positions in their peptide sequences. Note the identical positions of the lysines (K), phenylalanines (F), and the triplets of glycine, leucine, and amidated methionine (GLM*) at the right sides (or C-termini) of these peptides.

Categories of Neurotransmitter Receptors

Extensive research with the use of molecular cloning methods has led to the complete description of the genes that encode virtually every receptor for each of the neurotransmitters heretofore discussed—the amino acids, monoamines, and peptides. From these molecular characterizations, neuroscientists have drawn two important general conclusions:

1. All neurotransmitters bind and act at more than one kind of receptor. For example, serotonin may have more than eight distinct receptors, each with its own unique mode of responding to this transmitter to influence the postsynaptic neurons and each with its own unique pattern of circuits expressing these receptors. GABA and glutamate probably have even more than eight distinct kinds of receptor molecules, and they have many modes of responding.

2. Despite the large number of neurotransmitter chemicals and the even larger number of receptor molecules used by each of them, when the molecular structures of these receptors were established, all of the receptors could be separated into one or the other of two distinct structural patterns (scientists call them *structural motifs*).

One category of receptor is both an ion channel and a receptor and is always composed of either four or five subunits embedded as a unified assemblage in the neuronal membrane. Additional similarities between these receptors have been found in the structures of the subunits, each of which appears to be threaded back and forth across the plasma membrane four times and, like the peptides, to belong to families that have many of the same amino acid sequences in common. As already noted, such similarities suggest that over evolutionary time a basic set of building blocks (in this case, for receptors) was permitted extensive customization. The majority of the receptors for glutamate and GABA, about half of the receptors for acetylcholine (the ones termed nicotinic), and one of the serotonin receptors all belong to this *ion-channel receptor* category. This type of transmitter receptor generates rapid and brief changes in neuronal excitability by changing the membrane's permeability to ions that will excite or inhibit the postsynaptic neuron.

The other major category of receptor also has a very consistent structural motif: all its members consist of a single protein with, apparently, seven transmembrane domains (seven loops back and forth through the membrane). When activated by their transmitters, these receptors work indirectly to change the excitability of their neurons, either by changing calcium ion levels inside the neuron or by activating so-called intracellular second messengers. *Second-messenger molecules* work inside the cell to execute the "command" of the triggering neurotransmitter molecule bound to the outside of the cell. Second messengers include substances such as cyclic adenosine monophosphate (cAMP) and powerful lipid signals such as inositol triphosphate (see Figure 2.12). Receptors of this type activate the synthesis of the second messengers through a complex protein intermediate called a *G-protein,* and for this reason the entire class of receptors is sometimes called *G-protein–coupled receptors.* Such receptors are used by a few of the glutamate and GABA receptors, all of the catecholamine receptors, the rest of the acetylcholine receptors, all the other serotonin receptors, and all of the neuropeptide receptors. A few of the glutamate and GABA receptors are also G-protein–coupled receptors. The advantage of this structural motif is its use of an enzymatic process inside the receiving cell as an efficient way to amplify and extend the cell's response to the transmitter.

Patterns of Neuronal Circuitry

Three patterns of neuronal circuitry appear frequently in the brain's architecture: hierarchical-chain circuits, local-circuit neurons, and single-source–divergent circuits. The billions of neuronal circuits in the human brain can in large measure be simplified schematically so as to illustrate all three types of circuits by using just nine cells (Figure 2.13 on the following page). Although the number of neurons in these circuits varies, the three patterns are found reliably enough to make a useful classification scheme.

Hierarchical Circuits

The most common type of interneuronal circuitry, the hierarchical circuit, is found in the major sensory and motor pathways. In sensory systems, the hierarchy is an ordered chain of neurons through which information *ascends* from the external environment or from inside the body into the nervous system: primary receptors to secondary relays, to tertiary relays, and so on. The incoming sensory information enters and is then passed on "up" to where the information can be sorted, compared, and attended to. In contrast, motor systems are organized in a *descending* hierarchy in which commands come "down" out of the nervous system to the muscles: cells figuratively "on high" in the motor system "speak" to specific motor cells in the spinal cord that, in turn, speak to specific sets of muscles.

Hierarchical systems facilitate precise information flow because neurons in one location are speaking to neurons in another location with relatively little branching. Hierarchically connected neurons also show subpatterns known as *convergence*—in which several sets of neurons at one level converge on a smaller number of relays at the next

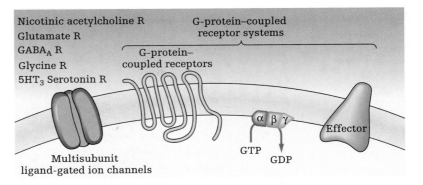

Figure 2.12 Receptors for neurotransmitters are of two main types: (1) ion-channel receptors, in which the receptor is composed of four or five subunits aggregated to compose the channel through the membrane *(left)* and (2) G-protein–coupled receptors, in which the neurotransmitter changes the excitability of the postsynaptic neuron by activating an associated G-protein–coupled complex of three proteins (alpha, beta, and gamma) that allow for transient changes in intracellular enzymes, which amplify the signal.

level—and *divergence*—in which the cells at one level speak to a larger number of cells at the next level. These patterns filter and amplify information (see Figure 2.2). Like all chains, hierarchical systems are only as strong as their weakest link: any inactivation at any level by injury, disease, stroke, or tumor can render the whole system inoperative. At the same time, convergence and divergence give the circuit some ability to continue operating in the aftermath of severe damage. If a small number of cells in the damaged area survive, they may be able to maintain the circuit's function.

Hierarchical systems are by no means restricted to the sensory and motor pathways. The same pattern is found in all the circuitry systems dedicated to a specific function, such as the memory systems and the central endocrine system, which are considered in more detail in later chapters.

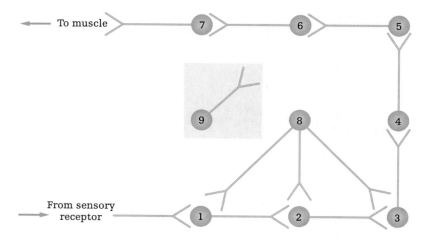

Figure 2.13 A "nine-cell" nervous system. Around the edge, neurons link in the one-to-one hierarchical connections typical of circuits in the sensory and motor systems. At center (8), the single-source–divergent pattern, typical of the monoamine systems, in which one neuron connects with a great many targets. At left center (9), a local-circuit neuron whose major connections are made within its immediate environment.

Local-Circuit Neurons

The neurons constituting a local circuit differ in character from other neurons: they have very short axons and thus can fire without the mechanism of an action potential. When a local-circuit neuron is triggered into action by synapses on its surface, the result is an almost immediate release of its transmitter. Portrayed in Figure 2.13 as an isolated neuron, a local-circuit neuron is one that receives and sends all of its synaptic messages within a spatially restricted location through which a hierarchical circuit passes.

Because of their short axons, local-circuit neurons are restricted in their tasks and range of influence. They essentially function as filters within one or more levels of a hierarchy to modulate the flow of information, and their effect can be either excitatory or inhibitory. As information passes through a hierarchical circuit, the local-circuit neurons can either broaden or restrict the flow.

Single-Source–Divergent Circuits

Some neural circuits consist of clusters of neurons in which one sending cell has many, many recipients, pushing the term "divergent" to the extreme limits of its meaning. Inquiry into this type of circuit began in the 1960s, but the only sites that we know much about so far are specific parts of the brainstem. The advantage of this pattern lies in its ability to influence a very large number of neuronal targets—communicating with all levels of a hierarchy simultaneously, for example—and thus to transcend the boundaries of specific sensory, motor, or other functional systems. Because divergent circuits are not confined to specific systems, such as sensory or motor, their paths are sometimes referred to as "nonspecific."

In general, the effects of the transmitters associated with single-source–divergent systems are "conditional"; that is, they depend on the conditions under which the transmission takes place. Being conditional does not mean that these systems are not vital to the operations of the brain. Because these circuits can influence many different levels and functions, they play a large part in integrating the diverse activities of the nervous system (see Chapter 6). In other words, divergent systems act like concert masters or athletic coaches to get the best performance possible out of a big group that must work together.

Single-source–divergent circuits are only a small fraction of all neural circuits, but, as already noted, their influence is widespread. They apparently play an integrative role in governing certain global behavioral states, such as sleep, arousal, and attentiveness (see Chapter 7).

Other Cells and Structures of the Nervous System

So far, we have dealt solely with the characteristics of neurons and their circuitry. But neurons are not the only cells making up the brain, even though they are the most important. To do its work, the cellular machinery of the brain depends on the active participation of the glia and other structures described in this section.

Glia

The extracellular space between the nerve cells is filled with specialized support cells called *glia*. By most counts, there are perhaps five or ten times as many glia as there are neurons, but, despite considerable effort by researchers, the actual functions of most glia are unknown. Scientists generally attribute to them some vague "housekeeping" chores. Unlike the neurons, glia do have the capacity to divide to form new cells.

The most common of the two major types of glial cell is called the *astrocyte* for its starlike shape. Astrocytes are thought to "clean up" excess transmitters and ions from the extracellular spaces, thereby helping to keep the interactions that take place on the neurons' surfaces free of background chemical "noise." Astrocytes may also contribute glucose to very active nerve cells; and they may redirect the flow of blood and therefore the transport of oxygen to especially active regions. These glia may also be important in providing some of the signals essential for the regulation of synaptic function. Individual astrocytes seem to mark off specific regions of synaptic connections on a target cell. Although none of these proposals is as yet certain, scientist do know that, after minor damage to the brain, astrocytes scavenge the dying neurons, an

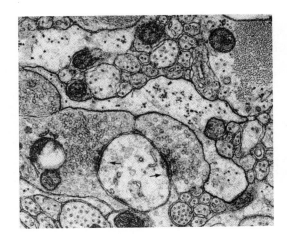

Astrocytes, one of the major types of glial cells, contribute glucose on demand to the neuronal elements that they surround. *Above:* An electron micrograph of an astrocyte (outlined in cross section) containing glycogen granules. Arrows indicate two synapses on the same dendrite. *Below:* A light micrograph of fibrous astrocytes (dark brown) surround the dendrites of cerebellar neurons.

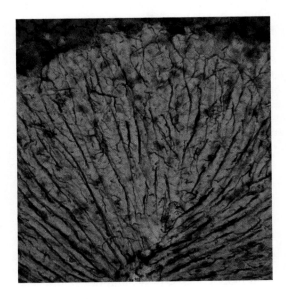

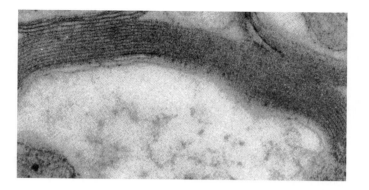

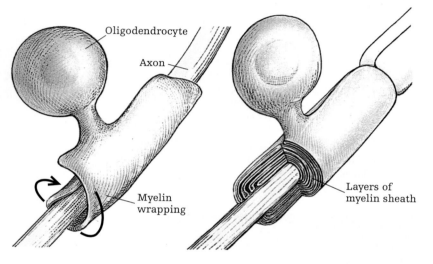

lular insulation, called *myelin*, is a compact wrapping material consisting of layers of membrane that project from the oligodendrocyte's cell body (see Figure 2.14). In diseases such as multiple sclerosis, the myelin insulation around the axon becomes unhealthy, exposing ion channels in parts of the axon surface that are normally covered. The result has been likened to short-circuiting in electrical equipment: contact occurs between normally unconnected neurons, delaying the proper transmittal of signals from one brain region to another. It explains why patients with multiple sclerosis experience sensory dysfunction and loss of muscular control. In the peripheral nervous system, the glial cell that forms myelin is known as the *Schwann cell* and has slightly different synthesizing abilities and chemical properties from those of the oligodendrocyte.

Vascular Elements

Among the other nonneuronal cells of the nervous system are those of the blood vessels—the arteries, veins, and capillaries—which make an essential contribution to its vitality. The brain receives a privileged share of oxygenated blood; in fact, all the muscles of your body together, when fully active, draw only about 25 percent more oxygen than the brain does.

The blood vessels of the central nervous system are unlike those of the rest of the body in that they lack the ability to transport large molecules across their walls. These vessels are also more or less sealed off on the brain side by the solid attachment of astrocytes to their outer surfaces. These modifications limit the substances that can enter the brain from the bloodstream mainly to the blood gases (oxygen and carbon dioxide) and the small nutritional molecules, including glucose and essential amino acids, that

Figure 2.14 Oligodendrocytes, the other major type of glia, form myelin around axons, providing insulation to speed conduction of impulses. In the diagram at the left, an oligodendrocyte wraps its membrane around an axon to form a myelin sheath. Ions flow into the nerve membrane only at gaps in the myelin. At the right, the multiple layers of myelin (dark rings) surround a small axon.

action that perhaps limits the spread of toxic substances.

Glia of the other major class, *oligodendrocytes*, are better defined by their function than by their shape. Some axons are insulated in a way that customizes them for rapid conduction of electrical impulses. This cel-

the brain needs to operate properly. This restriction on the access of the blood's contents to the tissues of the central nervous system is so different from their access to other tissues that it has a special name—the *blood–brain barrier*. The existence of this diffusional barrier certainly suggests that it is to the brain's advantage not to be exposed to all of the different chemical signals that may be circulating in the bloodstream. Unfortunately, a few toxins, such as alcohol, nicotine, and nerve gases, are able to cross the barrier and enter the brain.

The exacting metabolic demands of the brain increase even further during certain mental activities, and the active regions can be partly visualized by modern techniques that spot changes in blood flow or in oxygen or glucose consumption (see box entitled "How Scientists Study the Brain" in Chapter 1). These techniques help physicians pinpoint small zones of epileptic activity or other pathological changes, such as cancers or vascular tumors. The same methods have also begun to provide information about which parts of the brain become especially active or quiet when a depressed patient or one with schizophrenia is behaving abnormally (see Chapter 12).

Connective Tissue Elements

The last nonneural cells that we will look at are those that line the outer and inner surfaces of the central nervous system. Within the bony confines of the skull and spinal

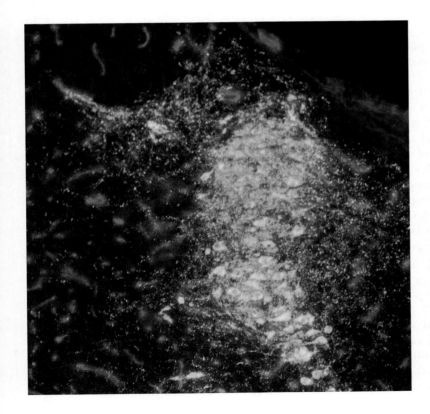

Injection of a dye that produces a red fluorescent image permits the rapid assessment of the degree of vascularization around neurons. Each red spot is a small arteriole, capillary, or venule. The degree of vascularity differs from one region to another, depending on the underlying metabolic demands of a region's neurons. The bright blue-green neurons are the norepinephrine-containing neurons of the locus ceruleus, fluorescent because of exposure to glyoxylic acid.

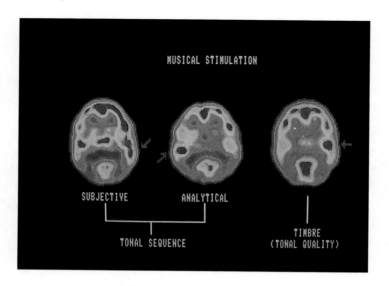

MUSICAL STIMULATION

SUBJECTIVE   ANALYTICAL

TONAL SEQUENCE

TIMBRE
(TONAL QUALITY)

After injection of a nonradioactive modified glucose molecule, the PET (positron emission tomography) scan detects the relative amounts of glucose being consumed in the cortex while the subject listens to music. This subject, a trained musician, shows increased metabolic demand over both the right temporal and the left parietal areas, suggesting focused attention to the details of the music.

cord, the CNS is sealed into a form-fitting, fluid-filled "stocking" of membranes called the *meninges,* made up of conventional connective tissues found elsewhere in the body. The fluid is the *cerebrospinal fluid.* The meninges and the cerebrospinal fluid act as a shock-absorber system to soak up the twists, turns, bumps, and other insults to the body that would severely hamper the integrity of the nervous system were they to be transmitted full force.

The cerebrospinal fluid also fills pockets of space extending from the outer surfaces of the brain and spinal cord into hollow internal chambers, the *cerebral ventricles* (see Figure 2.15). (As noted in Chapter 1, the ventricles received the lion's share of attention from the brain students of antiq-

uity.) The cells lining these inner ventricular spaces are also specialized, and, except for certain key spots, their edges are sealed together tightly, apparently to limit passage of anything across this layer of lining. The cerebrospinal fluid itself is produced from the passage of the blood through specialized blood vessels, the *choroid plexus,* which filter out the blood cells. The choroid plexus is attached to certain parts of the ventricular system, and the fluid that its cells yield circulates from the inner ventricles down into the space around the spinal cord and up over the surface of the cortex and cerebellum. After circulating, the fluid is reabsorbed into the venous channels of the meninges.

The function if any of this internal circulation of spinal fluid is not known, but physicians make use of it when trying to diagnose infections of the nervous system— bacterial meningitis, for example. When infection is present, white blood cells are found in the spinal fluid, and its protein content becomes much higher than normal. Because the spinal fluid also contains some of the by-products of synaptic transmission, diagnosticians and researchers frequently examine its content as they try to piece together chemical clues to the unsolved mysteries of brain disorders. The possibility that the cerebrospinal fluid might transport chemical signs of brain abnormality almost brings us back full circle to the view of the ancient Greeks and Romans, who considered the ventricles and their plumbing functions to be of premier importance.

Now that we have the elemental parts of the brain defined and their ways of working with one another briefly described, we turn in the next chapter to two topics essential to a beginning understanding of how the brain works: how the brain forms and what makes each of us so different.

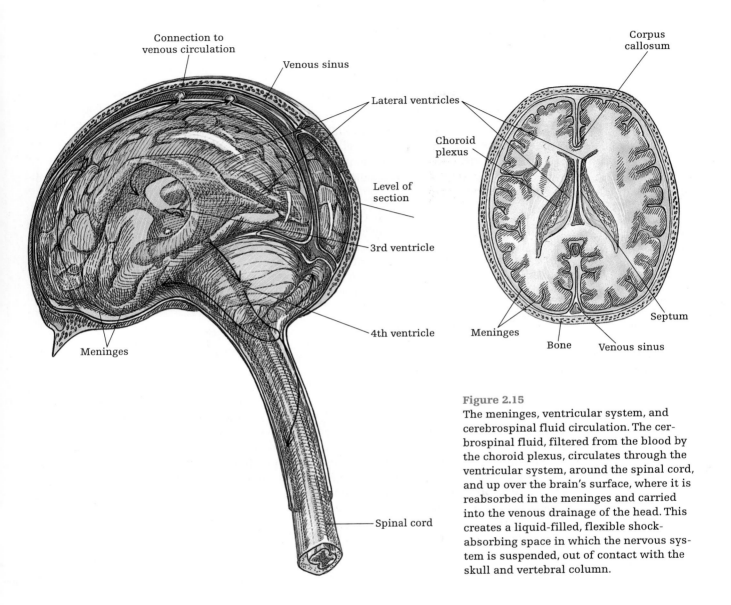

Connection to
venous circulation

Venous sinus

Lateral ventricles

Level of
section

3rd ventricle

4th ventricle

Meninges

Spinal cord

Corpus
callosum

Choroid
plexus

Meninges

Bone

Septum

Venous sinus

Figure 2.15
The meninges, ventricular system, and
cerebrospinal fluid circulation. The cer-
brospinal fluid, filtered from the blood by
the choroid plexus, circulates through the
ventricular system, around the spinal cord,
and up over the brain's surface, where it is
reabsorbed in the meninges and carried
into the venous drainage of the head. This
creates a liquid-filled, flexible shock-
absorbing space in which the nervous system is suspended, out of contact with the
skull and vertebral column.

Summary

1. The basic operating elements of the nervous system are the individual nerve cells, or neurons.

2. Neurons have certain universal cellular features in common with other cells in the body. All have a plasma membrane, a cytoplasm containing organelles, and a nucleus.

3. Neurons also differ from other body cells in several ways. They have characteristic shapes, with protrusions—the axons and dendrites—that connect with other neurons to form circuits. In addition, the arrangement of organelles within neurons differs from that of other cells.

4. The activity of neurons is regulated by the properties of the nerve cell membrane. When chemically stimulated, the membrane's electrical state changes from a resting potential to an action potential, and a nerve impulse is generated.

5. The chemical stimulation of a neuron by a synaptically connected neuron is accomplished by the release of a synaptic transmitter, manufactured by the connected neuron and released into the synaptic gap to affect the receiving neuron.

6. Synaptic transmitters may act either to produce a nerve impulse, to inhibit an impulse, or to modify the effects of another transmitter.

7. Generally, a receiving neuron requires a summation of many impulses in order for it to become sufficiently depolarized to initiate an action potential.

8. The three major classes of synaptic transmitters are amino acids, monoamines, and peptides.

9. There are three basic patterns of neuronal circuitry: hierarchical chains, local circuits, and single-source–divergent circuits.

10. Besides neurons, the nervous system contains two types of glial cells—oligodendrocytes, which form the myelin sheath covering many types of neural circuits, and a neurosupportive cell type called the astrocyte.

11. Other tissues found in the brain are the blood vessels and the membranes surrounding the brain and spinal cord.

Key Terms

axon	receptors
dendrite	amino acids
nerve impulses	monoamines
excitation	neuropeptides
inhibition	neuronal circuitry
conditional modulation	local-circuit neurons
synaptic transmission	glia

Further Reading

Bloom, F. E. 1996. Neurotransmission and the central nervous system. In J. G. Hardman, L. E. Limbird, P. B. Molinoff, and R. W. Ruddon, Eds., *Goodman and Gilman's The Phamacological Basis of Therapeutics*, 9th ed. (pp. 265–294). McGraw-Hill, New York. An overview for medically oriented students of the details of brain circuitry, chemistry, and physiology to define how and where drugs may act to influence brain diseases.

Cooper, J. R., Bloom, F. E., and Roth, R. H. 1997. *The Biochemical Basis of Neuropharmacology,* 7th ed. Oxford University Press, New York. A small but authoritative coverage, expanding on the principles developed in this chapter, with many examples of each chemical and phsyiological feature, intended for the entry-level graduate student.

Hökfelt, T., Castel, M.-N., Morino, P., Zhang, X, and Dagerlind, Å. 1995. General overview of neuropeptides. In F. E. Bloom and D. J. Kupfer, Eds., *Psychopharmacology: The Fourth Generation of Progress* (pp. 483–492). Raven Press, New York. A recent detailed review of progress in the identification and functional characterization of neuropeptides.

Iversen, L. L. 1986. Chemical signalling in the nervous system. *Progress in Brain Research* 68:15–21. A very readable introduction to the chemistry of the brain focused on synaptic transmission.

Keynes, R. D. 1979. Ion channels in the nerve cell membrane. *Scientific American* (March). A readable introduction to the ionic basis of neuronal excitability.

Kandel, E. R., Schwartz, J. H., and Jessell, T. M. 2000. *Principles of Neural Science,* 4th ed. McGraw-Hill, New York. The latest revision of the first comprehensive textbook in the neurosciences, emphasizing the needs of medical students.

Zigmond, M. J., Bloom, F. E., Landis S. C., Roberts, J. L., and Squire, L. R., Eds. 1998. *Fundamental Neuroscience* (pp. 41–416). Academic Press, New York. First edition of a comprehensive textbook written for the entry-level student of the brain sciences, with highly informative schematic depictions of current understanding.

Interactive Resources

The CD-ROM that accompanies this book offers various ways to visualize the material covered in this chapter. Its "Neural Communication" module includes graphic descriptions of neurons as well as animations of the action potential and synaptic transmission. In addition, its "Research Methods" module includes a description of a confocal microscope—an important tool for studying neurons—as well as images of neurons, including video clips of glial cells.

To learn even more about the cellular and chemical machinery of the brain, visit our Web site at www.worthpublishers.com/bloom. Click on "Chapter 2" for resources including practice quizzes, flash cards, simulations, links to related Web sites, and updates on new research.

Life-Span Development of the Brain

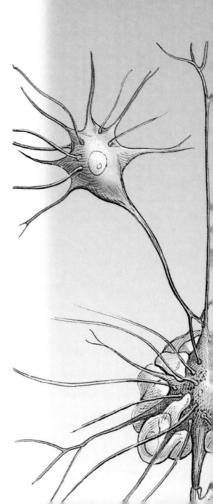

Virtually all of what we are and do depends on how our brains function, and normal functioning of the brain depends greatly on how the brain develops. By "development" we mean, among other things, the formation of neurons, glial cells, and synapses. Some of these processes—such as the formation of neurons—are completed very early in development, long before birth, whereas others—such as the cultivation of synapses—do not complete their development until many years after birth. Importantly, as we will illustrate in this chapter, many of the molecular and cellular modifications that take place in the initial construction of the brain do not cease once the brain is fully formed; rather, they continue throughout the life cycle.

In this chapter, we will consider what is known about the brain's development before birth, during childhood and adulthood, and in old age. Most of our information comes from studies carried out with animals such as monkeys, frogs, or chicks. Although we cannot state with certainty that the processes in animals are identical with those in human beings, the strong likelihood is that they are much the same across species.

Genes begin to direct brain development as soon as the egg and sperm join at fertilization. Thus, after outlining the overall course of the brain's formation, we will focus on an instructive example of the genes' role in development—how the genes that determine a person's sex affect brain and behavior and, in particular, the brain structures and behaviors that are not directly linked to sexual activities.

We have the least information about developmental changes during childhood and adulthood and thus cannot outline a sequence of changes like those seen in prenatal development and infancy—it is not clear that there is any such sequence. However, we will look at evidence that a child's interactions with the environment produce changes in brain struc-

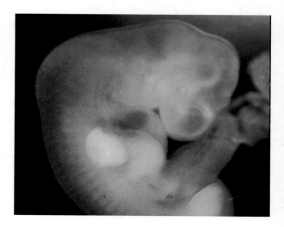

A fetus in the womb.

tures and that lack of certain interactions can alter normal developmental patterns.

Developmental changes in old age are another focus of much ongoing scientific study. What actually happens to the aging brain and why? What are the genetic and environmental factors that might affect aging? The most recent theories and data are reported in the final section of this chapter.

Prenatal Development

Gross Anatomical Changes

Scientists have learned about the general sequence of anatomical growth in the human fetus by examining fetuses that did not survive until birth. The most indispensable body parts—the heart and brain—begin to form first, within the first weeks after fertilization.

The First Month By about the fifth day after fertilization, the original *zygote* (the group of cells that are formed by the coupling of sperm and egg) has divided until there are about 100 embryonic cells, in the shape of a hollow ball, referred to as the *blastocyst* (see Figure 3.1). At about the eighth day, cells on

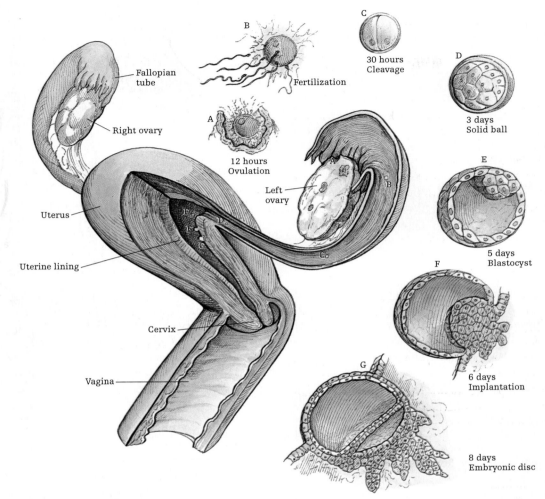

Figure 3.1 The first week of prenatal development. Most development during the first week takes place in the Fallopian tube, as the organism makes its way to the uterus. (A) The egg is released from the ovary and begins its journey through the Fallopian tube toward the uterus. (B) Sperm deposited in the vagina make their way to the far end of the Fallopian tube. As soon as one sperm penetrates the egg, chemical changes make it impossible for other sperm to enter. The sperm's genetic material combines with the egg's to form the zygote, a new cell with the full human complement of 46 chromosomes. (C) Cleavage, or cell division, first takes place about 30 hours after fertilization, as the zygote continues its passage through the Fallopian tube toward the uterus. Cell division continues until (D) a solid ball of cells has formed. This ball is no larger than the original egg. (E) As cell division continues, the spaces between the inner cells of the ball become larger until the ball becomes the blastocyst, a hollow sphere of cells with a small mass of cells adhering to one point on its inner surface. (F) Now within the uterus, the blastocyst makes contact with the uterine lining, where it implants itself. (G) By the eighth day, the thickened cell mass that was evident inside the blastocyst at five days has become the embryonic disc, from which the baby will develop. The outer part of the blastocyst will eventually become the support structures, such as the placenta, umbilical cord, and amniotic sac, for the embryo and fetus.

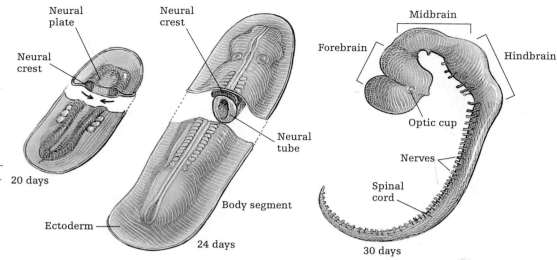

Figure 3.2 Stages of development in the embryonic human brain. At 30 days, the major regions can be recognized in primitive form. By 2 months, most of the subcortical regions are fairly well along in their development. The cerebral and cerebellar cortices continue to develop throughout gestation and beyond the time of birth.

Neural plate

Neural crest

Neural crest

20 days

Ectoderm

Body segment

24 days

Neural tube

Midbrain

Forebrain

Hindbrain

Optic cup

Nerves

Spinal cord

30 days

the inside of this ball detach themselves and form a flat plate across the inside—the *embryonic disc*. Within another week, some of the cells in this homogeneous cluster begin to lose their uniform character—that is, cell differentiation begins—and the disc is soon made up of two distinct layers, the ectoderm and the endoderm. The *ectoderm* will become the nervous system (as well as skin, hair, and fingernails), and the *endoderm* will go on to form the respiratory and digestive tracts and related organs. Later, a third layer, the mesoderm, forms between the first two layers. Although the *mesoderm* does not become nervous tissue, it contributes to the formation of the nervous system.

Shortly after the ectoderm has become differentiated, it thickens and builds up along its midline. At this point, it is identifiable as the primitive neural plate. (Figures 3.2 and 3.3 show details of these developmental processes.) Experiments have shown that even at this primitive point in development—three to four weeks after conception—specific segments of the neural plate are assigned to form specific brain parts. Early in the formation of the neural plate,

such assignments are still capable of being modified; that is, if some parts of the neural plate are removed, the remaining tissues can make up for the lost pieces, and a complete brain will still develop. However, only a few days further into the developmental program, missing pieces can no longer be replaced, and the brain that is formed will be incomplete.

As the neural plate continues its growth, parallel ridges begin to form along its length and, within a few days of their development, these ridges fold over toward each other and fuse to form the neural tube (this process begins by approximately the 18th day after conception). The top of this hollow tube soon thickens and begins to show three bulges, which eventually become the forebrain (*prosencephalon*), the midbrain (*mesencephalon*), and the hindbrain (*rhombencephalon*). The remainder of the neural tube becomes the spinal cord. In rare instances (approximately 1 percent of all pregnancies), an error in the closing of the neural tube produces a so-called *neural-tube defect*. In the most severe case, the top (rostral) end fails to close, and the child, if it survives to full term, is born

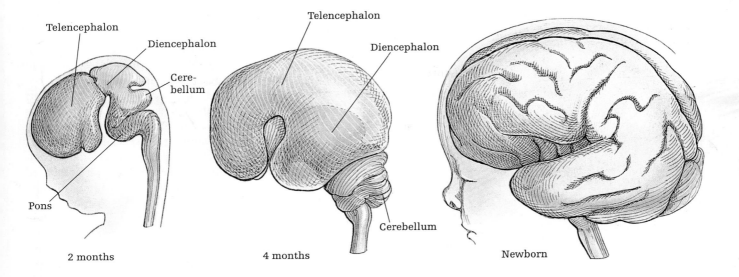

Telencephalon

Diencephalon

Cere-
bellum

Pons

2 months

Telencephalon

Diencephalon

Cerebellum

4 months

Newborn

without a cortex. However, such *anen-cephalic* infants usually die within the first weeks or months of life. When the neural-tube defect is farther down along the tube (such as at the level of the spinal cord), the child is usually intellectually normal but suffers from motor impairments.

As Figure 3.3 shows, a cluster of young neurons, or *neuroblasts*, remains outside the neural tube when it folds and fuses. This cluster, the *neural crest*, will give rise to the peripheral autonomic nervous system.

Figure 3.3 The earliest development of the nervous system, occurring during weeks three and four of prenatal life. Two views of each developmental stage are shown: at left an external view of the developing embryo and at right a cross section as indicated by the dashed line. From the top down, you can see how the primitive ectoderm thickens and differentiates to form the neural plate, which folds to become the neural groove and, finally, the neural tube. Note, at bottom, the group of cells remaining outside the neural tube—the neural crest, from which the peripheral nervous system develops.

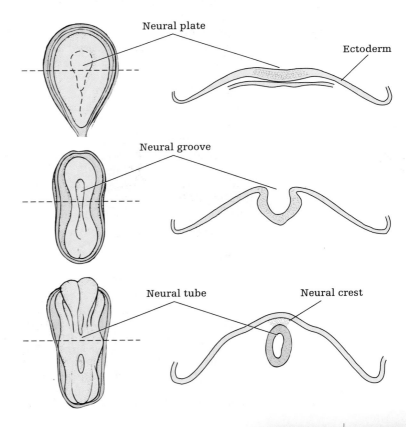

Neural plate

Ectoderm

Neural groove

Neural tube

Neural crest

The Second Month Soon after the three primary bulges form, what can now be called the brain begins to undergo the first of a series of folds and bends. This process results in further differentiation of the three major divisions; moreover, it creates the large internal cavities within the brain, the cerebral *ventricles* (see Figure 3.4).

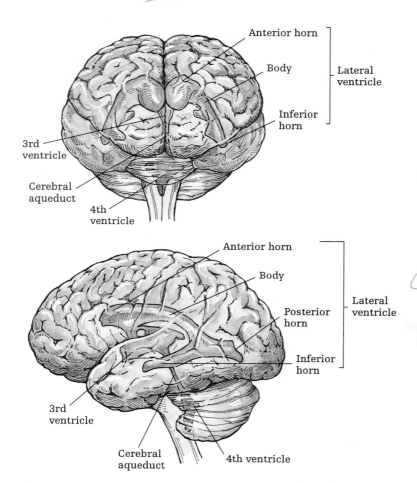

Figure 3.4 As the three vesicles that eventually give rise to the forebrain, midbrain, and hindbrain form, so, too, do the large internal cavities that come to be called the cerebral ventricles. *Top:* A coronal section of the brain that reveals the 3rd and 4th ventricles. It is through the 4th ventricle that cerebrospinal fluid flows into the spinal column, *Bottom:* A saggital view of the brain that shows the lateral ventricles.

The next major developmental specialization takes place when the large forebrain bulge undergoes yet another division, into the *telencephalon*, which later forms all parts of the cortex, and the *diencephalon*, which forms all structures of the thalamus and hypothalamus (see Figure 3.2). Various parts of the telencephalon are highly specialized in mammals, especially primates, accounting for the greater functional capacities of the human nervous system compared with that of nonprimates and nonmammals.

Further Development of the Telencephalon As the second month progresses, the telencephalon undergoes further refinement, eventually going through three distinct stages. First, the olfactory parts of the brain develop, which at this time include the hippocampus and other connected regions around the inside edge of the cortex. Next, the walls of the forebrain become thicker. The masses of growing cells that create this thickening are the basal ganglia, which will become structures such as the caudate nucleus, globus pallidus, and putamen, all critical to the coordination of sensory and motor-control systems and some forms of learning. The amygdala, which plays a critical role in emotion and in integrating sensory signals from different regions of the brain with internal adaptive responses, also is derived from this same group of cells. Finally, the cerebral cortex itself develops, with all of its specialized regions. The product of this stage of development has historically been referred to as the neocortex, or "new cortex," although more recently some have argued that the term "isocortex" is more accurate. In this book, we shall continue to use the term *neocortex*, referring to the several-millimeter-thick layer of neurons situated between the olfactory cortex laterally (to the side) and the hippocampal cortex medially (to the middle).

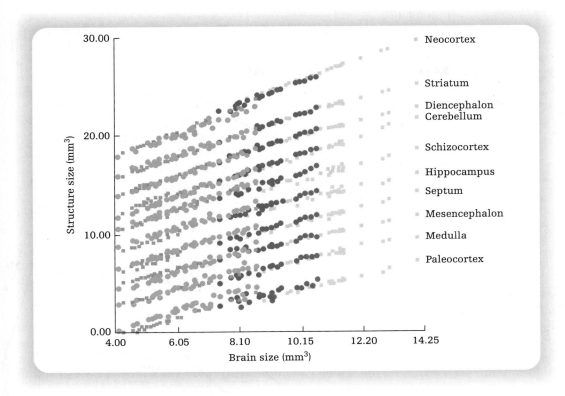

Sizes of 10 measured brain subdivisions from 131 species plotted as a function of total brain size (orange squares, simians; green circles, prosimians; red circles, insectivores; and blue squares, bats). This method of representation emphasizes the linearity of the relation between brain sizes and structure sizes across mammalian groups on logarithmic scales. Each scatterplot of data points corresponds to a brain subdivision.

The neocortex is unique to mammals, and it has grown so large in human beings that its surface becomes intricately folded as it develops in order to fit inside the skull. The infolding begins as the neocortex achieves its maximum growth rate, about 250,000 cells per minute (an event that takes place in humans about halfway through the gestation period). When development is complete (in humans, at the sixth to seventh prenatal month), 70 percent of the billions of neurons that make up the brain are found within the cerebral cortex.

Having outlined the major developmental stages of the first two prenatal months, we shall now take a step back and examine some of these events in more detail. Specifically, let us look at the developmental processes responsible for the production and distribution of neurons and glia in the various parts of the brain.

Processes of Neuronal Development

The eight major processes by which neurons develop to form all parts of the brain are outlined in Table 3.1 on the following page and discussed in some detail in the following sections.

TABLE 3.1 Processes of neuronal development

Process	Description
Induction	Process that allows some parts of the ectoderm of the neural disc to become transformed into the neural plate
Proliferation	The cell division throughout which the few cells making up the neural plate and neural tube multiply to become the billions of cells of a complete brain
Migration	Movement of newly formed cells from the region in which they proliferated to their final destination in the brain
Aggregation	Mutual adhesion of similar cells as a first step in the formation of functional brain parts
Differentiation	Process by which each neuron acquires its given size, shape, location, connections, and mode of transmitting messages—for example, excitatory versus inhibitory
Circuit formation	Establishment of synaptic connections with other neurons through growth of axons and dendrites
Apoptosis	Elimination of redundant or extraneous cells and of some cell-to-cell connections accompanied by synapse refinement

Induction This term refers to the process that causes some cells in the neural plate to form the nervous system while others go on to form skin, hair, and fingernails. Although the precise mechanisms that underlie *induction* are not known, we do know that the crucial initiating event is an interaction between the ectoderm and the mesoderm underlying it. Scientists believe that the mesoderm produces neural-inducing factors and modifiers that help to establish the *neuraxis* (the longitudinal axis that will represent the neural tube once it is formed) of the ectoderm. Although the precise mechanism underlying this interaction is unknown, the induction of forebrain development is believed to differ from the induction of the development of the hindbrain.

Interestingly, the order in which the mesoderm is formed determines which parts of the ectoderm will develop into each of the three major parts of the brain (forebrain, midbrain, and hindbrain) and the spinal cord. The first part of the mesoderm that forms under the ectoderm induces the development of forebrain structures. The next part cues the formation of midbrain and hindbrain. The final part causes the ectoderm associated with it to produce the spinal cord.

Even though neuroscientists are convinced that the mesoderm must transfer some chemical substances to the ectoderm to work its effects, no one has yet been able to isolate them definitively or identify them. These substances are called *trophic factors* from the Greek word for "nourishment." Among the substances that might prove to be trophic factors are three proteins called *follistatin, noggin,* and *chordin,* all of which are known to be able to influence the so-called bone morphogenic (BMP) family of molecules, which in turn may stimulate development of the anterior part of the neural plate.

Proliferation Cells begin to *proliferate* (increase in number through cell division) soon after the neural tube is closed off (a process referred to as *neurongenesis*). Experiments with mice have shown that there are most likely two phases of cell proliferation. The first takes place before embryonic day 11 (E11). In this phase, all progeny of proliferating cells undergo a single division, with the result that the number of cells in the original epithelial layer of the neural tube is doubled. After E11 (with the normal gestational period being 21 days), the daughter cells produced by the original population of cells join one of the two groups. One group consists of cells that will continue to proliferate but remain where they are, and the second group consists of cells that leave their zone of origin as young neurons. Development in the rhesus monkey, a favorite of neuroscientists, follows a similar pattern. Before E40 (the monkey's normal gestational period is 165 days), each progenitor cell produces two new daughter cells for each cycle of division. After E40,

some progenitor cells remain where they are and continue to reproduce, whereas others begin changing into neurons, leave their zone of origin, and never reproduce again. In mouse, monkey, and human being, the cells that are destined to become neurons detach themselves from the ventricular surface of the neural tube and migrate toward the pial surface (that is, toward the pia matter, the canvaslike material that covers the surface of the brain; see Figure 3.5). What is particularly interesting about this scenario is that the duration of the first phase of cell division, 10 days in the mouse and 40 in the monkey, appears to determine the ultimate number of cells in the cortical surface, leading indirectly to the size of the cortical surface itself (because more cells result in a larger cortical surface).

In the second phase of neurongenesis, the daughter cells that become mobile move by forming processes along which the cell bodies

Figure 3.5 Cytological organization of the primate cerebral wall during the first half of gestation. (A) The surface of the brain of 60- to 65-day-old monkey fetuses is still smooth and lacks the characteristic convolutions (gyri and sulci) that will appear in the second half of gestation. (B) Coronal section across the occipital lobe at the level indicated by the vertical broken line in (A). The lateral ventricle at this age is still relatively large, and only the identification of the incipient calcarine fissure (a sulcus demarcating the occipital lobe) marks the position of what will be the visual cortex. (C) A block of the tissue dissected from the upper bank of the calcarine fissure. At this early stage, six embryonic layers can be recognized from the ventricular surface *(bottom)* to the pial surface *(top):* ventricle zone (V); subventricular zone (SV); intermediate zone (I); subplate zone (SP); cortical plate (CP); and marginal zone (M).

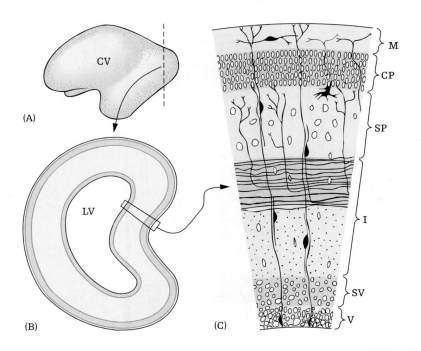

travel up to the neural tube's outer surface. There they synthesize DNA, and then they move back down again to divide. After a number of such cycles, some as-yet-unknown mechanism turns off the cell's ability to synthesize DNA and, consequently, to proliferate. Some of these cells are neurons; some are glial-cell precursors. With the exception of cells in the olfactory bulb,

the dentate region of the hippocampus, and possibly some regions of the frontal cortex, none will divide again.

The period of proliferation (first and second stages combined) differs for different populations of cells; each population appears to follow its own rigid schedule for ending division. Moreover, the end of each mobile cell's proliferative cycle seems to trigger that cell's migration toward its final functional location.

Migration The cells that are going to migrate do so by moving up and down between the ventricular zone and the marginal zone of the neural tube. These cells eventually come to rest and form a layer between these two zones—called the *intermediate zone*—thereby thickening the developing cortex (see Figure 3.5). In some parts of the brain, an additional layer of cells forms between the ventricular zone and the intermediate zone. This new zone is called the *subventricular zone* (see Figure 3.6). In contrast with cells that occupy the intermediate zone, the cells of the subventricular

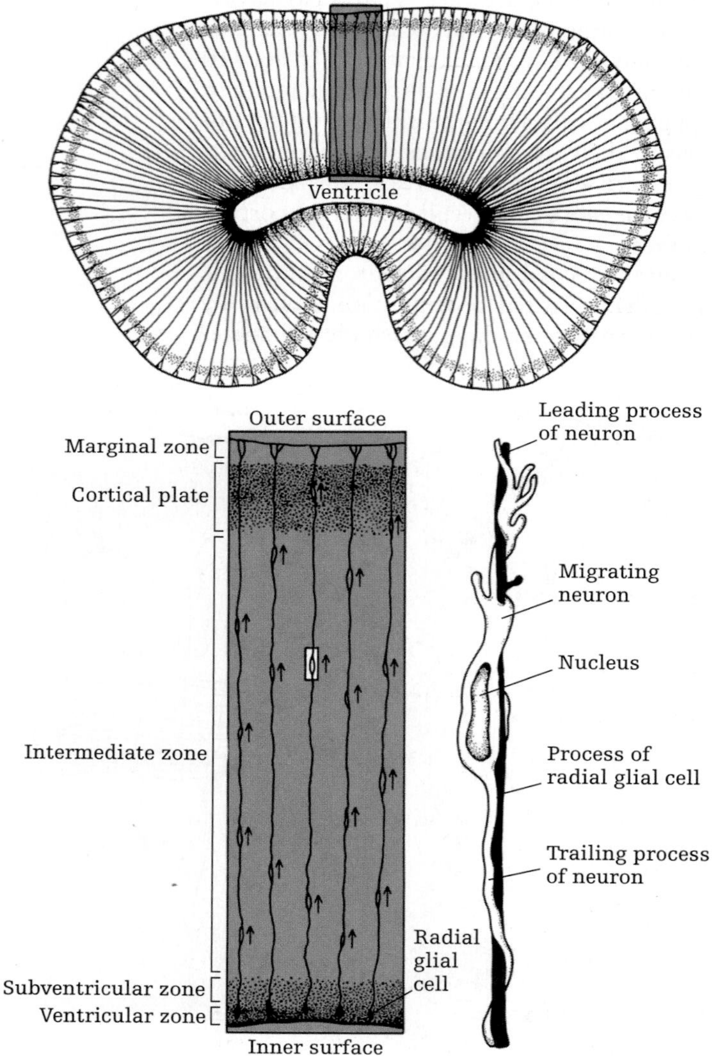

Figure 3.6 *Top:* Drawing of a Golgi-stained section through the wall of the cerebral hemisphere of a fetal monkey; the specialized supporting cells, the radial glial cells, can be seen clearly. *Bottom left:* The processes of these glia are very long, extending from the inner surface to the outer surface of the developing neural tube and its derivative structures. The arrows indicate that the cells migrate along the processes from the inner surface of the cerebral hemisphere to the marginal zone at the outer surface. *Bottom right:* From the close relation between the processes of the migrating neuron and the radial glial cell, it is clear that the migrating neuron depends on the glial substrate for guidance. When the radial glial fibers have guided their migrating cells to the correct location, they undergo a second mitotic division and become *astrocytes*.

zone continue to proliferate, giving rise to many of the neurons and glial cells that migrate to form the forebrain.

The glial cells of the subventricular zone play a prominent role in directing the migration of many neurons to their ultimate destinations. The bodies of these specialized glial cells—called *radial glial elements*—lie inside the subventricular zone, but their cell processes radiate out to the surface of the developing brain. Neurons seem to use these long glial processes as a kind of scaffolding, in much the same way as the vine of a bean plant grows along a string that the gardener sets out for it (see Figure 3.6).

Our understanding of the events described in the preceding paragraphs has profited enormously by studies of an unusual strain of mouse, called the *reeler*. In the reeler mouse, the migrating neurons come to populate the normally underpopulated cellular marginal zones of the forebrain structures; in addition, the positions of the major classes of cortical neurons are inverted. In the normal brain, the earliest-formed neurons occupy the deepest layers of the cortex, whereas the later-formed neurons occupy more superficial layers. Exactly the opposite occurs in the reeler mouse brain. However, equally remarkable about the reeler mouse is that, after the cells have taken up their (incorrect) positions in the cortex, they go on to establish normal connections with other cells.

These discoveries, coupled with recent reports concerning the molecular bases of the reeler-mouse phenomenon, have done much to enhance our understanding of the processes that give rise to the normal brain. It is a common theme in biology: by understanding the consequences of a genetic mistake, we are often able to infer how the normal genes function (or vice versa). As you continue to read this book, you will see many examples of how the study of an abnormal process can enhance our understanding of how the normal brain works.

Given the number of cells that must travel to their target destinations, and the great distances that many of them traverse, it is not surprising that some should go astray. It happens even in normal development. Studies indicate that as many as 3 percent of cells may migrate to incorrect locations. Almost all of these cells, however, degenerate during the stage of programmed cell death (discussed in a later section), and thus do not cause any problems. Unfortunately, there are instances in which migration errors are not benign but lead to grossly abnormal outcomes, such as disorders in which entire parts of the cortex are missing or in which the brain lacks *gyri* (the convolutions that cover the surface of the brain). Such problematic errors are believed to occur between the 13th and 15th weeks of gestation. Children suffering from these disorders are always mentally retarded.

Aggregation After a neuron has migrated to its final location, it may attach itself, or adhere, to cells of a similar kind. This process creates aggregations of similar neurons that later become functional units. Such is the origin of the thalamic nuclei and the layers of the cortex. The mechanism that causes certain cells to "recognize" and to "prefer" each other is the interaction of specific classes of large molecules on the cells' surfaces, so-called *cell adhesion molecules,* or CAMs, that bind to similar molecules on adjacent cell membranes. This mechanism resembles that which allows cells of the immune system to differentiate between "self" and "not self" in their quest to destroy invading bacteria or other microorganisms.

Differentiation Cell differentiation begins early, when germinal cells in the neural tube become identifiable as either young neurons or young glia. The precise mechanism that tells a cell to stop dividing and begin to differentiate into a glial cell or a specific type of neuron is not yet known. It appears, however, that as soon as a neuron emerges from its proliferative phase, much of its destiny is set. It not only begins its migration, but also seems to head for a definite location. The pattern of connections that it will ultimately make seems to be set at this early time.

As stated earlier, different populations of cells begin and end their proliferative cycles at different times. The timing of these events within a given population of cells depends on their ultimate location and function. For example, the cells that form the deepest layer of the cerebral cortex are always the first group to stop proliferating; the next set to complete mitosis forms the layer above that, and so forth. Thus, a wave of cortical maturation proceeds "from the inside out" (except, of course, in the reeler mouse). The sequence is different in other brain structures, but the general rule appears to be that cells destined for similar locations are always generated at the same time. Thus, a neuron's "birth date," the time at which it undergoes its final cell division, seems to determine many of its ultimate characteristics.

It is likely that the neurotransmitter that a neuron will manufacture also is decided when proliferation stops, but some experiments have shown that a cell's environment also may influence that function. In one experiment, young neurons from lower parts of the neural crest were transplanted into the developing brainstem. Normally, they would have developed into parts of the autonomic nervous system and would have produced norepinephrine as their transmitter. Instead, they produced acetylcholine, like the other cells in that brainstem area. It may be that some neurons have the potential to produce several transmitters and that the local environment stimulates the production of one or the other during differentiation.

Circuit Formation: Development of Axons and Dendrites One of the most intriguing problems in neural embryology is, How do axons find their way to their destinations? Some axons have to travel more than a thousand times the diameter of the cell body (several centimeters), and some have to make right or left turns as they grow in order to find their appropriate target on the opposite side of the brain.

Usually, a neuron will not grow axons and dendrites until after it has migrated to its final destination. The initial growth of these cell extensions and their orientation appear to be genetically determined, because cells that have been experimentally moved or rotated nevertheless show initial growth patterns indicative of the cells' original place and orientation. The trajectory of a given axon is not a smooth line or a curve; rather, it appears to be divided into short segments that were grown in spurts. Thus, an axon does not need to make one big leap to its final target; instead, it finds its way by making successive approximations.

After their initial growth, however, the axon and dendrites can be influenced by a number of factors in their environment, primarily mechanical and chemical ones. It appears, for example, that the axons of young neurons require contact with a certain underlying surface, or substrate, to help guide their growth. Accordingly, the experimental disruption of the *reeler* gene in the reeler mouse creates a disturbance in the cortical layers described earlier. This disturbance, in turn, results in a mouse that walks with a reeling gait (for which the mouse strain is named).

The growing end of most axons (named the *growth cone*) emerges from an undulating membrane whose constantly moving, fingerlike extensions are called *filopodia*. The filopodia expand and contract, seeming to explore their environment for "the right" surface to which they can adhere. The molecules on the substrate surface are believed to act as directional guides for the growth cones. Research suggests that this directional guidance depends on two types of cues: substances that attract the growing axon and substances that repulse the axon. Axons that move only short distances and axons that must move long distances can all be influenced by both kinds of cues.

The chemical that guides the growth cone by means of attraction perhaps diffuses in such a way that it forms a concentration gradient ranging from weaker to stronger, the stronger concentration being "upstream." The growth cone would be attracted toward the stronger concentration. In the other mode of guidance, repulsion, chemicals that are inhibitory to the neuron's growth are perhaps arranged in such a way as to create a pathway that the growth cone has no option but to follow (see Figure 3.7 on the following page).

Several substances have been identified as possibly playing a role in the directional guidance of growing axons. One group of candidates are the CAMs mentioned earlier. Another possible guidance substance is called *nerve-growth factor* (NGF). Italian neuroscientist Rita Levi-Montalcini was awarded the 1986 Nobel Prize in physiology or medicine for discovering it. In one experiment, for example, scientists injected NGF into the brain of young rats, and it caused the dorsal root ganglia (the neurons that lie alongside the spine) to send their axons into the spinal cord and up toward the brain, a completely abnormal pattern of growth. The axons had followed the path of the injected NGF. In the explosion of knowledge that followed the initial discovery of NGFs, entire families of those substances have been identified. These families include *neurotrophins* (such as brain-derived neurotrophic factor, or BDNF) and *neuropoletic factors* (such as *cholinergic*

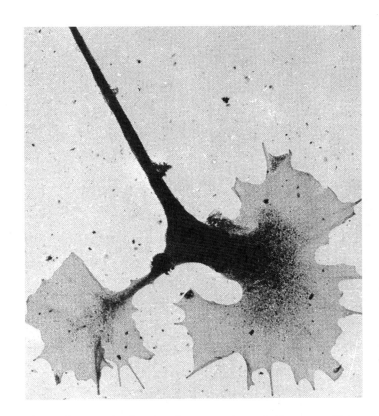

Photomicrograph of a growth cone at the end of an axon. Note the filopodia—the fingerlike extensions.

differentiation factor/leukemia inhibitory factor, or CDF/LIF).

One research strategy aimed at discovering how axons find their way and make the right connections is to rearrange the brain anatomy of embryo frogs or chicks and then examine either the innervation pattern that develops or the behavior of the animal. In one set of experiments, researchers rotated the developing eye of a frog through 180 degrees. When the rotation was done at an early stage of development, the images reflected on the frog's retina were normal. When the rotation was done later, though, the resulting images on the retina were rotated to the same degree as the eye. These

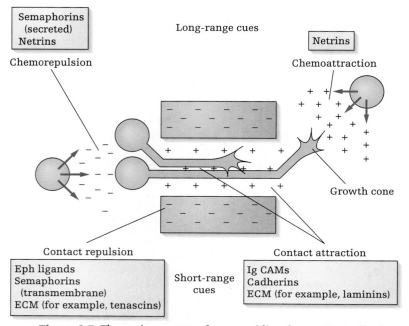

Long-range cues

Semaphorins (secreted)
Netrins

Chemorepulsion

Netrins

Chemoattraction

Growth cone

Contact repulsion

Eph ligands
Semaphorins
(transmembrane)
ECM (for example, tenascins)

Short-range cues

Contact attraction

Ig CAMs
Cadherins
ECM (for example, laminins)

Figure 3.7 The various types of axon-guiding forces. Basically, four types of mechanisms interact to guide the growth cone: contact attraction, chemoattraction, contact repulsion, and chemorepulsion. The term *attraction* is used to refer to a range of permissive and attractive effects, and the term *repulsion* to a range of inhibitory and repulsive effects.

Figure 3.8 Scientists have many ways of studying how neurons make specific connections in the developing brain. One strategy is to rotate or transplant the eyes of frogs or tadpoles at various stages of development and then see what effect the procedure has on the animals' visual behavior. The top drawing shows the behavior of a control frog, which had developed normally; the frog sees an insect ahead and above and strikes ahead and above. In the second drawing from the top, the frog's eye has been rotated 180 degrees (at a late stage in its development); the frog strikes forward and down when the insect is behind and above. In the third drawing from top, the left eye has been substituted for the right eye (again at a late stage in development) and the dorsoventral axis reversed; the frog strikes down when the insect is above. In the bottom drawing, the left eye has again been substituted for the right (also late in development), this time with the anteroventral axis reversed; the frog strikes up but in the wrong direction.

results indicate a great deal of plasticity at the early stage of the developing system; that is, early on, it has a great capacity for adjusting to change. After further development, however, that plasticity weakens or disappears. (Figure 3.8 shows how scientists knew that the image on the frog's retina was rotated. They placed a tasty-looking fly in the frog's field of vision and observed where the frog directed its attack.)

The discovery of developmentally regulated proteins in the chick retina may explain such changes in plasticity. Two of these proteins are present during early development but disappear later, and three are present in later stages of development but are absent earlier. This program of timed

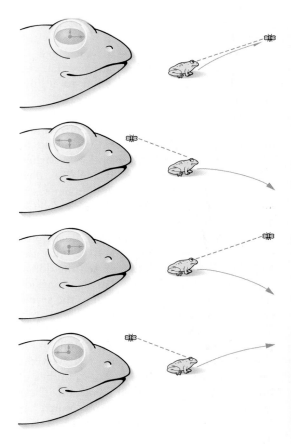

gene expression could mean that the surface molecules in the chick retina change in the course of development. Axons seeking to connect with certain proteins can find them at earlier stages but not later, after the early proteins disappear.

Circuit Formation: Formation of Synapses

As axons grow and travel, they eventually make connections, either with other neurons or with the anatomical structures that they will innervate and whose function they will regulate. As you know, the connections between neurons take the form of synapses, where one neuron releases a neurotransmitter that affects the activity of the receiving neuron. Each class of neuron in the central nervous system is able to form a synapse with only a very limited repertoire of cell types.

The development of most synapses in the primate neocortex takes place after birth. Nevertheless, the brain at birth already contains an overabundance of synapses. Starting soon before birth, the cortex continues to overproduce synapses, a process that is then followed by a reduction in the number of synapses until adult levels of synapses are obtained. Scientists have studied the formation of synapses in the visual, somatosensory, motor, prefrontal, and hippocampal cortex in monkeys. Because the behaviors controlled by each of these areas develop on different time frames (for example, we acquire basic visual functions, the ability to see, before we acquire certain cognitive functions, such as the ability to plan), scientists expected that synapse development would show the same timing differences (that synapses would be observed in sensory areas before cognitive areas). The researchers were surprised to observe, instead, that the timing and rate of increase in the formation of synapses were similar for each area studied. Thus, synaptic density increased rapidly during the last third of gestation in every area that was studied, and this increase continued until the fourth postnatal month (possibly equivalent to the maturity of a one-year-old human child). Furthermore, each area passed through a phase of excess synapses, higher than adult levels, at roughly the same postnatal age. This synapse overproduction was particularly high from two to four months after birth. After four months, synapse elimination increased, until the number of synapses declined to adult numbers. The decline was steepest in the first year and more gradual in the next several years.

The pattern just described for monkeys is slightly different for humans. The human visual cortex undergoes a rapid burst of synapse creation at postnatal months 3 to 4, with maximum density reached at four months. In the auditory cortex, synaptogenesis follows a similar timetable. However, in the middle frontal gyrus (an area comprising a variety of high-level cognitive functions), a similar early overshoot occurs, but its maximum density is not reached until one year. Importantly, the reduction in synapses also differs for these three areas: in visual and auditory areas, adult levels of synapses are reached early in childhood (between two and six years of age); whereas, in the middle frontal gyrus, adult levels of synapses are not attained until adolescence. Nevertheless, most synapse elimination in the human appears to occur late in gestation and early in the postnatal period. As we shall see in a subsequent section, in this stretch of time, the nervous system seems to be critically sensitive to environmental events and can take advantage of the abundance of synapses.

Apoptosis and the Refinement of Synapses

Apoptosis refers to the programmed cell death (often regulated by genes) that occurs during embryo formation or in the turnover of senescent (dying) cells. The developing nervous system produces many more neurons than are found in the final product (similar to its production of many more synapses than are seen in adults). This super-abundance of cells (in some areas, as much as 85 percent excess) is reduced by a kind of sculpting action that accompanies the formation of synaptic connections between populations of neurons and their targets. The process allows for the formation of necessary neural circuits and for the elimination of redundant or improperly connected ones, until the neural network has adjusted to match the size of the area it is to govern.

Some superfluous neurons die early in their development, but others develop fully before being eliminated. They may differentiate, send forth axons, and make contact with a target before they give up the ghost. One possible explanation for why some neurons survive and other, identical neurons die is that they require certain life-sustaining factors that they can receive only from their proper synaptic targets. That is, a neuron that succeeds in making a synaptic connection with an appropriate target—and thereby receives sufficient exposure to an appropriate growth factor—will survive. Those that make inappropriate or nonfunctional connections or no connections will be eliminated. Experimental manipulations of embryos in which, for example, a third leg is grafted onto an animal support this theory. Under these circumstances, scientists observe much less cell death in the spinal cord than normal. The extra limb provides an additional opportunity for the cells to develop working connections and survive.

Another mechanism that may act in regard to motor neurons to eliminate some cells while promoting the survival of others is muscle movement at the appropriate stage before birth. When the limb of a chick embryo is treated with a paralyzing agent, cell death in that area is greatly reduced, and the limb ends up being innervated with an abnormally large number of neurons. It appears that, in the normal development of a limb, axons seek acetylcholine (ACh) receptors on muscles as their targets for synapse formation: the limb's degree of physical activity *in utero* ("in the uterus") ordinarily determines the number and distribution of these receptors on the muscle; then axons compete to make synaptic connections with the receptors. Because each receptor site can support only one synapse, neurons that are smaller or less mature lose out in the race to connect. In the paralyzed limb, the cell membranes on the muscle do not undergo the changes that would have been stimulated by activity, and therefore many nonfunctional ACh receptor sites are retained. The presence of these extra sites prevents the normal pruning of neurons by programmed cell death.

In short, the activity of muscle–neuron connections before birth may also act to hone and sharpen the nervous system, at least at the level of spinal cord and subcortical brain connections. Human fetuses are very active before birth. They move their limbs against the tension of the amniotic fluid; they swallow; they perform breathing-like movements. This activity most likely serves to strengthen certain neural connections while contributing to the death of cells that the system does not need.

In the past few years, we have learned a great deal about the genetics of apoptosis. For example, mice made deficient in one of the interleukin-1β-converting enzyme (ICE) proteases not only died within a few weeks of birth, but, more importantly, possessed brains that had too many cells, some of which were disorganized. This important discovery will likely lead to further insights into the genetics of apoptosis, which will in turn assist us in understanding what regulates cell death in the developing brain.

A Summary of Early Brain Development

Let us quickly review the highlights of prenatal brain development. The formation of the brain begins shortly after conception, with the development of a pseudostratified layer of epithelial cells that gradually thickens to form a neural plate and then a neural tube. As the cells proliferate, the forebrain, midbrain, and hindbrain appear. The neocortex (which is derived from the forebrain) will eventually form six layers of cells. These layers are created by immature neurons that migrate along radial glial fibers to occupy genetically specified locations. When the cells have reached their target destination, they begin to aggregate (adhere to cells of a similar kind) and differentiate (mature) and then to develop axonal and dendritic processes and form synaptic connections. Both neurons and synapses are overabundant at birth, but, through the processes of cell death (apoptosis) and synaptic pruning, they eventually arrive at adult numbers. Most likely, these adjustments are not completed until mid- to late adolescence.

The Genetic Plan

As the fetus and embryo develop, the plans encoded in the genes are revealed. The fact that we do not yet know the exact molecular mechanisms of most developmental phenomena should not obscure the more striking fact that, generation after generation, the brains of developing animals grow the right neurons in the right places.

The genes determine a neuron's size and shape and the transmitter that it will manufacture. (Even though the neuron's immediate environment may have some influence on what that transmitter will be, structural or secretory proteins produced by specific genes normally guide each neuron to a specified environment.) The neuron's intracellular operations (those within a given neuron) and its intercellular operations (those between two or more neurons) also are programmed by proteins encoded by the genes.

Sometimes, though, the genetic program is incomplete or scrambled in some way. For example, in the disorder known as Down's syndrome, the affected person inherits more than the normal complement of genes on a part of the 21st chromosome. The scrambled genetic program results in a number of physical abnormalities, some of which are reflected in the mental retardation that is part of the syndrome. In other disorders, the lack of a single gene or the mutation of a single gene severely affects development. The box on pages 76 and 77 describes how a single-gene mutation affects the brain development and the observable behavior of the Siamese cat, as well as producing the beautiful pattern of coloring that characterizes the breed.

It is important to realize that the absence of a normal gene or genes need not always result in a disability. For example, in the single-gene defect *phenylketonuria* (PKU), the afflicted person lacks an enzyme that helps metabolize the amino acid *phenylalanine*. Because this amino acid is commonly found in the diet (one form of which is the sugar substitute *aspartame*), persons with PKU build up abnormally high levels of phenylalanine, which eventually results in severe mental retardation. However, because screening for PKU is now mandatory in the United States, infants with this genetic defect are identified at birth. They are then placed on a diet low in phenylalanine, which enables most of the affected population to develop normally.

The Siamese Cat: How a Single Gene Affects Brain Development

The distinctive markings of the beautiful Siamese cat and its characteristic cross-eyed look result from mutation of a single gene. This mutant gene also results in a serious miswiring of the cat's visual pathway.

The cross-eyed look of the Siamese cat results from a miswiring in the cat's visual pathway.

How does this occur? A gene, as you probably know, specifies the manufacture of a given protein. (Genes also program the initial proliferation, differentiation, and migration of neurons, although the manner in which they do so remains a mystery.) In regard to the Siamese cat, the single gene that malfunctions would normally produce an enzyme (tyrosinase) that is a necessary step in the proper synthesis of the dark pigment melanin. The result of this missing step is that melanin cannot be synthesized by the cat's body at its normal body temper-ature. Only the cooler areas of the body—the paws, the tips of the ears, and the snout—are darkly pigmented.

This missing step in a metabolic pathway also disrupts development of the visual pathway—the normal neural connections between eye and brain (see drawing at right). Some growing axons end up on the wrong side of the brain, and so the cats do not have a normal binocular field of vision. One type of miswiring produces cats that can see only objects appearing in the part of their visual field nearest their nose; another miswiring produces monocular rather than binocular vision.

Impaired development of the visual pathway is also present in albino mammals (such as some tigers, mice, or mink)—animals with a different mutant gene that also prevents normal synthesis of the pigment melanin.

It is clear that the absence of the pigment somehow produces the aberrant growth pattern of visual-path axons, even though the cells themselves do not normally contain melanin. Neuroscientists and geneticists do not yet know how this happens. Because another set of cells developing in the eye's retina do normally contain melanin, it could be that some interaction between the visual-path cells and the retinal cells is needed for normal development.

The case of the Siamese cat is a source of tantalizing insight into genetic mechanisms in the developing nervous system. It helps demonstrate the role that genes play in development. Genes most likely do not contain a complete program for the laying

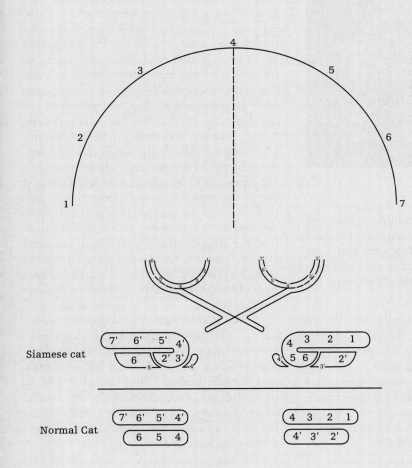

Siamese cat

Normal Cat

The map of the visual field on the lateral geniculate nucleus in Siamese cats *(top)* and normal cats *(bottom)*.

down of all the brain's neural circuits; rather, they produce the elements that begin the orderly process of development. Many steps in the developmental process are governed by intracellular events and intercellular interactions; these events and interactions take place in a context that is almost always the same for members of a given species—except in cases like that of the Siamese cat, where one abnormal gene produces a number of unexpected developmental outcomes.

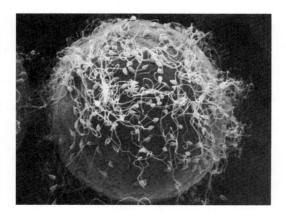

Sperm surrounding an egg.

In the next section, we look at how the genes that determine a person's sex produce differences in brain development and how these physiological differences may be related to behavioral differences between the sexes.

Sex and the Brain When egg and sperm unite at the moment of conception, a person's sex is determined. Each parent contributes a set of 23 chromosomes to the new cell, one of which is the chromosome that determines sex. Women always contribute an X chromosome, because a female's cells contain two of them; a male's cells contain one X chromosome and a smaller Y chromosome. If the impregnating sperm carries an X, the offspring will be female (XX); if it carries a Y, the embryo will develop into a male (XY). Before the third month of gestation, there is little difference between the sexes. Every embryo, whether male or female, possesses three undifferentiated sexual structures at that stage. These structures are the *genital tubercle,* which will develop into the external genitalia; the *bipotential gonad,* which develops into ovaries or testes; and the *Mullerian* and *Wolffian* ducts, which differentiate into internal sexual structures.

Beginning at the third month, however, a decisive change takes place. First, the *SRY* gene (the sex-regulating gene of the Y chromosome whose gene product is called *testis-determining factor*) facilitates the production of hormones that will cause the testes to develop from the bipotential gonad. In turn, the testes produce *androgens* (male hormones such as testosterone) that will stimulate the development of the Wolffian duct system, while another hormone (the Mullerian-inhibiting substance) discourages the development of the Mullerian duct system (which is the precursor to female organs). In contrast, if the Y chromosome is *not* present, and thus there is no *SRY* gene, the testes will not develop, and there will be no androgens to stimulate the development of the Wolffian duct system. Instead, the Mullerian duct system (which otherwise would have been inhibited) is permitted to develop, leading to the creation of a girl.

Given that the sex chromosomes produce such impressive physiological differences between male and female bodies, do they also produce any differences between male and female brains? They certainly do in many animals, and, although the anatomical and physiological evidence for similar effects in human beings is not abundant, significant differences have been found.

Among canaries, it is the male that sings—as a part of the courting ritual and to lay claim to its territory. The song is controlled by a nucleus of cells in the bird's left hemisphere, and this nucleus is much larger in males than in females. This difference between male and female anatomy and behavior is without doubt the result of hormonal influences. Early implantation of the male hormone testosterone in a female bird plus later treatment with androgens cause the female to sing, as well as enlarging her cortical nucleus, making it more nearly the size seen in males. In the course of normal development, the male gene complement directs the production of testosterone.

In the canary, then, male and female brains are organized differently; the difference is anatomically obvious and is clearly linked to differences between male and female behaviors. How can a hormone—in this case, testosterone—work to produce such differences?

When the male gonads begin to manufacture testosterone, it is secreted into the embryo's general circulation and travels to the brain. Certain target cells in the brain are able to recognize and retain the hormone by virtue of specialized receptors. As the testosterone accumulates within these cells, it binds directly to specific sites in the cell's nucleus to regulate genetic mechanisms (see Figure 3.9). In this way, testosterone is able to increase the expression of selected gene products.

Such changes in genetic expression have at least two major consequences. First, the testosterone-induced gene products (probably some structural proteins or some enzymes, not yet fully characterized) "sensitize" the cell so that in the future it will respond to increases in the hormone's presence (for example, at puberty). This kind of prenatal effect of hormones on the brain is called an *organizational effect*. The effects that the hormone will have later on as a result of this sensitization—such as its effects at puberty—are called *activational effects*. Second, the changes in genetic expression can produce the sort of anatomical differences that we noted between the brains of male and female canaries. Similar *dimorphisms,* or male–female anatomical differences, have been found in the brains of hamsters and rats.

Human Differences in Brain and Behavior

The *corpus callosum,* the large bundle of

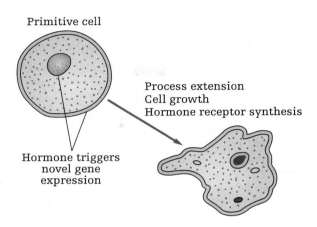

Figure 3.9 Ways in which testosterone can alter a cell's development: by promoting or inhibiting growth; by inducing development or extension of axon branches or dendrites and influencing their direction; by sensitizing receptors to respond to the future presence of the hormone.

fibers connecting the left and right sides of the brain, is the most talked about sexually differentiated structure in psychology—possibly because it provides a fertile testing ground for hypotheses about the sexually dimorphic brain. This structure has three main regions: the *genu,* which is the most anterior part; the *splenium,* the most posterior part; and the *body* (the middle part). Some neuroanatomists now think that the splenium not only is larger in women than in men, but also differs in shape. Some studies have found that these differences can be seen as early as the 26th week of gestation.

A second anatomical difference is seen in the *anterior commissure,* a band of fibers connecting the two halves of the brain. Although this structure is only 1/100 the size of the corpus callosum, a number of researchers report that the anterior commissure is larger in women than in men and is larger in homosexual than heterosexual men.

A third region of the brain receiving attention from neuroanatomists is the *massa intermedia*, which is a small band of fibers connecting the left and right regions of the thalamus (see Figure 3.10). Some reports claim that the massa intermedia may be larger in women than in men. Interestingly, some men entirely lack a massa intermedia; such men typically have lower nonverbal (that is, spatial) IQ scores.

A final region of the brain that may differ in men and women is the *planum temporale,* the upper surface of the temporal lobe (see Figure 3.11). In the left hemisphere, this area overlaps Wernicke's area, a major language center. In most brains, the left planum temporale is larger than the right, with rare exceptions; it is only in female brains that the right is occasionally found to be larger.

Given these differences in the brains of men versus women, it makes sense to ask how they translate into *behavioral* differences. Psychologists have reported certain statistical differences for many years. In other words, they have found that the *average* scores of men differ from the *average* scores of women when the following behaviors are measured:

1. Males are more aggressive than females. This difference appears in all cultures and at an early age.

2. Females have greater verbal fluency than males.

3. Males have more acute visual-spatial abilities than females.

On closer inspection, however, these differences are found to be more subtle than the

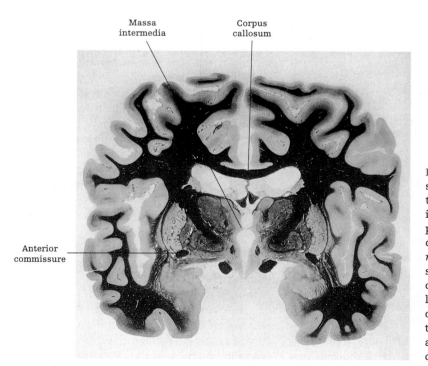

Massa intermedia

Corpus callosum

Anterior commissure

Figure 3.10 Here you see a coronal section of the brain that is stained in such a way so as to provide a great deal of detail. The *massa intermedia* is a midline structure that sits in close proximity to the lateral and third ventricles (also displayed are the anterior commisure and the corpus callosum).

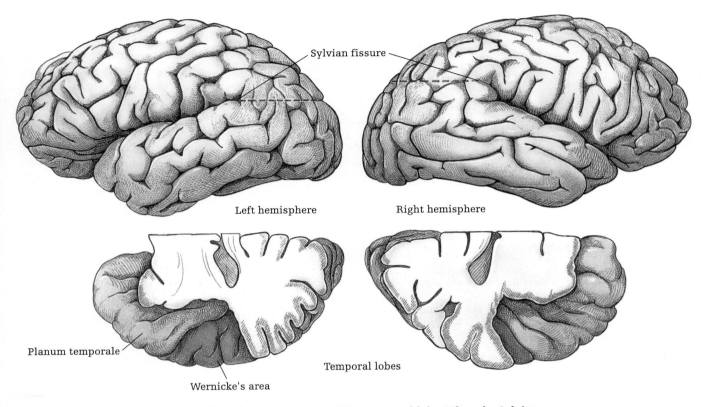

Figure 3.11 The Sylvian fissure defines the upper margin of the temporal lobe. When the Sylvian fissure is opened and the cut completed along the dashed line, the planum temporale (light purple), which forms the upper surface of the temporal lobe, can be seen. It is usually much larger in the left hemisphere, and the enlarged region is part of Wernicke's area (dark purple). For the most part, the only exceptions (brains with a larger right planum temporale) are found in women.

laboratory data might suggest. To illustrate this point, we will focus on verbal and visual-spatial differences between the sexes. The differences in aggression are discussed in Chapter 7.

To begin with, let us stress again that the male–female differences just listed are statistical (see Figure 3.12 on the following page), by which we mean that these effects apply to *groups* of subjects, not to an individual subject. For example, it is not unusual for an individual male to have greater verbal fluency than do most females or for an individual

female to be better at visualizing objects in space than are most males. Nevertheless, studies have found that, on average, there are consistent differences between groups of males and females in these characteristics. (Figure 3.13 on the following page gives examples of the types of problems on which females and males score differently.) But how do we explain these statistical differences? For most people, the parts of the brain responsible for language lie in the left hemisphere. The right hemisphere is mainly responsible for the processing of visual-

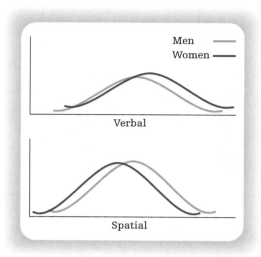

Figure 3.12 These idealized curves illustrate that, whereas on the average females show higher verbal abilities and males show higher spatial abilities, the differences are quite small.

spatial information. Could there be some difference in the organization of the two hemispheres and their interconnections in males and females that would account for the differences in ability in these two areas?

On the basis of the known differences in the responsibilities of the two hemispheres—language, left; visual-spatial, right—we might predict that left-hemisphere damage would produce verbal deficits and right-hemisphere damage would produce spatial deficits in adult patients. This outcome was predicted for a study on the effects of partial removal of one temporal lobe in both males and females. (The subjects were patients who had undergone surgery to remove tumors or repair injuries.) The prediction held true for the males but not for the females. This surprising result caused the researchers to speculate that the distribution of abilities may be different in male and female brains.

Subsequent studies lent some support to this conclusion. In one study of 85 patients who had suffered damage to one or the other

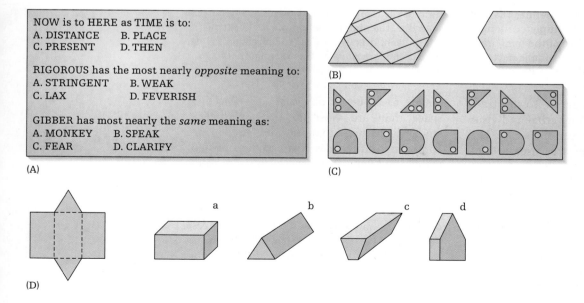

Figure 3.13 (A) An example of a verbal problem that females, on the average, solve more easily than do males. The drawings represent visual-spatial problems that males, on the average, solve more easily than do females. (B) Find in the figure at the left the shape shown at the right. (C) The figures at the left are models: from the six choices at the right, pick the rotated figure identical with the model. (D) Does a, b, c, or d represent the sample figure when folded along the dashed lines?

hemisphere, left-hemisphere damage was found to produce aphasia (a type of language disorder) in three times as many males as females; the males also showed much greater impairment in the high-level verbal tasks tested by the Wechsler Adult Intelligence Scale, one of the standard IQ tests. The Wechsler scale also includes a set of tasks that require very little language for their solution; several are tests of visualization. The men with *right*-hemisphere damage showed greater impairment in the performance of these tasks relative to the verbal ones, and those with *left*-hemisphere damage performed worse on the verbal tasks than on the visual ones. For women, the side on which the damage had occurred seemed to make little difference. Their abilities were impaired, but the impairment did not correlate with right or left damage.

We must be cautious in interpreting results based solely on the performance of people with brain damage. First, the number of people in a study is usually small, which increases the possibility that some unknown factor will interfere with the results. For example, if one person in a small sample has other, unknown problems, these abnormalities could significantly change the average test scores. Second, we have no way of knowing whether the results obtained from such subjects would apply to normal persons. Indeed, more recent work testing normal people does not so readily suggest male–female differences in verbal ability, at least not all kinds of verbal ability.

One study compared a number of experiments that had examined verbal differences between the sexes, ultimately comprising nearly 1.5 million subjects. The researchers concluded that, in general, there were *no* differences in verbal ability between men and women. Nevertheless, when other studies have looked closely at rather specific types of verbal ability, some differences have become apparent. For example, women do generally outperform men in verbal fluency (tests in which, for example, a subject might be told, "You have one minute to name all the mammals you know"). Note, however, that this advantage in verbal fluency does not extend to other domains of language use: there are no differences between men and women in vocabulary, reading comprehension, or essay writing. One researcher has argued that women outperform men only in the motor (talking) aspects of speech.

Other researchers have looked for differences in people of different sexual orientation. A number of those studies report a *slight* tendency for heterosexual women, as a group, to score highest on certain motor aspects of verbal fluency, followed by homosexual men, with heterosexual men coming in last.

If there is relatively little difference between men and women on verbal ability, what about spatial ability? As a rule, there are rather large differences between men and women on mental rotation tasks, of the sort illustrated in Figure 3.14 on the following page, with men outperforming women. In addition, men seem to outperform women in other tasks of spatial perception, such as spatial relations (see Figure 3.15 on the following page). Moreover, consistent with the studies correlating verbal skills and differences in sexual orientation, there are reports suggesting that heterosexual men outperform homosexual men on tasks of mental rotation and spatial relations.

On the whole, the research indicates that there are subtle differences in the verbal and spatial abilities of men and women and possibly of homosexuals and heterosexuals. The effects are small, however, and generally confined to narrow domains of functioning (such as mental rotation). Furthermore, it is unclear whether these behavioral differences

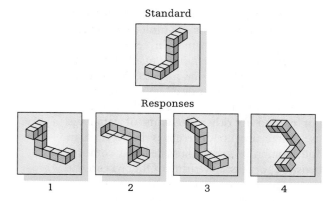

Standard

Responses

1 2 3 4

Figure 3.14 A mental rotation task requiring the subject to examine the top (standard) stimulus and then decide which of the other stimuli (responses) matches it.

are due to anatomical differences, those previously discussed and others, such as the reported possible differences in the hypothalamuses of gay and straight men. Finally, the few studies that have included children report that sex differences in performance typically emerge during adolescence, and scientists know very little about when in development most of the aforementioned

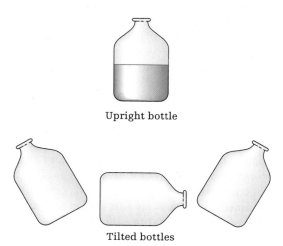

Upright bottle

Tilted bottles

differences in neuroanatomy appear. Nevertheless, certain anomalies of sexual development shed further light on the subject, and we turn to them next.

Experiments of Nature Hormones are known to play powerful roles in the behaviors of males and females. One way of studying their effects on behavior has been to examine the consequences of genetic malfunctions or of harmful substances in the prenatal environment that influence prenatal hormones and, subsequently, behavioral development.

Sometimes, genetic accidents occur at the chromosomal level. In the process of *meiosis*, when the paired chromosomes in the male or female reproductive cell separate to form sperm or egg, the division may go awry, leaving one daughter cell with one too few or one too many of an entire chromosome. When one of these cells impregnates or is impregnated (and survives), the resulting offspring will suffer some abnormality in his or her development.

Three abnormalities in the sex chromosomes have been extensively studied. One is *Turner's syndrome*, in which the person has only one X chromosome and no Y or second X to make a pair (this configuration is designated as XO). Fetuses with Turner's syn-

Figure 3.15 Subjects are told that the upper image shown here is "a picture of a bottle." They are then told that the horizontal line drawn across the middle of the bottle represents its water line—that is, that the bottle is approximately half filled with water. They are then shown the lower three images (pictures of more bottles), which are tilted to the left or right. However, water lines do not appear in these bottles. Finally, subjects are asked to draw, using a pen and straight edge, where they think these bottles' water lines would fall if each of the bottles were approximately half filled with water.

drome, though female, do not develop ovaries. All such females are unusually short and have short necks and widely spaced nipples. They never menstruate and do not develop breasts. As a result, from the eighth week of prenatal life, they do not have the level of sex hormones that the ovaries ordinarily manufacture and release into circulation. (Besides the female hormone estrogen, the ovaries also normally produce small amounts of testosterone.)

The most interesting behavioral deficit that women with Turner's syndrome show, in light of our earlier discussion of sexual dimorphism and the brain, is their poor performance on tests of visual-spatial ability. Their scores are generally much lower than those of the average female, although their performance on verbal tests is about average. It may be that the total absence of male hormone in these women affected brain organization.

Another chromosomal aberration, *Klinefelter's syndrome,* produces a male with an XXY genotype. These males show some feminization as adolescents and adults: an XXY male generally has little beard growth, he has a small penis and testes, his voice is unusually high, and he may have some breast development at puberty. However, the visual-spatial skills of XXY males fall within the normal male range. Evidently, the hormones produced under direction of the Y chromosome are sufficient for masculinization of the brain in this area.

In contrast, some chromosomally normal XY males have a rare genetic deficiency called *idiopathic hypogonadotropic hypogonadism* in which testosterone is not produced at puberty. These males score well below the average for men on tests of visual-spatial ability. Perhaps the flow of hormones at puberty that activates parts of the brain controlling male sexual development is also responsible for activating the development of brain areas required for visual-spatial tasks.

Although the existing data allow few uncontestable assertions about human behaviors as developmental products of sex-linked genes, future studies will no doubt verify and explain some of the proposed relations between genes, brain physiology, and behavior. Because these relations are easily demonstrated in a number of animal species, there is good reason to believe that they also exist in the human species.

Postnatal Development

At birth, the human brain weighs, on average, about 25 percent of its adult weight. It reaches half its adult size by six months and almost 75 percent by age two. Because no new neurons are created after birth (with the exception of the dentate region of the hippocampus, the cells in the olfactory bulb, and possibly cells in some regions of the frontal cortex), the increase in brain size is explained by an increase in the size of neurons and in the number of connections that they make through axon growth and dendritic branching. New glial cells and the growth of myelin (which is produced by a specific type of glial cell, the oligodendrocyte) around many neurons accounts for some of the increase.

After birth, a person's genetic program begins to interact with his or her unique environment, and thus that person begins to accumulate experience; as a result, each individual brain is in some ways different from all others. Experience affects the course of brain development in several ways. Of particular importance is that the brain's processing of sensory and cognitive inputs determines the cultivation of synapses and the growth of dendrites. Experiments in which an animal is denied some sensory or cognitive input help show how this development takes place.

Sensory Inputs

A mouse's whiskers (or vibrissae) are very important sources of sensory input: they give the animal information about place and movement. Each whisker sends its input to a grouping of neurons—called a *barrel*—in the mouse's cerebral cortex, on the side opposite the whisker. The fibers that innervate the whiskers are linked to the barrels through at least two synaptic relays (that is, by a circuit of at least three neurons).

If one row of whiskers is removed shortly after birth, the cortical barrels that would have innervated those whiskers will fail to develop. The subsequent lack of normal sensory input to those cortical cells results in their shrinkage and loss of function. At the same time, the barrels of adjoining rows become larger than normal, a development that demonstrates the system's *plasticity*—its ability to make up for a loss (see Figure 3.16).

When one eye of a kitten is kept closed from soon after birth until it is several months old, the kitten will no longer be able to see out of that eye, not because of deficits in any eye structure or in the retina, but because the visual cortex of the brain fails to

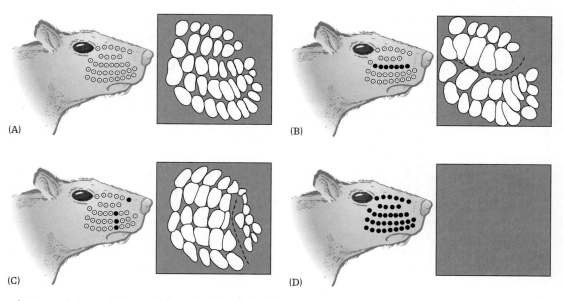

Figure 3.16 Experiments with mouse whiskers demonstrate not only the importance of sensory inputs to the brain's development, but also the brain's plasticity. The boxed drawings represent the barrels of neurons in the mouse's cerebral cortex that receive input from the whiskers; each barrel receives its input from a single whisker on the opposite side of the mouse's snout. A normal mouse and its barrels (A). When one row or column of whiskers was destroyed shortly after birth (B and C), the corresponding barrels failed to develop, but the adjoining barrels became enlarged, to compensate for the loss. When all the whiskers were destroyed (D), there was no cortical development.

develop. The same thing happens to young monkeys, whose visual system more closely resembles that of human beings.

In Chapter 4, you will read about the columnar organization of the cortex. In layer IV of the primary visual cortex, columns of cells receiving input from the left eye alternate with columns receiving information from the right eye. These columns are called *ocular dominance columns* (further discussed in Chapter 4). The effect on these columns of using only one eye can be seen clearly in Figure 3.17, prepared by T. Wiesel during research for which he and David

Figure 3.17 Ocular dominance columns—the columns of neurons that alternately receive input from the right and the left eye. The importance of sensory inputs for cortical development can be seen clearly when these two photos are compared. *Top:* A relatively normal pattern (from a monkey whose right eye was closed after the monkey had reached maturity). *Bottom:* The pattern in a monkey whose right eye was closed at two weeks of age and was kept closed for a year and a half; the columns for the functioning left eye obviously dominate.

Hubel were awarded the 1982 Nobel Prize in medicine or physiology. The upper photograph shows the columnar organization of a monkey whose right eye was closed after the monkey was 14 months old; the organization closely resembles the pattern that would be seen in monkeys reared under normal circumstances. The lower photograph is the cortex of a monkey whose right eye was closed at 2 weeks of age and kept closed for 18 months. The columns representing the functioning left eye obviously dominate. Figure 3.18 on the following page diagrams the process.

It appears that, during the infant monkey's development, the neurons from the two eyes compete for dendritic connections in layer IV, but the lack of visual stimulation for the right eye results in retarded growth of its axons. The left-eye neurons, which receive plenty of stimulation, then take over many more of the available synaptic connections that, under conditions of normal binocular vision, would have been connected to the right eye.

Human neural development has a similar need for sensory input. One study demonstrated abnormal cortical development in adults who were astigmatic as infants and whose astigmatism had not been corrected by glasses. *Astigmatism* refers to poor vision resulting from an abnormal curvature of the cornea (the clear outer covering of the eyeball), either in a vertical or horizontal direction. It causes visual input to the eye to be blurred in the direction affected. The researchers measured neural activity (evoked potentials) in the visual cortex as these subjects looked at patterns of lines at various orientations through a viewing apparatus designed to compensate for the eye's abnormality. Even though each of the subjects reported being able to see all the patterns through the apparatus, they showed less

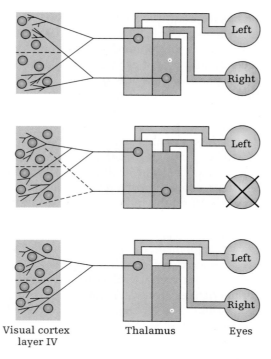

Figure 3.18 How the closing of one eye affects the development of the visual cortex. The green boxes represent the visual cortex; the blue boxes represent the thalamus. *Top:* With both eyes open, neurons from the two eyes compete for connections in layer IV of the visual cortex; neither eye dominates. *Middle:* Right eye is closed early in life; growth of that eye's axons and therefore of cortical connections is retarded. *Bottom:* Axons from the left eye then take over many of the available synaptic connections in layer IV.

cortical response to lines running along the direction that had always been blurred by their astigmatism.

The process of organizing sensory inputs to the brain does not necessarily end in early development. For example, one group of scientists studied a group of monkeys 12 years after disconnecting the afferent fibers from one of the monkey's upper limbs (the fibers had sent sensory signals from the limb to the somatosensory cortex). When the animals were examined, it turned out that the area of the brain that normally would have been occupied by the limb fibers was now occupied by fibers coming from the face. This outcome meant that the face region had essentially moved as much as 10 to 14 mm to occupy the limb region.

This type of sensory reorganization is not limited to animals. For example, similar effects have been noted in human adults who had undergone amputation of an arm. One such person, whose arm was amputated above the elbow, reported periodic sensation that seemed to come from the missing part of the limb (*phantom limb phenomenon*). Being familiar with the work described earlier, the scientist examining the person decided to test the patient's sensitivity to being touched on the face (which is known to innervate a region of the brain near the limb region). When the face was lightly stimulated, the patient reported sensation in both the face *and* the missing limb. In short, this patient, and others like him, demonstrated cortical reorganization similar to what had been observed in monkeys.

Most normal human environments provide the sensory stimuli necessary for normal development. However, in one classic study that examined infants in several orphanages in Iran, the effects of a severely deprived environment were all too evident. The infants in two of these orphanages spent virtually their entire first year of life just lying in their cribs. The babies were fed by means of bottles propped in their cribs and were picked up only once every other day to be bathed. The sides of their cribs were covered with a cloth (to prevent drafts), so they could not see out. Whereas virtually all normally reared babies can sit unaided by 9 months of age, some of these orphans still could not sit at 21 months. Fewer than 15 percent of them could walk at 3 years of age, whereas almost all normally reared children walk well before their second birthday.

When children are picked up, cuddled, and played with, they receive not only emotional and social stimulation but also stimulation of nerves and muscles. They learn to adjust their bodies to various ways of being held. Their sense organs and brains process the great variety of information that they receive from looking at things from different perspectives and from feeling different skin pressures and muscle tensions. All kinds of normal experience stimulate development of the brain.

Cognitive Inputs

In the preceding section, we considered how the brain can be altered by sensory experiences, including negative ones such as having a limb amputated. But what about the role of cognitive experience—thinking and remembering—in influencing the brain? Perhaps the best example is how learning promotes brain development. Learning is discussed at length in Chapter 8, but we present a short, general description here of some of the ways in which the brain profits from cognitive stimulation. Again, studies with animals give us the clearest indication of these phenomena.

Synaptic Remodeling May Be Possible Throughout the Life Span

William Greenough and his colleagues reported dramatic demonstrations of the

Stimulation of sense organs is a key element in normal development.

effects of cognitive experience on brain function and structure. For example, Greenough raised some rats in complex environments, such as cages that are full of toys and other rats (something like a school playground for rats) and that provide ample opportunity for exploration (see Figure 3.19). When these rats were compared with rats reared in conventional cages, the former did far better on a variety of cognitive tasks, such as maze

Figure 3.19 To examine the effects of different rearing conditions on synaptic remodeling in the developing and developed brain, rats are reared in a "complex" environment—that is, cages filled with lots of toys and other rats.

running. When he examined the animals' brains at autopsy, Greenough also found interesting physical differences in the rats reared in the complex environment: (1) certain regions of the neocortex were thicker and heavier and had more synapses per neuron, (2) dendritic spines and branching patterns were greater in number and length, and (3) there was increased blood flow to certain regions of the brain.

The effects of positive learning experiences on the brain are not limited to the rat. For example, experiments have been done with children who suffer from a rather specific language problem: they have a hard time telling the difference between certain sounds. A group of elementary-school-age children with such language problems were given four weeks of intensive training in speech discrimination. Amazingly, at the program's end, some children showed gains of two years in this ability, gains that were still evident weeks later (and presumably would never be lost). Clearly, then, the areas of the brain in which sound discriminations are made (perhaps the auditory-thalamocortical pathway) underwent some reorganization.

These effects, too, are not necessarily limited to early development. A group of investigators in Germany studied the somatosensory cortex in adults with and without experience in playing a stringed instrument, such as a violin. The cortex was examined through the use of magnetoencephalography, which, as already mentioned, measures the magnetic activity associated with neuronal firing. The scientists found that, among musicians, the area of the brain that represented the fingers of the left hand—the hand used on the finger board—was larger than the area that represented the right hand (which was used to bow, a movement considered less complex than those used on the fingerboard). And, needless to say, the area of the brain representing the left hand in musicians was larger than the area for the same hand in nonmusicians. Interestingly, although these effects were observed in all musicians, they were somewhat more obvious in those who had started their musical training before age 10. These observations clearly suggest that experience played the critical role here, although *when* the experience occurred also seems to have been important.

Overall, then, it appears that the human brain—even the brain of an adult—is capable of undergoing reorganization after certain kinds of experience. Moreover, it appears that much of the development during childhood and adulthood depends on an individual's interactions with his or her environment. Thus, it is clear that, although the brain grows less plastic with increasing age, it continues to be able to learn, and new learning changes it. Brain development is a lifelong process. Therefore, a challenge facing both behavioral and neuroscientists is to discover precisely what *kinds* of experiences are capable of influencing changes in the brain throughout the life span and what mechanisms are responsible for these changes.

Development of the Mind

The brain develops structurally during the nine months of prenatal life—and perhaps for a few months after that, because human beings seem to be born in a physically unfinished state. In the process, billions of cells proliferate, differentiate, and migrate to make connections and to form operational systems. Equally remarkable in human beings is the development of complex mental and psychological processes in the first decade or two of life. Some of these mental and psychological changes appear to depend critically on experience, whereas others do not. For example, many aspects of emotional development, such as an infant's attachment to its mother or father, appear to depend heavily on experience. Thus, infants who receive sensitive, responsive, and consistent caretaking are generally observed to be more confident in their relations with their parents. Further, such children are often more confident in themselves and mature in their social relations than others, and some even show advantages in intellectual functioning. Likewise, some advanced aspects of language, such as speaking in full sentences and understanding the words of others, depend heavily on experience; thus, children who have been deprived of normal language input typically fail to develop normal language. In contrast, there are aspects of language that appear to develop relatively independently of experience, such as the ability to discriminate speech sounds from foreign (that is, nonnative) languages in the first 6 to 12 months of life.

Mental development becomes even more heavily dependent on experience as infancy and early childhood are left behind. The changes undoubtedly occur through interactions of the environment with the excess number of synapses that are present in many regions of the brain well beyond the childhood period. For example, as already mentioned, it is not until mid- to late adolescence that synapses in the prefrontal cortex begin to decline to adult numbers. Scientists have speculated that this overabundance of synapses plays a critical role in capturing experience and, in turn, influencing the course of behavioral development. Given the role of the prefrontal cortex in solving problems and performing other "executive" functions (such as working memory, planning behav-

ior, and so forth), it seems likely that experience in such domains would promote mental development through the creation of new synaptic contacts. This, then, would be the phenomenon responsible for the success of many types of early intervention programs such as Headstart for children who are otherwise deprived of the experiences that their minds need in order to "grow."

Overall, the fascinating changes that take place as children grow to adulthood are greatly influenced by both the status of the brain at birth and the changes that take place in the brain owing to experience.

Aging and the Brain

All organisms age and die; however, whereas mayflies are born and die in the same day, great tortoises can live for a century and a half. In mammals, a species' average life span is generally related to the animal's size. Smaller animals, whose breathing rate and heartbeat are faster than those of larger animals, live a shorter chronological time. But, in terms of biological time, all mammals, regardless of their size, tend to breathe about 200 million times during their lives, and their hearts beat about 800 million times. *Homo sapiens* is an exception to this body-size–life-span ratio. Human beings live almost three times as long as mammals of our body size "should," even though our rate of breathing and heart rate are correctly scaled to our mammalian size. Nevertheless, some have speculated that the average upper limit to the human life span is 85 years.

The agents of aging remain as much a mystery as the agents directing development. Most hypotheses about why we age focus on genetic mechanisms, which are likely to be complex and act indirectly. (For example, we know that heredity accounts for only a relatively small percentage of the variability in the life span, in contrast, for example, with life style.) According to one hypothesis, the genetic program contains specific "aging" genes that are switched on at a certain time of life, just as the genes initiating puberty are switched on at a certain age. According to another hypothesis, in later life the organism simply runs out of genetic information (that is, the DNA is used up). This deficiency, in turn, is responsible for the biological changes that follow. A third hypothesis states that the genetic program is subject to random damaging events over time that eventually lead the cells to produce too many inactive or even harmful proteins and too few that function properly. Other theories implicate the immune system as well, suggesting that it attacks the body's own dysfunctional proteins as if they were foreign substances, producing antibodies that eventually cause the changes seen in aging.

How is the aging process revealed in the structure and functioning of the brain? And how are these brain changes manifested in behavior?

Neurobiology of Aging

To date, scientists know more about the *aged* brain than they do about the *aging* one. Most of the changes discussed in this section have been found in the brains of very old organisms, but it is difficult to say when such changes might have begun or how rapidly they occurred. Many of the data on human brains are difficult to interpret because researchers were not able to discover the health status of the elderly people whose brain tissue was under study. Still, a number of developments seem to be universal in the brain as it ages. The aging brain loses size, weight, and volume. For example, between the ages of 35 and 60, 10 percent of the brain's volume may be lost. This atrophy

is a result of the loss of neurons and their replacement by fibrous astrocytes. (In fact, 40 years ago, it was proposed that the cortex loses as much as 40 percent of its neurons during the aging process; however, that drastic percentage has since been revised.) On the other hand, recent studies that carefully screened for brain pathology reported that there may be relatively little loss of cortical neurons in the normal aging brain, although these neurons do shrink in size (with perhaps male brains shrinking more than female brains).

Whether each person actually loses cortical neurons depends heavily on many factors, not the least of which is whether our brains become diseased. For example, among elderly people with *dementia* (a condition characterized by a progressive loss of higher cognitive abilities, which eventually leads to confused or delusional thinking or both), 50 percent of the cells in the entrorhinal cortex (part of the temporal lobe dealing with memory) have been lost; for those with advanced *Alzheimer's disease* (a disorder characterized by progressive mental deterioration, which also results in dementia), the loss approaches 60 percent. In addition to cell loss, some aged brains show *neurofibrillary tangles* and *senile plaques.* The tangles consist of skeins of microtubules that proliferate inside a neuron and eventually replace it, making the cell nonfunctional. The plaques are amorphous structures made up of granules and filaments, thought to be a sort of debris from degenerating neurons. They appear in large numbers in brains of people who have died of Alzheimer's disease (see Chapter 10 for elaboration).

Aging and Behavior

A universal finding about mental changes in old age may be related to the kinds of physiological changes just discussed: cognitive processes slow down in older people. In tests where speed of response is an important component, such as some of the subtests in commonly used IQ tests, elderly people do not score as well as younger ones—or as well as they themselves scored when they were younger.

The loss of myelin (which speeds the transmission of nerve impulses) might contribute to a more general decline in cognitive function. This loss might particularly affect the prefrontal cortex, which is critical in problem solving. In addition, there is reportedly as much as a 30 percent drop in the density of the N-methyl-D-aspartate (NMDA) receptor for the neurotransmitter glutamate, which plays a prominent role in learning and memory.

In spite of the clear effects of aging on the brain, it is still difficult to make many generalizations about age-related losses in intellectual functioning. Variability seems to be greater among older people than at any other time of life. Some 60-year-olds already show a noticeable decline in abilities, whereas some 90-year-olds are as sharp as ever, though a bit slower.

Several longitudinal studies (studies that test the same persons repeatedly over a number of years) have shown that, on the average, scores on the verbal parts of IQ tests decline little or not at all until the mid-70s. Vocabulary, comprehension, factual knowledge, recognition of similarities, and arithmetic ability show almost no change from scores obtained earlier in life. There is some decline for tasks that require simple motor movements (some of which are timed); but, though the decline is statistically significant, it is not dramatic or disabling (see Figure 3.20). Perhaps most encouraging is a report

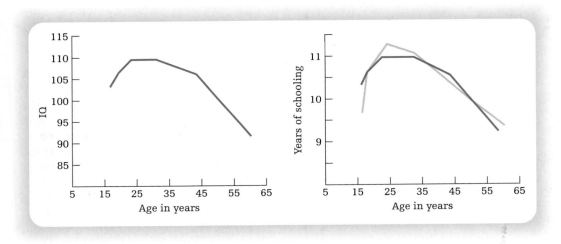

Figure 3.20 Cross-sectional data relating age and IQ is shown on the left. People in different age groups from 15 to 60 years old were given IQ tests at about the same time. (The data were collected by the developers of the widely used Wechsler Adult Intelligence Scale.) The curve connecting the data points seems to show that IQ declines after age 30—that people become less intelligent beginning at about the thirtieth birthday. However, as shown on the right, we are forced to alter that conclusion after plotting the education level of each of the tested age groups and superimposing that curve over the one shown at the left. Now it seems clear that the first curve represents not a decline in IQ with age but an increase in amount of education received by different age groups over the years.

suggesting that remaining intellectually active into old age protects against some aspects of cognitive decline. For example, a range of intellectual tasks were administered to young (average age 38 years) and old (average age 65 years) college professors and to a control group of young and old subjects drawn from the college community. Only on tests of reaction time (where speed is of the essence) and of paired-associate learning (the ability to remember arbitrary associations, such as a name and a face) did the elderly professors and elderly control subjects perform the same (in both cases, worse than younger subjects). Whereas the elderly professors showed relatively little decline in a variety of other intellectual tests, such as prose recall (the ability to remember a written passage) and working memory (the ability to hold information in mind long enough to act on it, such as the ability to dial a telephone number just received from the operator), the elderly controls showed a significant decline. Whether the brains of the professors differed physically from the control subjects was not examined.

Some part of this decline may be due to age-related changes in hearing and vision. In most people, visual and auditory acuities deteriorate with age. Such sensory losses can decrease both the amount of information received and the rate at which the information can be processed.

The aging body is also subject to a number of diseases that can affect mental functioning. Foremost among them is *atherosclerosis,* hardening of the arteries, which affects the blood vessels that nourish the brain, along with the body's other vessels. Obstruction of circulation in the brain's vessels can produce *infarcts,* or injury of the brain tissue (destruction of neurons), in the area of the obstruction. Atherosclerosis, in fact, is a major producer of dementia in the aged, but there are other cases of dementia whose causes are not known. In any case, fewer than 5 percent of people age 65 and older (the group usually defined as aged) suffer from any form of dementia, and only 1 to 2 percent are severely impaired.

Even when faced with the body's increasing inadequacies as it ages, the brain finds ways to deal with the new problems. It comes up with alternative solutions for how to get the groceries home when the arms no longer have the strength to carry two big bags (pull a wheeled cart or ask for a ride). It devises intricate reminder systems (lists over the stove, calendars on the bathroom door, and lists of lists) for when the memory can no longer be counted on to recall upcoming events and appointments. Generally speaking, it appears that, if we take care of our brains (for example, by not subjecting them to teratogens such as smoking, alcohol, and so forth), we can expect our brains to last for a long time.

Summary

1. Formation of the nervous system begins about two weeks after fertilization, when cells in the embryonic disc differentiate into endoderm and ectoderm. Cells of the endoderm will form the respiratory and digestive systems. Cells of the ectoderm will form the nervous system, which begins as the neural plate and then thickens and folds over to form the neural tube. The top of the tube becomes the brain; the rest becomes the spinal cord. Ectodermal cells remaining outside the tube as it forms constitute the neural crest, which develops into the peripheral nervous system.

2. In the second month after fertilization, the three major divisions of the brain— hindbrain, midbrain, and forebrain—

begin to differentiate, and the forebrain divides into the diencephalon and telencephalon. Development of telencephalon structures proceeds from the inside out, with the cerebral cortex, or neocortex, developing last. In human beings, the cortex comprises 70 percent of the brain's neurons.

3. The eight processes of neural development are described in Table 3.1. Although these processes are under genetic control, certain environmental conditions seem necessary for normal development. For example, neurons aggregate to form specific brain structures through the agency of certain adhesion molecules on the neuronal surface, but some migrating neurons also require a particular biochemical substrate in the environment to guide them.

4. Males and females inherit different gene complements on the chromosomes that determine sex—XY for males and XX for females—and these differing sets of genes produce differences in anatomy and physiology of both body and brain. The agent of such differences is the male hormone testosterone, which male embryos begin secreting early in prenatal development.

5. Prenatally, hormones have an organizational effect on the brain: they change its anatomical development by entering cells and altering their genetic message, sensitizing the cells so that they later respond to the presence of the hormone. This later effect that hormones have on a sensitized cell is called an activational effect.

6. Human males and females have been shown to differ from each other in brain function, particularly in the verbal and spatial domains. There is some evidence that these differences are also true for heterosexual and homosexual people. However, these differences, though statistically significant, are less pronounced than popular stereotypes might have us believe. Because the two hemispheres of the brain are known to have different responsibilities in information processing in most people—the left hemisphere for language and the right for visual-spatial information—it has been suggested that the two hemispheres are organized differently by sex and by sexual orientation, with verbal and spatial functions more widely distributed in both hemispheres in females and in homosexual males, whereas the heterosexual male and possibly homosexual female have brains that are more specialized bilaterally.

7. The course of brain development after birth appears to depend crucially on an organism's interaction with its environment. Sensory and cognitive inputs promote dendritic growth and strengthen synapses. When certain inputs are denied an organism, as when one eye is covered in infancy, normal development of relevant brain areas fails to take place.

8. As organisms age, certain brain changes take place: the brain decreases in size, weight, and volume through loss of neurons and a decrease in the size of some types of neurons. Perhaps the most significant change is a decline in the firing rate of some neurons, because the most significant behavioral change in old age is a slowing down of information-processing abilities. This slowing down accounts almost entirely for the lower scores attained by elderly people on IQ tests. Importantly, however, brains that are "exercised" intellectually throughout the life span may be somewhat protected from other cognitive declines.

Key Terms

apoptosis	migration
synaptogenesis	aging
axon guidance cue	Y chromosome
induction	X chromosome
ectoderm	plasticity
proliferation	

Further Reading

Knudsen, E. I. 1999. Early experience and critical periods. In M. J. Zigmond, F. E. Bloom, S. C. Landis, J. L. Roberts, and L. R. Squire, Eds., *Fundamental Neuroscience* (pp. 637–654). Academic Press, New York. A chapter written for neuroscientists that focuses on what is known about the effects of experience on brain development, with particular emphasis placed on *when* experience most matters.

Kuida, K., Zheng, T. S., Na, S., Kuan, C., Yang, D., Karasuyama, H., Rakic, P., and Flavell, R. A. 1996. Decreased apoptosis in the brain and premature lethality in CPP32-deficient mice. *Nature,* 384, 368–372. The normal process of programmed cells death and its implications are studied in a genetically engineered mouse.

Nauta, W. J. H., and Feirtag, M. 1986. *Fundamental Neuroanatomy.* W. H. Freeman, New York. See Section 111, "Anatomy," Chapter 10, "Ontogeny; Spinal Cord." A classic text that provides detailed illustrations of brain anatomy, including histopathological studies and studies that employ magnetic resonance imaging.

Nelson, C. A., and Bloom, F. E. 1997. Child development and neuroscience. *Child Development* 68:970–987. Written primarily for psychologists, a review article that introduces the reader to major advances in those aspects of neuroscience that are of greatest relevance to those studying child development. Included is an overview of brain development, neuroimaging methods, and neural plasticity.

Science. 1996. November 15, Volume 274, Issue 5290. Within this scientific weekly is a special section on developmental neurobiology.

Shimamura, A. P., Berry, J. M., Mangels, J. A., Rusting, C. L., and Jurica, P. J. 1995. Memory and cognitive abilities in university professors: evidence for successful aging. *Psychological Science* 6:271–277. The authors of this study report a number of experiments performed on "older" college professors and control subjects of comparable age. A major finding is that using one's intellect appears to confer some protection against decline in cognitive performance as one ages.

Tessier-Lavigne, M., and Goodman, C. S. 1996. The molecular biology of axon guidance. *Science* 274:1123–1133. Seminal article that describes the molecular means by which axons grow to reach their target destination.

Wickelgren, I. 1996. For the cortex, neuron loss may be less than thought. *Science* 273:48–50. Written for a lay audience, this brief news clip describes recent evidence that calls into question the myth that we lose brain cells as we age.

Interactive Resources

To learn even more and make sure you've mastered the material covered in this chapter, visit our Web site at www.worthpublishers.com/bloom. Click on "Chapter 3" for resources including practice quizzes, flash cards, simulations, links to related Web sites, and updates on new research.

Sensing

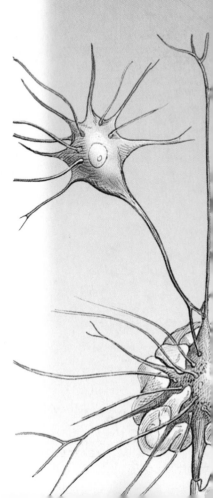

We monitor our environment at all times, our bodies and minds checking continuously for external and internal changes. Our very lives depend on our success in sensing the world through which we move and on the accuracy with which our sensations guide our movements. We move ourselves away from danger—extreme heat, the sight, sound, or smell of a predator—and toward the necessities of life—food, comfort, and protection. Our capacities to sense and to move, as noted in Chapter 1, are two basic properties of all living animals, from the simplest to the most complex. Creatures with nervous systems, however, have sensing and moving abilities far beyond the capacities of simpler, nerveless ones.

The intricate cellular machinery of the sensing and moving systems relies on many interconnected cells working together like an assembly line. The brain continually interprets sensory information and directs the body to make the best response—to seek shade from the heat or shelter from the rain or to relax on deciding that a stranger's stare poses no threat. All sensing systems operate on a similar organizational plan. Before looking at the specific workings of vision, hearing, taste, and smell, let us quickly survey the features that they have in common.

A General Model for the Sensing Systems

Through the ages, people have developed ingenious ways to communicate across distance. These methods have ranged from flashes of reflected sunlight, to more complex codes beaten on drums, to complete sentences carried over telegraph wires, to telephone or electronic waves bounced off communications satellites. All these systems have the same function, but the advantages of the more sophisticated methods are that they can carry more information faster and with less interference. Achieving these improvements in communication required the addition of components for detecting, filtering, and amplifying the signals.

The nerve cells in the sensory systems also must communicate for these systems to operate properly. And just as the electronic communication systems of the twenty-first century operate powerfully thanks to subtle but complex features that were added through the years, our body's sensing and moving systems have been refined as new controlling features were added through the eons of evolution. As these complex elements evolved, they enabled certain species to collect and interpret information more effectively than others, contributing to their survival.

As we examine what is known about the operations of the sensing and moving systems of the brain and spinal cord, keep in mind that we currently know enough to recognize that their organization is much more complex than we can explain. These still-mysterious complexities are almost certainly due to undiscovered principles of sensory integration that somehow demand special biological components. In this chapter, we examine the systems of neurons whose function is to sense the world around us and within us and, in the next chapter, those that control movement. The numerous similarities in the structural organization of the sets of brain structures responsible for sensing and moving tasks will ultimately make them easier for readers to understand.

All the known sensing mechanisms in both simple and complex nervous systems seem to have at least the following components:

1. A *stimulus-detector unit* consisting of a specialized sensory receptor neuron

2. An *initial receiving center* where neurons receive convergent information from groups of detector units

3. One or more *secondary receiving and integrating centers* where neurons receive information from groups of initial receiver neurons

In more complex nervous systems, the integrating centers are also linked to one another.

At some point in the sensory-integration process, the brain begins to compare the incoming information about the world being examined with other information that was received previously. The combination of currently sensed information and recollections of previously experienced similar objects, events, or entities allows us to *perceive;* that is, to infer the nature and meaning of what has just been sensed.

The process of sensing begins when an environmental event, or *stimulus,* is detected by a sensory neuron through its sensory receptor (another name for component 1 in the preceding list). The stimulus detector converts the sensory event from its original physical form (light, sound, heat, and pressure) into action potentials. These action potentials, or nerve impulses, now represent the sensory event in the form of cellular signals that can be further processed by the nervous system.

The nerve impulses produced by the stimulus-detection receptors travel along the sensory neuron to the *receiving center* responsible for that form of sensing (component 2 in the list). The mere arrival of the impulses signals the occurrence of an event in that sensory information channel. This first processing area in a sensory system is therefore termed the "primary" sensory relay. When the impulses are received in this processing area, certain details are abstracted from the specific qualities of the impulses. From the stimulus events of your ability to sense a flower through vision or smell, for example, color, shape, size, distance, and fragrance are abstracted. This information is then transmitted from primary processing areas to secondary processing areas (component 3). In those areas, further judgments about the flower—or whatever the sensory event happens to be—are made and sent on. At some point, the nature and importance of what has been detected is determined by the process of conscious identification that we call "perception." Finally, an appropriate response may be initiated.

All the systems specialized for sensing are organized to operate in this general way. To some extent, therefore, when we have examined one sensory system, we can apply its operating principles to any of the others.

What Do We Sense?

Like other animals, we perceive the world around us through our sensing systems. Each system is named for the kind of sensory information that it is specialized to detect: sight, sound, touch, taste, smell, and gravity, for example. (Information about gravity gives us our so-called sense of balance or equilibrium.) Other senses are less apparent, such as *proprioception,* the internal monitoring of body and limb positions, and *kinesthesis,* the continuous monitoring of movements. These senses help guide our limbs so that we can walk without stumbling or scratch our noses without poking our eyes. Even less obvious "senses" collect information from deeper sources in the body: temperature, blood chemistry and volume, and the chemical adjustments controlled by our endocrine organs. (These internal senses and the adjustments that the body makes to them are considered in Chapter 6.)

Some animals have yet other sensory systems. Snakes sense objects by detecting infrared signals, and certain sea animals detect the electrical signals given off by their predators, their prey, and their local social groups.

All forms of sensing carry information about *time*—when the detection of the stimulus began and how long it has lasted. Sight, sound, smell, and touch also carry information about *location,* where in space the signal arose. By comparing the strengths of the signals detected by each of our two ears or by comparing the differences in the images recorded by each of our eyes, the brain can determine the source of the signal in the environment.

Beyond simply alerting us to the fact that "something" is "out there," each of the sensory systems also distinguishes one or more qualities of the signal that it detects. We see light as color and brightness. We hear pitch and tone. We taste sweetness, sourness, and saltiness. We distinguish sensations on our body surface by the shape of the stimulus (sharp or dull), by its temperature (hot or cold), and by how it contacts the skin (a steady pressure or a vibrating or moving pressure). Each of the stimulus qualities distinguished by the senses indicates the existence of a cell (or cells) specialized to detect it, a *sensory receptor.* The activity level of these receptor cells depends on the intensity of the signal being detected—the brighter the light, the louder the tone, the sharper the sting, or the stronger the taste, the greater the receptor activity. The reverse is also true: less-intense signals produce less receptor activity. Signals that are too weak for sensory detection are termed "subthreshold." The frequency of the impulses and the total number of sensory receptors transmitting them also depends on the size of the object being sensed. Fingers do a better job of sensing size and shape than your back does because they

have more sensing receptors per millimeter of surface than your back. (Try distinguishing coins laid on your back. The sensory receptors on your back are too far apart to detect the coin's edges.)

The duration and intensity (or quantity) of a sensation also influence other aspects of its evaluation. A playful tickle turns painful if it goes on too long or gets too rough. Although we commonly speak of "sensing pain," it would be more appropriate to say that we "interpret" a sensation as pain from the quality and quantity—that is, the intensity and duration—of certain sensory signals that touch, sound, and even light can produce. Pain is therefore considered a "subjective" sensation. That is, decisions about whether a stimulus is or is not painful require an evaluation by the person experiencing it. People also differ in their sensitivity to painful stimuli. (The subject of pain and reactions to it are described at greater length in Chapter 8.) Table 4.1 lists the six major human sensory systems, the specialized organs that detect the stimuli peculiar to each, the qualities detected, and the receptor cells in each that pick up the quality and quantity of the stimuli.

Fine-Tuning of the Receptive Process

The role of sensory receptors is to alert us to change in the external world. Some sensory-receptor neurons respond most intensely when a stimulus begins, but, as the stimulus continues, the response fades. This diminishing responsiveness is termed *adaptation.* The rate and degree of adaptation to a prolonged stimulus vary for each sense and with the conditions of the moment. We scarcely remember a tight shoe as we dash off to work or school. The sound of street traffic fades away until a siren or rumbling truck catches our notice. We can detect a persistent gas leak or the lingering scent of a pleasant

TABLE 4.1 The fundamental properties of the six major sensing systems

Sensation	Sensing system	Quality	Receptors
Vision	Retina	Brightness Contrast Motion Size Color	Rods Cones Rods and cones Rods and cones Cones
Hearing	Cochlea	Pitch Tone	Hair cells
Equilibrium	Vestibular organ	Gravity Rotation	Macula cells Vestibular Cells
Touch	Skin Internal organs	Pressure Temperature Vibration	Ruffini corpuscles Merkerl discs Pacinian corpuscles
Taste	Tongue	Sweet Salty Sour Bitter	Taste buds at tip of tongue Taste buds at tip of tongue Taste buds at base of tongue Taste buds at base of tongue
Smell	Olfactory epithelium	Floral Fruity Musky Pungent	Olfactory receptors

perfume only when we breathe in deeply to see if it is still there.

Adaptation is essential for the proper perception of change. Our initial detection of a stimulus serves to bring the novel event into the pool of information that we are using to interpret the current status of our world. The fading of the response then allows us to update our interpretation as new sensory signals come along (see Figure 4.1 on the following page). If the sensing of new and old signals were always equally strong, the flood of sensory information pouring in from all of our receptors would drown our ability to cope with any of it.

We use our capacity to gain refreshed information about the world in everything that we do. If you close your eyes and try to identify an object placed in your hand, the task becomes much easier as you fondle the object because, when it just lies there, your palm's sensory receptors adapt and quickly lose detection of its edges. By turning it over and moving your fingers on its surface repeatedly, you begin to form a pattern of collected information that tells you what kind of a thing it is. Each new touch provides a new angle of analysis, giving you new information to add to the image you have been forming gradually from the first and subsequent touches before you adapt to them. When you awaken in a strange room, you need a few seconds to quickly remap the location of the doors, windows, and major objects even though you had sensed and adapted to all those objects before you fell asleep.

Another general mechanism facilitating the process of perception is *information*

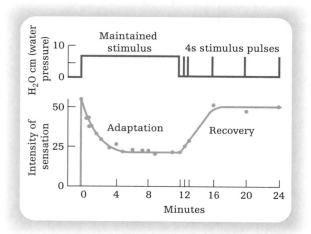

Figure 4.1 When a sensory event first occurs (the square wave at the top, for example, indicating application of pressure to the skin, represents the onset and ending of the pressure), the sensory receptor responds very vigorously. As the event continues, the receptor adapts to it, and activity in the nerve fiber diminishes to a lesser level of sustained activity. If stimuli are brief and periodic, or pulselike, the receptor responds fully each time without adaptation.

channeling. Each activated sensory receptor feeds sensory information into a chain of synaptic relays specific to that sense. These relays carry the signal higher into the nervous system hierarchy. In each leg of the relay, the signal receives additional processing. Whatever the actual physical stimulus may be—light waves, sound waves, odors, heat, cold—after it has been transduced by the receptor into nerve impulses, those signals have no distinct quality themselves. From that point on, the message initiated by the physical event exists only in its coded patterns of nerve impulses within the specific circuits of each sensory system. These systems therefore provide discrete sensory channels in the nervous system.

The brain, then, reconstructs an image of the external world by piecing together all of the information that it receives at any given time from every active sensory channel. It is this collection of information that the brain interprets to make the fluid mental construct that is our perception of our ever changing world.

Table 4.2 names the major sensory-processing locations along the channels for each kind of sensory information. The table shows only the main relays, to highlight the general pattern of level-by-level information processing that is common to all sensory systems. Within each system, the information entering a given level may or may not undergo special processing at that point. For example, the information may be heavily processed peripherally, as visual information is in the retina. (The retina contains not only the sensory receptors for light, but also several linked initial-processing neurons; it is the only specialized sensory organ that both detects and processes information locally in this way.) Or the information may be transferred in its original state to be processed by the other processing stations awaiting it down the line. (Equilibrium-sensing information goes directly to the brainstem for processing, for example.)

Every synaptic connection affords an opportunity for processing sensory information. For example, information becomes concentrated and has greater impact on higher integrating centers when many sensory-receptor neurons converge on a few common initial receiving neurons. Conversely, information may be diluted by the divergence of a few receptor neurons onto many receiving neurons. Although the physical connections do not change, modulatory systems can sharpen or diminish the impact by changing the functional responses of the common initial receiving neurons. More

TABLE 4.2 Channels for specific forms of sensing

Sensation	Primary (level 1)	Secondary (level 2)	Tertiary (level 3)
		Relay level	
Vision	Retina	Lateral geniculate Superior colliculus Hypothalamus	Primary visual cortex Secondary visual cortex
Hearing	Cochlear nuclei	Lemniscal, collicular, and medial geniculate nuclei	Primary auditory cortex
Equilibrium	Vestibular nuclei	Thalamus Spinal cord Oculomotor nuclei Brainstem Cerebellum	Somatosensory cortex
Touch	Spinal cord or brainstem	Thalamus	Somatosensory cortex
Smell	Olfactory bulb	Piriform cortex	Limbic structures, hypothalamus
Taste	Medulla	Thalamus	Somatosensory cortex

complex alterations can also occur at synapses. To see how these modifications take place, recall two of the basic neural connection patterns described in Chapter 2: the *hierarchical circuits,* which relay information from one level of a sensory system to the next and connect the various levels of a sensory system, and the *local circuits,* which operate within each level to expand or restrict the number of integrating neurons. Within each sensory-processing center, local-circuit neurons can either partially excite the relay neurons, making them more likely to fire when sensory information arrives, or partially inhibit them so that much more sensory input will be required to make them fire. Were you ever alone in a strange place, with your listening "turned up" to be able to hear any possible intruder immediately?

Every somatosensory-receptor cell monitors a limited area of the body's surface over which it detects the external event to which it is sensitive. This area is called its *receptive field.* Each sensory receptor in the skin sends its main signal to one select subset of primary relay neurons at the initial receiving level in the spinal cord (see Figure 4.2 on page 105). Because of the linkage of specific regions of the body surface to specific subsets of sensory processing neurons in the spinal cord or medulla, the sensory information can immediately be shared with other neurons, such as movement neurons, needed when the sensory signal represents a serious alert—for example, "hot" or "sharp." Sensory neurons in each of the other sensing systems also have limited receptive fields. In the visual and auditory systems, the receptive field is determined by the physical

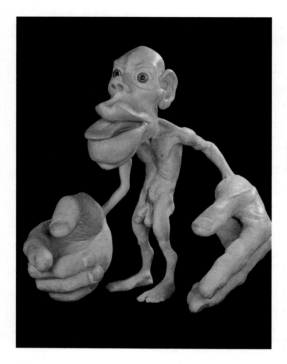

The misshapen appearance of this little man (a "homunculus") represents the disproportion in size of the areas of the somatosensory cortex dedicated to different surfaces of the body. Note that tongue, lips, face, and digits of the hands are represented by a far greater proportion of the cortex than would be represented by their proportion of the body's surface area.

location of the sensory neuron. If we monitored one visual receptor in the retina, we would see that it becomes active only when light passing through the lens of the eye falls on that cell's receptive field. In the olfactory system, odorant detectors are limited to certain discrete chemicals and register no responses except to the compounds for which they are programmed.

In short, information processing takes place every time a message is relayed from one neuron to another at any hierarchical level and during interactions between cells at each level. To gain a more detailed understanding of how this allows a specific sensory system to operate, we shall now examine some of the properties and principles of vision, the sense about which investigators currently know the most.

Seeing: A Detailed Look at the Visual System

The visual system responds to stimulation by light, electromagnetic radiation that has wavelengths ranging from very short (blue) to very long (red). We see objects because they reflect light into our eyes. An object's color depends on which wavelengths of visible light are reflected or absorbed by the object. Apples are red because they reflect red wavelengths and absorb blue. Isaac Newton, the famous seventeenth-century English physicist, used prisms to show that what appeared to be "white" light was actually made up of lots of colors mixed together.

When the German medical physicist Hermann von Helmholtz dissected animals' eyes in the last half of the nineteenth century, he discovered that visual information was displayed on the retina much as it is in any simple camera with a compound lens: upside down and reduced in size. The retina sees the world through the lens of the eye, much as the film in a camera sees the world through the camera's lens. On this simple foundation, scientists have constructed a towering body of information about the visual system. In fact, we are closer to understanding how our visual image of the world is reconstructed than we are to understanding any other sensory experience.

To examine the structure and operations of the visual system, we first need to know its principal components and how they are

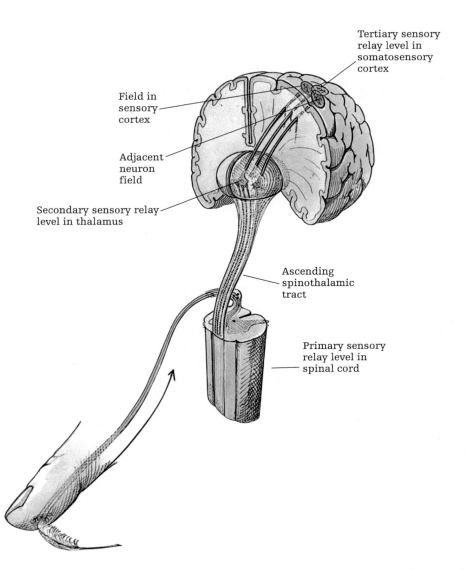

Tertiary sensory
relay level in
somatosensory
cortex

Field in
sensory
cortex

Adjacent
neuron
field

Secondary sensory relay
level in thalamus

Ascending
spinothalamic
tract

Primary sensory
relay level in
spinal cord

Figure 4.2 The several levels of sensory information processing. The sensation of a feather's touch travels from the receptive field at the tip of the index finger to primary sensory neurons in the dorsal horn of the spinal cord. The second link carries the tactile information upward through the spinothalamic tract linking the dorsal horn to sensory centers in the thalamus, and the third link projects the activity of the thalamic neurons onto the somatic sensory region of the cerebral cortex, specifically to that area onto which is mapped the surface of the tip of the index finger. Adjacent fields in the sensory cortex will detect touch on adjacent parts of the index finger and on adjacent fingers. The receptive fields on the tips of the fingers are highly specialized, so we can experience tactile stimuli that are only millimeters apart as distinct. The receptive fields on the back of the shoulders are quite large, and most people have less ability to discriminate closely grouped stimuli there as distinct.

organized into circuits. Then we will see how external visual stimuli are processed into "sight" by neurons working at different integrating levels. Finally, we explore some of the conclusions that psychologists have drawn about how humans view the world.

The Structure of the Visual System

The major structural components of the visual system (see Figure 4.3) are:

1. The *eye*, whose *lens* focuses the image and whose *retina* detects and transmits it

2. The *optic nerves*, which carry visual information from the output neurons of the retina to their initial relay targets in the thalamus and hypothalamus

3. Several *second-level neuronal targets:* specifically, three pairs of vision sensing nuclei—the *lateral geniculate nuclei* and the *superior colliculi* within the thalamus and the *suprachiasmatic nuclei* in the hypothalamus; and the paired motor-neuron nuclei that control the extraocular muscles

4. The *primary visual cortex*, which receives information from the thalamic nuclei

Even though it is the third processing level of the visual system, the primary visual cortex is called "primary" because it is the first *cortical* target to receive visual information. Information from the primary visual cortex is then distributed throughout a hierarchy of other vision-related regions in the cerebral cortex, termed secondary, tertiary, and so on.

The Eye The eye is the only visual-response organ in mammals. It consists of an "image focusing" unit and an "image detection" unit (see Figure 4.4 on page 108). The parts of the image-focusing unit are the *cornea*, a thin, curved, transparent membrane that starts the focusing process; the *lens*, an adjustable structure that completes the focusing process; and the *iris*, a circular muscle that alters the amount of light entering the eye by dilating or constricting the opening in its center, called the *pupil*.

The lens lies suspended like a hammock within a flexible lens capsule. When the muscles attached to the capsule contract or relax, the changing tension in the capsule

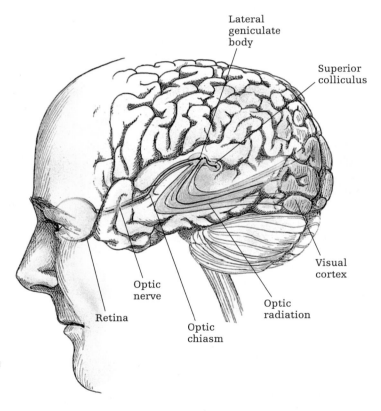

Figure 4.3 The component parts of the visual system beginning with the primary receptive component in the retina, the second-level neurons in the lateral geniculate or superior colliculus, and the third-level neurons in the visual cortex. The optic radiation consists of the fibers that connect the neurons of the lateral geniculate to the neurons in the visual cortex.

changes the curvature of the lens. The lens becomes either thinner and flatter or thicker and more rounded, depending on what is required by the distance between an object and the viewer. The size of the pupil also influences what and how we see. Hand your friend a small object to look at and see what happens. When he or she brings the object closer, the size of the pupil shrinks. Smaller pupil size excludes the peripheral rays of light that are being reflected from the object and helps produce a sharper image (the lens will also change shape to focus on an approaching object). Now ask your friend to close his or her eyes for a half-minute or so and then open them. You will see that the pupils are relatively dilated just after the eyes open, then rapidly close down to adjust to the room lighting. Autonomic nerve fibers to the involuntary muscles of the iris control these changes in pupil size automatically (see Chapter 6). These adjustments of the pupil (which you can observe) and of the lens (which your friend can experience) are termed *accommodation*.

The image-detecting unit of the eye is the retina. Your first thought on reading a description of the retina may be that its construction is all wrong. Its visual receptor cells, the rods and the cones, not only are situated as far as possible from the lens, but also point away from the incoming light, with their light-sensitive tips tucked between darkly colored epithelial cells, the *choroid pigment layer*.

Although this structural organization may initially seem backward, it does in fact serve a very useful purpose, as you shall see. The neuronal layers that intervene between the incoming light and the receptor cells are essentially transparent, which means that light could diffuse from adjacent regions of the retina. However, by detecting only the light that reflects off the choroid pigment

just beyond the tips of the rods and cones, each of these light receptors reacts to a very small illuminated area. The more independent light receptors per unit area of retina, the higher the visual resolution. The pigment epithelial cells also serve a metabolic support role for the highly active rods and cones. In some animals, such as dogs and cats, however, the choroid layers have highly reflective pigment that can increase the sensory cells' ability to detect dimly illuminated objects.

Under the microscope, the retina displays a very highly organized three-layered structure (see inset in Figure 4.4 on the following page), with each layer containing characteristic neurons. The outermost layer, the one next to the choroid epithelium, contains the cell bodies of the *rods* and *cones,* the primary light sensory receptors; this layer is termed the *outer nuclear layer*. The rods and cones connect with the *bipolar neurons,* whose cell bodies are in the *inner nuclear layer* along with those of the inhibitory and excitatory interneurons of the retina, the *horizontal* and *amacrine* neurons. The bipolar neurons in turn connect with the *ganglion cells,* whose cell bodies constitute the *ganglion cell layer*. The synapses between these three cell-containing layers, referred to as the *inner* and *outer plexiform* layers, are where almost all of the retinal synapses are located. The ganglion cells send their axons by way of the optic nerve to the initial visual relay neurons in the thalamus. Each rod and cone connects with several bipolar cells, and each bipolar cell can connect with several ganglion cells. The horizontal cells and the amacrine cells act as inhibitory local-circuit neurons within the retina, restricting the spread of the visual signals so that they converge onto the ganglion cells. This hierarchical pattern maximizes image detection through the divergent processing of light, ensuring that even small visual stimuli will reach ganglion cells.

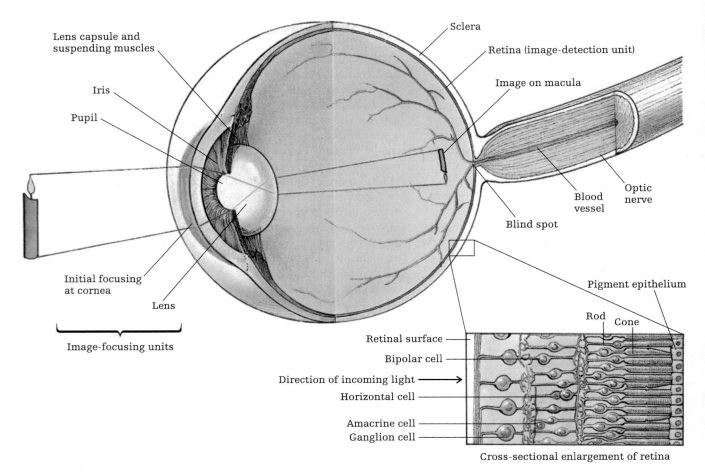

Figure 4.4 A cross-sectional drawing of the eye as seen from the side. The lens, its suspensory apparatus, and the iris are shown, as are the light-sensing detectors within the retina. The inset shows the cells of the retina in greater detail, with the initial-detector cells—the rods and cones—facing away from the iris and the incoming light. The primary receptors converge on the bipolar cells, which converge on the ganglion cells. The axons of the ganglion cells converge on the optic disc, or blind spot, where there are no primary receptors. These axons form the optic nerve, which carries information into the visual system. The local-circuit horizontal and amacrine neurons expand or constrict the activity that arises from images detected by the primary receptors.

Using fine electrodes, scientists have been able to record the activity of single ganglion cells as a light beam stimulus is moved over the retina. They have discovered that each ganglion cell responds to light falling on a unique, precisely demarcated *receptive field*— a small region on the retina where light detected by rods and cones most intensely activates or inhibits that particular ganglion cell through convergence. A ganglion cell does not respond at all to light falling outside the perimeter of its receptive field. Some ganglion-cell receptive fields are "center-on"; others are "center-off." A *center-on ganglion cell* is activated by light in the center of its receptive field but is inhibited by light at the perimeter. A *center-off ganglion cell* is turned off by activity in the center of its field but is activated by light at the borders. The functional lateral synaptic interactions between center-on and center-off ganglion cells make possible the sharp contrasts between the details of an image that are critical for visual acuity.

The distribution of the rods and cones on the inner layer of the retina also is organized in an orderly fashion. Cones are most dense on that part of the retina where images are most sharply focused by the cornea and the lens. This spot where visual acuity is the highest, called the *macula lutea* (literally, "yellow spot"), has a yellowish color and a high density of cones. Within the center of the macula is a rounded depression, at the point on the retina where images in the center of the field of visual focus will fall. No other retinal neurons are situated in this small zone; so, in cross section, the cone-enriched macula looks like a small pit, which gives it its name, *fovea centralis*. Away from the fovea, a small number of cones are spread evenly over the rest of the retina. Cones respond to light of different colors, some being sensitive mainly to blue, some to red, and some to green light. Rods are sensitive to reflected brightness but not to color. They are densest around the edges of the fovea but are more numerous than the cones over the rest of the retina. At night, when light is dim, the world becomes colorless and the rods do most of our seeing.

The prevailing layered cell structure of the retina picks up just outside the fovea. The layer first crossed by the incoming light consists of the axons of the ganglion cells. The ganglion-cell axons from all over the retina converge at a point slightly below the fovea, where they form a bundle of axons—the *optic nerve*—that carry visual information to the brain. The convergence of the ganglion-cell axons, however, leaves no room for any receptors or other retinal neurons in that spot. Any light that falls on the retina at the base of the optic nerve is, therefore, invisible. We are never aware of this hole, or "blind spot," because higher visual processing centers help us reconstruct a solid world. But Figure 4.5 will convince you that the hole is there.

The Optic Nerve and the Optic Tract The collected axons of the ganglion cells, bundled together in an optic nerve from each eye, travel to the base of the front of the hypothalamus, where the two bundles meet in the *optic chiasm*. Here, a partial crossover of fibers, called the *optic decussation*, takes place. The continuations of these axon bundles, separated again, are given a different name, the *optic tracts*.

Imagine that you are looking up at the human visual system from below with a microscope that permits you to see each of

Figure 4.5 To discover the blind spot of your right optic disc, close your left eye and stare at the spot on the left as you move the figure closer. When the figure is about 12 inches from your eye, King Charles will "lose his head."

the cellular relay levels—primary, secondary, and tertiary—and the synapses that link them. From this vantage point, you can see that all of the ganglion-cell axons on the half of the retina closest to the nose cross to the opposite side of the brain at the optic chiasm. As a result of this crossover, everything seen by the inside, or *nasal,* half of the retina of the left eye crosses over to the right optic tract, and everything seen by the nasal half of the retina of the right eye crosses over to the left optic tract (see Figure 4.6). The information seen by the outside, or *temporal,* half of the retinal field remains uncrossed. From the optic chiasm on, all stimuli in the left side of the world that you see are processed by the components of the visual system on the right side of the brain, and all stimuli in the right side of the world that you see are processed by the components of the visual system on the left side of the brain.

Axons of the optic tract run to one of four second-level receiving and integrating centers. Each center is in fact a pair of centers, one for the right side of the brain and one for the left. The two lateral geniculate nuclei and the two superior colliculi (see Figure 4.6) are the targets most critical to carrying out the function of seeing. A third target pair, the *suprachiasmatic nuclei* in the hypothalamus, uses information about light intensity to coordinate our internal rhythms (see Chapter 6). A fourth set of targets, also paired, are the *extraocular muscle,* or *motor nerve nuclei,* that keep the movements of the eye coordinated as we shift our gaze.

The Lateral Geniculate Nucleus The optic tracts carry the ganglion-cell axons to their secondary target neurons in the lateral geniculate nuclei (see Figure 4.6), and these neurons, in turn, pass the information on to the tertiary target cells in the primary visual cortex. Half of the ganglion-cell axons reaching

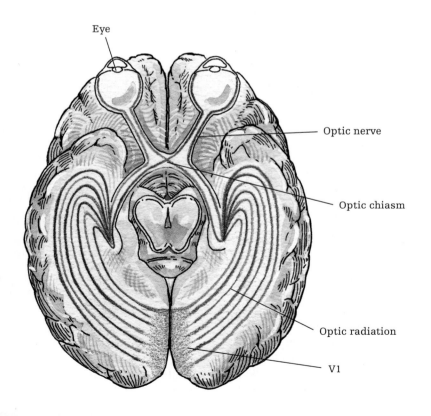

Eye

Optic nerve

Optic chiasm

Optic radiation

V1

Figure 4.6
A view of the components of the visual system as viewed from beneath the brain which has been partially cut away to reveal the internal components. Images detected by the rods or cones in the nasal (inside) halves of each retina reach ganglion cells whose nerve fibers cross over at the optic chiasm to reach their level two target neurons in the lateral geniculate and superior colliculus. The images detected by receptors in the temporal (outside) half of the retina connect to ganglion cells whose axons project to the level two neurons without crossing over. Thus, the right side of the visual system detects objects to the left of the midline and the left side of the visual system detects objects to the right of the midline.

the lateral geniculate nucleus come from the right eye and half from the left; their synapses are organized to provide a complete map of the visual field. In monkeys and humans, the lateral geniculate has six distinctive layers, named for the sizes of the neurons in these layers: two large neuron-containing layers, called *magnocellular,* and four layers with smaller sizes of neurons, called *parvocellular.* Each type of lateral geniculate neuron receives input from specific categories of retinal ganglion cells that differ in their sensitivity to color, their speed of transmission, and their sensitivity to brief visual stimuli. Between these six major layers are still smaller geniculate neurons that seem mainly to respond to color information.

Consider what happens when you gaze straight ahead: a visual stimulus that is just off center will fall on a group of receptors in the nasal half of one visual field and on a corresponding set of receptors in the temporal half of the other visual field. Both the nasal and temporal groups of receptors are displaced by about the same angle from the center of their respective retinas. When the nasal-field axons cross over in the chiasm, these corresponding nasal- and temporal-field fibers come to lie near each other within the optic tracts, and they travel to their secondary relay targets in tandem. Thus, the optic nerve fibers carrying information about a particular point in space arise from ganglion cells that are located in similar parts of the right and left retina. Their axons synapse with neurons that are near each other within the lateral geniculate. As the secondary-target neurons in the lateral geniculate project onto the visual cortex, these maps of the retinal world are passed on to the cortex as well. Thus, the retina represents a map of the visual field, and so do the lateral geniculate nuclei as well as the right and left primary visual cortices. In the primate lateral geniculate, the cells within the six layers are stacked in a precise vertical overlapping registration such that all of the neurons along a line that runs across the layers would be responsive to images in a single direction in space (see Figure 4.7 on page 114).

These "retinotopic" maps have diagnostic importance. They can help clinicians to map defects in the central parts of the visual system and determine the most likely locations of tumors or other damage that affects parts of the visual field. (See box entitled "Disturbances of Vision" on the following two pages.)

The Superior Colliculus We now come to a very interesting and important anatomic feature of the visual system. Many of the ganglion cell axons branch before reaching the lateral geniculate nuclei. While one branch connects the retina to the lateral geniculate, the other branch goes to another second-level relay target, the neurons in the superior colliculus (see Figure 4.6). This branching creates two "parallel" paths between the retinal ganglion cells and separate thalamic receiving centers. Both branches retain the retinal map specifics—nasal, temporal, left, right, up, down, and so on. However, the fibers reaching the superior colliculus are thought to represent retinal receptive fields from the rod-rich peripheral zones where visual acuity is weaker but where detection of movement may be stronger, whereas the fibers reaching the lateral geniculate represent cone-rich areas of high visual acuity.

The neurons of the superior colliculus also receive auditory information and vestibular information (about head position), as well as visual information that has already been processed by the neurons of the primary visual cortex and fed back to the superior colliculus. Because of the kinds of input that it receives, the colliculus is thought to

Given the numerous components and the complex organization of the visual system, the ability to see clearly, in color, with both eyes, and to the limits of our visual fields, is susceptible to a number of disruptive conditions. To understand such conditions, it is helpful to categorize them either as problems at the periphery (in the eye itself) or as central problems (problems within the optic nerve, optic tracts or projections, or the visual cortex).

Peripheral Disturbances of Vision

Visual problems in the eyeball are generally tended by an *ophthalmologist,* a medical doctor whose duties may include prescribing glasses or contact lenses, which are then constructed by an *optician,* a visual specialist who is not medically trained. *Optometrists,* also trained vision specialists who are not medically trained, can measure visual acuity and prescribe corrective lenses, but they do not deal with other problems of the eyeball apparatus.

Visual problems may arise from abnormalities of eyeball shape, from the inability of the lens to change its shape, from the inability of the pupil to constrict or expand, or from problems of the neuronal elements within the retina. The most common disorders, nearsightedness *(myopia)* and farsightedness *(hyperopia),* are caused by eyeballs that are too deep or too shallow, respectively, so that the image coming through the lens does not fall sharply on the retina. These problems can be corrected by lenses that refocus the image at the correct depth.

As we age, it is normal for growth of the facial bones to help correct modest degrees of nearsightedness. At the same time, age brings another visual change that is not so welcome. The lens of the eye becomes harder and less malleable, and this change makes it difficult to focus on objects close to the face even though the eyeball itself does not undergo any change of shape. The progressive loss of near vision with age, *presbyopia,* is only correctable by wearing reading glasses or by increasing the distance from the eyes to the object being looked at.

Astigmatism is a visual problem arising from irregularities in the surface of the cornea. These irregularities cause images entering the eye from certain angles to be more distorted than images entering the eye from other angles. Astigmatism is readily corrected by contact lenses that essentially float on a shallow layer of tears and smooth out these irregularities. The surface of the cornea is also subject to physical damage, and, if infected, the resulting damage can significantly impair vision.

Abnormalities of color perception arise from a congenital absence of one or more of the genes that control the expression of the pigments that allow the cones to distinguish blue, green, or red light. The genetic defects of red and green color blindness are recessive traits linked to the X chromosome. (The gene for blue color is located on a different chromosome and rarely affected.) Because females have two X chromosomes, one from the mother and one from the father, they rarely express the defect. However, males have only one X, so an X chromosome with the defective gene will result in color blindness.

Other, less common causes of visual disturbance arising within the eye include the development of *cataracts,* opaque areas in the lens capsule, usually as a result of aging. In *glaucoma,* the normal movement of fluid from the space behind the iris (the posterior chamber) to the space between the iris and the cornea (the anterior chamber) becomes obstructed, and the posterior chamber develops excessively high pressure. This high pressure compresses the retina and can destroy the ability of the rods and cones to function. Typically, the visual-field loss begins at the periphery, and spreads inward, making the field of view increasingly narrower as the disease progresses. In many cases, glaucoma can be treated by topical medications that facilitate the movement of the fluid between the chambers or reduce the rate of fluid production; surgical treatment is also possible to improve outflow.

The function of the retina can also be disturbed by direct trauma (producing the retinal separations that end the careers of promising athletes). Because of its high metabolic activity, the retina is very susceptible to the vascular problems that may accompany diabetes mellitus and certain forms of sickle-cell anemia. When the optic nerve itself is damaged, as can occur with multiple sclerosis—a disease characterized by progressive disturbance of myelinated nerve-fiber function throughout the central nervous system—vision may be patchy, with no signs of physical disturbance to the retina. Lastly, imbalances in the opposing strength of the extraocular muscles may cause double vision, because the eyes do not track in parallel. These muscles, as well as the eyelid-opening muscle, are found to be weakened early in the course of *myasthenia gravis.*

Central Disturbances of Vision

When strokes, tumors, or trauma affect the visual pathways beyond the retina, the degree and location of the peripheral vision loss help to diagnose the location of the damage. Tumors that arise in the area of the pituitary frequently cause pressure on the optic chiasm, and the effects include a loss of the lateral (or temporal) visual half of the field *(bitemporal hemianopsia),* the half of the visual field where ganglion-cell axons cross over at the chiasm. When both eyes have lost vision on the same side of the body *(homonymous hemianopsia),* the problem must lie beyond the chiasm, either in the optic tract or in the visual cortex, and, given the circuitry of the visual system, must be on the side opposite that of the peripheral field lost. If the tumor is benign, the visual loss may be temporary. Finally, strokes or trauma affecting levels of the visual cortex beyond the primary visual cortex may result in very subtle visual disturbances, as happened to the man who mistook his wife for a hat (see Chapter 11).

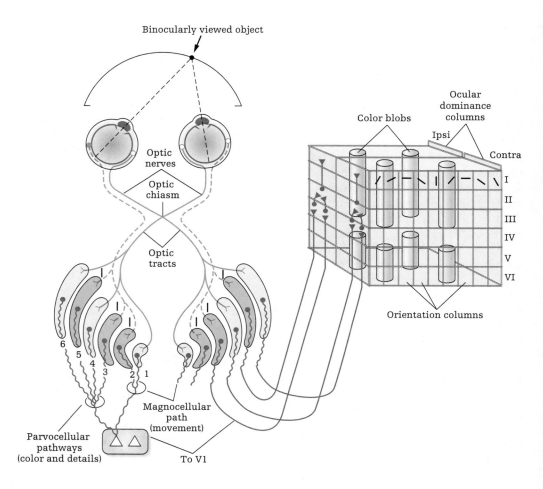

Figure 4.7 The retino-geniculo-cortical circuits of a primate brain are here illustrated schematically to show how the various categories of information are segregated and projected onto the cortex. Information about an object appearing in the right half of the visual field and viewed by the left hemiretina of each eye travels within the optic nerves to the optic chiasm. At the chiasm, retinal fibers from the temporal half of the left retina remain on the left side and project to layers 2, 3, and 5 of the left lateral geniculate. Retinal fibers viewing the same object from the nasal half of the right retina cross over to innervate layers 1, 4, and 6 of the left lateral geniculate. Layers 1 and 2 of each geniculate are the magnocellular layers, which receive information about object motion. Layers 3 through 6 are the parvocellular layers, which receive information about object details and color. The neurons in these layers project to the primary visual cortex (V1). At right, the output of these layers is shown in slightly greater detail to reflect how information from the ipsilateral and contralateral geniculate layers converges on neurons of layer IV of the ipsilateral and contralateral ocular dominance columns in each visual cortex. Also indicated schematically are the color blobs that span layers I to III and V to VI (but not IV), and the perpendicular arrangement of the orientation columns, with each column reacting preferentially to an object with a specific spatial orientation (as indicated by the lines in layer I).

serve as a subcortical integrating center for information used to orient the body spatially in a moving world.

The superior colliculus neurons receiving retinal input connect to a large nucleus in the thalamus called the *pulvinar*. In this ancillary path of visual processing, the pulvinar would be level 3. The size of the pulvinar in mammals increases as their brains become increasingly complex, and it is biggest of all in the human brain. Its large size suggests that it serves some peculiarly human visual function, but its actual role remains unknown.

Visual Areas of the Cerebral Cortex From each lateral geniculate nucleus, the retinotopic maps of the visual world are transmitted intact along the "optic radiation," the path taken by the level-2 lateral geniculate neurons to the primary visual cortex (the main level-3 visual processing station). At the cortical level, however, the retinotopic maps no longer represent that external world with the same exactness of proportion. The volume of cortex dedicated to input from the macula, the region of highest visual acuity, is approximately 35 times as great as the amount of cortex dedicated to the periphery of the retina. This disparity in cortical representation of input from different parts of the retina gives information from the macula far more significance and provides us with higher resolution—that is, greater detail—from the parts of the visual field on which we may be focused.

The primary visual cortex is also called the "striate cortex." The term "striate" refers to a unique "stripe" seen in slices of this area that is produced by a wide zone of myelinated axons. The primary visual cortex displays a system of orderly layering that is unequaled anywhere else in the nervous system. The entire cerebral cortex has a general pattern of layering that normally numbers about six layers, I through VI, starting at the outer surface.

The layers are distinguishable because of differences in the size and the density (the number of neurons packed within comparable cubes of cortex) of their neurons. In the visual cortex of human beings and monkeys, however, the six layers are even more elaborately subdivided, especially layers IV and V. Primate brains have more than 12 distinct layers of visual cortex, with layer IV, for example, subdivided into layers IVA, IVB, and IVC, and then subdivided again, as the sharp eyes of the microscopists noted patterns within the patterns (see Figure 4.8).

Cortical Representation of Vision

Observations of patients with head injuries and experimental studies in animals have shown that there are many cortical areas

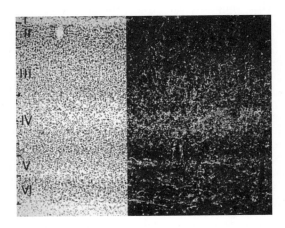

Figure 4.8 The most highly layered region of the primate cerebral cortex is the primary visual cortex. As seen in this micrograph, the six general layers are composed of cell-rich and cell-sparse populations; such layers are seen in almost all cortical regions. However, in the primary visual cortex, layer IV, the layer to which the level-2 neurons in the lateral geniculate make their connections, is further subdivided into five distinct layers that are seen only in the visual cortex.

engaged in visual processing other than the primary visual cortex. Moreover, many of these areas are "reciprocally interconnected." Most of the information about these connections has been acquired in the past few years, as scientists developed methods for specifying precisely which cells in which layers of each part of the cerebral cortex are in contact with one another. These interconnections have suggested some important principles of visual and other cortical organization.

Because of circumscribed visible differences superimposed on the six general layers of the cortex, scientists in the 1920s and 1930s recognized unique differences in the patterns of thickness and density of the cellular layers for small regions of the cortex. These so-called cytoarchitectonic differences between adjacent cortical areas seemed to indicate that each region of cortex had a specific function for which the differences in neuron numbers and sizes must be critical. Lacking any functional means to characterize these different regions, the early neuroanatomists gave each distinctive cytoarchitectonic area a numerical name. For this reason, the primary visual cortex was called area 17; the area immediately adjacent to it, called area 18, receives much of the output of area 17. Today scientists who study vision are more likely to call these functional hierarchical cortical regions for vision V1, V2, and V3. Whatever names are used, the new information on precise intracortical interconnectivity has revealed considerable mutual interconnection between the regions of the visual system, as well as in other sensory systems. The forward (or hierarchically upward, away from the eye) connections consistently link source neurons in layer III to targets in layer IV, whereas the reverse (backward or downward, back toward the thalamus) connections link source neurons in layer V to targets in layers I and VI.

On the assumption that these interconnection patterns could predict still higher visual integrating areas of the cortex, scientists have identified at least five more hierarchical levels. The "highest" integrating level that has been traced is in visual fields within the frontal cortex. These cortical areas are adjacent to the so-called association cortex, where several forms of sensory information are assembled. Relatively direct connections to the emotion-regulating systems (described in Chapter 8) also are made from this area of frontal cortex.

Analysis of such networks suggests that each level of reciprocal interconnections between these visual cortical regions provides an increasing degree of abstraction in perceiving the general features of the visual world. The question now is which features of the visual world are detected and analyzed by neurons of the primary visual cortical regions and which by the higher ones. Before we answer these questions, however, we need to describe some general features of cortical organization.

Signal-Processing Properties of Cortical Neurons The impressive horizontal layering of the cells and cell connections within the cortex originally suggested to scientists that the main action within the brain takes place in horizontal planes. In the 1930s, however, the first close looks at the orientation of cortical neurons persuaded the Spanish cytologist Rafael Lorente de No that cortical events take place locally within vertical assemblies, or *columns,* of neuronal units that span the cortex from top to bottom. In the early 1960s, this view was dramatically confirmed. By observing the responses of cortical cells to tactile (touch) stimuli as fine recording electrodes were slowly moved through the thickness of the cortex, the American physiologist Vernon B. Mountcastle was able to compare response patterns within vertically related units. His original work was done on the cortical regions that map the body's surface, receiving information from touch receptors in and below the skin, but the conclusions about cortical structure that this work generated were later confirmed for the visual system. The basic finding was that sensory stimuli from the same general receptor site activate neurons that are vertically adjacent.

These vertically related columns of cells extend through all layers of cortex and exist in roughly similar form throughout the regions of cerebral cortex dedicated to the visual, somatosensory, and auditory systems. We will see in Chapter 5 that columns exist in the motor system as well, although the sizes of the cells and the densities of their occurrence vary. Consequently, scientists believe that information processing in the cortex depends on (1) the information that reaches a cortical region and (2) how the information received there is transformed by the connections among the cells within a given vertical column. The output of any one such column might be roughly compared to the result of a multistepped mathematical calculation in which the same operations are performed in the same order on whatever starting data are fed in. For example, to average your test scores, you add up all the scores and divide the total by the number of tests that you took. You follow these same steps whatever the course, scores, or numbers of tests.

The information on which the cells within a cortical column operate—visual input for the visual cortex, somatic sensation for the sensory cortex, auditory data for the auditory cortex, and so on—has already been partly processed by initial receiving and integrating centers. The products of one cortical column's operations are handed on, by means of specific intracortical synaptic relays, to another cortical column for yet another operation on the data.

Most cortical columns have about the same number of cells, roughly 100 or so, in a rat's brain, a cat's brain, a monkey's brain, or the brain of a human being. (There is one exception: columns in the visual cortex have nearly double this number.) What makes the difference in the mental abilities of different mammals is the number of columns in the cortex. A greater number of columns in the cortex and a greater number of nerve fibers that link columns within cortical regions result in increasingly greater abilities.

With this concept of vertical connections among the cells of a horizontally layered cortex in mind, we can now return to our explorations of the specific cells of the visual system.

Neurons That Respond Selectively to Visual Features As noted earlier, some retinal ganglion cells are activated by light in the center of their receptive field and inhibited by light around the periphery; others show the opposite response. We might say that donuts excite some retinal cells and that donut holes excite others. In addition, and very critically, cells activated by donut-shaped light are also inhibited by hole-shaped light, and vice versa. Exposed to a solid circle of light, they might not be activated at all because the inhibiting force of light in the center balances out the activating force of light at the edges.

Experiments conducted by the American physiologist Steven Kuffler in the mid-1950s revealed why scientists could not analyze how the retina "sees" when they used diffuse light as a stimulus. Diffuse light stimulates many neighboring neurons that have different receptive fields (both center-on and center-off), and the homogenization that results weakens the response of the retinal ganglion cells under study. But, Kuffler found, very discrete light stimuli yield highly consistent patterns of individual ganglion-cell activation.

A few years later, David Hubel and Torsten Wiesel used the same discrete visual stimuli to activate lateral geniculate neurons of the cat and the monkey and found response patterns very similar to those found in retinal ganglion-cell receptive fields. The geniculate also had cells with receptive fields shaped like small donuts in which either the center or the "surround" was the activating factor. Inhibitory effects of the surround on the center, or vice versa, were linked directly to the ganglion cell activating the target neuron in the geniculate. From these results, Hubel and Wiesel reasoned that the visual process begins with a comparison of the amount of light striking any small region of retina with the light level around it.

As they moved their electrode vertically down through the neuronal layers of the lateral geniculate, Hubel and Wiesel observed another consistent finding. The vertically adjacent neurons all seemed to be activated by light falling on the same specific region of the retinal field, with adjacent layers in the vertical array being maximally activated by the corresponding fields in the right eye *or* the left eye (see Figure 4.8). This vertical layering of information from corresponding points in each retina further clarified the nature of the retinotopic maps at the level of the lateral geniculate.

Hubel and Wiesel then extended their analysis to layer-IV cells in the primary visual cortex, the next receiving station for the information passed along by the lateral geniculate. These cells showed patterns of responsiveness similar to the patterns observed in the retina and geniculate cells. Cells above and below layer IV, however,

appeared not to recognize the simple, small, donut-shaped retinal receptive fields at all. Visual stimuli consisting of black dots on white backgrounds, or vice versa, produced only weak or inconsistent responses. What accounted for the differences in responsiveness in different parts of the same vertical column?

An accidentally observed response in one cell began to clarify the mystery. The circle (actually a spot painted onto a microscope slide and projected onto a screen in front of the cat) that had caused vigorous response in layer IV did little or nothing to stimulate cells in layer V. However, as the slide was removed from the projector, the dark line of the slide's edge produced a brisk response in layer V. Soon the response pattern became clear. Almost all cortical cells above and below layer IV preferred stimuli in the shape of slits, bars, or edges. Once this shape factor was evident, subsequent studies showed that different cells even preferred edges at particular angles. Some specialized cells preferred that the edges be moving, and some preferred movement in a particular direction. Particular cortical cells above and below layer IV also reacted to different-sized edge lines and to whether the edge was black-on-white or white-on-black. Subsequent studies in monkeys have shown that one region in the midtemporal cortex may be entirely dedicated to motion detection.

Hubel and Weisel categorized the responses of the shape and motion response neurons into two types. "Simple" cortical cells respond only in a retina-like (or geniculate-like) center-on or center-off manner and tend to be in layer IV. "Complex" cells either above or below layer IV respond with preferences in regard to orientation, contour, and motion-related or field-ground features. Simple cells are almost certainly activated by the combined excitatory and inhibitory data coming to them from their sources in the geniculate. Complex cells are apparently able to extract other information from the layer IV neurons about the size, shape, and movement of the signals.

How do the interactions between all these neurons yield the actual solid images that we see? If you looked at a photograph in your newspaper under a magnifying glass, you would "see" that the image there is made up of dots. In dark areas, the dots are very close together and, in light areas, they are farther apart. When you look only at the dots and the open spaces, you probably cannot tell what the picture shows. At the proper distance, however, you lose the dots and see the picture. At a very basic level, the responses of the ganglion cells in the retina, of their targets in the geniculate, and of the simple cells of the visual cortex are the brain's dot-detection system. In contrast (literally), bars and edges are handy images for describing what a complex neuron in the visual cortex detects.

Two Eyes, One World Many aspects of how we see can be described, but our understanding still lacks biological precision. In fact, although much of the human brain processes visual information, scientists cannot yet say, even in general terms, *how* much. We do know that we have two eyes, but we almost always see only one world. This ability to merge the information from both of our eyes rests on three underlying features of the visual system.

First, our eye movements are intricately coordinated as we scan our surroundings. If you gently push against the side of your eyeball while looking at the sharp edge of an object, you will briefly see the image that each eye contributes to the picture. The neurons in the superior colliculus are critical to the merger of these two images. They, too,

are arranged in vertical columns whose cells respond to stimuli in the same parts of the retina's visual field. Cells at the bottom of the column begin to fire just before a spontaneous eye movement.

Suppose, for example, that while you are driving your car and looking straight ahead, you become aware of something flashing off to one side. The rods at the periphery of your vision field activate neurons in the superior colliculus that drive the extraocular muscles to rotate the eyeball and shift your gaze precisely to the point in space where you detected the flashing object. Thus, you "turn your attention" by moving both eyes in tandem to the spot where a small flicker of light or motion occurred so that you can inspect it closely.

Cells in the deep layers of the colliculus also receive auditory information, and these cells respond to sound as well as to light stimuli. The combination of such information in these deep collicular cells provides signals to motor neurons in the midbrain that drive the muscles of the eyeball. These muscles are responsible for your shifting your gaze to the spot where you heard something happen.

The second feature critical to binocular vision arises from the way in which retinal maps of the world are transferred onto identical maps in each primary visual cortex. In anesthetized monkeys, cells in layer IV of area 17 respond to input from both eyes in varying proportions. In general, some cells respond better to one eye than to the other— that is, in some cortical neurons, input from one eye "dominates" input from the other. In fact, when the nerve fibers from a single part of the visual field of one eye are traced across their geniculate connections all the way to the visual cortex, they form alternating "ocular dominance" columns. (These columns coexist with the orientation and movement columns previously discussed.) The columns dominated by one eye or the other extend across the entire thickness of the visual cortex. If we were to look down on the ocular-dominance columns in area 17, the columns dominated by one eye would merge together to form swirled ridges that look much like a fingerprint (see Figure 4.6).

Animal experiments have revealed some surprising facts about cortical organization. If one eye is kept shut from birth, neither the neurons of the geniculate to which that eye's retinal ganglion cells connect nor the dominance columns in the cortex that would have been influenced by that eye will develop properly. Even though the retina of the closed eye is fully responsive when the eye is opened, the retinal connections never command their full measure of geniculate or cortical responsiveness. The cortical-dominance columns for the closed eye never develop properly and remain abnormally narrow. Meanwhile, the other eye, left open from birth, influences cortical cells over an area that is much larger than normal. This finding demonstrates that the level of activity can regulate the influence of sensory neurons over their cortical targets in that sensory system. In fact, activity-dependent expansion and contraction of cortical representation, readily demonstrated in the developing brain, continues well into adulthood.

The third feature critical to our binocular vision is the way in which the visual connections from our right and left eyes provide two separate but parallel pathways. (Later in this chapter, we will see that our ability to pinpoint the source of a sound comes from similar parallel circuitry in our auditory system.) As you saw in Figure 4.6, visual input from receptor cells in each retina travels along virtually parallel routes, although in mirror-image shapes, from retina to visual cortex. Obviously, the two eyes, with their dual visual pathways, do more than contribute to the symmetry of the face and provide a "backup" system against blindness in one eye. They also work together to add something.

Because of the distance between the right eye and the left eye, each records slightly different images of the object being seen. To prove that this is so, hold your hand in front of you against a complex background. Using one of your fingers as a reference point, look at your fingertip first with one eye, and then with the other. As you do this, your finger will appear to jump back and forth across the objects in the background. With both eyes open, you will see your finger in a fixed location, and you will be able to see more clearly that your finger is closer to you than the objects in the background. The alternating one-eyed views of your finger reveal the difference, or visual disparity, between the ways in which each of your two eyes views the same object. This difference allows our eyes to see one world in three dimensions.

The closer an object is, the greater the difference in each eye's view of it and the greater the apparent distance between the object and its background—that is, the greater the depth of the field. As objects get farther away, the difference in each eye's view decreases, and so does our ability to tell which objects are farther away than others. In these circumstances, we judge relative distance largely on the basis of what we infer about the relative sizes of different objects. For example, we might mistake a model airplane flying nearby for a commercial plane flying at a great distance.

Although it is not fully understood exactly how the brain combines, or fuses, the individual views of the two separate retinal images, it is clear that this fusion happens well along the visual processing pathway—and certainly in the visual regions beyond the primary visual cortex, because there the points of view of the two eyes are still separate. When the right and the left retinal images do become fused within the cortical visual system (wherever that takes place), we see one world in depth. People with only one good eye can achieve only limited depth perception of nearby objects.

The workings of other parallel visual circuits also contribute to the richness of what we see. Within each visual pathway, different pieces of retinal information are channeled into three parallel subroutes. Object information goes through the lateral geniculate to the primary visual cortex. Information about motion is carried by different retinal axons to the colliculus and area 17 of the visual cortex. Information about diffuse light levels enters the suprachiasmatic pathway. This information, processed along these separate but parallel routes, is eventually recombined somewhere in the integrating circuitry of the cerebral cortex to provide the complete "picture."

This general scheme by which primary information is divided into separate processing channels for later recombination is, as we shall see, one that is also generally used by both the somatosensory and the motor systems.

Color: The Special Quality of Vision

Color is one of the qualities of vision that hardly seems to need description. Everyone knows the difference between a black-and-white movie and one in color. There is quite a bit to say about color detection, however.

We have briefly noted the presence of three types of cones, the specialized color receptors of the retina. The biological representation of color begins with these cells. Their more numerous colleagues, the rods, respond to light—as little as a single photon, the smallest quantum of light energy—by converting the electromagnetic radiation into a biochemical signal that forces the receptor cell to discharge. Cones use a similar biochemical process, but their response to light is color coded: each cone will respond to only one of three colors—red, green, or blue—depending on which visual pigment it expresses, and which color of light that pigment can absorb. This discovery took scientists aback. In most other contexts, colors are described in terms of a different set of primary colors—red, blue, and yellow, not red, blue, and green. Even stranger though, when physiologists started to study how the output cells of the retina—the ganglion cells—responded to color, what they found did not match any three-color code. As a whole, the retina, responded to monochromatic light signals (that is, light signals composed of only one part of the color spectrum) as though it could detect four colors: red, blue, green, and yellow. Because no cone has been found that can detect yellow light, the fact that yellow is detected requires some further understanding.

An early clue to the origin of yellow perception came from questioning people about the colors that they could see under different testing conditions. If you stare at a gray shape surrounded by a bright green ring, the gray area will start to take on a reddish hue. If you stare at a bright red object and then close your eyes, you will see an "afterimage" of the shape in green, an event termed the "chromatic successive-contrast effect." The afterimage of a blue object is yellow (you may need to put the blue object on a black background to see this effect). It would seem, then, that blue and yellow are somehow linked, as are red and green. But these combinations may not seem correct to you. You know that, to get green paint, for example, you mix blue and yellow pigments. How does green reception come about?

One of the theoretical explanations best supported by the data is called the *opponent process theory,* first proposed in the nineteenth century by the German physiologist Emil Herring. In Herring's view, certain colors were "opponents": yellow versus blue, red versus green, and black (no color) versus white (all colors). Single-cell recording experiments 100 years later gave the very results predicted by this model. Cells (recording either from ganglion cells in the retina or, more easily, from the neurons in the lateral geniculate to which they connect) with red center-on receptive fields have green center-off surrounds, and vice versa. Cells with yellow-sensitive center-on receptive fields are activated by blue center-off surrounds, and vice versa. The cones are activated by light of a specific color—red, blue, or green. Interactions of the horizontal cells combine, modify, and integrate these color-coded cone messages as they converge on the retinal ganglion cells. As a result, opponent colors are detected at the ganglion cells; green emerges as the opponent of red, yellow as the opponent of blue (see Figure 4.9).

Recent studies indicate that the color coding of input from the retina is retained in the visual cortex. Cells in the upper layers of the visual cortex have color-coded receptive fields and show opponent-color reactions, but they lack any preferred-edge orientation. David Hubel has suggested that the system for processing color information is separate from but parallel to the system for processing form and spatial orientation. What is known at this time, at least from studies of the monkey visual system, is that the cones project to specific small neurons in the lateral geniculate. The small lateral geniculate color-response neurons project into so-called blobs of cytochrome oxidase (an enzyme found within the energy-producing organelles, the mitochondria) in layer I of the visual cortex.

Object Vision and Spatial Vision

We do not usually categorize sight as "one eyed" or "two eyed," "color" or "black and white," until something goes wrong. In the main, we just "see." Other visual qualities go unnoticed as well. One such quality has to do with determining "where" something is in the space around us and "what" that something is. For a long time, the processing of these two visual qualities was thought to

Receptive field of a red/green system neuron

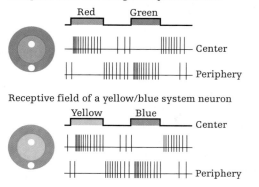

Receptive field of a yellow/blue system neuron

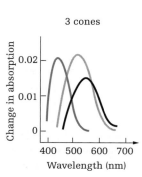

Figure 4.9
Probable patterns of color coding within the retina. *Upper left:* A ganglion cell is activated by red center-on cones and green center-off cones. *Lower left:* Activity of ganglion cells receiving input from yellow center-on and blue center-off cones. The center and periphery of these color-specific fields are organized in an opposing manner. (There are no yellow-sensitive cones. This quality arises from the convergence achieved by the horizontal, local-circuit neurons within the retina.)

become separated at an early stage of the visual process. Spatial information, at least in regard to depth perception, was attributed to the superior colliculus as it signaled muscles to move the eyes around to gaze at objects. Feature-detection functions, it was thought, resulted from progressive analysis of the objects being viewed. Recent investigations suggest that neither of these explanations is correct. Rather, both kinds of visual analysis appear to depend on the input of the geniculate to the primary visual cortex and on the different systems to which this area then sends its information for further processing.

Feature Detection and Recognition The most recent studies explored the ability of monkeys to remember rather subtle qualities of objects to get food pellets. They must choose a wooden square with stripes versus one without stripes, for example. When experimental monkeys had learned these discriminations, they underwent surgery in which a different small segment of the cerebral cortex was removed from each animal; in every case, it was part of a cortical region to which circuits carrying visual information have been traced. When they recovered, the monkeys were tested again. If a certain part of the temporal lobe receiving visual information had been removed on both sides, the animal could still see—it would pick up the objects to try to get to the food pellets—but it was no longer able to discriminate the striped blocks from the solid ones. This surgical procedure, used in combination with circuit tracing and electrophysiological recording, placed the visual function of "feature detection" in the temporal lobe area near the lower edge of the cortex.

The American neuropsychologist Mortimer Mishkin suggested that cells in this visual temporal lobe area retain some "trace" of a previously seen object. This trace is then used as a pattern against which to compare the next object. A match gives one kind of response ("I know that object"), and a non-match gives another ("I've never seen that before"). While recording the activity of single cells in this part of the brain, scientists found cells that responded specifically to some monkey faces but not others, regardless of their angle of presentation. If the monkey's distinguishing facial features—its mouth, nose, or eyes—were hidden, the incomplete face did not trigger any response in these cells.

Some researchers refer to a cell that seems to have this large a number of specific requirements as a "grandmother" cell. Such a cell becomes active only when the sum of certain shapes, edges, and contours allows the cell to identify an object as one that it has seen before, for example, as a "grandmother." A conclusion that there are too many different objects in the world for too few visual cells misses the point. At this high level of visual detection, the final features being detected are probably arrived at after many lower-level interactions, each of which filters a lot of information out and lets only a little through. The visual temporal cortex cells receive other sorts of sensory input besides visual, including sounds and, perhaps, smells. The convergence of these several different inputs also can help us distinguish between the objects in the world outside the laboratory.

Thus the "grandmother" cell can be viewed as the target of a series of integrated detections and abstractions of a complex object. When the full array of details defining an object of importance have been "learned," only a few of these details need to be subsequently detected to match the object being viewed now with one seen before. Thus, no cell that recognizes grandmother actually exists; rather, recognition is only through sequences of processing cells able to receive progressively higher order details until a match has been made with a previously seen pattern of details. In this manner, the brain can register an almost infinite variety of objects.

Spatial Discrimination The monkeys with the temporal-lobe lesions may have lost their ability to distinguish objects according to what they looked like, but they did not lose their ability to discriminate among objects according to place. A monkey trained to point at whatever movable object is closest to any given fixed object performs quite well after the bilateral temporal-lobe operation. Performance of location tasks, however, suffers after removal of a different region of visually connected cortex, one at the upper edge of the parietal lobe just in front of layer V1.

These results suggest that two parallel systems of visual analysis, one for spatial discrimination and another for object discrimination, do operate simultaneously higher up the processing ladder. Each system uses different routes and different combinations of cell circuitry. Each depends on the information received from earlier relays in the visual assembly line, and each uses that information in a slightly different way, even integrating it, in later processing, with inputs from other sensory systems. Finally, the end results of all these parallel visual processes are combined later in the construction of the complete visual image of the world, but the exact point in the brain where this happens remains to be discovered.

How Does Our Visual System Develop?

Both developmental neuroscientists and developmental psychologists (the branch of psychology concerned with behavioral development) have extensively studied the visual system. Although this system is a major focus of research, we must confine ourselves to only the briefest of summaries.

Most of the structures that form the layers of the retina differentiate in the first trimester of fetal life. This differentiation begins near the posterior pole of the eye (which eventually becomes the fovea) and then proceeds centrifugally to the extreme periphery. By the time a child is born, all layers in the periphery (which consists mostly of rods) are distinct and adultlike. In contrast, the fovea remains relatively immature. Thus, in the first 4 months after birth, ganglion cells and the inner nuclear layers (such as bipolar, amacrine, and horizontal cells) continue to separate from the foveal depression. By 4 months, the foveal cones are thinner and longer and packed more densely than they were at birth, but they are still not adultlike. The infant fovea is believed to begin to resemble what is seen in the adult by about 11 or 12 months of age.

As you learned earlier in this chapter, the lateral geniculate nucleus is the next major structure in the ascending visual pathway, the second level of visual information processing. It appears that the lateral geniculate of the human newborn has many characteristics of the adult lateral geniculate. For example, all six layers are readily observed, although the cell bodies in each layer are somewhat smaller than in the adult. Neurons in the four parvocellular layers grow rapidly from birth to 6 months and then more slowly until 12 months when they become adultlike. Neurons in the two magnocellular layers grow more slowly and do not reach adult size until the second year of life.

Considering the data presented in Chapter 3 concerning the generation of neurons that will become the cerebral cortex, it comes as no surprise that the full complement of prospective neurons in the visual cortex is produced well before birth in the ventricular and subventricular zones of the cortical plate. Like the rest of the fetal cortex, visual neurons migrate in an inside-out pattern; so, in the end, the oldest layers are the deepest layers. This radial pattern of development facilitates the formation and orientation of the ocular dominance columns mentioned earlier in this chapter.

After birth, the axons and dendrites of visual cortex neurons can be identified, but they are not yet mature. A large increase in dendritic branching is observed at 6 postnatal months, and then a decrease is observed over the next several months. Apparently, the neurons in the lower half of layer IVc of V1 start and then complete this cycle before the upper half, suggesting that cells receiving input from the parvocellular layers of the lateral geniculate develop more rapidly than those receiving inputs from magnocellular layers.

The two *superior colliculi* are a bilateral structure near the surface of the midbrain, a structural feature quite prominent in fish, amphibia, and birds. The superior colliculi are less predominant in humans, owing to the greater elaboration of the pathway from the lateral geniculate to the visual cortex. As a result, the superior colliculi are considered to be older in evolutionary terms, perhaps a more primitive module of the mammalian visual system.

Relatively little is known about the development of the superior colliculi in humans or monkeys, although a great deal is known about them in the cat. By the time a cat is born, the pathways bring in direct retinal information and indirect feedback loops from the visual-cortex pathway have reached the colliculi, although these pathways are not yet functional. After the animal's birth, the development of the superficial and deep layers of the colliculi continues through the second postnatal month.

The visual cortex appears to develop before the superior colliculi. Moreover, development of the superior colliculi depends heavily on cortical development. For example, when neither eye is allowed to see, the resultant superior colliculi are clearly abnormal, but this abnormality is secondary to the effects of visual deprivation on the cortex.

The development of vision lags behind that of our other senses. A human newborn infant's visual acuity is well below that of even a one-year-old child. In part, the lack of visual acuity comes from a lack of ability to accommodate visual images, and thus a newborn sees best those objects that are about 12 inches from the newborn's face (think of a camera with a fixed lens that can accommodate only certain distances). However, development proceeds rapidly after birth, particularly between 3 and 6 months when visual information helps drive and refine the system's development. By 6 to 12 months, acuity is so much closer to normal vision, so-called 20/20 vision, that infants can easily track moving objects and glance quickly at stimuli presented in the periphery. Moreover, by 6 months, their color vision and depth perception are well developed. By a year, nearly all aspects of visual development are complete.

How General Is Parallel Processing?

Evidence of parallel processing comparable to that noted in the visual system has been found in at least two other sensory systems: touch and hearing. Early studies attempting to trace peripheral sensory nerves from their body-surface locations to the cerebral cortex produced distorted maps of the body surface on the somatosensory cortex, the region of cortex that receives integrated information about touch (see Figure 4.10). These "little man" maps, or "little monkey" maps (see illustration on page 104) assigned much greater space to the face, lips, tongue, and fingers than to the legs, trunk, and back. Presumably the areas of skin with greater cortical representation have a greater ability to detect touch accurately.

More recent studies, however, using finer techniques of recording and tracing, suggest that, in fact, *multiple* body-surface maps exist within the sensory cortex. A method known as magnetoencephalography has detected such maps with great precision in human subjects. These additional maps extend beyond the sensory-cortex zones originally thought to be contacted by the thalamic sensory nuclei that receive and integrate pressure and touch stimuli (see Table 4.2). The existence of these additional maps of the body's surface suggests that additional features of tactile sensation—awareness of pressure, temperature, and movement, for example—may be recombined within the somatosensory cortex through reassembly along parallel processing routes in the same manner as that proposed for vision.

Had we been searching for simplicity in a sensing system, we would be most unhappy with so many "bells and whistles." But even these brief sketches of how we see or feel suggest that it is this very complexity that gives us the power to discriminate among subtle variations in stimuli, recognize them in different combinations, and, eventually, to decide whether we have encountered this or that sensory picture in the past. When you answer the telephone, how many words does it take before you recognize the voice? A close friend may establish herself with a single word, whereas a more remote acquaintance may need to give you several clues before you recognize his identity.

On the other hand, when you listen to a recording, you may not be able to pick out one voice from another. Nevertheless, in the recording studio, each voice and each instrument was probably recorded on a separate channel and then mixed by the director to create the full, balanced sound. Our sources of primary sensory information also are kept separate, independently filtered, and available for final recombination. We depend on the rapidity of parallel processing operations to increase our capacity for analysis. A system designed to process information qualities "serially," or consecutively (image shapes, then color, then movement, then location, and so on), would be too slow to keep us current with a rapidly changing world.

These insights into the function of parallel processing in the visual and somatic sensory systems provide a general model for the basic workings of all the senses. Now we will look briefly at three other senses: hearing, smell, and taste. As with vision and somatic sensation, we will consider the receptors for each of these senses, their neural pathways from receptors to cortex, and the qualities that are perceived through these systems.

Hearing: A Brief Look at the Auditory System

Although humans usually consider vision their most important sense, hearing is the sense that allows members of our sociable species to communicate—to hear and interpret speech. It is almost impossible for

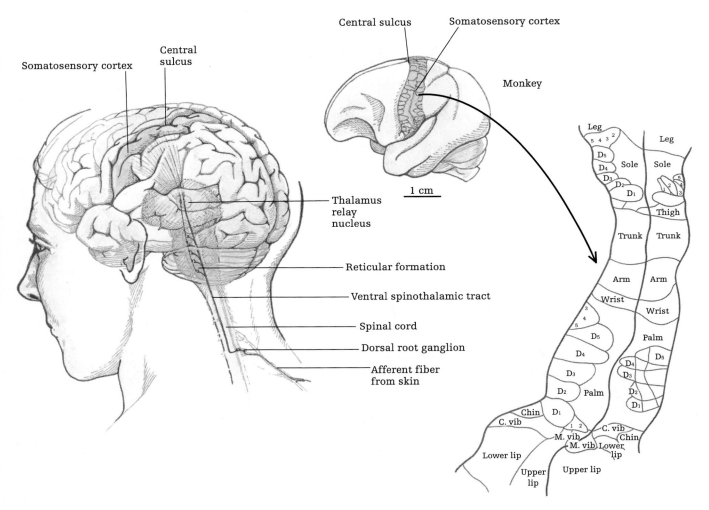

Figure 4.10 The components of the somatic sensory system in the human brain are shown at the left. Sensory fibers arising from receptors in the skin enter the spinal cord through the dorsal root ganglia and synapse on neurons within the dorsal horn of the spinal cord. Those dorsal-horn neurons send their axons through the spinothalamic tracts to synapse on neurons in the sensory nuclei in the thalamus. The thalamic neurons then project the map of the body's surface onto neurons within the so-called somatosensory region of the cerebral cortex, located just behind a major surface landmark, the central sulcus. In all mammals, the location of the somatosensory cortex relative to this "postcentral" gyrus is similar. In experimental studies of the responses of neurons to discrete sensory activation of points on the body surface, a dual mapping of body points can be defined, as illustrated for the owl monkey's brain at the right. Each bounded area defines the rough limits of responsivity of the cortical neurons to skin stimulation. Note that the amount of cortical volume dedicated to the lips and digits of the hands is disproportionately large compared with the actual surface area of the proximal limbs and trunk.

babies born deaf to learn to speak, even when their speech apparatus is completely intact. Such babies make the same speech sounds as hearing infants for the first few months of life, but, because they cannot hear their own vocalizations, they soon stop producing those sounds. (Luckily, the language-processing areas of the brain are able to process visual symbols, so even people who have never heard speech can communicate with others by sign language.)

Hearing also gives us other information about the world that is vital to our survival. Like vision, it is a multilevel system, with primary receptors, intermediate-level relays, a primary cortical representation, and many higher integrative areas as well (see Figure 4.11).

Sound

The stimulus that human beings perceive as sound begins when some object in the environment vibrates. The vibration causes the molecules making up the air to move as well, alternately pressing together and pulling apart. This molecular movement produces waves, or variations in air pressure, that travel away from the vibrating object at 700 miles per hour. When the *frequency,* or rate of repetition, of these air-pressure variations in a wave ranges between 30 and 20,000 cycles per second, it stimulates the receptor cells in the human auditory system and produces the sensation of sound.

Like the visual system, our hearing system distinguishes several qualities in the signal that it detects. We hear variations in *pitch,* the high or low quality of sound. Pitch is determined by the number of cycles per second of the sound wave—many cycles in high sounds, fewer in low sounds—and is measured in units of cycles per second, also called hertz (Hz). We also hear variations in the loudness of sound, a quality that results from the contrast between the alternating maximum and minimum air pressures that make up the wave. Large contrasts are perceived as loud, smaller ones as soft. Loudness, then, is determined by the intensity of the stimulus; it is measured in units of decibels (dB).

Figure 4.12 depicts these differences for a pure tone as produced in a laboratory by a tuning fork or an oboe. Such pure tones do not represent the kinds of sound people hear

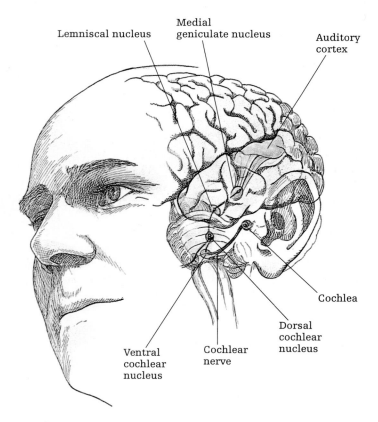

Figure 4.11 The components of the brain that participate in the function of hearing: the primary receptors are located in the cochlea, in the inner ear. The cochlear nerve conducts the auditory messages through intermediate-level neurons in the medial geniculate and the inferior colliculus within the thalamus. These second-level neurons then transmit to third-level neurons in the primary auditory cortex.

Lemniscal nucleus

Medial geniculate nucleus

Auditory cortex

Cochlea

Dorsal cochlear nucleus

Ventral cochlear nucleus

Cochlear nerve

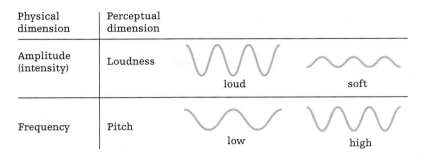

Physical dimension	Perceptual dimension		
Amplitude (intensity)	Loudness	loud	soft
Frequency	Pitch	low	high

Figure 4.12 The physical differences in sound waves that produce the different qualities of sounds, such as the pitch and loudness that we perceive.

every day, however. We hear sounds with *timbre;* that is, with a rich mixture of frequencies (see Figure 4.13). This mixture occurs because most sound-producing objects have several vibrating parts. Even a single violin string, when bowed or plucked, vibrates along its entire length. The timbre lets us distinguish between a violin and a cello and between voices; often, the pitch and timbre of just one word on the telephone is enough to tell us who is calling.

In fact, our hearing system is usually sorting through a rich mixture of complex sounds—an orchestra or a rock band; a voice on the telephone along with the jumble of sounds from a television program and the family dog barking in the background; the car radio, traffic sounds, and the voice of the person in the passenger seat. Our hearing system does not blend these different sounds, as our visual system does when two different wavelengths of light are mixed. We can usually follow the line of several different instruments as we listen to a group play.

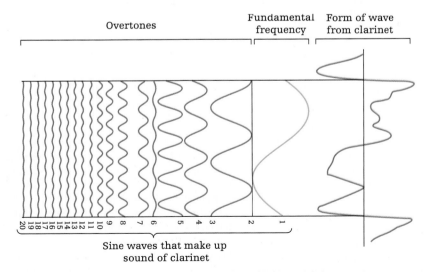

Sine waves that make up sound of clarinet

Figure 4.13 The "pure" timbre of a note played on a clarinet is actually composed of multiple frequencies as shown here.

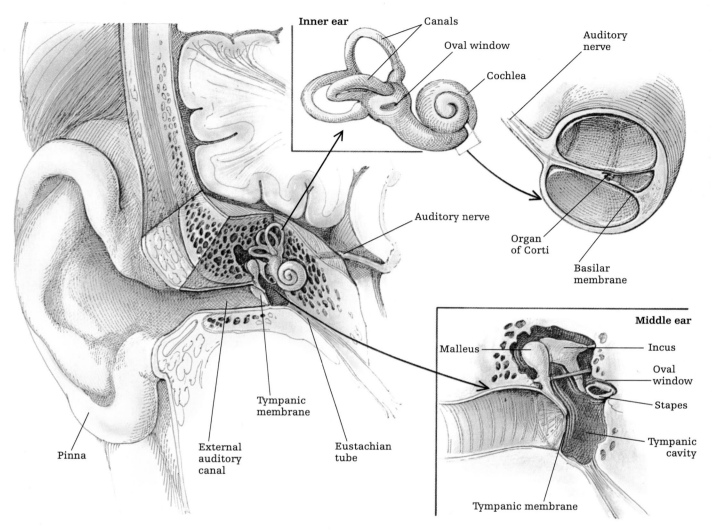

Figure 4.14 The structure of the ear, showing the relation of the external ear (pinna) to the middle and inner ear. The inset at the lower right shows the structure of the sound-detecting elements of the inner ear, indicating the physical connection between the ossicles and the detecting movements of the tympanic membrane that result from sound waves. Sound waves are transmitted to the hair cells of the cochlea through the oval window. The inset at the upper right shows a cross section through the cochlea revealing the inner structure of the organ of Corti. On the facing page, an enlargement of the cochlea shows how movement of the endolymph resulting from movement of the ossicles at the oval window disturb the primary auditory receptor neurons, the hair cells, which are too small to be seen at this magnification (see Figure 4.15 on page 132). The hair cells are embedded in the basilar membrane with their upper surfaces extending upward to the tectorial membrane (not visible in diagram). When the basilar membrane vibrates as a result of the sound waves transmitted by the ossicles to the oval window, the hair-cell upper surface is distorted, initiating activity within these neurons. This activity is then transmitted to level-2 auditory neurons through the cochlear nerve, which then merges with the auditory nerve.

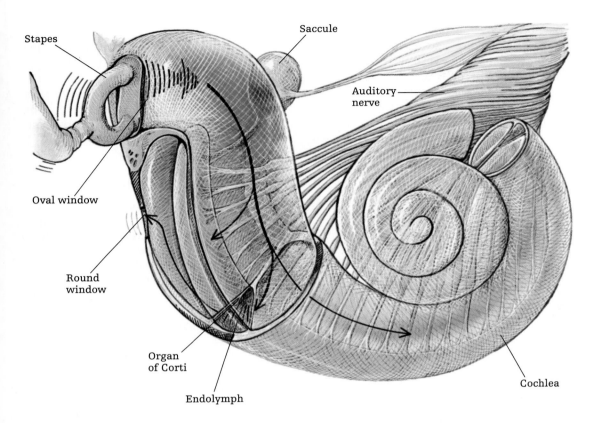

Stapes

Saccule

Auditory nerve

Oval window

Round window

Organ of Corti

Endolymph

Cochlea

The Structure of the Ear

The outer parts of the ear—the external ear, or *pinna,* and the *external auditory canal*—serve mostly to funnel auditory stimuli to the middle ear. The sound waves travel through these structures to the *tympanic membrane* (eardrum) and cause it to vibrate. These vibrations are passed on to the three tiny bones—the *ossicles*—of the middle ear: first to the *malleus,* commonly called the hammer; then to the *incus,* or anvil; and then to the *stapes,* or stirrup (see Figure 4.14).

The bottom of the stapes (the part that looks like the footrest of a stirrup) passes the vibrations to the *cochlea,* the snail-shaped, fluid-filled organ that transforms the mechanical energy into neural energy. The cochlea is surrounded by bone, except where the stapes contacts it, at a membrane-covered opening, the *oval window,* and at another such opening, the *round window.* The fluid within the cochlea is set into motion by the pistonlike action of the stapes on the oval window.

The cochlea, when uncoiled and stretched straight, is seen to be a tapering cylinder, divided lengthwise into three fluid-filled sections (see Figure 4.14, upper inset). Two of these sections, the *vestibular canal* and the *tympanic canal,* are joined by a small hole at the narrow end of the cochlea and filled with the same fluid. Each inward push of the stapes on the oval window moves fluid down the vestibular canal and then up through the tympanic canal to the round window, whose membrane covering bulges to relieve the pressure. The middle fluid-filled section is the *cochlear canal*. The two membranes separating the three sections are the *basilar membrane* and *Reissner's membrane*.

The neurons that serve as receptor cells for sound are anchored in the basilar membrane within the cochlear canal. These neurons are called *hair cells* because *cilia*—fine hairlike filaments—project from their tops. The motion of the liquid in the cochlea causes the basilar membrane to move relative to the membrane. (The hair cells and their supporting membranes are sometimes referred to as the *organ of Corti*; see Figure 4.15.) This relative movement exerts a shearing force on the hair-cell cilia, causing them to bend. The bending movements of the cilia physically open small potassium ion channels to produce action potentials in the receptor neurons of the hearing system. If potassium ions are removed from the fluid in the cochlear canal, the hair cells can no

longer fire. Recently, several different inheritable deafness genes were identified. Some deafness can now be seen to result from defects in the flexible proteins within the cilia of the hair cells and others to defects in the membranes that transmit the shearing force when sound waves vibrate the tympanic membrane.

The Pathway from Ear to Cortex

The hair cells have no axons; the base of the cell synapses directly with processes of bipolar neurons whose axons form a branch of the auditory nerve called the *cochlear nerve*. The auditory signals take the complicated path sketched in Figure 4.16, branching several times at relays as they wend their way to the primary auditory cortex in the temporal lobe. This primary auditory cortical area is not on the surface of the temporal lobe but is enfolded deep within the Sylvian fissure. As a consequence of the branchings at these relays along the auditory pathway, every structure along the pathway receives input from both ears. This difference between visual and auditory pathways may explain the comparatively greater difficulty of locating a sound in space than of locating an object visually.

The Neural Coding of Sound

The qualities of sound—pitch, intensity and timbre—are more readily studied as separate physical qualities. Scientists studying the components of auditory physiology have been able to reveal how these elementary features of sounds are detected and encoded in the brain.

Figure 4.15 Hair cells on the surface of the organ of Corti (see Figure 4.14). A single row of inner hair cells runs across the right side of the photograph; three rows of outer hair cells, with their upward-pointing cilia arranged in V-shaped configurations, run across the left half of the photograph.

Pitch Lifelong studies by the American auditory physiologist Georg von Bekesy, of Harvard University, revealed that the basilar membrane within the cochlea reacts to the vibration that it receives at the oval window with selective distortions. That is, the membrane bulges, and the bulge travels, wavelike, some distance along the membrane. The point of maximum deflection of the bulge corresponds to the frequency of the sound stimulus: high-frequency sounds produce distortions of the membrane at the narrow end of the cochlea, near the oval window; low-frequency sounds produce distortions toward the other end (see Figure 4.14). Very low frequency sounds produce an almost uniform bulge along the entire membrane. The various displacements of the membrane stimulate various combinations of hair cells. These sensory receptors then, firing from specific places on the basilar membrane, send the brain a specific message about the frequency of the auditory stimulus.

Location along the basilar membrane may not be the cue for coding sounds of very low frequency, because the entire membrane becomes distorted and vibrates. Rather, it may be the timing of neural firing that encodes the message about these low sounds; the rate at which the hair cells fire seems to be synchronized with the membrane's rate of vibration.

These neuronal messages follow an organizational pattern similar to the retinotopic design of the visual system. In this *tonotopic* system, adjacent neurons respond to tones that are only a note apart, and this relation extends from the cochlea through all the relays to the cortex. Besides such neurons, each of which responds to only a small range of frequencies, there are neurons that react to a wide range of frequencies and are thus not tonotopic. Others respond only to the beginning of a sound or only to the end of a sound or to both the start and the end of a sound; in regard to the selectivity of their responses, these units seem to correspond to

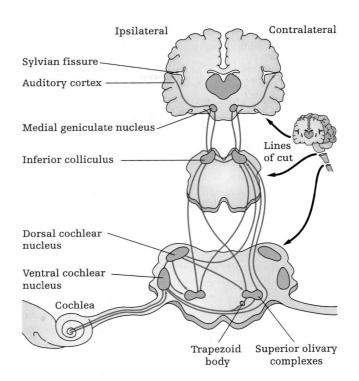

Figure 4.16 The pathway of the cochlear nerve. The first relay is at the cochlear nuclei in the medulla. Here some of the cochlear nerve fibers branch and ascend to the dorsal cochlear nucleus, whereas the others descend within the hindbrain to the ventral cochlear nucleus. The second auditory relay is at the superior olivary nuclei in the pons. Fibers from the the ventral cochlear nucleus go to the dorsal cochlear nucleus and to both the right and the left superior olivary nuclei; projections from the dorsal cochlear nucleus also go to both olivary nuclei and to the lemniscal nucleus, from which arise fibers making up the lateral lemniscus, an important sensory and motor pathway. The lemniscal tracts travel to the next higher level relay, at the inferior colliculi in the midbrain; here another bifurcation takes place, with auditory information from each ear mixed and transferred to neurons on the opposite side. The last subcortical auditory station is the medial geniculate nucleus, in the thalamus. The medial geniculate then projects to the first cortical auditory level in the temporal lobe enfolded deep within the Sylvian fissure.

the center-on, center-off cells in the visual system.

Loudness Whereas the pitch of a sound is cued by place—that is, where the bulge on the basilar membrane is greatest—loudness is cued by how big and expansive the bulge is. Sound waves of larger amplitude (louder sounds) produce bigger bulges over a wider area, with more intense vibrations. The intensity of the vibrations causes the shearing force on the hair cells to be greater. This greater force, in turn, presumably causes more neurotransmitter to be released. More neurotransmitter causes axons in the cochlear nerve to fire at a greater rate, and their rate of firing seems to determine our perception of loudness—at least for sounds of higher pitch.

Because rate of firing determines pitch for low-frequency sounds, it cannot also code for loudness of these sounds, because a higher firing rate would make the pitch higher. Many scientists believe that low-frequency sounds are perceived as louder when a stimulus causes a greater number of neurons in the cochlear nerve to fire simultaneously.

Two small muscles attached to the ossicles in each ear can contract to protect the ear automatically from very loud noises. The muscles displace the tiny bones, so the signal that the stapes transmits to the cochlea is less intense. Parents of teenagers might wish for these muscles to be under voluntary control, but they are not.

Location The fact that we have two ears separated by the width of a head and can easily swivel the head on its neck accounts for our ability to locate a sound in space accurately. Most sounds arrive at one ear before the other, and the hair cells and higher-level relay neurons on each side respond selectively to these different arrival times. Besides this time difference, there is a phase difference in what each ear hears; that is, different parts of a sound wave arrive at both ears simultaneously. With some neurons responding only during a particular phase of a sound wave, the two ears will detect the difference and pass it along the auditory pathways.

The time-difference cue works for locating an isolated sound, such as a click or a footstep. The phase-difference cue helps us in locating the source of continuous sounds, such as a low-pitched hum. Intensity differences also help to locate the source of a sound, particularly with high-frequency sounds. The bones of the head and ear, casting a sort of "sonic shadow," absorb some of the high-frequency sound waves on the side where the sound originates. The intensity of sound reaching the far ear will therefore be smaller.

With the several bifurcations and crossovers within the cochlear nerve and the secondary and tertiary levels of auditory processing, these codings for sound localization are carried through all the relay stations up to the cortex.

Feature Detection

The features of sound—its pitch, loudness, and location—are processed in parallel by specialized receptors and relay neurons. These sets of sensory data may undergo some processing at subcortical branchings and relay stations in the neuronal hierarchy of the auditory system. Still, when the auditory cortex of cats or monkeys is removed, the animals cannot locate a sound in space, cannot detect changes in a tone's duration, cannot discriminate between different sound patterns, and cannot detect changes in complex sounds. Although they can still detect differences in pitch and in loudness, their perception of sounds in their world requires processing at the cortical level.

One question about primate auditory feature detection that remains open to discussion is whether human beings process speech sounds in some special way. Investigations of squirrel monkey auditory neurons found that some neurons in the auditory cortex are activated best by voices of other squirrel monkeys. Perhaps, our auditory system processes all the signals that it receives in the same way until the point at which the sound is perceived as possibly a speech sound. Scientists think that this point is probably not reached until after a level of integration at the primary auditory cortex. At that point, the neural signal is shunted to the left hemisphere for processing in the language centers there (these centers are discussed in Chapter 11).

We have seen that the auditory system transmits the qualities of the sounds heard in separate but parallel pathways to higher subcortical centers, where they are processed, integrated, and then passed along toward the primary auditory cortex. Thus we begin to see some of the remarkable similarities in the nervous system's general methods of processing auditory, visual, and somatic sensory information.

How Does Our Auditory System Develop?

During the third to sixth week of human gestation, a thickening on the side of the head splits off from the overlying ectoderm to form the auditory vesicle, or *otocyst*. All of the structures of the inner ear, including the cochlea and vestibular apparatus, are derived from this primitive otocyst.

Before the end of the third prenatal month, one of the components of the inner ear, the *saccule,* will give rise to the cochlea. As is characteristic of most neurons, the hair cells of the cochlea do not continue to prolif-erate throughout life; they are essentially produced only prenatally. As is also typical for neurons in general, these cells are over-produced; for example, the 4.5-month-old fetus has more hair cells than the newborn. The loss of hair cells begins at midgestation and continues through old age.

The middle ear (containing the three ossicles, which transmit sound vibrations to the inner ear) appears to develop at about the same time as the cochlea. When the middle ear has formed, the ossicles begin to ossify and then change shape; for example, during the last two months of gestation, the stapes gets smaller.

On the whole, the auditory system is quite well developed before the infant is even born and, indeed, many experts assert that fetuses begin to hear some of the things that go on in the outside world in the last two months of gestation. Certainly newborns are capable of quite remarkable feats of hearing. For example, they can distinguish the sound of the human voice from other sounds. When researchers monitored changes in heart rate, respiration, and muscle activity of newborns while playing different sounds for them, they found the sound with the greatest effect to be a human voice.

In a now classic study, pregnant women were instructed to read a nursery rhyme out loud for a period of weeks before their babies were born. Within a day or so of being born, not only could these infants tell the difference between the mother's voice and a stranger's voice, but they could also recognize the particular nursery rhyme that they had heard as fetuses.

Not surprisingly, the auditory system develops rapidly over the next weeks and months of life, in no small measure owing to the experience that this system accumulates before birth. Thus, by the time infants are 6 months old, they possess many of the hearing abilities of an adult. One notable exception is that they are not able to localize sounds as well as the adult, in part because their heads are smaller and thus the temporal cues provided by the interaural separation are not as well developed. As head size increases, so, too, does the ability to localize sounds precisely.

Taste and Smell: A Briefer Look

The stimuli that trigger sight and sound are physical energy in the form of light or motion. The stimuli for smell and taste are chemical. To produce a taste, a substance must be soluble in water—that is, in saliva—so that its component chemicals can stimulate receptors on the tongue and palate. To produce a smell, a substance must be present in the form of a gas or vapor.

Taste

If you have ever had a bad head cold, you already know that smell and taste work closely together. When your nose is completely blocked, foods are virtually tasteless. With your nose in working order, however, the number of flavors seems almost infinite.

Actually, the *chemoreceptors* in the mouth record only four qualities of taste: sweetness, sourness, saltiness, and bitterness. The many flavors that we perceive come from various mixtures of these tastes with the odor of the food. The tip of the tongue is most sensitive to sweet and salty substances; the sides are most sensitive to sour things; and the back of the tongue, the throat, and the soft palate are most sensitive to bitterness (see Figure 4.17). A fifth quality of taste detection, known as *umami-*, accounts for the accentuated taste attributed to L-gluta-

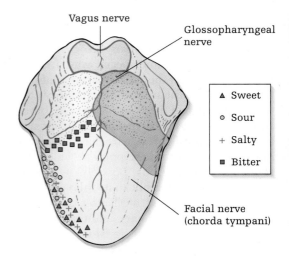

Figure 4.17 The location on the tongue's surface for detection of the major qualities of taste detection for sweet, sour, salty, and bitter stimuli.

mate. This receptor has just been characterized as a modified form of a metabotropic glutamate receptor with very low sensitivity to the amino acid.

The chemoreceptors for taste are called the *taste buds*. Most people think that the small bumps on the tongue, the *papillae*, are the taste buds, but the taste buds actually lie buried around the papillae, in moatlike indentations that trap the saliva (see Figure 4.18). These receptor cells have hairlike processes that project into the moat. There, the chemical components of food stimulate the hairlike parts of the appropriate receptors (sweet, sour, salty, or bitter), and the chemical stimulus is transformed into neural energy, although the molecules that do this are not known. No obvious structural differences have been detected between the types of taste buds specialized for the four modalities of taste, even with high-resolution microscopes. Just how their location on the

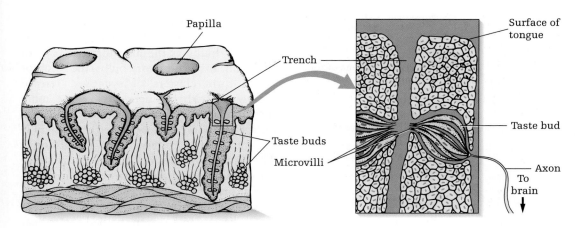

Figure 4.18 A drawing of a microscopic view of the internal structure of the taste-detecting receptors (the papillae) and the special primary taste-receptive cells (the taste buds) that line their surface. In the expanded drawing at right, the cells of the taste buds, buried within trenches on the sides of the papillae, send their axons into one of the cranial nerves (facial, glossopharyngeal, and vagus) that carry gustatory information centrally.

surface of the tongue allows them to detect these taste differences remains unclear. Also not known are exactly what properties of the tasted chemicals trigger the neurons' action potential.

A branch of the facial nerve innervates the taste receptors toward the front of the tongue; called the *chorda tympani*, it travels through the middle ear just beneath the tympanic membrane. Receptors toward the back of the tongue are innervated by the *glossopharyngeal* nerve. Receptors on the palate and in the throat are innervated by the *vagus* nerve (see Figure 4.19 on the following page). Sensory information traveling along these three nerves passes through a single synaptic relay station in the medulla, the *nucleus of the solitary tract*. From there, it travels up through a thalamic nucleus, the *arcuate nucleus*. From the thalamus, it travels to the somatosensory cortex. Some fibers from the nucleus of the solitary tract also project to the lateral hypothalamus and to parts of the

emotion-regulating system, pathways that might play a role in the pleasurable, or reinforcing, effects of sweet and salty foods.

Although the neural pathway for taste follows the general pattern of the routes for sight and sound, there is probably little interaction among these modalities below the cortical level. Because of the richness of cortical associations, however, we are able not only to savor the taste of an apple, but also to delight in its shiny red color and to enjoy the crisp sound as we bite into it. In fact, some neurons in the taste pathways react to mechanical stimulation of the tongue and to temperature changes as well as to taste, an association that is not too surprising, given that the texture of food is such an important part of the taste experience. However, the routes that keep these gustatory qualities segregated and then eventually integrate them are not as obvious as the analogous routes within the other major sense systems are.

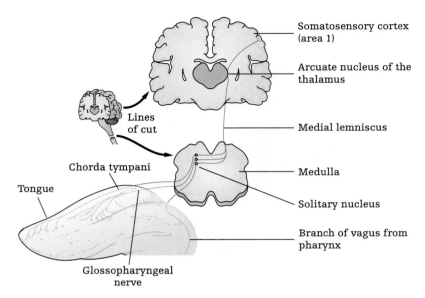

Figure 4.19 An overview of the neuronal components of the taste-detection system, in which the primary receptors neurons are located in the tongue and the level-2 neurons are located within the medulla, in the nucleus of the solitary tract, and from which higher connections carry this information to the thalamus and ultimately to the cerebral cortex.

The different taste qualities appear to be represented in different parts of the cortex. Sour and bitter substances stimulate neurons in adjacent areas at one end of the cortical taste area, whereas sweet substances stimulate neurons at the opposite end of the cortical taste area. Salty substances trigger a reaction from neurons all over the cortical taste area.

Smell

The anatomy of the olfactory sense differs radically from that of the other senses in that no hierarchical thalamic relay system intervenes between the receptors for olfaction and the olfactory cortical levels of the brain. Rather, axons from the olfactory receptors, which lie in the olfactory epithelium at the top of the nasal cavity, terminate in the olfactory bulbs at the anteriormost base of the brain. In the olfactory bulbs, the receptor axons form clusters of synapses (termed *glomeruli*) with the dendrites of the main output neurons of the olfactory bulb, the *mitral cells* (so called because they resemble the hats, called miters, worn by bishops). The synapses within the glomeruli are made up of millions of olfactory-receptor axons. The axons of the mitral cells leave the olfactory bulb and travel through the olfactory tracts directly to a region (named for its pear shape the *piriform cortex*) of the cerebral cortex on the medial and ventral surfaces of the temporal lobe. Olfactory information from branches of the mitral-cell axons is also transmitted to various parts of the emotion-regulating system, primarily to the amygdala, the hippocampus, and the hypothalamus.

To reiterate, in all the other sensing systems, the neuronal pathways pass through the thalamus on their way to the cortex, but, in olfaction, neurons go first to the olfactory cortical areas and then project from there "down" to subcortical structures. This olfactory wiring diagram is not quite as perverse as it sounds. The olfactory cortical regions accessed by incoming olfactory messages are the most primitive levels of cortex. This cortex does not have the specialized six-layered structure that we have been dealing with as we studied the other senses; rather, it has a more primitive arrangement that may in fact explain the close relation between taste and smell.

The inclusion of the amygdala and hypothalamus in this olfactory-response pathway helps explain why, in particular, smells elicit emotion-related behaviors such as sexual activity and aggression. Many species of animals identify potential mates and possible predators or prey by smell. Mothers identify their young by smell. Your dog or cat marks out its territory at home by spraying urine or more specialized scent-laden secretions on objects around its boundary in the hope that other animals will smell its marker and keep out.

For human beings, smells seem to have the power of quickly calling up memories—often emotion-laden ones—associated with those smells. Why do so many of us respond positively to the smell of freshly mowed grass or find ourselves thinking of that "special person" when a particular perfume is in the air?

Our olfactory powers are highly developed, responding to seemingly unlimited numbers of olfactants, and with extreme sensitivity, down to a very small number of molecules of the stimulus. However, much of the molecular basis of olfaction remains a mystery. One problem is the lack of a coherent scheme for classifying odors and explaining the differences between them, even a scheme as simple as the one for classifying tastes. In spite of this and other difficulties, however, recent work has identified a very large group of genes (perhaps as many as a thousand), all encoding olfactory receptors with a very high degree of overall structural similarity in the genes and in the protein receptors that they encode. Interestingly, the proteins of these odorant-detection receptors all belong to the same general class of proteins, the G-protein–coupled receptors described in Chapter 2, which are also used by most hormones and many transmitters. Perhaps this is another example of nature sticking with a good design, especially if it can be modified quickly as new variants are needed. Now that scientists know the nucleic acid sequences of these olfactory receptor genes, they are able to use this information to determine how widely the receptor proteins are expressed in the receptor cells of the nasal epithelium and how those cells project

to the olfactory bulb. The best-accepted current hypothesis for olfaction is that each receptor cell in the nasal epithelium contains only a few kinds of olfactory receptors on its surface. Although receptor cells containing the same type of olfactory receptor may be dispersed over wide stretches of the nasal epithelium, their axons seem to converge on common glomeruli. If so, this convergence would suggest that the olfactory bulb may discriminate odors on the basis of which sets of olfactory receptors have been activated, a kind of zone-defense detection system. Even if this hypothesis proves correct, however, a deeper mystery remains. The olfactory-receptor neurons die and are replaced every 60 to 90 days throughout our lives. If our ability to detect odors depends on the precise convergence of like neurons on common glomeruli, how do the replacement neurons find their proper targets?

How Do Our Senses of Taste and Smell Develop?

Much less is known about the development of the senses of taste and smell than about the senses of vision and hearing, in part because taste and smell are so difficult to study. Not surprising, however, given that these senses are old in evolutionary terms, is that both are quite well developed early in life

Scientists know that the taste buds appear on the tongue by the 13th week after conception, and all are fully developed and innervated by birth. Thus, infants come into the world with a well-developed sense of taste. (By "well developed," we do not mean a refined aesthetic sense, such as preferring one imported French cheese over another; rather, we mean that they are sensitive to a wide range of "tastants.") For example, we know that newborns prefer sweet substances to nonsweet substances and, in fact, within a class of sweet things, prefer those that are the sweetest. Newborns can also easily distinguish a range of other substances from one another, such as those that are bitter from those that are sour or salty.

A typical problem for developmental researchers is to find safe and ethical ways of testing what an infant can do; for example, one cannot allow infants to drink large amounts of sweetened water to prove their preference for sweets. Several clever investigators realized that infants, like children and adults, often convey what they think of a given taste by a change in facial expression. When infants are presented with drops of water (neutral taste), sucrose (sweet), urea (sour), and quinine (bitter) on their tongues, they produce four different facial expressions. Note that the cortex appears not to be necessary for this behavior. An anencephalic infant (the victim of a neural tube defect that resulted in the lack of a cortex) made the same faces in reaction to taste tests as were seen in healthy infants with a cortex.

What about our sense of smell? Most of the research on the development of smell has focused on the very young infant. It appears that, within the first weeks of life, infants are able to detect the presence of certain smells and to discriminate a variety of smells from one another. Moreover, infants remember smells after very short acquaintance. For example, within a day or two of birth, infants who are nursed by their mothers are able to recognize the smell of their mother's breast milk and underarm odor. Clearly, experience played a role in this ability, because as infants who were not nursed were unable to recognize these smells.

With these several examples of sensing systems and their main component principles of organization and integration, we are well positioned to look at the moving systems, whose job it is to guide us through the world that we are constantly sensing.

Summary

1. The systems responsible for sensing the external world are composed of hierarchically organized, interacting neuronal groups.

2. Sensory perception begins at peripheral receptors specialized to detect particular types of physical stimuli (light, sound, pressure, or temperature) or chemical stimuli (molecules of sugar or the smells of car exhausts).

3. The receptor cells synapse on neurons that relay the information through sensation-specific pathways that eventually reach the thalamic nuclei for each kind of sensing (except olfaction) and then proceed to a primary cortical sensory area.

4. The component qualities of visual information that are recognized by the activity of different rods and cones are separated out and sent along through separate, parallel thalamic and cortical structures. Auditory information derived from hair cells transmits complex qualities of acoustic signals, also separated through parallel processing into tone, pitch, loudness, and timbre through separate, parallel auditory thalamic and cortical structures.

5. Through the integrative actions of connections within the cortex, information processed by the primary sensory cortical areas is further processed and combined with other information in numerous association fields. The recombined information then constitutes our perception of the events in the world around us.

6. Specific lesions of the association fields can produce partial losses of selected types of sensory information (for example, the inability to distinguish objects by subtle visual cues).

7. The prenatal development of the sensory systems varies with the category of sensing. Hearing is well developed before birth, taste and smell are certainly well developed at birth, but vision, especially near vision and color vision, requires several months to mature.

Key Terms

receptors
receptor cells
receptive fields
hierarchical
  processing
integrative processing
parallel processing
feature detection
color vision

object vision
spatial vision
binocular vision
sound detection
  and discrimination
spatial localization
taste
smell

Further Reading

Axel, R. 1995. The molecular logic of smell. *Scientific American* (October): 154–159. A distinguished molecular immunologist defines the fascinating properties of the olfactory system that drove him to search for the olfactory receptors.

Casagrande, V. A., and Kaas, J. H. 1994. The afferent, intrinsic, and efferent connections of primate visual cortex. In A. Peters and K. S. Rockland, Eds., *Cerebral Cortex* pp. 201–259 Plenum Press, New York. An advanced look at the detailed comparative anatomy among monkeys and humans.

Garcia-Anoveros, J., and Corey, D. 1997. The molecules of mechanosensation. *Annual Review of Neuroscience* 20:567–594. An up-to-date comprehensive review of the proteins that make up the different forms of sensory receptors of our skin and joints.

Hildebrand, J. G., and Shepherd, G. M. 1997. Mechanisms of olfactory discrimination: converging evidence for common principles across phyla. *Annual Review of Neuroscience* 20:595–631. A comprehensive recent review of the olfactory mechanisms used across the array of living creatures.

Hubel, D. H., and Wiesel, T. N. 1979. Brain mechanisms of vision. *Scientific American* (September): 150–162. The team of Nobel Prize winning visual physiologists describe their views of the organization of the mammalian visual system.

Neisser, U. 1968. The processes of vision. *Scientific American* (September) :204–214. The details of the biochemical process by which photons are detected and converted into activity in retinal neurons.

Steel, K. P., and Brown, S. D. 1998. More deafness genes. *Science* 280:1403. A recent compilation of the many molecules needed to hear properly as disclosed by families in which these proteins are defective.

Interactive Resources

The CD-ROM that accompanies this book offers various ways to visualize the material covered in this capter. Its "Visual System" module includes a rotatable, three-dimensional view of the eye; detailed anatomical diagrams of several sections of the eye; several interactive activities; several animated segments; and six video clips showing the effects on human patients of lesions in the visual cortex. In addition, the subsegment on functional neuroanatomy in the "Central Nervous System" module includes several three-dimensional diagrams of sensory systems in the brain. Finally, the "Research Methods" module contains a segment and a video clip on optical imaging.

To learn even more and make sure you've mastered this material, visit our Web site at www.worthpublishers.com/bloom. Click on "Chapter 4" for resources including practice quizzes, flash cards, simulations, links to related Web sites, and updates on new research.

The Motor System

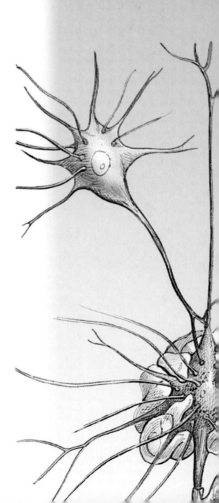

We now shift our attention from the sensory system to the motor system. It is an appropriate point at which to revisit the philosophy behind this book. As you will have already discovered from earlier chapters, a certain amount of intellectual investment on the reader's part is required to appreciate the beautifully coordinated complexity with which the brain runs the body and mind. You have already had to learn many new names and to study the relation between the named parts. The reward, when all these facts come together for you, will be a new level of insight into the marvel that is your brain.

Some people just want their "machinery" to work, never bothering to understand the underlying principles. They drive their cars without caring to know how the gas that they put in the tank eventually makes the car move. They operate their computers without understanding how their word-processor or spreadsheet programs work or how their files are stored for future editing. Likewise our brains generally function quite well without our knowing the first thing about how and why. On the other hand, those who are curious about the brain and behavior must peer intently into the black box inside our skulls, collecting hard facts and tracing connections in wiring diagrams. Nowhere is this approach better exemplified than in the consideration of how the brain makes the body move.

The motor system is organized on the same hierarchical principle as the sensory system, with multiple levels connected to each other in a precise order. In both sensory and motor hierarchies, each level performs certain aspects of information processing and then sends the necessary commands and details to the next level in the chain. In the sensory systems (summarized in Table 4.2 on page 103), the flow of information moves from the outside to the inside. Sensing starts with the primary sensory receptors on the body's surface (the retina, the auditory hair cells, and the sensory receptors in the skin), which send information to the spinal cord and brain stem. From there, the information ascends to the thalamus and is relayed to the primary sensory cortex responsible for each sensory modality (visual, auditory, somatosensory). Then, within each modality, additional streams of intracortical processing take place.

Although both sensory and motor systems are hierarchical, the flow of information in the motor system generally travels from the inside to the outside, the reverse of the sensory examples. The motor process originates centrally in the motor associational equivalents of the sensory cortices. These premotor areas plan and generate the movements necessitated by a given environmental condition. When the plans have been laid, motor commands are sent to the *primary,* or main, *motor cortex,* loop through the thalamus, and travel down to the spinal cord. In contrast with sensory events, the motor process ends at the periphery, when the muscles contract. The center–out, or top–down, flow of information produces the series of muscle commands that lead either to single movements or to sequences of movements, from the simple automatic act of scratching an itchy nose to the complex elegance of an Olympic diver's flight from the high platform (see Figure 5.1). Although the motor system thus operates in a top–down fashion, we are going to work our way backward. We will start with the muscles and consider how they move the bones and joints, then move back into the spinal cord, and lastly consider the three major "supraspinal" components of the motor system: the motor cortex, the basal ganglia, and the cerebellum. Not only is it somewhat easier to understand

Figure 5.1 A perfect 10. Diving is one of three ways to enter the water from dry land. Executing a reverse one-and-a half somersault with three-and-a-half twists from the 10-meter platform, however, exceeds all practical purposes. Such a dive is an exquisite, highly complex series of motions executed for the sake of its own difficulty and beauty. In the pursuit of perfection, Greg Louganis's body and brain must achieve a command and coordination that push human neurobiological capacities to their outer limits.

by moving backward, but you will also see that we know a lot more about how the motor system operates at the lower levels than we do about how it operates at the upper levels.

Another major difference between the sensory and the motor systems should be noted. The several sensory systems described in Chapter 4 can perform all their functions properly in a totally stationary body. Certainly, seeing (at least staring straight ahead), hearing, and sensing the surface of the body require no motion at all. Smelling and tasting require only the smallest of sniffing or swallowing movements. However, as this chapter will point out, the systems operating to guide the smooth, powerful, and purposeful movements of the limbs, digits, eyes, head, and trunk require continuous sensory feedback for their proper execution. We can sense without moving, but we cannot move precisely without sensing. The sense organs that make smooth coordinated movement possible are a vital, if less obvious, component of the motor system.

Muscles and Joints

The movement of part or all of the body is generated by the contraction of muscles. The study of how muscles contract and how they can do so with very significant strength is one of those exciting areas of biomedical research in which molecular explanations have been achieved for what was once considered a mysterious, magical act. Moreover, knowing the molecular basis for how normal muscles can contract and develop their strength when properly exercised has also helped explain some of the more perplexing muscular diseases of children and adults.

Muscles

Voluntary movements are performed by *skeletal muscles,* sometimes called *striated muscles* because of their internal composition: each skeletal muscle is composed of

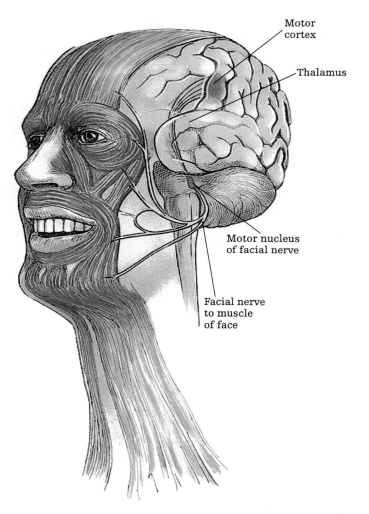

Motor cortex

Thalamus

Motor nucleus of facial nerve

Facial nerve to muscle of face

Figure 5.2 The voluntary muscles of the face are activated when neurons in the facial zone of the motor cortex excite the motoneurons of the facial nerve. The beginning and final positions of the muscles are conveyed through internal muscle receptors to thalamic and other neurons that alter the movement program to achieve the desired final positions.

multiple (often hundreds) of fibers, running in parallel along the muscle's long axis (see Figures 5.2 and 5.3). In short muscles, these fibers may extend from one attachment site on a bone to the other. (The attachment of muscle to bone is referred to scientifically as an "insertion" because the connective tissue of the muscle literally inserts itself into the connective tissue surrounding the attachment surface on the bone.) Involuntary movements (such as the contraction of your heart or stomach wall or bladder) are performed by a different kind of muscle called *smooth muscle;* these muscles and their control will be considered in Chapter 6.

Each striated muscle fiber is itself a merger of several embryonic muscle cells, or *myoblasts,* that combined in prenatal development to form a cylinder-shaped multinucleated giant cell. Within the fiber, the nuclei of those once-independent cells are displaced to the periphery. This configuration leaves room down the center of the cylinder for two specialized components: (1) the contractile elements of the muscle and (2) an internal

Figure 5.3 Internal organelles and structural relations of critical protein ensembles within striated muscle depicting the myofibrils, their internal filaments, the formation of the sources of the bands within the myofibrils, as well as the transverse tubules and sarcoplasmic reticulum forming (see inset at upper right) the tubular triads. Also shown are the mitochondria lying at the periphery of the bundles of myofibrils. The inset at the lower right shows at higher magnification a schematic diagram of the conceptual molecular mechanisms of contraction as the actin thin filaments and myosin thick filaments slide along through the chemical interactions of the tropomysin and troponin proteins. See also Figure 5.5 on page 150.

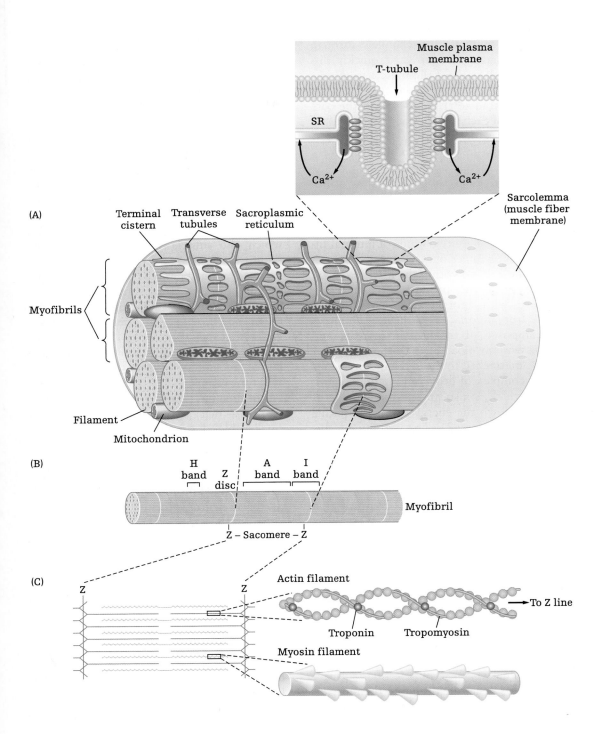

(A)

Muscle plasma membrane

T-tubule

SR

Ca²⁺   Ca²⁺

Sarcolemma (muscle fiber membrane)

Terminal cistern   Transverse tubules   Sacroplasmic reticulum

Myofibrils

Filament

Mitochondrion

(B)

H band   Z disc   A band   I band

Myofibril

Z – Sacomere – Z

(C)

Z   Z

Actin filament

To Z line

Troponin   Tropomyosin

Myosin filament

series of communicating channels through which the signal to contract is quickly distributed to all parts of the muscle to initiate its contraction.

The contractile elements within the core cytoplasm of each muscle fiber are a series of identical repeating subunits, each only a few microns long, linked end to end to make a *myofibril* that runs down the length of the muscle fiber. Each subunit of a myofibril begins and ends with a platelike structure, called a *Z band*, that runs perpendicularly across the muscle fiber. Running from Z band to Z band are two kinds of internal filaments. The thinner ones, connected at each end to the Z band within the myofibrils, are composed of the protein *actin* and are wrapped with another contractile protein called *tropomyosin*. The thicker filaments are composed of the protein *myosin,* and they essentially float next to the actin filaments, unattached to the Z bands. Myosin is itself a complex of heavy and light proteins, one of which is also an enzyme capable of breaking down the energy-storage molecule ATP (see Chapter 2). The activity of this enzyme increases considerably when the actin and myosin molecules come into contact. The electrical, chemical, and protein–protein interactions between actin and myosin cause an activated muscle to contract in a complex process in which the thick filaments slide along the thin filaments and pull the Z bands closer together.

The second set of intracellular components required for smooth contraction of the entire muscle's set of muscle fibers is a specialized form of intracellular channels called the "T-tubular system" because of their shapes. This intracellular system consists of numerous transverse "invaginations" (infolded surfaces) of the muscle fiber surface. The *T tubes* penetrate deep into the muscle's cytoplasm and at many points directly contact the smooth endoplasmic reticulum (see Chapter 2) of the muscle, called the *sarcoplasmic reticulum* (SR). These points of contact are called *triads* because of their triangular shape, formed by one T tube and two channels of SR (see Figure 5.3). The SR is specialized for Ca^{2+} binding and accumulation; it fills most of the internal cytoplasm of each muscle fiber, surrounding the myofibrils. The small amount of cytoplasmic space left is filled with mitochondria and the energy-storing resources stored in particles of the complex carbohydrate *glycogen,* which the muscle manufactures between bouts of activity.

Skeletal muscles come in two major types that differ in their blood supply, in their number of mitochondria, and in the amount of the muscle-specific oxygen-binding protein *myoglobin* that they contain. Red muscles have a liberal blood supply, many mitochondria, and lots of myoglobin; these muscles—thigh muscles, for example—can contract for long periods of time but do not need to be fast. White muscles—such as finger muscles—have a smaller blood supply, less myoglobin, and fewer mitochondria; they generally move more quickly than do red muscles.

Skeletal muscles are innervated by spinal neurons called *motoneurons,* and the axons of those neurons form bundles of *motor nerves* in the peripheral nervous system. The motoneurons and their axons, together with the muscles that they control, are termed *motor units.* The motor-unit complex is roughly analogous to the first part of a sensory system in that its position is closest to the outside world. When motoneurons are activated, they release their transmitter, *acetylcholine* (ACh). The secretion of ACh from the motor nerve to the muscle transmits the signal to the muscle to contract. (Many other neurons also use acetylcholine as their neurotransmitter.)

The sites on the muscle fiber where the nerve fibers end are called *neuromuscular junctions* or *end plates* (see Figure 5.4). The presynaptic part of such a junction is the specialized terminal of the motoneuron's axon with its synaptic vesicles and mitochondria. The postsynaptic component, the muscle side of the junction, possesses large clusters of acetylcholine receptors that allow the muscle to respond to the ACh signals.

The proteins that act as neurotransmitter receptors on muscle (and on neurons) are very different in molecular structure from the proteins that act as receptors in sensory neurons (the neurons described in Chapter 4 that respond to touch, heat, pressure, light, and sound). The muscle's ACh receptor is the prototype of the ionophore receptor described in Chapter 2; that is, a receptor that is also an ion channel. Each muscle ACh receptor (and other ionophore receptors) is a complex of five similar, but not identical, subunits mounted in the membrane of the muscle cell and anchored together to form a central pore or channel that penetrates the membrane. When the activated motor nerve releases ACh into the neuromuscular junction, the ACh diffuses to the receptor cluster, which then reacts by changing its shape (conformation), allowing sodium ions (Na^+) and calcium ions (Ca^{2+}) to enter the cytoplasm of the muscle cell through the ion channel.

The actions of acetylcholine at its muscle receptors can be mimicked by the drug *nicotine*. (In other words, nicotine molecules can bind to ACh receptors and activate them just like ACh, causing their ion channels to open.) On the other hand, molecules of the plant poison *curare* can bind to ACh receptors and prevent their ion channels from opening. (It was for this property that curare gained its reputation as a hunting weapon: animals struck with a curare-dipped dart are

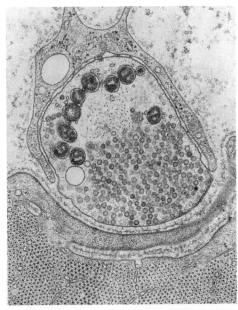

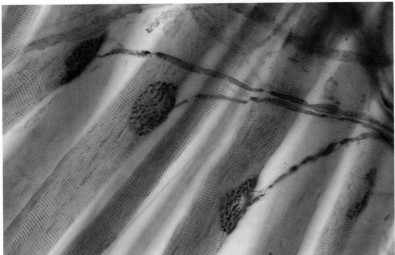

Figure 5.4 (*Bottom*) At the light microscopic level of resolution, several neuromuscular junctions can be seen across the surface of a muscle fiber. (*Top*) An electron micrograph of a typical neuromuscular junction, with the presynaptic axon filled with synaptic vesicles and mitochondria, the specialized undulating surface of the postsynaptic muscle, and the underlying sarcoplasmic reticulum through which the cholinergic receptors transmit the command to contract.

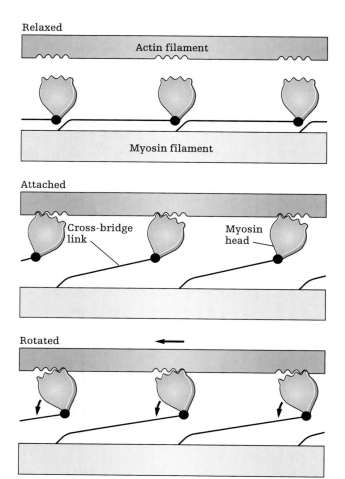

Relaxed

Actin filament

Myosin filament

Attached

Cross-bridge
link

Myosin
head

Rotated

Figure 5.5 Schematic illustration of the molecular interactions during muscle contraction as tropomyosin engages actin to move those filaments across the myosin.

paralyzed and cannot run away.) In the disease called *myasthenia gravis,* the muscles lose their ability to respond to acetylcholine because the acetylcholine receptors on the muscle cells are destroyed by an inappropriate attack of the immune system.

When ACh binds to its receptors on the muscle surface, Na^+ and Ca^{2+} enter the cytoplasm as the depolarization of the muscle fiber is initiated. The depolarization further

activates the voltage-sensitive calcium channels within the T-tubule membranes. This effect in turn releases Ca^{2+} into the cytoplasm of the muscle fibril that had previously been bound by the SR. Within the myofibril, Ca^{2+} binds momentarily to the actin and myosin proteins, allowing them to interact. This interaction takes place because the attachment of Ca^{2+} to the proteins actin and myosin triggers the transient formation of cross bridges between the thick and thin filaments.

The same protein–protein interaction that creates the cross bridges between the thick and thin filaments also activates the ATP-cleaving activity of myosin, which then breaks the cross bridge to actin. If the depolarization persists, however, because of multiple action potentials from the motoneuron to the muscle, and the cytoplasmic Ca^{2+} concentration remains elevated, new cross bridges will form (see Figure 5.5).

When the flexible neck of the myosin element repeatedly forms and breaks the cross bridges, the myosin head swivels and pulls itself along actin. Because the ends of actin are anchored at the Z bands, this process shortens the distance between the Z bands, thereby shortening the overall muscle length and creating muscle tension. When the nerve stops signaling the muscle, the contractile process abates and the muscle relaxes. Calcium ions now reaccumulate in the SR, and the muscle prepares for the next workout whenever that may be.

Moving

Each muscle in your body (but not all of them) connects two bones across a joint common to both bones. When a motor nerve activates a muscle to contract, the shortening of the muscle brings the far end of the bone (the end farther from the body) closer to the body. When this motion causes the angle of the joint to become more "acute" geometrically, we call the motion *flexion,* and, when the angle of the joint becomes less acute, we call it *extension.* The contraction of muscles need not always result in motion. For example, when opposing muscles exert equal tension across a joint such as the wrist or the elbow, they stabilize the joint's angle against gravity and allow you to hold a weight in your hand. The activated muscle develops tension, but the joint angle does not change. Such contractions are called *isometric.*

There are several exceptions to the "two-bone rule": the extraocular muscles that move the eyeball, the muscles that extend or retract the tongue or wiggle the ears, and muscles that you may be aware of depending on whether you are male or female. Even these exceptions, however, conform to another general rule: every muscle that pulls a bone (or an eyeball or a tongue) in one direction is opposed by another muscle, an antagonist, whose contraction leads to an opposing movement. In simple terms, there is an *extender* muscle across every joint for which there is a *flexor.* Often several muscles will insert onto the same bone to work together cooperatively *(synergistic muscles),* and that set of muscles also has its opposing antagonistic set. The opposition of sets of muscles is essential for human beings or their four-legged friends to stand erectly or maintain any steady position against the pull of gravity. Astronauts put this principle to work for them when they learn to move in the zero gravity of space to carry out their experiments (gravity is zero, but without opposing muscle sets they still could not stand erectly). The astronauts then have to relearn their movement coordination tricks when they reenter our gravity fields.

A muscle fiber can be activated only by a command from its motor nerve. Therefore, we speak of the motoneuron—that is, the

motor axon and the spinal motoneuron from which it originates—as the final common path for movement. The same equivalent components—the motoneuron, its axon, and the muscle fiber that it innervates—are always the last circuits in muscle innervation. Any single muscle fiber is controlled by only one motoneuron, but one motoneuron may control many muscle fibers through branches in its axon. When physicians attempt to determine the cause of a weakness, they first probe the function of the final common path.

The number of muscle fibers controlled by a given motoneuron varies, depending on how coarse or how fine the movements of a muscle or group of muscles need to be. The muscles that move the eyes (the extraocular muscles) have about one neuron for every three muscle fibers and are capable of very precise movements; the muscles that move the thigh may have one neuron for every hundred muscle fibers. The amount of strength that a single muscle can exert depends on the number of contractile fibers that it contains. Motoneurons that control single large muscles, such as your biceps or your calf muscles, have many branches in their axons to serve all of the fibers in that muscle, and those axon branches are proportionately larger than those that control the small muscles of your fingers. When athletes train, their muscles react to the repeated stress of exercise by adding myofibrils, and so the mass of the muscle increases.

In a healthy person, striated muscles move only when the person want them to move. Therefore, we call such action *voluntary movement* (see Figure 5.2). In some muscle disorders and problems of the motor system, spasms and other unwanted movements of the skeletal muscles can be seen. Even with voluntary movement, however, we are not usually aware of the deployment of specific individual muscles as we move. With few exceptions, we do not have the ability to move only one muscle at a time. Nevertheless, in a general way, the term "voluntary" distinguishes this class of movements from the wholly unconscious category of *reflex movements,* the kind that occurs, for example, when you inadvertently touch a hot stove and then jerk your hand away before you consciously experience any pain. Reflex movements are considered in greater depth in the next section.

The Spinal Cord

The next higher level of the motor system's hierarchy is the spinal cord, which contains all the motoneurons (the final common output link to the muscle) and their afferents, the pathways bringing the information from higher motor centers and from the sensory units in the periphery, the proprioceptors.

Within the motor system, the spinal cord has a hierarchical position roughly like that of the retina in the visual system. Both are ensembles of neurons one step removed from the periphery, and both perform substantial integrating and filtering functions by using long-distance axons as well as local-circuit neurons. The relatively simple kinds of integration possible at the spinal-cord level, however, are just a token of the more powerful and complex motor acts that the spinal cord can direct when it follows commands from motor centers in the cerebral cortex.

The different motoneurons have functional properties appropriate to the kinds of muscles that they innervate. Thus the slow, enduring actions of high-myoglobin red-muscle fibers arise from relatively small motoneurons whose electrical properties allow them to be active at low rates for long periods of time. Conversely, white muscles are innervated by faster motoneurons that tend to be larger, with larger-diameter axons. Axons, motor and sensory, are classified on the basis of their rate of conduction of action potentials down their axons *(conduction velocity).* The axons of motoneurons that innervate skeletal muscle all belong to the "alpha motoneuron" category; smaller neurons with smaller axons whose action potentials travel more slowly are assigned letters farther along the Greek alphabet. The latter motoneurons innervate very special kinds of muscles within the muscles themselves that have to do with the needed sensory feedback from within the muscle (proprioception).

Motoneurons that innervate the same muscle are arranged in a cluster within the ventral horn of the spinal cord; such clusters may extend over several segments (vertebrae) of the spinal column. Each cluster is a functional pool of motoneurons for a given muscle. Sensory information and voluntary commands from higher centers activate some or all of a given functional pool and make the motoneurons fire more or less rapidly, depending on the amount of muscle tension needed for a given task.

Spinal Reflexes

Muscle fibers also contain sensory nerves of a type known as *proprioceptors. Proprioception,* a term that means "self-detection," is the sense of awareness of a muscle's position and tension. The proprioceptors either lie buried within the muscle, in a special complex called the *muscle spindle* (because of its shape), or are found in the tendon, where the muscle attaches to a bone, in a complex known as a *Golgi tendon organ* (which is not necessarily spindle shaped; see Figure 5.6).

Muscle spindles are distinctly elliptical or "fusiform" objects lying parallel to the mus-

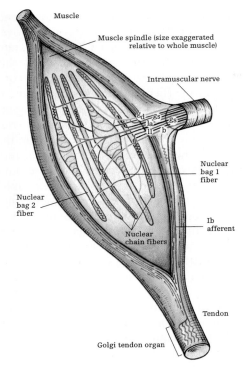

Figure 5.6 Schematic diagram of the intrafusal and Golgi tendon organ, sensory, and motor elements.

cle fibers. Each spindle has its own internal muscle fibers, called *intrafusal fibers* to distinguish them from the main skeletal, or *extrafusal,* muscle fibers. The intrafusal muscle fibers have their own motor and sensory neurons: the spindle's motor nerves are fine, slow-conducting *gamma* motor nerves; the one main sensory nerve is a larger, fast-conducting axon.

These sensory detector spindles and tendon organs inform the spinal cord and other higher motor centers of how much tension is being developed in the muscle as a movement is being carried out against gravity. The information from the tendon organs also helps establish the current degree of joint angle. All this information combined provides a three-dimensional description of how the limbs and digits are currently arranged in space. The monitoring of limb position in space is continuous; so, if a change is needed (say, you suddenly need to grab an approaching baseball), you have the information needed to alter your trajectory.

When the doctor tests your reflexes in a physical examination, the tap to your kneecap stretches a tendon where the thigh muscle attaches to the top of the patella. This stretch activates the sensory fiber in the tendon, and that, in turn, excites spinal motoneurons that cause the thigh muscle to contract and the foot to fly up (see Figure 5.7). The whole reflex takes place very quickly, usually in less than a second, indicating how quickly these neurons conduct their local affairs. When you stand, this reflex helps the spinal cord maintain the proper angle on the knee joint. In both cases, the spinal cord is operating without additional commands from higher motor centers.

The spinal cord makes other local decisions as well—for example, the automatic withdrawal response to a painful stimulus. If you have ever received an electrical shock while prying a stubborn piece of bread out of your toaster, you probably found your arm "flying" away even before you experienced any pain. Under spinal-cord control, a hurt extremity automatically withdraws by flexion of the joints in that limb. A problem encountered in the neurological disorders multiple sclerosis and amyotrophic lateral sclerosis (the latter is sometimes called Lou Gehrig's disease) is that the sensory nerves do not properly activate flexion withdrawal reflexes. As a result, patients suffer the consequences of frequent prolonged encounters with damaging objects and substances.

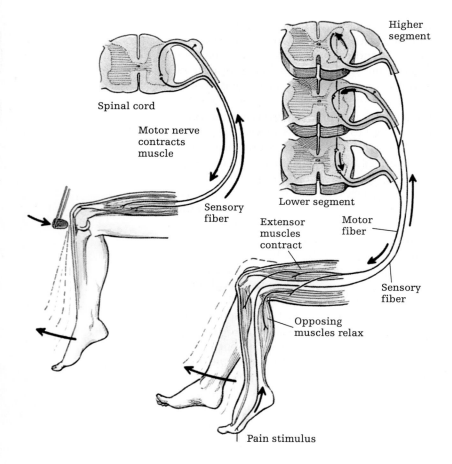

Spinal cord

Motor nerve
contracts
muscle

Sensory
fiber

Higher
segment

Lower segment

Extensor
muscles
contract

Motor
fiber

Sensory
fiber

Opposing
muscles relax

Pain stimulus

Figure 5.7 When a simple reflex action takes place, sensory stretch receptors of an extensor muscle directly activate the motoneurons of that muscle, causing extensor contraction. In a crossed reflex action, the connections within a given segment of the spinal cord enable skin and stretch receptors in the periphery to produce coordinated muscle contractions with no added input from higher motor levels. Instructions to the motoneurons activate opposing flexors and extensors, depending on the connection patterns.

Reciprocal Control of Opposing Muscles

If you put your foot on a tack while in a sitting position, you may not even notice that the injured foot withdraws by flexion. You may well notice, however, that your other

leg responds with the opposite movement, extension of the foot. This opposing movement of the limbs is called a "crossed extension." The motoneurons that control this reflex are wired together in the spinal cord before birth. (Even a very young infant, if suspended vertically with legs free to move, exhibits walking movements that are triggered mainly by the sensory receptors in the skin and the stretch receptors in the tendons.) In a crossed-extension reflex, sensory nerve fibers react to a pinprick, for example, in the sole of one foot, by directly activating spinal motoneurons that cause the flexor muscles of the insulted leg to contract. Simultaneously, branches of the same sensory fibers also excite the spinal motoneurons controlling the extensor muscles of the other leg.

These reciprocal muscle controls and cross-innervation patterns in the spinal cord produce the counterbalancing arm and leg movements that keep us steady when walking or performing almost any other physical activities. The brain systems, called *central program generators* (CPGs), that generate these locomotor behaviors are quite old evolutionarily and have been found in every known form of vertebrate. A CPG consists of interconnected modules of sensory and motoneurons that automatically generate specific movement sequences, such as a walking sequence or a swimming sequence, by using their own internal sensory feedback to assess the ongoing performance. CPGs are found in the spinal cord very early in prenatal development and probably account for the semicoordinated kicking movements that a fetus makes while still in the uterus. The early maturation of CPGs explains why certain mammalian newborns can get up and walk immediately after birth.

The CPGs are in turn commanded by a relatively primitive brain structure in an evolutionarily old part of the brain, the lower brain stem, or *mesencephalon*. The command region is called the *mesencephalic locomotor region*. Its responsibilities include the arousal of life-threatening sensory stimuli to activate escape behaviors well before the import of the sensory information can be deduced by the higher sensory systems of the cortex.

Polysynaptic Adaptations and Reflexes

So far, we have seen that muscles are controlled by spinal motoneurons and that, within the spinal cord, the motoneurons are organized to respond to sensory information concerning limb and joint position and to generate sequences of movement responses under appropriate stimuli. These features of muscle control and tension work together to ensure smooth voluntary muscle control. What goes on, for instance, in your arm and shoulder muscles and spinal cord that enables you to hold a flag out in front of you with your arm extended at exactly the proper height? The muscles that hold your arm up are opposed by other muscles that keep the arm from flying up too far. Reports from the proprioceptive nerves concerning the muscles' relative tension and length inform the spinal cord of the moment-to-moment status of this balancing act between opposing muscle groups.

Sensory proprioreceptors within the contracted muscle are activated when the muscle is stretched by the muscle opposing it. Tension proprioreceptors in the tendon are activated by the tension developed in the muscle as it pulls on the bone. If your shoulder muscles tire, the drooping of your arm stretches the shoulder muscle fibers and excites the motor neurons controlling them. At the same time, the drop in tension of the opposing muscles decreases activity in the tendon receptors, and their constant inhibition on the opposing motor neuron is relaxed. The result is increased contraction of the shoulder muscle and a restoration of its pull on the arm.

The internally wired local systems of the spinal cord control all of these adjustments automatically once a movement program is selected. A change in program, such as a decision to lift the arm and raise the flag to a higher point, however, has to be initiated by a higher center. The primary source of commands to the motoneurons of the spinal cord consists of the neurons of the motor cortex. If the spinal cord is damaged by penetrating wounds or trauma, the body parts controlled by the spinal cord below the damage will be permanently paralyzed even though the spinal motoneurons themselves remain intact. Eventually through disuse, the muscles will atrophy. An exciting experimental treatment uses stimulating electrodes placed over paralyzed muscles and activating them in the sequences that the normal spinal cord would use to stand or walk.

The Motor Cortex

The parts of the cortex that initiate movements were first detected in investigations of paralysis in patients with localized brain injuries or strokes. One strip of cortex in each cerebral hemisphere is dedicated to motor function. These two motor strips lie adjacent to the strips of cortex dedicated to somatosensory maps of the body surface in each of the hemispheres. Between the motor and sensory cortices in each cerebral hemisphere lies a deep sulcus, referred to as the *Rolandic fissure* or *central sulcus* (see Figures 1.5 and 1.6).

At one time, the motor regions of the cortex were thought to be organized like the adjacent sensory regions—that is, they were thought to be organized according to a map corresponding to the surface of the body. This notion arose from the observation that, when small regions of the motor cortex were stimulated, small muscle movements could be detected in certain parts of the body. The motor-cortex map, like the map for touch (see the homunculus illustration on page 104), was disproportionate to the surface of the body, with the lips, hands, and fingers taking up much more of the cortical area than the legs, trunk, and back muscles. Furthermore, traumatic wounds to the cortex, such as ruptured or plugged blood vessels that produce small strokes and give restricted zones of damage to the motor cortex, can leave the arms or legs of the opposite side of the body permanently paralyzed.

More recent microelectrode recordings of individual nerve cells in the motor region suggest a different interpretation of the motor cortex's arrangement. The recent data show that neurons of the motor cortex, like those in the somatosensory cortex, have a vertical columnar organization extending below the surface of the two-dimensional map. Fine-electrode recordings indicate that vertically related cells in the motor cortex form a functional motor column that seems to control related muscle groups. Other studies show, however, that adjacent neurons in a given motor column behave differently when their muscle groups are performing: some neurons are activated, some are inhibited, and some are not affected at all.

Neuroscientists currently believe that the basic function of each cortical motor column is to control the positioning of a specific joint in space, not simply to activate a group of specific related muscles. To start a movement, the motor system needs to sense the current angle of the relevant joint, the angles of all the other joints in the relevant limb or body part, and the current tension in the relevant muscles. For example, to bring a given joint to the desired angle, a given motor column might need to activate either flexor muscles or extensor muscles, depending on the starting positions of the hand and arm. Thus, a cortical motor column is a small ensemble of motoneurons that influence all the muscles acting on a particular joint. To extend the idea just a little, we can say that the cortex codes our movements not by instructing a series of muscles to contract, but by giving them a command to achieve a certain series of joint positions.

The cortical neurons that communicate directly with the motoneurons of the spinal cord are called *Betz cells,* after the nineteenth-century Russian anatomist who first described them. Betz cells are a special subset of the cortical neurons, called the pyramidal neurons, that project out of the cortex. Lying deep in the motor cortex (layers V and VI), Betz cells are among the largest neurons in the brain, and their axons converge in two large nerve-fiber bundles, called the *pyramidal tracts,* at the junction between the pons and the medulla. The tracts were named for their shape, not because they contain the axons of the pyramidal neurons, which was not then known. As the Betz-cell axons descend to the spinal cord, this bundle crosses over from the side of the cortex in which its fibers originate to the other side of the spinal cord (see Figure 5.8). That is why a stroke or lesion in the right motor cortex paralyzes the left side of the body.

Where does the excitation that drives the motor cortex units come from? The electrical and blood-flow patterns detected when people think about performing a series of movements but do not actually begin to do them (see Figure 5.9) are sources of insight concerning this once almost philosophical question. These observations suggest that premotor activity arises from the prefrontal and somatosensory cortex, regions that are

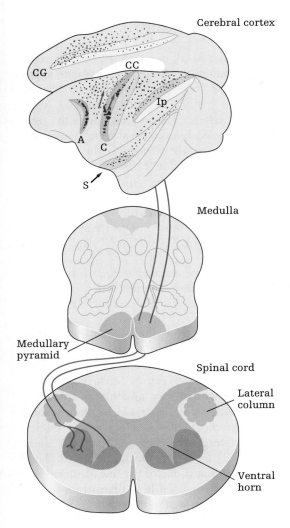

Cerebral cortex

Medulla

Medullary pyramid

Spinal cord

Lateral column

Ventral horn

Figure 5.8 Schematic depiction of the descent of the pyramidal tracts and their crossover to control motoneurons on the opposite side of the spinal cord, thereby controlling muscles on the opposite side of the body. The dots in the cerebral cortex indicate the location of neurons whose axons form the pyramidal tracts. Although concentrated in the pre-central gyrus anterior to the central sulcus (C), neurons of the primate corticospinal tract extend as far forward as the arcuate gyrus (A), ventrally to the Sylvia fissure (S), and into the infraparietal area (Ip), extending medially as far anterior as the cingulate gyrus (CG). (After Toyoshima and Sakai.)

informed more abstractly about the position of the body's limbs and more fully about current joint angles and muscle tension. Thus, when there is an urgent need to initiate movement rapidly, the prefrontal and sensory cortex can guide the motor cortex in selecting the best way to achieve the desired specific movements. One last point concerns the concept of the motor-control hierarchy, in which the premotor and prefrontal regions would appear to be near the top of the chain of command. Within these regions, however, one may also recognize that the motor-control system is widely distributed and that motor-control neurons residing in many cortical regions can

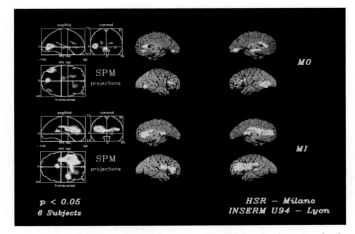

Figure 5.9 Using Positron Emission Tomography (PET) to look at changes in regional cerebral blood flow, researchers exposed young adult subjects to visual stimuli using a virtual reality helmet. They investigated the brain regions in which blood flow changed significantly as subjects stared at a stable visual stimulus, or at two sets of stimuli in which the same hand movements (clenching an object) were either observed (MO) or mentally imaged (MI). The colors (white → yellow) indicate the degree to which these changes in blood flow differed as a result of a particular observed scene. During MO, blood flow increased bilaterally in the occipital, parietal, and temporal lobes, as well as in subcortical regions like the basal ganglia and substantia nigra. During MI, the pattern was markedly different, involving regions directly related to motor activity, especially the pre-motor cortex and frontal lobes, the caudate nucleus, and cerebellum. (Decety, et al. *Nature*, 1994.)

control the same muscle groups, depending on the movements required.

To complete our survey of the motor system, we need to look at two other important structures in the regulation of specific, directed voluntary movements: the basal ganglia and the cerebellum.

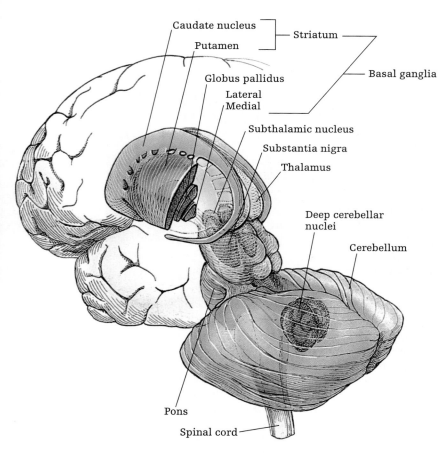

Caudate nucleus
Putamen
Striatum
Globus pallidus
Lateral
Medial
Subthalamic nucleus
Substantia nigra
Thalamus
Basal ganglia
Deep cerebellar nuclei
Cerebellum
Pons
Spinal cord

Figure 5.10 The basal ganglia, an alliance of brain units linked together within the so-called extrapyramidal component of the motor system. The information flowing through the basal ganglia coordinates the initiation and termination of large muscular movements.

The Basal Ganglia

The name "basal ganglia" is less obscure than it sounds. It simply refers to the location (at the *base* of the cortex) of certain collections of nerve cells *(ganglia)* that appear early in brain development (see Chapter 2). Within the basal ganglia are four separate units: the *striatum,* the *pallidum* (also called the *globus pallidus*), the *subthalamic nucleus,* and the *substantia nigra* (see Figure 5.10). These names refer either to the location of the structure (*subthalamic,* "under the thalamus") or to its appearance (*striatum,* "striped"; *pallidum,* "pale"; *nigra,* "black").

The striatum receives input from almost all regions of the cerebral cortex, including all kinds of sensory information as well as the state of activity in the motor system. Its "stripes" come from the heavily myelinated axons of incoming connections from the motor and sensory cerebral cortices. The striatum also receives raw sensory information from the sensory and motor thalamic nuclei before it is processed by the sensory cortex. A third source of input is a single-source–divergent neural connection (see Chapter 2) from the substantia nigra. This last neural link is one of the few affecting the motor system whose neurotransmitter, *dopamine,* is known to be important because of the symptoms that arise when this transmitter is lost in Parkinson's disease. The several neurological diseases that affect the basal ganglia do so in distinctly different ways, and each has helped scientists understand the role that these structures play in movement control.

One of the earliest diseases recognized to affect the basal ganglia is *Wilson's disease,* whose signs of muscular rigidity, tremor, and weakness are accompanied by loss of liver function, all now known to be due to problems with copper metabolism. At postmortem examination, it was observed that, despite the several signs of disturbed movement, the cortical areas were unaffected, whereas the globus pallidus and striatum were affected. From these observations, the British neurologist Wilson, for whom the disease was named, suggested that there were two parallel motor systems. One directed by the motor cortex, controlling the spinal cord through the pyramidal tracts, Wilson called the pyramidal system. The other presumably directed by the basal ganglia extraneous of the pyramidal system he called the extrapyramidal motor system. As more precise methods for clarifying the complex circuitry of the brain were applied to the basal ganglia, it became clear that much of the output of the basal ganglia was directed toward nuclei in the thalamus. In the analysis of their targets, these thalamic nuclei were found to provide abundant connections to the premotor and prefrontal cortical regions that are believed to guide the motor cortex (see Figure 5.11). Instead of "extrapyramidal," a more appropriate designation for the motor controls of the basal ganglia would be "prepyramidal."

Parkinson's disease (named for the first physician to describe it) is a progressive movement disorder characterized by rigid limbs and a coarse tremor of the hands and face. Except for the absence of the liver problems, it was confused with Wilson's disease. After more than a hundred years of vain efforts to help patients suffering from Parkinson's disease, scientists discovered the main cause of the disease to be the death of the dopamine-transmitting neurons of the substantia nigra. Early in the twentieth century, patients who succumbed to Parkinson's disease were found on postmortem examination to have lost the black pigment for which the substantia nigra is named. Eventually, the neurotransmitter made by these dying neurons was identified as dopamine, and the loss of color was attributed to the loss of these neurons and of dopamine. Further research then directly connected these losses with the onset of symptoms: an inability to initiate voluntary movements, accompanied by tremulous motions of the head, hands, and arms when the patient sits quietly.

Although the dopamine innervation is denser in the striatum than in any other brain region, it still accounts for probably less than one-fifth of the synaptic connections there. Nevertheless, the loss of dopamine fibers and dopamine-mediated control is devastating to the smooth operation of the motor system. Patients can, however, be successfully treated for a while by bolstering their declining stores of dopamine with the drug L-DOPA (dihydroxyphenylalanine).

Recordings from neurons in the striatum show that their activity begins just before the initiation of a particular kind of movement, a slow, directed movement of a limb from one large region of space to another. When you close your eyes and try to touch the tip of your nose, for example, the largest part of the movement—bringing the hand from where it was to a position very close to your nose—is what draws on activity in the basal ganglia. This kind of movement is lost by patients with Parkinson's disease.

When investigators destroy the dopamine-transmitting neurons running to the striatum in experimental animals, the animals go through a critical period during which they seem unable to initiate motor acts, even vital ones such as eating and drinking. On the other hand, if the animals are offered strongly scented food, the increased sensory activation helps them overcome this deficiency to some degree. Similarly, human patients with Parkinson's disease can temporarily overcome their motor defects if confronted with

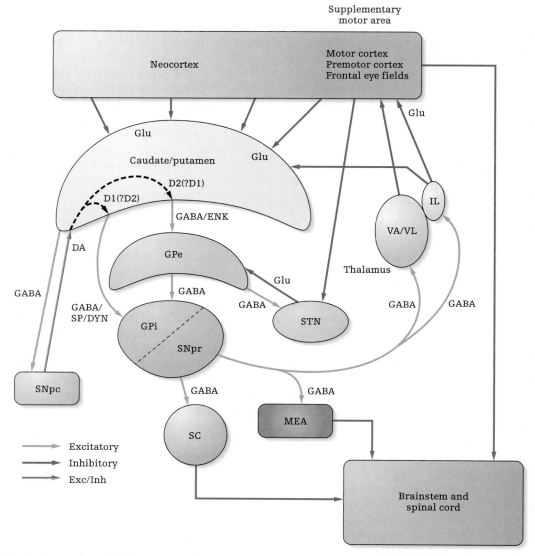

Figure 5.11 Schematic diagram showing the several components of the basal ganglia and the neurotransmitter systems that link them to each other [via GABA interneurons containing the neuropeptides enkephalin (ENK), substance P (SP), or dynorphin (DYN)] and to their afferents (glutamate, GLU) and efferents in the neocortex; and motor cortical areas, the Substantia Nigra pars compacta (SNpc), from which the dopamine neurons innervate the striatum through type 1 (DAD1) receptors as well as type 2 (DAD2) receptors. Also shown are the efferent from the Substantia Nigra pars reticulata (SNpr) via GABA connections to the thalamic nuclei (ventral anterior, VA, ventral lateral, VL, and Intermediolateral, IL) and to the subthalamic nucleus (STN), the superior colliculus (SC), and to the midbrain extrapyramidal area (MEA), and finally to the brainstem (mesencephalic motor area) and spinal cord.

an emergency—a car coming toward them as they are about to step off the curb, for example. The fact that patients with Parkinson's disease also have problems in initiating speech or eye movements suggests that dopamine is needed generally for proper motor control within other parts of the motor system. Dopamine is also a major transmitter within much less well studied components of the basal ganglia—in particular, the ventral pallidum, which connects directly with emotion-regulating regions such as the amygdala (see Chapter 8). The loss of dopamine from such *subcortical motivational systems* probably accounts for the observation that Parkinson's patients frequently have severely depressed emotional status.

Parkinson's patients must take L-DOPA for the rest of their lives. Experimental treatments to replace the dead and dying dopamine-transmitting neurons with transplants of dopamine-producing cells have been under investigation for more than a decade after some early pioneering trials in Sweden, but the success rate remains low and variable. This approach holds some promise of a more effective treatment in the future, but, so far, the explanations for the variable responses of the transplantation and of finding an ethically acceptable source of the good dopamine-producing cells remains unsolved.

On the basis of the now well-defined circuitry of the basal ganglia (see Figure 5.10), scientists have made recordings from neurons in monkeys in which the dopamine-transmitting neurons were destroyed experimentally. Activity within the globus pallidus was significantly altered in pattern, with the neurons firing in short bursts rather than in their normal slow and regular pattern. Based in part on these findings, a new experimental treatment, in which precise lesions are made

in a small part of the globus pallidus, has proved to be effective in reducing the tremors and rigidity in some drug-resistant Parkinson's patients.

In another neurological disease called *Huntington's disease,* the loss of a large subset of neurons of the striatum leads to progressive incapacitation characterized by rapid, random muscular contractions in the limbs, which early observers called "chorea" (a dance). The choreiform movements eventually render the patient rigid, weak, and wasted as a result of the uncontrolled energy expenditure. Huntington's disease has an autosomal dominant inheritance pattern, which means that, if one parent has the disease, the children have a 50–50 chance of inheriting it. The mutant gene, abbreviated *HD,* has been mapped to chromosome 6; tests based on the differences between the normal gene and the forms found in patients with Huntington's disease can predict which children have inherited the disease. The protein encoded by the *HD* gene is apparently expressed in many neurons and other cell types throughout the body. However, only neurons of the striatum whose axons project to the external zone of the globus pallidus are lost for reasons that remain to be determined. Because the cause of their death remains unknown, the disease remains untreatable.

What have scientists learned from these studies of diseases of the basal ganglia? For one thing, very small parts of the basal ganglia can cause severe problems; but, when one studies them in the diseased state, it is quite difficult to understand what the dysfunctional parts do. On the other hand, in experimental animals, very discrete lesions can be made in specific parts of the brain, and, in regard to the basal ganglia, this strategy has led to some presumptive functions for specific components. Lesions, especially large lesions, of the striatum or lesions within the globus pallidus lead to very slow movements, but with normal initiation delays. Damage to the subthalamic nucleus produces dramatic, involuntary wild flinging movements *(hemiballismus)* of the arm and leg on the side of the body opposite that of the lesion in the brain. Lesions of the substantia nigra outside the areas containing dopamine-transmitting neurons lead to involuntary eye movements due to loss of control over the superior colliculus. And, as noted previously, lesions of the parts of the substantia nigra that contain dopamine-transmitting neurons reproduce the findings of Parkinson's disease.

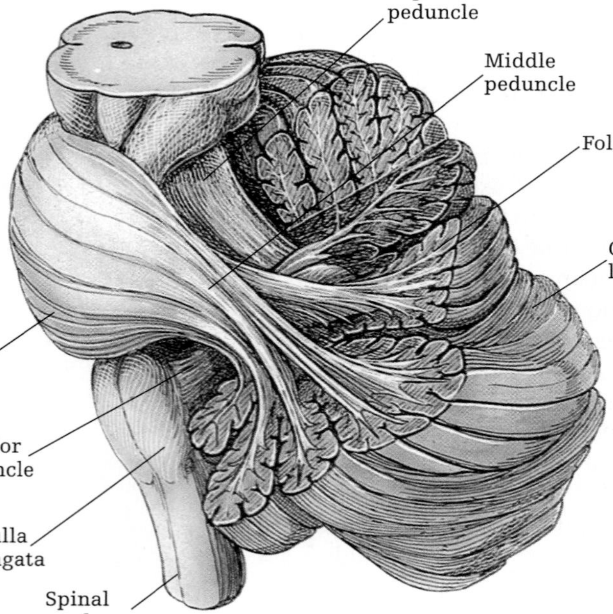

Still unanswered is the question, What do the normal basal ganglia do? Initial ideas, probably influenced by what patients had trouble with, suggested that the basal ganglia were critical for the initiation of movements, as though motor programs were stored in the basal ganglia and sent to the motor cortex for implementation. However, a comparison of the time when neurons in the basal ganglia become active relative to those in the cortex reveals that the basal ganglion neurons seem to become active too late for this explanation to be pursued. Currently, scientists are considering three hypotheses of basal ganglion function: First, the basal ganglia could be responsible for performing some sequences of motor steps, such as writing. Second, the basal ganglia could be organized in two parallel pathways: one for the striatum and the other for the other components of the basal ganglia—one pathway being excitatory and the other inhibitory. Under normal conditions, these two pathways would be in balance, but when they were not, either excessive or defective movement would result. Third, the basal ganglia could function as a tonically active inhibitory force over the pattern generators of the motor cortex and mesencephalon, which would be selectively turned on when one or another of those pattern generators was activated.

Figure 5.12 The midline surface of the cerebellum as viewed from the left, showing the leaflike subdivisions, or folia. Within each folium, a highly redundant layered structure of fiber-rich and cell-rich zones is found. Each folium directs muscular activity within specific muscular groups and specific regions of the limbs and trunk. The superior, middle, and inferior peduncles are the routes by which axons from the pons and medulla enter the cerebellum and by which cerebellar fibers exit.

The Cerebellum

The word *cerebellum* is a diminutive form of *cerebrum*, and the "little cerebrum" is indeed a small brain. It has an extremely regular structure, the surface of which is greatly expanded relative to its volume by virtue of its many folds (see Figure 5.12).

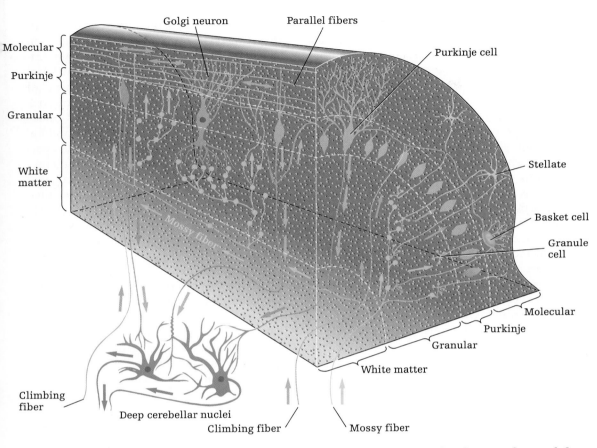

Molecular
Purkinje
Granular
White matter

Golgi neuron
Parallel fibers
Purkinje cell
Stellate
Basket cell
Granule cell
Molecular
Purkinje
Granular
White matter
Mossy fiber
Climbing fiber
Deep cerebellar nuclei
Climbing fiber
Mossy fiber

Figure 5.13 Schematic illustration of the four layers of the cerebellar cortex (see lower and upper left edges), the terminations of the afferents to the cortex, the mossy fibers within the granule cell layer, and the climbing fibers within the molecular layer on the apical dendrites of the Purkinje neurons. Also shown are the ascending intracortical axons of the granule cells which become the parallel fibers synapsing of the Purkinje neurons outer dendritic branchlets and spines. Lastly, the diagram also illustrates the interneurons of the molecular layer (stellate and basket cells) and of the Purkinje layer (Golgi cells), and the terminations of the Purkinje neurons onto the neurons of the deep cerebellar nuclei.

Sliced and viewed from the side, it consists of many small, folded lobes, which look something like leaves, and are accordingly called *folia*. An identical four-layered cellular structure curves through every folium (see Figure 5.13) Two of the layers of this structure, the Purkinje-cell layer and the granule-cell layer, are packed with neurons, whereas the third (the molecular layer) con-

tains relatively few neurons and the fourth contains mainly white matter of the axons entering or leaving the cortex. The Purkinje-cell layer is only one-cell thick, but the Purkinje cells are very large neurons. Immediately beneath the layer of Purkinje neurons are the granule neurons, several-cells thick and so named because they have very thin rims of cytoplasm.

The cerebellum receives information from the cerebral cortex, from the brainstem, and from the spinal cord. The spinal-cord information reveals the positions of the limbs, trunk, head, neck, and eyes, all of which is integrated by the Purkinje cells. Purkinje neurons seem to fire very rapidly, usually in bursts, perhaps an indication of their constant surveillance of trunk, limb, and head location and position. The Purkinje neurons' output travels to the nuclei of large neurons buried deep within the cerebellum and called the *deep cerebellar nuclei* (see Figure 5.11). Information transmitted from these nuclei modifies the activity of neurons in the motor cortex.

Despite its elegant structure and its well-characterized cellular circuitry, the exact role of the cerebellum in motor function is far from certain. Observations of subjects in whom the cerebellum has been injured or is stimulated (in an attempt to relieve abnormal postures) suggest that this structure is important for controlling the muscle tone needed to hold a posture. Tests given to people suspected of drunkenness—walking a straight line or standing still with their eyes shut—directly evaluate the cerebellum's success at this task.

Research also suggests that, during programs of fine movements, the cerebellum monitors the positions of the body parts at any given moment and compares their actual positions with their desired positions according to the ongoing motor program. It is very much as if the cerebellum possessed a carbon copy of the planned pattern of activity containing both the instructions for the neurons of the motor cortex and the intended positions of the trunk and limbs at each stage of the program's execution. The cerebellum then adjusts the activity of the motor cortex and spinal cord to smooth out the finer motions and alerts the cortex of any failures to attain the necessary positions on schedule. Thus, when you move your finger to touch the end of your nose, the basal ganglia activate the large movement of your hand toward the general area of your nose, but it is the cerebellum that guides the final approach to a perfect landing. The cerebellum is also required for the performance of rapid, consecutive, simultaneous movements, such as the sophisticated coordination of the trained typist or musician, or the somewhat coarser task (rarely required except in neurological examinations) of patting your head and rubbing your tummy at the same time.

Recent research has added something new to the list of possible responsibilities for the cerebellum. The noninvasive functional imaging studies of the brain mentioned in Chapter 1 and considered at greater length in Chapter 11—namely, PET and fMRI—have been the source of much of this new insight. In these studies, scientists have observed that the cerebellum is activated during a number of cognitive tasks—such as mental imaging, shifting attention, modulating emotion, and processing language—in addition to the expected activation as a subject learns a new motor skill. Moreover, subjects whose cerebella have been damaged have impairments of memory, emotion, and reasoning ability, the net effect of which is to lower overall intellectual capacity. Thus, in addition to its roles in motor performance, the cerebellum may have a more general error-detection function in other mental operations.

In this chapter, we have seen that the systems of the brain that allow us to move smoothly through our environments are composed of two essential streams. One stream is the coordinated conscious movement that we employ to change posture, to walk, and to grasp. The second consists of the more automated sequences of movements that we employ to perform long programs of motor events, often at speeds too rapid to decide each and every one. In the next chapter, we will consider other internal operations of our bodies governed by the brain that are essential to health and well being and almost never brought to our conscious awareness.

Summary

1. Like the sensory system, the motor system operates on a vertical hierarchy. Commands to move arise in the motor cortex and stimulate selected neurons in the spinal cord and the muscles to which they are connected.

2. The motor system operates in a sequential ordered fashion. Movement is initiated in the motor cortex, which communicates with the spinal motoneurons, which in turn activate muscle fibers controlling joint position and stability.

3. Programmed sequences of movement rely on modulatory systems in the cerebellum and basal ganglia to provide coordinated and polished movements.

4. Although the sensory and motor systems are independent of each other, sensory information concerning limb position and muscle tension is critical to the performance of complex movements.

5. Lesions of the primary motor system in the cortex or spinal cord produce total paralysis of muscle groups. Lesions of the basal ganglia or cerebellum produce uncoordinated and often involuntary movements.

Key Terms

muscle	Betz cell
actin	Purkinje cell
myosin	cerebellum
proprioception	Parkinson's disease
motor unit	Huntington's disease
motoneuron	dopamine
central program generator	paralysis
basal ganglia	stroke

Further Reading

Beiser, D. G., Hua, S. E., and Houk, J. C. 1997. Network models of the basal ganglia. *Current Opinion in Neurobiology* 7:185–190. Hypotheses of how information flows through the basal ganglia, aimed at the advanced student with a strong mathematical background.

Evarts, E. V. 1979. Brain mechanisms of movement. *Scientific American* (September): 164–179. The differences between the brain's role in reflex and in voluntary movement are revealed by studies using microelectrodes implanted in the brains of active monkeys. The importance of feedback signals from muscles to brain is explained.

Floeter, M. K. 1999. Muscle, motor neurons, and motor neuron pools. In M. E. Zigmond, F. E. Bloom, S. C. Landis, J. L. Roberts, and L. R. Squire, Eds., (pp. 863–887). *Fundamental Neuroscience.* Academic Press, New York. An excellent comprehensive description of muscles and motor units, aimed at the level of the beginning advanced student.

Houk, J. C., and Wise, S. P. 1995. Distributed modular architectures linking basal ganglia, cerebellum, and cerebral cortex: their role in planning and controlling action. *Cerebral Cortex* 5:95–110. An advanced, comprehensive examination of integrated motor-system function.

Kandel, E., and Schwartz, J., Eds. 1991. *Principles of Neural Science,* 3d ed., Part VI: Motor Systems of the Brain: Reflex and Voluntary Control of Movement (pp. 548–563). Elsevier, New York. An advanced textbook coverage.

Marr, D. 1983. A theory of cerebellar cortex. *Journal of Physiology* 202:437–470. One of the first comprehensive analyses of how the circuitry of cerebellar cortex analyzes its afferent activity.

Thach, W. 1999. Fundamentals of motor systems. In M. E. Zigmond, F. E. Bloom, S. C. Landis, J. L. Roberts, and L. R. Squire, Eds. *Fundamental Neuroscience,* (pp. 855–862). Academic Press, New York. An excellent brief overview of the components of the motor system and their coordination, aimed at the level of the beginning advanced student.

Interactive Resources

The CD-ROM that accompanies this book includes various ways to visualize the material covered in this chapter. Its "Control of Movement" module includes detailed diagrams of the motor system, and video clips and animations on reflexes and muscle movement.

To learn even more and make sure you've mastered the material covered in this chapter, visit our Web site at www.worthpublishers.com/bloom. Click on "Chapter 5" for resources including practice quizzes, flash cards, simulations, links to related Web sites, and updates on new research.

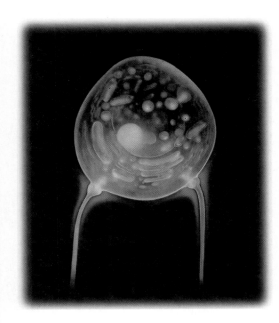

CHAPTER SIX

Homeostasis: Maintaining the Internal Environment

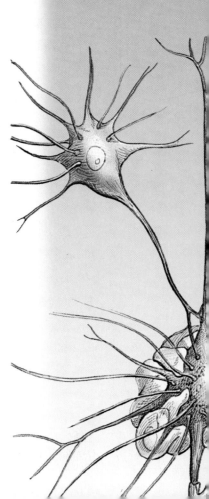

The world around us is constantly changing. Winter winds force us to wear heavy jackets and gloves. Central heating forces us to take them off. Summer sun reduces our need to preserve body heat until efficient air-conditioning turns the tables on us. Yet on any given day, whatever the temperature outside, the individual body temperatures of all the healthy people you know are probably identical to within a tenth of a degree. The bodies of human beings and other warm-blooded animals regulate their temperatures to a constant internal value of about 99°F, although that temperature rises and falls a few tenths of a degree in a regular daily rhythm (see Chapter 7).

People differ in their eating habits. Some like a good breakfast, a light lunch, and a hearty dinner, with dessert. Others take their largest meal at lunch and then a nap in the afternoon. Some people snack all the time; others skip meals and scarcely care about eating at all. Yet again, if you measured the blood-sugar level of everyone you know, their individual measurements would probably all be about one-thousandth of a gram (1 mg) per milliliter of blood, despite the wide range in dietary habits.

The regulation of body temperature and of blood glucose to such precise levels are just two examples of the many crucial body functions that fall under the command of the nervous system. The fluids surrounding all our cells also are continuously monitored by the nervous system, and their levels of essential salts and minerals are regulated to an extraordinary degree of constancy.

This ability of the body to keep its internal environment constant is known as *homeostasis* (*homeo*, "same" or "similar"; *stasis*, "stability" or "balance"). It is accomplished largely by the autonomic and diffuse enteric segments of the peripheral nervous system, in concert with the central nervous system,

acting directly on the body through the pituitary gland and the endocrine organs. Together, these systems integrate the needs of the body with the demands of the external environment. (That statement should sound familiar. We have used just those words to describe the main responsibility of the brain. The central and peripheral nervous systems work together to sample and regulate our *internal environment* as well.)

The nineteenth-century French physiologist Claude Bernard, who spent his career studying the process of digestion and the regulation of blood flow, viewed the fluids of the body as the *milieu interne,* the "internal environment." In every individual organism, the concentrations of specific salts and the normal range of temperatures may be slightly different from those of other individuals, but, within a species, the internal environments of all members conform to certain standards. Only momentary and modest deviations from the standard range can be tolerated if an organism is to remain healthy and contribute to the survival of its species. Walter B. Cannon, one of the leading American physiologists of the mid-twentieth century, expanded on Bernard's concept of the internal environment. He recognized that an individual organism is freed from the tyranny of continuous change in its external world by the *homeostatic mechanisms* that work to maintain a uniform internal environment.

The capacity of an organism to survive in spite of changes in its external environment varies considerably from species to species. Human beings, who have the capacity to perform highly complex behaviors in addition to having internal homeostatic mechanisms, appear to have the greatest freedom of all. Even so, many animals outstrip human beings in certain species-specific abilities: some, such as the polar bear, withstand more cold; some, such as desert spiders and lizards, withstand more heat; and some, such as the dromedary, tolerate longer periods of water deprivation. Nevertheless, none have quite the ability that humans have to purposefully invent new ways of adapting to a changing world. In this chapter, we will examine some of the nonconscious and autonomic structures responsible for endowing us with a measure of freedom from the changing physical demands of the world. In the process, we will look closely at the regulatory mechanisms that keep our internal environment so remarkably stable.

The Autonomic Nervous System

Certain organizational features of the autonomic nervous system make a good place to start our examination of internal regulation. (Recall that the autonomic nervous system is a part of the peripheral nervous system, as noted in Chapter 1.) Much like the systems examined in Chapters 4 and 5, the autonomic nervous system has both "sensory" and "motor" components. The sensory components monitor the internal world, whereas the motor components activate or inhibit the target structures (blood vessels, glands, and some smooth muscles) that do the actual adjusting. In the autonomic nervous system, we might more appropriately term these two elements the "sensing" and "effector" components.

The classical autonomic nervous system has two large divisions: the *sympathetic* and the *parasympathetic*. Both divisions have an architectural feature that we have not encountered until now. The neurons that direct the internal muscles and glands are located entirely outside the central nervous system in small encapsulated clusters of cells called *ganglia*. In the autonomic nervous sys-

In the gravity-free, oxygen-free environment of outer space, astronauts wear special suits that constrain heat loss, substitute for the pull of gravity, and maintain adequate oxygen pressure for brain function. On earth, these functions are achieved automatically by the brain and peripheral and autonomic nervous systems.

tem, therefore, an additional structure exists between the spinal cord and the final target structure. The diffuse *enteric nervous system* is still more remote from the spinal cord and contains its own ganglia onto which the sympathetic and parasympathetic nervous systems can convey information. Because it is now one extra link more remote, some investigators consider the diffuse enteric nervous system to be a third division of the autonomic nervous system.

In Chapter 5, you learned that intramuscular sensory receptors, along with sensory receptors in tendons and elsewhere, detect pressure and stretch. Together they constitute a kind of internal muscle-sensing system that helps to guide our movements. Receptors of the sensory systems used in homeostasis are more heterogeneous in structure and mode of operation: some detect chemical variations in blood composition, others recognize tension changes in the vascular system or in the "hollow organs" (intestinal tract, urinary bladder, and gall bladder). In many ways, these "sensory" components of the autonomic nervous system, which pick up information about the body's *internal* environment, are more like the sensory system that collects information from the *external* surface of the body. In both the sympathetic and parasympathetic nervous systems, the incoming sensory receptor neurons *(visceral afferent nerves)* make their first synaptic relays within the spinal cord. In some cases, information from major blood vessels such as the aorta and carotid arteries is conveyed directly to special autonomic integrating regions of the medulla.

Sensory information from the viscera and other sources is transmitted directly to the efferent autonomic neurons in the spinal cord. In turn, these efferent autonomic neurons regulate the activity of the neurons of the autonomic ganglia. The spinal-cord-to-ganglia axons are called *preganglionic fibers.* Therefore, these preganglionic autonomic neurons in the spinal cord are loosely analogous to the spinal motor neurons of the somatic motor system. The neurotransmitter for this link from the spinal cord to the autonomic ganglion neurons in both sympathetic and parasympathetic ganglia is *acetylcholine,* the same transmitter used by the motor neurons in the spinal cord to exert direct control over the skeletal muscles. The axons that emerge from the neurons of the autonomic ganglia, the *postganglionic fibers,* then run directly to

their target organs, where they branch extensively and innervate their target tissues. The postganglionic neurons that innervate the muscles of the heart, blood vessels, and gut cause them to constrict or relax. Other postganglionic neurons innervate glands and cause them to secrete (for example, tears, saliva, bile, and sweat).

In spite of their organizational similarities, the sympathetic and parasympathetic divisions of the autonomic nervous system also differ in the following important respects:

1. The spinal-cord region from which their preganglionic fibers emerge

2. The proximity of their ganglia to their target organs

3. The neurotransmitter used by their postganglionic neurons to regulate the activity of their targets

4. Their functions

It is to these points that we now turn our attention.

The Sympathetic Nervous System

The sympathetic division receives its preganglionic control from neurons in the thoracic and lumbar areas of the spinal cord (see Figure 6.1). Its ganglia lie relatively near the spinal cord (and are therefore called *paravertebral ganglia*), and its postganglionic fibers diverge over great distances to reach the cells in their respective target organs. The major transmitter for the postganglionic sympathetic nerves is *norepinephrine,* one of the catecholamines discussed in Chapter 2. Norepinephrine is commonly encountered as a neurotransmitter in the peripheral nervous system as well as in the central nervous system.

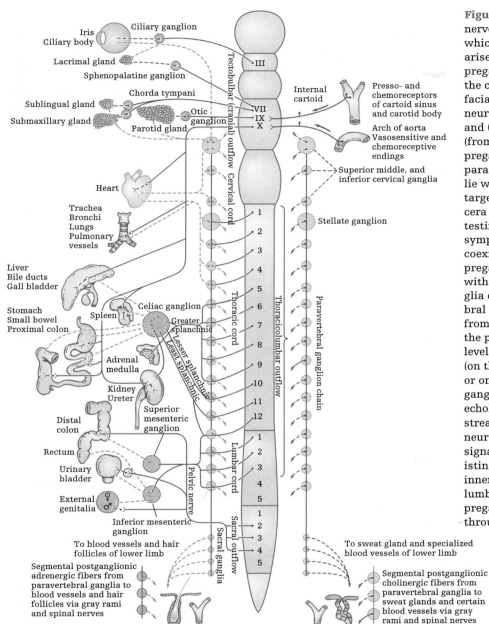

Figure 6.1 Basic elements of the autonomic nervous system. Preganglionic neurons, which use the transmitter acetylcholine, arise in two major divisions: (1) craniosacral preganglionic parasympathetic fibers from the cranial nerve nuclei (oculomotor [III], facial [VII], hypoglossal [IX], and vagus [X] neurons) and from the sacral spinal cord; and (2) thoracolumbar sympathetic fibers (from indicated spinal-segment levels). These preganglionic fibers are quite long for the parasympathetic fibers, whose target ganglia lie within or adjacent to their limited visceral targets (note the vagus nerve innervates viscera from the heart to the lower gastrointestinal tract). The postganglionic parasympathetic fibers also are cholinergic, with coexisting neuropeptides in many cases. The preganglionic sympathetic fibers connect with postganglionic neurons within the ganglia closest to the spinal cord (the paravertebral chain) or converge (see fibers emerging from thoracic cord) and penetrate through the paravertebral ganglia from several spinal levels onto one of the more distant ganglia (on the cervical, celiac, or mesenteric ganglia or onto the adrenal medulla, a sympathetic ganglion that secretes its postganglionic catecholamine message directly into the bloodstream). The postganglionic sympathetic neurons and their long fibers all transmit signals with norepinephrine and have coexisting peptides. For simplicity, sympathetic innervation of the skin is shown only for the lumbar ganglia but occurs at all levels. The preganglionic parasympathetic fibers through their distal postganglionic neurons and short postganglionic parasympathetic fibers also link directly to the diffuse enteric neurons of the gastrointestinal tract. The visceral afferent sensory fibers that bring information from the viscera back to the brain travel largely within the vagus nerve bundle (labeled X) but are not shown.

A simple way to remember the target organs of the sympathetic nervous system and its effects on them is to think of what happens to an aroused animal that must mobilize for "flight or fight." The pupils dilate to allow more light to enter. The heart rate picks up, and the heart muscle contracts more strongly, driving more blood to the muscles. Contractions of selected vascular channels shift blood away from the skin and intestinal organs and toward the muscles and brain. Motility of the gastrointestinal system decreases, and digestive processes slow down. The muscles along the air passages of the lungs relax, and respiratory rate increases, allowing more air to be moved in and out. Liver and fat cells are activated to furnish more glucose and fatty acids—the body's high-energy fuels—and the pancreas is instructed to release less insulin. The reduction in insulin allows the brain to draw off a sizable fraction of the glucose entering the bloodstream because, unlike other organs, the brain does not require insulin in order to utilize blood glucose. The neurotransmitter that triggers all these changes is norepinephrine. When tobacco smokers inhale, part of their pleasurable response depends on nicotine stimulating the preganglionic acetylcholine neurons that activate the sympathetic nervous system.

At the same time as the sympathetic neurons are activating these target organs, an additional element of the sympathetic nervous system acts more generally to promote the same effects; that is, it activates the two adrenal glands, sitting like small caps on top of the kidneys. In the middle, or *medulla*, of each adrenal gland is a group of cells innervated by preganglionic sympathetic fibers. The cells of the adrenal medulla are embryologically derived from the same neural crest cells that produce the sympathetic ganglia, a clue that the adrenal medulla is a component of the sympathetic nervous system. When activated by their long preganglionic fibers, adrenal medullary cells secrete their own norepinephrine and epinephrine directly into the bloodstream for general distribution to sympathetic targets (see Figure 6.2). Blood-borne chemical signals such as these are referred to as hormones. Later in this chapter, we consider a number of other important hormone signals and the general endocrine system that secretes them.

The Parasympathetic Nervous System

The parasympathetic division receives its preganglionic information from the *brainstem* (the "cranial component" of the parasympathetic system) and from the lower, or *sacral*, segments of the spinal cord (the "sacral component" of the parasympathetic system), as diagrammed in Figure 6.1. The parasympathetic preganglionic fibers include an especially important nerve trunk called the *vagus nerve*, which is also the tenth cranial nerve (X in Figure 6.1). The numerous efferent branches of the vagus nerve supply all of the parasympathetic innervation to and from the heart, lungs, and intestinal tract. (The vagus nerve also carries sensory information from these regions back to the preganglionic level. In fact, there are more sensory fibers coming from the viscera in the vagus than there are efferent fibers.) The preganglionic parasympathetic axons are very long because their ganglia are generally located very close to or within the tissues that they innervate.

Like the preganglionic fibers, the postganglionic fibers in this division use the transmitter acetylcholine. But unlike the targets of the other autonomic acetylcholine-producing neurons—the preganglionic neurons in both sympathetic and parasympathetic divisions—the targets of

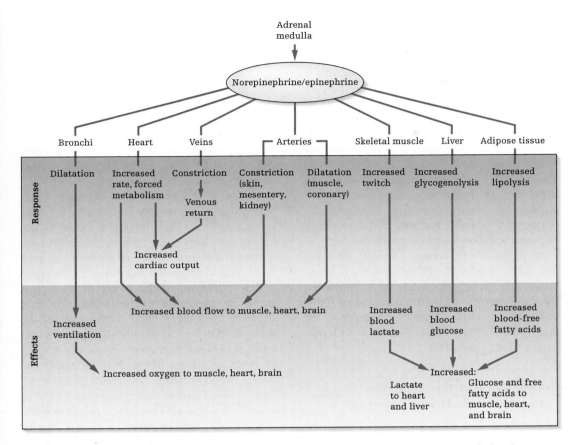

Figure 6.2 When autonomic nerve activity leads the adrenal medulla to secrete catecholamines, these messengers circulate through the bloodstream to influence the activity of several different target tissues. These global signals ensure a coordinated response from widely separated organs. (Glycogenolysis is the process by which glycogen is broken down to glucose; lipolysis is the breakdown of fat.)

the postganglionic parasympathetic fibers are not sensitive to nicotine. They respond to the acetylcholine message through a different class of cholinergic receptors called *muscarinic cholinergic receptors*. As the name indicates, these receptors are activated by the drug muscarine, and they are blocked by the drug atropine. These differing target-response patterns allow physicians to pre-scribe drugs designed to selectively stimulate or block only those acetylcholine signals that are recognized by parasympathetically inner-vated glands or muscles. For example, mus-carine will constrict the pupils and slow the heart just as the activated parasympathetic nerves do, whereas atropine blocks the parasympathetic cholinergic signals to the iris, heart, and other cholinergic targets.

Parasympathetic activity in the body sets the stage for "rest and recuperation." At the extreme, its overall effects resemble the state of lassitude and inactivity that follows a heavy meal. Stepped-up blood flow to the intestinal tract increases the movement of food through the gut and the secretion of digestive enzymes. Heart rate and the strength of heart contraction diminish, the pupils of the eyes constrict, and the airways narrow, while their mucosal secretions increase. (Atropine-like drugs are often employed when patients require anesthesia for surgery to reduce secretions of the trachea and bronchi that might otherwise restrict the flow of air into the lungs.) The urinary bladder also constricts. Taken together, these actions "restore" the body to the relaxed state that it enjoyed before a period of fight-or-flight activity. (These phenomena are illustrated in Figure 6.1 and from different perspectives in Chapter 8.)

Coordination of the Sympathetic and Parasympathetic Divisions

As we have just seen, the sympathetic and the parasympathetic nervous systems differ organizationally and functionally. The sympathetic nervous system has very long postganglionic fibers and prepares the body for fight or flight, whereas the parasympathetic system has very long preganglionic fibers to ganglia located near or within its target organs and prepares the body for rest and recuperation. Many internal organs, such as the lungs, the heart, the salivary glands, the bladder, and the genital organs, receive innervation from both of these major autonomic divisions. These organs are said to be "dually innervated." Other tissues, such as some of the smaller arteries, receive only sympathetic innervation. It is tempting to generalize by saying that the two divisions work in alternation: one or the other dominates, depending on the current needs of the body and the commands of the higher autonomic centers.

This generalization is not completely correct, however. Both systems are active to some degree all the time. The fact that a target organ such as the heart or the iris can respond to both systems is simply due to the complementary organization of the autonomic nervous system as a whole. For example, if you become very angry, the sympathetic component of the ANS raises your blood pressure, activating the pressure receptors in your carotid arteries. The integrating center of the cardiovascular system in the lower medulla detects the change in blood pressure. Output from this center then activates the preganglionic parasympathetic fibers of the vagus nerve to slow down the heart rate and decrease the force of heart contraction. At the same time, other outputs from this same vascular coordinating center depress the activity of the sympathetic fibers and counteract the rise in blood pressure. The result of the autonomic coordination is to allow the body to operate at a new level of blood pressure while not allowing blood pressure to rise out of control. (When this feedback is deficient, elevations of blood pressure can persist—a general disease termed *hypertension*.)

To what degree is either division essential to adaptive response and, ultimately, to survival? Surprisingly (because of its apparent essentiality), both animals and humans can tolerate an almost complete surgical removal of the sympathetic nervous system without any apparent ill effects, as long as the subjects are kept in carefully controlled environments. This form of surgical treatment was once advocated for certain forms of unremitting hypertension. However, outside the protective setting of a hospital or laboratory, subjects who have undergone such surgery can tolerate very few environmental demands. They cannot regulate their body temperatures when exposed to heat or cold, they cannot regulate their blood pressures when they lose blood, and they generally tire quickly in response to any increase in muscular workload.

The Diffuse Enteric Nervous System

A third major division of the autonomic nervous system—independent of, but modifiable by, the sympathetic and parasympathetic systems—is called the *diffuse enteric nervous system* (see Figure 6.3). This division is responsible for gastrointestinal innervation and coordination. It seems to act as a third, separate, neural control unit placed between the autonomic postganglionic nerves and the glands and muscles of the gastrointestinal system.

The neural ganglia of the diffuse enteric system innervate the muscular walls of the gut. Axons from these ganglionic cells directly activate the contractions of the circular and longitudinal muscles that propel food through the digestive system, a process called *peristalsis*, governing the local patterns of peristaltic movements. A food mass signals its presence at a specific location in the intestine by stretching the wall of the gut slightly. In response, the diffuse enteric

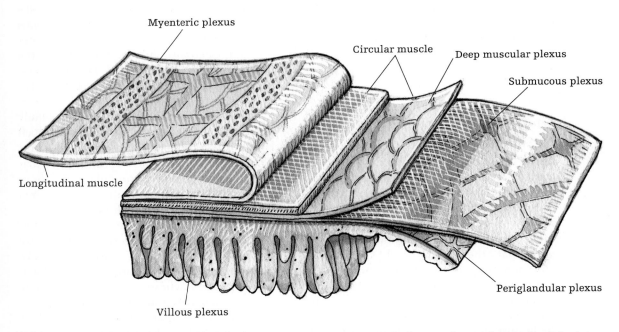

Figure 6.3 The diffuse enteric nervous system is contained between the layers of smooth muscle of the intestinal wall. Two large networks of neurons in ganglia and their interganglionic connections can be seen: (1) the myenteric plexus lies between the outer longitudinal muscle layer and the circular muscle layer, and (2) the submucous plexus lies between the circular muscles and the inner mucosal layer. These neurons control peristalsis and enteric secretions.

system causes constriction of the segment immediately above the mass and relaxation of the segment immediately below, resulting in the mass of food being pushed downward. Parasympathetic or sympathetic innervation in the gut, however, can modify enteric ganglionic activity. Parasympathetic activity increases peristalsis, whereas sympathetic activity decreases it.

The diffuse enteric system uses acetylcholine as the neurotransmitter that excites the intestinal smooth muscle. Inhibitory commands leading to relaxation, however, appear to be transmitted by several different neuropeptides, only a few of which have been identified. These neurotransmitters in the gut include at least three neuropeptides that also act as neurotransmitters for neurons in the central nervous system, and those central actions have nothing at all to do with the gastrointestinal actions: the endorphins (see page 47), somatostatin (see page 44), and substance P (see page 46).

Central Regulation of the Autonomic Nervous System

The degree of hierarchical control that the central nervous system exerts over the autonomic systems is far looser than the control that it exerts over the sensory and skeletal motor systems. This more relaxed control is implicit in the name autonomic, which suggests that these peripheral systems are "autonomous" from central control. The brain regions that connect most directly with autonomic functions are the *hypothalamus* and the *brainstem*, especially that segment of the brainstem just above the spinal cord, the *medulla oblongata*. From these regions, we can trace the major connections carrying input to the sympathetic and parasympathetic preganglionic autonomic neurons.

The Hypothalamus In general, the hypothalamus is thought to be the principal location for the integration of visceral functions, which it achieves in two ways. First, neuronal systems in the hypothalamus feed directly into the circuits that activate the preganglionic limbs of the autonomic nerves. Second, the hypothalamus exerts direct control over the entire endocrine system (described in the next section of this chapter) through specific neurons in the hypothalamus that regulate the hormones secreted from the anterior lobe of the pituitary gland, a gland that is situated directly beneath the hypothalamus. The hypothalamus is also one of the brain regions whose overall structure and organization appear to have remained fairly constant in the brains of vertebrates in many widely separated phyla (see Figure 6.4). Functionally, the hypothalamus can be considered a collection of three zones without clear-cut physical boundaries: the periventricular, medial, and lateral zones. Each zone contains several clusters of neurons, or nuclei (see Figure 6.4).

The *periventricular zone* is immediately adjacent to the third cerebral ventricle, which runs through the center of the hypothalamus. The cells lining the ventricles deliver information to cells in the periventricular zone about important internal conditions that may require regulation: temperature, salt concentration, and levels of hormones being secreted by the endocrine system, under the control of the pituitary gland. Surrounding the periventricular zone is a group of hypothalamic structures whose neurons constitute a *medial zone*. This zone contains most of the neuronal nuclei that regulate the pituitary gland's instructions to the endocrine system. In a crude sense, cells in the periventricular zone check on whether the commands issued to the pituitary by neurons in the medial zone were, in fact, carried out.

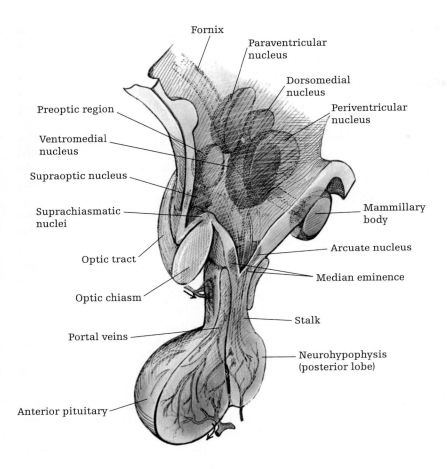

Fornix

Paraventricular
nucleus

Dorsomedial
nucleus

Periventricular
nucleus

Preoptic region

Ventromedial
nucleus

Supraoptic nucleus

Suprachiasmatic
nuclei

Optic tract

Optic chiasm

Portal veins

Anterior pituitary

Mammillary
body

Arcuate nucleus

Median eminence

Stalk

Neurohypophysis
(posterior lobe)

Figure 6.4 Structures of the hypothalamus and pituitary. The major functional zones of the hypothalamus are illustrated in simplified form. The various nuclei and other neuronal structures within each zone are shown as if the boundaries of the hypothalamus (in reality a relatively narrow and oblong envelope running from front to back) were a transparent interior brain space.

The endocrine-regulating neurons of the hypothalamus—those in the medial zone—send their axons to a highly vascular structure called the *median eminence* on the lower surface of the hypothalamus. This point is directly adjacent to the stalk of the pituitary gland (see Figure 6.3). A special closed system of blood vessels, called the *pituitary-portal circulation,* links the median eminence with the anterior pituitary. When endocrine-regulating neurons of the hypothalamus are active, their nerve terminals in the median eminence release their transmitter signals into this very limited circulatory system, to be carried directly and exclusively to the anterior pituitary.

The posterior lobe of the pituitary is made up of the terminal axons of another set of medial-zone hypothalamic neurons. The transmitters from those axons—vasopressin and oxytocin—are released from the posterior pituitary directly into the general bloodstream as hormones. *Vasopressin* increases blood pressure during extreme emergencies when fluid or blood is lost and decreases urinary excretion of water (vasopressin has also been called the *antidiuretic* hormone). *Oxytocin* activates the contraction of the uterus during the final stages of labor and helps the breasts eject milk when suckled.

Through diffusely placed neurons in the *lateral zone,* the hypothalamus receives higher-level control from the cerebral cortex and limbic system, as well as sensory information coming up from the centers in the medulla oblongata that coordinate respiratory and cardiovascular activity. The lateral zone provides a place where higher brain centers can override the otherwise more or less automatic hypothalamic responses to variations detected in the internal environment. For example, various kinds of information from both the internal and the external environments are compared in the cortex. If the cortex concludes that the time and place are inappropriate for, say, feeding, sensory information indicating low blood sugar and an empty stomach will be consciously filed away until a more opportune moment, although children often have a hard time making this determination. Input from the limbic structures, however, is less likely to override the hypothalamus. Instead, it is likely to add emotional and motivational qualities to the cortex's interpretations of external sensory signals or to compare a current status report on the world with information from similar situations in the past.

In concert with its cortical and limbic connections, the hypothalamus also manages a variety of routine integrating activities that occur according to schedules over much longer periods of time than its moment-by-moment homeostatic activities. For example, the hypothalamus anticipates what the body will need on a normal daily schedule, such as getting the endocrine system ready to be fully active just as we wake up. It also anticipates the body's needs on monthly or seasonal schedules. It monitors the hormones that the ovaries release as the reproductive cycle progresses, and it issues the commands that prepare the uterus to receive a fertilized ovum. In migrating birds and hibernating mammals, the hypothalamus—able to detect day length—coordinates activity over cycles lasting many months. This form of anticipatory regulation—the ability to initiate well in advance the changes that will be needed for future demands—is termed *allostasis.* Some of these aspects of the central control of internal functions are considered in greater detail in Chapter 7.

The Medulla Oblongata The entire hypothalamus makes up less than 5 percent of the mass of the brain, yet it regulates virtually all the body's functions except spontaneous respiratory movements, blood pressure, and cardiac rhythm. These last functions are controlled by the *medulla oblongata* (see Figure 6.5). In patients with severe brain trauma to the cortex, a legal status termed "brain death" is defined by the cessation of all signs of cortical electrical activity and the loss of hypothalamic and medullary controls over respiration. Before this state of reduced life was accepted by the legal system, some patients were maintained on life-support systems for many months to years because artificial respiration can maintain adequate oxygenation as long as the heart continues to beat and spontaneously circulates blood.

The Endocrine System

An *endocrine organ* is one that secretes a substance directly into the bloodstream to regulate the cellular activity of certain other organs. (The name derives from *endo,*

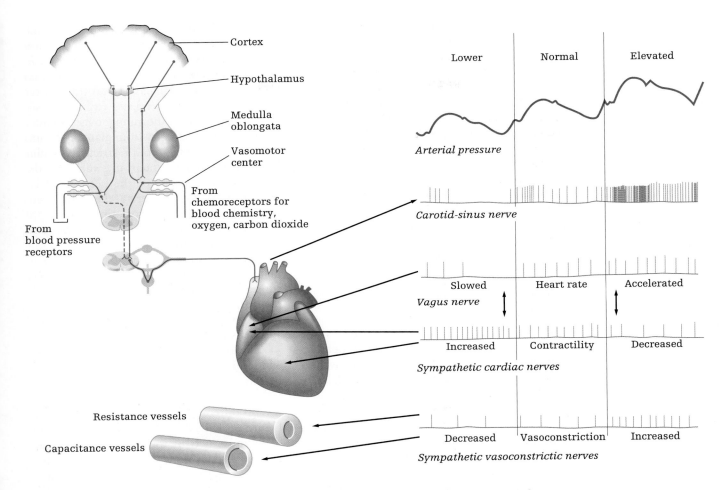

Figure 6.5 A diagrammatic view of the actions of the medulla oblongata, showing connections from various internal organs to the brainstem and reticular formation. Note how the activity of the carotid sinus nerve reacts to changes in blood pressue, dropping when blood pressure drops and rising when blood pressure rises. Sensory signals from these visceral organs regulate the integrative centers in the medulla, which in turn adjust the autonomic divisions concerned with cardiovascular control. Also shown at the right are the changes in the sympathetic nervous system and heart rate reacting to oppose the changes in blood pressue: rising when blood pressure drops and slowing when pressure rises. The medullary integrating center also responds to descending cortical and pontine system information that reflects the degree of arousal and attention that the brain focuses on external events.

"within," and *krinein*, "to separate" or "secrete.") Endocrine organs are called *glands*, and the substances that they secrete are called *hormones*, from the Greek word for "messenger." Each hormone adjusts the level of performance of its specific target-cell systems, usually increasing their rates of activity on a temporary basis.

Hormones are very potent—only small amounts are needed to do the job. Cells that respond to hormones are genetically endowed with special surface receptors that detect even very low hormone concentrations. The binding of a hormone to its target cell initiates a predetermined series of internal adjustments.

The Endocrine Organs and Their Hormones

The glands that make up the endocrine system are the *pituitary*, with its independently functioning anterior and posterior lobes, the *gonads* (ovary and testes), the *thyroid*, the *parathyroid*, the *adrenal cortex* and the *adrenal medulla*, the *islet cells of the pancreas*, and the *secretory cells that line the intestinal tract*. Table 6.1 presents the fundamental features of the system.

Traditionally, the endocrine system was viewed as separate from but parallel to the nervous system in its regulating and integrating activities. Neurons secrete their chemical messengers, neurotransmitters, into the synaptic gap to regulate the activity of their synaptic target cells. Endocrine cells secrete their chemical messengers, hormones, into the bloodstream, which carries them throughout the body so that they encounter all the cells that have receptors for them (see Figure 6.6).

However, these distinctions are clearly challenged by cumulating data that show that some substances work in both systems,

as hormones secreted by certain endocrine cells and as transmitters secreted by certain neurons. Norepinephrine, somatostatin, vasopressin, and oxytocin all serve this dual purpose, each working as a neurotransmitter near the region of its release from synapses and working as a hormone over broader domains when released from gland cells into the bloodstream or into a restricted vascular bed. Hypothalamic neurons, such as the somatostatin neurons of the periventricular zone, for example, secrete the same neuropeptide as do somatostatin neurons of the cerebral cortex and hippocampus. Somatostatin is also made and used in the pancreatic islets as a "local hormone" to regulate insulin and glucagon secretion. Other substances perform similar dual functions in the diffuse enteric nervous system and in the brain, such as cholecystokinin (CCK) and vasoactive intestinal polypeptide (VIP).

The traditional view of an independent endocrine system also held the pituitary to be the "master gland" of the endocrine system. The anterior pituitary gland contains several different types of endocrine cells (see Figure 6.6). Each type of cell produces one or at most two of the pituitary hormones. However, data collected in the 1970s and 1980s established that each type of pituitary cell is directly regulated by a specific hypophysiotropic hormone from the hypothalamus (see Figure 6.7). As we have seen, this hypothalamic–pituitary communication is routed through a very restricted network of blood vessels—a vascular bed—called the pituitary-portal circulation, which carries blood exclusively between the base of the hypothalamus and the anterior lobe of the pituitary. The growing recognition that anterior pituitary cells are themselves subject to control by hypothalamic neurons has forced a revision of the traditional view of the pituitary as master gland.

TABLE 6.1 The endocrine system

Tissue	Hormone	Target cells	Action
Pituitary, anterior lobe	Follicle-stimulating hormone	Gonads	Ovulation, spermatogenesis
	Luteinizing hormone	Gonads	Ovarian or spermatic maturation
	Thyrotropin	Thyroid	Thyroxin secretion
	Adrenocorticotropin	Adrenal cortex	Corticosteroid secretion
	Growth hormone	Liver	Somatomedin secretion
		All cells	Protein synthesis
	Prolactin	Breasts	Growth and milk secretion
Pituitary, posterior lobe	Vasopressin	Kidney tubules	Water retention
		Arterioles	Increases blood pressure
	Oxytocin	Uterus	Contraction
Gonads	Estrogen	Many	Secondary sexual characteristics, breast growth
	Testosterone	Many	Secondary sexual characteristics, muscle growth
Thyroid	Thyroxin	Many	Increases metabolic rate
Parathyroid	Calcitonin	Bone	Calcium retention
Adrenal cortex	Corticosteroids	Many	Mobilization of energy fuels
			Sensitization of vascular adrenergic receptors
			Inhibition of antibody formation and inflammation
	Aldosterone	Kidney	Sodium retention
Adrenal medulla	Epinephrine	Cardiovascular system, skin, muscle, liver, and others	Sympathetic activation
	Norepinephrine		
Pancreatic islets	Insulin	Many	Increases glucose uptake
	Glucagon	Liver, muscle	Increases glucose levels
	Somatostatin	Islets	Regulates insulin, glucagon secretion
Intestinal mucosa	Secretin	Exocrine pancreas	Digestive enzyme secretion
	Cholecystokinin	Gall bladder	Bile secretion
	Vasoactive intestinal polypeptide	Duodenum	Activates motility and secretion; increases blood flow
	Gastric inhibitory peptide	Duodenum	Inhibits motility and secretion
	Somatostatin	Duodenum	Inhibits motility and intestinal secretion

Thus far, seven hypothalamic hormones, each secreted by a specific group of neurons located in the hypothalamus, have been identified as having selective actions on cells of the anterior pituitary. Four of these hormones activate secretion and regulate the rate of synthesis of their target cells' hormones (thyrotropin-releasing hormone, luteinizing-hormone-releasing hormone, corticotropin-releasing hormone, and growth-hormone-releasing hormone). The other three inhibit secretion (dopamine; somatostatin—also sometimes called growth-hormone-release inhibitory hormone; and the hormone discovered most recently, but not yet accepted by all of the experts, that inhibits prolactin release).

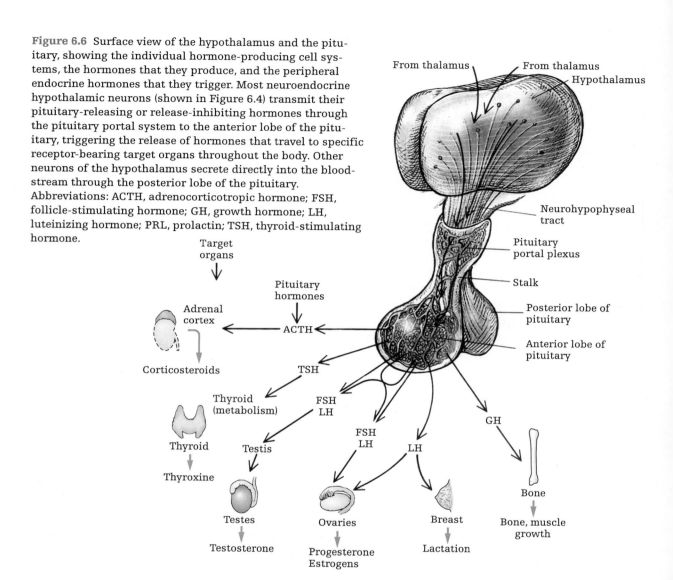

Figure 6.6 Surface view of the hypothalamus and the pituitary, showing the individual hormone-producing cell systems, the hormones that they produce, and the peripheral endocrine hormones that they trigger. Most neuroendocrine hypothalamic neurons (shown in Figure 6.4) transmit their pituitary-releasing or release-inhibiting hormones through the pituitary portal system to the anterior lobe of the pituitary, triggering the release of hormones that travel to specific receptor-bearing target organs throughout the body. Other neurons of the hypothalamus secrete directly into the bloodstream through the posterior lobe of the pituitary. Abbreviations: ACTH, adrenocorticotropic hormone; FSH, follicle-stimulating hormone; GH, growth hormone; LH, luteinizing hormone; PRL, prolactin; TSH, thyroid-stimulating hormone.

A Neuroendocrine Perspective

The fact that the pituitary is under the control of the brain in general and the hypothalamus in particular makes the brain the real "master gland" of the endocrine system. Thus, it may be more accurate to refer to the overall process by which the brain integrates the needs of the body with the demands of the environment as a set of *neuroendocrine functions*. Adjustments made on a local basis are coordinated by autonomic neurons and specific local hormone actions, whereas more global adjustments are brought about by hormone messengers secreted into the bloodstream.

The traditional description of homeostatic processes at the molecular level focused on endocrine secretions traveling to all parts of the body through the bloodstream so that any cell possessing the proper hormone receptor on its surface will respond. In contrast, the neuroendocrine view recognizes that, in principle, the release and subsequent binding of a neurotransmitter is operationally identical with the secretion and subsequent binding of a hormone, except for the diffusion distance between the releasing site and the responding site. A messenger molecule, whether a transmitter or a hormone, is defined only by its ability to cause a response on a cell other than the one that made and released or secreted it and not by the route that it traveled from the source to the target.

Precise Control of Secretion

Most aspects of homeostasis depend on tight control of a hormone's rate of secretion. Concentrations of the thyroid hormone thyroxin, for example, vary only minimally in a healthy body. By the same token, most other endocrine hormones must fluctuate widely in their concentrations to maintain a steady level of cell performance in the face of constantly changing physiological demands on the organism. For example, insulin and glucagon secretions vary considerably to maintain blood-glucose concentration within an acceptable range. Varying levels of the adrenal cortical hormone aldosterone (see Table 6.1) and the posterior pituitary peptide vasopressin are needed to maintain constant plasma volume and to regulate plasma salt and water concentrations. Epinephrine and norepinephrine levels vary with the level of

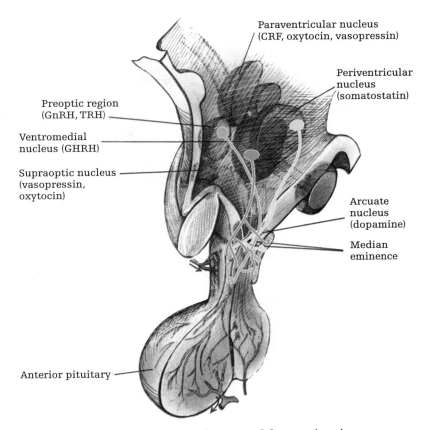

Figure 6.7 Each of the specific cell groups of the anterior pituitary controls specific endocrine organs throughout the body by means of its hormones. Each of these pituitary cell groups is under the command of activating or inhibiting factors secreted by hypothalamic neurons into the pituitary-portal circulation. Abbreviations: ACTH, adrenocorticotropic hormone; CRF, corticotropin-releasing hormone; FSH, follicle-stimulating hormone; GH, growth hormone; GnRH, gonadotropin-releasing hormone; GRH, growth-hormone-releasing hormone; LH, luteinizing hormone; TRH, thyrotropin-releasing hormone; TSH, thyroid-stimulating hormone.

overall physical activity, and their levels within local vascular beds may differ from their levels in the general circulation. This variability allows them to alter cardiac rate and force and to adjust vascular channels selectively to keep the blood supply to specific organ systems appropriate to demand. Whether the level of a given hormone varies is therefore not the most critical feature. As we will see next, what is more important is to envision neuroendocrine operations in terms of setpoint values around which the system strives for constancy. Moreover, these operations show how the CNS and endocrine system work together to control the internal environment.

Physiological Setpoints

Body temperature, blood-glucose level, blood pressure, and salt concentration in the blood are some of the physiological properties that must be finely tuned in healthy people. The concept of the setpoint helps us to understand how the central nervous system, the autonomic nervous system, and the neuroendocrine components act in unison to regulate these factors and others.

Let us assume, then, that the body operates in such a way as to maintain a constant value, or *setpoint*, in temperature, blood glucose, salt, oxygen, and so on. Whenever deviations occur, sensors detect them and activate adaptive mechanisms that work to recover the normal setpoint. These systems operate by means of "positive feedback" and "negative feedback" from the peripheral sensors to a central controller. Positive feedback activates the central controller, whereas negative feedback inhibits the central controller. Figure 6.8 illustrates the feedback controls for the series of neurons and endocrine cells that regulate the critical hormone cortisone. Examples from three physiological systems—temperature regulation, blood pressure control, and appetite control—should help to illustrate the general features of such feedback arrangements.

Temperature Regulation

Body temperature is monitored by external thermoreceptors in the skin and by internal thermoreceptors on neurons in the periventricular zone of the hypothalamus. The internal sensing components measure the actual temperature of the blood and seem to be critical for automatic adjustments of body temperature. Insertion of small thermal probes directly into the hypothalamus of experimental animals revealed that neurons near the front of the periventricular hypothalamus can be activated by a drop or rise in the temperature of arterial blood. Commands from the hypothalamus to the autonomic nervous system activate heat-gain or heat-loss mechanisms, and the skin and brain sensors provide the positive and negative feedback. The heat-gain and heat-loss systems are reciprocally interactive as well: turning up the heat-gain system turns down the heat-loss system and vice versa.

When the hypothalamus senses a drop in body temperature, peripheral autonomic ganglia act to shunt blood away from the skin toward deeper structures and to erect fur or feathers in order to trap a layer of warm air next to the skin. The so-called goose bumps that you get when you are chilled are a vestigial attempt to activate this mechanism. The heat-gain mechanisms also lead directly to shivering, an activity that generates heat in the muscles.

When the hypothalamic detectors sense an elevation in arterial blood temperature, heat-loss mechanisms are activated and heat-gain operations are curtailed. To lose heat, the body shunts blood from its interior to the skin so that heat radiates out into the external environment. From the skin, excess heat can also dissipate by evaporative cooling during perspiration.

When the body does exceed its normal upper temperature limit, as may occur in

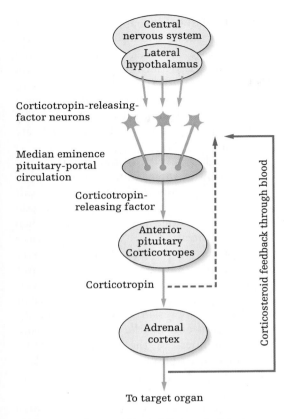

Figure 6.8 The coupling of the central nervous system and the endocrine system. Neurons in the hypothalamus produce corticotropin-releasing factor, which travels to the anterior pituitary by means of the pituitary-portal circulation. Cells, called corticotropes, in the anterior pituitary then release corticotropin, also known as adrenocorticotropin hormone, or ACTH, which stimulates the secretion of corticosteroids by the adrenal cortex. Corticosteroid levels in the bloodstream feed back to the pituitary and to corticosteroid-responsive neurons in the brain to perpetuate or terminate this secretory sequence.

response to a viral infection, for example, heat-gain mechanisms have been overactivated. The white blood cells of an infected subject release a series of very large peptides (called cytokines) and complex lipids (called prostaglandins) that in turn activate heat-gain mechanisms and drive body temperature up. A rapid rise in body temperature is often paradoxically associated with a person's feeling cold, hence the "shaking chills" that frequently accompany the onset of a fever.

The "purpose" of fever is unclear. Some, but by no means all, bacterial infections are actually conquered in part because the invading organisms are vulnerable to heat. (The spirochetes that cause syphilis are one example. The viruses that cause head colds, however, survive because they remain in the nose, where the local temperature remains below 99°F in spite of a fever in the body.) Elevated body temperature also helps to activate certain antibody-producing cells and thus may increase the rate at which white blood cells move toward sites of infection, where they engulf the infectious agents.

Perhaps you have noticed that your tolerance for cold weather increases in the winter, as does your tolerance for hot weather in the summer. Your body literally comes to anticipate the demands of the outside world. A similar process of adaptation takes place when a person who exercises frequently comes, in time, to perspire more readily: the brain has learned to put into action more and more quickly the coordinated programs associated with the "exercise" condition.

Control of Blood Pressure and Volume

Every hierarchical level of the central and peripheral nervous systems to some extent maintains constant circulatory function. *Pressure*, or *baro-*, *receptors* monitor the actual pressure of the blood within the large arteries above the heart, in the carotid arteries, and in the arch of the major artery, the aorta. When excess pressure activates neuronal receptors woven into these arterial walls, the fibers of these neurons carry that information to the primary relay nucleus in the medulla oblongata, called the *nucleus of the solitary tract*. From there, inhibitory commands (*negative feedback* commands) are sent to vasomotor centers (which control the expansion and contraction of blood vessels), and the activity of the peripheral sympathetic nervous system is depressed. At the same time, the parasympathetic system assumes control over the cardiovascular structures.

Normal blood pressure results from a continuous competition between the sympathetic and parasympathetic systems for control of the cardiovascular system. The sympathetic nerves control the major blood vessels, and both sympathetic and parasympathetic divisions can regulate the rate and force of heart contractions. The pressure-detecting baroreceptors, which provide sensory afferent information to the medulla, appear to be primarily responsible for setting the normal point around which the cardiovascular coordinating system operates. The baroreceptors show most sensitivity to deviations from normal pressure of the blood on the vessel walls (that is, a pressure equal to that exerted by a thin column of mercury 100- to 120-mm high). When blood pressure gets outside of the normal range, too high or too low, this system produces less-accurate feedback.

In addition to the baroreceptors in the aorta and the carotid arteries, there are other stretch receptors sensitive to the pressure of the blood in the upper chambers, or *atria*, of the heart. Because the pressure of the blood entering the right atrium from the venous system is a more accurate indicator of the blood's volume than its average pressure is, the atrial receptors use the former as an information base. When blood volume becomes excessive, as happens when salt is retained or under conditions of early "congestive heart failure," the atrial stretch receptors become activated. This activation causes cells in the walls of the atrium itself to release one or more neuropeptides from a family of hormones called *natriopeptides* that act on the kidney tubules to accelerate salt loss.

At higher levels in the hierarchy of information of integration, the neurons of the hypothalamus monitor relative salt concentration in the plasma and activate water-gain or water-loss mechanisms. When salt concentration in the plasma rises above a certain setpoint, large neurons in the medial zone of the hypothalamus secrete vasopressin from their axons directly into the venous blood of the posterior pituitary. Vasopressin carried through the bloodstream acts on the cells of the distal collecting ducts of the kidney, markedly increasing their permeability to water. This increased permeability conserves fluid, and salt concentration decreases.

Another brain–kidney interaction also affects the process of water-volume regulation. Special cells in the kidneys, called *juxtaglomerular cells,* are activated when blood pressure goes down, as it does, for example, subsequent to substantial loss of blood and especially in the presence of increased sympathetic nervous system activity. These kidney cells then secrete the enzyme *renin* into the bloodstream, where it acts on a small protein made by the liver, *angiotensinogen*. This conversion process is continued through the action of other enzymes in the lungs and brain and eventually produces a protein fragment called *angiotensin II* with powerful ability to constrict arterioles.

By causing the arterial muscles to constrict, angiotensin II induces a prompt, large rise in blood pressure. It also acts on certain vascular-volume receptor cells in the hypothalamus. Through cellular systems not fully understood, this action of angiotensin II causes the organism to drink prodigiously, which raises the fluid level in the body. In fact, direct injection of extremely small amounts (a millionth of a millionth of a gram) of angiotensin II into the cerebral ventricles causes animals already sated on water to stop whatever else they may be doing and proceed to drink heavily. This desire to drink is frequently observed in wounded soldiers and other trauma victims who have suffered large losses of blood.

Other transmitters are used by vascular pressure receptors and by vascular chemoreceptors that sense the levels of oxygen and carbon dioxide in the bloodstream to relay information to cardiovascular centers in the lower medulla oblongata. On the basis of their positive or negative feedback, these centers then act to increase the firing rate of neurons in the respiratory and cardiovascular control systems. In response to the drop in blood pressure as a positive feedback, activity in some of the more laterally placed of these medullary centers leads to peripheral sympathetic activation and an elevation of blood pressure. In contrast, in response to elevated blood pressure positive feedback, activity in centers in the more medial lower medulla leads to parasympathetic activation and a fall in blood pressure. Like the heat-gain and heat-loss nuclei of the hypothalamus, these medullary centers are reciprocally interactive.

The primary relay cells of the medulla also pass their information about blood pressure and flow to higher centers in the hypothalamus and the reticular activating system (see Chapter 8), from which connections go to the cerebral and cerebellar cortices. These structures, in turn, can exert considerable influence in coordinating blood flow to the muscles that require it.

Human subjects with chronically elevated blood pressure appear to have setpoints that are set too high. The ultimate causes for this abnormality are difficult to determine in most cases. All levels of the vascular control system have been implicated. In some cases, kidney disease accounts for elevated pressure; in other cases, the sympathetic nervous system may be overactive. The doctor selects the most appropriate treatment on the basis of the probable site of the problem: surgery to replace a damaged kidney, diuretics for the overloaded kidneys, or other drugs to reduce vascular reactivity.

Eating and Eating Behavior

Because the intake of nutrients is vital to all living creatures, most higher organisms have developed physiological mechanisms that produce the motivation to eat—the motive that we call *appetite* or hunger. They have also developed equally important mechanisms that tell them what to eat and when to stop eating. Because it is the job of the brain to guide the organism in its search for appropriate foodstuffs—whether they are tasty grasshoppers or Big Macs—the brain must be the ultimate recipient of these hunger or satiety signals. This signaling system works very well for most animals living in their natural habitats. Human beings may be the exception.

Although we cannot describe the entire process of digestion here, some of the basic facts about these metabolic activities should be mentioned to help explain the brain's role in eating.

1. All nutrients absorbed by the digestive system pass through the intestinal walls

in one of three forms: glucose (derived from carbohydrates), amino acids (derived from proteins), and fats. Calories (food energy) ingested in any of these forms and not immediately expended for tissue needs will be converted into fat or into glycogen (an insoluble glucose polymer) and stored. If the individual exercises, the amino acids will be converted into muscle proteins. The stored fat or the amino acids of muscle protein are later converted into glucose as required. If the amount of amino acids ingested exceeds that required for normal cellular turnover of proteins, it is generally excreted in urine. However, excess carbohydrates are stored as fat and body weight increases.

2. Glucose is the major source of energy for all tissue. The liver plays a vital part in converting stored fat and proteins into glucose.

3. For most cells to take up and use the glucose available in extracellular body fluids, insulin must be present. Only the cells of the nervous system are able to take up and use glucose without insulin. Insulin is manufactured by the *islet cells* in the pancreas. These islet cells are sensitive to a variety of circulating hormones and other circulating neuroregulators, all of which, taken together, constitute a complex regulatory system worthy of more attention than we are able to give it here.

Appetite Control: When to Eat

What causes a person to think, "I'm hungry," or induces a rat to search for food? Until relatively recently, most textbooks answered this question by pointing to the hypothalamus. Experiments that had been done many years ago showed that, when the ventromedial nucleus of the hypothalamus (a nucleus in the lateral zone) in rats had been destroyed, the animals ate much more than normal rats did and became extremely obese, often doubling their original weight. Such results were interpreted as demonstrating that the ventromedial nucleus acted as a "satiety center."

In other experiments, destruction of the lateral hypothalamus produced animals that would not eat or drink. This part of the brain was then dubbed the "hunger center." Thus it appeared, for a while, that the answer to hunger and satiety lay in the activities of these two centers in the hypothalamus. As more precise experimental techniques were developed, however, and as knowledge of the brain's anatomy and chemistry grew, it became clear that the mechanisms controlling hunger and satiety were not quite so simple or quite so localized. The surgical procedures performed in those early experiments had actually disrupted a number of important neural pathways and had produced subtle but widespread metabolic changes and behavioral deficits.

In 1955, the American nutritionist Jean Mayer proposed that glucose levels in the blood provided the hunger signal. In Mayer's theory, low glucose levels were sensed by special sensory neurons, called *glucostats*, which fired at a higher rate when glucose levels fell. Subsequent research did verify the presence of glucose receptors in the lateral hypothalamus, but investigators found that they did not play a crucial role in regulating eating. The liver is also known to contain glucose receptors that monitor glucose levels in the blood passing through the hepatic portal vein and apparently send information to the brain through a branch of the vagus nerve. However, when that branch of the vagus nerve was cut in experimental animals, their eating behavior was not significantly affected. In fact, glucose levels generally remain within a relatively narrow range, no matter what the timing and amount of food intake, because the metabolic system is so efficient at converting and storing excess nutrients and at calling up and reconverting those stores.

More recent research indicates that motivation to eat results from a complex interplay of physiological mechanisms. The process is not well understood but is generally viewed as an interaction between two distinct systems: a "metabolic need" system that works to restore depleted energy stores on the one hand versus a "caloric homeostasis" system that works to induce animals, including humans, to eat when food is available unless inhibited by signals generated by a full stomach. Detailed examination of the eating patterns of laboratory rats has shown that, although the amounts that they eat at meals are quite unpredictable, the intervals between meals are closely related to how much the animal ate in the previous feeding. These observations, which have been replicated by different laboratories, suggest that the strength of satiety signals generated by eating is in direct proportion to the size of meals. Additional evidence suggests that the neuropeptide cholecystokinin is released from the walls of a distended stomach (a stomach full of food or water, which is why drinking eight full glasses of water a day can lead to reduced food consumption). Cholecystokinin provides negative feedback to the brain by acting on sensory afferent nerves of the vagus. This effect seems to be more pronounced in young animals and is probably only one of many such feedback systems.

The Setpoint Hypothesis of Eating

Scientists long assumed that the size of an animal's store of fat was determined, on the one hand, by what it ate and, on the other hand, by its metabolic rate. In other words, stored fat, or *adiposity*, was held to be a secondary effect of one or more other, primary regulators of feeding and digestion. It now appears that adiposity itself is the primary regulator of eating behavior. New evidence appears to show (1) that the amount of an animal's fat store is somehow represented in its brain, and (2) that the brain directs metabolic processes and eating behaviors to defend that store (see Figure 6.9).

When an experimental animal is starved until it loses weight and is then allowed to feed freely, it will overeat until it has gained back the fat that it lost. When an animal is force-fed until it gains weight and is then allowed to feed freely, it will undereat until it has lost the excess fat. These and other observations indicate that total body adiposity is maintained at a relatively constant level in adult animals and that this maintenance is achieved through changes in food intake. Therefore, some representation of total body-fat level must exist in the brain, along with some type of signaling system to alter eating behaviors or metabolic processes or both. The nature of this representation and of the signals that allow the brain to read it have recently been defined. Insulin secreted from the pancreas appears to be the key.

Both the aroma and the taste of food activate third-order and higher olfactory processing structures, which, by descending circuits through the hypothalamus, initiate insulin secretion. This sequence of events is termed the *cephalic stage of eating*, because it happens when the brain anticipates that food is coming and acts to get the whole system of digestion going. This advanced secretion of insulin prepares the body to make quick use of the digested carbohydrates. Additional insulin secretion is stimulated by the absorption of carbohydrate in the gut. The state of a person's body fat (adiposity)

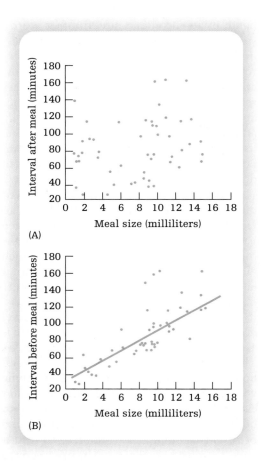

Figure 6.9 (A) When rats are allowed to feed on liquid food as they wish, the amount consumed at any specific meal bears no relation to when they last ate. (B) However, the amount eaten does predict approximately when they will eat again.

has an effect on these insulin secretions. Healthy people show a reciprocal relation between the secretion of insulin and the sensitivity of the insulin-responsive cells. Lean people have more insulin receptors on their fat and muscle cells than obese people do. Because their muscles are more sensitive to insulin, a given carbohydrate load will pro-

duce less insulin secretion in lean people than in obese people. Because obese people are less sensitive to insulin, more of their ingested carbohydrate goes unused and becomes deposited as fat. Adiposity also seems able to determine how quickly food passes through the gut, how long nutrients remain in the circulation, and how the liver handles the metabolic load. The next section deals with one of the molecular signaling systems that may determine adiposity.

Long-term regulation of food intake (that is, how the brain controls food absorption, distribution, and usage), then, seems to depend on the brain's representation of the body's fat stores, with insulin as the primary agent signaling the state of those stores to the brain. On the other hand, short-term regulation—when to stop eating at a specific meal—seems to depend on several digestive hormones, or gut peptides. Figure 6.10 presents a simple model of the entire regulation process. Its appetite-suppressing and psychological aspects are explored next.

Appetite Control: When to Stop Eating

The stretch receptors in the stomach wall serve the purpose of preventing an animal from injuring itself by overfilling its stomach. But these receptors play only a minor role in the normal experience of satiety. The major signals of satiation are digestive hormones secreted in the gut during a meal. There are a number of such hormones, and exactly which ones are secreted depends on the specific foods being consumed and their amounts. For obvious reasons, these substances are called *satiety factors*.

The study of experimental animals joined surgically in such a way that their vascular systems become connected was a source of significant insight into these processes. Two lean rats joined in this manner ate similar amounts,

Figure 6.10 In this model representing the regulation of food intake and body weight, initiation of eating is influenced by psychological factors (the appearance and taste of food, learned associations with time and place of eating, and so forth) as well as by signals from the hypothalamus to the cortex. The end of eating—the feeling of satiety—is influenced when gut chemoreceptors sense the chemical composition of the food consumed. These chemoreceptors stimulate the production of hormones, which feed back to the hypothalamus, which, in turn, influences the consumption decisions of the cortex. This process is ultimately regulated by the brain's monitoring of the body's fat stores, the monitoring signal presumably being insulin.

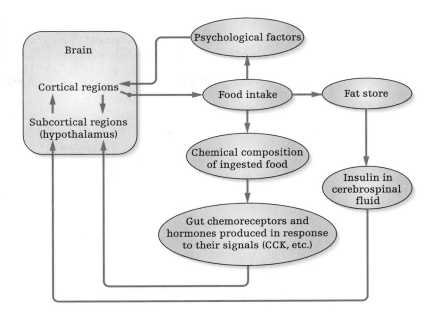

as did two animals made experimentally obese by prior lesions in the ventromedial hypothalamus. However, when a lean rat was linked to an obese rat of that type, a very surprising result was obtained: the lean rats lost interest in eating and would lose substantial amounts of weight unless separated again. Such experiments led scientists to search for appetite-inhibiting factors whose effects may have been blocked by the hypothalamic lesions, resulting in uncontrollable appetite.

Subsequently, the study of genetically transmitted obesity in a mouse with a mutation called *ob/ob* led to the discovery of a large peptide hormone called *leptin* made by fat cells. When such mice were injected with synthetic leptin, their appetites were reduced and their weight gain reversed, suggesting that the mutation consists of an inability to produce functional leptin. In a related mouse mutant showing comparable obesity, leptin production seemed normal, but leptin receptors were deficient.

Leptin injected into the cerebral ventricles of *ob/ob* mice also reduces their appetites and body weight. This observation leads some investigators to conclude that circulating levels of leptin released by adipose cells can directly influence leptin detectors in the brain. Even though the size of the peptide would normally not permit it to penetrate the blood–brain barrier, it is possible that the brain can detect leptin levels in the cerebrospinal fluid. Other research shows that the injection of leptin into the cerebral ventricles reduces the expression of the gene for an appetite-stimulating neuropeptide called "neuropeptide Y" (so called because both ends of the peptide have the amino acid tyrosine, whose one-letter symbolic representation is "Y").

Appetite Control: Psychological Factors

For human beings—at least those lucky enough to live in a society where food is plentiful and readily available—a number of factors besides hunger lead people to eat. We are strongly influenced by learned associations having to do with time and place. For example, when the clock says that it is lunchtime, we are apt to feel hungry, no matter what we may have eaten earlier in the day. We have learned that noon or one o'clock spells lunchtime. Certain places also are associated with food. Many of us find it almost impossible to sit through a movie without popcorn or a candy bar. As children, we learned to associate the movie theater with these snacks—it is a place where eating is done.

Socialization in the ways of our culture also plays a part in when and what we eat. Surrounded by others who are eating at a party, for example, we eat, no matter what our current energy needs might be. But our culture has also given us certain food preferences. If the caterers at a Rotary Club gathering in Wichita, Kansas, set out a buffet of squid cooked in its own ink (Spanish), fried grasshoppers (African), and sheep's eyes (Arabic), most of the members would not feel that same "hunger." Such learned preferences soon weaken, however, when food is scarce and the physiological factors signaling hunger become urgent.

The interaction of psychological and physiological factors are poignantly illustrated in two types of human eating disorders—anorexia nervosa and bulimia—and in what factors may cause some people to exhibit obesity.

Eating Disorders: Anorexia Nervosa and Bulimia

Most human beings, like most other animals, eat enough food to satisfy their energy needs and to maintain their fat store at a relatively stable level. Some, however, eat so little that their weight becomes dangerously low, and some eat so much that their weight becomes dangerously high.

Anorexia means simply "loss of appetite," and *anorexia nervosa* is the name given to a clinical disorder in which loss of appetite is presumably caused by psychological factors. The vast majority of anorectics are female, and they are usually young—between 12 and 18 years of age. An anorectic may eat so little food that her body weight drops to 70 or even 60 percent of what is considered normal for her height, which can be lethal. In a sense, "loss of appetite" does not truly describe the psychological state of such patients, because the symptoms that make up this clinical syndrome include an obsession with food. The anorectic experiences hunger, but the appetite is denied in the pursuit of being thin. The anorectic also typically has such a severely distorted body image that, even when she is emaciated, she sees herself as "too fat." Other symptoms include depression and social isolation.

Some anorectics indulge in food binges on occasion, eating prodigious amounts of food—thousands of calories—within a short period of time. Then they force themselves to vomit or they purge themselves with laxatives and diuretics so that the calories will not be absorbed. This binge–purge behavior is called *bulimia nervosa*. Bulimia is the most common form of the two eating disorders, estimated to affect some 3 percent of women over their lifetimes. However, many patients with bulimia have prior histories of anorexia. The major difference between the two disorders is that patients with anorexia are very thin, whereas those with bulimia have normal body weight.

Figure 6.11 presents a theory of the interacting causes and self-perpetuating effects of anorexia nervosa. One contributing factor is the social climate. In Western countries, for

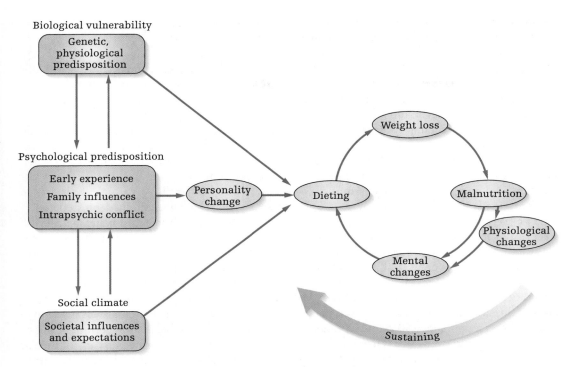

Figure 6.11 A model depicting the interacting causes of anorexia nervosa and its self-perpetuation in a "vicious cycle." That is, after the patient has undergone significant weight loss, the physiological effects of malnutrition (for example, slower emptying of the stomach) and the psychological effects (for example, increasing social isolation) help sustain the disorder.

example, over the past four decades the "ideal" female figure—the one that appears in ads, movies, and television programs—has been growing thinner. One need only compare the pin-up girls of the 1950s and 1960s with those of the 1980s to see the difference. The idealization of the boyish figure, with small breasts and narrow hips, is one force working on the psyche of anorectics. Of course, this ideal image is held up for all women in our society, and most of them do not become anorectic, so there must be some predisposing factors that make certain young women especially vulnerable to it. Malnutrition affects a number of physical functions in ways that tend to aggravate the

disease. For example, emptying of the stomach is much slower in malnourished persons. Furthermore, the social isolation that is common as the disorder progresses allows for less and less reality testing. In other words, there are fewer people to remark that "you're nothing but skin and bones."

Whatever the cultural, psychological, and physiological disposing factors may be, once the weight loss has become significant and the young woman becomes malnourished, the disease becomes self-sustaining. Most emphasis has gone toward the psychological rather than prior biological vulnerabilities because most of the biological alterations that have been observed in bulimic and anorectics

Heidi is a 17-year-old girl who lives with her parents and is a senior in high school. She was first referred for a diagnostic consultation six months after she began dieting in order to be more attractive. Heidi is 170 cm (5 feet 7 inches) tall and weighed 61 kg (135 pounds) before dieting. The lowest acceptable weight range for a woman at this height is between 54.5 and 57 kg (120–128 pounds). Heidi gradually lost weight to a low of 40.5 kg (90 pounds), which she weighed two weeks prior to the consultation. She had never induced vomiting or abused laxatives, but she did exercise a great deal. She started menstrating at the age of 14, and her last period occurred just at the time she started dieting. She emphatically stated that she would like to weigh about 50 kg (110 pounds) and not one pound over that. When Heidi's dieting behavior began, she also began to have difficulties in school. She started to skip classes and go out with friends. After a few months, however, she began to have arguments and altercations with her friends. Then she began to stay at home; for several months prior to the consultation, she had isolated herself from her peer group and stayed in the house most of the day. She became very interested in cooking and started collecting recipes and cooking for her family. She admitted to feeling depressed and to having occasional crying spells. About two months before Heidi began to diet seriously, she broke up with her boyfriend, who had told her she was too fat and should lose weight.

Treatment Heidi was mildly depressed and preoccupied with the fear of being fat. She stated that she had an obsession with counting calories and was not able to stop her dieting behavior. Heidi was referred to an experienced therapist in her area for outpatient therapy. Heidi was completely uninterested in treatment. An attempt was made to set up a variety of behavioral contracts, but Heidi refused to cooperate with any of them. After 10 sessions, she refused to see the therapist, stating that she would gain her weight back alone. She then began a pattern of eating nothing during the day and then, late at night, eating 10 to 15 pieces of Kentucky Fried Chicken with an extensive amount of salt over about a two-hour period. Eventually she stayed up through the night, going to sleep at

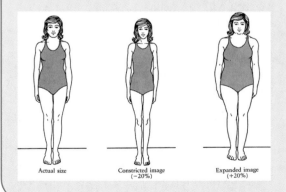

Actual size   Constricted image   Expanded image
                        (−20%)   (+20%)

The perception of body shape and size can be evaluated through the use of special computer-drawing programs that allow a subject to distort the width of an actual picture of a person's body by as much as 20 percent larger or smaller. Both anorectics and normal subjects adjusted the figures of other people's bodies to normal dimension. However, each anorectic consistently adjusted her own body picture to a size 20 percent larger than its true form, suggesting that an anorectic has a major problem with the perception of her own image.

5:30 A.M. and then sleeping until about 1:00 or 2:00 P.M. For a short period, Heidi tried to stop this pattern and attended school all day to make up credits; however, her eating difficulties prevailed, and she eventually stopped going to school entirely.

One year after the initial consultation, Heidi reluctantly went to the hospital for treatment. After the hospitalization, it became obvious that Heidi's mother had a severe problem with alcohol abuse and that there was a strong history of alcoholism and depression in her mother's family. During the first few days after hospitalization, Heidi was very upset and wanted to leave the hospital; however, when her parents supported the continued hospitalization, she became less agitated and more cooperative. Her weight on admission was 40.5 kg (90 pounds). She was placed on a liquid formula, Sustacal, with enough calories to maintain her weight plus 50 percent for activity. She was given this in six equal feedings throughout the day. The amount of calories was increased every five days until she reached her target weight.

Heidi needed a great deal of encouragement to interact with her peers. One week after hospital admission, she started attending the hospital school. Because of her desire to isolate herself, a program was put into effect that allowed Heidi access to her room for several hours each day if she gained weight on that day. She gradually became more involved with her peers and her school program and, by the time she reached her target weight, was able to eat fairly normally.

During individual sessions, it became obvious that Heidi had had to stay at home to take care of her alcoholic mother. The mother's alcoholism was discussed in the fam-

Pop singer Karen Carpenter died in 1983 of the effects of anorexia.

ily threapy sessions, and the mother entered a treatment program. Heidi eventually requested to be removed from her single room into a four-bed girls' dorm room on the unit. After a series of visits to her family, Heidi was discharged from the hospital program and transferred to an outpatient therapy program. Heidi also signed a behavioral contract, which she helped design with her outpatient therapist. In this contract, she agreed to go to her family doctor's office to be weighed once a week. She agreed to eat three meals a day and not to eat at night. Every week that she had been able to maintain her weight within a normal weight range, she would reward herself by buying some new painting or drawing materials. The family agreed that Heidi could not be responsible for her mother's care. Alternative care programs were set up for the mother.

normalize when they begin to eat normally and restore their normal body weight. There is some evidence that bulimic and anorectics may have abnormalities in the manner in which their hypothalamic appetite-regulating nuclei respond to the pontine and medullary raphe innervation mediated by serotonin. Some subjects respond to antidepressant medications that act to bolster serotonin synaptic function. However, a larger proportion respond to a psychological treatment known as *cognitive behavioral therapy,* in which the patients are encouraged to closely monitor their feelings and situations surrounding episodes of binge–purge and to decouple body image from self-esteem. In the best of cases, fewer than half of the patients respond to either treatment, so much more work is necessary. Various other psychotherapeutic approaches have been used in treating the disorder, but all of them include some management of the patient's food intake to provide adequate nourishment and so break the vicious cycle shown in Figure 6.11. When anorectics have ingested enough calories and nutrients to replace some of the lost weight, their sleep disturbances are eased and the depression often lifts, at which point they are more capable of benefiting from psychotherapy.

Obesity

Both psychological and physiological factors contribute to obesity. Obesity is defined on the basis of the relation between height and weight, called the body-mass index (BMI), calculated by dividing a person's weight in kilograms by his or her height in meters squared. An index above 30 currently defines a person as being obese, and a BMI above 25 defines a person as being overweight. Data from the National Health and Nutrition Examination Surveys carried out by the National Center for Health Statistics on U.S. residents suggests that the incidence of obesity has risen significantly, affecting about 13 percent of the population in 1962 and nearly doubling by 1994. More than half the U.S. population met the definition for being overweight.

An important physiological factor seems to be a difference in metabolic rate, the rate at which the body converts nutrients into energy, either for immediate use in cell operations or for storage as body fat. In a study that measured food intake in subjects matched for age, weight, height, and activity, some subjects were found to eat twice as much as their counterparts. With all other factors equal, it was clear that those subjects who ate less and maintained their weight had metabolisms that converted calories into tissue very efficiently. In view of the fact that the subjects were matched for levels of physical activity, those who ate a great deal more to maintain the same weight must have been losing heat to the environment. People who gain excess weight, then, are likely to be efficient converters; to keep slim, they would have to eat a lot less than someone whose metabolic rate was higher.

A single fat cell is called an *adipocyte,* and obese people generally have larger adipocytes and more of them than do thin people. In light of our discussion of the set-point hypothesis, we might well ask what role, if any, these cells play in the signaling system between brain and fat tissue. As noted in the preceding discussion of genetically obese mice, current theory suggests that what the brain ultimately regulates is the total combined volume of individual fat cells and that fat cells emit leptin (negative feedback) to inform the brain about their volume. When an obese person diets, the leptin signal would be reduced, signaling the brain to call for more food (and insulin) to bring adipocyte volume back up. This might explain why losing weight and keeping it off is so difficult. So far, however, there has been virtually no support for the view that leptin can help obese but otherwise normal humans reduce their adiposity.

A number of psychological reactions to food and eating also seem to differentiate obese from normal-weight people. Obese people are more finicky about food. They will drink less of a doubtful-tasting milkshake, for example, than will a normal-weight hungry person and more of a milkshake that tastes good. The obese seem to be more susceptible to cues relating to food—the odor from a bakery or the textures and colors of a pyramid of fruit outside a greengrocer's. Yet they appear to be unwilling to work hard for food. When normal-weight and obese subjects in one study were left alone in a room with a bowl of nuts in their shells, only 1 of 20 obese people used the nutcracker and ate a few, whereas 10 of 20 normal-weight subjects did. Parallels have been drawn between the food-related behavior of obese people and that of mice with lesions in the ventromedial hypothalamus, but there is no evidence that obese humans have ventromedial abnormalities. Perhaps these behavioral idiosyncrasies are simply due to the fact that obese people feel chronically hungry because of elevated abnormal hormone levels or because social pressures are preventing them from satisfying their hunger.

Obesity is not only a socially disapproved condition. It is also a health hazard. Death from cardiovascular diseases rises significantly above BMI levels of 30. And, for most obese adults, permanent weight loss is a tremendously difficult—almost impossible—undertaking. The recidivism rate—the number of people who regain lost weight—is well over 90 percent in almost all forms of treatment. A regular exercise program along with regulation of food intake seems to offer the best chance for success.

Other Setpoint Systems

Most of the body's other internal regulatory systems are every bit as intricate as the temperature, blood pressure, and appetite control systems just described. Because extracellular calcium ions participate in so many intracellular events, their levels, too, are extensively regulated. Cells in the parathyroid glands that secrete calcitonin and parahormone and cells in the kidneys, the liver, the bones, and even the skin, which synthesizes the vitamin D necessary for dietary calcium absorption, all participate in this almost, but not completely, nonneural regulation. Neural participation in this regulatory sequence comes in part from the capacity of exercise to strengthen bone structure, (inaction can lead to bone weakening) and in part from the selection and consumption of calcium-rich food resources.

One other setpoint system that deserves special attention is the way in which the brain handles stress. When you feel "emotional heat"—anger, excitement, nervousness, or fear—inappropriate sweating responses may occur to "cool you off." During extreme anxiety, your hands and feet may grow "ice cold," as though your body were retreating inward from the anxiety-producing stimulus. To date, however, speculations about the psychological "meaning" of physiological responses that accompany departures from emotional setpoints remain just that—speculations. The increase in activity of the sympathetic nervous system that prepares you physically for fight or flight when you confront a tense situation provides a more than adequate explanation for your cold hands and feet, the increased rate and contractile force of your heartbeat, your dry mouth, and your fixed, wide-eyed stare. To understand this system more thoroughly, Chapter 7 explores another intricate control system that causes an elevation of corticosteroid secretion during periods of stress and then promptly suppresses it when the need has passed.

Within the reproductive system, as a last example, an intricate series of endocrine feedback signals interact with direct influences from the central and peripheral nervous systems to prepare for reproduction, select a mate, and consummate sexual relations.

Reproductive Behaviors and Human Sexual Response

The hypothalamus is responsible for those complex forms of integrative behaviors that result in maintenance of the species through sexual reproduction. Although the human desire for pleasurable reproductive behaviors can sometimes be viewed as one of those setpoint kinds of regulations for which satiety is rarely reached, for most species, reproduction seems to be far more banal and merely required.

Whatever a person's sexual orientation, means of attracting partners, or favorite sexual techniques, the sexual act produces a sequence of predictable physiological reactions that are very similar in males and females of all animal species. Table 6.2 describes these phases of the human sexual response. But what physiological mechanisms produce the motivation and the behaviors? For some animals and some behaviors, scientists are now able to provide fairly complete models describing most of the neural mechanisms and hormonal actions. One such model explains why and how female rats perform the postural behavior called *lordosis,* a crouching, rump-raised position that not only facilitates intercourse, but is necessary for fertilization.

Lordosis in Female Rats

The lordosis behavior requires the use of many neural circuits in the rat, including touch receptors in the skin; neurons driving the muscles required for assuming the sexually receptive posture; and many neurons in the brainstem, the midbrain, the hypothalamus, and even the forebrain. (A rat whose forebrain has been disconnected from the lower brainstem and spinal cord does not perform lordosis, so this behavior cannot be a simple spinal reflex, triggered by touch in the proper place.) The actions of certain hormones—estrogen, progesterone, and luteinizing hormone releasing hormone (also called gonadotropin-releasing hormone), which is released by the pituitary—also are necessary.

Environmental inputs—namely, the presence of a male and the stimulation provided by his mounting behaviors—also are necessary. In the natural course of mating behavior in rats and mice, the male repeatedly grasps the flanks of the female and mounts her while thrusting his lower body against her rump, tail base, and perineum. Stimulation of the skin in these regions causes a barrage of action potentials in most of the primary sensory neurons in the area, but only certain pressure-sensitive neurons give the sustained responses that can initiate lordosis. If enough of these neurons fire, the sequence that can initiate lordosis begins.

Input from these primary sensory neurons converges on pressure-sensitive local-circuit neurons in the lumbar area of the rat's spinal cord. If the sum of the stimuli is large enough, the message to induce lordosis will be passed along through fibers that carry the message to

TABLE 6.2 The human sexual response

Phase	Reactions of the sex organs		General body reactions	
	Male	Female	Male	Female
Excitement	Penile erection. As phase is continued: thickening, flattening, and elevation of scrotal sac; partial testicular elevation and size increase	Vaginal lubrication. As phase is continued: thickening of vaginal walls and labia; expansion of inner 2/3 of vagina and cervix; tumescence of clitoris	Nipple erection	Nipple erection; sex tension flush
Plateau	Increased size of penis head and testicular tumescence; full testicular elevation and rotation; purple hue on penis head; mucoid secretion	Outer 1/3 of vagina narrows; congestion of blood vessels; full expansion of inner 2/3 of vagina; full elevation of cervix; darkening of labia; mucoid secretion; clitoral withdrawal	Sex tension flush; muscle spasms in hands and feet; generalized tension of skeletal muscles; hyperventilation; increased heart rate	Sex tension flush; muscle spasms in hands and feet; generalized tension of skeletal muscles; hyperventilation; increased heart rate
Orgasmic	Ejaculation: contractions of accessory organs of reproduction; relaxation of external bladder function; contraction of penile urethra; contractions of anal sphincter	Pelvic response: contractions of uterus; minimal relaxation of external cervical opening; contractions of outer 1/3 of vagina, external rectal sphincter, and external urethral sphincter	Specific skeletal muscle contractions; hyperventilation; increased heart rate	Specific skeletal muscle contractions; hyperventilation; increased heart rate
Resolution	Refractory period with rapid loss of penile congestion; loss of penile erection	Retarded loss of vasocongestion; ready return to orgasm; loss of clitoral tumescence; loss of skin color	Sweating reaction; hyperventilation; increased heart rate	Sweating reaction; hyperventilation; increased heart rate

structures in the brainstem. These brainstem centers may be able to exert some control over the postural changes in lordosis, but they cannot do so over a long period of time; that is, they cannot sustain the behavior for the time required for the sexual act. The control necessary to achieve this part of the behavior comes through fibers descending to the spinal cord from cells in and around the ventromedial nucleus of the hypothalamus. When these cells are destroyed in experimental animals, lordosis does not take place.

These ventromedial hypothalamic neurons, however, must be primed by prior exposure to estrogen to work their effects. Estrogen is required for lordosis to occur. In fact, to facilitate the behavior, estrogen blood levels in the female must have been raised for at least 20 hours prior to stimulation by the male. Unless this happens, the female is unresponsive regardless of the amount of male thrusting behavior.

In all vertebrate species, specific groups of neurons in the medial hypothalamus (as well as in other brain regions) respond to estrogen. Estrogen can increase the electrical activity of these cells. This heightened output travels down to the midbrain and facilitates lordosis. In addition, these medial hypothalamic cells integrate the behavioral responses of lordosis with other aspects of the animal's physiology; for example, they coordinate the behaviors with controls exerted by the autonomic nervous system, controls having to do with rate of respiration, heartbeat, and so on, as described earlier in this chapter. Progesterone enhances the action of estrogen. It does so by inhibiting activity in a group of serotonin-containing neurons that ordinarily act to inhibit responses to touch stimuli. The effect of the progesterone inhibition, then, is to enhance the animal's response to touch stimulation and thus to facilitate lordosis.

Several groups of axons descend from the medial hypothalamic and preoptic areas to the central grey and reticular formation central-program-generating neurons of the midbrain (see Figure 6.12). Then axons from these neurons in the midbrain descend through the reticular formation to the spinal cord. As described in Chapter 5, these descending central-program-generating neural tracts constitute the pathways to the spinal motoneurons, the final common pathway controlling the muscles that must flex or stretch to produce lordosis.

Even though the primary stimulus for lordosis is the male's pressure on the female's rump, a female rat engages in courtship behaviors before ever being touched by the male. She does some characteristic hopping and darting about and displays some irresistible ear wiggling.

When she goes through such routines, it is clear to all onlookers, whether rodent suitors or human researchers, that the rat is in an excited state. This excitability depends on the actions of estrogen and progesterone and prepares her to perform the specific lordosis behavior in response to the pressure stimulus from the male rat. This is another way in which the hormones have a preparative role, as well as a reactive neural and behavioral one.

To ensure that offspring have a good chance of survival, preparation for mating must be carefully timed. The female's peak of excitability and receptivity should coincide with ovulation, and ovulation should be timed for propitious birth seasons. This timing requires the integration of multiple neurotransmitters and hormones acting across neuronal and nonneuronal cells in the central nervous system (including the hypothalamus), the pituitary, the ovary, and the uterus. The seasonal aspect of breeding behaviors is discussed at greater length in Chapter 7. Sufficient for now is to note that the rat's hypothalamus receives much of the information needed to regulate reproduction and reproductive behavior according to environmental rhythms.

The hypothalamus does its job of regulation both through the release of hormones and by controlling behavior. In the female rat, the hypothalamus signals by secreting gonadotropin-releasing hormone into the pituitary-portal circulation; the pituitary, in turn, sends luteinizing hormone and follicle-stimulating hormone as signals to the ovaries to begin ovulation. The ovaries then manufacture and release estrogen and progesterone, which travel to the hypothalamus and prepare the animal for mating. These hormones also feed back to the brain and pituitary to regulate further hormone release. The job of GnRH-secreting neurons is to integrate these happenings so that ovulation will take place at the time that the rats mate, given that fertilization is the goal.

Sex and the Cerebral Cortex

The hormones that influence sex-related physiological events and behaviors seem to be much the same in all vertebrates. For example, the mechanisms governing ovulation in human females do not differ markedly from the mechanisms in mice. Estrogens and androgens are present and circulate in all vertebrates, and they seem to be accumulated by, and influence the activity of, certain medial hypothalamic and limbic nerve cells in every species The principles of feedback from hormone-producing cells to the neurons that control the hormone-producing cells also seem to be much the same.

Even though the principles of neural control of behavior apply across species, the sheer size and complexity of the human cerebral cortex mean that sexual behavior, like many other behaviors, will long remain an object of study. Even in other vertebrates, the cortex appears to play an important role in sexual behavior. For example, a dog whose spinal cord has been cut so that the cortex plays no part in the behavior will have erections of the penis and will ejaculate if its penis is mechanically stimulated. But a normal, intact dog will not have such a reaction to mechanical stimulation unless a receptive female dog is present. The dog's cortex, then, inhibits the sexual reaction to mechanical stimulation and decides what is or is not sexually arousing.

The human cortex can be endlessly inventive in its ideas about what is sexually arousing and in its search for and enjoyment of sexual activity. For some people, at least some of the time, simply imagining—fantasizing about a sexual encounter—can bring

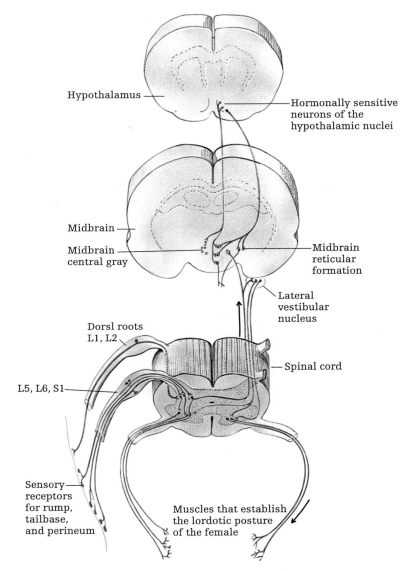

Figure 6.12 Cascades of axons descending from hypothalamic and preoptic areas to midbrain, to reticular formation, and eventually to spinal motoneurons that control the muscles necessary for lordosis.

about sexual arousal and even orgasm. Human males can send sexual signals to human females by a variety of media, including fast sports cars, poetry, and athletic

A Blow to the Head

I am a man, and I wanted to live as I viewed a normal man. . . .

Mitch Heller grew up normally—played hockey, graduated from college with a degree in engineering, got married. After an automobile accident in which he struck his head, however, everything began to change.

After about a month I realized I didn't have as much interest in sex. I couldn't perform as well. . . . It was very scary. . . . I knew something was going on inside my body and I didn't know what.

Not only was sex drive impaired. Mitch also began to lose secondary sexual characteristics—chest and facial hair, for example—and his sperm count dropped and continued to drop. All these signs indicated testosterone loss, but what could connect that to a bump on the head?

Dr. William Crowley at Massachusetts General Hospital had some tentative answers. Apparently the blow, taken on the side of the brain away from the impact, had traumatized those neurons in the hypothalamus that secrete gonadotropin-releasing hormones (GnRHs). With these signals to the pituitary lost, the testes no longer received their signals from the pituitary to secrete testosterone. Crowley prescribed a mechanical pump through which the hypothalamic hormone that starts this process, GnRH, could be administered automatically every two hours through a needle inserted subcutaneously in the abdomen.

With the pump in place, positive results followed. Sexual interest and chest hair gradually returned. Within six months, Mitch's sperm count was almost normal, and his wife became pregnant. In the future, his hypothalamus may regain normal function.

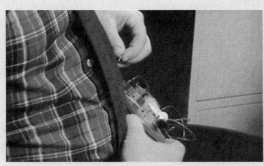

Top: Mitch with his wife before treatment.
Middle: Dr. Crowley explains the hormone pump.
Bottom: Mitch attaches the pump.

prowess. Females can send signals to males in a single meaningful glance, a long philosophical conversation, or a perfect serve at tennis—all far more subtle than ear wiggling. Each male or female will react to such signals idiosyncratically, depending on his or her cultural mores, social class, upbringing, and individual psychological and biological characteristics—that is, depending on his or her experiential history.

Homosexuality

Some men and women are sexually attracted to members of their own sex; they are homosexual rather than heterosexual. It is estimated that 2 to 4 percent of men and 0.5 to 1 percent of women engage in exclusively homosexual behavior. At one time, most of the proposed explanations to account for sexual orientation were attributed to psychological theories, such as various childhood experiences—for example, having a weak or absent father and a strong, domineering mother. Others were attributed to the idea that early learning experiences—homosexual episodes that produced reward in the form of sexual pleasure—are responsible.

A large-scale study of hundreds of male and female homosexuals, however, failed to support either of these premises, causing researchers to conclude that a biological basis for homosexuality was likely. Although many studies over the years have attempted to find some such biological basis, none was successful—until recently. The most compelling evidence emerged in postmortem evaluations of neuronal populations of the hypothalamus. *Morphometric analysis* of human brains—that is, analysis of quantitative changes in neuron number and shape—first disclosed distinctions related to sexual orientation in the *suprachiasmatic nucleus* (SCN). (The SCN is a hypothalamic brain region that was included briefly in our consideration of the visual system and that will be examined in greater detail in Chapter 7.) In comparison with that of 18 age-matched heterosexual males, the SCN of 10 homosexual men was nearly twice as large and contained more than twice as many neurons. Such differences had to have been present since early postnatal life, which would rule out most of the learned behavioral hypotheses of homosexuality. Not only was the SCN twice as large and the number of neurons twice as high, but also virtually all of the extra neurons produced the neuropeptide vasopressin, which is normally found in only 8 percent of the neurons of the human SCN.

Subsequent postmortem studies of homosexual brains revealed two other significant differences. The interstitial nucleus of the anterior hypothalamus is smaller in homosexuals, only about half the volume found in age-matched controls. In addition, the *anterior commisure*, a myelinated bundle composed largely of axons connecting the olfactory bulb and the left and right temporal lobes, has been reported to be larger in homosexual men than in heterosexual men. These results do not prove conclusively that homosexuality is biologically based. However, given what is known about the organizational effects of androgen on the developing brain, it does seem possible that the brains of homosexual men (the pituitary-hypothalamus complex, at least) may have received abnormal signals during a sensitive period of prenatal development.

Maintenance of the Internal Milieu

In this chapter, we have so far looked at the two major systems used by the brain to integrate the needs of the body with the moment-to-moment demands of the external environment: the autonomic nervous system and the endocrine system. The autonomic nervous system does its regulating through small shifts in predominance between two of its generally balanced divisions, the sympathetic and the parasympathetic nervous systems. Each of these divisions has a sensing component that monitors specific internal physical or chemical factors and an effector component that produces the changes necessary to maintain a constant internal environment. Within the endocrine system, the hypothalamus regulates a variety of internal organs through intermediate hormones secreted by the pituitary. Under the active control of neurons in the hypothalamus, the anterior lobe of the pituitary regulates the endocrine glands throughout the body. The posterior lobe of the pituitary allows other hypothalamic neurons to secrete their hormones directly into the bloodstream. The activity of both sets of hypothalamic neurons can also be modified by current and recalled sensory information that has been processed by cortical and subcortical systems.

Both the autonomic and endocrine systems function as though they were monitoring a specific physical or chemical "setpoint" for every component of the internal environment. These systems activate or inhibit internal activity to keep each internal property component within a very narrow range, despite wide variations in the external environment. For example, blood pressure is normally set to fixed standards, as is the body's utilization of calories.

In the next chapters, we turn our attention to the interplay between these global systems and the predictable patterns of life. By considering the organized oscillations—or rhythms—of the operations of our internal regulatory systems, we can begin to see how the brain anticipates the cyclical demands of our daily and seasonal activities.

Summary

1. The brain regulates the internal environment of the body through the autonomic nervous system and the endocrine system.

2. The autonomic nervous system has two major divisions that serve the entire body and a third division that provides additional regulation of the gastrointestinal system. The parasympathetic division of the autonomic nervous system is, in general, balanced by the activity of the sympathetic division of the autonomic nervous system. A change from one dynamic state to another (such as from the excited state of taking an examination to the more placid state that follows a good meal) requires an increase in the activity of one system and a concomitant decrease in the activity of the other.

3. Through the anterior pituitary and its hormones, the brain can also speak to selected target cells throughout the body through the secretion of blood-borne messenger molecules, the hormones.

4. The several different hormones regulate: overall metabolism; the activity of the gonads, liver, and adrenal glands; and, in some stages of our lives, the rate at which we grow.

5. The regulation of these hormone messages from the pituitary is also

tightly monitored by the brain to match the strength of the messages to the demands of the body in what-ever environment we are forced to exist.

6. Through the combined action of the autonomic nerves and the endocrine system, we are able to make short-term and long-term adjustments to alterations in our environment—for example, to remain cool when the weather is hot and vice versa.

7. The brain also regulates the replenishing of energy supplies by eating, although as human beings we are able to override these internal controls and eat even if we are not particularly hungry, because we enjoy eating or find it relaxing.

8. Similarly, the brain is able to regulate every one of the major visceral systems, including heart rate, blood pressure, and salt and water balance.

9. By establishing a normal value, or setpoint, the dynamically opposed systems regulated by the brain are able to maintain an exact balance in a wide variety of internal chemical and physical properties.

10. Similarly, the brain is able to regulate reproductive behaviors in concert with appropriate endocrinological preparation and the demands of seasonal breeding.

Key Terms

homeostasis
internal environment
setpoint

hormones
neuroendocrine
    integration

autonomic effectors
visceral afferents
acetylcholine
muscarinic receptors
nicotinic receptors
norepinephrine

pituitary-portal
    circulation
central coordination
    of autonomic
    function

Further Reading

Kandel, E., and Schwartz, J., Eds. 1991. *Principles of Neural Science,* 3d ed., Chapter 47: Hypothalamus, limbic system, and cerebral cortex: homeostasis and arousal (pp. 735–749) and Chapter 49: The autonomic nervous system (pp.761–775). Elsevier, New York. A comprehensive textbook written mainly for the interests of advanced medically oriented students.

Kiberstis, P. A., and Marx, J. 1998. Regulation of body weight. *Science* 280:1363–1364. The introductory essay overview for a special issue dealing with the subject of obesity and eating disorders.

Pawley, T. L. 1998. Central control of autonomic functions. In M. J. Zigmond, F. E. Bloom, S. C. Landis, J. L. Roberts, and L. R. Squire, Eds., *Fundamental Neuroscience* (pp. 1027–1050). Academic Press, New York. A comprehensive textbook aimed at advanced college-level biologists, with excellent schematic representations of the complexity of the autnomic nervous system.

Sved, A. F. 1998. Cardiovascular system. In M. J. Zigmond, F. E. Bloom, S. C. Landis, J. L. Roberts, and L. R. Squire, Eds., *Fundamental Neuroscience* (pp. 1051–1062). Academic Press, New York. Another chapter from the same comprehensive textbook aimed at advanced college-level biologists.

Stunkard, A. J., and Stellar, E., Eds. 1984. *Eating and Its Disorders.* Raven Press, New York. A collection of papers presenting research on obesity, anorexia nervosa, and other eating disorders.

Swaab, D. F. 1997. Neurobiology and neuropathology of the human hypothalamus. *Handbook of Chemical Neuroanatomy* 13:39–117. An advanced review article that deals with morphometric evidence about changes in human hypothalamic neurons associated with sexual orientation and selected medical diseases.

Woods, S. C., and Stricker, E. M. 1998. Food intake and metabolism. In M. J. Zigmond, F. E. Bloom, S. C. Landis, J. L. Roberts, and L. R. Squire, Eds. *Fundamental Neuroscience* (pp. 1091–1109). Academic Press, New York. Another chapter from the same comprehensive textbook aimed at advanced college-level biologists.

Interactive Resources

To learn even more and make sure you've mastered this material, visit our Web site at www.worthpublishers.com/bloom. Click on "Chapter 6" for resources including practice quizzes, flash cards, simulations, links to related Web sites, and updataes on new research.

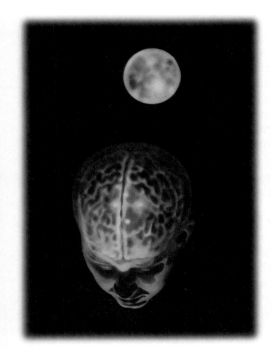

Rhythms of the Brain

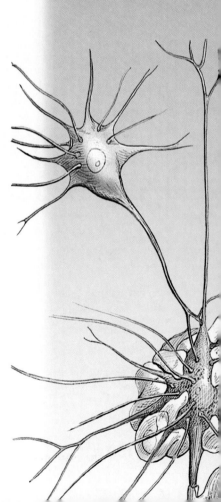

The world is governed by rhythms that we cannot ignore: spring, summer, fall, and winter follow their familiar cycle; the sun rises every day, moves across the sky, and sets; the moon waxes and wanes; the tides ebb and flow. Long before anyone knew anything

Long before scientists learned that many biological rhythms are adaptations to earth's seasonal rhythms and light–dark cycles, human beings marked the significance of seasonal changes with rites and celebrations. This illustration of such rites is from a medieval book of hours, *Les Trois Riches Heures of Jean, Duc de Berry* (ca. 1413).

about the turning of the earth and the movement of the planets around the sun, people witnessed these changes, speculated on their meanings, created rites and festivals to mark them, and planned their activities accordingly. In medieval Europe, "books of the hours" depicted appropriate seasonal and daily activities and furnished prayers for each of the different occasions.

The body also has its rhythms, and many of them appear to be adapted to the earth's cycles. Most of these rhythms follow their course without our ever being aware of them: ebbs and flows of hormonal tides, shorter cycles of high and low body temperature, and rapid cycles of fast and slow brain activity. Until recently, we knew very little about the molecular nature and cellular location of the actual biological "clocks" on which these rhythms depend. Now we know that, in mammals, the brain coordinates these rhythms of the body with the temporal events of the environment.

Daily rhythms are also seen in animals with less-elaborate brains and even in organisms with no brain at all. Living in the sands of a beach on Cape Cod is a species of golden brown algae. During the high tide, these single-celled, plantlike organisms stay under the sand. But, as the waters begin to recede during each daylight outgoing tide, the algae travel upward between the grains of sand and bask in the sunlight, recharging their photosynthesis machinery (see Figure 7.1). Moments before the returning tide reaches them, they scurry back down into the safety of the sand.

Tides do not come in at the same clock time every day. Our clocks measure the 24-hour solar day (see Figure 7.2). Tides, on the other hand, ebb and flow according to the lunar day, which is 24.8 hours long. One Monday, therefore, the algae on the Atlantic coast of the northeastern United States must

Figure 7.1 These golden brown algae remain about 1 mm below the surface of the sand during high tide. Each day, they propel themselves upward to the surface when the tide ebbs, bask in the sun, and burrow again just before the tide returns.

retreat below the surface at 2:01 P.M., on Tuesday at 2:57 P.M., on Wednesday at 3:55 P.M., and so on.

Are the algae responding to environmental cues in keeping to their intricate schedule? Samples of them were scooped up with their beach sand, taken to a laboratory, and kept in a tub maintained under continuous light, with no simulated tides. Without those environmental cues—no days, nights, or tidal changes—the algae continued to climb to the surface of the sand just as the tide receded at their old beach and to withdraw to the depths just before the tide returned. They were so punctual that the experimenters could accurately assess the level of the tide at a beach 27 miles away. Clearly, some biological clock, set on lunar time, directs this activity.

Types of Rhythms

The golden brown algae show a daily activity rhythm, even though that day is 24.8 hours long. Such rhythms are called *circadian* (Latin *circa,* "about," and *dies,* "a day"). The human sleep–wake cycle is a circadian rhythm, as are rhythms in body temperature, hormone levels, urine production, gastrointestinal motility, and levels of cognitive and motor performance. These variations in

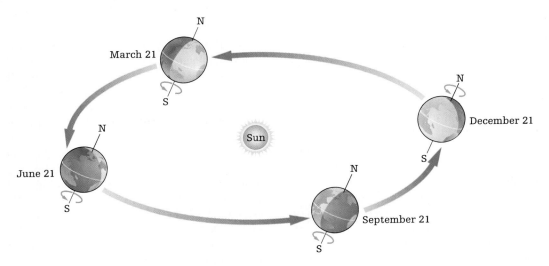

Figure 7.2 The earth's light–dark cycle, which drives most human rhythms, is a result of the earth's revolution around the sun and its daily rotation on its axis.

physiological activity with time of day are stable within a given species. In humans and in many other species of diurnal animals—visually oriented animals that are most active in the daytime—levels of physiological function begin to rise just before the time of awakening and decline in the late afternoon. In nocturnal animals—animals that depend on olfactory and auditory clues to monitor their environments—physiological activities peak at night and decline during the day when those animals rest. In both kinds of animal, the brain operates a circadian timing system that serves to keep the physiological functions tied to the changes in the environment.

Rhythms that require a period longer than a day are called *infradian* (*infra*, "below") because their frequency is less than once a day. Some squirrels and bears, for example, hibernate every year. Their body temperatures drop, and they become completely inactive for several months. This annual pattern is an infradian rhythm, as are the cycles of ovulation and menstruation in females—every few days for mice and rats and monthly for humans.

Rhythms that repeat more than once a day are called *ultradian* (*ultra*, "beyond") because their frequency is greater than once a day. The cycle of stages observed within the normal 6- to 8-hour period that human beings sleep is one example, and there are many more.

Scientists are interested in these rhythms not only out of curiosity about how living organisms function, but also because of the realization that certain medications are more effective when taken at a given time of day. For example, mice, which are nocturnal, vary dramatically in their susceptibility to toxic agents: a dose of bacterial toxin that is well tolerated at night might kill or incapacitate them during the day. Knowledge of the ebb and flow of chemicals produced by the human body has great potential for enhancing the quality of health care.

Much of the research on biological rhythms has been carried out with plants, birds, and laboratory animals. Occasionally, when conditions are safe and proper, the conclusions are tested in humans as well. Researchers hope to discover answers to the following questions:

1. How is a biological rhythm functionally organized—that is, which neurons in what circuits are required to operate the rhythm?

2. Where in the body is the *pacemaker,* or clock, that drives the rhythm?

3. What are the cellular and molecular mechanisms that cause the pacemaker to generate the rhythm?

Studies of Rhythms in Nonhuman Organisms

More than 260 years ago, the French astronomer Jean-Jacques d'Ortous de Mairan, having noted that his heliotrope plant spread its leaves open during the day and closed them at night, decided to see whether this unfolding and folding was a response to light and dark. He put the plant in a dark closet and observed it. Not only did the plant continue to open and close in the absence of light, its cycle of opening and closing corresponded to the day–night cycle outside. The plant's rhythms, he concluded, must be governed by an inner mechanism.

Flowers show such regularity in unfolding and folding their petals each day that the great biologist Linnaeus created a garden plan for a flower clock. Each species of

The opening of the morning glory over a four-hour period is timed by a circadian biological clock.

flower opens and closes in its turn, starting at 6 A.M. and ending at 6 P.M.

Simple Organisms

The algae that perform with such clocklike regularity in the Cape Cod sands consist of only one cell, so the mechanism that produces their circadian rhythm of activity must exist within that cell. So far, however, attempts to identify the pacemaker or any of its parts, anatomically or functionally, have been unsuccessful. Researchers have exposed these organisms to high temperatures and a number of potentially disruptive chemicals, but their rhythms continue, undisrupted.

Another single-celled organism, an aquatic plant called *Gonyaulax,* has four different known circadian rhythms, each relating to one of four different functions: photosynthesis, luminescence, irritability, and cell division. Are these different rhythms driven by a single pacemaker or four different ones? The answer has not yet been found. Even when the cell's nucleus is removed by microsurgery, some of the rhythms continue.

One well-studied multicelled organism is *Aplysia californica,* a sluglike animal that adjusts its activities to the tides of the Pacific beaches. *Aplysia* makes a good subject for neuroscience because the connections and functions of its large neurons are relatively easy to discover. Certain neurons in the

A photograph of the sea slug *Aplysia californica,* whose large neurons make it an excellent subject of study. Neurons in the outer rim of its eye act as pacemakers, keeping *Aplysia's* feeding and resting cycles attuned to cycles of light and dark.

outer rim of the *Aplysia* eye maintain a circadian rhythm in the frequency of their firing, discharging faster in the light and more slowly in the dark. Furthermore, these neurons maintain that rhythm even when removed from the eye and kept in complete darkness. These neurons apparently act as pacemakers to keep the daily feeding and resting cycles of *Aplysia* in tune with the cycles of dark and light and of tidal comings and goings. Their rhythm is evidently set by some process taking place within the neurons themselves.

All these circadian rhythms are clearly genetically based. Astute observers have noted that plants such as the bread mold *Neurospora* and insects such as the fruit fly *Drosophila* occasionally produce offspring with genetic mutations that cause their clocks to malfunction, giving them abnor-

mally long or short periods. The offspring of these mutant forms pass the same abnormal timing traits to their offspring, so scientists accept them as having been inherited. Detecting the nature of these clock-gene mutations has been a source of stunning insight into the molecular process by which circadian rhythms are generated. Some of these discoveries are described toward the chapter's end.

Birds and Mammals

Every fall, the willow warblers migrate from central and northern Europe, where they have bred, to the warm climate of central and southern Africa. Many species of birds follow such migration patterns: the Atlantic golden plover flies from as far south as Argentina to breed in the Yukon, a trip of about 7000 miles; the Arctic tern breeds in northern Europe, Asia, and North America, and migrates to the Antarctic. What triggers migration? Do these birds sense the days getting shorter or the temperature gradually dropping?

To answer such questions, scientists took fledgling warblers from their European nests in the spring and divided them into four groups. One group was left in its natural environment. The second was kept in a laboratory near its home territory but at a constant temperature of 53°F and a constant cycle of 12-hour alternating periods of light and darkness. The other two groups were flown by airplane to their usual wintering quarters in Africa. One of these groups was kept under the same laboratory conditions as the second group in Europe while the other lived outdoors in natural conditions. All four groups of birds, it turned out, went through the same yearly cycle of behaviors. No matter where they were, they tended to show a migratory urge, manifested by night activity not seen at other times, in the spring and fall and to shed their feathers in the summer and spring (see Figure 7.3).

Another infradian cycle of behavior, seen in many species of mammals, is hibernation. The golden-mantled ground squirrel, a native of the Rocky Mountains, hibernates during the hard winters there. Scientists investigated what triggered their hibernation behavior by keeping the squirrels in a laboratory under constant temperatures below body temperature (some at 32°F and others at normal room temperature) and alternating 12-hour periods of light and dark. These laboratory-bound squirrels did exactly as their cohorts in the wild: they increased their food consumption and gained weight in September and October and then went into hibernation, with their body temperatures dropping to near freezing (see Figure 7.4 on the following page). They awakened to feeding and activity in the spring. This annual cycle seems to be innately programmed in the golden-mantled squirrel. Squirrels raised from birth in the laboratory under light and temperature conditions that were held constant showed the same cyclical behavior for 3 years.

The Role of Environmental Cues

The genetic heritage that causes willow warblers to prepare for migration and golden-mantled squirrels to prepare for hibernation at almost the same time each year undoubtedly has a long evolutionary history. If the animals waited for certain environmental events before preparing their bodies for these activities, their survival would not be so certain. A prolonged Indian summer in the Rockies, for instance, might lead a squirrel to put off fattening up, and a sudden blizzard would be disastrous for it. Therefore, the squirrel's biological time clock must override most environmental cues.

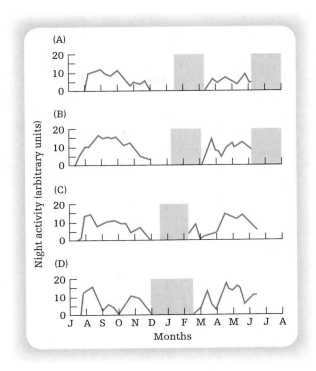

Figure 7.3 Night activity (graphed in blue) in experimental groups of willow warblers: in laboratories in Germany (a) and Africa (c) and in natural settings in Germany (b) and Africa (d). Colored bars represent periods of feather molting.

On the other hand, most species' biological clocks do respond to certain environmental cues. Two physical environmental signals seem to be especially important: *temperature* and *light*. Squirrels kept close to their normal body temperature will not hibernate but do show normal annual cycles of weight gain and loss. Heliotropes that have been moved indoors to be kept in total darkness show normal cycles of leaf folding and unfolding; but, if these heliotropes' seedlings are raised in darkness, they remain arrhythmic until they receive their first exposure to light.

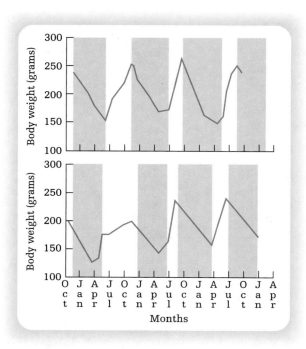

Figure 7.4 *Facing page:* As the golden-mantled ground squirrel comes out of hibernation during a 2-hour period, its body temperature rises from near freezing to normal. *Above:* Evidence that ambient temperature does not determine hibernation patterns. The 4-year record shows patterns at room temperature of 53°F *(top)* and at just above freezing *(bottom)*.

The rhythms displayed by some species of birds also are influenced by the amount and intensity of light. Like most birds, finches are normally active during the daylight hours and rest at night. If they are kept in constant dim light with only 15 minutes of bright light a day, the timing of the bright light influences their activity cycle. When the period of bright light comes early in their waking period, the birds become active earlier, accelerating their cycle. If it comes later, their period of most intense activity is delayed.

Scientists use the German word *Zeitgeber,* which literally means "time giver," as the general term for environmental cues that affect biological rhythms. What are the mechanisms by which Zeitgebers affect an organism's biological clock?

The Pineal Gland

Any biological clock that is influenced by light must have three elements: (1) an input pathway through which light energy sends a message to the pacemaker and stimulates it, (2) a pacemaker to generate and regulate the rhythm, and (3) an output pathway through which the pacemaker signals travel from the pacemaker to the appropriate tissues and organs. In birds and certain nonhuman animals, a small circumventricular gland called the *pineal gland* seems to serve as just such a biological clock. Moreover, its location, just beneath the top of the skull in all species suggests that this function has been preserved through evolution.

In birds, the pineal gland extends on a thin stalk from the top of the bird's thalamus and lies just beneath the semi-transparent skull. Here it acts as a light detector, and serves as a primary pacemaker of avian

The chicken's pineal gland senses light directly through the skull, which may explain why the cock's crow is the first sound in the barnyard every morning.

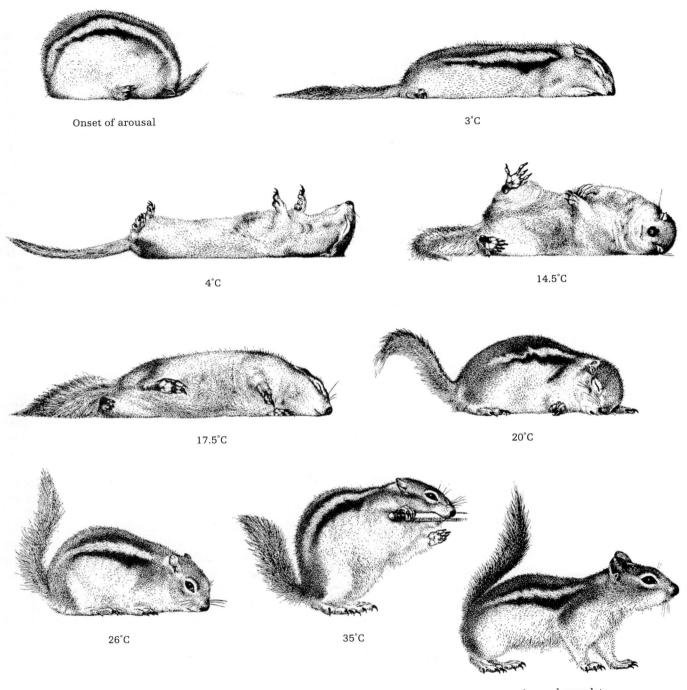

Onset of arousal

3˚C

4˚C

14.5˚C

17.5˚C

20˚C

26˚C

35˚C

Arousal complete

rhythms. If sparrows have their pineal glands surgically removed, they lose their circadian rhythms. However, the rhythm can be fully restored if the pineal is transplanted into the anterior chamber of the eye. Here pineal cells can detect environmental lighting and inform the brain of it by secreting a serotonin-like hormone called *melatonin* (because the hormone was first discovered in frogs, where it has the ability to cause melanin granules to disperse and the skin to lighten in color).

Input Pathways The light-input pathways to the pineal gland appear to vary in different animals. Birds sense light directly through their skulls, as well as through their eyes. In rats and all other mammals, the pineals have lost their ability to detect light directly. Nevertheless, information on environmental lighting conditions still reaches the pineal very indirectly, through changes in activity within the branches of its sympathetic innervation.

Pacemaking Activities The amino acid tryptophan, the raw material for serotonin, can be converted by the pineal gland into melatonin. The biochemical pathway is the same as that for serotonin production except for two additional steps. One of the two enzymes that accomplish these steps is serotonin N-acetyltransferase. The activity level of N-acetyltransferase determines the amount of melatonin released by the pineal gland into the bloodstream. In turn, the amount of melatonin circulating in the blood controls such physiological rhythms as the cycle of body-temperature changes and such behavioral rhythms as the sleep–wake cycle. Therefore, some scientists believe that N-acetyltransferase acts as a pacemaker for these functions.

In many species of animals, both diurnal and nocturnal, N-acetyltransferase activity is always highest in the dark. In chickens, the activity of N-acetyltransferase is 27 times as high at night as during the day, and the amount of melatonin is 10 times as high, peaking at about the same time as the amount of enzyme peaks. The increased melatonin causes the chicken to roost (sleep) and lowers its body temperature.

Because the number of hours of light and darkness varies during the year, light must somehow influence the activity of the N-acetyltransferase clock. In constant darkness, chicks have normal 24-hour rhythms in N-acetyltransferase activity, but, when they are kept in constant light, the amount of N-acetyltransferase is reduced. Interestingly, when chicks raised with normal light cycles are suddenly exposed to light in a dark period, their N-acetyltransferase enzyme activity drops rapidly (see Figure 7.5). No such effect occurs when chicks get a sudden "lights out" in a regular light period, suggesting that the pineal can sometimes remain impervious to changes in environmental lighting.

Apparently, then, the pineal gland is sensitive to changes in light in the dark periods—nighttime in the barnyard—and may somehow provide the means by which chickens measure the different lengths of successive nights. The light of morning causes the activity of N-acetyltransferase to be reduced. This reduction reduces the amount of melatonin released. With less melatonin in circulation, a chicken's body temperature rises, and the chicken begins its daily activity of feeding and scratching. Because dawn may arrive at 4:30 A.M. in the summer and 6:30 A.M. in the winter, the chicken's pineal-gland clock is reset every day while still maintaining its 24-hour period.

Great differences exist in the way in which light reaches the pineal gland in different species, in the neural mechanism of enzyme regulation, and in the chemi-

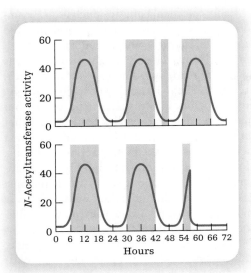

Figure 7.5 When chicks raised in alternating 12-hour periods of light and dark were exposed to darkness early in a light period *(top)*, there was no increase in *N*-acetyltransferase activity. But, when light was introduced in a dark period *(bottom)*, enzyme activity decreased dramatically.

cal processes that govern the activity of *N*-acetyltransferase. In rats, for example, *norepinephrine* released from the sympathetic nerves innervating the pineal gland stimulates activation of the enzyme; in chickens, norepinephrine inhibits the enzyme. The mechanisms of this pineal biological clock in chickens and some mammals are clear, but no such timekeeping function of the pineal gland in human beings has been established. In fact, in most adult humans, the pineal becomes calcified. Nevertheless, in some congenitally blind people, daily rhythms of blood-melatonin levels correlate well with other circadian functions.

Pacemakers in the Mammalian Brain: The Suprachiasmatic Nuclei

In the late 1960s, the physiologist Curt Richter performed a series of experiments on rats in an attempt to find the brain sites responsible for circadian rhythmicity. Richter destroyed parts of hundreds of animal brains—more than 200 different sites—and then looked for disturbances in each animal's circadian eating, drinking, and activity patterns. As a result of this lengthy series of trials, he discovered that he could disrupt rats' daily rhythms by destroying a part of the hypothalamus.

During those same years, related research was presenting neuroscientists with an intriguing puzzle. Rats with circadian rhythms timed to a light–dark cycle in the laboratory showed no disruption in their rhythms when the visual pathways between their retinas and their brains were destroyed. Clearly, the rats' biological-clock mechanism, which Richter had located in the hypothalamus, was not getting its information about light and darkness through the normal visual pathways.

The puzzle was eventually solved by anatomical studies that revealed a second, separate set of neural pathways linking the retinas to the hypothalamus. These pathways lead directly from the eyes to a part of relatively small cell clusters in the hypothalamus (one on each side) called the *suprachiasmatic nuclei (supra,* "above") or SCN. These nuclei lie just above the optic chiasm, where half the nerve fibers from each eye cross to the other side. Armed with this clue, two research groups soon proved that the suprachiasmatic nuclei are the crucial hypothalamic structures for normal circadian rhythmicity in rats.

Structures analogous to the suprachiasmatic nuclei have been found in all mammalian species subsequently studied, from platypus to chimpanzee to human (see Figure 7.6). Birds possess them as well, incorporated into circadian control systems that are far more complicated than those of mammals. So far, four different patterns of retina–brain–pineal connectivity have been seen in bird species. In birds such as the sparrow, the SCN can be bypassed by direct connections from extraretinal photoreceptors of the pineal, but the SCN is still required for melatonin secretion to regulate daily locomotor behaviors. In the quail, the retinal light sensors seem to have the important role; whereas, in the pigeon, the retina and the pineal gland are (co)dominant.

Each suprachiasmatic nucleus is composed of about 10,000 small, densely packed neural cell bodies whose dendrites branch sparsely. Many closely neighboring neurons synapse on one another in a mesh of local circuitry. Such mutual synapsing among close neurons is unusual in the brain, but many scientists had earlier conjectured that our neural clocks might be composed of just such closely packed interacting neurons. Modern analyses indicate that the suprachiasmatic nuclei have two distinct regions: (1) a dorsomedial division with relatively small neurons and (2) a ventrolateral division in which the larger neurons express GABA, vasoactive intestinal polypeptide, and gastrin-releasing peptide. The ventrolateral division, thought to be the main clock core, receives projections from both the retinohypothalamic circuits (mediated by glutamate signals) and from an intense GABA-mediated feedback loop in the region of the lateral geniculate visual relay region, termed the *intergeniculate nucleus*. It also receives an intense innervation from the serotonin-transmitting neurons of the raphe nuclei through one of the single-source–divergent monoamine circuits described in Chapter 2.

The neuronal pathways emerging from the suprachiasmatic nuclei have been difficult to trace because of the dense packing of the neurons. Currently, neurons with cell bodies in the suprachiasmatic nuclei are known to send axons to other nuclei in the hypothalamus, to the pituitary gland, to the pineal gland (through a multisynaptic circuit), and to parts of the brainstem known to take part in the timing of sleep.

The suprachiasmatic nuclei generate rhythms themselves. Electrical recordings of nerve cell activity in the suprachiasmatic nuclei of rats have established that these neurons produce spontaneous firing rhythms

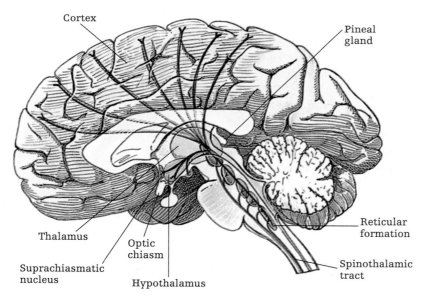

Figure 7.6 The suprachiasmatic nucleus appears just above the optic chiasm in the base of the hypothalamus in this midline view of the right hemibrain. The highly divergent axons of neurons arising from single sources in the reticular formation also are seen.

that parallel the animals' circadian sleep–wake cycles. When all of the neuronal connections between the suprachiasmatic nuclei and the rest of the brain were surgically severed, nerve cell firing persisted in a circadian rhythm within the suprachiasmatic nuclei but disappeared elsewhere in the brain. Similar studies in very young rats show that these cells fire in synchronized repeating waves of higher and lower activity, suggesting that they are somehow able to coordinate their local activity. This evidence points strongly to the role of these nuclei as pacemakers, at least in rats. Apparently, for circadian timing to occur, the neurons of the suprachiasmatic nuclei in the ventrolateral division must in some manner work together. Their oscillatory behavior can be detected long before synapses occur and is maintained even if all action-potential generation is blocked by the Na$^+$ channel inhibitor tetrodotoxin. In humans, tumors within the region of the SCN have been associated with serious disorders of sleep or of waking from sleep.

Multiple Pacemakers

Although the suprachiasmatic nuclei are clearly important components of the circadian timing systems in mammals, additional evidence has long suggested that other mammalian pacemakers also must exist. A squirrel monkey subjected to lesions in the suprachiasmatic nuclei, for instance, loses its feeding, drinking, and activity rhythms, but its daily body temperature cycle remains unaltered. This finding could indicate that some other pacemaker might be guiding its fluctuations in temperature. Furthermore, records of physiological cycles in human subjects living in environmental isolation indicate that while on free-running time their circadian temperature rhythm desynchronized from their sleep–wake cycles.

Faced with such evidence, some investigators have suggested that different clusters of physiological rhythms might be driven by different pacemakers. One such cluster would include rhythms of sleep–wake activity, skin temperature, and levels of certain chemicals, such as levels of growth hormone in the blood and levels of calcium in the urine (see Figure 7.7). This cluster is the set of rhythms most strongly linked to the activity of the suprachiasmatic nuclei. Another cluster of functions that seem always to vary together, even when other body functions fall out of synchrony, consists of the cycles of sleep, internal body temperature, level of cortisol in the blood, and level of potassium in the urine (also shown in Figure 7.7). The pacemaker that controls these rhythms appears to be more stable than the one controlling the sleep–wake rhythm. In case studies where rhythms are allowed free run—where the environment offers no

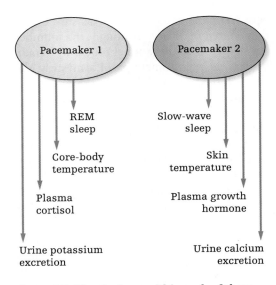

Figure 7.7 The rhythms within each of these clusters do not uncouple under free-running conditions; therefore, each cluster appears to be driven by a different pacemaker.

Zeitgebers—this second cluster rarely breaks away from its 24.8-hour cycle.

Other investigators point out that some of these clusters of physiological circadian rhythms could be explained by "secondary pacemakers," each controlling a different set of timed functions in its own way but all obtaining their timing information from the suprachiasmatic nuclei. In such an explanatory scheme, for mammals, the suprachiasmatic nuclei would be the primary pacemaker, delegating command over specific physiological variables to specific integrative output systems. As usual, research has a way of forcing logical hypothesis to be revised, as we shall see in the final section of this chapter.

Molecular Properties of Biological Clocks

The biological clocks that we have examined here have the same function as any clock: they measure time. Although the number and location of these timekeepers in human beings has been something of a mystery, the best established candidates for this function so far, the neurons of the hypothalamic suprachiasmatic nuclei, have clocklike behavior in common with pacemaker neurons found in sea slugs, flies, and frogs. Scientists describe this cellular behavior as "oscillatory," meaning that, for short periods of time, the neuronal discharge rate fluctuates in a precisely timed cycle of higher and lower activity. Almost all the rhythms that we have examined are tied directly or indirectly to the earth's circadian cycle of day and night, something that all living creatures have to live with. Even seasonal rhythms, such as migration and hibernation, appear to be driven by daily rhythms (such as a change in the respective length of day and night).

Until recently, researchers trying to discover the mechanisms by which some neurons are able to maintain a clocklike oscillatory activity were armed only with the knowledge, based on the heritability of biological clocks, that protein synthesis was somehow required for this function to be maintained. Mutants of *Neurospora* and *Drosophila* were known whose biological rhythms deviated substantially from the 24-hour period or were totally nonexistent. Thanks to advances in molecular genetics, the genes and gene products of such mutations were finally identified. Their properties are sources of surprisingly complete and unexpectedly pervasive insight into the nature of biological clocks.

The first of these mutant gene products to be analyzed were FRQ, encoded by a "frequency"-determining gene in *Neurospora;* PER, encoded by a clock-period-determining gene in *Drosophila;* and TIM, encoded by a gene mutated in "timeless," or arrhythmic, *Drosophila.* When these genes were cloned and their protein products characterized, certain molecular features of their expression pertinent to clock function were recognized. For example, the three putative clock genes all code for proteins that regularly change in abundance over the 24-hour day, building to a peak and then seemingly turning their genes off to start a new cycle. However, if these proteins were some of the biological cogs in a pacemaker mechanism, some essential wheels were still eluding detection—namely, the proteins that would turn the genes back on when the gene products are not turning the genes off.

Then, within a single month in the spring of 1997, the picture was enormously enhanced by discoveries from two separate teams, each pursuing separate lines of research. One team isolated the *Neurospora* proteins necessary to activate the expression of FRQ. The other discovered a mutant mouse gene, which they named *clock*, that seemed to produce mice with abnormally long (longer than 25-hour) circadian periods. When eventually deciphered, this mutant gene was found to produce a protein with two important features: one domain of the protein was specialized for interacting with other large proteins, a feature also found in the FRQ gene activator (the protein discovered by the other team), and a second domain bore all the necessary attributes of a gene-activating protein. Apparently, the CLOCK protein interacts with an as yet undiscovered protein partner to form a complex that activates a gene.

One other component was missing: a gene product whose job is to delay the turnoff of the *per* and *tim* genes until critical levels of PER and TIM proteins are reached. Not much later, such a protein, named DOUBLETIME (DBT), was indeed discovered from studies of a rapidly oscillating mutant *Drosophila*. With this molecule revealed, researchers constructed the following scenario: DBT binds to PER and causes it to lose its ability to bind with TIM until enough TIM begins to accumulate to compete with DBT for PER. The complex consisting of TIM bound to PER is then imported into the nucleus where it can bind to the appropriate sequences of DNA and turn off the expression of the *per* and *tim* genes. The levels of PER and TIM then decline (in fact, the degradation of TIM is accelerated by light in cells that are near enough to the body surface to receive any) until CLOCK and its partner restore the production of PER and TIM.

What is particularly appealing about these discoveries is the degree to which nature has retained very similar versions of these genes and gene products across species. Genes similar to the *Drosophila* clock genes have since been found in mouse neurons, and genes similar to the mouse genes were recognized in *Drosophila*. But, in *Drosophila*, the clock genes seemed to be expressed in cells all over the body surface, not just in their neurons. Amazingly, researchers following up on the implications of that fact found that the biological clocks of humans can be reset by shining light on parts of the body surface—for example, on the back of the knee—totally remote from the light-detection systems of the pineal gland and hypothalamus. Perhaps airline seats of the future will be equipped with special lamps that can adjust your biological rhythms en route to your destination.

Human Circadian Rhythms

Every person is aware of at least one daily rhythm: the cycle of sleep and wakefulness. The human body actually has more than a hundred circadian rhythms, although many of them appear to be coordinated with the sleep–waking cycle. Body temperature, for example, fluctuates about 3 Fahrenheit degrees in a 24-hour day. It is higher during the daytime, peaking in the afternoon, and reaches its lowest point between 2 and 5 A.M. You may recall times when you stayed up particularly late studying for an exam or traveling by plane. If you felt chilled, it was not only because you were more tired than usual, but also because your body temperature was at its lowest point. The essential hormone *cortisol*, manufactured by the adrenal cortex, is secreted in its greatest quantity just before dawn, readying the body for the activities of the coming day. In nocturnal animals, these adrenal hormones peak in the early evening.

Urine flow also is rhythmic, being lowest at night during sleep. This is an important conservation mechanism. Because we spend about 8 hours of every day lying flat and ingesting nothing, we would run the risk of depleting blood volume and bone mass if we excreted fluid during the night. The rate of urine excretion is probably determined by the rhythmic output of different hormones in the body. For example, scientists have found a pronounced circadian rhythm in concentrations of the neuropeptide *vasopressin,* also called the antidiuretic hormone; this peptide is produced by the large neurons of the hypothalamus whose axons constitute the posterior lobe of the pituitary gland. Dehydration leads to increased activity of these neurons and secretion of vasopressin into the blood of normal people. At the kidney, vasopressin causes the reabsorption of water from early stages of urine formation.

All of these rhythms are obviously in synchrony with the sleep–wake rhythm.

Sleep–Wakefulness

Sleep is a specific state of the nervous system, with its own characteristics and cycles of brain activity. A person does not fall asleep gradually; the changeover from the waking state to the sleeping state is instantaneous. If human volunteers allow themselves to be put to bed in a sleep laboratory with their eyelids taped open, they can demonstrate very consistent button-pushing responses to flashes of light. The button-pushing responses cease immediately when the subjects fall asleep, with no warning or gradual slowdown. The actions, and therefore perceptions, stop abruptly at this point, even though the eyes are wide open.

Scientists do not yet know the purpose of sleep, but it is obviously a biological requirement for our species. Conventional wisdom holds that sleep is essential for good health, but people clearly differ substantially in their sleep requirements, with no obvious relation to recent physical or mental activity. Although it is still unclear what essential processes are served by the rest our brains get during sleep, we know a great deal about the neuronal circuits whose activity changes before and during sleep.

Sleep seems to be regulated by the interaction of clusters of neurons at several sites within the brain, including the cholinergic neurons of the upper brain stem, the noradrenergic neurons of the pons, and the serotonergic neurons of the pons and medulla. These diffuse systems, described in earlier chapters, regulate the activity of cortical neurons—neutralizing the actions of sensory information coming to the cortex by means of the thalamic sensory systems described in Chapter 4. The mechanisms of these interactions are presented later in this chapter, when we consider the cycles of sleep, an ultradian rhythm.

Most of us arrange our lives on the basis of certain patterns. We find, or create, many timing cues, or Zeitgebers, in our environments besides the cycle of dark and light. We eat our meals at certain times; we go to work or school at certain times; and we return home at certain times. Our social activities, too, are patterned: we usually go to parties or the movies in the evening and almost never in the morning. Most of us wear a watch or keep an eye on the clock "to keep track of time." What effect do these outside cues have on our biological rhythms? What would our days and nights be like if we had no access to cues?

A number of experiments have been carried out with subjects who volunteered to spend long periods of time in isolation, not only away from other people but also away from all environmental time-giving cues. Most strikingly, all such subjects when isolated from the normal cues of daily living for only a few weeks tended to shift to cycles close to that of the 24.8-hour lunar day.

When a person's time is entirely freed from time-giving cues, sleep experts say that it is "free running." Humans without watches and without environmental cues turn out to be very bad judges of the passage of time and show a surprising amount of variation as they adapt to such unusual environments (see box on page 224). Furthermore, in the total absence of time-giving cues, human sleep–activity cycles also become irregular. Nevertheless, people who live in the Arctic, where darkness is virtually continuous during the winter and daylight is continuous in the summer, keep regular sleep–activity cycles, testifying to the strength and importance of social time-giving cues.

Several circumstances of modern life introduce irregularities into our sleep–wake cycles: jet travel, changing work shifts, insomnia. Do these changes have any effect on the body's other rhythms? Do they cause loss of synchrony between rhythms, and, if so, what are the physical or psychological consequences of such a loss?

When Rhythms Fall out of Phase

In the long-term cave experiments, the subjects on free-running time lengthened their "days" well beyond the usual 24-hour cycle, and this departure did indeed break the synchrony between the rhythms of body temperature and the sleep–activity cycle. In fact, this interplay among the thermal regulatory systems and the sleep regulatory systems in retrospect may have led to the misinterpretation of the length of the normal human daily cycle duration. Ordinarily, you recall, the body temperature reaches its highest point in the afternoon, when most people are very active. The lowest temperature is between 2 and 5 A.M., when most of us are asleep.

One cave dweller's "days" lengthened to an average of 33 hours, but his temperature cycle remained much closer to a 24-hour pattern (see Figure 7.8 on page 225). Therefore, he sometimes experienced both a high and a low temperature in the course of his period of wakeful activity. On day 12, in fact, he experienced two highs and two lows in the course of one sleep–wake cycle.

In spite of the break in synchrony, body temperature dramatically affected the length of the sleeping period in the subjects of these cave experiments. When a subject's retirement time coincided with his lowest body temperature, he slept for a relatively short time—about 8 hours. In contrast, if he retired when his body temperature was at its high point, he slept as long as 14 hours. People on a 24-hour cycle of daytime activity and nighttime sleep normally fall asleep when their body temperatures begin to drop and awaken when they have started to rise. Evidently, the daily rhythm of body temperature affects how long a person sleeps, but most of us, because our lives are carefully scheduled, do not perceive that influence. If we occasionally happen to sleep for 12 hours, we generally ascribe it to being overtired or to that extra glass of wine. Perhaps the long sleep actually results from going to bed when our body temperature is at its high point.

Jet Lag One very common experience in the modern world that disrupts the schedules of many people is long-distance airplane travel. We fly from coast to coast in the United States in about 5 hours, but, by jumping over time zones, we gain or lose 3 hours in the process. A flight from San Francisco to London takes about 10 hours, and we step off the plane into a day that is 8 hours ahead of our circadian clock. If our plane leaves at noon, we arrive at 10 P.M. by our internal time but at six o'clock the next morning London time.

A Man Out of Time

Most of Siffre's "days" were much longer than 24 or 25 hours, and very few were shorter.

In the spring of 1972, French cave-explorer Michel Siffre lived deep in a Texas cave for six months while researchers observed his brain rhythms.

You live following your mind . . . it's all your brain, your functions. It's black—you have not the alternance of day and night. The cave where I was, it's a semitropical cave, you know, no sound, nothing . . . darkness completely.

Siffre lived in a carefully prepared cave that no outside light could enter. He ate whenever he was hungry. He slept when he wished, attaching electrodes to his scalp so that his sleep cycles could be recorded. He took his temperature several times a day and sent urine samples to the surface for analysis. He phoned up to announce when he was ready for sleep, and the researchers turned off his artificial lights. When he awoke, he phoned, and they turned the lights back on. Siffre called each of his sleep–wake cycles "one day."

During Siffre's stay in the cave, his "days" lengthened so that his cycle 151 was actually the 179th day—the last day of his stay below ground. He had "lost" a month of solar time. Here is his diary entry.

Cycle 151: Sullenly, mechanically, I stumble through my battery of tests. Just as I finish my laps on the hated bicycle, the telephone rings. Gerard tells me that it is August 10, a stormy day, and the experiment has concluded; I am confused; I believed it to be mid-July. Then, as the truth sinks in, comes a flood of relief.

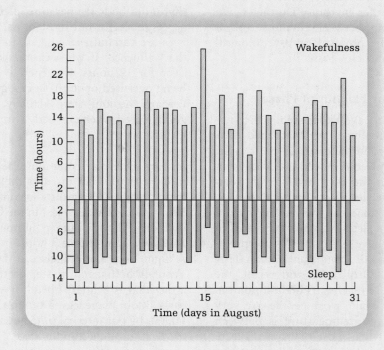

Most of us have experienced at least the jet lag that comes from a coast-to-coast flight. For a while, we are tired and irritable; we have trouble sleeping; our digestive systems may bother us; we feel a little dull—not quite mentally or physically fit. These problems result from the *desynchronization* of our body rhythms—the uncoupling of two or more rhythms that ordinarily work in harmony. Desynchronization occurs because of a *phase shift*; that is, a disengagement of our biological clocks from the clock time around us. Whereas ordinarily we go to bed when our body temperatures start to drop, we may now be trying to go to sleep when our body temperatures are rising. Normally our adrenal glands pour out cortisol just before we awaken, but, when we are desynchronized, that wave of cortisol may now be rushing through us in the middle of the day or just as we go to bed. For a few days after the flight, we may wake up feeling sluggish and find ourselves wide eyed at bedtime.

Eventually these rhythms adjust to the new sleep–wake cycle and become resynchronized. But because some rhythms adjust more quickly than others, it takes a while for full biorhythm synchrony to return. How long that takes depends on several factors. For one, speed of readjustment depends on whether you have lost or gained time. After westbound flights, in which biological clocks lose time relative to the 24-hour day, rhythms must *phase-delay*—that is, repeat an earlier phase—to adjust to schedules in the new locale. After eastbound flights, they must *phase-advance,* or jump ahead to a later phase. Phase-delay is evidently easier for the body than phase-advance: it takes less time for people flying westward to synchronize (see Figure 7.9). For another, the time that it takes to adjust to a new time frame depends on a person's physiology. People vary widely in their adaptive abilities.

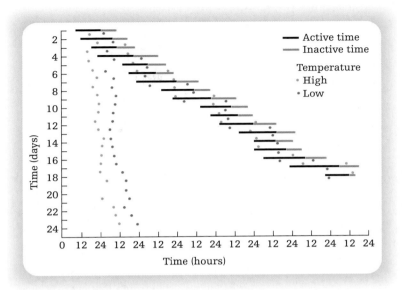

Figure 7.8 Desynchronization of body rhythms in an isolated cave dweller. Black bars represent the hours during which the subject was awake and active. Green bars represent sleep. High body temperatures are dots above the line; low body temperatures are below.

The best way to deal with jet lag is to adjust your schedule to that of your locale as soon as possible, so that the local time-giving cues—Zeitgebers—will begin to work on your rhythms right away. In one study, subjects were flown across six time zones. Some had to stay in their hotel rooms, and some went out and joined in the life around them. Those who stayed inside adjusted to the new schedule much more slowly. If you arrive in London at 6 A.M.. London time, you should try not to go to bed, even though it is 10 P.M. for you. You should have breakfast and stay out in the daylight. If you go to bed about the same time as Londoners do that night, you stand a better chance of waking up feeling like a Londoner rather than like a sleepless San Franciscan.

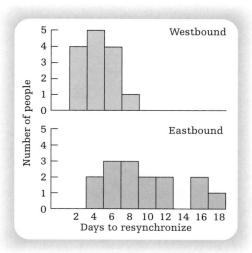

Figure 7.9 Resynchronization of body rhythms after jet lag resulting from flight over six time zones. Fourteen subjects flew westbound *(top)*, and fourteen flew eastbound *(bottom)*. Although there are wide individual differences in resynchronization, it generally takes less time to readjust after westbound flights.

One factor in determining the effect of Zeitgebers on human beings is unique to our species. That factor is an individual person's motivation. The effectiveness of one strident Zeitgeber, the alarm clock, depends on the day of the week and what the consequences may be of ignoring its message. People almost always follow the clock's dictate to get out of bed on a weekday, but on the weekend they can, and usually do, go back to sleep. In fact, "Monday morning blues" may be a sort of jet lag resulting from going to bed and getting up progressively later on Friday, Saturday, and Sunday. By Monday morning, our circadian systems may have become significantly phase shifted with respect to environmental time.

Shift Work Some industries and organizations run 24 hours a day. Airlines, for instance, often have pilots and flight attendants on different, staggered shifts (see Figure 7.10). Hospitals and airports must have personnel on duty at all times, and many factories operate with three 8-hour shifts a day. Because many workers dislike permanent swing-shift work (4 P.M. to midnight) or graveyard-shift work (midnight to 8 A.M.), they choose instead to

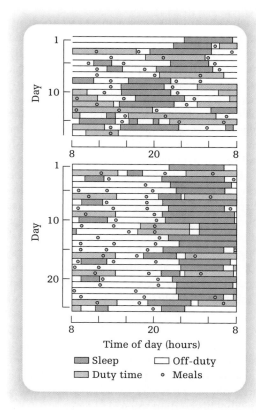

Figure 7.10 Plots of the sleep time, duty time, and meals of two pilots show little correspondence with circadian time. The airlines schedule pilots' off-duty time solely on the basis of work time.

rotate shifts, working one week on swing shift, one on graveyard, one on days, and then back to graveyard.

Changes in work schedules require changes in sleep schedules, so the results of shift rotation are often just like those of jet lag. They bring about desynchronization of biological rhythms, with a consequent decrease in efficiency. Because some people require 5 or 6 days to readjust their body rhythms and get them back into phase after an 8-hour change in the sleep–wake schedule, some shift workers on 1-week rotations never have a chance to readjust.

Air-traffic controllers usually rotate shifts—every few days in some towers, every two weeks in others. Certain shifts always

The same work goes on round the clock at this salt-flats plant near Ogden, Utah.

handle peak traffic, with takeoffs and landings every few seconds, and rotation means that this nerve-wracking burden is shared all around. The controllers are prime candidates for the disease processes caused by prolonged stress—stomach ulcers and hypertension, for example (see Chapter 8). Although it is difficult to say which features of the job contribute most to their problems, shift rotation, with its rhythm desynchronization, undoubtedly plays its part.

A number of near-fatal air accidents were traced to the lowered efficiency of pilots who had not adapted to their new shifts. The effects of shift rotation also were seen as an important factor in the near disaster at the Three Mile Island nuclear plant. Increasing knowledge about the human circadian system and greater understanding of the potential health hazards of rotating shift-work schedules have encouraged the aviation and trucking industries to take biological rhythms into account in designing work schedules.

As with jet lag, individual workers differ greatly in their speed of adjustment to shift work and in their tolerance for it. Some people suffer persistent fatigue, sleeping problems, irritability, decreased efficiency, and digestive problems after only a few months of shift work; even after many years, they continue to suffer. Others adjust with apparent ease. Researchers have found that workers with high tolerance for shifting schedules have a greater range of body temperature in their circadian cycles than do workers with low tolerance.

The physiological problems that result from jet lag and shift work highlight the fact that our lives are normally adapted to our planet's cycle of light and dark. Even though electricity and jet travel give us the ability to turn night into day or to add hours to a day, violating the earth's circadian rhythm takes its toll. By desynchronizing our own biological rhythms, we make ourselves miserable for a while.

Human Ultradian Rhythms

Several hormones, such as luteinizing hormone and follicle-stimulating hormone, are

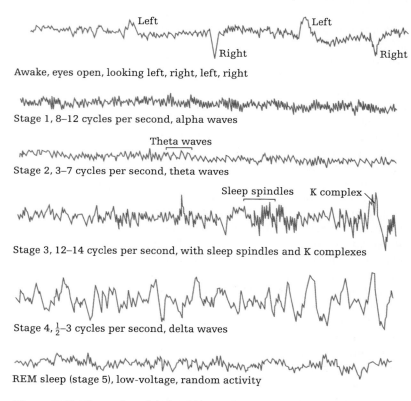

Awake, eyes open, looking left, right, left, right

Stage 1, 8–12 cycles per second, alpha waves

Stage 2, 3–7 cycles per second, theta waves

Stage 3, 12–14 cycles per second, with sleep spindles and K complexes

Stage 4, $\frac{1}{2}$–3 cycles per second, delta waves

REM sleep (stage 5), low-voltage, random activity

Figure 7.11 The various levels of arousal, somnolence, and sleep are indicated by changing patterns and amplitudes of brain activity as recorded by electrodes placed on the scalp. The electroencephalogram is a record of the activity of large numbers of neurons within the brain region closest to the surface electrodes. REM sleep resembles waking activity, except that electrodes record no muscular activity other than that of the eye muscles.

secreted into the bloodstream in an ultradian rhythm. Careful measuring techniques can chart the episodic release of these hormones.

Some of the other ultradian rhythms that punctuate our days, however, are difficult to discern and even more difficult to explain. One subtle ultradian rhythm recurs approximately every hour and a half, whether we are awake or asleep. Day in, day out, as EEGs show, human adults experience a cycle in brain activity every 90 minutes or so, a rhythm so subtle that we are not aware of it. However, special tests consisting of verbal and spatial matching tasks also reveal that human alertness and cognitive performance appear to run in 90- to 100-minute cycles. Research into such cycles in daytime brain function has only begun, even though the nighttime part of this ultradian rhythm has been known almost since the first sleep research was done.

Sleep Cycles

In human beings, five stages, or levels, of sleep can be identified by electroencephalography (see Figure 7.11). People sitting or lying down quietly show *alpha rhythms,* in which electric activity oscillates with a frequency of 8 to 12 cycles per second (stage 1). (The scientists who studied early electroencephalograms named the rhythms according to the letters of the Greek alphabet, but the order in the alphabet is not logical and can be understood only in a historical context.) As the sleep period begins, the basic rhythms slow (the rhythms of 3 to 7 cycles per second are termed *theta* because they were presumed to arise from the thalamus), and the amplitude of the individual peaks of electrical activity decreases (stage 2). Sleep researchers interpret this neuronal activity as more or less random. Deeper stages of sleep are marked by the appearance of synchronized bursts of electrical activity that interrupt the low-voltage, slow activity (stage 3). These events are called *sleep spindles,* bursts at about 12 to 14 cycles per second but lasting for less than 1 second at a time and slightly longer large waves, called *K complexes* (for "kompound shape"), in response to arousing stimuli. Still deeper stages of sleep show even more marked slowing of activity and the appearance of *delta waves* (at $\frac{1}{2}$ to 3 cycles per second), called stage-4 sleep. Finally, as the deepest stage of sleep is entered, electroencephalographic activity changes to a pattern of faster, low-amplitude activity punctuated by occasional bursts of phasic events during which the eye muscles show rapid movement. This fifth stage, called *rapid-eye-movement* or *REM sleep,* is accompanied by almost total relaxation of the skeletal muscles. People awakened in the course of REM sleep say that they have been dreaming, and therefore REM sleep has been regarded as synonymous with dream sleep. Other studies have suggested that dreaming can also occur during deep, slow-wave sleep, such as that of the delta-wave stage.

Some studies attempting to determine which brain systems generate sleep and its stages have used the standard strategies of brain research: stimulation of specific brain regions or the study of brains with lesions in specific regions.

In the early 1950s, work done by the Italian physiologist Giuseppi Moruzzi and the American physiologist Horace Magoun identified structures at the core of the pons and brainstem as constituting a critical region in sleep and consciousness (see Figure 7.12). Anatomical studies had previously been interpreted to show that fibers from this area of the brainstem project to the cortically directed nuclei of the thalamus. Such circuitry means that this reticular core is in an efficient position to influence the cerebral cortex. In experiments, electrical stimulation of the core in the pons did indeed lead to activity that could be seen in the cortical electroencephalogram. In addition, when researchers induced lesions in the pons of laboratory animals, the animals went into a permanent coma.

Recordings of the activity of specific neurons of the pons and midbrain within the reticular formation have subsequently established that some of these neurons make specific shifts in their activity just before the transitions between sleep stages. Some of these pontine cells increase their discharge rate dramatically just before deep REM sleep begins, at that point firing some 50 to 100 times as rapidly as they did during the quiet waking stage. The fact that these cells begin to increase their rates of discharge well before the EEG shifts from slow-wave to REM sleep suggests that these cells participate in the events leading to the transition to REM sleep.

Two other groups of pontine neurons tend to show characteristic patterns of discharge in association with sleep-stage transitions. The investigation of these neurons was serendipitous, occurring only because scientists happened to know something about the identity of their neurotransmitters and thus were curious about the possible role of those transmitters in sleep-stage regulation. The two groups of cells are (1) a cluster of norepinephrine-containing neurons in the locus coeruleus and (2) a cluster of serotonin-containing neurons in the dorsal raphe nucleus (see Figure 7.12). Recordings from single neurons in these nuclei show maximal activity during waking, progressive slowing through the earlier stages of slow-wave sleep, almost complete silence before the end of slow-wave sleep, and persistent silence throughout REM sleep.

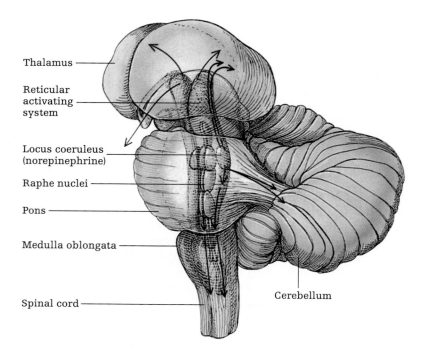

Thalamus

Reticular activating system

Locus coeruleus (norepinephrine)

Raphe nuclei

Pons

Medulla oblongata

Spinal cord

Cerebellum

Figure 7.12 The major brain areas implicated in sleep stages and waking: the reticular activating system, the raphe nuclei (transmitter, serotonin), and the locus coeruleus (transmitter, norepinephrine).

The pontine neurons that become active during REM sleep and the neurons of the locus coeruleus and the raphe nuclei that become silent during REM sleep are, in fact, now thought to be connected to each other. One hypothesis was that early activity in the "REM on" cells (the cells active during REM sleep) turns down the activity in the "REM off" cells (the cells inactive during REM sleep). But this hypothesis does not explain what makes the REM-on cells pause near the end of a REM episode or what eventually restores their activity once they have turned "off." Moreover, it is possible that many other, as-yet-unrecorded neurons in the pons show similar patterns and that these patterns of activity fit even more closely with the timing of sleep–wake stages.

These studies did serve to suggest that the transmitters serotonin and norepinephrine play a role in the regulation of sleep and waking. So did related studies in which lesions of the locus coeruleus and of the dorsal raphe nuclei temporarily caused severe disruption of normal sleep stages, depressing REM sleep especially. These transmitters may also play a role in human attentiveness, because certain tranquilizing drugs that affect behavior by making the person drowsy and unresponsive also deplete the brain's stores of serotonin and norepinephrine.

The circuits of both norepinephrine- and serotonin-secreting neurons are of the single-source–divergent pattern (see Chapter 2). The cells in each nucleus send their axons to many regions of the brain and thus appear to influence a large number of other neurons. This would give them the potential to generate global behaviors such as sleeping and attentiveness.

Detailed observations of the activity patterns of neurons in the locus coeruleus lend support to these hypotheses. In animals that are awake and interacting with their environment, the neurons of the locus coeruleus show brief periods of increased activity when the animals are experiencing novel sensory events in the external environment, whether touch, light, sound, or smell. Because these data suggest that activation of the locus coeruleus is linked to the onset of brief states of heightened responsiveness, or attentiveness, it seems reasonable to suppose that slowing in the activity of the locus coeruleus could be a prerequisite for sleep to begin.

Other single-source–divergent systems probably also participate in regulating the transitions between sleep and wakefulness and between stages of sleep. The cholinergic neurons of the upper pons, projecting onto the thalamus, form one such system. Other acetylcholine neurons, in the diencephalon, project to the cerebral cortex and hippocampal formation. Neuronal systems such as these, connecting many target locations in the brain, could serve to integrate the activity of the different targets, and perhaps that is one of the still undocumented means by which brain circuits turn on and off with sleep.

REM Sleep

According to the EEG pattern of brain activity, REM sleep resembles the waking state more than a sleeping one. Several other physiological functions also are surprisingly active during REM sleep, including increases and irregularities in heart and respiration rate, elevation in blood pressure, and erection of the penis. The eyes move quickly back and forth, as if the sleeper were watching things.

At the same time, REM sleep is a very deep sleep during which most major body muscles become virtually paralyzed. It is during REM sleep that vivid dreams occur. As mentioned earlier, when sleep researchers awaken people in the midst of a REM period, almost all report that they were dreaming and can describe the interrupted dream in detail. Only about 20 percent of the time do sleepers report that they were dreaming when awakened from non-REM sleep.

The first REM period lasts about 10 minutes, but, as the night wears on, REM periods become longer and are interrupted only by transitions into stage-2 sleep (see Figure 7.13). In other words, sleep becomes lighter

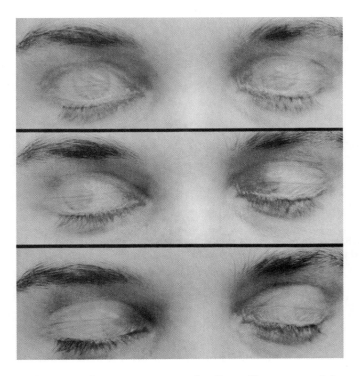

During REM sleep, our eyes move busily as if we were watching images moving in our dreams.

after the first few hours. An adult who sleeps $7\frac{1}{2}$ hours each night generally spends $1\frac{1}{2}$ to 2 hours in REM sleep.

All mammals appear to have REM sleep. You may have seen your cat's or dog's eyes moving in its sleep, along with twitches of its whiskers and paws. Reptiles do not have it, but birds do have occasional, very brief episodes of something resembling REM sleep. This difference might suggest that REM sleep is a characteristic of more highly developed brains and that the more complex the brain, the more REM sleep there is. But among mammals, the amount of time spent in REM sleep seems to follow no such rule. Opossums have more REM

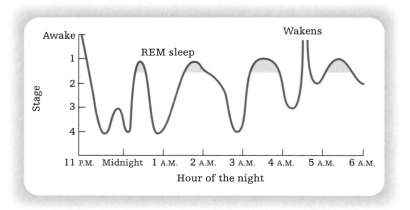

Figure 7.13 Pattern of a night's sleep. Sleep increases and decreases in depth, and periods of REM sleep get longer as the night progresses.

sleep than human beings do. Newborn human beings spend 50 percent of their sleeping time in REM periods, whereas infants born prematurely spend about 75 percent.

So the purpose of this paradoxical kind of sleep—an aroused, alert brain but a paralyzed body—is hard to pin down. Some investigators have suggested that REM sleep facilitates neural growth, especially in the young. It seems quite certain that it is mainly during the periods of delta sleep in the early night that the pituitary secretes natural bursts of growth hormone. Protein synthesis in the brain also is at its highest during REM sleep.

Human Infradian Rhythms

Rhythms that span long time periods are generally more difficult to analyze and study than are daily rhythms or those with cycles less than 24 hours. In many animals, seasonal swings in hormone levels are sig-

naled by clusters of behavioral events and physical changes. The stag, for example, grows antlers in the spring and summer, which subsequently turn into horn. It uses these antlers to challenge other stags as it fights for a harem during rutting season and then loses its antlers when rutting is over. Clear signs such as these tell researchers when to study the male animal's cyclical testosterone levels.

Human beings do not grow horns, and monthly or quarterly or annual patterns of small changes in human hormonal levels or in localized neuronal activity may go on undetected. That is why we have less information about these rhythms.

The Human Female Reproductive Cycle

The period of the human female reproductive rhythm is about 28 days. Each cycle begins when certain neurons in the preoptic area of the hypothalamus begin to secrete *gonadotropin-releasing hormone* (GnRH; see Chapter 6). GnRH travels directly to the anterior pituitary through the pituitary portal veins, and it stimulates the pituitary to produce and release two hormones into the bloodstream, separately, at appropriate times: *follicle-stimulating hormone* (FSH) and *luteinizing hormone* (LH; see Figure 7.14).

FSH acts on the ovary to stimulate the growth of the *follicle*, the hollow ball of tissue containing the *ovum*, or egg. (All the eggs that a woman will produce are present in her ovaries at the beginning of her fertile years; the eggs mature there, and one egg is released each month.) As the follicle grows, it secretes increasing amounts of the female hormone *estrogen*. This estrogen, in turn, feeds back to the pituitary, inhibiting it from sending out more FSH. Estrogen also stimulates the pituitary to release LH, which causes the walls of the follicle to break and

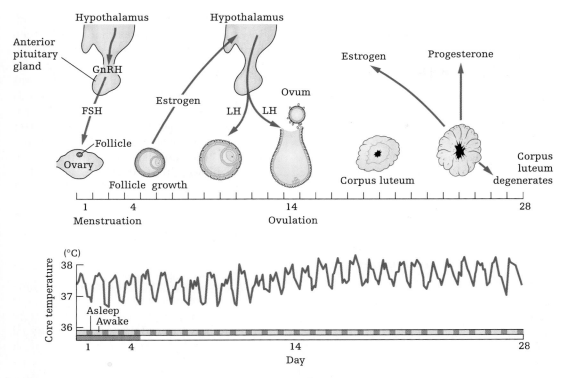

Figure 7.14 *Top:* The hormonal events of the human female reproductive cycle, an infradian rhythm. *Bottom:* Temperature is elevated during ovulation, an example of a circadian rhythm apparently linked to an infradian rhythm.

release the mature ovum. The whole process, called *ovulation,* takes about 10 to 14 days.

After the release of the egg, the remaining follicular tissue undergoes changes and becomes a small endocrine body called a *corpus luteum.* Luteinizing hormone causes the corpus luteum to secrete large quantities of the hormone *progesterone.* Progesterone increases blood supply to the uterine wall, preparing it for the egg's implantation in case fertilization takes place. Progesterone also feeds back to the pituitary and signals it to inhibit the secretion of LH. If fertilization does not take place, the level of progesterone decreases,

the corpus luteum shrinks, and the uterine lining that had been built up to receive the egg is expelled in menstruation.

The mechanism that controls the infradian reproductive cycle in human females is not well understood. In some animals, the estrous cycle is tied to circadian rhythms. (The female reproductive cycle is called *estrous* in species whose uterine lining is absorbed; in species whose uterine lining is expelled, it is called *menstrual.*) Female hamsters, for example, normally ovulate every 96 hours. But, if they are kept in constant dim lighting, their circadian sleep–wake cycles lengthen from 24 to 25 hours, and their estrous cycles lengthen to 100 hours. Because the lengthening of the circadian rhythm results in a longer estrous cycle, the two cycles must be connected.

Some relation between circadian rhythms of body temperature and the infradian reproductive cycle in women does exist, as any woman knows who has tried to conceive a child or who has used the rhythm method of birth control (see Figure 7.14). An increase in body temperature, taken upon awakening, of 0.4 Fahrenheit degrees or more above the average daily early morning temperature of the five preceding days indicates that ovulation is taking place. This rise, on top of the normal morning circadian rise, is interpreted as an important overshoot.

Seasonal Rhythms

The seasonal rhythms observed in migrating birds and hibernating squirrels are now quite well understood. As we saw, these rhythms are genetically set, but, in some cases, they can be influenced by environmental factors such as light and temperature. Do humans display seasonal rhythms, and if so how are they regulated?

Although they do not migrate or hibernate, some human beings do seem to experience a seasonal rhythmic depression. During the summer months, their moods are happy and their energy levels high, they are productive, and their outlook on life is positive. When winter comes, however, their mood plummets—they become extremely depressed, lethargic, and pessimistic—and they feel unable to cope with the demands of daily life. These people are said to have a form of recurrent depression, called *seasonal affective disorder*. In some cases, this condition responds to therapy consisting of exposure to very bright lights in the early morning. Researchers conjecture that unspecified dysfunctions of the human pineal gland and related brain structures may be responsible for these winter depressions and that artificial extension of the day is the solution. Clinicians' theories concerning these problems are very speculative and the therapies are very experimental because the mechanisms that govern human biological rhythms are so hard to discover.

Sexual Behavior: Rhythms and Cycles

For all animals except humans, sexual behavior has one purpose: to produce offspring. For many animals, including humans, nature seems to have cleverly arranged for sexual behaviors to be pleasurable so that motivation to engage in them is abundant. The mechanisms of some well-studied sexual behaviors were described in Chapter 6. Here, we briefly examine the rhythms underlying sexual motivation and behavior.

Hormones and Sexual Behavior

An animal's sexual life has to be in synchrony with the animal's environment to ensure that offspring will be born into circumstances that favor their survival. They should not be born, for example, at a time of year when food supplies are low or when extreme temperatures could endanger them or when short days may curtail their parents' food-hunting time. For most animals other than humans, therefore, the motivation to engage in sexual behaviors occurs in cycles that are tied to the earth's rhythms— the cycle of seasons, the lengthening and shortening of days, the rise and fall of temperature. This synchronization is accomplished by hormonal secretion.

Of Mice and Men

One outstanding difference between human beings and other animals is that human females do not normally have cycles in which periods of high sexual receptivity alternate with periods of total nonresponsiveness. That is, sexual responsiveness in women does not seem to be strongly tied to hormonal levels. Removal of the ovaries, for example, has little or no effect on human females' sexual desires. On the other hand, in human males, sexual reproduction is critically dependent on relatively constant production of testosterone. Without sufficient testosterone, there can be no spermatogenesis nor penile erection. However, because the production of testosterone is relatively constant, that hormone cannot explain seasonal reproductive behaviors, or can it?

In animals living under conditions of extreme seasonal cycles of temperature and food availability, the evidence seems clear that the activity of the pineal gland, controlling the levels of circulating melatonin, provides an essential means of monitoring the length of day and hence the changes in seasonal conditions. As observed earlier in Chapter 4 and again in Chapter 6, the control of pineal activity by light depends on a link between light-sensing cells in the retina and neurons in a subdivision of the hypothalamic nucleus—the suprachiasmatic nucleus—and then a series of circuits between those neurons and the neurons of the superior cervical sympathetic ganglion, which directly innervate the pineal.

In the hamster, breeding is triggered by long daylight periods, ensuring that the relatively short gestation will be completed well before the onset of winter. The control system is relatively simple but remarkably effective. When daylight periods begin to shorten, the longer nocturnal period presents the hamster's pineal gland with more time in which to secrete melatonin. The prolonged exposure to melatonin causes the hamster's testes to shrink and sperm formation to stop. As the days lengthen in the spring, the nocturnal melatonin secretion diminishes, and sperm formation is restored.

Variations consisting of similar elements are seen in the cyclical reproductive regulation of numerous other species. Sheep, for example, have a longer gestational period than that of hamsters. If sheep are to give birth in the spring (the optimal season), they must become sexually active in the fall and winter. Thus, the sheep's reproductive function is diminished by long daylight intervals and enhanced by short daylight intervals.

Rhythms and Psychological Disturbance

As we have seen, disruption of daily rhythms can affect physiological variables such as body temperature, salt and water balance, and endocrine secretions. In addition, there are important connections between these daily rhythms and the regulation of emotional status. These effects are both direct, through the regulation of sleep onset and waking, and indirect, through the influence of environmental lighting conditions on subjects vulnerable to depression.

Delayed Sleep-Phase Insomnia

Readers may well identify with the following description: A 24-year-old male student

Some scientists believe that a number of people undergo seasonal depression, the symptoms coming on during the short days of winter. Such patients may find relief from their symptoms when treated by exposure to full-spectrum lights. These lights at the right times of day produce sufficient illumination to alter the subject's circadian rhythm and achieve a day-lengthening effect.

came to the student health office complaining that he has had difficulty falling asleep since childhood. As a teenager, he was rarely able to doze off before 1:30 A.M., and he awakened only with great difficulty in the morning, despite an alarm clock and his mother's insistence. When he entered college, he was unable to fall asleep until 5:30 or 6:00 A.M. even though he consistently turned out the lights by 1:00 or 2:00 A.M. On weekends and holidays, he often slept until three o'clock in the afternoon. At age 23, extreme sleepiness and fatigue during the day were taking a toll on his education, he finally sought medical help.

Unlike people with other types of insomnia, sufferers of delayed sleep-phase insomnia can sleep soundly for a full 8-hour period and awaken refreshed if their sleep periods are not confined to a strict schedule. They just cannot move their late bedtimes to an earlier hour, and they suffer constant insomnia and fatigue when they try to conform to a socially acceptable schedule. As noted earlier, sleeping later on weekend mornings and then staying up even later on weekend nights probably compounds the problem when normal class schedules resume on Mondays.

In some extreme cases, in which sleep onset is severely delayed, a semblance of normality can be achieved by helping the circadian timing system resynchronize with a more normal sleep–wake cycle. In such cases, sleep specialists prescribe *delaying* bedtime 3 additional hours each day for a week until patients reach a sleep onset hour nearer to the desired bedtime. Then they must adhere strictly to the new time in order to set their clocks permanently.

Seasonal Depression

Although little is known about the biological basis of emotional regulation (explored in Chapter 8) or the biological role of sleep in the maintenance of mental health or health in general, some researchers conjecture that desynchronization between circadian rhythms, sleep, and emotional state may be a causative factor in emotional disorders. Pathological depression is almost invariably cyclic in human patients, although the cycles vary considerably from person to person. (Chapter 12 considers depression and manic-depressive disorder more fully.) Moreover, many depressed patients enter REM sleep much earlier in their sleep cycles than do normal people. In fact, in some depressed subjects, sleep deprivation has been observed to cause a temporary respite from the depressed state. Treatment based on biological rhythms, however, has had more success in helping people who suffer from a specific type of insomnia.

Summary

1. All organisms, even those consisting of just one cell, exhibit physiological processes that occur in regular cycles, adapted to the earth's cycles. These rhythms may be circadian, occurring daily; infradian, occurring less often than once a day—monthly, for example; or ultradian, occurring more than once a day.

2. The seasonal hibernation patterns of animals such as squirrels and the migrations of birds are genetically set, but these rhythms may be affected by extremes of temperature and by the amount and intensity of light that the animal experiences.

3. The pineal gland appears to act as a key component of the circadian timing system. The pineal gland produces the hormone melatonin from the amino acid tryptophan. One of the participating enzymes, *N*-acetyltransferase, controls the key rate-limiting step in melatonin production and is the most likely pacemaker for avian circadian rhythms.

4. The suprachiasmatic nuclei, in the hypothalamus, have been identified as the primary biological-clock component of the circadian timing system in mammals.

5. The key genes and gene products underlying the pacemaking oscillatory rhythms of living organisms have been identified and may be expressed far more ubiquitously throughout the body than was previously recognized.

6. Human beings display a number of biological rhythms, such as circadian sleep–wake and body-temperature rhythms. Usually, these rhythms are in phase with each other. For example, the body's lowest daily temperature is during night sleep.

7. One human ultradian rhythm comprises the cycles in brain activity during sleep. The brain structures and transmitters that participate in the transitions between sleep–wake states have been localized to discrete neurons in the reticular formation, including cholinergic, noradrenergic, and serotonergic nuclei.

8. The menstrual cycle is a human infradian rhythm, closely linked to the circadian rhythm of body temperature.

9. In many nonhumans, the reproductive cycle is tied to the cycle of annual seasons so that infants will be born at times of year when their chance of survival is best.

Key Terms

circadian	sleep cycles
ultradian	alpha rhythm
infradian	delta waves
pacemaker	rapid-eye-movement sleep
biological clock	seasonal reproduction
pineal gland	

Further Readings

Barinaga, M. 1998. Clock photoreceptor shared by plants and animals. *Science* 282:1628–1630. The pigments for detecting the various colors of light are common to plant and animal cells; this is a news feature based on an original research article in the same issue but far easier to read for those unfamiliar with the jargon of the field.

Campbell, S. S., and Murphy, P.J. 1998. Extraocular circadian phototransduction in humans. *Science* 279:396–399. The astonishing report demonstrating that the skin may contain important light-detection responsibilities that can also regulate circadian rhythms.

Czeisler, C. A., et al. 1999. Stability, precision, and near-24-hour period of the human circadian pacemaker. *Science* 284:2177–2181. The human circadian rhythm appears to follow a daily pattern very much like that of the other mammals, despite what the original analysts of cave dwellers seemed to reveal.

Darlington, T. K., et al. 1998. Closing the circadian loop: CLOCK-induced transcription of its own inhibitors *per* and *tim*. *Science* 280:1599–1603. For those of stout spirit, this report describes some of the most recent discoveries in clock proteins and their interactions.

Moore, R. Y. 1998. Circadian timing. In M. J. Zigmond, F. E. Bloom, S. C. Landis, J. L. Roberts, and L. R. Squire, Eds., *Fundamental Neuroscience* (pp. 1189–1206). Academic Press, New York. An excellent overview chapter, with plenty of detail, written for advanced college students and early graduate students.

Moore, R. Y. 1996. Entrainment pathways and the functional organization of the circadian system. *Progress in Brain Research* 111:103–119. A more comprehensive and detailed review of circadian timing; readers who compare this review and the preceding reading will note how rapidly the details change.

Interactive Resources

To continue your study of rhythms of the brain online, visit our Web site at www.worthpublishers.com/bloom. Click on "Chapter 7" for a number of resources which will help you master this material. These include practice quizzes, flash cards, simulations, links to related Web sites, and updates on new research.

Emotions: The Highs and Lows of the Brain

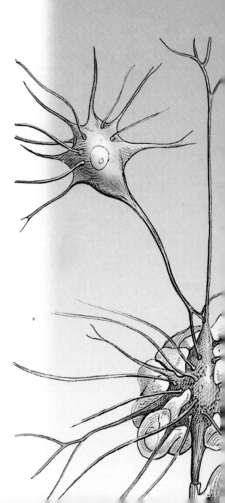

It had started the night before when he had wakened and heard the lion roaring somewhere up along the river. It was a deep sound and at the end there were sort of coughing grunts that made him seem just outside the tent, and when Francis Macomber woke in the night to hear it he was afraid. He could hear his wife breathing quietly, asleep. There was no one to tell he was afraid, nor to be afraid with him. . . . Then while they were eating breakfast by lantern light out in the dining tent, before the sun was up, the lion roared again. . . .

They were driving slowly along the high bank of the stream. . . . The car stopped. "There he is," he heard the whisper. "Ahead and to the right. Get out and take him. He's a marvelous lion."

Macomber sat there, sweating under his arms, his mouth dry, his stomach hollow feeling. . . . He stepped out . . . and down onto the ground. . . . His . . . hands were shaking and as he walked away from the car it was almost impossible for him to make his legs move. They were stiff in the thighs, but he could feel the muscles fluttering.

Thirty-five yards into the grass the big lion lay flattened out along the ground. His ears were back and his only movement was a slight twitching up and down of his long black-tufted tail. . . . Macomber heard the coughing grunt, and saw the swishing rush in the grass. The next thing he knew he was running, running wildly, in panic in the open, running toward the stream.

In "The Short Happy Life of Francis Macomber," from which this excerpt is taken, Ernest Hemingway portrays an emotion all of us have felt at one time or another—fear. Although few of us face a lion about to charge, soldiers face battle, women face childbirth, and children face bullies (and bul-

lets) on the playround. Even sitting in the dentist's waiting room or hearing the coughing grunt of a plane's engine in midair can produce the dry mouth, the hollow gut, the racing heart, the shaking hands, and the experience, "I'm afraid."

We all recognize the physiological changes that accompany strong emotion—Macomber's parched mouth and shaking hands. Most of these physiological changes are mediated by our brains and can be measured and verified. "Lie detectors" record just such alterations in blood pressure, skin moisture, and breathing rate. Milder emotions—appreciation, affection, irritation—are accompanied by less-apparent changes, but changes nonetheless occur. Every time we perform an act or have a thought, a feeling, or a memory, some physiological change takes place in our brains and nervous systems.

There exists, however, no one-to-one correspondence between discrete neural events and the states that we experience and describe to ourselves as "emotions." Nevertheless, we do feel afraid or elated or sad because of neural events and processes taking place within the systems of the brain that regulate emotion. In this chapter, we use the common vocabulary of emotion to describe how we feel and the language of neurobiology to describe how it is that we have the experiences we call "emotion."

Emotion and Motivation

Even though our common vocabulary allows us to converse about emotions and feel fairly certain that we understand each other when we describe being "afraid" or being "overjoyed," scientists have not yet been able to agree on a clear definition of *emotion,* one that excludes subjective assessments and does not rely on a list of examples. Therefore, we will not attempt a definition here but instead will proceed on the assumption of a common understanding of what human beings experience when they describe themselves as feeling angry, sad, or happy.

William James was an American psychologist whose theory of emotion was among the first attempts to relate the experience of emotion to observable physiological functions. Here he describes the powerful role that emotions play in human experience.

Conceive yourself, if possible, suddenly stripped of all the emotion with which your world now inspires you, and try to imagine it as it exists, purely by itself, without your favorable or unfavorable, hopeful or apprehensive comment. It will be almost impossible for you to realize such a condition of negativity and deadness. No one portion of the universe would then have importance beyond another; and the whole collection of its things and series of its events would be without significance, character, expression, or perspective. Whatever of value, interest, or meaning our respective worlds may appear imbued with are thus pure gifts of the spectator's mind.

Emotion and motivation are closely linked. Psychologists generally define *motivation*—which is not an observable process and therefore cannot be measured directly—as a hypothetical state that is inferred from goal-directed behavior. If an animal directs its behavior toward obtaining water, we infer that it is motivated by thirst. If the animal works hard to obtain that goal, ignoring tempting food and bypassing attractive potential sexual partners along the way, we can infer that its motivation is strong.

Many goal-directed behaviors, especially those performed by human beings, are performed because the goal has an incentive value for the person—in other words, because he or she expects that attainment of the goal will produce some positive emotion or will at least reduce some negative emotion. You study hard for a test because getting a good mark will make you happy; additionally, the act of studying and preparing for the test allays your anxiety about passing the course and getting a degree.

If we assume that even the fulfillment of such basic needs as drinking when we are thirsty produces a positive feeling—call this mild emotion "satisfaction"—then it is clear, as James says, that emotion is all-pervasive in our lives. Emotion gives value and interest to our immediate actions and motivates us to undertake actions in the future.

Emotional behavior is a means for one animal to communicate its motivational state to another of its species. Squirrel monkeys, for example, make specific vocal calls to seek contact with another monkey, to indicate that they are in a state of high excitement, to regulate the distance between themselves and other monkeys, and to express aggression.

Theories of Emotion

People have always been aware of the visceral changes that accompany emotional arousal—changes in heart rate, breathing, stomach and intestine contractions, and the rest. For at least the past 100 years or so, scientists have known that such changes are commanded by the brain. But how the brain functions to produce these changes and how the changes produce the emotions that a person experiences have been, and remain, a matter of controversy.

The James-Lange Theory

In the late 1800s, William James, drawing on the ideas of Carl Lange, a Danish psychologist, spelled out what came to be known as the James-Lange theory of emotion (see Figure 8.1).

Common sense may tell us that someone staring into the open jaws of a lion first says to himself, "I'm in danger. That's scary," and then experiences the autonomic arousal that accompanies fear. But have you ever sat alone at home reading in the evening and suddenly had a sense that something nearby had moved? You probably were unsure about what you saw or, indeed, that you had seen anything. But your heart sped up and your mouth went a little dry. The James-Lange theory proposed that a person sitting very still after such a puzzling event would take note of his or her racing heart and dry mouth and then conclude, "Wow, that scared me!" In essence, the theory proposes that, after the initial perception, the experience of emotion results from the perception of one's

own physiological changes. In other words, the physical sensations are the emotion. As James said, "We feel sorry because we cry, angry because we strike, afraid because we tremble."

Although his theory attempted to ground the emotions in physiological functions, James could not produce evidence to support it. However, more recent experimental evidence, described later in this chapter, supports some of his contentions.

The Cannon-Bard Theory

In 1929, the physiologist Walter Cannon pointed out that the James-Lange theory erred in its assumption that each emotional experience has its own particular set of physiological changes. Cannon's studies gave evidence that similar patterns of physiological arousal accompany a number of emotions. Even a simple physical experience—scalp tingles, for example—can occur while listening to a beautiful piece of music or while watching an autopsy. Thus, emotions have to be more than just the sensations of arousal. More recent studies seem to support Cannon's contention.

Cannon constructed a theory, later modified by Philip Bard, saying in essence that, when a person faces an emotion-arousing event, nerve impulses first pass through the thalamus. From there, the theory goes, the message splits: half goes to the cerebral cortex, where it produces the subjective experience of fear or anger or happiness; the other half goes to the hypothalamus, which commands the body's physiological changes. According to the Cannon-Bard theory, the psychological experience of emotion and the physiological reactions are simultaneous (see Figure 8.2).

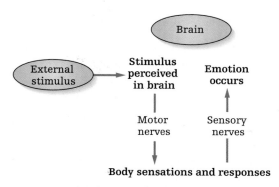

Figure 8.1 The James-Lange theory of emotion holds that the psychological experience of emotion follows the perception of one's own physiological reactions.

The physiology of the Cannon-Bard theory was not correct in its particulars. But it did bring the origination of emotion back into the brain from the peripheral organs, where the James-Lange theory had placed it.

The Papez Circuit

The Cannon-Bard theory focused on the role of the thalamus as a "center" for emotional experience. We know today, thanks largely to the work of anatomist James W. Papez in 1937, that emotion is a function not of specific brain "centers" but of circuitry.

Papez called this circuit the "stream of feeling." He also proposed a "stream of movement," relaying sensations through the thalamus to the corpus striatum, and a "stream of thought," relaying sensations through the thalamus to the major parts of the cerebral cortex. In the merging of these streams, Papez said, "sensory excitations . . . receive their emotional coloring." Papez's contribution stands even today as a basic outline for what scientists know about the neuroanatomy of emotion. Unfortunately, as is often the case with fast-moving sciences such as neuroscience, many of the details of his outline have proved to be incorrect. This is particularly true of the connections between brain structures that Papez originally proposed, which have been shown to be more complex than he ever envisioned. For example, we now know that the fornix (a fiber system described in the next section) is derived from multiple populations of neurons and that the projections of these neurons can act directly and indirectly on the hypothalamus (through direct and indirect connections). Figure 8.3 (on the following page) illustrates this complexity just in the context of fear.

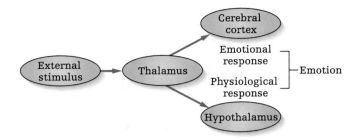

Figure 8.2 The Cannon-Bard theory, in contrast with the James-Lange theory, says that the psychological experience of emotion and the corresponding physiological reactions are simultaneous.

Brain Structures That Mediate Emotion

Many of the structures responsible for the homeostasis and rhythms of the body (see Chapters 6 and 7) also produce emotion, which is not too surprising. A hungry animal must be motivated by aggressive impulses to stalk, attack, and eat a smaller animal, all in the interest of supporting the requirements of its internal systems. At the same time, it must be motivated by fear to stay constantly alert to danger and ready to defend itself against attack by larger predators.

The most important of the brain's structures that produce emotion are called, collectively, the *limbic region* (the term "limbic" simply refers to its position at the inner edge of the brain). This system is also known as the "animal brain" because its parts and functions appear to be essentially alike in all mammals. The limbic region sits above the brainstem and under the cortex. A number of structures in the brainstem and parts of the cortex also participate in producing emotion. All these limbic, cortical, and brainstem structures are connected by neural pathways.

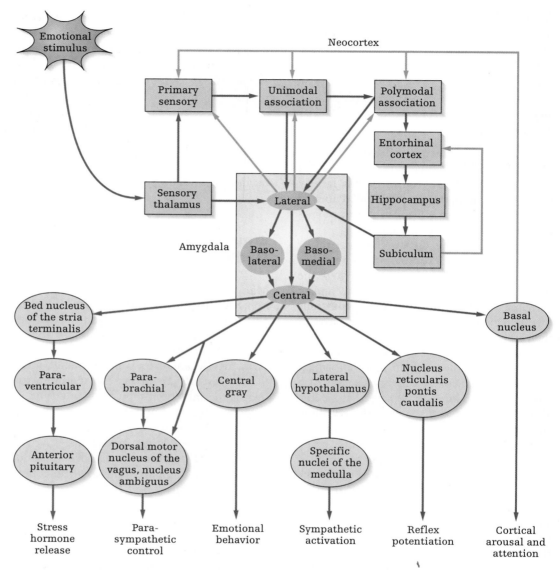

Figure 8.3 A model of the neural circuit for conditioned fear. A hierarchy of incoming sensory information converges on the lateral nucleus of the amygdala. Through intraamygdala circuitry, the output of the lateral nucleus is transmitted to the central nucleus, which serves to activate various effector systems taking part in the expression of emotional responses. Feedforward projections are indicated by solid lines, and feedback projections are indicated by dashed lines.

The Limbic Region

The limbic region includes a number of interconnected structures (see Figure 8.4). For example, certain nuclei in the *anterior thalamus* participate in the limbic alliance. Under that brain region lies the small but potent *hypothalamus,* another participant—the one whose neurons produce the familiar changes in the autonomic nervous system (in heart rate, respiration, and so forth) that accompany strong emotion. Deep in the lateral forebrain lies the *amygdala,* a walnut-sized mass of gray cells. Animal experiments have shown that the amygdala is active in the production of aggressive behavior and fear reactions. In addition, it appears to play a key role in the ability of an animal to recognize facial emotion, particularly negative emotion such as fear, and, as discussed later in this chapter, to play a role in emotional memory. Adjacent to

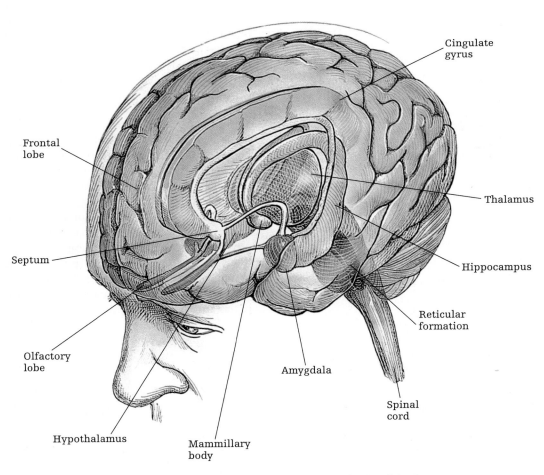

Frontal lobe

Cingulate gyrus

Septum

Thalamus

Olfactory lobe

Hippocampus

Reticular formation

Hypothalamus

Amygdala

Mammillary body

Spinal cord

Figure 8.4 The major structures forming the limbic region of the brain. This view shows their locations around the inner edge, or limbus, of the brain.

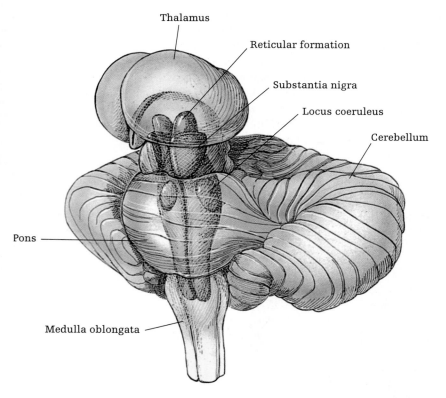

Thalamus

Reticular formation

Substantia nigra

Locus coeruleus

Cerebellum

Pons

Medulla oblongata

Figure 8.5 Structures in the brainstem that play a role in emotion. Dopamine fibers from the substantia nigra and norepinephrine fibers from the locus coeruleus arise to innervate the entire forebrain. Both of these neuron groups and several others form discrete structures contributing to the reticular activating system.

(a term that means "dividing wall" or "membrane"), receives neural input through the fornix from the hippocampus and sends neural output to the hypothalamus.

When we trace the course of the neural pathways in the brain, we can see why all our interactions with our environment have an emotional quality of some sort. Incoming neural messages from all the senses, after traveling through pathways in the brainstem or the various processing levels in the cortex or both, pass through one or more of the limbic structures: the amygdala, the hippocampus, or part of the hypothalamus. Outgoing messages sent down from the cortex also pass through these structures.

Structures in the Brainstem

Within the brainstem, the *reticular formation* plays an important role in emotion (see Figure 8.5). It receives sensory information through various neural pathways and acts as a kind of filter (in fact, "reticulum" means "little net," which the structure resembles) that transmits only information that is novel or persistent. Its fibers project widely to areas of the cerebral cortex, some by way of the thalamus. Most neurons in the reticular formation are thought to be "nonspecific." That is, unlike neurons in a primary sensory pathway (visual or auditory, for example; see Chapter 4), which respond to only one type of stimulus, neurons in the reticular formation can respond to information from many sources. These neurons pass along messages from the eyes, the skin, and the viscera, among other organs and structures, to the limbic region and the cortex.

Some structures within the pons and some midbrain components of the reticular formation have particular functions. The *locus coeruleus*, or "blue area," in the pons is a concentrated collection of cell bodies of neurons

the amygdala is the *hippocampus*, which plays a key role in memory (see Chapters 9 and 10), including emotional memory. Encircling the hippocampus and the other structures of the limbic region is the *cingulate gyrus* ("cingulate" means "girdling" or "encircling"). A two-way fiber system, the *fornix*, follows the curve of the cingulate gyrus and connects the hippocampus to the hypothalamus. Another structure, the *septum*

with single-source–divergent circuitry that secrete the neurotransmitter norepinephrine. As you learned in Chapter 6 in connection with REM sleep, some neural pathways from the locus coeruleus travel up into parts of the thalamus and hypothalamus and many parts of the cortex. Other pathways travel down to the cerebellum and into the spinal cord. The product of these specialized neurons, the transmitter norepinephrine (also secreted as a hormone by the adrenal medulla), triggers emotional arousal. It has been suggested that too little norepinephrine action in the brain results in depression, whereas too much norepinephrine action for too long a time is implicated in severe stress reactions. Norepinephrine may also play a part in producing feelings that an organism experiences as pleasure.

The *substantia nigra,* or "black area," in the midbrain is a concentration of cell bodies of neurons, again of the single-source–divergent type of circuit, that secrete the neurotransmitter dopamine. Among other things, dopamine appears to facilitate some pleasurable sensations, including the exhilaration that people seek in taking cocaine and amphetamines.

The Cerebral Cortex

The parts of the cerebral cortex thought to be most active in emotion are the *frontal lobes,* which receive direct neural projections from the thalamus and amygdala. Because emotion colors thought, the temporal lobes (which coordinate memory with emotion, among other functions) are likely to figure in emotion too, but little is known yet about how the mechanisms linking thought and emotion interact.

The importance of the frontal lobes to temperament and personality has been known since at least 1848. In that year, an explosion blew a 3-foot-long, 13-pound metal rod up through the skull of Phineas Gage, a 25-year-old railroad construction foreman. The accident removed his left frontal lobe. Miraculously, the man survived, but he was greatly changed. Before the accident, Gage had been dependable, industrious, and well liked. When he recovered, he was restless, loud, profane, and impulsive. His doctor described him as "manifesting but little deference for his fellows, impatient of restraint or advice when it conflicts with his desires, at times pertinaciously obstinate, yet capricious and vacillating, devising many plans of future operations, which are no sooner arranged than they are abandoned. . . ." (Harlow, 1868).

It is impossible to reconstruct an exact clinical picture of this case after the fact. Part of Gage's character change may have been an emotional reaction to his damaged looks. Indeed, he did travel around for a while with P. T. Barnum, carrying his rod and displaying himself as a freak. But subsequent scientific evidence has shown that the frontal lobes, perhaps because of their associations with the thalamus, play an important part in emotional experience and expression. Indeed, one critical role thought to be played by the prefrontal cortex, the *orbitoprefrontal cortex* in particular, is in inhibition. Thus, although the amygdala is thought to be the seat of emotion, it is the prefrontal cortex that is instrumental in regulating the emotion produced by the amygdala. Researchers Hanna and Antonio Damasio and their colleagues were able to reconstruct Gage's injury by using modern neuroimaging techniques. These scientists took detailed x rays of Phineas Gage's skull, which had been preserved (subsequent, we should add, to the exhumation of his body 5 years after burial). What they observed was quite consistent with the picture that was painted of Gage's injury by John

Harlow, a physician who reexamined the case 20 years after Gage's death. Harlow argued that the damage to Gage's brain must have been restricted to the frontal lobe. What the Damasios reported was even more precise than that: the area of the frontal lobes most affected was the orbitoprefrontal cortex, whereas the motor cortex, including Broca's area (an area in the frontal lobe involved in speech), was spared. Thus, there was no damage to the amygdala itself, but there was a disconnection between the prefrontal cortex and the amygdala, thereby permitting the amygdala to produce emotion that then went unchecked. (Some of this damage is illustrated in the adjoining reconstruction of Gage's skull and brain.)

Much is known about the anatomy of these limbic, brainstem, and cortical structures and the neural pathways that connect them to each other and to other parts of the brain and nervous system. But exactly how they function in emotion—especially human emotion—is still largely a matter of inference.

The Role of the Autonomic Nervous System in Emotion

The brain does its work through its control

Phineas Gage's accident took place on September 13, 1848.

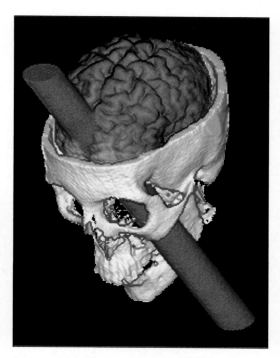

A computerized reconstruction of Phineas Gage's skull after the accident. Note the damage to the frontal lobe.

Strong emotions may include pleasure or pain and arise from the numerous interactions of daily life.

of the body's systems. The arousal that you experience with fear or rage is triggered by your brain, but it is implemented by your autonomic nervous system.

The *autonomic nervous system* has two anatomically distinct divisions (see Figure 6.1): the *sympathetic division* mobilizes the body's resources and energy—the "fight or flight" response; the *parasympathetic division* generally works to conserve bodily energy and resources. As you have learned, the two divisions work together, even though their functions may seem antagonistic. The balance among their various activities at any given moment depends on an interaction between the demands of the external situation and the body's internal state.

To illustrate how the two divisions work in emotion, suppose that you have just finished eating a big meal. The parasympathetic nerves slow your heart rate and enhance your digestive activity. But if a stranger suddenly breaks into your dining room—or even if you merely hear an unusual noise outside the window—your sympathetic nerves take over. Your digestive processes slow down; your heart rate increases; blood is diverted from arteries in the skin and digestive organs to provide more oxygen to muscles and brain; your lungs expand to take in more oxygen; the pupils of your eyes dilate to let in more light; and your sweat glands become active, preparing to cool your body during its coming exertion. Activation of the sympathetic nervous system also causes your adrenal medulla to secrete epinephrine (sometimes called adrenaline) and causes other sympathetic nerves to release the transmitter norepinephrine, which acts directly on the heart and blood vessels. Together, these chemical signals tell the circulatory system to increase blood pressure. Epinephrine circulating through the blood increases heart rate and heart output directly. Norepinephrine released from the sympathetic nerves constricts certain blood vessels, decreasing the volume of blood going to areas not essential for quick response—the gut, skin, and kidneys—and increasing blood flow to areas that must prepare the brain and the muscles for action.

When a person is faced with an event that calls for mobilization, the ANS responds within 1 to 2 seconds, which may seem very fast. But consider what happens when you see a car in front of you on the highway come to a sudden stop. In less than $\frac{1}{2}$ second you automatically step on your brake, and you have probably also checked your rearview mirror to see the proximity of the car behind you. The experience of arousal—the pounding heart, shaking hands, and so forth—comes after the emergency is over. Your brain apparently dealt with the situation without help from the elaborate but relatively slow backup equipment.

This timing difference is due to a difference in "wiring." The hierarchical neural pathways from the sensory receptors to the cortex and back are fairly direct. The messages go through the reticular system, through the thalamus, and up to the cortex. Within a split second you take appropriate action: you step on the brake. Meanwhile, the same messages are also going on a longer journey, along neural pathways connecting the thalamus and hypothalamus and those connecting the hypothalamus and the frontal region of the cortex by way of the amygdala and hippocampus. If these systems all agree that danger is imminent, the hypothalamus sets off the ANS arousal mechanisms, which go into effect after a second or so. The hormonal messages from the now-alerted pituitary are blood-borne, however, and travel more slowly than messages speeding along neural pathways. Hence the delay in physiological response. In regard to species adaptation, the arousal occurred in time to help you to fight, to flee, or to take other action had the danger been an attack. That may explain why so many fender benders are followed by vociferous arguments about who was to blame.

The emotional reaction that follows a fender bender has an obvious cause. But it sometimes happens that we feel anxious or uneasy or exalted without having had, in the immediate past, some experience that we can point to as the cause of that feeling. The James-Lange theory says that we examine our physiological reactions and decide from them what emotion we feel. The studies described in the next section examine the role of cognition in the experience of emotion.

Cognition and Emotion

In 1924, Gregorio Maranon published an important but essentially anecdotal study bearing on emotion. When he injected patients with epinephrine, Maranon wrote, about one-third of them said that they experienced something like an emotional state. The rest said that they felt no emotion but described a physiological state of arousal. The people who reported feeling emotional, however, carefully specified that they felt "as if" they were afraid or "as if" something exciting were about to happen. When Maranon happened to talk with a few of these people about some important life event in their recent past—a death in the family or an upcoming wedding—their feeling lost its "as if" status and became full emotion,

whether grief or joy.

On the basis of Maranon's report and other evidence, Stanley Schachter theorized that, to experience an emotion, both physiological arousal and a cognitive evaluation must be necessary. Neither one alone could produce a true emotional state.

In the best known of Schachter's experiments testing this hypothesis, some subjects received an injection of epinephrine, which they were told contained vitamins that would have an effect on visual skills. Control subjects received only a placebo, a saline injection, which they too were told contained vitamins. After the injection, subjects from both groups were treated in one of three ways:

1. Some were told about the physiological effects of epinephrine. That is, without naming epinephrine, the researchers warned them that they might feel palpitations, tremors, and the like.

2. Others were given no information.

3. Still others were misinformed. They were told that their hands and feet might feel numb, for example, or that they might have a slight itch or a headache.

After the injection and the explanation, each subject waited in a room with a person who claimed to be a subject in the same experiment but who was actually a *confederate*—part of the experimental setup. Some confederates behaved euphorically, chuckling to themselves, playing basketball with the wastebasket, and so forth. Others were highly irritable and insulting, acting increasingly angry until finally leaving the room in a fit of rage.

The experimenters observed the pairs through a one-way mirror, and later they questioned the subjects about their feelings.

The epinephrine-injected subjects who had been informed correctly about the drug's effects showed and reported the least reaction to the confederate's behavior. Those who had been misinformed, who had physiological symptoms different from those they had been told to expect, were most influenced. Each began to act like the confederate in the waiting room and reported that they felt very happy or very angry, depending on the confederate with whom they had been paired. Those who received no information after injection also imitated the emotions displayed by the confederates, but to a much lesser extent.

These results appear to confirm Schachter's thesis. If physiological arousal is induced (by injection or by an event) in someone who has no immediate explanation for it, the person will give an emotional label to the induced state based on his or her perception of what is going on at the time.

A 1966 study of patients who had suffered spinal-cord injuries lends support to Schachter's thesis. Subjects were divided into five groups according to how high on the spinal cord the injury was. (The higher the damage, the less visceral sensation a person experiences.) Then the patients were asked to compare the emotional reactions they had had before their injuries with those they had afterward. Those patients with injuries high on the spinal cord reported the greatest difference in their before-and-after emotional reactions, whether the reaction was grief, fear, or joy. In fact, their descriptions of emotional states after injury resembled those given by Maranon's subjects: the subjects reported feeling "as if" they were afraid or "as if" they were joyful. Maranon's subjects had these "almost" feelings when they had no appropriate cognitive cues to help them interpret their physiological arousal. The patients who suffered injuries to the spinal cord experienced the "as if" feelings even though the right cognitive cues were there, because they were not capable of feeling any physiological arousal.

Other findings also support the conclusion that, in human beings, the thinking and learning areas of the brain interact with the limbic region to influence emotion. The psychologist George Mandler makes the point that even events that would seem to trigger "wired in" autonomic responses in us—a sudden loss of support for our weight, for example—can be modified by our cognitive analysis of the event. Some people react euphorically to the feeling of the ground falling out from under them on a roller coaster. The same people, experiencing the same feeling of release from gravity when an airplane suddenly drops in an air pocket, would probably be terrified. One difference between these reactions lies in our sense of whether we are in control of the situation. If you choose to ride on the roller coaster, you expect the sensations, and you have some sense of control. As an airplane passenger, you are—and feel—helpless if the plane drops. This particular cognitive factor—the belief that one has some control of a situation—turns out to be significant not only in emotional arousal, but also in the experience of pain and stress, as discussed in later sections of this chapter. The interaction of cognitive and physiological arousal is also related to another phenomenon: the keenness with which we remember emotionally charged events (as distinct from our ability to remember events that have no emotional context or theme).

Neuroscientist James McGaugh and his colleagues suggested that emotional arousal activates the amygdala, which in turn modulates the function of the hippocampus. For example, in a stressful situation (such as preparing for a forthcoming test), the brain releases glucocorticoids and epinephrine, which influence memory storage through their effects on the amygdala (the basolateral nucleus in particular). Patients with damage to the amygdala but not the hippocampus often appear to have intact memory for nonemotionally arousing events and relatively poor memory for emotionally arousing ones. Thus, there are strong ties between the cognitive (memory) functions subserved by the hippocampus and the emotional functions subserved by the amygdala.

Of all the research on emotion, perhaps the studies receiving most attention have been on aggression, the topic to which we turn next.

Aggression

Animal studies performed in the past four or five decades have given rise to a vast body of literature on what has been called "aggression." Like emotion in general, aggression is difficult to define. Some earlier theories assumed that aggression was a unitary concept—that animals possessed an aggressive drive or instinct and that it operated pretty much the same way in all members of a species and under all circumstances. Instead, experiments eventually showed that, even in mice and rats, "aggression" differs from individual to individual and from one situation to another.

The different types of aggressive behaviors found in animals include:

1. *Predatory aggression*—a hungry animal stalks and kills the prey that it feeds on.

2. *Competitive aggression*—males of a species threaten or attack each other for position in a dominance hierarchy—for females or for food.

3. *Defensive aggression*—an animal faced with an inescapable threat responds with fear-motivated threat or attack.

4. *Irritative aggression*—a laboratory animal threatens or attacks in response to some aversive stimulus, such as an electric shock.

5. *Territorial aggression*—an animal actively responds to an intruder violating the boundaries of the group's or its own established living area.

6. *Maternal protective aggression*—a female threatens or attacks another animal perceived as endangering her infants.

7. *Female social aggression*—a female attacks a juvenile or a strange female.

8. *Sex-related aggression*—a male whose normal sexual advances have been rebuffed turns and attacks the female who rebuffed him.

9. *Instrumental aggression*—an animal repeats threat or attack behavior that has worked in the past to achieve a similar outcome; for example, the dominant monkey in a hierarchy might use threats to affirm and consolidate his position even when no other animal is being provocative or competitive.

Electrode Studies

Early research using implanted electrodes pointed to the hypothalamus as the brain site responsible for aggression.

In the early 1950s, W. R. Hess, a Swiss neuroscientist and Nobel Prize winner, conducted the pioneering studies using electrode placement. Hess found that, when he stimulated a specific area of a cat's hypothalamus, the cat showed behaviors typical of aggression in the face of threat: it spat and growled, it lashed its tail, it extended its claws, and its fur stood on end (see Figure 8.6). The subject showed all the behaviors shown by any cat when confronted by a barking dog—but in the absence of a dog or any other environmental cues. Neural activities alone, arising from the hypothalamus, appeared to produce this expression of fear-provoked aggression.

Undoubtedly, the most dramatic exhibition of electrical stimulation apparently affecting emotional behavior was staged by Jose Delgado. He implanted an electrode in the hypothalamus of a bull bred specifically to fight aggressively in the ring. Delgado claimed that stimulation would turn off the bull's aggression. Standing in the bullring himself at the moment of the bull's charge, Delgado pushed the button that fired the electrode. The bull stopped in its tracks. However, a one-time study with just one subject offers drama but little in the way of scientific verification.

Later electrode studies indicated that stimulation of different areas of the hypothalamus and parts of the amygdala can elicit behaviors typical of one or more of the nine types of aggression described in the preceding section. Nevertheless, the interactions of these structures are quite complex, and no complete picture has yet emerged of how the parts interact in stimulating or inhibiting aggressive behaviors in animals, especialy as animals behave in their natural environments.

Hormones

Hormones also appear to play a part in aggressive activity. In most species, males are more aggressive than females, a characteristic that seems to result from the organizational effect of prenatal androgen on the developing brain (see Chapter 3). Female animals injected prenatally with androgen become more aggressive than other females when they are given androgens later in life. If females have had no prenatal exposure to the hormone, an injection of androgens later in life has no effect on aggressive behavior.

It is important to note, however, that the nature of the link between hormones and aggressive behavior is unclear. For example, although males with very high levels of circulating testosterone are reported to be more aggressive than those with lower levels of testosterone (a relation observed in adolescent males as well as in adult males), there are also data to suggest that dominance and achievement status in general correlate with high levels of testosterone. For example, a study of testosterone levels in male judo competitors seemed to show that the highest levels accounted for success

Jose Delgado stops the charge of a fighting bull by sending a pulse through the electrode implanted in the bull's hypothalamus.

Figure 8.6 With an electrode implanted in one area of its hypothalamus, this cat postures aggressively when electrical stimulation is applied (Hess, 1957).

in competition. Similarly, in a sample of 13-year-old boys, a strong relation was found between testosterone and social dominance, but not between testosterone and aggression in particular. Thus, boys rated as both tough and social leaders had the highest levels of the hormone, even though these boys were not rated as particularly aggressive. In contrast, boys rated as tough but *not* leaders had levels no greater than nontough boys.

Neurotransmitters

Neuroscientists were able to breed mice for high levels of aggressive behavior. They selected a strain of mice notable for its willingness to attack a strange but docile neutral mouse and then bred the most aggressive of these mice so that the trait grew stronger generation after generation.

When compared with mice from the original generation, the later-born, more aggressive mice were found to have a somewhat lower brain concentration of the neurotransmitter serotonin (one of the transmitters implicated in human depression; see Chapter 13). This finding is supported by studies in which experimental animals are given drugs that deplete the brain's ability to make serotonin; these animals become more likely to attack neutral targets. In other experiments, when certain serotonin-rich tracts in the brains of cats were electrically stimulated, the cats showed intense rage during the stimulation period.

Similar findings have been observed in humans. For example, depressed patients who commit suicide by violent means (such as guns) have been found to have lower levels of serotonin. Likewise, children with conduct disorder or oppositional defiant disorder have been observed to have lower levels

of this transmitter than those of healthy control subjects. Although serotonin appears to play some part in aggression, many other transmitter systems and circuits probably take part as well. For example, rats bred for their willingness to attack mice are found to have increased blood levels of the enzymes that produce norepinephrine and epinephrine, the circulating hormones released by the adrenal medulla. (In contrast, when norepinephrine in the brain is measured after electrode stimulation to the brain has produced aggression, its level is lower than before the stimulation.) Aggressive behavior is also more likely after normal animals are given some of the drugs used to treat human depression. These drugs work in part by prolonging the effects of norepinephrine in the brain. (To refresh your memory about serotonin, norepinephrine, and other neurotransmitters, see Chapter 2.)

Animal Studies and Human Aggression

Aggression, as we have seen, is variable enough in animals. In human beings, the behaviors that might be classified as aggressive are so variable that no classification is likely to be sufficiently comprehensive. In fact, some scientists feel that aggression in human beings should be considered apart from aggression in other animals.

When you consider the most damaging sorts of human aggression—the Nazi policy of exterminating whole population groups, for example, which required the full-time support of an immense bureaucracy devoted to filling out order forms for poison-gas dispensers and keeping the trains full of victims running on time—it appears somewhat fruitless to try to find animal models for such behavior. In fact, as Nobel Prize–winning philosopher and writer Arthur Koestler

(1969) suggests, "The trouble with our species is not an overdose of self-asserting aggression but an excess of self-transcending devotion, which manifests itself in blind obedience and loyalty to the king, country, or cause. . . . One of the central features of the human predicament is this overwhelming capacity and need for identification with a social group and/or system of beliefs, which is indifferent to reason, indifferent to self-interest, and even to the claim of self-preservation." Although many animals have similar needs for social affiliation, none possess them to the degree of our own species.

Pain

Pain is not an emotion, but painful sensations can undoubtedly *elicit* emotions. Like emotion, pain usually energizes an organism into action. Just as fear prepares you to fight or flee, pain signals you, in no uncertain terms, to break contact with a potentially damaging agent and to begin restoring the injured part.

A very small number of people are insensitive to pain, and they often suffer severe tissue damage from cuts and burns. One such woman died at an early age of spinal damage because she did not receive the normal discomfort signals from her joints telling her to change her posture—she never moved in her sleep, for example.

How Pain Is Sensed

Pain receptors in human beings are located in the skin, in sheath tissue surrounding muscles, in internal organs, and in the membranes around bone. These receptors in animals are called *nociceptors* (from the same root as that for "noxious," meaning harmful

or destructive) rather than pain receptors, because neuroscientists cannot, with certainty, establish that what an animal feels is pain. Animals, after all, cannot say what they feel. Adult human beings can report pain reliably, so the nerve endings that sense pain are called "pain receptors." (The reader will recognize that this is a paradox: we know what pain is because we have all experienced physical damage and the sensations that go with it, yet none of us can know exactly how somebody else experiences the same kinds of damage— do they hurt more or less than we do? Nevertheless, we are generally more confident in interpreting emotional signals, including pain, from members of our own species than from members of other species.)

Pain receptors and nociceptors have a much higher threshold for firing than do receptors for temperature and touch and react mainly to physical stimuli that distort them or to chemical stimuli that, in essence, "irritate" them into activity. Inflamed joints or sore, torn muscles produce natural substances called *prostaglandins,* which irritate the receptors and cause the experience of traumatic pain. Drugs such as aspirin and other over-the-counter pain treatments seem to fight pain by acting to stop the body's synthesis of prostaglandins.

The simplest responses to noxious stimuli take place reflexively—that is, the impulses travel only to the spinal cord, which commands the muscles to make a quick response. If you step on a thorn while walking barefoot, impulses from receptors at the injury site activate the flexion withdrawal reflex, and you lift your foot. (Meanwhile, the crossed-extension reflex causes you to straighten the other leg, taking your weight off the injured foot—see Chapter 5 for a refresher on this aspect of the motor system.) Other branches of the same sensory neuron that contains the pain receptors synapse on an intermediate neuron, which sends the message to your brain for processing. But you will have lifted your foot before your brain registers any pain message.

Pain receptors in the skin are excited by cuts and scrapes, heat, chemical substances released when tissue is damaged, and lack of proper blood circulation to an area. Most of these receptors are not specific: they can respond to several noxious stimuli. It also appears that they can signal not only the presence of a stimulus, but also its location and its intensity.

The action of most pain receptors within the body is less well charted. The workings of a few are known, such as lung-irritant receptors that signal pulmonary congestion or the presence of dust particles.

Pain Pathways to the Brain

Two different neural pathways transmit pain messages to the brain. One is a system of myelinated, fast-conducting, thin fibers that give a sensation of fast, bright pain (see Figure 8.7). The other is a system of unmyelinated, slow-conducting fibers that produce diffuse, nagging pain.

In the spinal cord, the fibers of the *fast pathway* connect directly with the thalamus, where they make synaptic connections with fibers that project to motor and sensory areas of the cortex. This system appears to allow the organism to discover exactly where the injury is, how serious the damage is, and how long the pain has been going on.

The fibers of the *slow pathway* project to the reticular formation, the medulla, the pons, the midbrain, the hypothalamus, and the thalamus. Some fibers contact neurons that connect with the hypothalamus and amygdala, whereas other fibers connect with diffuse neural networks to many other parts of the brain. The many synapses in this system, the lack of myelination of its neurons, and the narrow diameter of its conducting pathways explain its slower speed.

The fast system may function as a warning system, providing immediate information about the presence of injury, its extent, and its location. The unpleasant, nagging pain characteristic of the slower system may serve to remind the brain that an injury has occurred, that normal activity should be restricted, and that continued attention is required.

In a way, the fast system is "free of emotion," whereas the slower timing of the other system allows the injured person to attribute qualities to the painful sensation. Apparently, both the limbic region and prefrontal cortex mediate this emotional coloration (in addition to collaborating in other emotions, as we have seen). Patients who have undergone a frontal lobotomy, an operation that severs the connections between the frontal lobes and the thalamus, rarely complain about severe pain or ask for medication. In fact, they typically report after the operation that they have pain but that it does not "bother" them. Phineas Gage, you recall, appeared to suffer little pain after the accident that severely damaged his frontal lobe, despite the enormous physical damage that he sustained. Patients under hypnosis also can acknowledge that something is painful, yet they, too, report that the pain does not bother them. The neural mechanism for this phenomenon is not known but is likely to be a means of "turning off" the frontal lobe.

Chemical Transmission and Inhibition of Pain

An important synaptic relay in the transmission of pain impulses to the brain takes place in the parts of the spinal cord called

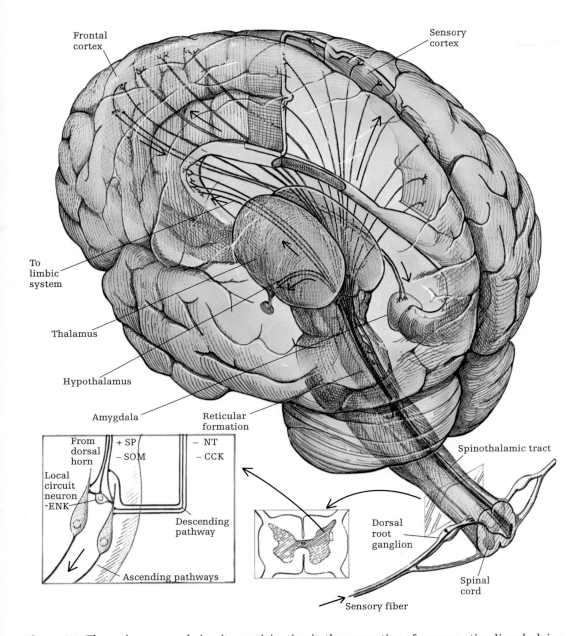

Figure 8.7 The major neuronal circuits participating in the perception of sensory stimuli underlying the experience of pain extend from sensory receptors in the skin through synaptic relays in the spinal cord, thalamus, sensory cortex, and limbic region. The arrows indicate the paths taken by sensory information moving along the fast, or specific, pathway. Information moving along the slow, or nonspecific, pathway is disseminated largely through fibers in the reticular formation.

the *dorsal horns,* the gray matter forming a butterfly-like outline within the cord's white matter. Many fibers from pain receptors synapse there with other ascending neurons. Discharges of these spinal neurons can be 10 times as strong as the discharge of a single pain receptor, indicating that the dorsal horns provide a place where many of the fibers from receptors of the slow pathway converge. These spinal fibers also display a buildup of responsiveness during painful stimulation, and their high level of activity can continue for as long as 100 seconds after the painful stimulus has been removed.

The buildup of responsiveness, along with the continuation of firing after removal of the stimulus, indicated to some researchers the presence of a neurotransmitter that, after release, is inactivated relatively slowly. The transmitter, a neuropeptide called *substance P,* has now been isolated. Found in neurons on each side of the spinal cord, substance P appears to be a specialized transmitter that relays pain-related information from peripheral pain receptors to the central system. It is also widely distributed in neurons in the brain, so it probably has other functions as well.

Luckily for us, the mammalian nervous system not only manufactures a substance that transmits pain sensations, but also provides us with painkillers. In 1972, researchers studying the biological basis of drug addiction began to identify the precise locations of receptor sites where opium and its derivatives, morphine and heroin, produce their specific effects on animal and human brains. What were these receptors doing in the body? Surely there could be no evolutionary advantage in a mammalian addiction to drugs. The most likely explanation for the existence of such receptors was that the body itself produces opiate-like

substances and that these substances work through receptors that morphine only borrows. In fact, a number of such natural opiates have now been identified. They are called *opioid peptides* or *endorphins,* the latter coined from the phrase "endogenous morphine" (which means a morphine produced by the body).

Early in the 1960s, psychologists at McGill University, Ronald Melzack and Patrick Wall, investigated the fact that acupuncture subjects generally report little pain or discomfort from the insertion of the needles. From there, they conjectured that the kind of stimulation caused by the needles' insertion triggers impulses in the reticular formation that travel down the spinal cord and, in essence, close a spinal "gate," shutting down the perception of pain. Their elaboration of this work led to what is called the *gate-control* theory of pain. Although Melzack subsequently abandoned the original conception of the gate-control theory, we now know that the turning on and off of pain signals is a chemical process that is probably the work of endorphins.

Both endorphins and opiates, such as heroin, are believed to work in the following way to regulate the perception of pain. A pain signal starts impulses up the spinal cord, through the slow pain pathway just described. These neurons contain substance P and synapse onto neurons in the dorsal horns within the spinal cord (see Figure 8.7 on page 257). When substance P is released at these synapses, the neurons that are sensitive to it transmit the pain message to the brain. However, the dorsal horns also house endorphin-containing neurons, which synapse onto the substance P-releasing neurons. When these dorsal-horn neurons release endorphin, it inhibits the release of substance P. Thus the receiving neuron at the

Pain is blocked in a variety of ways. Marathon runners may gain relief through a pathway that does not include endorphins but is integrated at the highest levels of the nervous system. Evidence shows that pain relief provided by acupuncture comes from endorphins that the body produces in response to the punctures.

synapse gets less stimulation because it now receives less substance P, and fewer pain impulses go to the brain.

Endorphin-containing neurons and opiate-receptor sites exist in many other areas of the nervous system as well. One such area, which lies along the slow pain pathway, is the *periaqueductal gray* area, a cluster of neurons lying in the thalamus and pons. Injection of morphine directly into the periaqueductal gray reduces pain. Electrical stimulation there causes endorphins to be released and produces relief. In fact, stimulation by means of implanted electrodes has been used experimentally to treat people suffering from pain that does not respond to any other treatment.

Scientists have been able to study the action and its location of both manufactured and natural opiates by using the antagonist drug naloxone. The shape of naloxone molecules allows them to bind to opiate-receptor sites, although the drug itself has no painkilling properties. When naloxone occupies an opiate-receptor site, neither an opiate nor an endorphin can get in to activate the receptor (see Figure 8.8). None of the pain-inhibiting activities that would normally take place at those synapses can therefore take place. Naloxone is often given to heroin addicts who have overdosed, to halt the action of the heroin.

Researchers looking into the pain-killing properties of cells in the periaqueductal gray area first electrically stimulated that area in laboratory mice. They saw that mice so stimulated became relatively insensitive to the pain of being placed on a hot surface; at least they did not run away. When naloxone was administered before the electrical stimulation, however, the mice were more sensitive than normal to the heat-produced pain. These observations suggested that the elec-

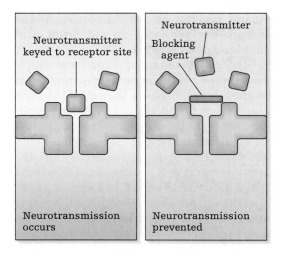

Neurotransmitter keyed to receptor site

Neurotransmission occurs

Neurotransmitter

Blocking agent

Neurotransmission prevented

Figure 8.8 Neurotransmitters and their antagonist drugs act through the same receptors. *Left:* The neurotransmitter molecule fits the receptor-recognition site precisely. *Right:* In the presence of an antagonist drug, the neurotransmitter molecules are denied access to the receptor. In practice, antagonist drugs often bind more tightly to the receptor than do transmitter molecules, thus preventing transmission for long periods of time.

trical stimulation of the periaqueductal gray had caused endorphins to be released and that naloxone occupied the receptor sites that the endorphins would have otherwise found. Other studies of the periaqueductal gray matter have revealed that cells located in this area contain high amounts of endogenous opioid.

Studies using radioactively labeled opiate drugs have shown that opiate receptors populate the limbic region in high concentrations. The discovery of these receptors in the limbic region amounts to a physical confirmation of the psychological hypothesis that the perception of pain comprises both the sensation of pain and an emotional reaction

to the sensation. The euphoria so desired by heroin users probably arises from the binding of the drug to sites in the limbic region. The fact that heroin and endorphins bind to the same sites in the limbic region suggests that endorphins also play a role in aspects of emotion not directly related to pain.

The Role of Endorphins in Pain and Emotion

The role of endorphins in modulating pain seems clear. Although the perception of pain is necessary to warn us of danger to flesh and bone, constant intense pain would incapacitate us. Endorphins regulate the degree of pain that we feel, enabling us to remove ourselves from the pain inducer and to begin nursing any wounds. Endorphins seem to play a similar modulating role in emotions. The arousal that occurs during fear or rage can be so intense that it prevents animals or people from behaving in ways that would save them from injury or loss. Endorphins seem to modulate the arousal so that the organism can more readily adapt its behavior to the situation.

Research into the nervous system's use of endorphins is in its infancy, and evidence concerning the role of endorphins in emotion is scarce. It does appear, though, that fear can call endorphins into action. Mice trained to expect that a certain warning signal would be followed by an electric shock evidently released endorphins at the sound of the signal, even when no shock followed. Fear of the pain seemed to be sufficient to make a mouse's nervous system prepare for its onslaught.

A number of other studies have also shown that stress and anxiety can cause the release of endorphins from neural circuits in experimental animals. For example, their "perception of pain," as measured by their movement away from a pain-inducing stimulus, declines after stress causes them to secrete endorphins. Perhaps human beings do the same sort of thing. It would be nice to think that the sight of a dentist's drill, for instance, could cause streams of endorphins to rush to our aid. In one study using human subjects, pain to the foot in the form of electric shocks was evaluated not by subjective means—by people recounting how much it hurt—but by measuring the reflex actions of leg muscles, the muscles that react when you step on a thorn, for example. The experimenters introduced stress into this situation by sounding a warning signal 2 minutes before a shock might or might not be delivered. The subjects were tested under three conditions: (1) with no injection (control condition), (2) with injection of a painkiller, and (3) with injection of naloxone. The initial pain-reflex sensitivity was identical under all three conditions. But repeated stress—hearing the warning signal several times—caused sensitivity to decrease under both the no-injection and the painkiller-injection conditions. This result indicated that the subjects had indeed produced endorphins under stress. Proof of endorphin action came from the finding that, with the naloxone injection, pain-reflex sensitivity immediately increased by 30 percent. In other words, when naloxone occupied the endorphin receptor sites, no modulation of the pain by stress-induced endorphins was possible.

Some people's everyday experience of stress or fear is so extreme and unfounded that it is considered symptomatic of mental disorder. These *anxiety disorders* include the *phobias*—extreme, irrational fears of particular objects or situations. People who suffer from claustrophobia, fear of enclosed spaces, cannot get on elevators, for instance, without suffering severe anxiety.

Just thinking about the objects of such fears causes victims to experience arousal of the autonomic nervous system: racing heart, sweating, dry mouth. Some researchers believe that these people may not experience the normal regulation of arousal provided by endorphins. We will examine the experience of anxiety again in this chapter and in Chapter 12.

Individual Perception of Pain

Pain perception, like most functions of the brain, is a complex phenomenon that differs from person to person and, within any single person, from time to time. The pain experience depends partly on physiology. Some rare people never feel any pain at all, whereas, at the opposite extreme, others who are perhaps deficient in endorphin production feel extreme pain from even minor bumps or scrapes. Physiological differences aside, however, the way in which a person experiences pain depends on past experience—on what that person has learned from his or her culture and family. It depends on the meaning that the person assigns to a pain-inducing event. And it depends on such moment-to-moment psychological factors as attentiveness, anxiety, and suggestability.

Cultural learning, or *socialization*, clearly shapes human perception of pain. In some societies, women do not dread childbirth; they go about their business until shortly before a baby is born, have the baby, and go back to their tasks a few hours later. In other societies, women have learned to expect terrible pain and so they have it, as if childbirth were a severe illness. The Lamaze method of training for "natural childbirth" starts with the premise that women in most Western cultures have been conditioned to expect pain in childbirth and to fear it. The fear produces changes in their muscle tone and breathing patterns that hamper the process and make it more painful. The Lamaze method teaches breathing control and provides exercises to strengthen pelvic muscles. It also explains the entire process of birth so that women know what to expect. Thus, learning, which takes place in the higher cortical regions, can modify the experience of pain, just as it modifies the experience of emotion.

Learning appears to modulate the experience of pain in nonhuman animals as well. In one of a series of conditioning experiments begun at the beginning of the twentieth century, Ivan Pavlov discovered that when dogs were consistently given food immediately after an electric shock to the foot—a shock strong enough to cause the dogs to react violently before conditioning—the animals stopped showing any signs of pain. Instead, they salivated and wagged their tails after the shock.

Even mere suggestion can alter pain perception. When *placebos*—nonactive sugar or salt pills or injections—are given to experimental subjects who believe they are being given a painkiller, some people actually experience pain relief. Just the expectation of relief appears to cause the release of endorphins.

Other currently accumulating evidence points to the existence of pain-relief systems within the body that are separate from the endorphin system. The first work suggesting the existence of nonendorphin pain-relief systems was done by D. S. Mayer. When testing the pain-relief and anesthetic effects of acupuncture, Mayer found (1) that acupuncture does produce such effects and (2) that, because these effects can be blocked by naloxone, they are the work of endorphins. But, when he then tested the effects of hypnosis, a powerful form of suggestion, he found (1) that it, too, produces protection

from pain and (2) that naloxone does *not* block its effects. Mayer suggested that hypnosis works through another pain-relief pathway, integrated at the highest levels of the nervous system and including cognitive and memory factors.

Perhaps this pain-relief pathway is put to use by people such as long-distance runners or football players, whose intense concentration on their goals enables them to ignore or subdue pain. Ballet dancers, too, can execute triumphant performances on bloody feet. But research into this pathway has only begun.

What is more baffling in many cases is the experience of chronic pain. On the one hand, there are persons suffering intractable but understandable pain as a result of a debilitating accident or illness; some cancers serve as examples. But there are also mysterious cases in which, say, a person has been treated for an injury—a broken neck or back, for example—with seeming success and yet continues to experience pain long after the injury has healed. Such cases led Ronald Melzack to revise his gate-control theory. Although Melzack acknowledges that many forms of pain originate in signals coming through a spinal-cord gate, he also feels that, ultimately, the brain generates the experience of pain. Moreover, the brain can generate pain even in the absence of external stimuli. Melzack postulated the existence of what he calls "neuromodules," little pain centers in the brain that, when stimulated exogenously (that is, through external events) or endogenously (internally), give rise to the experience of pain. These neuromodules are not pieces of neural tissue; rather, they are neural networks that link several brain regions, including cognitive and emotional regions as well as sensory regions. When some stimulus (again, either externally or internally generated) passes the threshold of the neuromodule, pain is experienced.

Pleasure

Like pain, pleasure in animals can only be inferred from their behavior. If a stimulus is rewarding, animals will quickly learn whatever tasks are required to give them access to that reward. (Pain also produces quick learning; animals need very few trials to learn how to avoid aversive, pain-giving stimuli.)

In 1953, neuroscientist James Olds and his colleagues used electrodes to stimulate an area of a rat's hypothalamus. The animal not only quickly learned to press a lever to receive the stimulation but, once having learned, continued to press the lever—as many as several thousand times per hour for 10 hours. Because the rat worked so hard to produce the experience, its behavior has

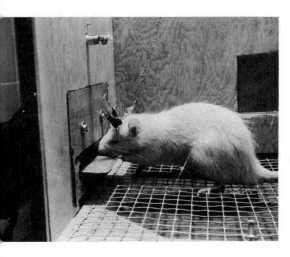

h an electrode implanted in an area of the othalamus that has come to be known as a asure center," this rat pushes a lever to apply trical stimulation to its own brain.

been taken to mean that it "liked" the feeling. Certain areas of the hypothalamus therefore came to be called "pleasure centers."

Subsequent studies of pleasure centers in animals have identified a number of areas that cause animals to work for repeated stimulation. This "reward pathway" follows virtually the same route as that of the dopamine-transmitting neurons from the substantia nigra and the norepinephrine-transmitting neurons from the locus coeruleus. Because stimulation by electrodes is known to increase the synthesis and release of these two neurotransmitters, it may be fair to infer that one or both of them are activated by the electrical stimuli that produce the rewarding sensations in rats. However, it is not possible to conclude that these circuits actually "produce" the sensation.

Some researchers, hypothesizing that endorphins have a role in the experience of pleasure (as well as in the abatement of pain), have used naloxone to see whether normal people, enjoying normal activities that they consider pleasurable, owed any of this pleasure to endorphins. Each subject is brought into a laboratory setting and invited to engage in activities that he or she likes. Some eat good food; some listen to their favorite music. Those who are runners run on treadmills to the point of getting the runner's "high"; some are asked to masturbate. The subjects are asked to repeat the pleasurable experience on more than one occasion; each time, before beginning the activity, they receive an injection, sometimes of naloxone and sometimes of a placebo. The subjects do not know which is which.

Later, the subjects are asked to rate their pleasurable sensations. If endorphins play a major role in their pleasurable reactions, their reported enjoyment under naloxone should be less intense. But the subjects' reports do not differentiate between the naloxone and placebo conditions. Evidently, endorphins are not a major contributor to everyday pleasures.

For a number of reasons, much less has been learned about the positive emotions—the highs—than about the negative ones—the lows. Recently, however, work by psychologist and neuroscientist Richie Davidson at the University of Wisconsin revealed that the experience of positive emotion is represented in the brain differently from the experience of negative emotion. Using electroencephalographic recordings, Davidson observed that the left prefrontal cortex is activated during the experience of positive emotion (including pleasure), whereas the right prefrontal cortex is activated during the experience of negative emotion. Interestingly, people who suffer from depression have, on the whole, greater right hemisphere activation relative to left hemisphere activation; conversely, people considered to be upbeat or happy most of the time have the reverse pattern. What these patterns mean, however, remains to be determined.

Unfortunately, less attention has been paid to positive emotions than to negative emotions. Indeed, in recent years, much study has focused on a particular negative emotion, that of stress. It is this topic to which we next turn our attention.

Stress and Anxiety

The word "stress" appears frequently—and often incorrectly—in many popular magazines and books. Thousands of self-help "experts" promise to teach us how to avoid or manage it. But *stress,* according to Hans Selye, a scientist who played a prominent role in the field of stress research, is "the nonspecific response of the body to any demand." You *want* your brain and body to respond in ways that help you meet the demands made by disease or by events such as a final exam, the opportunity to break Roger Maris's home-run record (as did Mark McGuire and Sammy Sosa in 1998), or an important job interview. Stress, in other words, is not always bad; it is an important part of everyone's life. Challenges and changes, which often engender stress, provide opportunities for developing new strengths and skills.

Stress itself, then, is not harmful. In fact, one study found that young mice exposed from time to time to mild stresses—to handling or to weak electric shocks—became better able to tolerate stressful events than did their more sheltered littermates. As adults, they were also stronger and larger—and their adrenal glands were bigger.

What *is* potentially harmful to animals, including human beings, is a prolonged experience of stress or an onslaught of many stressful events—called "stressors"—that makes it difficult or impossible for the organism to adapt.

Selye's General Adaptation Syndrome

In 1956, Selye described an animal's stress reaction, which he called the "general adaptation syndrome," as having three phases: (1) alarm, (2) resistance, and (3) exhaustion.

In the alarm reaction, the sympathetic nervous system is aroused, just as described on page 249. The hypothalamus sends a chemical signal to the pituitary, causing it to increase its release of adrenocorticotropic hormone. ACTH, in turn, travels in the bloodstream to the adrenal glands and causes them to secrete corticosteroids, hormones that prepare organs all over the body to engage in action and to deal with potential injury. Sympathetic nerves and the adrenal medulla secrete norepinephrine into the bloodstream. Increased levels of norepinephrine, ACTH, and corticosteroids are the signs that researchers typically use to measure stress arousal.

In the resistance stage, the body mobilizes its resources to put an end to the stress-producing event. When the stressor is a disease or an injury, antibodies rush to the affected site. In psychological stress, the sympathetic system prepares the animal—or person—for fight or flight.

Everybody goes through the alarm and resistance stages many, many times in life. When resistance is successful, the body returns to normal. But, if the stress is not relieved, the body may reach a stage of exhaustion. In the mice that Selye originally studied, for example, unrelieved exposure to extreme cold first caused the adrenal glands to discharge all their microscopic corticosteroid-containing fat granules (the alarm stage). The glands then became laden with an unusually large number of fat droplets containing more corticosteroids (resistance). Finally, though, after all those droplets were discharged and the mice could produce no more, the animals died (exhaustion). When stress is psychological rather than physical, exhaustion equals breakdown—sometimes in the form of mental illness and sometimes as psychosomatic disease.

Stress, Disease, and Perceptions of Control

In a song from the musical *Guys and Dolls*, Adelaide, sneezing and coughing, laments

her lover's many delays in marrying her. "Just from waiting around for a plain little band of gold, a person," she says, "can develop a cold." Many psychological and physiological studies have corroborated this connection between emotion and disease.

In one large-scale study, 5000 patients were questioned about the events in their lives that preceded their physical illnesses. The researchers found that dramatic life changes had preceded illness in a large number of cases. The patients were asked to report events such as the death of a spouse, divorce, marriage, change of residence, being fired from a job, or retirement that had happened within two years before the onset of illness. In a subsequent study of a group of physicians, researchers quantified such life changes by giving them point ratings and, on the basis of the subjects' recent histories, categorized some as being at high risk for illness. Of these high-risk subjects, 49 percent reported having contracted some sort of illness in the eight months of the study; only 9 percent of those rated as being at low risk reported being ill. The psychologists concluded that the struggle of coping with life crises, especially when a person's coping techniques are faulty, can lower resistance to disease. Although unsubstantiated by physiological evidence, this conclusion fits Selye's description of the stages of resistance and exhaustion.

Many scientists believe that stomach ulceration, for example, is caused by psychological factors. Ulcers can be induced not only in people but also in rats and monkeys. A series of studies with rats as subjects, conducted by psychologist Jay Weiss, demonstrated such a psychological dimension to the effects of environmental stress. These rats were put in an experimental apparatus that controlled all movement (see Figure

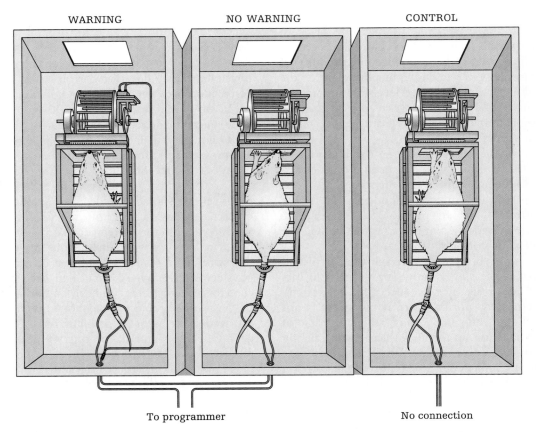

WARNING   NO WARNING   CONTROL

To programmer   No connection

Figure 8.9 In this experimental setup, the control rat received no shocks. The other two rats got identical shocks, but one heard a warning tone 10 seconds before each shock. The ability to predict shock resulted in fewer stomach ulcers than did random shocks.

8.9). As part of the manipulation, two rats received simultaneous electric shocks of equal intensity to their tails; a third, the control rat, received no shocks. One of the shocked rats consistently heard a beeping tone 10 seconds before the shock, whereas the other heard only random beeps with no predictive meaning. The rat that heard the warning beep, and so could predict the arrival of the shocks, had very little ulceration. The shocked rat who had no way of predicting the arrival of the shocks developed rather severe ulcers.

With the original experiment complete, Weiss then arranged the setup so that one of the rats could prevent the shock for itself *and* its partner by jumping onto a platform during the warning signal (or, if it had been a bit slow to react, it could terminate the shock for both by jumping onto the platform after the shock began). The rats that were able to cope with the shocks by preventing them or escaping from them developed much less ulceration than did their helpless partners, even though both groups had received identical amounts of shock.

These results lend support to the researcher's hypothesis that the predictability of events in one's environment, feedback from that environment about the outcome of one's actions, and the consequent sense of being able to cope help prevent stress from having deleterious effects.

Studies using human subjects produced similar findings. When volunteer subjects were given inescapable shocks, those who had been told (falsely) by the experimenters that they could terminate (not prevent) a shock by clenching a fist or pressing a button showed less emotional arousal (measured by amount of skin moisture) than did subjects who knew that they had no control. The shocks were brief, so the subjects who pressed the button believed that their actions were responsible for ending the shock. Because they got feedback in the form of termination of the shock, they felt that they had a means of coping with the situation.

What happens to a lone animal given a series of shocks that it believes it has no power to escape? Psychologist Martin Seligman gave a series of shocks to two groups of dogs. One control group of dogs was permitted to learn how to escape; they could jump a hurdle into the other side of the box in which they were placed, where no shocks were delivered. The other group was first given a series of inescapable shocks and then given an opportunity to learn the escape mechanism. They could not learn it. They did not even try. Seligman calls this phenomenon "learned helplessness."

Jay Weiss's research may have light to shed on Seligman's findings. When Weiss sacrificed a number of rats used in his experiment and studied their brains, he found that the helpless rats, even though they had received fewer shocks, had decreased levels of norepinephrine in their brains. Weiss believes that the helplessness of Seligman's dogs—their inability to learn an escape mechanism when it was finally made available to them—resulted from a temporary depletion of norepinephrine in their brains. The "executive rats," those that had been able to jump on the platform and avoid or escape the shock, had normal brain levels of norepinephrine.

Brain Function and Everyday Stress

The leap in logic from laboratory situations in which electric shock is administered to situations that generate stress in ordinary human lives may seem difficult to justify. However, a study with monkeys conducted by researcher Jay R. Kaplan and his colleagues shortens that leap. In this study, which showed that social stress can contribute to atherosclerosis (hardening of the arteries), all of the monkeys had been fed from birth with a "prudent" diet, one low in saturated fats and containing almost no cholesterol. Over a two-year period, some of the monkeys were subjected to a number of stressful conditions arising from interruptions of the usual social organization of monkey life. For instance, individual monkeys were repeatedly taken from their own social group and put into a new one, where they had no rank in the dominance hierarchy and had to fight for position. Groups of the male monkeys were also housed for two-week periods with one female in heat and so were subjected to the stress of fighting for her favors. The stressed monkeys ended up having significantly more numerous and more severe arterial lesions (the signs of atherosclerosis) than did the monkeys whose social life was stable.

Is it too far-fetched to draw an analogy between the stresses of these monkeys' social lives and the stresses encountered by, say, a middle-management executive or a single working mother? The executive receives directives from her superiors that she must carry out, yet she probably had no control over the decision making that produced them. Most of the time she is acutely aware of being in competition with others for promotion—and of the efforts of those below her who are competing for her job. Much of her social life revolves around other employees of the corporation, so work tensions carry over into her private life. Add the frustration of rush-hour commuter traffic and the necessity of travel, with attendant jet lag, and you have a formula for stress.

The single working mother's life often requires her to balance at least three conflicting claims: the requirements of her job, the psychological and social needs of her children, and her desires for personal fulfillment. How serious does a child's cold have to be for the mother to stay home from work? What does she do when she has to work late on the same evening that her son has a Little League game? In a way, she loses the feeling of control whatever she decides. Something important always remains undone.

Prolonged stress of this kind produces the psychological state that we commonly call *anxiety*. In a modern, complex culture, many people experience it. The limbic region does its job in producing emotional arousal, and the cortex monitors and modulates that arousal. This is a fine balance. But, if we feel that things have slipped out of our control, if stressors seem to pile up endlessly, the fine balance may be disturbed. Anxiety may represent tensions between limbic and cortical impulses.

One widely used means of allaying anxiety is to take tranquilizers. The most popular among them is Valium, a benzodiazepine thought to work by promoting the effectiveness of the neurotransmitter gamma-aminobutyric acid, whose primary function is to inhibit the firing of neurons. GABA has its own receptors, and Valium receptors are very close to them; when the drug is present, it actually promotes the binding of GABA to the GABA receptors. The more GABA bound to a neuron, the less likely the neuron is to fire.

The discovery of opiate-binding sites led to the discovery of endorphins, so the discovery of tranquilizer-binding sites has led to a search for the body's own tranquilizers. As noted in Chapter 2, GABA receptors are made up of several similar but distinct subunits, only a few of which can recognize benzodiazepines. Exactly why those GABA-receptor subunits have surface features to which the benzodiazepine-drug molecules can bind selectively is unknown. Perhaps there is another neuropeptide system like the endorphins to be found. Although benzodiazepines make GABA messages stronger, the first candidate for this neuropeptide site had the opposite effect: its action proved to antagonize the effects of benzodiazepines.

The limbic region contains many neurons on which GABA acts. It seems likely, then, that tranquilizers do their job by inhibiting the flow of messages through the limbic region, thereby dampening emotional arousal.

One psychopharmacological study produced findings in rats that seem relevant to human anxiety. Rats were trained to run a maze for food rewards. In one group, the rats were rewarded every time they correctly negotiated the maze; another group found the food reward only some of the time. Then, for both groups, all rewards ceased. The rats that had been rewarded each time they ran the maze soon stopped searching. In the language of classical conditioning, the behavior was extinguished. But the rats that had found the food reward only occasionally—that is, who had received only partial reinforcement—took much longer to stop their searching. The uncertainty of reward during training was thought to create an anxiety state, which was revealed by their purposeless running of the maze long after the reward had been withdrawn and long after the other group of rats had given up the search.

The researcher, using implanted electrodes, had noted that in the "anxious" rats, a certain level of electrical activity occurred in the hippocampus. When these rats were given barbiturates, alcohol, or tranquilizers, the frequency of electrical activity in the hippocampus decreased, and the animals stopped their fruitless, anxious searches for the reward, their anxiety apparently reduced. Such findings suggest why so many people elect to use alcohol and tranquilizing drugs despite their potential dangers, because these substances temporarily reduce anxiety levels and modulate the stresses of living in a complex modern society.

After all this discussion of the brain's lows, one might be tempted to ask why human beings have evolved in a way that makes them subject to such emotional storms. Why have we inherited this capacity to feel so awful? Perhaps fish are better off. The poet T. S. Eliot once said as much: "I should have been a pair of ragged claws, scuttling across the floors of silent seas." Luckily, we have also inherited the capacity for feeling wonderful—for experiencing such emotions as joy, tenderness, affection, and exultation. There appear to be some logical reasons for our emotional lives being more variegated than those of fish or crustaceans.

The Development of Emotions: An Evolutionary Perspective

Animals low on the evolutionary scale—fish and crustaceans, for example—have no limbic region, only an elaborated brainstem. The limbic region evolved in higher species. As evolution progressed, the cortex became larger relative to body size. This progressive enlargement continued up the phylogenetic scale to human beings.

The brainstem and other hindbrain structures are the sources of the rigidly programmed—or "hard wired"—behaviors necessary to survival. All lizards of a certain species, for example, turn sideways and display their dewlap in threat. Among human behaviors, smiling in greeting seems to be a genetically wired expression. Newborns in all cultures show a smilelike expression, and infants only two or three months old smile at nearby faces. In human infants, this smilelike expression helps elicit the caregiving that these helpless creatures require for survival. Indeed, it was this observation that led John Bowlby, a British psychoanalyst and ethologist, to develop his theory of attachment. In brief, Bowlby proposed that infants are biologically predisposed (through evolutionary pressures) to emit signals that enhance the likelihood of adults responding to their needs. One of these signals is the social smile, which, as just stated, emerges around the second month of life. The other is the cry, which emerges at birth. Bowlby proposed that the cry signal is designed to elicit approach behavior from a caretaker, whereas the smile signal is designed to keep the caretaker with the infant. A great deal of research has largely supported Bowlby's claims. Thus, most adults and even most children cannot resist approaching a smiling infant, and most are also highly motivated to reduce an infant's crying, often by picking the infant up. Sadly, we also know from seemingly daily reports in the newspaper that not all people are motivated in the same way by these signals; child abuse and neglect are two exceptions to the rule.

Bowlby proposed that over the first 2 years of life, the infant forms a strong emotional

The monkey shows a "fear grin," a submissive gesture. The human smile, shown even by very young infants, may have its origins in such a gesture.

bond—referred to by most psychologists as *attachment*—with its primary caretaker, be it the mother, father, or daycare provider. It is believed by a number of theorists that this early relationship is the harbinger of all future emotional relations, including intimate relations with other adults.

The Neurobiology of Attachment Behavior

Although developmental research on the neurobiology of emotional behavior, including attachment behavior, is still in its infancy, most scientists feel that the limbic region plays a strong role in such behavior. Many mammals other than human beings have well-developed limbic regions, whereas reptiles and amphibians do not. Clearly, mammals show more emotional behavior than do reptiles or amphibians. Your turtle, for example, is unlikely to let you know that he's happy to see you coming home after work in the same way that your dog or cat does, and, when threatened, he will freeze, not flee, unless he is underwater. In fact, the higher up the evolutionary scale an animal is, the more emotion it can display. Human beings are the most emo-

tional creatures of all, with many highly differentiated emotional expressions and, at least according to subjective reports, a wide variety of emotional experiences.

It is because the human limbic region interacts with the cortex and because the frontal association cortex is so highly developed in humans that our emotional life is so variegated. Because of this relatively high cortical development, human beings have the ability to abstract and to remember. Therefore, we can feel intense anger over an idea, such as injustice, or shame at not living up to some cultural notion of how we should behave.

What is essential for normal adult functioning, however, is that we learn to master our emotions, including how we express emotion. For example, we are not surprised when a 2-year-old throws a temper tantrum, whereas we would be surprised if a 15-year-old did. The critical difference between these two children likely resides in the differences in their prefrontal cortex. As outlined in Chapter 3, this region of the brain matures slowly, not reaching adultlike functioning until adolescence. Because the prefrontal cortex is the overseer of the limbic region, we are not surprised that young children are less in control of their emotions than older children are.

Social Communication

The naturalist Charles Darwin also studied emotion. His studies, as summarized in *The Expression of the Emotions in Man and Animals* (1872), led him to believe that many facial and gestural expressions of emotion are the result of the evolutionary process. A number of our expressions bear a strong resemblance to those of our distant primate kin, and Darwin saw these expressions as remnants of attack and defense sequences from earlier evolutionary stages. Ethologist Niko Tinbergen calls them "intention movements"—fragments from the process by which an animal prepared for action. As social animals evolved, these expressions, which had earlier only heralded actual behaviors, developed functions of their own—functions that made a system of social communication possible. An animal could convey information to others about its own internal state or about certain events in the environment, a highly useful ability that enables a social species to build an increasingly complex society.

There is good evidence that a number of fundamental abilities of the human emotional system have an evolutionary basis—that is, they have been "wired" into our limbic region by means of our genes, through selection pressures. First, it is well known that the primary emotions of fear, anger, sadness, happiness, surprise, and disgust are universally recognized, regardless of which culture is being evaluated. More importantly, even children as young as 6 or 7 months are capable of discriminating these expressions from one another. The amygdala appears to be responsible for this ability, particularly for the recognition of negative emotions such as fear. Second, most people throughout the world universally produce these same emotions. And, most of these emotions can be observed in infants younger than 1 year of age. Collectively, this evidence provides some support for the evolutionary significance of emotion.

Summary

1. Because scientists have been unable to come up with a satisfactory definition of emotion, it is not defined here. Instead, we assume that all readers can agree on what constitutes discrete emotions such as happiness, anger, and sadness.

2. Motivation, which is closely linked to emotion, is inferred from an organism's goal-directed behavior. If the organism works hard to attain a specific goal, we assume that it is motivated. For human beings, we can make the further assumption that goal-directed behaviors are performed because the goal has an incentive value for the performer and that attainment of the goal will therefore produce a positive emotion.

3. Early theories attempting to relate physiological change to the experience of emotion include (1) the James-Lange theory, which suggested that the experience of emotion results from perception of one's own, preceding, physiological reactions; (2) the Cannon-Bard theory, which inferred a neural pathway through which nerve impulses would simultaneously give the cerebral cortex the experience of

emotion and would command, through the thalamus, the body's physiological changes; and (3) the Papez circuit, which suggested that a number of linked brain structures were responsible for emotion.

4. Many parts of the brain are now known to be responsible for emotion. One is the limbic region, which consists of a number of interconnected structures. Another is the brainstem: specifically, the reticular formation; the locus coeruleus and its widely disseminated transmitter norepinephrine; and the substantia nigra and its widely disseminated transmitter dopamine. Of the parts of the cerebral cortex, the frontal lobes appear to be most important in the experience of emotion. The autonomic nervous system, especially the sympathetic division, mobilizes the body's resources for emergency actions—the "fight or flight" response.

5. If the physiological changes of "fight or flight" take place in a person who has no immediate explanation for them, the person will identify his or her emotional state on the basis of environmental evidence, which indicates how the thinking brain interacts with the limbic region in human beings.

6. Aggression in animals is of various types, some of which can be invoked by electrical stimulation of several areas of the hypothalamus and parts of the amygdala. Animals bred for aggressiveness have lower brain concentrations of the neurotransmitter serotonin. Human aggression remains largely a puzzle.

7. Pain is sensed through receptors in the skin, in sheath tissue surrounding muscle, in internal organs, and in the membranes around bone. These receptors react mainly to physical stimuli that distort them or to chemical stimuli that irritate them, such as the prostaglandins released by sore muscles.

8. Pain messages from the receptors travel to the brain by two different pathways: the fast pathway, whose fibers make direct connection with the thalamus and then synapse with fibers going to motor and sensory areas of the cortex; and the slow pathway, whose fibers project to the reticular formation, the medulla, the pons, the midbrain, the hypothalamus, and the thalamus. The fast system permits immediate action to withdraw from further danger, and the slow system, along with the limbic region and prefrontal cortex, mediates the emotional reaction to the pain.

9. A neurotransmitter, substance P, is a specialized transmitter of pain-related information from peripheral pain receptors to the brain. It is secreted by fibers in the dorsal horns of the spinal cord. The effect of substance P can be modulated by endorphins, which bind to pain-transmitting neurons and inhibit its release. Endorphin-containing neurons exist in many areas of the nervous system.

10. Endorphins also appear to play a role in modulating the arousal that accompanies fear, rage, or stress.

11. Studies using implanted electrodes detected "pleasure centers" in several brain areas of animals; the animals press levers to give themselves long periods

of electrical stimulation there. Because these areas coincide with pathways followed by the dopamine-transmitting neurons from the substantia nigra and the norepinephrine-secreting neurons from the locus coeruleus, release of these transmitters likely plays a part in the pleasurable sensations.

12. A stress reaction, according to Selye's general adaptation syndrome, includes the three phases of alarm, resistance, and exhaustion. In the alarm phase, the sympathetic nervous system is aroused. In the resistance phase, the body mobilizes its resources to return to its prestress state. If stress continues despite resistance, the result can be exhaustion, either physiological or psychological, in the form of mental illness or psychosomatic disease.

13. Predictability of environmental events and feedback from the environment, allowing an animal a sense of having control over what happens to it, are important to stress prevention.

14. The limbic region is not very elaborate in animals lower than mammals on the evolutionary scale. In humans, the early development of the limbic region is probably responsible for an infant's ability to produce and recognize most, if not all, of the basic emotions. On the other hand, the prolonged developmental trajectory of the prefrontal cortex, well into adolescence, is responsible for a young child's relatively poor ability to control his or her emotions.

Key Terms

limbic region
amygdala
orbitofrontal cortex
emotion
Papez circuit
hormones

stress
attachment
pain
pleasure
EEG
aggression

Further Reading

Cooper, J. R., Bloom, F. E., and Roth, R. H. 1996. *The Biochemical Basis of Neuropharmacology,* 7th ed., Chapter 12: The peptides (pp. 410–458). Oxford University Press, New York. An easy-to-read account of the opioid and other peptide systems that act within the central nervous system.

Damasio, A. 1994. *Descartes' Error: Emotion, Reason, and the Human Brain.* Putnam, New York. Dr. Damasio, a distinguished neurologist, draws on his experiences with brain-damaged patients and shows how the absence of emotion and feeling can break down our ability to think rationally. Other topics discussed include the nature of emotions and consciousness.

Davidson, R. J., Abercrombie, H., Nitschke, J. B., and Putnam, K. 1999. Regional brain function, emotion and disorders of emotion. *Current Opinion in Neurobiology,* 9:228–234. In this article written for scientists, Dr. Davidson and his colleagues describe how modern methods of imaging the brain have been used to characterize the circuitry underlying disorders of emotion. Particular emphasis is placed on the prefrontal cortex, anterior cingulate, parietal cortex, and the amygdala, largely because of their roles in depression and anxiety.

Kagan, J., Snidman, N., Arcus, D., and Reznick, S. J. 1997. *Galen's Prophecy: Temperament in Human Nature*. Basic Books, New York. Drawing on their extensive laboratory and observational studies of children, Dr. Kagan and his colleagues describe the roots of temperament and personality. Also included are discussions of the implications of his findings, wherein he argues that the existence of inborn temperamental biases neither excuses asocial behavior nor undermines free will.

Ledoux, J. 1998. *The Emotional Brain: The Mysterious Underpinnings of Emotional Life*. Touchstone Books, New York. An in-depth look at the seat of our emotions, with particular emphasis placed on the origin and neural bases of negative emotions such as fear.

Interactive Resources

To continue your study of the emotions online, visit our Web site at www.worthpublishers.com/bloom. Click on "Chapter 8" for resources including practice quizzes, flash cards, simulations, links to related Web sites, and updates on new research.

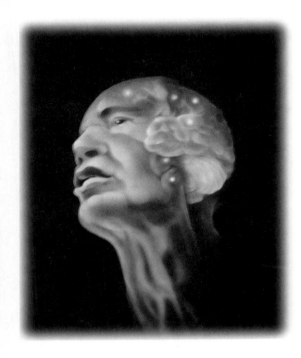

The Human Memory System

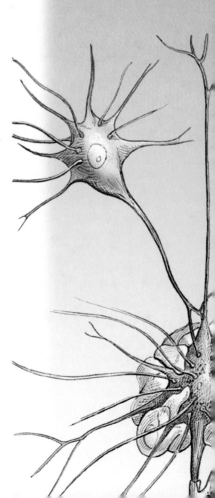

Five decades ago, psychologist Karl Lashley, a pioneer in experimental studies of brain and behavior, attempted to answer the question of how memory is organized in the brain. He taught animals a specific task and then removed a different piece of cerebral cortex from each, one by one, to find where the memory was stored. No matter how much cortex he removed, however, he could not find a specific part in which the memory trace, or the "engram," as he called it, seemed to be located. In 1950, he wrote:

This series of experiments . . . has discovered nothing directly of the real nature of the engram. I sometimes feel, in reviewing the evidence on the localization of the memory trace, that the necessary conclusion is that learning just is not possible.

In this chapter, we examine our knowledge of memory from a variety of perspectives. We begin by tracing the history of this exciting discipline, whose earliest experimental studies—begun in the late 1800s—bear an uncanny resemblance to studies carried out today. We then turn our attention to different types of memory and the different neural systems on which each type seems to depend. Embedded in the discussion of memory "types" is a consideration of how we know what we know about memory. Thus, we will also look at studies of brain-damaged patients and the latest tools for imaging the living brain. We conclude with the phenomenon of neural plasticity—how the brain can be modified by experience—of which learning is a key example.

Revolutions in the Study of Memory

Subsequent research made the reasons for Lashley's failure clear: many regions and structures in the brain in addition to the cerebral cortex are critical to the formation of memory. Moreover, although memories appear to be stored in the cortex, that storage seems to be "organized" in a distributed and redundant way.

One of Lashley's students, Donald Hebb, went on to construct a theory of memory processes that has guided subsequent research for more than four decades. In his theory, Hebb distinguished between short-term and long-term memory. Short-term memory, he said, was an active process of limited duration, leaving no traces, such as what might be entailed in remembering an address long enough to write it on an envelope but with no memory of the address beyond that. In contrast, long-term memory (for example, remembering the name of your eighth-grade English teacher) was produced by structural changes in the nervous system.

Hebb thought that these structural changes resulted from repeated activation of a loop of neurons (one loop per memory). The loop might run from the cortex to the thalamus or the hippocampus and back to the cortex. Repeated activation of the neurons composing the loop would cause the synapses between them to become functionally connected. Once connected, these neurons would constitute a *cell assembly,* and an excitation of neurons in any part of the assembly would activate all of it. Thus a memory could be retrieved by any sensation, thought, or emotion that activated some of the neurons in the cell assembly. The structural changes, Hebb believed, were probably at synapses and took the form of some growth process or of some metabolic change that increased each neuron's effect on the next. What is truly impressive about this theory is that, in devising it, Hebb intuited a number of structures and mechanisms that were unknown at the time but that have since been shown to exist. He would surely be delighted to know the extent to which modern research supports his ideas.

The idea of cell assemblies recognized that memories are not simply static "records," products of a change in a nerve cell or a molecule in the brain, but that memory is a process requiring the interaction of many nerve cells. This remains the best neurological explanation for what psychologists have discovered about how people normally process information.

Memory Basics

To remember something, a person must do three things successfully: acquire a piece of information, retain it, and retrieve it. If you fail to remember something, the problem may lie in any of these three processes.

But memory is not quite this simple or this automatic. We do not merely learn and remember discrete pieces of information; we actively process the information that we receive, constructing the frameworks of knowledge whose organization then guides our learning, storing, and retrieval of new knowledge. In other words, memory is an active process: our existing knowledge is always changing and always being examined and reformulated by our thinking, and its properties are not easy to capture.

Long before Lashley and Hebb entered the picture, Herman Ebbinghaus (1850–1909) was paving the way. Considered to be the foundation of the experimental study of

memory, his studies (begun in 1878) are particularly remarkable in view of the historical context in which they appeared. Before Ebbinghaus, the dominant method of studying memory was *introspection*. A person would simply be asked to concentrate on what he or she was thinking and report those thoughts to the experimenter. This method was also the dominant technique in Freudian psychoanalysis being developed at the same time: patients were encouraged to reflect on their early life experiences—in other words, their early memories. In the last half of the nineteenth century, what a person reported about his or her memory was assumed to be reliable, and thus such reports could be taken as the truth.

Rather than accept the dogma of the times, Ebbinghaus developed his own methods for studying memory that flew in the face of his colleagues' thinking. His methods were ingenious and in all respects revolutionized the science of memory.

Ebbinghaus proposed that three principles be applied to experimental studies of the brain. The first principle required that unobservable mental processes be translated into observable behavior. The goal here was to move away from a dependence on what the subject *said* happened and instead make a direct observation of some behavior that corresponded to the process in question. A present-day example might be for an experimenter to ask you what kind of cereal you had for breakfast by asking you to point to the correct cereal box. The second principle required that this behavior be measured reliably; for example, that two independent observers would report the same behavior (thus, two of your friends confirm and validate what you had for breakfast). Finally, Ebbinghaus required that the behavior be shown to vary systematically with other variables and experimental conditions. To return to our breakfast example, the experimenter might present the subject with different cereal boxes over multiple trials and determine whether the subject consistently picked the same cereal box. If these requirements could not be fulfilled, then the *veridicality,* or truthfulness, of the memory would be called into question.

Ebbinghaus devised experiments to test his principles, using himself as his sole subject. For example, to evaluate the process of acquiring memories (an *unobservable* mental process), he made himself read a series of nonsense syllables (for example, two consonants separated by a vowel forming a syllable that has no meaning, such as *wix*) until he could reproduce the series flawlessly (an *observable* behavior). He would then vary the learning conditions by increasing or decreasing the list length (thereby satisfying his third principle). His measure of learning was the amount of time required to master the series of words. At some later point in time, he would vary the conditions by forcing himself to relearn the series of "words" (which, because they were meaningless, were easily forgotten). He would then compare the original learning with the relearning. The difference between these two trials, referred to as *savings,* was the measure of retention of the original learning.

Using this general method, Ebbinghaus made a number of important discoveries about learning and memory. One discovery in particular that warrants mentioning was that, in the course of learning a series of nonsense syllables, a person begins to recognize associations not only between the syllables that are immediately adjacent to one another, but also between syllables that are more distantly separated from one another in time (for example, the second and the tenth). A related finding was that items presented in the beginning of a list and at the end of a list are better remembered than those in the middle (respectively referred to as *primacy* and *recency* effects). This last finding proved particularly important in that it tells us that people must be using strategies to remember the material (such as rehearsing the syllables). As discussed later, the use of strategies is probably a function of the frontal lobe.

For all intents and purposes, this early work ushered in the modern experimental study of memory. Currently, the study of memory remains one of the most actively pursued areas of investigation in *cognitive psychology* (the study of "thinking") and in *cognitive neuroscience* (the study of the relation between brain and thinking).

The Stages of Memory

The creation of a memory, as Hebb discovered, seems to consist of several stages. One stage is of extremely short duration and today is referred to as *working memory* (Hebb referred to this stage as short-term memory). Information is held "in" working memory for only a few seconds, just long enough for you to do something with that information. An example of working memory is when you call directory assistance to ask for a friend's telephone number. After the operator gives you the number, you can probably remember it by saying it over and over again ("rehearsal") just long enough to actually dial the number. But, if you are distracted—if someone speaks to you or you drop the coin that you were about to put in the slot of the pay phone—you will probably forget the number or mix it up. As a rule, information can be held in working memory for just a few seconds.

A second stage, or form, of memory that can last a bit longer than working memory is *short-term memory.* This stage is a repository for information that needs to be remembered for a short time (seconds, minutes, or possibly longer) but not necessarily manipulated. An example of short-term memory is the "mental" grocery list that you create but that you then pass along to your roommate, who will actually do the shopping. Researchers have found that the limit of such memory tends to be approximately seven (plus or minus two) items; thus, if you were presented with a list of 20 words, you would most likely remember from 5 to 9 of them, and only for a few minutes at most.

Importantly, one of the factors that determines how many words we can hold in short-term memory is how skilled we are in the conscious use of our memory—that is, our use of strategies. As a rule, people who use more sophisticated strategies remember better than people who use simpler ones. For example, "chunking" the material (seeing the first three digits of a telephone number—the exchange—as one piece of information, or "chunk") works better than straight rehearsal (saying the seven numbers of the telephone number again and again). This use of strategies most likely relies on areas of the prefrontal cortex, which is also the location of our ability to plan our behavior and engage in abstract thought, as well as the site, as just mentioned, of our working memory. Collectively, these abilities are referred to as examples of *executive functions* because they represent higher-order cognitive behaviors that in some ways oversee the operation of the brain as a whole.

The third stage of memory, *long-term memory,* is thought of as permanent information storage. Examples include remembering the names of your best friends, the name of your elementary school, or the name of the dog that you had as a child. As a rule, information is transferred into long-term memory from short-term memory, although the precise neural mechanism is not known. This is the process that you likely experience when you study: you listen to lectures and take notes; later, you review your notes and possibly even rewrite them (a practice that Donald Hebb encouraged his Introductory Psychology students to adopt). Finally, in advance of an exam, you review the notes yet again, as well as review the material by reading the textbook. This repetition essentially transforms the information that you may have remembered initially for only the short term into knowledge residing in your long-term memory. Not surprisingly, as we shall see, the areas and circuits of the brain that participate in short-term and long-term memory differ.

The case of a patient referred to as H. M. illustrates the differences between short-term and long-term memory. It is one of the most studied cases in the history of cognitive neuroscience. His story will illustrate why.

As a young man, H. M. suffered from a type of epilepsy sometimes referred to as *temporal-lobe epilepsy.* Epilepsy (a seizure disorder) is a condition in which the brain generates inappropriate electrical activity that interrupts its normal operation. Symptoms of a seizure include involuntary chewing movements and sounds, staring, and convulsing. Temporal-lobe epilepsy, specifically, is a seizure disorder that originates in the temporal lobe, often in or around the hippocampus. The *hippocampus* is believed to play a very important role in our ability to encode new information and form new memories of this information. It may also play a role in transferring that information to long-term memory. People with untreated or poorly controlled temporal-lobe seizures generally have poor memories, in part because of damage done to the hippocampus by the seizures themselves (which starves the brain of oxygen and thus kills neurons).

Researchers working with monkeys in whom epilepsy was experimentally induced found that removal of the temporal-lobe brain tissue could completely or largely reduce the seizures themselves. Because of H. M., however, we now know that the temporal lobe of only one hemisphere should be removed. In H. M.'s case, the medial part of *both* temporal lobes was removed, with the result that H. M. lives entirely in the present. He can remember events, objects, or people only for the time that they remain in his short-term memory. If you chat with him, leave the room for a few minutes, and then return, he will have no recollection of ever having seen you before. We will return to H. M. and what scientists have learned about memory from studies of him and similar cases of memory loss later in this chapter.

The Neuroanatomy of Memory

Earlier in this chapter, we said that different parts of the brain subserve different types of memory. We will now elaborate on this point with a look into those different regions.

Working Memory

It is now believed that working memory is an operation performed largely by parts of the frontal lobes. If the material to be held in working memory has to do with *where* objects are *(spatial working memory)*, the dorsolateral prefrontal cortex is called into action. In contrast, if you must remember *what* the objects are, then regions of the

orbitoprefrontal cortex come into play. These areas are illustrated in Figure 9.1.

Spatial working memory can be illustrated with the *delayed-response task*, originally developed for use with monkeys. As Figure 9.2 on page 282 illustrates, a monkey sits facing a window that has two wells in it. A piece of food is placed in one of the wells and then covered up. Naturally, the monkey is motivated to find the food; so, it immediately reaches for and removes the cloth covering the well. However, to make the task more difficult, as soon as the food is hidden, a barrier comes down to hide the wells and delay retrieval of the food for 5 or 10 seconds. The barrier is then removed, and the animal is allowed to reach. The question is whether the animal reaches for the correct well. Normal animals have no trouble with this task. However, if the dorsolateral prefrontal cortex is damaged, the animal usually cannot remember the food's location for more than a few seconds; after that, the monkey will reach indiscriminately, seemingly with no awareness of where the food was hidden. Interestingly, the same pattern of behavior is observed in monkeys just a few weeks old. The fact that infant monkeys behave like adult monkeys with brain damage suggests that this region of the brain—the dorsolateral prefrontal cortex—is not yet developed. A version of this task, referred to as the "A not B" task (see Figure 9.3 on page 283), has been used with human infants, fashioned after one developed by the late child psychologist Jean Piaget. In this task, the human infant or child watches while attractive toys or bits of cereal (Cheerios work well) are placed first in one hiding place and then in another. The infant or child is then prevented from retrieving the objects for a certain period of time (the delay period). The imposed delay usually causes the

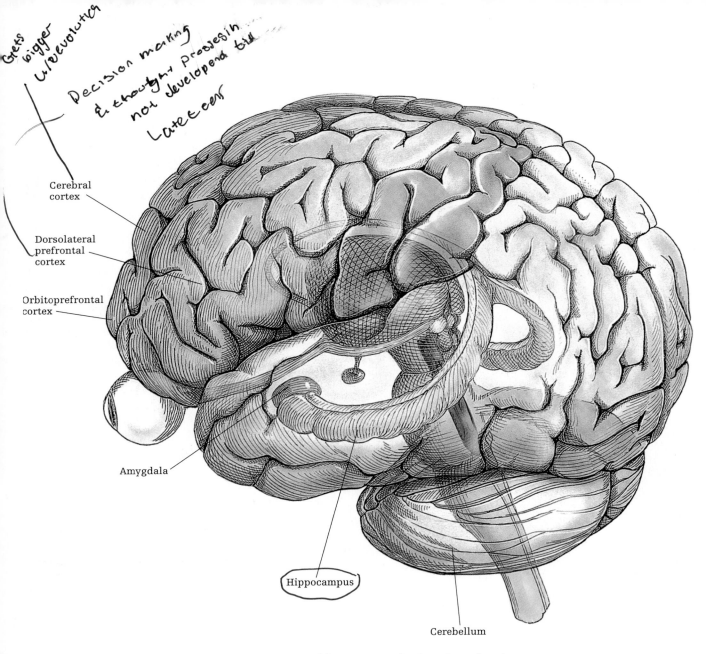

Gets bigger w/evolution

Decision making & thoughts processing not developed till late teens

Cerebral cortex

Dorsolateral prefrontal cortex

Orbitoprefrontal cortex

Amygdala

Hippocampus

Cerebellum

Figure 9.1 The prefrontal cortex is responsible for working memory: the dorsolateral region seems to know where objects are, and the orbitoprefrontal region seems to know what the objects are.

youngest infants to forget that the object was moved. Sometime after 8 months of age, the infants begin to be able to tolerate very short delays (1 or 2 seconds), but not until close to 1.5 years of age can they tolerate delays of 8 or 10 seconds (still far less than

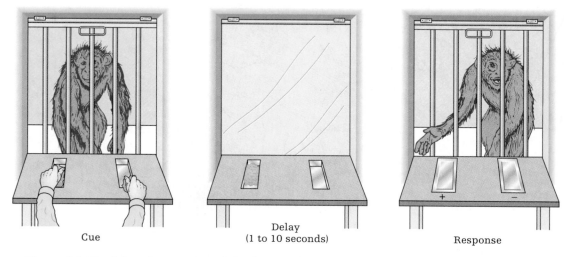

| Cue | Delay (1 to 10 seconds) | Response |

Figure 9.2 The delayed-response task is often used to evaluate the spatial working memory of monkeys. In the cue period, the monkey watches an experimenter place food in one of two wells. During the delay phase, a screen is lowered for 1 or more seconds. In the response phase, the monkey must select the well containing the reward.

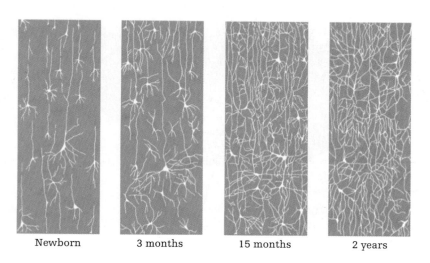

| Newborn | 3 months | 15 months | 2 years |

The development of neurons in the cerebral cortex from birth to 2 years of age. The neurons grow both in size and in number of connections between them.

what an older child or an adult could do). These findings are consistent with the monkey work, suggesting that the dorsolateral prefrontal cortex matures slowly in the first years of life.

Short-Term and Long-Term Memory

As H. M.'s experience demonstrates, short-term memory seems to depend on the medial parts of the temporal lobe, such as the hippocampus and the entorhinal cortex (see Figure 9.4 on page 284). Scientists have long suspected the critical involvement of the hippocampus in this function, but the entorhinal cortex is now also known to have a significant role. These same regions—the hippocampus in particular—also play a prominent role in *memory consolidation*, the physical and psychological changes that transpire as the brain organizes and restructures

Location A

Location B

Figure 9.3 The well-known child psychologist Jean Piaget developed what he referred to as the "A not B" task. In the neuropsychological modification of this task, the infant is presented with two hiding wells. An object is placed in one of these wells and then both wells are covered. As the infant watches, the object is then moved to the other well and covered again. After a short delay (about 5–10 seconds) the infant is "asked" to retrieve the object. Even with very short delays, 8-month-old infants will reach for the old location (A not B), as though they have "forgotten" the most recent hiding place and, instead, persevere in expecting to retrieve the object from the first hiding place. As they grow older, infants can tolerate increasingly long delays, and so by 14 to 18 months they can perform correctly with delays as long as 10 seconds.

information that may eventually become a part of permanent (long-term) memory.

As a simple example of consolidation, think back to when you learned to read. At first you had to be able to recall that the difference between "d" and "b" was that the "loop on the "b" goes on the right." After you had mastered letter recognition, your reorganized memory permitted you to recognize the letters without retrieving such cues. Still later, after you had learned to read with ease, your memory for sounds, shapes, and combinations of letters became a coherent and stable whole. Skilled readers never read letter by letter or even word by word; they process chunks of words at a time.

The hippocampus and the medial temporal area appear to act in the formation and development of memory rather than being sites of permanent storage. Thus, in spite of the surgical removal of these areas, H. M. has a good memory of events in his life that preceded his operation. The memories already in his long-term storage—at least those that were stored 1 to 3 years before his

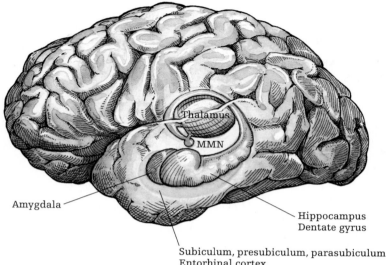

Medial temporal lobe memory structures

Thalamus

MMN

Amygdala

Hippocampus
Dentate gyrus

Subiculum, presubiculum, parasubiculum
Entorhinal cortex
Perirhinal and parahippocampal cortices

Figure 9.4 Some of the structures thought to be involved in explicit or declarative memory, including the hippocampus and surrounding cortex (particularly the entorhinal cortex). As discussed in the text, the amygdala may play an important role in modulating the function of the hippocampus when the material to be remembered is of an emotional nature.

surgery—were not lost. The fact that H. M. suffered some amnesia for events that preceded his surgery by a year or two but not for earlier events suggests that memory may undergo changes—consolidation—for some time after learning.

Memory expert Larry Squire speculates that, at the time something is learned, the region of the temporal lobe establishes a relation with memory-storage sites elsewhere in the brain, primarily in other parts of the cortex. Interaction between these areas may be required for as long as several years while reorganization of the memory continues. In this reorganization, neural circuitry is physically remodeled in some way, Squire believes. At some point, though, when reorganization and remodeling are complete—when the memory is permanently stored in the cortex—the temporal region is no longer required to support that memory's retention or retrieval.

The role of the cortex in long-term memory may explain an intriguing observation that experts have talked about since Freud first started treating patients—the phenomenon of *infantile amnesia*. As a rule, people are unable to recall the events of their lives much before the age of 3 or 4 years. You may test this yourself by reaching back in your memory as far as you can go. How old were you at the time of the earliest recollection? Although Freud attributed infantile amnesia to repression, claiming that the early memories are stored but not accessible because they are troubling in some way, a simpler explanation may be that the regions of the cortex that take part in long-term storage are immature early

I'll Always Remember

Most of us will remember our high-school graduation day for the rest of our lives—even the middle-aged Beach Boys sing about it. Most middle-aged adults, in fact, remember a surprising number of things about high school, once their memories are jogged. After all, they had at least 4 years to acquire and use a fairly constant body of information. Such recall, however, is due to long-term memory.

In 1974, a research team set out to test people's long-term memory of their high-school experience. Working with a sample population of 392 high-school graduates, the investigators tested their subjects with recall and recognition tasks by using names and photographs from high-school yearbooks.

Not surprisingly, they found that people recognize better than they recall. Those for whom 35 years had passed since graduation could recognize the pictures of 9 of 10 classmates. More recent graduates did just as well at recognizing names alone, but,

after 30 years or more, the success rate for that task dropped slightly to 70 or 80 percent. At least 10 to 15 years after graduation, the subjects could match 90 percent of names with faces, but this rate dropped to 60 percent after 20 to 25 years—still, a decent success rate.

In all the cohorts studied, women did better than men, with the exception that men out of school 20 years or more exceeded their female classmates on all but one recall test. Specifically, these men remembered significantly more boys than girls, whereas women remembered only slightly more girls than boys. Both men and women remembered best the people whom they had dated or their close friends.

A look at your own high-school yearbook will probably confirm these observations. The study reiterated what most of us already know: the human brain stores more than most of us want or need to remember. It is access and retrieval that cause our problems.

in life. This immaturity may result in a deficit in forming long-term memories or retrieving them after they have been stored. This long-term memory ability improves dramatically throughout the preschool years. For example, from the box above, we learn that adults are quite good at remembering pictures of their high-school classmates from 25 or more years ago. But, in a clever study performed with children, 10-year-olds were shown pictures of their preschool classmates who were no longer their friends at the time of the test. On average, the children had not seen each other

for nearly 6 years. In contrast with adults, the children performed only slightly better than chance. Thus, even as old as 4 years, children still suffer from poor long-term memory.

To summarize, our ability to remember things is strongly influenced by (1) how long we must remember them (seconds, minutes, months, or years), (2) what it is we have to remember (places, objects, names); and (3) how old we are when we are first exposed to whatever it is we have to remember. Moreover, the neural bases of working,

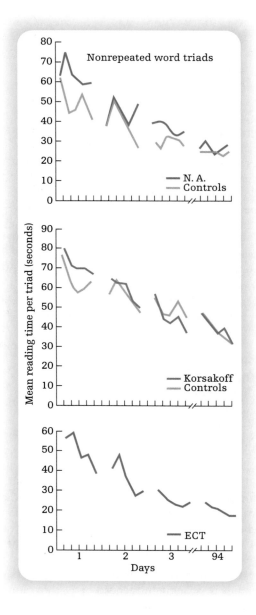

Figure 9.5 The procedural skill of mirror reading groups of words was acquired at a normal rate by amnesiac patients and was retained at a normal level for 3 months after learning. "N. A." is patient N. A.; Korsakoff patients have Korsakoff's syndrome; "ECT" represents patients who had undergone electroconvulsive therapy. The curves demonstrate that each time the patients were given new words to read, they deciphered the words more quickly.

term memory depends on the cortex (after the information has been processed further by the temporal lobe).

In addition to the roles played by working, short-term, and long-term memory processes in human remembering and failing to remember, we appear to have two other distinct mechanisms of learning, depending on what is being learned and remembered.

Procedural and Declarative Memory

Even though they cannot remember facts about the world, H. M. and other patients with brain damage like his can learn how to do things and retain that learning. For example, in one study, groups of such patients with damage to the medial temporal lobe were taught the skill of mirror reading—that is, reading text that has been transposed by being reflected in a mirror (see Figure 9.5). They took 3 days to become skillful at the task, about the same number of days that normal people take, and they retained a high level of skill for the 3 months during which they were tested. Yet, when tested, many of the patients did not remember ever having worked at the task before, and none of them could later remember the words that they had read.

short-term, and long-term memory differ. Working memory relies on the prefrontal cortex, short-term memory relies on structures in the medial temporal lobe, and long-

Another example of this type of learning is observed in the serial reaction-time task, illustrated in Figure 9.6. Here subjects might be presented with a panel of lights: 10 rows of lights with 4 lights per row. One light blinks on and off in each row, one row at a time, and the subject is required to push a key corresponding to the blinking light as quickly as possible. The sequence of 10 lights makes a pattern, and, after the 10th light blinks, the sequence begins again. To assess learning, the investigator examines whether (1) the subjects' reaction times decrease over trials (that is, do they get faster and faster at pushing the buttons as they learn the pattern?) and (2) whether their reaction times increase when the pattern unexpectedly changes. In one such study, the subjects were elderly adults with Alzheimer's disease and a healthy elderly control group. Both groups showed decreased reaction times as the 10-light sequence was repeated, and both groups showed increased reaction times when the sequence of lights was unexpectedly changed. Thus, both groups learned the sequence. Only the control subjects, however, seemed aware that the sequence of lights formed a pattern; the Alzheimer's patients seemed oblivious to this fact, even though both the patients and the control group showed exactly the same kinds of changes in their reaction times, responding faster and faster as they learned the sequence and more slowly when the sequence changed.

Such studies suggest to investigators that the brain processes information in at least two separate ways—one mechanism is conscious and the other is unconscious—and each kind of information is stored differently and in different regions of the brain. *Declarative knowledge,* knowledge that is consciously retrievable, is described by Squire as providing "an explicit, accessible record of individual previous experiences, a sense of familiarity about those experiences." *Procedural knowledge,* in contrast, is knowledge of how to do something, even if we lack awareness of what it is that we are doing. The former requires processing in the temporal region, whereas the latter apparently does not.

Procedural learning probably developed earlier in evolution than declarative learning. The learning processes known as habituation and classical conditioning (both covered in Chapter 10) take place without awareness that learning has occurred and are therefore examples of procedural learning—as are mirror tracing (copying text

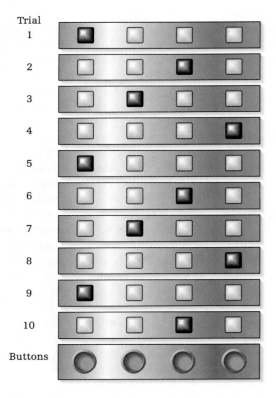

Figure 9.6 A typical sequence in the serial reaction-time task

that is reflected in a mirror) and the type of learning acquired in the serial reaction-time task. Another example may be what is called *priming*. Suppose that you are shown a list of words (cat, apple, monkey, hippocampus, fruit) presented one at a time on a screen and are asked to remember them. You are then shown a second list with some of the same words as well as different ones, but this time the words are presented with letters missing: C_t or M__k_y. You are asked to push a button whenever you see a familiar word. Subjects will respond much faster to words repeated from the first list, although they may say they have never seen the words before. That is, they lack awareness of what they have learned.

The distinction between procedural and declarative memory may help to explain why certain *mnemonic devices*—schemes to aid in storing and recalling memories—work so well. Basically, anything that helps you become *consciously* aware of something that you have just learned will make it more likely you will remember that information at a later time. One of the most commonly used of such devices, the *method of loci* (places), was invented by the Greek orators, and it has worked well ever since (see Figure 9.7). The technique consists of visualizing a familiar location and then, in your mind's eye, placing things to be remembered—the points that you want to make in a speech, for example—at prominent places along the route. When the time comes, you mentally revisit the place, retrace your path, and find at each location the item you placed there. This device uses a context for organizing declarative information. By retrieving the context, you are more likely to retrieve the specific points to be remembered.

Thus, we have two major memory systems. One, the *declarative* system, enables us to consciously recall and recognize events in our lives. It is responsible, for example, for everything from being able to retrieve the names and faces of childhood friends to mastering the complicated material presented in this book and flawlessly demonstrating this knowledge on essay or multiple-choice exams. The other, the *procedural* system (sometimes referred to as *implicit* memory), includes different types of remembering (motor-skill learning, priming, conditioning) that collectively are beyond conscious awareness. Examples include learning to ride a bike, play a musical instrument, and perform a new dance step. They may also include the ability to recognize things seen so briefly that we are not even aware of having seen them before (although research shows that we behave as though we had). And, as stated earlier, these different behavioral systems appear to operate through different neural systems. We have already seen that the declarative system uses structures in the medial temporal lobe (which were destroyed in patient H. M.), whereas the procedural system does not. There are different types of procedural learning, and each one uses a slightly different circuit. What they have in common is that they do not, apparently, involve the temporal lobe and do not consist of conscious memories (the topic of consciousness is taken up in Chapter 11). For example, visual word priming probably takes place in areas of the visual cortex, whereas skilled motor learning probably takes place in the basal ganglia. The intact basal ganglia of the patients with Alzheimer's disease explain why they did well on the serial reaction-time task. By the same token, they were not consciously aware that they had learned a pattern or even that there was a pattern,

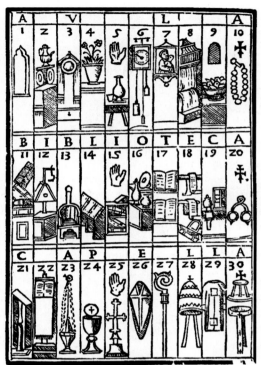

Figure 9.7 The "method of loci," or "places," as an aid to memory dates back to the Greeks and Romans. The guide shown here was written and illustrated by Dominican friars in the sixteenth century to aid in the memorization of speeches. At the left are the abbey and its outbuildings—the courtyard, the library, the chapel. Each object in each row at the right is associated with an idea in the speech and then "placed" along the route through the abbey. Every fifth item is coupled with a hand or a cross so that the speaker can keep track of items on each hand. When the speaker needs to recall the speech, he retraces the route through the abbey, finding each object (or idea) in the order in which he wishes to use it (Johannes Romberch, *Congestorium Artificia Memoriae,* Venice, 1553).

because they had pathology in the temporal lobe.

Besides the functional differences between these various aspects of memory, there is one other important qualitative factor in learning that influences the storage and retrieval of information: whether an action is followed by either rewarding or punishing consequences.

Reward and Punishment in Learning and Remembering

Learning theorists propose a mechanism called *operant conditioning* to explain how behavior is shaped by its consequences. This form of learning deals with what B. F. Skinner, its major theorist, calls *operant behaviors*—that is, behaviors that an animal or person

Figure 9.8 No one knows why, but Joey jumps on the fire hydrant every time he passes it and stays there as long as he is allowed to. Joey's behavior has somehow been operantly conditioned by the promise of a reward that only Joey knows about.

voluntarily and spontaneously performs. Operant and classical conditioning (the latter of which will be explored in Chapter 10) are likely forms of implicit memory, because we have no conscious awareness of having been conditioned.

According to the theory, an operant behavior that results in the attainment of something that the organism likes tends to be repeated (see Figure 9.8), and an operant behavior that results in something that the organism dislikes tends not to be repeated. This basic principle is extremely important in determining what behaviors an animal or a person will learn and remember. The survival of an animal depends on its doing things that are rewarding. Behaviors that procure food, for example, are rewarded by something to eat, and, if the animal remembers the behaviors that produced the reward and repeats them, it can enhance its chances of survival. The animal also learns to avoid behaviors that result in its being hurt or frightened. To say that an animal tends to repeat a behavior that results in attaining something that it likes is to say that learning and emotion interact. We learn to repeat behaviors that are accompanied by positive emotions, and we learn to avoid repeating behaviors that are accompanied by fear or discomfort (even though we may have learned how to perform them). But what brain mechanisms might account for this interaction?

James L. McGaugh, a neuroscientist who, as you may recall from Chapter 8, studied the effects of emotional arousal on the amygdala, suggests possible physiological bases for the effects of operant conditioning. Many studies have shown that an animal's memory of a behavior that it was trained to do in the laboratory (usually through classical conditioning) can be disrupted by a number of different treatments administered soon after the training—electrical stimulation of various parts of the brain (similar to electroconvulsive shock in humans, perhaps) or the injection of various hormones. The fact that memory retention is so readily altered by these posttraining treatments suggested to McGaugh and his colleagues that memory consolidation could be influenced by the physiological effects of everyday experiences. More specifically, McGaugh has suggested that the amygdala—an almond-shaped structure in the temporal lobe that is the seat of emotion—mediates the function of the hippocampus. We touched on this relation in Chapter 8, because it is particularly important when learning has an emotional context. For example, if you are in a strange city and are suddenly frightened by a seemingly threatening person or a narrow miss by a car, you will be likely to retain a clearer memory of where the frightening event occurred than of some other part of the city where nothing special (emotionally charged) has happened to you. The exact mechanism of how the amygdala mediates the hippocampus and thus learning and memory is not known, but it is likely to include a complex interplay of hormones (such as cortisol) and neurotransmitters (such as norepinephrine), about which more will be said in a moment.

If the physiological consequences of an experience are considerable—a pounding heart, profuse sweating, and so forth, all brought about by the cascade of hormones and neurotransmitters responsible for the flight-or-fight response—it would be adaptive for the organism to remember that experience for a long period of time, the better to avoid a similar experience in the future. If the consequences are trivial, the experience is best forgotten quickly. Thus, the time-dependence of memory processes may be the result of a mechanism that has evolved to let organisms select which of their experiences should be permanently stored.

To illustrate this possibility, McGaugh conducted an extensive series of studies in which rats engaged in a variety of learning tasks, some including high levels of emotional arousal (for example, fear). One of McGaugh's conclusions was that the amygdala exerts a powerful effect on stress-related hormones such as cortisol and norepinephrine and that these hormones, in turn, can exert a powerful effect on memory. For example, he found that memory can actually be enhanced by infusing into the amygdala drugs that activate these hormones. McGaugh proposed that by modulating emotional arousal, the amygdala, through its connections to the hippocampus and other declarative memory-related structures, can actually influence memory. This may well explain why we remember things best that have strong emotional content (whether the emotion is pleasant or painful).

These studies have shown us some of the structures and processes taking part in memory and how they might operate together, but they have not yet, by any means, provided a complete blueprint for the workings of the human memory system. Another set of studies, which looked at the specific deficits of damaged brains, furnished some of the missing details.

What Can We Learn from Damaged Brains?

In movies, characters who have amnesia usually wake up in hospital beds without a single recollection of their past lives. Will he recognize his wife when she walks into the room? Will he remember that he has witnessed a murder? Such depictions are far from accurate. Amnesia can take many forms, but rarely, if ever, are all of a person's memories erased.

Amnesia is important for scientists to study and understand because very often studying what happens when the brain is damaged can be a source of great insight into how the normal brain functions. For example, we may hypothesize that a certain region of the brain is implicated in a particular ability. One way to test this hypothesis is to examine the brain by using one of the new neuroimaging tools (see box on page 334). However, such tools provide only a piece of the puzzle because they often cannot localize brain function more precisely than within a few millimeters of tissue. To complement this approach, it would be useful to test our hypothesis by studying people who have had brain damage. If some part of the temporal lobe is responsible for some forms of memory (as the hippocampus plays a role in declarative memory), then it follows that people with damage to that area of the brain should show deficits in the ability in question. Importantly, it is often helpful to prove that other abilities are left intact (to show, for example, that patients with Alzheimer's disease perform well on the serial reaction-time task).

The brain can be damaged in a variety of ways. Accidents account for most cases, but rarely is the resultant damage specific to one part of the brain. More revealing would be illnesses, such as encephalitis, that can attack specific regions of the brain or diseases, such as epilepsy, that require neurosurgery. Strokes also account for many instances of discrete brain damage. The next section includes a series of case studies and conditions that illustrate the value of studying "broken" brains.

Four Types of Amnesia

A number of things can happen to a person's brain that can lead to amnesia (such as a stroke or an interruption of the blood supply to the brain due to choking or even neurosurgery, in which some part of the brain is cut out). Through the years, a handful of selected patients such as patient H. M., have been talked about in the scientific literature. Some brain disorders, such as Korsakoff's

syndrome or Alzheimer's disease, can consistently lead to the same type of brain damage in different patients. As stated earlier, the study of such patients and disorders is instructive in what it tells us about the neural bases of memory.

Amnesia Due to Damage to the Medial Temporal Lobe H. M., the patient with epilepsy mentioned earlier, is an amnesiac, although his memories for events that preceded his surgery by 3 years are intact. H. M.'s problem is an inability to transfer declarative memories from short-term to long-term memory. He can learn how to do things, but he cannot remember facts about the world. H. M.'s amnesia resulted from surgery that removed most of both hippocampi and amygdalaes.

Another patient (R. B.) with the same clinical signs of memory impairment as that of patient H. M. died, and a detailed examination of his brain at autopsy showed bilateral damage to a very small part of the hippocampus. (The damage might have been a result of insufficient blood flow during a stroke.) Loss of these relatively few cells produced the same sort of amnesia suffered by patient H. M.

Amnesia Due to Damage to Thalamic Structures Another well-known clinical case of amnesia is that of N. A., who suffered a penetrating brain injury when a fencing foil went up his nose. N. A.'s long-term memory for events preceding his accident also appears to be unimpaired. N. A.'s amnesia, like H. M.'s, takes the form of an inability to learn new material, but his inability is most evident when the material to be learned is verbal (see Figure 9.9). He quickly forgets lists of words but seems to be able to remember faces and spatial locations. N. A.'s injury occurred in the left dorsomedial nucleus of the thalamus.

Amnesia Due to Korsakoff's Syndrome The amnesia of patients with *Korsakoff's syndrome*, a disease of chronic alcoholics, who often go for long periods of time without eating, results from a deficiency of vitamin B$_1$ (thiamine) and is usually progressive. If discovered early enough, it can be treated with massive doses of vitamin B$_1$. Patients with Korsakoff's syndrome not only have trouble forming new memories, but also suffer amnesia for events that took place earlier in their lives (so-called retrograde amnesia), before the disease process set in.

Unlike H. M. or N. A., these patients show other deficiencies in thinking and problem solving. Given a series of problems whose solution requires a change of strategy, Korsakoff patients persevere in using a failed strategy long after its uselessness becomes apparent.

For example, one type of problem used in testing patients—the *Wisconsin Card Sort*—offers them an array of cards containing geometrical shapes. Not told which of the shapes is the correct solution, the patients pick shapes one at a time until they happen to pick, say, the triangle, at which point they are told, "Yes, the triangle is correct." One simple test of thinking abilities is to see whether a subject will pick the triangle on the next few trials. In the next phase of the test, the experimenter changes the solution to a different shape—a circle, for instance. After picking a triangle and being told that it is the wrong answer, normal people—and H. M. and N. A.—try other shapes until they pick the circle. A Korsakoff patient keeps on choosing the triangle.

Another characteristic that normal people display is *proactive inhibition*. When a person is trying to learn successive groups of words that all belong to the same category (animal names, for example), the content of lists learned earlier interferes with the learning of later ones. When the later word groups are changed to a different category (vegetable names, for example), proactive inhibition disappears and learning improves. Korsakoff patients show no improved learning when a new category of words is presented.

The brain damage in Korsakoff's syndrome appears to be widespread and in most cases includes damage to the same thalamic nucleus that N. A. lost. There is also neuronal loss in the cerebellum and cerebral cortex, often in the frontal lobe. In fact, studies have shown that patients without amnesia who have sustained injuries to the frontal lobes persevere in their mistakes during problem solving, just as Korsakoff patients do. This kind of failure, then, may not be directly related to the amnesia. It may just be an additional cognitive dysfunction caused by the vitamin deficiency or by other brain damage.

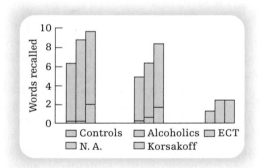

Figure 9.9 In this study, 10 word pairs were presented to different kinds of amnesiacs and to controls. After each presentation, the subjects were shown the first word of each pair and were asked to recall the second. Each test was then repeated two times. The results show the severe handicap that amnesiacs suffer in regard to new learning.

Alcoholics frequently fall down, for example, and trauma to the head may do some of the damage. Thus, more studies are needed before we can draw any conclusions concerning the causes and effects associated with this syndrome.

Amnesia Due to Electroconvulsive Shock Therapy A fourth kind of amnesia that is clearly identifiable and easily studied (the patient can, in fact, be studied both before and after treatment) is the amnesia that follows electroconvulsive shock therapy (ECT). When ECT is used to treat severe cases of depression (see Chapter 12), treatments are usually scheduled every other day in a series of 6 to 12 sessions. Each shock causes a certain loss in memory, which is then recovered to some degree before the next treatment. Nevertheless, memory deficits accumulate throughout the series.

Whereas ECT induces seizures in the brain and disrupts memory of recent events, long-term memory remains intact. It is not possible to say precisely which brain structures are most affected, but it is likely that insult to the temporal area and the hippocampus, which is very sensitive to seizures, produces the amnesia.

The distinct characteristics of each of these types of amnesia and the different brain areas implicated in each suggest to brain researchers that two regions of the brain are at work in the normal operation of memory and that each region has a separate function.

Two Brain Regions and Their Functions

We have seen that amnesia takes several forms. Some victims have trouble retrieving old memories; some victims have trouble forming new ones. Two studies of the rate of forgetting in patients with amnesia (using normal subjects as controls) indicate that the two different brain regions identified as injured in these patients contribute in two different ways to memory function.

In the first study, normal controls, patient H. M., and patients with Korsakoff's syndrome were shown 120 slides of familiar objects, one at a time. Controls were shown each picture for 1 second; amnesiacs viewed each one for as long as 16 seconds. Then they were shown some of the pictures again, along with some new ones, 10 minutes, 1 day, and 1 week later and were asked to indicate whether they recognized each picture. At 10 minutes after viewing, patients with Korsakoff's syndrome forgot at a normal rate, but H. M. forgot at an abnormally rapid rate. A similar study found that Korsakoff patients forgot at a normal rate but that patients receiving ECT forgot at a very rapid rate. Other studies showed that patient N. A. forgot at a normal rate (Table 9.1).

N. A. and the Korsakoff patients, whose rate of forgetting new material was relatively normal, have injuries in the thalamic region. H. M. and patients receiving ECT, who forgot at an unusually rapid rate, have suffered injuries or disruption of the hippocampus and the temporal stem. These two different regions therefore appear to make essential but fundamentally different contributions to normal memory functions. Experiments with monkeys as subjects support this distinction. A monkey whose thalamus has been operated on does not show rapid memory loss, whereas a monkey whose hippocampus and surrounding (entorhinal) cortex have been bilaterally removed does.

The hippocampus and entorhinal cortex are apparently necessary in memory consoli-

TABLE 9.1 Rates of forgetting in brain-damaged subjects

Forget at a normal rate (Primary injury site: medial dorsal thalamic nucleus)	Forget at a rapid rate (Primary injury site: hippocampus and temporal stem)
Patient N. A.	Patient H. M.
Patients with Korsakoff's syndrome	Patients receiving bilateral ECT
Monkeys with medial thalamic lesions	Monkeys with amygdala and hippocampus lesions

dation, the transfer of declarative material to long-term memory (a process, by the way, that has been found to be facilitated by 8 hours of sleep). The thalamic region, on the other hand, appears to be necessary for the initial coding of certain kinds of declarative information. N. A., for example, has trouble coding verbal material, but he can learn skills—procedural material.

Studies of damaged brains, then, are sources of insight into the working of normal brains. Another approach is to examine how environment facilitates or hinders the development of memory and learning in normal brains.

Semantic Memory

The enormous libraries of facts and procedures to which our brains have access are organized and reorganized through experience into interlocking frameworks, so we can retrieve a piece of data from long-term memory along many different pathways. Our repository of facts and general knowledge is sometimes referred to as *semantic memory,* a subtype of the declarative memory system. Recently, some startling observations were made about the development of this type of memory based on case studies of three patients, ranging in age from 14 to 22 years at the time of testing, who had received brain damage early in life. Two of these patients suffered from severe oxygen deprivation at or near the time of birth (and one did so again at the age of 4 years), whereas the third had been deprived of oxygen at the age of 9 years. All now demonstrate bilateral pathology of the hippocampus, and all have severe *anterograde amnesia* (a type of amnesia in which the person cannot form new memories, although memories of the past are intact, as is the case with patient H. M.). Indeed, their amnesia is sufficiently problematic that the parents of all three patients report that their children (1) cannot find their way around familiar environments or remember where objects and belongings are, (2) are not oriented in place and time, and (3) cannot learn new information; thus, they cannot easily tell you, for example, what they saw on television today or to whom they talked on the telephone and what was said. Remarkably, however, all three patients have learned to read and write (something they have not forgotten how to do), have vocabularies and stores of general information that approach the normal range, and, finally, have gone through mainstream education.

What is particularly intriguing about these patients is that they have developed nearly normal semantic memory—for example, their vocabulary and general knowledge base—in spite of the severe impairment of their *episodic memory* (that is, their ability to remember specific instances or episodes in which both place and time are important). The researchers speculate that the intact, normal brain tissue that surrounds the hippocampus—specifically, the entorhinal cortex—may have permitted the children to develop a knowledge base that does not require *context* (the memory of "where" or "when" something was learned). In contrast, the hippocampal damage prevented the children from acquiring what the scientists called "context rich" memories; that is, episodic memories.

These case studies illustrate the remarkable plasticity of the brain early in life. Important to note is the fact that, although brain damage occurring earlier usually results in a better outcome, our brains have ways of compensating for injury—even in later life. Moreover, the human brain's ability to be modified by experience—learning—and to store this learning—memory—remains one of our greatest strengths. Indeed, the human memory and the information-processing capacities of the brain are so extraordinary that no computer can yet approach their complexity.

Perhaps the most extraordinary characteristic of this human memory and cognitive system is our capacity to think and to think about ourselves thinking—our capacity for consciousness. We turn to these "higher order" functions in Chapter 11. Before doing so, however, it is necessary first to dig a bit deeper into the neural bases of memory, a topic that we tackle in Chapter 10. There we will focus more on the cellular basis of learning and memory. Because more is known about this topic in the context of the simplest forms of memory—for example, conditioning—most of our attention will be focused at that level. Remember, though, that the biological principles underlying conditioning are also likely to apply to the forms of learning and memory that we have considered here.

Summary

1. Regions of the brain that appear to be important in learning and memory are the cerebellum, which may store some classically conditioned responses (see Chapter 8); the hippocampus and surrounding structures, which appear to be critical in short-term memory; the prefrontal cortex, which underlies working memory; and the cerebral cortex, which is where our long-term memories are stored.

2. There are several "types" of memory. The first is working memory, where information is stored for only a few seconds, just long enough to be used in some way. The second is short-term memory, where information may be stored for several minutes. The third type is long-term memory, to which information from short-term memory may be transferred to be held for hours or for a lifetime. The hippocampus is necessary for making the transfer from short-term to long-term memory; its bilateral destruction has been proved to prevent the formation of long-term memories.

3. The human brain seems to process and store different kinds of information in different ways. For

example, procedural knowledge (implicit memory), which is knowledge of how to do something, and declarative knowledge (explicit memory), which has cultural content and may have a linguistic basis, are two distinct kinds of learning. Declarative learning is processed in the temporal lobe and parts of the thalamus, whereas procedural learning apparently is not.

4. Learning and emotion interact, providing an explanatory basis for the theory of operant conditioning. An operant behavior is any voluntary behavior that an animal "naturally" performs. The theory says that behaviors that produce a rewarding experience for the animal tend to be repeated, and behaviors that result in punishment tend not to be repeated. One mechanism that may be responsible for the consolidation of memories of reward and punishment is the circulation of hormones that are released during emotion-arousing circumstances, especially norepinephrine and cortisol. These hormones could affect the activity of the amygdala, in a sequence of physiological processes that underlie memory storage.

5. Studies of victims of various types of amnesia indicate that at least two regions of the brain operate in memory storage and have separate functions. The hippocampus and entorhinal cortex seem to be necessary in the transfer of declarative knowledge to long-term memory. The thalamic region, in contrast, appears necessary to the initial coding of certain kinds of declarative information.

Key Terms

declarative memory
procedural memory
implicit memory
hippocampus
entorhinal cortex

short-term memory
long-term memory
working memory
semantic memory

Further Reading

Hilts, P. J. 1995. *The Strange Tale of Mr. M. and the Nature of Memory.* Simon & Schuster, New York. A good lay description of patient H. M., including his fascinating history.

McGaugh, J. L., Cahill, L., and Roozendaal, B. 1996. Involvement of the amygdala in memory storage: interaction with other brain systems. *Proceedings of the National Academy of Sciences,* 93:13500–13514. A report by a distinguished neuroscientist on how the amygdala plays a role in memory.

Nelson, C. A. 1995. The ontogeny of human memory: a cognitive neuroscience perspective. *Developmental Psychology,* 31:723–735. A proposal by one of the authors of this book on how memory develops through the first years of life.

Sacks, O. *The Man Who Mistook His Wife for a Hat.* 1998. Touchstone Books, New York. A distinguished neurologist reports on a number of fascinating cases of brain damage, including one in which a husband mistakes his wife for a hat and keeps trying to place her on his head.

Schacter, D. L. 1996. *Search for Memory: The Brain, the Mind, and the Past.* Basic Books, New York. An excellent lay description of why the study of memory is so important and how memory has been studied through the centuries.

Squire, L. R. 1994. Declarative and nondeclarative memory: multiple brain systems supporting learning and memory. In D. L. Schacter and E. Tulving, Eds., *Memory Systems 1994* (pp. 203–231). MIT Press, Cambridge, MA. Written by one of the leading authorities on memory, this chapter describes the major "types" of memory that we have considered only briefly.

Vargha-Khadem, F., Gadian, D. G., Watkins, K. E., Connelly, A., Van Paesschen, W., and Mishkin, M. 1997. Differential effects of early hippocampal pathology on episodic and semantic memory. *Science,* 277: 376–380. Three case reports of adults who suffered significant damage to the hippocampus as young children.

Interactive Resources

To continue your study online, visit our Web site at www.worthpublishers.com/bloom. Click on "Chapter 9" for resources including practice quizzes, flash cards, simulations, links to related Web sites, and updates on new research.

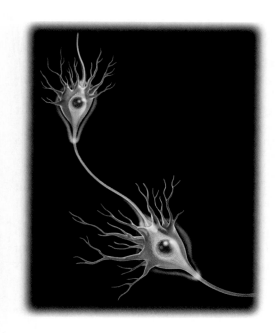

CHAPTER TEN

Cellular Mechanisms of Simple Learning and Memory

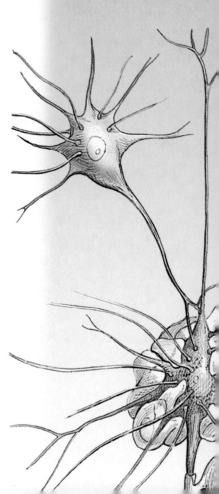

This chapter examines one of the great questions of neuroscience: how do life experiences modify the functional properties of our brain so that we are able to learn from our successes and failures? From the moment of birth—in fact, probably for some time before birth—we experience life as a collection of sensory stimuli: shapes, colors, sounds, textures, pressures, aromas, and tastes. These early sensory experiences can modify the nervous system directly. For example, if researchers deprive the brain of visual stimuli by sealing shut a newborn kitten's eye, neurons in the visual circuits will show fewer dendritic branches, fewer dendritic spines, and fewer synapses (see Chapters 3 and 4). Indeed, they show less development in every aspect than do visual neurons in animals receiving normal stimulation. Thus, vision and other types of sensory experience can drive neural development. Although that is interesting, an even deeper puzzle is how the developing nervous system learns to interpret the sensory events and acquires information from them to guide survival and other behavior.

In Chapter 9, we examined the information that has been gathered about memory and learning through two kinds of research: (1) the observation of normal subjects as they learn and then demonstrate their learning and (2) the observation of subjects in whom accidents and injuries have revealed the functional importance of specific brain structures in learning. In this chapter, we look at learning from a different perspective: what researchers have discovered about *cellular operations* of the nervous systems of subjects as they learn from sensory experience and use the learning to make new behavioral choices. In fact, most psychologists would define learning as a relatively permanent change in behavior as a result of experience.

Learning and remembering are, for all practical purposes, two sides of the same coin. *Learning* refers to the information-acquisition process and *memory* to the storage and retrieval process. Even the simplest kinds of learning imply that something has been remembered. Birds and deer learn to run from an approaching fire in the forest. Cats who repeatedly hear the sound of a can opener followed immediately by the sight and smell of food quickly learn that the can-opener sound reliably predicts their feeding. In fact, as you study this chapter, you will find that learning and remembering about the brain will in fact modify the structure and function of your own brain.

Clearly there are many kinds of learning, from the simplest kinds of survival reflexes learned by "lower" animals to the complex frameworks of abstract knowledge (such as mathematics, physics, philosophy, and art) that the human brain is capable of constructing. In this chapter, we shall look first at the cellular events of learning in animals with very simple nervous systems. In the neurons of these animals, researchers have been able to identify and explain some of the physical and chemical changes that constitute learning. The great pioneering analyst of the brain's cellular structure, Santiago Ramón y Cajal, regarded the synapse as the primary site of interneuronal communication and held strongly to the view that learning was a synaptic event. Accordingly, we shall consider data establishing that a change in a specific neurotransmitter's action at a specific synaptic location is both necessary and sufficient to explain a behavioral change in a living organism. It is not yet known with complete certainty that human memory and learning capacities are based on exactly the same kinds of molecular and cellular changes as those seen in the brains of other species. Nevertheless, the principles gleaned from these experimental systems are unquestionably essential to understanding the human memory and learning operations and perhaps to developing treatments that can be used to restore these properties when diseases interfere.

Simple Learning and Neural Changes

Two categories of learning—called "nonassociative" and "associative" learning—have been studied at the cellular level with particularly impressive results revealing specific short-term and long-term synaptic changes. *Non-associative learning* refers to the functional changes that ensue when an organism interacts with a single, repeating, inconsequential stimulus. For example, an organism may jump once or twice to a flash of light or loud sound, but, when there are no consequences, it soon learns to ignore the distraction. The decrease in response that occurs when a sensory stimulus is repeated serially without change is called *habituation* and is a nonassociative form of learning. This kind of adaptation is not due to the exhaustion of a sensory system's signaling capacity by prolonged overstimulation. Rather, habituation refers to a behavioral change that allows an organism to ignore a meaningless signal. Importantly, the original, unhabituated response can be restored by an unexpected difference in the sensory stimulus, either a different intensity or a different modality. This reversal of the habituated response is termed *sensitization,* and it, too, is a nonassociative learning event (in fact, it is also known as "nonassociative facilitation").

In *associative learning,* as the name implies, the subject comes to associate a previously neutral (meaningless) stimulus with a response normally generated by another previously learned cue. Associative learning is also called *classical,* or Pavlovian, *conditioning*. The cat's associative response to the sound of the can opener is of the same sort made famous by Pavlov's archetypal experiments demonstrating that, after sufficient exposure, a dog would begin to salivate when it heard the sound of a bell previously rung every time raw meat was offered (described in greater detail in a later section).

Habituation and sensitization—the two forms of nonassociative learning just described—and classical conditioning are three kinds of "simple" learning, so called to differentiate them from the more complex, nonreflexive, intentional forms of learning that require the formation of abstract concepts or the use of factual or object classification skills. Simple learning is accomplished without the subject's awareness of a change in behavior. Most animals—even animals with only ganglia for brains—can learn in these elementary ways.

In a fourth category of simple learning, *operant conditioning,* an animal learns—either by reward or punishment—to respond to a given stimulus with a specific act, often one that is unnatural for that animal. A rat that presses a steel lever to get a food pellet is demonstrating operant conditioning. All these types of learning play important roles in human behavior.

Habituation and Sensitization

To reiterate, habituation takes place when a stimulus that an organism originally responded to is presented so often that the organism stops responding to it. In sensitization, the opposite of habituation, an animal learns to respond vigorously to a previously neutral stimulus (see Figure 10.1 on the following page). An animal that has habituated

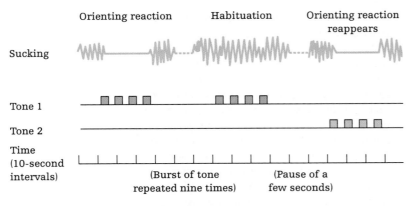

Orienting reaction   Habituation   Orienting reaction reappears

Sucking

Tone 1

Tone 2

Time
(10-second
intervals)

(Burst of tone repeated nine times)   (Pause of a few seconds)

Figure 10.1 A sensing device in a pacifier sucked on by a baby only 4 hours old produced the tracing at the top. The baby stopped sucking when a tone was first played but habituated to it—that is, resumed sucking—after hearing the tone 9 or 10 times. Sucking stopped again when the second tone was sounded.

to the sound of a chair rocking may again begin to react to that sound if the lights in the room suddenly go out.

Both habituation and sensitization have survival value. In sensitization, an animal generally experiences some noxious or irritating stimulus, learns to regard it as dangerous, and consequently attempts to avoid it. In habituation, a stimulus that originally aroused the animal is subsequently experienced several times without irritation or harm; the animal learns to ignore the stimulus and so is freer to attend to other stimuli.

Studies of the sea snail *Aplysia californica* by Eric Kandel and his colleagues have demonstrated the cellular changes that accompany habituation. Two notable characteristics of this creature made it a very promising model to study: (1) *Aplysia*'s nervous system is made up of only about 20,000 neurons, some of them so large they can be

seen by the naked eye; and (2) *Aplysia* has an easily induced reflex behavior, the gill-withdrawal reflex, that is vital to its survival (see Figure 10.2). When waters are calm, *Aplysia* extends its gill to breathe. In rough waters or if its siphon is touched by a piece of floating debris—or by experimenters in the laboratory shooting it with a jet of water—it withdraws the gill to protect it. This gill withdrawal is controlled by one ganglion, called the *abdominal ganglion,* containing 6 motoneurons and 24 sensory neurons. Some of the sensory neurons are in direct contact with the motoneurons through excitatory synapses; others are in indirect contact, through interneurons.

After repeated stimulation of the gill in laboratory training, *Aplysia* withdraws the gill less vigorously or not at all. Such a habituated response, created by as few as 10 stimulations, might last for hours. This form of learning is referred to as short term because it comes on quickly and lasts for a relatively brief period of time. Such learning is the result of a specific change that takes place at

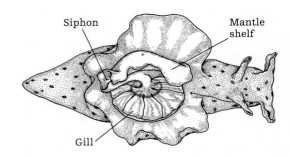

Siphon

Mantle shelf

Gill

Figure 10.2 After brief stimulation, *Aplysia* normally retracts its gill into the position shown in blue. Prolonged stimulation can produce habituation, so the gill-withdrawal response weakens or actually ceases.

the synapses between the sensory neurons and the motoneurons. Specifically, as stimulation continues, less neurotransmitter is released from the sensory neurons to activate synapses to the motoneurons. The motoneurons thus receive a lower level of sensory activation, and the behavior that they generate—the gill withdrawal—is performed less vigorously. In *Aplysia*, then, habituation results when excitation decreases at the synapses of an already existing neural pathway. If the stimulation ceases, however, the release of neurotransmitter will return to normal in a few hours, and the gill-withdrawal reflex will again be vigorous.

What is perhaps most exciting about the study of the habituation mechanism in *Aplysia* is that the responsible genes and gene products have been identified. This discovery has been a source of insight into similar molecular factors operating in much more complex nervous systems, such as our own.

In sensitization, the reverse of habituation, the effectiveness of synaptic transmission is enhanced. In *Aplysia*'s gill-withdrawal reflex, for example, strong electrical stimulation of the connections between the visceral ganglion (the abdominal ganglion described earlier) and the head ganglion (*Aplysia*'s most brainlike structure) facilitates gill withdrawal by increasing the amount of transmitter released by the sensory nerves taking part in the withdrawal reflex. This increased release of sensory transmitter thus counteracts any previously induced habituation of the reflex. The effects of sensitization, like those of habituation, can last from several minutes to hours and are regarded as short-term adaptations.

The sensitizing stimulation also has another effect in *Aplysia*. It has been found to increase the ganglionic content of the postsynaptic second messenger cyclic adenosine monophosphate (cAMP; introduced in Chapter 2). Exposure of the ganglion both to serotonin (known to activate cAMP production in this ganglion) and to cAMP (applied to the whole ganglion or injected intracellularly into the sensory nerve cell) replicated the effects of the sensitizing stimulation. These data shed further light on the process of sensitization by suggesting that the sensitizing stimulation activates a serotonin-secreting interneuron between the sensory neuron and the motoneuron (see Figure 10.3 on the following page). The release of serotonin by this interneuron leads to increased levels of cAMP in the sensory neuron and a consequent enhancement of the amount of transmitter that it is able to release. Eventually, this interneuron (and other sensitizing interneurons with comparable biochemical actions) was identified.

Habituation and sensitization are the simplest kinds of learning because they do not require the organism to make an association between one event or stimulus and another. In classical conditioning, the animal does have to learn such an association.

Classical Conditioning

In the early 1900s, Ivan Pavlov conducted the experiments that demonstrated what has come to be called classical conditioning. While studying dogs' digestive systems, he discovered that the animals began to salivate at the sight of the white-coated attendants who usually brought them food, well before the dogs actually had the food in front of them. Inspired by this observation, he went on to prove that the sound of a bell or a flash of light, if presented consistently before the arrival of food, could also be made to cause the dogs to salivate.

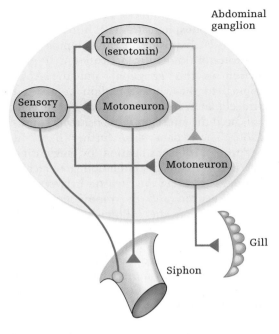

Abdominal
ganglion

Gill

Siphon

Figure 10.3 A simplified circuit diagram of the neurons taking part in the *Aplysia* gill-withdrawal reflex (similar withdrawal also occurs for the siphon, a small fleshy tube used to expel seawater and internal wastes). Sensory neurons from the siphon can excite the motoneurons that will withdraw the gill and the siphon into the internal mantle cavity. The sensory neurons also excite a serotonin-secreting interneuron that enhances the responses of the motoneurons to the sensory stimulation.

Classical conditioning, then, is the learning that occurs when a stimulus that naturally produces a certain reaction, as food naturally and automatically produces salivation, is paired a number of times with a neutral (meaningless) stimulus, such as the ringing of a bell. With classical conditioning, the neutral stimulus comes to elicit the same reaction as the primary stimulus. For condi-

tioning to take place, the two stimuli must be presented very close to each other in time, with the sound of the bell immediately preceding the presentation of food. In this example, the food represents what psychologists have come to call the *unconditioned stimulus* (US, the natural, automatic stimulus); the bell, a previously neutral stimulus, is called the *conditioned stimulus* (CS); the salivation when food is presented is called the *unconditioned response* (UR); and the salivation on hearing the bell is called the *conditioned response* (CR). (Pavlov himself used the terms "unconditional stimulus"—the stimulus with no conditions attached—and "conditional stimulus"—the stimulus that requires the condition of being paired with a primary stimulus.) In other words, an animal learns the association between an unconditioned stimulus (food) and a conditioned stimulus (bell) so that its behavior in response to the previously neutral stimulus (bell) changes. The cat that comes running to the kitchen when it hears the can opener operating has been conditioned to associate that sound with the presentation of food.

The same experimental methods that revealed the cellular events underlying habituation and sensitization also revealed some of the cellular activity that underlies a more complex form of memory plasticity. The gill-withdrawal reflex of *Aplysia,* for example, demonstrates classical conditioning when a weak touch is employed as a conditioned stimulus and a very strong electrical shock to the tail is used as the unconditioned stimulus. In other words, after a few pairings of a light touch with a strong shock to the tail, *Aplysia* learns to respond to a light touch by protectively withdrawing its gill. The simple circuits that operate in this response have also been identified and recreated in tissue culture.

Under these greatly simplified conditions, it is possible to show that the biochemical effects of the unconditioned stimulus (that is, of the shock) can be replicated by local exposure of the motoneurons to serotonin or cAMP. Like the activities of the *Aplysia* sensory neurons that would normally release serotonin to stimulate the synthesis of cAMP, these local responses interact with the excitatory effects of the conditioned stimulus. As in the intact ganglion, depolarization of the sensory nerve terminals leads to rises in intraneuronal calcium ions. The rise in calcium ions in turn synergizes with the rise in cAMP to initiate enduring changes in synaptic efficacy for the duration of the conditioned response. The combined changes in Ca^{2+} and in cAMP produce a long-lasting change in the response pattern of the motoneuron. These observations suggested that the associative, classically conditioned gill-withdrawal reflex is basically an extension of the nonassociative presynaptic sensitization. Ultimately, both forms of learning are represented by increased levels of the intracellular regulator cAMP.

Supportive evidence for the role of cAMP (and the consequent intracellular cascades of interacting proteins) in cellular learning came from a novel experimental system based on the fruit fly *Drosophila melanogaster.* Seymour Benzer (a pioneer in the study of fly behavior and its genetic basis) and his colleagues disrupted single unknown genes by exposing the flies to discrete doses of cancer-producing chemicals and then breeding them for a few generations to identify specific mutations. In this way, the scientists were eventually able to recognize behavioral mutations in some of the strains and to determine the gene product responsible for the abnormal behavior.

For example, in one set of experiments, the scientists used classical conditioning that paired odors with electrical shocks to teach flies to avoid certain odors. Flies that were genetically incapable of this learning were discovered to be deficient in one or another of the proteins needed to make cAMP, to metabolize cAMP, or to respond to changes in cAMP content. Researchers observed the same deficiencies in association with other long-term memory problems as well. As described in a later section, similar changes were observed in cellular models of memory and learning in the rodent central nervous system.

Thus, similar biochemical and biophysical changes during learning have been discovered in organisms as widely disparate as fruit flies, sea snails, and rodents. This fact suggests that the fundamental aspects of these adaptive events have been conserved through evolution. One of the principles of biology is that nature builds on and reuses important functional building blocks. In all likelihood, the same molecular processes—regulation of intracellular cAMP and Ca^{2+}—are key components of the basic learning process in larger mammals as well. Although this likelihood is not yet known with certainty, the following examples will illustrate current understanding.

Brain Systems and Memory

Do animals with brains demonstrate the same learning-associated cellular changes seen in lower organisms? Are these changes concentrated in the parts of the brain that clinical and experimental studies have shown to be essential for memory (see Chapter 9)? Recent research has been able to provide some important clues.

The Rabbit Nictitating-Membrane Reflex and Associative Learning

The rabbit's eye has a feature not seen in many other mammals, an extra internal eyelid in the inner angle of the eye that can quickly be extended to protect the cornea. This structure is called the *nictitating membrane*. Investigation of how the reflexive movement of this membrane can be conditioned has provided another molecular and cellular model for scientists to use in the study of memory and associative learning. Using this mammalian neuronal system, scientists can observe the performance of the animal during tests of learning and memory and at the same time discover exactly where in the brain the learning events have taken place.

Normally, a rabbit will automatically blink its nictitating membrane every time a puff of air blows on the cornea. Basic studies accomplished independently by John Harvey and Richard Thompson showed that this reflex could be associatively (classically) conditioned. For example, a loud tone presented just before the air puff can condition rabbits to blink to the tone alone. Eventually, the rabbits blink every time they hear the tone, with no air puff at all. Scientists describe this procedure as "conditioning the eye-blink reflex."

The sensory and motor pathways of this reflex response were already well known from earlier research. By making experimental lesions in different parts of this circuitry and by stimulating different relay points, researchers eventually defined which sites in which pathways produce the unconditioned (air puff-induced) blink and the conditioned blink triggered by the tone (see Figure 10.4). The critical site for producing the associative response was identified as the *interpositus nucleus*, one of the deep cerebellar nuclei.

Most of the transmitters operating in this system have not yet been defined, but, within the interpositus, GABA antagonists have been observed to block the conditional reflex. At the same time, chemical lesions of the *inferior olivary nucleus* (the source of the climbing fiber projection to cerebellar Purkinje neurons, described in Chapter 5) will also completely disrupt the acquisition and retention of the conditional reflex. Because glutamate is presumed to be the transmitter of this climbing fiber pathway, this experimental result implies that glutamate is the transmitter for this step, which is the final link in the circuit.

In more recent experiments, forebrain regions, such as the hippocampus, also have been implicated in the nictitating-membrane associative reflex. For these experiments, the rabbits received similar classical conditioning of the nictitating membrane response, but the tone stimulus and the air puff were separated by a pause, or *trace*, of approximately 500 milliseconds between the end of the conditioned stimulus and the start of the unconditioned stimulus to make the simple learning task just a bit more complicated. The extra time delay allowed the investigators to distinguish nonspecific arousal such as the rabbit's exhibiting fear or reacting to the voices of the investigators (which could possibly sensitize the reflex) from more specific interactions. Macroelectrodes placed in the hippocampus showed a substantial increase in activity there during the tone and persisting through the trace interval, even before the rabbit showed any consistent association between the tone and the unconditioned response (see Figure 10.5 on page 308). As the rabbit learned the association, hippocampal neurons became active later and later in the trace interval. These observa-

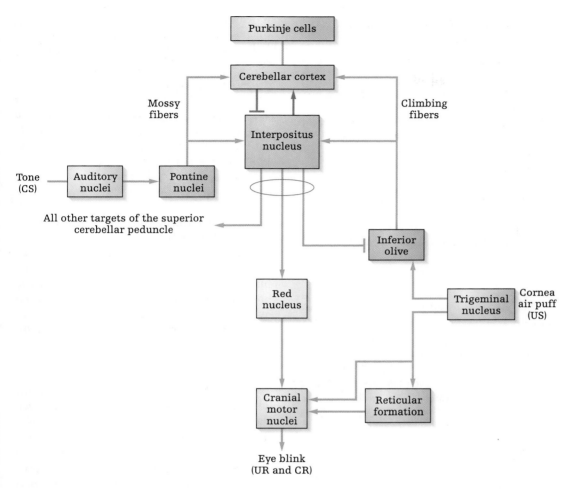

Figure 10.4 Schematic diagram of the principal brain structures and circuitry analyzed for the rabbit eye-blink conditioning response. The unconditioned stimulus (the air puff) is applied to the cornea and enters the circuitry through the sensory fibers of the trigeminal ganglion. The conditioned stimulus (a neutral tone) enters through the auditory system. With training, synaptic adaptations between the cerebellar Purkinje neurons and their targets in the deep cerebellar nuclei allow the conditioned stimulus to elicit the eye blink, which is then both the conditioned and unconditioned response.

tions point to some specific, but unknown, interactions between the hippocampus and the cerebellum. Perhaps the hippocampus is learning the context of the conditions for the unusual sensory event that now pro- duces movement of the nictitating mem- brane. The findings also suggest that cer- tain types of associative memories can be stored within the cerebellum, a fact that earlier research had overlooked.

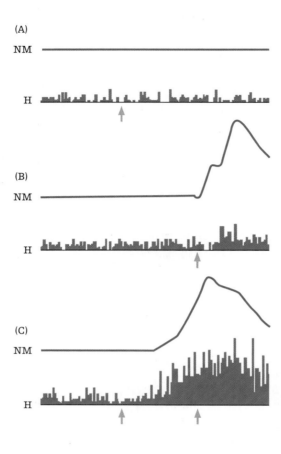

(A)

NM

H

(B)

NM

H

(C)

NM

H

Figure 10.5 The use of the hippocampal trace-stimulation method shows the responses of the nictitating membrane (NM) and of neurons recorded in the rabbit hippocampal formation (H) to the the tone alone (A), to the air puff (B), and to the tone followed by the air puff (C) after the conditioning training has taken place.
Note that the hippocampal neurons and the nictitating membrane begin to respond after the tone but before the air puff. Arrows indicate the applications of the stimuli.

The results of these experimental studies on rabbits have important implications. For example, patients with cerebellar injuries (say, due to strokes, cancer, or surgery for these problems) demonstrate severe impairment in acquiring a conditioned eye-blink response. It is interesting that these patients can be consciously aware that a tone will be followed by a puff of air, but the reflex still cannot be conditioned. In contrast, patient H. M., the well-known neurosurgical case who suffered damage to the hippocampus but not the cerebellum and who was dis-cussed at length in Chapter 9, *can* acquire the conditioned eye-blink response, although he is *not* aware of having done so. Collectively, it would appear that the human literature is in agreement with the animal literature: acquiring the conditioned eye-blink response requires the cerebellum and does not require structures of the medial temporal lobe.

The Hippocampus

The hippocampus (see Figure 10.6) has been the subject of much research in the past four decades, but we still cannot say precisely what functions it performs in learning and memory (see Chapter 9). The numerous studies have taken various approaches and discovered several roles that the hippocampus might play.

The few human patients who are known to have suffered severe damage to both left and right hippocampi have serious learning problems. They are unable to store memories of anything new that they learn, even the name or the face of someone whom they encountered only minutes earlier. Their memories of events that occurred before the brain damage, however, appear to be unimpaired. (See pages 325–327 for a discussion of these patients and their problems.)

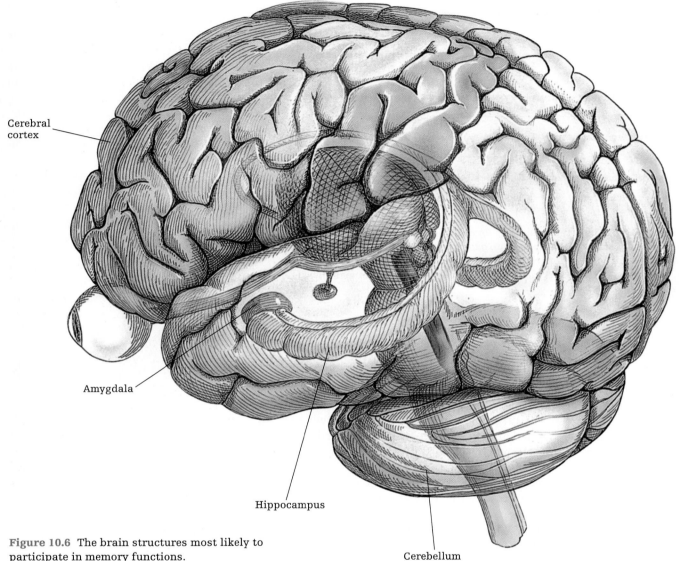

Cerebral cortex

Amygdala

Hippocampus

Cerebellum

Figure 10.6 The brain structures most likely to participate in memory functions.

More than 20 years ago, researchers who implanted electrodes in single neurons of rats' brains learned that some neurons in the hippocampus seem to respond only when the animal is at a certain place in a familiar environment (O'Keefe and Nadel, 1978). The cell remains quiet until the animal reaches a certain location. Then, and only then, the neuron fires rapidly, only to become quiescent again when the rat moves away. In rats, at least, the hippocampus apparently plays an important role in the learning of a "spatial map."

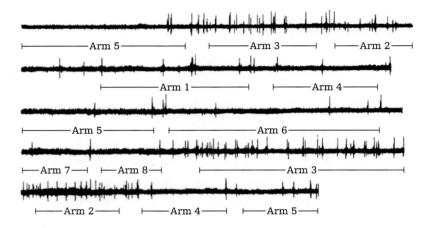

Arm 5 —— Arm 3 —— Arm 2

Arm 1 —— Arm 4

Arm 5 —— Arm 6

Arm 7 — Arm 8 — Arm 3

Arm 2 —— Arm 4 —— Arm 5

Figure 10.7 Activity recorded from an electrode implanted in one neuron of a rat's hippocampus in an experiment by John O'Keefe and Lynn Nadel. The neuron fires rapidly only when the rat is in arms 2 or 3 of the maze, places that evidently have some special spatial meaning to the rat.

Long-Term Potentiation Recent research has revealed that cells in the hippocampus, when stimulated repeatedly by electrodes or by the neurotransmitters of specific hippocampal pathways, will continue firing for as long as weeks after the stimulation stops. This technique, called *long-term potentiation* (LTP), produces neuronal firing resembling that found in an animal going about the ordinary business of learning something.

The expression "long-term potentiation" refers to a long-lasting enhancement of syn-

This phenomenon was demonstrated in a maze modeled after the way that rats forage in the wild (see Figures 10.7 and 10.8); every arm of the maze had food at its end, as would many routes in a natural setting. The rat's problem was to remember where it had already been in order to proceed to a place where it had not yet eaten the food. After only a few runs, normal rats learned the maze so well that they never retraced their steps. After the hippocampi of these rats were surgically removed, however, the animals frequently retraced their paths, apparently unable to remember where they had been and where they had not. It was as though the rats had lost their short-term "spatial memory." Perhaps, then, the hippocampus operates in "spatial memory" over the short-term, as indicated by its differing levels of neuronal activity during classical conditioning.

Figure 10.8 This radial arm maze was created by David Olton to test rat memory. Food was placed at the end of every arm, and, just as in the wild, the rat's problem was to find all the food without retracing its steps, wasting time running to places that it had already visited. The pattern shown here represents the perfect learning of normal rats: this rat visited each arm of the maze only once, eating whatever it found there; it did not go back to an empty arm even one time.

aptic transmission. The enhancement, which lasts minutes to days, depending on the conditions used to evoke it and on where it is tested, is manifested as an increase in the sizes of excitatory postsynaptic responses in specific circuits. It was first demonstrated by brief, high-frequency stimulation of the entorhinal cortex through the perforant path (see Figure 10.9), which resulted in an enhanced activation of granule cells of the hippocampal dentate gyrus. Studies in cats, guinea pigs, and rats confirmed that the enhanced transmission could last for days to weeks.

The conditions for expressing the phenomenon of long-term potentiation may sound familiar, because they are virtually the same conditions as those described in Chapter 9 for "Hebbian" synapses. In both LTP and Hebb's theory of synaptic plasticity, a postsynaptic neuron's connections can be enhanced and "remembered" only when a reinforcing pathway converges on the postsynaptic neuron simultaneously with the signal being facilitated by that neuron.

Long-term potentiation has also been observed at two other sites within the hippocampal formation: (1) at the synapses between the dentate granule cells and their mossy fiber synapses to CA3 pyramidal neurons and (2) between CA3 pyramidal neurons and their targets, the CA1 pyramidal neurons (see Figure 10.9). Although the basic phenomenon of long-term potentiation after high-frequency, high-intensity activation by an afferent pathway is similar in all three synaptic sites, the relative importance of specific transmitters and their receptors varies considerably.

Antagonists of N-methyl-D-aspartic acid will prevent LTP but will not affect previously potentiated transmission. Researchers therefore suspect that glutamate acting at the

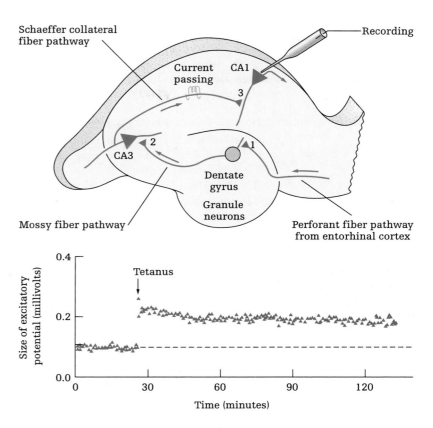

Figure 10.9 *Top:* A simplified diagram of the main excitatory circuits within the rat hippocampal formation, each of which is capable of demonstrating the basic phenomenon of long-term potentiation: (1) entorhinal cortex to dentate granule neurons through the perforant pathway, (2) dentate granule cells to CA3 pyramidal neurons through the mossy fiber pathway, (3) CA3 pyramidal neurons to CA1 pyramidal neurons through the Schaffer collateral fiber pathway. *Bottom:* A typical long-term potentiated response as would be seen if a long burst of frequent electrical stimuli were applied to any of these circuits.

NMDA receptor is responsible for starting the long-lasting synaptic enhancement. The required high-frequency, high-intensity stimulation of the NMDA receptor couples the postsynaptic neuron's depolarization with an increase in the entry of Ca^{2+}. For the potentiation to occur, however, the NMDA receptor must be biochemically prepared through the actions of glutamate or other transmitters at a convergent synapse. Mice with genetically induced mutations in their NMDA receptors have apparently normal brain-cell structure and normal brain growth and development, but their hippocampal LTP is significantly reduced.

The NMDA-regulated step alone, however, is not sufficient for long-term enhanced transmission. A cAMP-regulated process similar to those seen in the longer-term plasticity of *Aplysia* and *Drosophila* research models also has been noted in connection with hippocampal LTP. In the wake of pharmacological studies that strongly suggested a role for cAMP, transgenic mice with mutations in the cAMP response-element binding protein (CREB) learned a short-term conditioned fear response normally but could not retain their learned fear for more than 2 hours. LTP induction also was normal in these mice but was likewise shortened.

It is clear that the hippocampus plays a role in learning and memory, even if its exact function cannot yet be described.

Long-Term Depression Glutamate receptors and calcium ions also play significant roles in a related intrahippocampal and intracerebellar process called *long-term depression* (LTD), which has so far received much less scientific examination. If LTP is seen as the cellular and molecular model for learning, LTD could be considered the equivalent model for forgetting.

LTD has been most extensively studied at the synapses between the parallel fibers and the Purkinje neurons, but it is also seen in connections to hippocampal pyramidal neurons. The induction of LTD in Purkinje neurons requires the influx of calcium ions as well as the simultaneous activation of two other subtypes of glutamate receptors described in Chapter 2—an ionotropic glutamate receptor and a G-protein–coupled glutamate receptor. Transgenic mice whose gene for the G-protein–coupled glutamate receptor has been disrupted (so that they form only inactive receptors) do not exhibit parallel-fiber-to-Purkinje-neuron LTD.

Progressive accumulation of the kinds of evidence described in this chapter will one day explain with precision the functioning of the brain regions described in Chapter 9, and we will understand the brain's remarkable ability to learn, remember, and adapt. In the next chapter, we will consider still more complex aspects of brain function concerning our ability to communicate and to be aware of our own mental activity.

Summary

1. The cellular circuits for several models of nonassociative (reflexive) and associative learning have been described for both invertebrate and mammalian nervous systems. In mammals, the hippocampal formation and the cerebellum have received the most attention in these studies.

2. Within these circuits, the associative mechanisms seem to build on and extend the basic molecular events occurring in nonassociative learning.

3. In the invertebrate gill-withdrawal reflex, habituation has been explained as the adaptive reduction of transmitter released presynaptically from the sensory pathway conveying the stimulus to be ignored. The identity of the transmitter

for the sensory pathway is still unknown. The reversal of habituation by a sensitizing second stimulus activates the original level of transmitter release through changes in the intracellular second messenger cAMP, with its ability to alter the effectiveness of proteins mediating calcium-sensitive transmitter release.

4. When the gill-withdrawal reflex is subjected to classical conditioning by association with an initially irrelevant sensory stimulus, the intracellular mechanisms are similar—specifically, regulation of cAMP-mediated changes in proteins that influence transmitter release and levels of intracellular-calcium ions. Classical conditioning also requires changes in postsynaptic neuronal function in the cir-cuits that are conditioned.

5. In the rabbit, a conditioned modification of the nictitating membrane withdrawal reflex can be learned. This adaptation relies on GABA-mediated circuits in the deep cerebellar nuclei. The learning can be further modified by incoming information from the hippocampal formation.

6. One form of enduring long-term alteration in synaptic function in the hippocampal formation is termed long-term potentiation. LTP requires convergent interactions between any of several excitatory synapses reacting through a special glutamate receptor, the N-methyl-D-aspartate receptor. After the initial depolarization, NMDA-mediated responses allow the enhanced entry of calcium pre- and postsynaptically. Actions by other hippocampal afferent systems that enhance cAMP pre- and postsynaptically also are required.

Key Terms

learning
memory
nonassociative learning
associative learning
habituation
sensitization
short-term adaptation
long-term potentiation
long-term depression
cAMP

Further Reading

Cleary, L. L., Lee, W. L., and Byrne, J. H. 1998. Cellular correlates of long-term sensitization in *Aplysia*. *Journal of Neuroscience* 158:5988–5998. This review is intended for advanced students who wish greater exposure to the intricacies of long-term changes in invertebrate neurons during nonassociative learning.

Daniel, H., Levenes, C., and Crépel, F. 1998. Cellular mechanisms of cerebellar LTD. *Trends in Neurosciences* 21:401–407. A brief review of the phenomena underlying cerebellar synaptic changes during long-term depression.

Kandel, E. R. 1979. Cellular insights into behavior and learning. *Harvey Lectures,* Series 73, pp. 29–92. A comprehensive, but early, overview of the *Aplysia* ganglionic connections that mediate the withdrawal reflex.

Kandel, E. R. 1995. Cellular mechanisms in learning and memory. In E. R. Kandel, J. H. Schwartz, and T. M. Jessell, Eds., *Essentials of Neural Science and Behavior* (pp. 667–694). Appleton and Lange, East Norwalk, CT. A more recent overview of the invertebrate learning phenomena and their similarity in vertebrate nervous systems.

Lechner, H. A., and Byrne, J. H. 1998. New perspectives on classical conditioning: a synthesis of Hebbian and non-Hebbian mechanisms. *Neuron* 20:355–358. An excellent brief review of the phenomena of classical conditioning from the perspective of an invertebrate physiologist.

Squire, L. R., and Knowlton, B. J. 1994. Memory, hippocampus and brain systems. In M. Gazzaniga, Ed., *The Cognitive Neurosciences* (pp. 825–837). MIT Press, Cambridge, MA. A definitive analysis of the various categories of memory from the learning of facts to skills and of the simpler forms of associative and nonassociative learning described in the present chapter.

Thompson, R. F., and Kim, J. 1996. Memory systems in the brain and the localization of memory. *Proceedings of the National Academy of Sciences* 93:13438–13444. A recent brief review of the rabbit eye-blink reflex experimental memory system.

Interactive Resources

The CD-ROM that accompanies this book offers various ways to visualize the material covered in this chapter. Its "Electrical Brain Stimulation" module includes a video clip on self-stimulation in rats.

To continue your study online, visit our Web site at www.worthpublishers.com/bloom. Click on "Chapter 10" for resources including practice quizzes, flash cards, simulations, links to related Web sites, and updates on new research.

Thinking and Consciousness

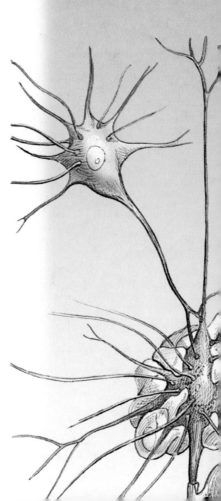

△○△○△__

You probably solved this problem—you put a circle in the blank—even before you consciously saw this row of symbols as a problem. During the second or so that this response took, you were *thinking*—engaging in structured mental actions. But how much of that thinking were you aware of?

Thinking, or mental action, is sometimes conscious and often not conscious. The concept of consciousness itself is so rich and complex that it has no simple definition. We all know what we mean when we say that a person is "conscious": we are referring to the condition that is turned off when we go to sleep or is lost when we suffer a severe blow to the head. But that simplest state of consciousness is not our subject here. Rather, we shall examine *active consciousness,* the state of being aware of our thoughts and behaviors. As a working definition, let us say that *consciousness* is awareness of one's own mental or physical actions or both.

Most scientists agree with this definition. However, they do not necessarily agree about the nature, source, or substance of the awareness to which it refers. Because neuroscientists cannot yet blueprint the brain mechanisms responsible for this focused awareness, the nature of human consciousness remains at the center of an ancient and ongoing debate. Participants in the debate include physiologists, philosophers, theologians, and computer scientists in the field of artificial intelligence, as well as neuroscientists of all stripes. One point of controversy is whether consciousness is an integral, material process of the brain or a separate, nonmaterial function—a spirit, or soul. Our position has already been stated. Just as sensing, moving, adapting, learning, and feeling can ultimately be explained in relation to the structure and workings of the brain, so will consciousness ultimately be explained in this same light.

Another point of controversy is whether consciousness is the exclusive province of human beings. Are other animals capable of consciousness? Some argue that their behavior indicates that they do engage in conscious thinking. The behavior of the monkeys that wash sand off corn kernels given to them by anthropologists on the beaches of northern Japan is often cited as an example of animal thought. So is that of the "creative" crows that drop shellfish onto the rocks to break them open while other crows look on and learn from them. We know that these monkeys and crows are capable of procedural learning—they can learn and remember *how to do* some things without being aware of the fact that they have learned. But such animal behavior does not necessarily indicate conscious thinking.

As stated in Chapter 9, *declarative learning*—the learning of facts—requires both that we store our previous experiences in memory frameworks and that we have access to those memories when a situation reminds us that they are on tap. Declarative knowledge combines a record of one's previous experiences, a sense of familiarity with those experiences, information about the time and place that they occurred, and factual knowledge derived from those experiences. To make their declarative knowledge accessible, human beings use language. We even use language to classify objects and events that we have never experienced or been conscious of before. Once we name new experiences, we can file them in their appropriate frameworks. All of this is to say that we use language to name and describe the things that appear in consciousness. There are few aspects of conscious thought that do not depend on language. One such aspect is the mental representation and rotation of objects in space. Generally speaking, language is the basic means by which human beings structure their experience. Therefore, consciousness depends largely on language.

If consciousness does depend primarily on language, then human consciousness is obviously not present at birth. It develops as we gain experience in the world and as we build a vocabulary that allows us to think about things and their relations, to plan and decide, to select and act. Having the capacity for conscious awareness does not mean that we are aware all the time. We often act—or even think and solve problems like the one at the beginning of this chapter—without our consciousness being engaged. Later, though, when we think back on what we did, mentally reconstructing the behavior or the event and focusing our conscious mind on our actions, we are able to fit those actions into a rational or at least plausible pattern that coincides with our consciously held goals, self-image, and values.

We can perform some actions without conscious planning because, as the psychologist Julian Jaynes says, "Our minds often work much faster than consciousness can keep up." *Mind*, as we use the term, is not synonymous with consciousness but with the working of the brain as a whole—mind is a product of what the brain does. The brain events that we experience consciously are only those events that are processed through the brain's language system.

You have seen how the brain carries out its responsibilities for directing specific behaviors—how we move, how we sense, how we learn and remember, how we regulate our internal systems, how we feel. We do some or all of these things simultaneously, and our brains integrate and organize all of them. These same high-level integrative and organizational abilities also make thinking and consciousness possible. Although we are far from having a thorough understanding of how such integration takes place, in a gross

sense we do at least know something about *where* much of it takes place. That place is the cerebral cortex.

Anatomy and Mind

What we call thinking and consciousness appear to depend on the quarter-inch thickness of the cerebral cortex that covers the four lobes of the brain. Its intricate and highly ordered architecture contains about 75 percent of the brain's approximately 50 billion neurons. You are already familiar with some regions of the cortex that are dedicated to specific functions. The primary visual cortex, located in the occipital lobe, for example, processes visual stimuli and is instrumental in producing our sense of sight. Many areas of the cortex, however, do not have such specific, wired-in functions.

Association Cortex

The large "uncommitted" areas of the cortex have been called *association cortex* (see Figure 11.1 on page 320). Traditional brain science has held that associations between the specialized areas of the cortex are formed here, integrating the data from those various parts. Here, too, it is believed, new information is integrated with past emotions and memories, enabling human beings to think, decide, and plan.

Association areas in the parietal lobe, for example, are thought to synthesize information from the somatosensory cortex (messages from the skin, muscles, tendons, and joints about the body's position and movement) with information about sight and sound transmitted from the visual and auditory cortices in the occipital and temporal lobes. According to the traditional model, this integrated information helps us to form

Altered Consciousness

Human beings in all known cultures throughout history have chosen to ingest substances that alter brain chemistry and, thus, alter consciousness. Many medicines prescribed by doctors into the 1950s contained some form of opium. Laudanum, a sleeping aid and potion "for the nerves" favored during the Victorian era, is a mixture of alcohol and morphine. The popularity of the first cola drinks owed something to the presence of cocaine in the formula. Common substances that alter consciousness range from the caffeine in coffee to alcohol—perhaps the drug of choice in Western cultures—to potent hallucinogens such as LSD.

Human beings seem to have two compelling but contradictory needs: we like things to stay the same (to be familiar) and we crave novelty. We search for substances that will get us out of our rut—drug abusers often report that they take drugs to relieve boredom—and substances that calm our anxiety when things become too unpredictable. The two drugs that have become increasingly common as boredom relievers are cocaine and marijuana.

The Indians of the Andes have for centuries chewed the leaves of the coca bush. When ingested, the cocaine in the leaves acts as a stimulant to the central nervous system. It acts to inhibit the reuptake of norepinephrine in the central nervous system and peripheral nervous system and of dopamine in the central nervous system after the release of those neurotransmitters into their synapses. Thus, more of these transmitters remain available to receiving cells for longer periods of time, and this excess produces the stimulation and energy that users feel. Drugs used for the treatment of depression (see Chapter 12) produce the same effect. Amphetamine, another stimulant, accomplishes the same result by forcing the release of norepinephrine and dopamine into their synapses.

The hallucinogens include mescaline, which comes from the peyote cactus; psilocybin and psilocine, which are present in certain mushrooms; and LSD, which is derived in the laboratory. Marijuana is also called a hallucinogen, but its effects are far

an accurate sense of our physical selves as we move through our environment. The blending of new sensory impressions with input from our memory stores allows us to assign meaning to specific sights, sounds, smells, and touches. The sensation of something moving and furry touching your arm means one thing if you hear a purr and see your cat but quite another if you hear a growl and see a bear.

Association areas in the frontal cortex are thought to mediate decisions about what action to take—in the presence of a cat or a bear, for example. An integrated sensory picture of the event would be transmitted to the prefrontal part of the frontal cortex. Through extensive reciprocal connections with the limbic system, emotional tone would be added, along with input from memory. Other connections would contribute information that would enable the frontal cortex to assess the current condition of the body and the environment and to assign priorities—to judge what is better or worse for the self in a given situation. The frontal cortex is also thought to be responsi-

less potent than those of the other drugs within this same category.

Marijuana comes from the hemp plant *Cannabis sativa* and is used extensively throughout the world. The principal active substances in marijuana are called tetrahydrocannabinols (THCs), but very little is known of how they act on the central nervous system. Marijuana users report initial feelings of euphoria and heightened sensitivities to sights, sounds, and tastes. They often experience a "splitting of consciousness," simultaneously feeling their intoxication and observing themselves having the experience. A pleasant lethargy follows the euphoria.

The long-term effects of these drugs on the central nervous system are not yet clear, but there is plenty of evidence that their use can, at the least, result in extreme psychological dependency. Warnings against the use of these drugs abound—on television, in magazines, and in newspapers. Nevertheless, it is not surprising that, in a species whose members choose recreation in

the form of jumping out of airplanes, climbing sheer rock precipices, or racing automobiles at incredible speeds, a significant number should choose to use such "recreational" drugs.

ble for generating our long-range goals and our judgments in light of those goals.

In normal healthy people, the *prefrontal* cortex in particular (the strip of tissue anterior to the motor cortex) is thought to provide for a range of functions that contribute to working memory, planning, foresight, time estimation, the use of strategies, and, importantly, cognitive flexibility (for example, the ability to develop a way of doing things—a so-called set, or mindset—and then to change that set easily). These abilities develop slowly. For example, you may recall

as a child driving somewhere with your parents and asking every few minutes, "When are we going to be there?" Your ability to estimate the passage of time had not yet matured. Even children as old as 12 still need help in planning important behavioral activities such as homework (and even some teenagers have difficulty in time management). As discussed in Chapter 3, the synapses in the prefrontal cortex develop over a long time span, often not reaching the adult level until mid-to-late adolescence. Presumably, the change in connectivity of

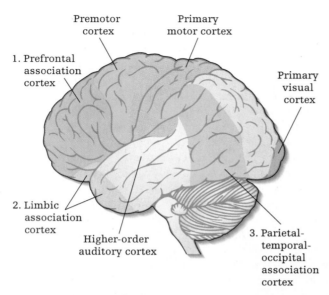

Figure 11.1 The association cortices occupy large areas on the surface of the brain, and integrate information from diverse sensory and/or motor regions. Such integration provides for more complex forms of behavior. For example, the *limbic association cortex* is concerned with memory and emotion, whereas the *prefrontal association area* is associated with planning movement.

this region of the brain is responsible for these changes in behavior.

After these cognitive behaviors (that is, planning, working memory) have developed, damage to the frontal cortex can easily disrupt behavior. For example, accounts of people with damage to the frontal lobes (a number of whom were described in Chapter 8) attest to the critical role of the frontal cortex in judging and planning. Such victims have great difficulty reconciling life's conflicting and shifting demands. Like Phineas Gage, they become irresponsible, unable to act appropriately or to carry out any consistent life plan. And recent data suggest that, if this

damage occurs in the first few years of life, the effects can be even worse.

The frontal cortex appears to cooperate, through massive nerve connections, with the temporal cortex in carrying out some of the brain's highest functions. The unique human ability to use language, for example, is believed to be the product of association areas in the temporal and frontal lobes, as well as in the occipital lobe. The temporal cortex is active in memory, both in deciding

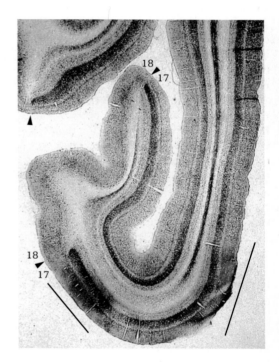

Very low power microscope view of a slice through the occipital lobe of a monkey's cerebral cortex. The tissue section has been retracted to reveal the layers of cells. One of those layers is interrupted at the boundary, indicated by the arrows, separating the primary visual cortex (area 17) and the secondary visual cortex (area 18).

what will be stored and in the storage and retrieval not only of the memories themselves, but also of whether the remembered events were evaluated as pleasant or unpleasant. Extensive damage in this area can produce loss of long-term memory (or at least an inability to retrieve such memories). The plan-making abilities of the frontal lobes depend greatly on access to relevant experiences from the past, and these data may be transmitted from the temporal cortex.

This traditional account of how association areas of the cortex operate is only hypothetical, because there are very few data to corroborate or refute it. It is based chiefly on neuroscientists' observations of the brain's gross anatomy—its hierarchical circuitry and observable division into lobes. Besides the lack of experimental verification for its hypotheses, the theory lacks an explanation of how all the brain's higher functions combine to produce a unified active consciousness. At least one more step seems to be required to explain the feeling that an "I" is perceiving and evaluating its environment and is choosing when and how to act. More recent discoveries about the detailed architecture and functioning of the brain have led to a theory of consciousness based on the cortex's columnar organization. One advantage of the newer theory is that it promises to provide scientifically testable hypotheses.

Columns of Neurons and Consciousness

As described in earlier chapters, the cells of the cortex are organized into columns. Chapter 3 described how the neurons of the developing brain migrate along glial cells to assume a regular vertical patterning that forms a sort of grid in combination with the horizontal layering of the cortex (see Figure 11.2). Chapter 4 explored the role of these vertical columns in the organization and

information-processing functions of the visual cortex, auditory cortex, and so on.

All parts of the cortex, including the so-called association areas, are organized in columns. The basic unit, or *minicolumn,* consists of 100 or so vertically interrelated neurons that span the cortex's horizontal layers. These minicolumns are virtually identical in size in all parts of the cortex. They consist of (1) target neurons that receive their major input from subcortical structures—the specific sensory and motor nuclei of the thalamus, for instance; (2) target neurons that receive their major input from other regions of the cortex; (3) local-circuit neurons that connect the cells making up the minicolumn; and (4) output neurons that send messages from the minicolumn back to the thalamus or to other cortical regions or to targets in the limbic system.

Several of these minicolumns may have connections with each other, thus functioning as a larger composite unit called a *column.* Although the structure of columns in different parts of the cortex may vary, according to the number of constituent minicolumns and their mode of packing, Vernon Mountcastle believes them to be the fundamental information-processing units of the cortex (see Figure 11.2). To get some idea of how such columns work, you might refer to page 119, which shows, through a special staining technique, the ocular dominance columns of the monkey's visual cortex. Alternating columns in the visual cortex process information alternately from the left eye and right eye. (Chapter 4 discusses the very complex nature of the cortical processing of visual information which combines binocular processing with many other kinds of information.)

By experimenting with the placement of microelectrodes in a functioning monkey's brain, Mountcastle discovered that cell

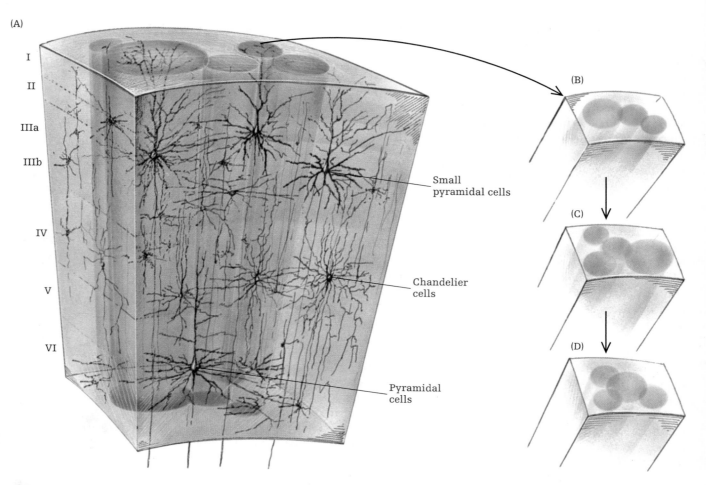

Figure 11.2 Diagrammatic representation of the columnar organization of the cortex. The larger, variously shaped, overlapping columns (A) are made up of minicolumns, vertically connected sets of single cells. The details at right (B, C, and D) show the shifting locations of vertically connected cells active at a given time.

columns in two areas of the parietal cortex are active when the animal performs actions on and within his immediate environment. Further examination showed that different sets of columns are active during (1) projection of the arm toward an object of interest; (2) manipulation of an object; (3) fixation of gaze and thus of visual attention; (4) movement of the eyes as a result of visual stimulation; (5) movement of the eyes in slow-pursuit

tracking of an object; and (6) the sudden appearance of an object in the periphery of the visual field. A given column might be active during several of these actions. The columnar organization is therefore what Mountcastle calls a *distributed system:* a system in which information flow may follow a number of different pathways and in which the dominance of one path or another is a dynamic and changing property of the system. He describes some pathways as processing information coming from the outside world, others as carrying information from other parts of the brain—the internally generated information (memories, emotions, cognitive skills) that Mountcastle calls *reentrant information*. The internally generated neural activity may cycle through a number of pathways, beginning with pathways handling primary sensory data but then proceeding successively to more general and abstract processing units of the cortex. The advantage of a distributed system that simultaneously handles both reentrant information and current information about external conditions is that a person can continuously update perceptual images of his or her self and self-in-the-world and can match that image against external conditions. In Mountcastle's theory, the match between internal "readout" and external world is the proposed mechanism for conscious awareness.

One other characteristic of this distributed system according to Mountcastle is that it has access to output pathways at many levels and therefore has many possible command levels—levels where an "I" may evaluate the environment and choose to act. Thus the command function is likely to take over in whatever part of the system is conveying the most urgent and necessary information. Pain and danger, for example, usually focus one's consciousness quickly on ways to escape or avoid them, no matter what one was focusing on when the pain or danger arose.

Mountcastle's explanation of the workings of consciousness is far from proved. Given the human brain's complexity and the impossibility of human experimentation, scientists may never be able to validate the hypotheses. Still, animal experiments, like the tests with monkeys mentioned earlier, in which sets of neurons are monitored in an animal that is moving about and performing certain tasks, offer some data as a basis for the conjectures. For example, in one such study of neurons in the parietal association area in monkeys, Mountcastle and his colleagues found that certain sets of neurons function to command the operation of the limbs, hands, and eyes, but do so only when the animal is motivated to obtain a certain nearby object that it sees (food or drink, in these experiments). These sets of cells are not activated by sensory stimuli alone, and they do not discharge when the hands or limbs are moved aimlessly. They represent a general command function that is exercised in a holistic fashion. Perhaps groups of cells that function in this manner betoken something approaching monkey consciousness.

One other aspect of brain anatomy critical to our understanding of consciousness and language is the hemispheric organization of the cerebrum.

The Cerebral Hemispheres

The two hemispheres that compose the forebrain are connected at several points by cables of neurons, the general term for which is *commissure*. The largest and most important of these is the *corpus callosum* (see Figure 11.3 on the following page). The right hemisphere controls sensing and moving on the body's left side, and the left hemisphere controls those functions on the body's right side. For hearing and vision, hemispheric control is a bit more complex. As discussed in Chapter 4, each eye has a left visual field and a right visual field. Information in the right visual field goes only to the left hemisphere, and information in the left visual field goes only to the right hemisphere (see Figure 11.4 on the following page). These visual areas of the left and right hemispheres normally communicate through the corpus callosum. In contrast to these contralateral functions, human language is usually localized in only one hemisphere of the brain.

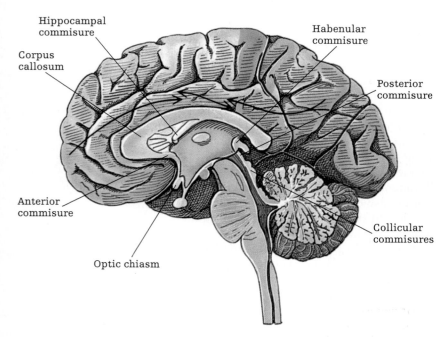

Figure 11.3 The major connectors between the brain's two hemispheres. The large size of the corpus callosum stands out relative to the other connectors. Here the brain has been sectioned at the midline.

The most promising insights into the physiological bases of mind and consciousness have been reached through clinical studies of people whose brains have been damaged as a result of accident or illness or who have undergone brain surgery—in particular, the operation that separates the brain's two hemispheres from each other.

The Bisected Brain

During an epileptic seizure, abnormal and progressively asynchronous neural firing spreads from the site of a brain lesion to other parts of the brain. When this asynchronous firing passes through the corpus callosum, the entire brain becomes involved in the seizure. In some life-threatening cases

of epilepsy that do not respond to any other type of treatment, neurosurgeons cut parts of the corpus callosum to contain the neural storm. (When this procedure was first developed many years ago, the entire corpus callosum was severed.) The procedure succeeds very well, and patients appear to be virtually

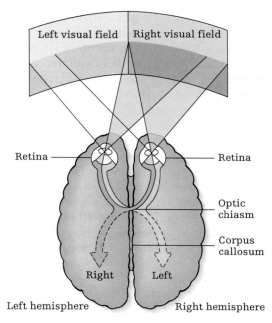

Figure 11.4 The visual pathways and visual fields. When the optic nerves travel from the retina on their way to the brain, they first come together at the optic chiasm. Here, a partial crossover of fibers takes place. The fibers coming from the half of the retina closest to the nose cross over to the opposite side; the fibers coming from the outside, or temporal, half of the retina do not cross over. Consequently, when a person fixates his gaze on a point, information from the right visual field goes only to the left hemisphere, and information from the left visual field goes only to the right hemisphere. Normally, the visual areas of the two hemispheres communicate through the corpus callosum. If that commissure is cut and if the eyes and head are kept still, each hemisphere can see only half of the visual world.

unchanged in personality, intelligence, and behavior after the operation. But ingenious tests, conducted by neurologists and psychologists, indicate that the brain bisection does indeed change the consciousness and thought patterns of these patients in profound but subtle ways.

In one specially designed test, patient N. G., a California woman whose corpus callosum had been completely severed, sits in front of a screen with a small black dot at its center (see Figure 11.5). The experimenter asks her to look continuously at the dot. Then a picture of a cup is flashed to the right of the dot with the use of a *tachistoscope,* a special device that allows the experimenter to control precisely how long a picture stays on the screen. Such presentations are very brief—about one-tenth of a second—so that subjects do not have time to move their eyes away from the dot. The experimenter wants only one hemisphere to view the picture, and eye movements could result in its being perceived by both hemispheres.

When patient N. G. is asked what she saw, she reports that she saw the cup. Again she is asked to look at the dot, and a picture of a spoon is flashed to its left. Asked now what she saw, she says, "Nothing." Then the researcher asks her to reach under the screen, where several small objects are scattered, and to choose, by touch only, an object resembling the picture that has just been flashed. With her left hand, she handles several of the objects and brings out a spoon. Asked what she is holding, she says, "A pencil."

In another such test, a picture of a nude woman is flashed to the left of the dot. N. G. blushes and begins to giggle. Asked what she saw, she says, "Nothing, just a flash of light." "Then why are you laughing?" asks the experimenter. "Oh, doctor, you have some machine!" N. G. replies.

When N. G. saw the picture of the cup in her right visual field, which was processed in

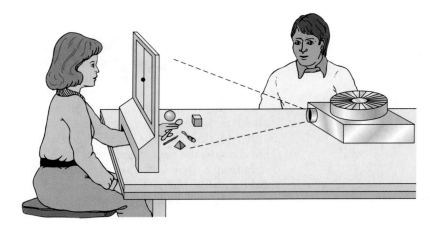

Figure 11.5 The experimental setup for tachistoscope studies. Images are projected through the screen either to the right or to the left of the central black dot on which the subject fixes his or her gaze.

the left hemisphere, she had no trouble naming the item. When she was shown the spoon in her left visual field, processed in her right hemisphere, she said she had seen nothing. Yet she had obviously processed that information because she was able to select the spoon by touch from an array of objects. In N. G., as in most people (some left-handers, as discussed later, are an exception), the left hemisphere is responsible for language and speech. With the corpus callosum intact, the left hemisphere and right hemisphere work together in perceiving and naming things. But each side of N. G.'s bisected brain is essentially blind to what the other side sees. Because her right hemisphere is mute, it recognized the spoon but could not name it.

N. G.'s reaction to the nude picture, which appeared to the left of the center of the screen, is especially interesting. Her right hemisphere had obviously processed the image because she blushed and giggled when the picture was flashed. But, because her left, verbal, hemisphere did not know what had happened, it tried to make sense of her general state of embarrassment by assuming that the machine must somehow have sparked her response.

In another tachistoscope study, the subject is first shown the four photographs seen in Figure 11.6. Then she sits in front of the screen, onto which is flashed a composite picture, half of one face (a woman wearing glasses) on the left side of the dot and half of another (a child) on the right. When asked what she saw, the patient answers, "a child," the half-face that she saw with her left, speaking, hemisphere. Later, the same composite picture is flashed, and she is asked to select the picture that she saw by pointing to it. This time she points to the woman, seen by her right, nonspeaking, hemisphere.

One interesting aspect of this study is that patients denied that there had been anything unusual about the pictures that they had seen. They perceived each half-face as a whole—that is, their brains completed the picture. This constructive aspect of perception helps explain why split-brain patients normally function well in their everyday lives. Another aid that they use, in both experimental and day-to-day situations, is *cross-cuing*. One hemisphere uses clues available to it to detect information supposedly accessible only to the other hemisphere. For example, if the left hand (controlled by the right hemisphere) is given a set of keys to identify, the left hemisphere might recognize the clinking sound and be able to say "keys," even though neither sight nor touch of the keys had been available to the left hemisphere.

In spite of the split brain's constructive and cunning ways, it appears that, as Roger W. Sperry (1974), a Nobel laureate pioneer in split-brain surgery, noted,

(A)   (B)   "Whom did you see?"   "It was a child."   (C)   "Point to the person you saw."

Figure 11.6 The composite-picture study. The subject becomes familiar with the faces in the photographs, then a composite picture is flashed by a tachistoscope so that the left hemisphere (right visual field) sees the child's half-face and the right (left visual field) sees the half-face of the young woman with sunglasses. When asked to say what she saw, the subject reports having seen the child. When asked to point to what she saw, she chooses the young woman.

Each hemisphere . . . has its own . . . private sensations, perceptions, thoughts, and ideas, all of which are cut off from the corresponding experiences in the opposite hemisphere. Each left and right hemisphere has its own private chain of memories and learning experiences that are inaccessible to recall by the other hemisphere. In many respects each disconnected hemisphere appears to have a separate "mind of its own."

Hemispheric Specialization and Dominance

Split-brain studies indicate that, in general, the left hemisphere is responsible for language and speech, and the right hemisphere directs skills related to visual and spatial processing. Other research reveals more subtle differences in the ways in which the two hemispheres process information. The left hemisphere is believed to process information analytically and sequentially. The right appears to process information simultaneously and as a whole. It tends to perceive an assemblage like those in the adjoining figure as a total construct rather than as the separate parts that make it up.

Figures like the two shown here are quickly and easily perceived as wholes by the right hemisphere.

Each hemisphere, then, appears to have particular strengths and weaknesses and to contribute in its own way to thinking and consciousness. In examining these different attributes, we shall look first at some more-specific evidence for left- and right-brain characteristics and then turn to some of the ways in which the two hemispheres may work together in thinking and consciousness when the corpus callosum remains intact.

The Left Hemisphere and Language

A patient, fully conscious, lies on the table, a tiny tube threaded into the carotid artery on one side of his neck. The physician asks him to raise both arms and to begin counting backward from 100 by threes. Sodium amytal, a barbiturate, is then injected into the artery, which quickly carries it to the hemisphere of the brain bathed by the blood carried through that artery. Within seconds, the arm opposite the side of the injection falls limp. Then the patient stops counting. If the hemisphere anesthetized is the one controlling speech, the patient will remain speechless for several minutes. If not, he will start counting again within a few seconds and be able to carry on a conversation, even though half his brain is anesthetized. This procedure, the *Wada test,* enables neurosurgeons to determine which hemisphere controls the speech of a patient scheduled to undergo brain surgery. With this information, the surgeon can try to avoid trauma to that area.

Results of the Wada test show that the left hemisphere controls speech and language in more than 95 percent of all right-handed people with no history of early brain damage. In the remaining 5 percent, speech is controlled in the right hemisphere. A majority of left-handers—about 70 percent—also have left-hemisphere control of language. About 15 percent of left-handers have speech in the right hemisphere, and 15 percent show evidence of bilateral speech control.

When the Wada test was administered to patients known to have suffered damage to the left hemisphere early in life (generally due to uncontrolled epileptic seizures), it showed that the right hemisphere either controls or participates in the control of speech in 70 percent of the left-handers and 19 percent of the right-handers. In these patients, the right hemisphere evidently developed language capacities to compensate for the early left-hemisphere damage. Shifts such as these give clear evidence of the plasticity of the brain in infancy and early childhood.

Brain Sites That Function in Language
Scientists have known for more than a century that, for most people, speech is controlled by the left hemisphere. In 1836, an obscure French physician, Marc Dax, presented a short paper at a medical society meeting in Montpellier in which he described 40 of his patients who had suf-

fered speech disturbances. All, without exception, showed signs of damage to the left hemisphere. As significant as these findings were, Dax's report went unremarked by contemporary scientists, perhaps because it came from someone practicing outside of Paris. Twenty-five years later, Paul Broca presented to the Anthropological Society in Paris a case study of a patient who had lost the ability to talk but who could nevertheless read and write normally and could comprehend everything said to him. Broca pointed to a lesion in the frontal lobe of the left hemisphere as the cause of the patient's speech problem. That specific area, adjacent to the area of the motor cortex that controls the muscles of the face, tongue, jaw, and throat, has come to be called *Broca's area* (see Figure 11.7). The specific impairment in producing the sounds of speech, even though language ability remains normal, is called *Broca's aphasia.*

Victims of another kind of aphasia produce well-formed speech sounds in essentially correct grammatical sequences, but some of the sounds are meaningless: "I think that there's an awful lot of mung, but I think I've a lot of net and tunged in a little wheat duh-vayden." Damage to the upper, posterior part of the left temporal lobe, named *Wernicke's area* after Carl Wernicke, who located it in 1874 (see Figure 11.7), produces this aphasia, called *Wernicke's aphasia.* Patients suffering from this type of aphasia have difficulty comprehending language, although their speech can appear quite normal.

Aphasia is the general term for a disturbance of language, and these disturbances can take many forms: difficulty in producing speech sounds; inability to produce meaningful speech even when the sounds are correct; a breakdown in comprehension of speech sounds, to mention a few (see Table 11.1). Studies of well-defined aphasias have

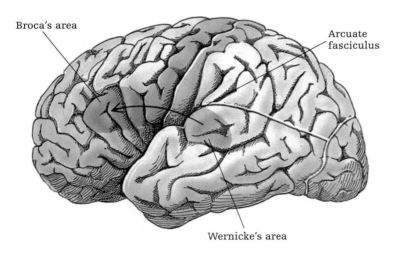

Broca's area

Arcuate fasciculus

Wernicke's area

Figure 11.7 Areas of the left hemisphere known to be active in speech and language. Wernicke's area and Broca's area are connected by a collection of nerve fibers called the arcuate fasciculus, indicated by an arrow because it cannot be seen from this angle.

TABLE 11.1 Aphasias

Name	Symptoms	Location of brain lesion
Broca's aphasia	Difficulty in the motor act of producing language; comprehension unimpaired; reading and writing unimpaired; patient aware of disability.	Frontal region of left hemisphere, especially Broca's area
Wernicke's aphasia	Comprehension of speech very impaired; production of speech fluent but odd or meaningless, full of nonexistent words; rhythm and intonation of speech and grammatical form preserved; reading and writing impaired; patients seem unaware of meaningless speech.	Posterior region of first temporal gyrus, or Wernicke's area
Conduction aphasia	Speech is fluent but somewhat meaningless; may show some comprehension and reading ability; unable to repeat phrases correctly.	Damage to fiber tracts connecting Wernicke's area to Broca's area
Word deafness	Comprehension of spoken language impaired; comprehension of written language normal; production of verbal and written language normal.	Lesion in the area connecting Wernicke's area to auditory inputs
Anomic aphasia	Inability to think of a specific word or the name of a person or an object; comprehension and conversation virtually normal.	Angular gyrus (junction of the temporal, parietal, and occipital lobes), left hemisphere
Global aphasia	Severe impairment of all language-related function.	Widespread damage to left hemisphere

SOURCE: Adapted from *Left Brain, Right Brain*, fifth edition, by S. P. Springer and G. Deutsch, W. H. Freeman, New York, 1998.

helped to identify the brain areas responsible for specific parts of the language process. As a result of this mapping of Broca's area, Wernicke's area, and other regions, neuroscientists have been able to construct a model of how the brain produces and processes language.

According to this model, the underlying structure of an utterance—its form and meaning—is produced in Wernicke's area. It then passes through a collection of nerve fibers, called the *arcuate fasciculus* (see Figure 11.7), to Broca's area. There, the impulses evoke a detailed and coordinated program for vocalization—a program for how each lip, tongue, and throat muscle must move. The program is then transmitted to the adjacent area of the motor cortex that controls the face, and the appropriate muscles are activated.

Wernicke's area is also important in language comprehension. The sound of a word is received in the primary auditory cortex, but the processed message must pass through the adjacent Wernicke's area if the sound is to be understood as language.

When words are read rather than heard, the information is thought to be transmitted from the primary visual cortex to the angular gyrus (another region of the temporal lobe) where the visual input is somehow matched with the sounds that the words have when spoken. The auditory form of the word is then processed for comprehension in Wernicke's area, as it would be if the words had been heard. Because spoken language long preceded written language in human evolution and because all human young learn to speak and to comprehend spoken language before they learn to read or write, the hypothesis that the processing of written language is sound based seems to make sense.

Although this general model of how the brain generates and processes speech is consistent with the symptoms characteristic of Broca's and Wernicke's aphasias, it is not universally accepted among neuroscientists as modeling the normal workings of the brain in producing language. Many neuroscientists believe that at least the entire left hemisphere and perhaps many other parts of the brain function in language. As John Hughlings Jackson (one of the nineteenth-century pioneers of neuroscience) warned long ago, "to locate the damage which destroys speech and to locate speech are two different things."

Studies using direct electrical stimulation of the brains of surgical patients support the idea that language capacity is widely distributed in the brain. Stimulation of many sites in the language region of the cortex interferes with reading ability, and stimulation at sites in the frontal, temporal, and parietal lobes disrupts the ability to speak and to understand speech sounds.

Among patients with command of two languages, stimulation at sites in the center of the language area of the cortex disrupts speech in both languages, but stimulation at some sites outside this central region disrupts only one or the other of the two languages. Because bilingual speakers who develop aphasia usually experience difficulties in both languages, however, it appears that the basic brain organization of most languages (including sign language) is the same. Support for this conclusion can be found in some very recent work using positron emission tomography (see box on pages 334–339). In persons completely fluent in two languages, regardless of how old they were when they learned the second language, the same neural representation was revealed for both languages (that is, the same parts of the brain "lit up" when they spoke either one). Interestingly, if a person spoke a second language but not fluently, then a *different* part of the brain was activated during use of the second language. Whether similar findings would be obtained for third, fourth, or fifth languages (not uncommon in many parts of the world) remains to be seen.

Greater overall understanding of how the brain processes language may shed light on a problem that exists only in literate cultures, the learning disability called dyslexia. In dyslexia, there is a disconnect, of sorts, between the sounds of a language and the written counterparts of these sounds (such as letters).

Dyslexia *Developmental dyslexia* is a disturbance in the ability to read that is not caused by mental retardation, physical injury, or lack of motivation. Dyslexics have normal intelligence, and their comprehension and production of spoken language are unimpaired. Their reading problems take several forms and may, in fact, be caused by a number of different factors. In some, the disturbance appears to be primarily visual and spatial; these people have difficulty in perceiving words as wholes and in knowing what words look like—they cannot differentiate between "lap" and "pal," for example. Other dyslexics are unable to match letter combinations with the sounds of those letters. They are at a loss when asked to read simple words that they have never read before. For example, they may be able to read the word "stone" correctly if it is familiar to them; however, at the same time, they may be unsuccessful at reading the word "stein" if they have not learned to read it before.

Unfortunately, those studying dyslexia have not yet formed a consensus about what causes this disability. Some think it results from damage to the magnocellular layer of the lateral geniculate pathway (a relay station in the thalamus that transmits information from the retina to the visual cortex). The magnocellular layer is part of the dorsal stream of visual information processing and has a role in motion detection. One hypothesis is that the magnocellular layer inhibits the parvocellular layer during *saccadic* (jerky) eye movements—the type of eye movement made during reading. In a recent test of this hypothesis, normal and dyslexic readers were asked to look at pairs of moving visual stimuli and judge which of the two members of each pair moved faster (that is, make speed-discrimination judgments). In functional magnetic resonance imaging scans that were made of the subjects' brains as they performed this task, greater activation in area V1 (Brodmann area 17) of the visual cortex and areas in and around a part of the magnocellular pathway was associated with lower thresholds for detecting the stimuli and with faster reading time. Although these findings do not prove a cause-and-effect relation, they do suggest an association between poor reading and deficits in the magnocellular pathway of the dorsal visual stream.

Other investigators currently view dyslexia as being a problem in *phonological coding*. A *phoneme* is the smallest unit of sound that can stand alone, such as /ba/, /ga/, or /pa/. A person with a phonological coding deficit is unable to hear the differences among these sound units and thus cannot recognize the written version of them—that is, they cannot "hear" the words on the page. Whether the problem has to do with the ability to differentiate between sounds (knowing that "ba" sounds different from "pa") or with the ability to think about and manipulate sound has not yet been decided. A test of the latter ability, for example, would be to ask subjects to remove the initial phoneme of a spoken word, move it to the end of the word, and add "ay." (Try this with the word "dog.")

Although the nature of the phonological problem is not yet clear, there is evidence that damage to the thalamus causes a problem in hearing the differences between phonemes. Support for this model comes from two sources. First, recordings of a type of brain activity thought to originate in the thalamus were abnormal in people who cannot easily distinguish among phonemes (people suffering from a language-learning disorder). Second, tissue sections from the medial geniculate nuclei (MGN) of the thalamus in dyslexics had an asymmetry that was not observed in control brains. The MGN are responsible for processing the inputs from the auditory nerves. Neurons in the left MGN of dyslexic brains were smaller than corresponding neurons in the right MGN. As suggestive as these findings are, we must remember that the subjects in the first study were not dyslexics, and other learning disabilities that may have plagued the subjects in the second study are unknown.

木	tree	き
林	woods	はやし
森	forest	もり
白	white	しろ
鳥	bird	とり
白鳥	swan	はくちょう
電話番号	telephone number	でんわばんごう
大統領選挙		だいとうりょうせんきょ

presidential elections

Figure 11.8 Two alphabets are written, and sometimes mixed, in Japanese. Kanji, at the left, uses symbols that are almost pictorial. Kana, at the right, uses symbols that stand for sound combinations, or syllables.

It seems reasonable to argue that dyslexia is a complex disorder and likely to involve higher regions of the brain as well, not just subcortical structures such as the thalamus. Evidence in support of this idea comes from fMRI scans made of the brains of dyslexics as increasing demands were made on their phonological awareness. During tests of understanding language and seeing letters and words, the dyslexic readers showed underactivation in posterior regions of the brain (Wernicke's area, the angular gyrus, and the striate cortex) and overactivation in the inferior frontal gyrus.

There is also evidence to suggest that the development and incidence of dyslexia may depend on the kind of language that a person learns to read. For example, whereas from 1 to 3 percent of the population in Western countries is dyslexic, the incidence in Japan is just one-tenth of that. Japan has two types of written language (see Figure 11.8). One is *kana*, which, like our alphabet, uses symbols that represent sounds. (In kana, each symbol stands for a syllable, or combination of sounds.) The other is *kanji*, in which the written symbols are ideographs, each representing a thing or an idea rather than a sound. It may be that the kanji ideographs are processed in a visual-spatial mode on the right side of the brain and thus are not subject to the processing problems that result in dyslexia. Evidence from Japanese stroke victims suggests as much: when damage occurs in the left hemisphere, a person may lose the ability to read words written in kana but retain the ability to read kanji. In fact, some dyslexic American children have successfully learned to read English represented by Chinese characters in a special system devised by researchers.

Another form of language that makes use of visual-spatial abilities is the sign language used by the deaf.

Sign Language Many deaf persons, especially those born deaf, find that a gestural language—such as the American Sign Language (ASL) in the United States—is their most effective vehicle for communication. ASL is a formal language with a complex vocabulary of some 4000 signs and a well-defined grammatical structure, even though it is based on spatial relations. Each sign represents a word. The word order is different from that of English: the most concrete or vivid element in each sentence comes first, followed by signs that explain or describe the situation (adjectives, adverbs, or verbs), followed by the outcome of the situation. An example is provided in Figure 11.9.

Because sign language is very much a visual-spatial activity, scientists thought for many years that it might be mediated by structures in the right hemisphere, given the importance of that hemisphere in visual-spatial analysis. However, a series of studies revealed that, in most respects, sign language is also mediated by the same regions of the brain that control spoken language. For example, one study examined six sign-language users suffering from aphasia and

e 11.9 Two individuals conversing in American anguage, a dominant method of communication hearing-impaired individuals.

discovered that three had damage to the left hemisphere and three had damage to the right. Right-hemisphere lesions led to the expected problems in visual-perceptual functions but had no discernible effect on signing. In contrast, left-hemisphere lesions led to Broca- and Wernicke-like aphasic symptoms, such as word fluency problems.

This study clearly supports the idea that sign language is mediated by the same neural structures that mediate spoken language. As with spoken language, however, the neural representation of this system may exist in the right hemisphere in some people or at least be different in left- compared with right-handers. The same researchers examined the signing speed of the left and right hands of ASL users who had been deaf since birth. As one might expect of normal hearing people, the right-handed subjects had inferior signing ability with the left hand. In contrast, the left-handed signers had greater flexibility in signing with their nondominant (right) hands than did the right handers. The researchers concluded that, as is the case with spoken language in left-handed subjects, left-handed signers may have bilateral representation of language in their brains (in a later section of this chapter, we return to the question of brain and handedness).

It is of interest to note that most readers of Braille—a writing system used by the blind in which symbols are read through touch—prefer to use the left hand to identify the symbols. This observation suggests an interesting type of coordination between the superior language skills of the left hemisphere and the normally superior spatial skills of the right.

The Right Hemisphere

The right hemisphere has long been thought to play an important role in many functions, including the ability to respond to wholes

The field of *cognitive neuroscience* is relatively new. It is a marriage of cognitive psychology—the branch of psychology concerned with *mentation,* or thinking, perception, and problem solving—with some of the tools of neuroscience—especially *neuroimaging* tools, the tools that permit visualization of the workings of the brain. Thus, a cognitive neuroscientist is one who is interested in examining not just behavior (as a traditional psychologist would do) and not just the brain (as a traditional neuroscientist would do) but rather the *relation* between brain and behavior. For example, a cognitive neuroscientist might use the newly available technology to try to discover what part of the brain is involved in recognizing faces. Although cognitive neuroscientists are particularly interested in cognitive behavior, some also study emotional behavior.

Cognitive neuroscientists depend on four broad classes of tools: neuropsychological tools, metabolic tools, electrophysiological tools, and magnetoencephalography.

Neuropsychological Tools

Neuropsychological tools are tests whose purpose is to study behavior for the purpose of clarifying which brain activities are regulated by which brain structures. These tests are given to human or animal subjects already known to have damage in specific parts of the brain. For example, researchers were aware that the removal of much of H. M.'s medial temporal lobe (see Chapters 9 and 10) had resulted in a severe deficit in explicit memory. On the basis of this observation, they devised a variety of ingenious behavioral tests that measured the severity of the memory loss and determined whether other cognitive abilities also were affected. These tests may now be applied to other patients (or animals) in whom damage to the medial temporal lobe or any other region of the brain is known or suspected. Thus, after a basic relation between structure and function has been established, neuropsychological tests can be used clinically to determine whether a person has damage to a certain region of the brain. They can also be used in developmental research to determine the approximate age at which areas of the brain develop. The virtues of neuropsychological tests include the fact that they are completely noninvasive and relatively inexpensive. However, because neuropsychological tools do not permit direct examination of the brain, but rather require that information about the brain's structure be inferred from its function, they provide at best an indirect assessment of structure–function relations.

Metabolic Tools

Two powerful imaging methods are capable of measuring variations in metabolic activity in the brain: *positron emission tomography* (PET) and *functional magnetic resonance imaging* (fMRI). PET uses radio-activity to track the utilization of certain substances that the brain requires for its work. For example, a radioactive form of oxygen (^{15}O) may be injected into a subject who is then placed in a PET scanner and asked to perform a specific mental task (say, to look at a series of faces and select those that are familiar or those that display a specific emotion). The part of the brain that is most active during the task will require the most oxygen. The PET scanner detects positrons emitted by the radioactive oxygen, determines where in the brain the largest numbers of positrons are coming from, and in that way reveals what part (or parts) of the brain are most active in the performance of a particular task. Because no two brains are created equal (even the brains of identical twins), brain structures tend to vary slightly in their location from one person to another. For this reason, researchers often display the PET images (basically splotches of color representing areas high in metabolic activity) superimposed on a structural view of the brain that is typically obtained by using magnetic resonance imaging.

One advantage of PET imaging is that it produces detailed "pictures" of the brain in the act of performing tasks; another is that its spatial resolution is on the order of centimeters (see below for an example). However, PET has its shortcomings: its mildly invasive nature (the injection of a radioactive isotope), its cost (a cyclotron is needed on site to create the isotope), its poor temporal resolution (generally on the order of minutes), and the fact that it cannot be done with normally developing children (who cannot give informed consent to have a radioactive substance injected in them solely for experimental reasons, although there are conditions under which it is permitted when children are suffering from some abnormality).

The other, relatively new technique for measuring metabolic activity in a working brain is fMRI. The most common form of fMRI (the so-called BOLD technique, which stands for "blood-oxygenation-level dependent") takes advantage of the fact that deoxygenated hemoglobin (hemoglobin with the oxygen removed) can be magnetized (much as a sewing needle can be made to act like a magnet by being rubbed on a magnet). Combining this property with the use of conventional magnetic resonance technology, scientists can measure subtle

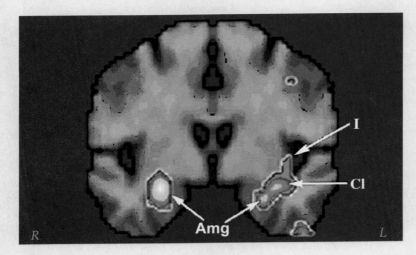

continued

changes in blood-oxygen levels. When a particular brain region is called on to perform some task, the flow of blood to that region increases, carrying more oxygen to the cells there. The fMRI scanner, by taking consecutive pictures of slices of the brain in various orientations, is able to reconstruct where in the brain these increases are taking place. An example is below.

fMRI has the following advantages: it is noninvasive, it does not require exposure to ionizing radiation, it is *relatively* inexpensive (assuming that an MRI scanner is already available), it has excellent spatial resolution (along the lines of millimeters), and it can be used with normally developing children.

However, like PET, the temporal resolution of fMRI is relatively poor (measuring changes in seconds). In addition, the subject must sit very still in a very confined space, which is problematic for some people (claustrophobic people, for example).

Electrophysiological Tools

Whereas PET and fMRI measures metabolic activity, the *electrophysiological imaging* tools permit neuroscientists to track synaptic activity. The best known is the recording of *event-related potentials* (ERPs). ERPs represent electrical activity generated by populations of neurons in response to some

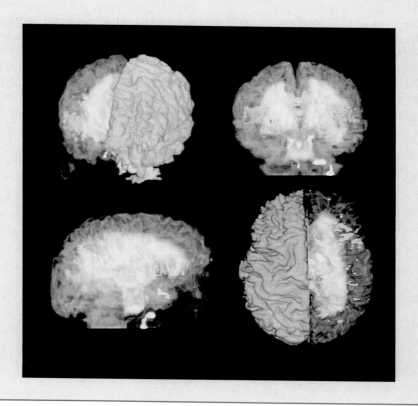

of the number of times a particular picture or sound is repeated. Many trials are administered, and averages of like trials are constructed. The result is an electrophysiological "signature" in the form of peaks and valleys that correspond to particular times in particular regions of the brain. Presumably, each peak and valley represents a distinct neural process; for instance, one represents attention, one memory, and so forth (see examples here and on the following page).

Unlike PET and fMRI, ERPs can resolve time on the order of milliseconds and can therefore be used to track exactly when certain neural events are taking place. In addition, the recording of ERPs is relatively inexpensive, can be done quickly (a typical task might take only 5 or 10 minutes), and is completely noninvasive (making its use in children particularly appealing). The spatial resolution of ERPs is not as precise as that of PET; but, because the spatial resolution is tied to the number of recording electrodes, it is expected to improve as scientists devise ways to use larger numbers of electrodes.

Magnetoencephalography

A general principle of electromagnetism is that every electric current is accompanied by an associated magnetic field. Thus, any site of electrical activity in the brain will also be producing magnetic activity. Unlike electrical activity, which takes a circuitous, intercellular route to the scalp surface (a principle referred to as *volume conduction*), magnetic activity follows a more direct path. As a result, it is often easier to determine the source of a magnetic field than the source of an electrical field.

discrete event (such as the presentation of a visual stimulus). They are detected by small metal electrodes placed on the surface of the scalp. ERP signals are very small—on the order of millivolts when they originate in the brain, and, by the time they have traveled through intercellular spaces to reach the surface of the scalp, where they are picked up by the electrodes, they have shrunk to microvolts. They must therefore be amplified before they can be recorded.

In a typical ERP experiment, a subject is presented with a series of discrete stimuli, such as pictures or sounds, and a task pertaining to them, such as keeping track

continued

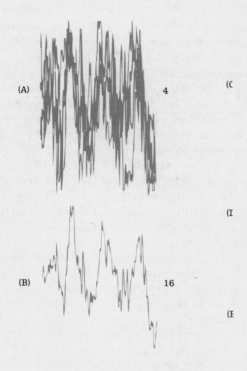

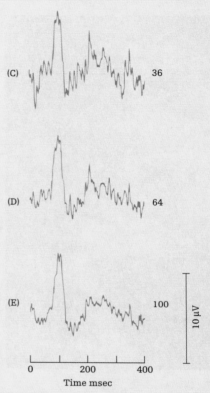

Magnetoencephalography (MEG) refers to the recording of the brain's magnetic activity. Because magnetic signals are small and therefore easily distorted by the earth's magnetic field, special equipment must be used to record them. The sensors (which otherwise resemble the electrodes used to record ERPs) are encased within a supercooled medium of liquid helium to reduce interference by other kinds of signals. As with ERPs, the subject is asked to perform some mental task, typically including a series of discretely presented stimuli, and the magnetoencephalograph is recorded as each stimulus is presented.

Similar trials are averaged, with the result being an MEG signature analogous to the signature produced by using ERPs.

MEG, like ERPs, has excellent temporal resolution and can be recorded fairly easily and quickly. It surpasses ERPs in having excellent spatial resolution if the source of magnetic activity lies tangential to the surface of the scalp. Unfortunately, if the source lies deep in a sulcus and is not optimally oriented (as would be the case for deep structures in the brain in general, such as subcortical structures), inferring the underlying source can be difficult. Unlike that of ERPs, the cost of MEG can be considerable, in part because of the sensitive equipment required to record clear signals.

Selection of Neuroimaging Tools

As may be apparent, there are advantages and disadvantages to each of these tools. Whereas some have better spatial resolution, others have better temporal resolution. Some are relatively invasive and others are noninvasive. Finally, some are expensive and others are less so. On the whole, the choice of imaging technique is determined by all these factors as well as by the specific question under consideration. For example, if one wishes to study normative processes, then the invasive nature of a technique may be a factor. The more invasive tools can be used only with animals or with certain special populations of human patients who require neurosurgery.

Such surgery may provide an opportunity for neurosurgeons to record the brain's electrical activity directly from brain tissue itself or to electrically stimulate the brain and observe the results. Wilder Penfield (1954) advanced the latter procedure by performing delicate brain surgeries on epilepsy patients while they were awake and able to talk. During these operations, Penfield (and some surgeons still today) placed small electrodes on the surface of the brain and applied small electrical currents in the hope of inducing some action, thought, or sensation on the part of the patient. When this procedure is applied to the motor strip (as it commonly is), the surgeon is able to identify what region of the body each part of the motor cortex represents and thus is able to spare important regions from damage when the neighboring tissue is removed. A complementary approach is to place electrodes on the brain's surface (or, in some cases, deep into the brain) and record brain activity. This approach permits the surgeon to identify what areas of the brain are generating seizure activity and, in so doing, precisely target that region for excision. These procedures are first performed on animals before they are extended to humans.

(for example, to see the outline of a house but not the individual features of the house, such as the windows and doors) rather than parts (for example, to see the windows and doors of a house but not the general outline). Several examples of its abilities are presented next.

Language In 1975, Eran Zaidel created an instrument called the *Z lens*, which serves the same function as the tachistoscope but is superior to it in several respects. The Z lens permits prolonged viewing of stimuli, whereas the tachistoscope flashes for only one- or two-tenths of a second (because, in the tachistoscope, any slight eye movement away from the center dot presents the stimulus to both visual fields). The Z lens ensures, with complete certainty, that only one hemisphere of a person's brain receives the visual information used for the test (see Figure 11.10). Studies with the Z lens subsequently caused neuroscientists to revise their earlier assertions that the right hemisphere was

woefully deficient in, if not totally lacking in, language comprehension.

Zaidel worked with two adult split-brain patients whose left hemispheres were dominant for language. In one test, the patients heard a word spoken by the experimenter, saw three pictures through the Z lens in the left visual field (thus, perceived by the right hemisphere), and were asked to select the picture corresponding to the word. Another test required them to follow spoken instructions, such as "Put the block with the yellow square on the block with the red circle" while the blocks that were to be used were shown in the left visual field.

Zaidel found that the right hemisphere could comprehend more words and more *about* words than had been thought. Earlier tachistoscope results had suggested that the right hemisphere could comprehend nouns but not verbs. Using the Z lens, which gives patients more than a fraction of a second to view words, Zaidel found that the noun–verb distinction was invalid: verbs took a bit

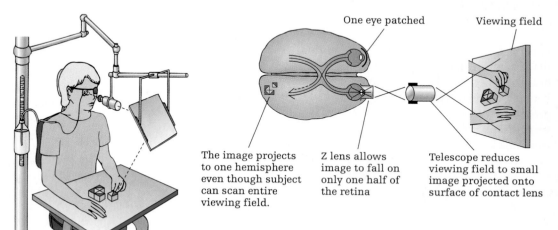

One eye patched Viewing field

The image projects to one hemisphere even though subject can scan entire viewing field.

Z lens allows image to fall on only one half of the retina

Telescope reduces viewing field to small image projected onto surface of contact lens

Figure 11.10 How the Z lens works. The lens fits directly on the eye and allows the image, which is fed directly through the lens, to reach only half of the retina. The other eye is patched, so there is no possibility of both hemispheres' viewing the material. Subjects can view images for much longer than the tachistoscope permits.

longer to process, but they were understood. The vocabulary tests showed the right hemisphere's comprehension of vocabulary to be roughly equivalent to that of a 10-year-old child. Its processing of the sequential strings of words that made up the spoken instructions was somewhat poorer than its comprehension of single words.

Even though the right hemisphere has these rudimentary comprehension abilities, it cannot produce speech. Evidently, the specialized brain regions, such as Broca's area and Wernicke's area, are required for language production.

Visual and Spatial Processes In a number of ways, the right hemisphere has proved superior to the left in the perception of spatial relations and in the manipulation of objects in response to those perceptions. To test this superiority, split-brain patients were shown cut-up drawings of shapes and then asked to choose, by touch alone and using one hand or the other, the solid shape that the drawing represented (see Figure 11.11). Choices by the left hand (right hemisphere) were correct between 75 and 90 percent of the trials; the right hand (left hemisphere) scored at about 50 percent, the level of chance, in six of seven patients.

In other studies, researchers have asked patients to arrange patterned blocks to match a design shown on a card (see Figure 11.12). Results for one patient in a series of trials are

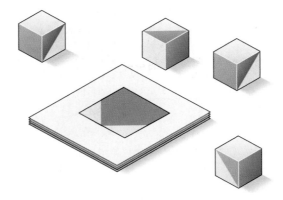

Figure 11.12 In the block-design task, subjects are asked to arrange the patterned blocks to match a specific design. Split-brain patients are asked to use one hand or the other. Performance by the left hand is far superior, as Table 11.2 shows.

shown in Table 11.2. The hand controlled by the right hemisphere was far superior to the hand controlled by the left, although the latter was not totally incompetent.

TABLE 11.2 Performance of left and right hands on block-design task		
Time (in seconds)		
Design	Left hand	Right hand
1	11	18
2	[a]	74[b]
3	13	36
4	12	69
5	15	95[b]
6	25	74[c]

[a] Design not completed within time limit (120 seconds).
[b] Subject gave up before end of time limit.
[c] Correct design was constructed but in wrong orientation.

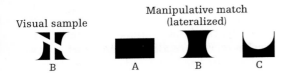

Manipulative match (lateralized)

Visual sample

B   A   B   C

Figure 11.11 Objects used to test spatial judgment. Split-brain patients manipulated the solid objects with one hand or the other and attempted to judge which one was represented in the fragmented sample picture. Left-hand scores were much higher.

3 children with left hemisphere injury

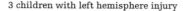

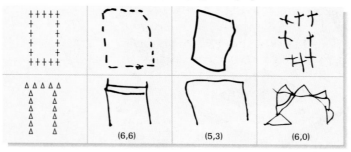

3 children with right hemisphere injury

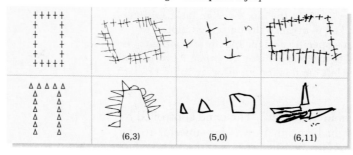

3 normal control children

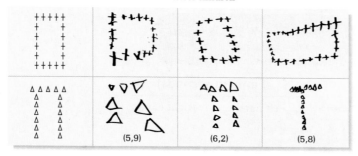

Figure 11.13 Children were asked to reproduce the figures that appear in the far left column of all three panels. Note that each of these figures is composed of smaller, individual units. The top panel reveals that children with damage to the left hemisphere respond most to the general overall shape of the figure, but miss the important details. Conversely, children with damage to the right hemisphere see the details but not the overall shape, as illustrated in the middle panel. These findings support the notion that the left hemisphere is most involved in detecting and analyzing individual component parts of a figure, whereas the right hemisphere responds best to the overall "gestalt" of the figure. The drawings of comparably aged children with no brain damage are shown in the bottom panel.

One study examined the role of the right hemisphere in visual-spatial analysis by testing children who as infants suffered a lesion to that part of the brain. As already mentioned, as a rule, the right hemisphere excels at recognizing whole scenes, whereas the left excels at analyzing the individual features of a scene. In this study, children with right-hemisphere damage (particularly in the right posterior) were asked to reproduce letters of the alphabet by using specific components, as shown in Figure 11.13. The difference between the two groups of subjects was dramatic in that children with left-hemisphere damage largely ignored the fact that the letters were made up of repeated smaller units.

Musical Processes At the age of 57, the French composer Maurice Ravel suffered severe damage to his left hemisphere in an automobile accident. The report of his subsequent condition stated that, although he could "still listen to music, attend a concert, and express criticism on it or describe the musical pleasure he felt, he never again was able to compose the pieces he heard in his head." After the accident, Ravel suffered from Wernicke's aphasia and could no longer play the piano, sing in tune, or read, much less write, musical notation.

There is no doubt that the right hemisphere also plays a role in the processing of music. In cases such as Ravel's, left-hemisphere damage does not eliminate the ability to hear music and to perceive discordant notes or rhythmic anomalies. There have been numerous reports of people who, with massive left-hemisphere damage and aphasia, could nonetheless still correctly carry the melody and sing the lyrics of a song.

Neither studies of musical abilities after brain damage nor studies of music perception in persons with normal brains have established the localization of musical ability in one or the other hemisphere. The components of music are numerous and complex in themselves—melody, pitch, timbre, harmony, and rhythm. These components are combined in an incalculable number of ways to produce music from Bach to rock. In addition, music listeners range from those who are highly trained to those who do not know what a musical phrase or a chord is. Consequently, most neuroscientists conclude that it would be premature, given current knowledge, to ascribe primary responsibility for music function to one hemisphere or the other. Nevertheless, there is some evidence that a very rare musical ability may be mediated more by the left than the right hemisphere. Magnetic resonance imaging has revealed that the left *planum temporale* (the upper surface of the temporal lobe) is larger

in musicians who have perfect pitch than in nonmusicians or even in musicians lacking perfect pitch. Perhaps this finding is not so surprising, however, considering that the left hemisphere excels in analytic processing, something that is clearly required to recognize individual notes.

Face Perception To recognize a face, we need to see more than the individual details of the mouth, the eyes, or the nose; specifically, we need to combine these pieces together to make a whole. Given that the right hemisphere seems to be in charge of recognizing wholes (rather than parts), it is not surprising that the right hemisphere has been implicated in perceiving and recognizing faces. On the basis of tests in which faces

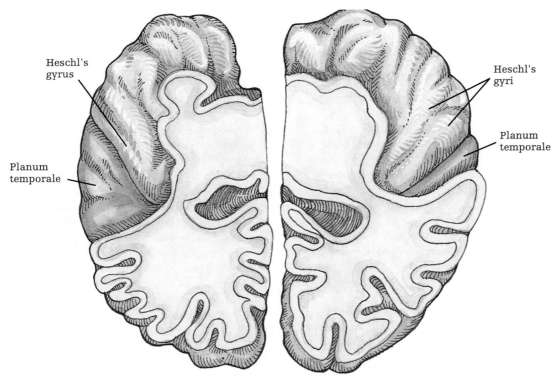

As discussed in the text, for most individuals the planum temporale is larger in the left hemisphere than in the right hemisphere. This potentially correlates with the finding that for nearly all right-handers and the majority of left-handers, the left hemisphere is dominant for language.

As discussed in an earlier chapter—and in a box within the present chapter—the ability to image the living brain has revolutionized our ability to link the structures of the brain with their functions. Moreover, the new imaging tools allow scientists to expand their studies, once limited to neurological patients (such as H. M. or R. B., considered in Chapter 9), to include neurologically normal adults and even children. The use of such tools has resulted in several important new insights into thinking and consciousness.

Mental Imagery

Mental imagery is the ability to envision in one's "mind" some scene, sound, or smell. We all have had this experience. For example, take a moment to imagine the sight or smell of your favorite food or the layout of your bedroom or the face of a close friend. Stephen Kosslyn of Harvard University has been studying mental imagery for many years and has recently discovered some important facts about this ability by using both PET and fMRI, including which region of the brain is activated when one simply *imagines* seeing. When subjects were asked to close their eyes and visualize objects, PET scanning revealed activation of the visual cortex, just as if the subjects were actually looking at an object. Moreover, the amount of metabolic activity varied, depending on the size of the mental image: the bigger the image, the greater the activity—again, the same thing that happens with the viewing of real objects. These exciting findings suggest that the visual cortex is activated even when there is no active seeing, but simply imagined seeing.

A similar phenomenon may also occur in the somatosensory system. In a recent study of healthy right-handed people,

magnetoencephalography was used to examine the somatosensory cortex during real and imagined finger movements. The authors of this work reported that both real and imagined motor movements activate this region of the brain in the same fashion.

Plasticity of Cortical Systems

We have repeatedly noted examples of our brain's remarkable plasticity, that is, its ability to change as a result of experience. An example of such change is what happens to the brain subsequent to a stroke. A stroke is generally caused by the interruption of blood flow (ischemia) to some region of the brain. If this interruption continues for too long, brain damage occurs. It is common for a stroke to affect the motor cortex and, in so doing, render the patient mildly or even severely paralyzed. Extensive physical therapy may restore much, if not all, of this function (depending on the severity of the stroke). However, until recently, it was unclear how this therapy worked its magic on the brain. A recent experiment using squirrel monkeys sheds light on what might be happening.

Monkeys were trained to retrieve food by using one of their forelimbs. A brain-mapping procedure known as *intracortical microstimulation* (ICMS) was used to map the motor cortex and reveal exactly how and where this arm movement was represented in the brain. An ischemic event was then introduced, after which the animals were no longer able to use the forelimb to retrieve food, as they had been trained to do. Correspondingly, ICMS revealed a lesion in the region of the motor cortex that represented the arm. Extensive rehabilitation was then undertaken, until eventually the animals' levels of performance were comparable to what they had been before the stroke. At that point, ICMS revealed substantial rearrangement of the area in the brain surrounding the damaged section.

In Chapter 3, we considered the phenomenon of the phantom limb, in which a person who has had a limb amputated will often experience sensation in the missing limb when another region of the body is stimulated. To understand this phenomenon, researchers used MEG to map the somatosensory cortex in amputees and found that the region of the brain that previously represented the missing limb expands to represent the area adjacent to the limb. For example, the region of the somatosensory cortex that represents the cheek may "invade" the region of the brain that previously (until the amputation) represented the forearm. This accounts for why, under some circumstances, stimulation of the cheek can cause the patient to experience sensation in the missing limb.

Explicit Memory

As described in Chapter 9, regions of the medial temporal lobe—the hippocampus and the rhinal cortex, in particular—play an important role in explicit memory. That settled, researchers were curious about why some things are remembered better than other things and whether brain-imaging tools could tell the difference. Thus, researchers use fMRI to monitor both the medial temporal lobe and the frontal lobe during a memory task. Subjects were asked to view photographs of objects. One half hour later, they were presented with pictures of the same objects again, along with pictures of novel objects. As might be expected, some people remembered the first set of pictures better than other people did. What was most intriguing,

however, was that fMRI was able to predict these differences in memory performance. Specifically, activation patterns in regions of the right prefrontal cortex and bilateral regions of the parahippocampal cortex predicted which photographs were later remembered well, less well, or not at all.

ERPs produced similar results in human infants. Nine-month-old infants were shown a series of actions in a logical sequence; for example, a small object was placed in a cup, which was then picked up and shaken to make a rattling noise. The infants simply observed this sequence but were not allowed to reproduce it. A week later, they returned to the laboratory and were presented with pictures of the objects that they had seen used a week earlier, along with pictures of novel objects, while their brain activity was recorded. Finally, *an entire month later,* the infants returned to the laboratory for the last time. At this session, they were given the objects to see if they would spontaneously reproduce the sequence that they had observed 5 weeks earlier. In accord with previous work, about half the infants could complete the sequences and half could not. What was most intriguing, however, was that the ERPs recorded a month earlier *predicted* which infants would later go on to reproduce the sequences accurately; specifically, the infants whose ERPs differed in regard to the novel and familiar objects (showing evidence of discrimination and recognition) were the same infants who recalled and mimicked the sequences a month later. Infants in whom there was no ERP differentiation showed no recall at the later date. Importantly, the topographic patterns of the observed ERPs pointed to the medial temporal lobe as a possible site of origin for the recognition-memory performance.

are presented selectively to the left or right visual fields (right and left hemispheres, respectively), many investigators have reported a left-visual-field/right-hemisphere superiority in processing faces. Thus, faces presented to the right hemisphere are recognized more quickly and accurately than faces presented to the left hemisphere. In addition, lesions of the right hemisphere, particularly of areas in and around the superior temporal sulcus and fusiform gyrus, seem to be especially disruptive to face recognition. Finally, the right-hemisphere bias for faces appears to be present in babies less than a year old. Whether this indicates the existence of an innate module for face recognition or is simply a process whereby one part of the brain becomes specialized on the basis of experience cannot be ascertained (in part because one cannot raise babies without allowing them to see faces). However, at the least, this developmental finding suggests that face recognition, like language, appears to require dedicated neural tissue. Considering how important the face is in communicating to infants who do not yet have language, this finding makes perfect sense.

Two Hemispheres, One Brain

We have seen that the study of specific hemispheric functions in patients with bisected brains is a source of insight into what each hemisphere might contribute in the intact brain. In addition, researchers use experimental means to study hemispheric function in normal brains. In tachistoscope studies of people with normal brains, for example, experimenters assume that faster responses from the left visual field reveal that the right hemisphere is best equipped to deal with the material presented and that faster responses from the right visual field are evidence of left-hemisphere superiority.

Another test often used with normal subjects is the *dichotic listening test*. Different

auditory stimuli are presented simultaneously to each ear, and subjects are asked to report what they hear. If they report more accurately what was presented to the left ear, the response is interpreted as indicating right-hemisphere superiority in processing the stimuli, and vice versa. The results of such studies seem to show a left-hemisphere advantage for language-related sounds—even for language played backward. The evidence for any right-hemisphere advantage is less clear-cut.

Studies of this sort support the theory that the two hemispheres of the brain have specialized functions, but, in an intact brain, the hemispheres work together and are part of the reason for the mental adaptability and extraordinary problem-solving prowess of human beings. Interest in different hemispheric functions has led some neuroscientists to wonder if there might be anatomical or physiological differences between the hemispheres that could account for such specialization. Until recently, the brain's two hemispheres were assumed to be anatomically identical. Research in the past two decades, however, has proved otherwise.

The Anatomy and Physiology of Hemispheric Differences

In 1968, after detailed postmortem examination of 100 human brains, neurologists Norman Geschwind and Walter Levitsky reported marked anatomical differences between the left and right hemispheres. In 65 percent of those brains, the upper surface of the temporal lobe—the planum temporale, a region overlapping Wernicke's area—was significantly larger in the left hemisphere. In 11 percent of the brains, the planum temporale was larger in the right hemisphere. The remaining 24 percent showed no difference between the hemispheres.

Since this original study, hundreds of other brains have been measured, and the findings are generally consistent: about 70 percent of all the brains studied have a larger planum temporale in the left hemisphere (see Figure 11.14). This difference is most likely indicative of the fact that the control of speech and language is, for most people, located in the left hemisphere.

Other studies have produced findings of additional hemispheric asymmetries, many of which are related to sex and others to handedness (see Table 11.3). (The box on pages 350–352 deals with the topic of handedness.) For example, there have been reports that Broca's area in the left hemisphere is, paradoxically, actually *smaller* than the corresponding area in the right hemisphere. There have also been reports that the right frontal lobe is wider and protrudes more than the left frontal lobe and that, conversely, the left occipitotemporal

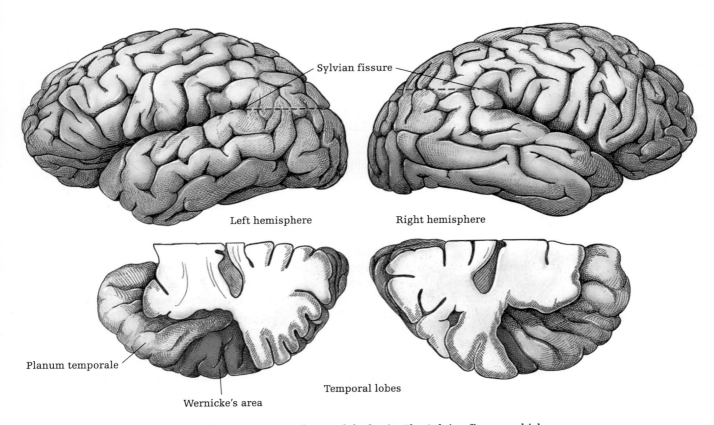

Left hemisphere　　　　Right hemisphere

Planum temporale

Wernicke's area

Temporal lobes

Figure 11.14 Anatomical asymmetries in the hemispheres of the brain. The Sylvian fissure, which defines the upper margin of the temporal lobe, slants upward more sharply in the right hemisphere. When the Sylvian fissure is opened and the cut completed along the dotted line, the planum temporale, which forms the upper surface of the temporal lobe, can be seen. It is usually much larger in the left hemisphere, and the enlarged region is part of Wernicke's area.

Asymmetry	Right-handers			Left- and mixed-handers		
	Yes	Equal	Reverse	Yes	Equal	Reverse
Sylvian fissure higher on right (Galaburda, LeMay, Kemper, and Geschwind, 1978)	67	25	8	20	70	10
Occipital horn of lateral ventrical longer on left (McRae, Branch, and Milner, 1968)	60	30	10	38	31	31
Frontal lobe wider on right (LeMay, 1977)	61	20	19	40	33	27
Occipital lobe wider on left (LeMay, 1977)	66	24	10	36	48	26
Frontal lobe protrudes on right (LeMay, 1977)	66	20	14	35	30	35
Occipital lobe protrudes on left (LeMay, 1977)	77	10.5	12.5	35	30	35

SOURCE: *Human Laterality*, by M. C. Corballis, Academic Press, 1983, p. 72.

region is wider and protrudes more than the right frontal lobe. Interestingly, in both cases, these differences exist in infant and fetal brains as well as adult brains. Additionally, there have been reports that parts of the corpus callosum are smaller in men than in women and are larger in people who use their right hands inconsistently than in those who always use their right hands. Finally, there is some evidence that the asymmetry of the planum temporale is greater in right-handed people than in left-handed people. On the whole, such differences might provide a physical basis for the different functions of the two hemispheres.

When the evidence of hemispheric asymmetry first became known, some scientists suggested that the asymmetry in the language area could be an effect of language learning, but such asymmetries have also been detected in the human fetus. Thus, the anatomical difference is more likely a cause than an effect. Another asymmetry was discovered in the course of *carotid angiography*—x-ray examination of the brain by means of dyes injected into the carotid artery: the paths of large blood vessels in the brain are also somewhat different in the two hemispheres, a result of the anatomy of the surrounding tissue. These differences revealed to researchers the fact that the Sylvian fissure (sometimes called the lateral fissure), the large groove in the cortex that divides the temporal lobe from the rest of the cortex, is longer and straighter in the left hemisphere. It slants more sharply upward in the right hemisphere (see Figure 11.14). Fossil skulls of Neanderthal man show evidence of this same asymmetry, which suggests that it may be part of the evolutionary heritage of *Homo sapiens*.

Evidence that the anatomical asymmetries in the brains of newborn infants are indicative of functional differences comes from studies of *evoked potentials* produced by speech sounds in infants as young as one week old (see page 370). In 9 of 10 infants presented with speech sounds, records of electrical activity in their brains showed that the responses from the left hemisphere were of markedly greater amplitude. When nonspeech sounds were played—a burst of noise or a musical chord—all 10 infants showed evoked potentials of greater amplitude in the right hemisphere.

Our brains, then, seem anatomically and physiologically prepared to process language as part of our species' inheritance. In most of us, the cortex of the left hemisphere is the part of the brain programmed for this function. Unlike that of most sensory and motor functions, however, the development of the language function shows plasticity. That is, if the language areas in the left cortex are damaged early in life, areas in the right cortex are able to take over their responsibilities. On rare occasions, when a cancerous tumor has spread throughout a hemisphere of the brain, for example, surgeons must remove the cortical covering of the entire hemisphere in a procedure called a *hemispherectomy*. Adults whose right hemispheres are removed show little language impairment. Adults who undergo such operations on their left hemispheres suffer severe aphasia, which seldom shows improvement. However, when infants undergo the same left-hemisphere surgery or are born with significant left-hemisphere damage, the outcome is much different. The language development of children whose left hemispheres were removed in infancy has few deficits. Standard tests of verbal intelligence reveal few differences between these children and normal children—and no difference between the children who had left hemispherectomies and those who had right hemispherectomies.

On more careful evaluation, subjects whose left hemispheres were removed early in life do reveal some subtle shortcomings. In particular, they have a problem in the use of so-called *reversible passives*: patients with left hemispherectomies reveal deficits in understanding sentences such as "the cat isn't chased by the dog" (though they do understand "the dog isn't chasing the cat"). This subtle deficit notwithstanding, such children do remarkably well in the day-to-day use of language, perhaps the ultimate measure of the brain's plasticity.

Even in the absence of overt brain damage, experience may affect the distribution of brain activities between the hemispheres. For example, in the 1970s, a horrible case of child neglect was reported in southern California. A 13-year-old girl named Genie had spent long periods of time by herself, severely deprived of normal social contact with others. Genie was found to be unable to speak or comprehend speech. After she had learned some language, psychologists used evoked-potential studies (see page 370) to see which part of her brain was processing that language. They found that she was using her right hemisphere for both language and nonlanguage functions.

Susan Curtiss, the psycholinguist who worked with Genie, suggests that the acquisition of language triggers the normal pattern of hemispheric specialization; if language is not acquired at the appropriate time, "the cortical tissue normally committed for language and related abilities may functionally atrophy." This interpretation is

The connection between handedness and consciousness has long been recognized. For example, left-handedness may correlate with specific talents and skills. There is evidence that left-handers may excel in visual-spatial analysis (see the section on right-hemisphere function), and certainly two of the best-known artists who ever lived, Michelangelo and Leonardo da Vinci, were both left-handed. In addition, some types of mathematics have been associated with right-hemisphere superiority; in particular, theoretical mathematicians may be overly represented among the left-handed population. Moreover, lefties in general appear to be overly represented among people of very high IQ: for example, in a longitudinal study of exceptionally bright high-school students, those scoring in the top 0.1 percent on the SAT (Scholastic Aptitude Test) were more than twice as likely to be left-handed as right-handed. Higher levels of education also are correlated with left-handedness. Alas, lefties are also overly represented at the other end of the IQ distribution (that is, the other extreme of intelligence). Here, however, it is likely that these people are left-handed for pathological reasons, such as pre- or perinatal insults (which are major contributing factors to a range of disabilities).

Why are there are differences in handedness? As will be clear, there is more speculation in this field of neuroscience than there is fact; nevertheless, the speculation is intriguing.

Most human beings write with the right hand and use it almost exclusively for tasks requiring skillful manipulation of objects. This is true of all cultures, and archeological evidence points to it having been true since prehistoric times. The paintings on the walls of Egyptian tombs often depict people engaged in everyday activities—eating, pouring, counting—and most are seen using the right hand in these activities. Even drawings of hunters found on cave walls show the weapons being wielded by the right hand. And the Paleolithic weapons and tools that have been found appear to have been made for the right hand. No such overwhelming preference is found in the rest of the animal kingdom. Why, then, are approximately 8 percent of human beings left-handed? And what relation exists between hand preference and the two hemispheres of the brain?

Cultural Influences

Although the incidence of left-handedness is about 8 percent worldwide, there are some differences across cultures. For example, in some Asian cultures, the incidence is lower, perhaps only 3 to 5 percent, and, among some aboriginal societies, it may be as low as 0.5 to 2 percent. On the other hand, among the Alaskan Inuit, it may be as high as 15 percent. These differences might be interpreted as being due to the influence of culture. Nevertheless, not many modern writers attribute the right-hand preference to cultural influences alone. Although it is true that some cultures—the Taiwanese, for example—put pressure on children to perform important activities with the right hand, it is possible that there is an underlying physical reason for this bias. After all, no culture has ever been found in which a similar left-hand bias predominates. Even chimpanzees are largely right-handed for some tasks (but no animal shows the consistency for preferring one hand over another—or one eye or one leg for that matter—that humans show).

Biology and Pathology

On the biological side of the argument, there are many hypotheses. One school of thought holds that right-handedness is a universal human trait and that all left-handedness is a result of some prenatal or perinatal damage to the brain, most likely caused by a lack of oxygen. The incidence of left-handedness in twins is 20 percent, much higher than that in the rest of the population, and some experts attribute it to damage that they may have suffered as a result of intrauterine crowding and difficult birth processes. One must exercise caution in accepting such an argument, however. Increasing numbers of very premature and sick infants are being kept alive today (many more than even a decade ago). If pre- and perinatal brain damage causes left-handedness, one would expect to have seen a corresponding increase in the number of lefties over the same period. Thus far, no such increase has been noted. Furthermore, there are no data to support the assertion that perinatal damage to the left hemisphere occurs with any greater frequency than perinatal damage to the right hemisphere. Thus, there should, in theory, be as many right-handers who use the right hand because of brain damage as there are left-handers who use the left hand because of brain damage. Current models of handedness fail to address this observation. Finally, although there is strong evidence to support the claim that perinatal left-hemisphere damage can produce left-handedness, the number of people who have become left-handed for this reason is unclear.

Genetics

Genetics has also been proposed as the determinant of handedness. For example, 25 percent more males than females are left-handed. In addition, the probability of being left-handed is twice as high if your mother is left-handed as if she is right-handed. However, even if both of your parents are left-handed, it does not necessarily mean that you will be left-handed (given how low the base rate of left-handedness is in general). No simple genetic model seems able to explain all the data, including the fact that the incidence of left-handedness is about the same in both identical and fraternal twins. Because identical twins have 100 percent of their genes in common and fraternal twins have 50 percent, the incidence should not be the same.

An interesting genetic model describes most people as inheriting a gene called the "right-shift factor." According to this model, most, but not all, of these people will become right-handers. Those who do not inherit this gene may become right-handers or left-handers or be ambidextrous (with similar dexterity in both hands), depending on chance factors—training or injury, for example. Evidence to support this hypothesis comes from the fact that left-handers show much less consistency than right-handers in other measures of laterality. Right-handers usually have dominant right eyes, ears, and feet, and they gesture almost exclusively with their right hands when they speak. Left-handers tend to gesture about equally with both hands, and they show mixed patterns of eye, ear, and foot dominance.

In one test of this theory, a group of children of two left-handed parents were given a peg-sorting task, and their performance with each hand was timed. About half the children did better with the right hand, and about half did better with the left. These results upheld the prediction that hand preference in this group would be determined by chance (because presumably none had inherited the right-shift factor). The parents were interviewed to determine whether any of them had suffered trauma during their own births. Those who reported such traumas had significantly more right-handed children. These left-handed parents may, then, have inherited the right-shift gene but were forced, because of the birth-trauma injury, to use the left hand. Nonetheless, they were able to pass along the right-shift gene to their children.

Other data in support of the right-shift theory have been questionable. Overall, it may be reasonable to assume that right-handedness may be genetically fixed, but left-handedness is not. In any case, the central cause of left-handedness remains a mystery.

based on the findings of Nobel laureates David Hubel and Torsten Weisel, which show that neurons not exposed to normal visual input fail to develop the normal number of connections with other cells and so become functionally inactive. No evidence exists to show that neurons in the language areas would fail to develop connections in this way, however. Furthermore, the findings obtained by Hubel and Weisel came from animal experiments, and animal brains cannot be used to demonstrate the development of human language.

Language and Cognitive Dissonance

One case stands out as apparently unique among all patients with bisected brains. Early in life, epileptic lesions had evidently caused damage to the left hemisphere of patient P. S., and the brain's plasticity had allowed the development of some language-processing ability in his right hemisphere. After a brain bisection had been done to control P. S.'s epilepsy, researchers made an unusual discovery: they could communicate with the patient's left and right hemispheres. This happenstance has been the source of some valuable insights into the nature of consciousness and the role that language plays in it.

P. S.'s right hemisphere not only possessed the ability to understand single words, but could also understand complex verbal instructions and could direct his left hand to spell out responses to questions by using the letters from a Scrabble game. The testing of P. S.'s separated hemispheres produced an amazing result: two discrete spheres of consciousness seemed to be operating side by side within him. When psychologist and researcher Michael Gazzaniga asked P. S.'s left hemisphere, "What do you want to be?" P. S. responded, "Draftsman." When the same question was posed to the right hemisphere, P. S. spelled out, "Automobile racer." Gazzaniga (1970) describes the moment when he and his associates discovered P. S.'s two "selves":

We stared at each other for what seemed an eternity. A half-brain had told us about its own feelings and opinions, and the other half-brain, the talkative left, temporarily put aside its dominant ways and watched its silent partner express its views. . . . Paul's right side told us about his favorite TV star, girlfriend, food, and other preferences. After each question, which we had carefully lateralized to the right hemisphere through our testing techniques, we asked Paul what the question was. He (that is, his left brain) shot back, "I didn't see anything." Then his left hand, controlled by the right hemisphere, would . . . proceed to write out the answer to our question. . . . Here was a separate mental system that could express mood, feeling, opinion.

P. S. was able to act in response to verbal commands presented exclusively to one hemisphere or the other. When his left hemisphere was asked to explain the actions that P. S. had carried out in obedience to commands presented to his right hemisphere, the responses were fascinating. When, for example, the command "rub" was flashed to his right hemisphere, he began to rub the back of his head with his left hand. Asked what the command had been, his left hemisphere said "itch." Apparently, his left hemisphere observed the right hemisphere's response and guessed what the command might have been.

An example from one particularly revealing series of tests is depicted in Figure 11.15. With the tachistoscope, each of P. S.'s hemispheres was simultaneously presented with a different drawing. Also before him were drawings of other objects from which he was asked to pick the drawings that were most closely related to the stimuli flashed by the tachistoscope. Each hand responded for its own hemisphere.

When shown a chicken claw in the left hemisphere and a snow scene in the right, P. S. quickly responded correctly by choosing a picture of a chicken with his right hand and a picture of a shovel with his left.

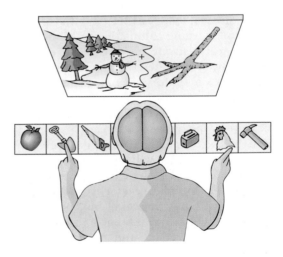

Figure 11.15 Simultaneous tachistoscope presentation of differing stimuli to P. S.'s right and left hemispheres. When he chose matching stimuli with each hand, each choice was appropriate to the corresponding hemisphere's stimulus. But his left hemisphere's verbal explanation of its choice consistently included a rationale for the right hemisphere's choice, even though the left hemisphere had no idea what, if anything, the right hemisphere had seen.

When asked, "What did you see?" he said, "I saw a claw and I picked the chicken, and you have to clean out the chicken shed with a shovel."

During an entire series of such choices, the left hemisphere consistently explained why it had made its choice and then went on to incorporate the right hemisphere's choice into the framework of its response, even though it had not been asked to do so. And, although the left hemisphere could construct only a plausible guess, its answers had an unmistakable ring of certainty.

The behavior of P. S.'s left, verbal hemisphere in justifying his right hemisphere's actions and in trying to make the actions of both consonant illustrates a well-known psychological theory called *cognitive dissonance*. According to this theory, all human beings feel a strong need to avoid disharmony between their actions and their beliefs. If a man, for instance, believes himself to be prudent and conservative yet is persuaded to invest in high-risk stocks, the cognitive dissonance between his beliefs and his actions will make him extremely uncomfortable. He will try to erase the dissonance either by changing his behavior, selling the speculative stocks and buying blue chips, or by changing his conception of himself, protesting that, although he may appear prudent and conservative in his personal life, he can be quite adventuresome in business.

Many experiments have confirmed the operation of this psychological principle in people with normal, intact brains. Its operation in P. S., with his separated hemispheres, however, revealed something new about the role of language in human consciousness. As Michael Gazzaniga (1970) concludes, "The environment has ways of planting hooks in our minds, and while the verbal system may not know the why or what of it all, part of its job is to make sense out of the emotional and other mental systems and, in so doing, allow man, with his mental complexity, the illusion of a unified self."

Conscious and Nonconscious Information Processing

Virtually everyone who drives a car has had the experience at least once of arriving at some destination and having no recollection of the last 10 or 15 minutes on the road. You might have been talking with a passenger or listening to music or just thinking about something else. In any case, you were probably a bit surprised to find yourself home safely, having paid so little attention to the traffic and the route.

Nevertheless, you must have been processing the necessary information at some level to have escaped accident and ended up where you wanted to be. You must have perceived the cars around you and the road signs or landmarks along your route to have safely navigated. And you must have acted on those perceptions without engaging the language-using, conscious, part of your mind.

There are ample experimental data demonstrating this kind of perception and processing below the level of consciousness. One interesting outcome of a certain kind of brain damage helps to throw light on the topic.

The Neglect Syndrome

Some patients with fairly extensive damage to the posterior area of the right hemisphere (parieto-occipital cortex) behave as if the left side of space, and even the left side of their bodies, had ceased to exist. A man may stand in front of a mirror to shave and yet shave only the right side of his face. A woman may eat all the food on the right side of her plate and ask for a second helping until someone points out that all the food on the left side of the plate remains uneaten. Such patients reproduce drawings like those in Figure 11.16. Patients with equivalent damage to the left hemisphere generally do not show this *neglect syndrome.*

Patients with this right-hemisphere damage do not suffer from blindness. When the tachistoscope flashes a picture of

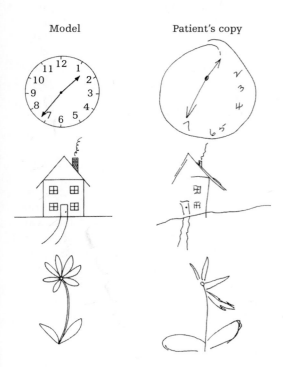

Figure 11.16 Drawings copied by a patient with neglect syndrome demonstrate total neglect of the left side of space.

an object to the left visual field, they can identify the object. Interestingly, however, when two stimuli are flashed simultaneously to both left and right visual fields, the patients will report seeing the picture in the right field and claim that it was all they saw. (Remember, these are not split-brain patients.) The patients evidently have no awareness of having seen anything in the left visual field. Did they, in fact, see the picture or not?

To answer this question, the task was changed slightly. Instead of being asked to name what they saw in the left visual field, the patients were asked to say whether the two pictures flashed to the right and left visual fields were the same or different. Patients answered this question with a great deal of accuracy. Obviously, then, they had perceived the object in the left visual field and they remembered it, but they were not conscious of processing the information.

One study made the same point with normal subjects by flashing pictures of nonsense shapes at speeds so fast that later recognition of the shapes was impossible. Later, when the subjects were given a number of nonsense shapes—some that had been flashed and some that they had never seen before—and were asked to indicate which shapes they preferred, many chose the shapes that had been flashed. They had gained familiarity with those shapes, even though they had never consciously "seen" them.

A similar study made use of patients in whom the left hemisphere had been anesthetized for medical reasons. With the anesthetic at work, these subjects were given an object to feel with the left hand. After the anesthetic wore off, they were asked to name the object. They could not. But, when shown an array of objects and asked to identify the object by pointing to it, they could do so accurately. The information had obviously registered, though not in verbal codes. Information coded in the absence of language proved to be inaccessible to consciousness, although it was readily accessible through behavior. In a sense, these subjects had "neglected" that incoming information.

One explanation of the neglect syndrome says that it occurs with right-hemisphere but not left-hemisphere damage because it results from the left hemisphere's use of language to rationalize the person's experiences to the conscious mind (as in the case of patient P. S.). The left hemisphere assumes that what it sees is all there is to see. Many patients with the neglect syndrome insist that there is nothing wrong with how they perceive and act in the world.

Other explanations of the neglect syndrome propose that the right-hemisphere damage has produced deficits in the mechanisms controlling perception. The following anecdote indicates, however, that the phenomenon does not depend on sensory processing. Physicians asked a patient with the neglect syndrome to imagine and describe a plaza in Milan that the patient had been familiar with *before* his illness. They asked him to imagine himself arriving from the north end of the plaza and to describe what he saw. The patient went on to describe the buildings one by one on the west side—that is, to the right of where he pictured himself entering. He did not mention any of the buildings on the left. Then he was asked to imagine himself entering from the south. This time he described all the buildings on the east side. The neglect syndrome appears to affect even the recall of images from memory.

Consciousness and Emotion

We human beings use many nonconscious systems of information processing to evaluate the world around us: in judging how far away from us a large dog is, for example, or in deciding whether a cup of coffee is too hot to drink. According to Joseph LeDoux (1985), these mechanisms are "direct descendants of comparable systems of our evolutionary ancestors . . . and reflect our biological heritage as vertebrates." Our emotional systems belong to this category of nonconscious systems. LeDoux makes the point that we find it much easier to consciously control our emotional *behavior* than our emotions themselves.

Piazza del Duomo, Milan.

For example, another person's actions may make us furious, but, even though we have the impulse to punch that person in the nose, we refrain from doing so most of the time. Nevertheless, the feeling of anger may persist for hours or even days, even if we wish it to go away.

LeDoux believes that the neural pathways between the mechanisms of emotion and the mechanisms of consciousness (both mechanisms, we have seen, being somewhat language dependent), are limited; so many emotional reactions take place without being consciously encoded. It is only after an emotion has arisen and we consciously examine the circumstances, our feelings, and our behavior that we decide the significance of an event. These speculations resemble the James-Lange theory of emotion and coincide with the experimental findings of Stanley Schachter, discussed in Chapter 8. His subjects, unaware that they had received an injection of adrenaline, felt an emotional arousal for which they had no explanation. Faced with this puzzle, they ascribed meaning to their feeling on the basis of the angry or euphoric behavior of those around them, deciding that they, too, were feeling the same thing. The behavior of patient P. S., when his left, verbal, hemisphere justified his right hemisphere's actions, also lends some support to this hypothesis.

The Cortex, Consciousness, and Self

We have seen that the brain's two hemispheres are not identical, either anatomically or functionally. For most people, the right hemisphere seems to process information as a unified whole, whereas the left hemisphere processes information sequentially. The most important sequential processing in the left hemisphere is the processing of language—a species-specific behavior unique to *Homo sapiens*.

Most of the evidence for separate hemispheric functions comes from brain-damaged individuals. In all normal people, however, the two hemispheres constantly interact, with neural impulses running through the several commissures connecting left side to right. Specifically, the cortices of both hemispheres are linked by many fibers passing through the corpus callosum.

It is our cerebral cortex—what has been called the "enchanted loom"—that produces the characteristics that set human beings apart from other animals. It has given us the power to create tools—from the stone axe to the nuclear reactor—and to invent vehicles that move us faster than the cheetah and fly us higher and farther than the eagle. And human language allows us to preserve and pass on information about our creations to future generations, something that no other animal can do.

The human cortex is probably more intricate in structure and more complex in functioning than anything else known to us. Its mechanisms, according to Vernon Mountcastle's model, are alike in all of us. Yet the operations of these ensembles of neurons create in each of us a unique consciousness, a self unlike any other. Mountcastle (1975) himself best describes this process:

Sensory stimuli reaching us are transfused at peripheral nerve endings, and neural replicas dispatched brainward, to the great grey mantle of the cerebral cortex. We use them to form dynamic and continually updated neural maps of the external world, and of our place and orientation, and of events, within it. At the level of sensation your images and my images are virtually the same, and readily identified one to another by verbal description, or common reaction.

Beyond that, each image is conjoined with genetic and stored experiential information that makes each of us uniquely private. From that complex integral each of us constructs at a higher level of perceptual experience his own, very personal, view from within.

Summary

1. Consciousness is defined as awareness of one's own mental or physical actions or both. Usually, language is the vehicle that makes thought and action available to conscious awareness.

2. The large areas of the cerebral cortex not committed to processing specific sensory or motor information are called association cortex. It is in these areas, according to some scientists, that primary information from all the senses is integrated and then further integrated with emotions and memories, creating consciousness.

3. Another theory, that of Vernon Mountcastle, says that consciousness is ultimately a function of the columnar organization of the cerebral cortex, which he characterizes as a distributed system. That is, the columns' internal and external connections allow for dynamic and changing information flow through the system, with different pathways used according to the organism's needs. Through such pathways comes not only information from the outside world, but also reentrant information—memories, emotions, and cognitive skills. This simultaneous processing of external and internally generated information allows a continuous updating of perceptual images of the self, which, when matched against external conditions, is the proposed mechanism for consciousness.

4. Patients who, for medical reasons, have had the two hemispheres of their brains disconnected by surgery that cuts through the corpus callosum have been sources of much insight into the workings of consciousness. Studies using specially designed equipment that allows only one hemisphere or the other to see objects reveal that each hemisphere processes information somewhat differently: the left analytically and sequentially; the right simultaneously and as a whole.

5. In more than 95 percent of right-handers and 70 percent of left-handers, the left hemisphere controls speech and language. The specific brain areas are: Broca's area, responsible for the production of the sounds of speech; Wernicke's area, responsible for the production and comprehension of meaningful language; and the arcuate fasciculus, a tract of nerve fibers connecting Broca's and Wernicke's areas. If the left hemisphere sustains damage early in life, control of language is developed in corresponding areas of the right hemisphere.

6. The right hemisphere appears to be superior for the perception of spatial relations. It plays a role in the processing of music and perhaps in the processing of faces. And it has, even in people whose left hemispheres are dominant for language, some slight ability to comprehend language.

7. A number of anatomical differences between the hemispheres have been noted. In about 70 percent of people, the planum temporale, the upper surface of the temporal lobe, is larger in the left hemisphere; this asymmetry in the language area has also been seen in human fetuses. The Sylvian fissure, which defines the upper limit of the temporal lobe, slants upward more sharply in the right hemisphere in most right-handed people. A number of anatomical asymmetries are related to handedness.

8. Studies conducted with one split-brain patient, P. S., whose right hemisphere had developed enough facility in language to communicate with researchers by spelling out answers to questions with Scrabble tiles, revealed that each hemisphere may have its own consciousness. P. S.'s hemispheres differed in their preferences for careers, foods, and favorite television stars. Studies with P. S. also showed that, if the left, language-dominant hemisphere became aware of discrepancies between the hemispheres' replies, it somehow incorporated the right hemisphere's choice into its response, constructing a rationale for that choice and thus preventing cognitive dissonance.

9. Some people with damage to the posterior area of the right hemisphere display the neglect syndrome, behaving as if the left side of space has ceased to exist. It initially appeared that these people do not process information presented to their left visual fields; but, when researchers probed, it became clear that the patients do process the left-field information but at a nonconscious level. Much information processed by normal persons is processed at a nonconscious level.

Key Terms

consciousness	right hemisphere
divided field	corpus callosum
dichotic listening	PET
visual neglect	fMRI
handedness	ERPs
face perception	MEG
left hemisphere	neuropsychology

Further Reading

Annett, M. 1985. *Left, Right, Hand and Brain: The Right Shift Theory.* London: Erlbaum Press. Discusses the origins of handedness.

Corina, D. P., Vaid, J., and Bellugi, U. 1992. The linguistic basis of left hemisphere specialization. *Science,* 255:1258–1260. A scientific study of the functions subserved by the left hemisphere.

Kosslyn, S. M., et al. 1995. Topographic representations of mental images in primary visual cortex. *Nature,* 378:496–498. An example of the use of neuroimaging tools to study how the brain performs mental imagery tasks.

Mountcastle, V. B. 1997. The columnar organization of the neocortex. *Brain* 120:701–722. A distinguished neuroscientist describes the columnar and thus modular organization of the cortex.

Shaywitz, S. E., et al. 1998. Functional disruption in the organization of the brain for reading in dyslexia. *Proceedings of the National Academy of Sciences,* 95:2636–2641. A neuroimaging study of people with dyslexia.

Springer, S. P., and Deutsch, G. 1997. *Left Brain, Right Brain: Perspectives from Cognitive Neuroscience.* Worth, New York. A short, well-presented compilation of research and theory into all aspects of the brain's two hemispheres.

Tallal, P., et al. 1996. Language comprehension in language-learning impaired children improved with acoustically modified speech. *Science,* 271:81–84. A scientific study reporting on the effectiveness of an intervention program for treatment of language-learning disorders, based on the premise that such disorders are due to the inability to parse the speech train into its constituent elements.

Interactive Resources

To continue your study online, visit our Web site at www.worthpublishers.com/bloom. Click on "Chapter 11" for resources including practice quizzes, flash cards, simulations, links to related Web sites, and updates on new research.

The Malfunctioning Mind

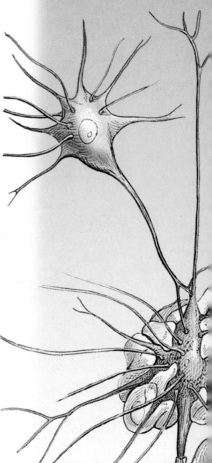

DOCTOR: *How are you doing?*

GERRY: *I'm not doing so hot. I think and feel as though people have called me here to electrocute me, judge me, put me in jail . . . or kill me, electrocute me, because of some of the sins I've been in.*

DOCTOR: *It must be very frightening for you, if it feels like you're about to get killed?*

GERRY: *. . . It's so scary, I could tell you that picture's got a headache.*

DOCTOR: *Can you tell me more about that—the picture . . . has a headache?*

GERRY: *Okay, when a sperm and an egg go together to make a baby, only one sperm goes up in the . . . egg, and, when they touch, there's two contact points that touch before the other two, and . . . then it's carried up into the air. And . . . when they fuse, it's like nuclear fusion, except it's human fusion . . . there's a mass loss of the proton . . . one heat abstraction spins around, comes back down into the proton to form the mind, and the mind could be reduced to one atom.*

DOCTOR: *At this point, what would you like us to do for you?*

GERRY: *I'd like you to get me off of cigarettes, get me dried out, cleaned up, so I can go home and get a job in a bakery and go to medical school.*

DOCTOR: *If you had to pick one or two things that you'd like us to help you with, what would they be?*

GERRY: *Schizophrenia.*

DOCTOR: *Schizophrenia. What does that mean? Different people use the word different ways.*

GERRY: *Schizophrenia is when you . . . you hear voices inside your head. You know?*

Like, inside your head, but I'm psychosomatic . . . I can . . . pantomime with people. Psychosomatic. That's what that means.

You may have only rarely, or never, encountered people who express abnormal thinking like this in their conversations. Gerry suffers from a severe mental disease, *schizophrenia*, which is characterized by disordered thinking and behaving, perceptual distortions, and gross delusions. He is, his doctor says, a "textbook case."

Depending on how old you are and how long it has been since you were last cooped up indoors with small children, you may or may not smile at the line "Insanity is hereditary—you get it from your children." The constant clamor, physical activity, and unending interruptions virtually "drive you crazy." You probably did not need to read about stress in Chapter 8 to realize that modern living can make you feel as if you, too, are "going crazy." But what does it really mean to be insane, or to "go crazy," and how different is a serious mental illness from a temper tantrum or a day of being "depressed"? How does Gerry's conversation differ from that of someone who is temporarily "not himself" or "not herself"?

The view taken in this book is that the biological science of the brain can give us a better and deeper understanding of the nature and causes of mental illness than any other available approach. Everything that the brain does is becoming explainable in relation to specific nerve cells, their circuits, and their neurotransmitters. We do not have room here for a comprehensive examination of the biological underpinnings of abnormal psychology and of the neurological diseases that are characterized by disordered thinking and loss of mental capacities, but we do believe it will be worthwhile to take a general look at the kinds of biological discoveries that help explain disorders of thinking and behaving.

Examining the roles of certain neuronal circuits, chemical signals, and cellular mechanisms in the diseased mind can lead us to a new understanding of how the normal brain works. Moreover, it may help us develop a deeper understanding of what goes wrong within the brain and lead to ways of predicting who may be most susceptible to mental problems.

Historical Views of Behavior Disorders

Current medical research on mental problems seeks not only to develop better understanding of their different causes and to provide more effective treatment, but also to find ways to prevent these problems in the future. Historically, however, the approaches to mental illness were often far less constructive.

Early Descriptions

Like most human problems, abnormal patterns of behavior, especially those that affect thinking or moving, were recorded in the Bible, as well as by ancient Greek and Chinese observers. The Old Testament, for example, reports that God punishes those who disobey Him with "madness, blindness and astonishment of the heart," mental states possibly equivalent to mania, dementia, and anxiety. Early Chinese writings in *The Yellow Emperor's Classic of Medicine* describe insanity, dementia, nine kinds of emotional disharmony, and convulsions.

Most early cultures treated behavioral problems of thinking and moving as though evil spirits had taken possession of people,

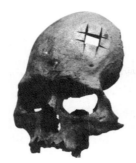

Ancient civilizations used trephination, the drilling of holes in the skull, to make exits for the evil spirits that had taken possession of the mentally ill.

and punishment was the only proper course of action. In addition to abandoning or beating such people, many cultures designed elaborate religious rituals to cast out the demons. Treatment strategy may also have

Trephination, or cutting the stone of folly, continued into early modern times. Jan Saunders van Hemessen painted *The Surgeon* about 1530.

included drilling holes in the skull to allow the evil spirits to escape.

Hippocrates' writings in the fourth and fifth centuries B.C. did much to bring attitudes toward mental illness out of the realm of superstition. He accurately described the depression that sometimes follows childbirth and gave more accurate descriptions of epileptic seizures than his predecessors had. Hippocrates is also known for having given the name "hysteria" to a disorder in women caused, he said, by "wandering of the uterus," but in general he espoused the then-radical view that mental illness arises in the brain.

Near the end of the eighth century A.D., Arab physicians, who had rediscovered earlier Greek medical writings, developed what we can call the first humane treatment centers for the mentally ill. They established what would later come to be called "asylums" where the ill, mainly "melancholic" patients, were cared for with special diets, rest, and music. In accord with the traditions of many cultures that a supernatural power spoke through the insane, Moslems believed that Allah had chosen these people to speak the truth.

With rare exceptions, no further lasting changes in concept or treatment occurred until well into the Renaissance. Instead, Western thought of the Middle Ages perpetuated the view that the mentally ill, being possessed of evil spirits, could be treated by exorcism, beating, or burning. Throughout the Inquisition and the era of witchcraft in the fifteenth and sixteenth centuries, madnesses and delusions were viewed as epidemics that could be spread by contact with the ill. Those who survived more formal social punishments were kept in dungeons. Such views held sway until the middle of the sixteenth century, when the Swiss physicians Weyer and Paracelsus proposed that abnormal mental conditions were really medical problems.

However, during the birth pangs of medical science in sixteenth- and seventeenth-century Europe, understanding of these diseases was still constrained by the weight of religious thought. Medical diseases might affect the body, but the soul—the realm of mind and spirit—was deemed to be the property of God. Nevertheless, royal sovereigns—engaged in power struggles with the Catholic church and the emerging Protestant religion—began at this time to accept responsibility for the well-being of their subjects. This led them to create large institutions for the mentally ill. Unfortunately, the mentally ill were more or less imprisoned in those institutions—largely ignored in the hope that they and their problems would disappear.

A major turning point in this rather dismal state of affairs occurred with the tragic illness of George III of England, whose reign included the years of the American Revolution. Beginning in 1788, the king suffered a recurring illness characterized by periods of intense abdominal pain, insomnia, and extreme restlessness, accompanied by confusion and irrational behavior. At times, George's behavior was so bizarre that a straitjacket was required to restrain him. In 1810, after the third or fourth recurrence, Parliament made his son (later George IV) regent.

For the rest of his life, George III remained the "mad king." However, his prominence and the severity of his illness led to the first systematic attempts by medical investigators to find a cure for a serious mental problem. Two of the king's sons set up the first research fund for the study of such disorders. The king's episodic disease, with its fluctuating cycles of apparent insanity and normality, was later identified as a

TEMPERANCE *enjoying a Frugal Meal.*

Contemporary cartoonists mercilessly caricatured the peculiar behavior of King George III. The royal physicians kept detailed notes of everything that the king did, making modern reexaminations of his case possible. The evidence suggests that the king was not in fact "mad," but rather that he suffered from a rare form of metabolic disease known today as acute intermittent porphyria. In this disease, the body is unable to construct proper hemoglobin molecules for red blood cells to transport oxygen. Large amounts of unassembled hemoglobin components are then excreted in the urine. The deep red urine (center test tube; its color resembles that of port wine, shown in the right test tube; the color of normal urine is shown in the left test tube) that characterized the king's episodes was described by contemporary physicians, without its significance being understood. To this day, however, medical investigators do not know how this very specific metabolic disease produces the pain and, in some cases, the mental problems that are sometimes its characteristics.

rare form of the metabolic disorder *porphyria*. (See illustration above).

The plight of the mentally ill changed little in the eighteenth and nineteenth centuries, except that their treatment in hospitals became somewhat more humane. Large general asylums for the insane, pioneered by the French superintendent Philippe Pinel in the late eighteenth century, improved their facilities, but these institutions remained, essentially, hiding places for the mentally ill throughout the Western world. Nevertheless, the eighteenth and nineteenth centuries were a time of scientific revolution, and, in

John Hughlings Jackson
1835–1911

Ivan Petrovich Pavlov
1849–1936

Emil Kraepelin
1855–1925

Sigmund Freud
1856–1939

Eugen Bleuler
1857–1939

the second half of the nineteenth century, the beginnings of a scientific understanding of the brain based on investigations of the structural consequences of strokes, tumors, and brain trauma emerged. Some of the most prophetic scholars of the brain, the mind, and behavior—all physician-scientists—began to do their most important work: Claude Bernard, the French physiologist noted in Chapter 6; the neurologist-anatomists Paul Broca, Franz Nissl, Korbinian Brodmann, Jean-Martin Charcot, and Carl Wernicke, some of whom were discussed in Chapters 4 and 11; Ivan Pavlov, introduced in Chapter 10; and Sigmund Freud, John Hughlings Jackson, Emil Kraepelin, and Eugene Bleuler, whom we will meet here.

The Past Century

By the 1920s and 1930s, medical science had eliminated two diseases that accounted for a sizable number of the patients imprisoned in asylums: pellagra and general paresis.

The first to go was *pellagra*, a disease caused by dietary insufficiency of the B vitamin niacin. (The individual B vitamins had first to be discovered before the differences and the foods containing the different B vita-

mins could be identified.) The foods richest in niacin were, it turned out, missing from the diets of many poverty-stricken and protein-deficient populations. Pellagra was once estimated to account for 10 percent of the admissions to state asylums in the southern United States, where corn was a major dietary staple. (Corn niacin is especially hard to digest.) The delirium, confusion, and general disorientation of the pellagra victim were often accompanied by periods of "mania": extremely excited behavior, loud and incessant talking, and constant movement. Because high fevers often appeared to precipitate these mental derangements, people had believed that some "germ," the common name for any unknown infectious agent, was being propagated among the squalor of the poor and causing these outbreaks of "insanity." It never occurred to them to wonder why the "insanity germ" did not spread to those who guarded the inmates. With adequate nutrition and niacin supplements, however, the "madness" promptly disappeared.

A germ does in fact cause a mental illness known as *general paresis*, actually a late stage in the infection of the brain by syphilis. Before the advent of antibiotics as a successful treatment for the primary infectious episode of syphilis, all patients went effectively untreated. Ten or so years after first being infected, as many as one-third of those with syphilis would undergo an increasingly pronounced loss of memory and concentration, progressing to chronic fatigue and lethargy accompanied by an emotional instability that alternated between depression and delusions of grandeur. Examinations of the brains of these syphilitic patients after death showed that large parts of their brains and spinal cords had been destroyed by the invading bacteria.

Shortly before the end of World War I, the Austrian physician Julius von Wagner-Jauregg devised a fever therapy for syphilis. Patients infected with syphilis were purposely infected with malaria in order that the high fevers from the malaria infection would kill the heat-sensitive syphilis bacteria. Later, the patients had to be given quinine drugs to treat the malaria, but this seemed a small price for avoiding the progressive mental deterioration of neurosyphilis. In 1927, Wagner-Jauregg received the Nobel Prize for this cure. Today, syphilis is fully cured by treatment in its early stages with antibiotics such as penicillin, so general paresis has been virtually eliminated. Even later stages are treatable with high doses of penicillin given intravenously.

Porphyria, pellagra, and general paresis are now known to be "organic" forms of mental illness. In other words, observable, verifiable signs of chemical or structural pathology are seen in these diseases, proving that the patient's abnormal behavior is caused by specific cellular changes within the brain. Elimination of pellagra and neurosyphilis have allowed clinical scientists to to focus on other serious mental illnesses for which there are no obvious "organic" signs. In such an effort, clinical neuroscientists believe that more accurate diagnosis is a nec-essary first step so that the general body of patients with some sort of behavioral problem can be separated into discrete categories of conditions with common origins and possibly distinct treatments.

Diseases of the Brain and Disorders of Behavior

In discussing abnormalities of the brain and the ways in which they affect the mind and behavior, scientists draw an distinction between the terms *disease* and *disorder*. Both diseases and disorders constitute malfunctions of some kind, but a disease is a specific set of signs and symptoms that are seen together often enough for doctors to consider them a consistent diagnostic entity. On the other hand, a disorder is a much softer concept, connoting that something is wrong, but without enough consistency in features to be recognizable from patient to patient. Thus, diseases have names (measles, rabies, diabetes) and arise from a variety of inherited, infectious, or toxic causes. When a disease is diagnosed, predictions can be made concerning the course that it is likely to take and the patient's probable response to specific treatments. A disorder, in contrast, is a problem that does not fit a clearly defined diagnostic category. Many disorders of thinking and behaving take highly variable forms, and their manifestations have no recognizable common foundation. In some instances, they consist of serious malfunctions. In others, they are defined as abnormal only because of what most people—or most doctors—define as normal. Whatever its cause, a disorder becomes a disease only when its manifestations are recognized as having a truly consistent form.

In a general sense, all diseases are disorders (malfunctions), but not all disorders are diseases. This discussion reserves the term "disease" for the most consistent, repeating forms of abnormal brain conditions, and uses the term "disorder" (or its more common synonym, "illness," the opposite of wellness) for various abnormal conditions that are still incompletely defined.

Understanding the difference between a disease and a disorder, in the context of abnormal behavior, is not just a matter of semantics. As asserted earlier, this text takes the view that biological explanations can be found for everything that the brain does, when it is working correctly and when it is not. Therefore, a search for those logical explanations requires that we define "not working correctly" very carefully. First, it is necessary to identify any biological and behavioral "abnormalities" in a patient at various stages in the progression of his or her illness and then to see if similar correlations between biology and behavior can be made in others with these same symptoms. Second, to gain a better understanding of the nature of the major psychiatric diseases, we must determine whether we can categorize groups of mentally affected patients according to discrete clusters of symptoms that might then constitute the basis for a definition of a specific disease. If we were to try to lump together everyone who falls outside of what we deem normal into one large category, we would be unable to find any consistent meaningful differences, even if we knew what to measure.

There is an additional distinction between disease and disorders. From the medical point of view, diseases by definition entail some degree of pathological change that seems to demand a treatment or prevention strategy whether that be a medication, a vaccine, or long, thoughtful conversations. On the other hand, behavior that is only mildly disordered might require behavioral adjustments on the part of the person without warranting treatment, whether in the form of drugs or psychotherapy. For example, being unable to fall asleep when one is nervous the night before a test or being unable to resist eating too much chocolate candy may require action on the part of the person who has the problem, but such "abnormal" behaviors are widespread among otherwise totally normal people. Furthermore, not all behavioral problems are likely to be reduced to a straightforward chemical or biological explanation either now or in the near future—for example, fascination with fire (*pyromania*) or obsessive hair pulling (*trichotillomania*). As students of the brain and behavior, we need to concentrate our efforts on those problems for which solutions may be possible—that is, on problems that have been classified as diseases.

Brain-Cell Dysfunction

How is a state of "unhealth" in the brain identified and studied? Virtually all the diseases of other organ systems—the lungs, the kidneys, or the skin, for example—can be explained as stemming from problems in the structure or function of the cells in those organs. Diseases of the brain also stem from problems in cell function. The study of the cellular dysfunctions that cause disease is known as *pathology*.

Pathologists find that the brain is susceptible to the same disease-causing factors as those affecting the other major body systems: abnormalities of development, inherited metabolic problems, infections, allergies, tumors, inadequate blood supply, injury, and the scars that persist after recovery. Such diseases, whose signs and symptoms can be identified under the microscope or can be shown to be side effects of a medical condition such as kidney, liver, or cardiovascular diseases, are often referred to as "organic." The organic diseases of the brain—including problems in sensing the world around us, such as blindness, deafness, or other loss of sensing or moving ability—are the province of the neurologist.

At times, however, no obvious organic pathology can be found to explain brain malfunction, particularly when the symptoms themselves are nonphysical—alterations in the patient's mood, thinking, or social interactions. To distinguish them from organic disorders, such problems are often termed *functional disorders*, a term that means that the person's abnormal behavior clearly interferes with his or her normal functioning, but no organic cause can be discerned. Psychiatrists (who are medically trained and therefore have an M.D. degree) or clinical psychologists (who are not medically trained and have a Ph.D. degree) specialize in treating patients with functional disorders. It is important to remember, in this context, that failure to find an organic cause for a brain problem does not mean that an organic cause does not exist but rather may mean that the right entity to measure has not yet been uncovered. Conversely, purely functional disorders may well exist in some people.

Diagnostic Tests for Identifying Brain Diseases

The examination of a patient with symptoms of disordered brain function by a medical doctor, generally a neurologist, consists of several phases. First, the doctor conducts a careful verbal interview of the patient, and sometimes of those with whom the patient lives, to determine when and how the problem began and how it manifests itself. Next, the patient receives an initial thorough physical examination to test the functioning of the sensory and motor systems. At this point, some tentative understanding of the nature of the problem and whether it is treatable may be possible. In some cases, an accurate diagnosis requires additional tests (see Figure 12.1 on pages 370 and 371).

By ruling out various possible causes of the pathology, the neurologist attempts to arrive at the best choice of therapy. For example, a patient may consult a neurologist because of a sudden "speaking" problem. Examinations reveal that the patient can understand speech but cannot initiate it. Further examination shows no deficits in tongue and lip movements or in vocal cord movement. The electroencephalogram is normal. However, a magnetic resonance image (MRI) of the brain or a computerized axial tomographic (CAT) analysis may reveal an abnormality of the left temporal cortex: for example, the neurologist and radiologist observe that the density of the brain mass in this area is reduced. If the causes are uncertain, an older, more invasive technique may be required. Injection of an opaque dye into the carotid arteries followed by an x ray normally produces an image, called an *angiogram*, of the entire vascular structure supplying the brain. In this case, the angiogram could reveal that some intracerebral blood vessels in the left cerebral cortex are closed. At this point, the diagnosis can be made: a limited stroke has occurred in the part of the left cerebral cortex that is responsible for speech.

Had the tests revealed increased brain mass and increased blood flow, the diagnosis might have been a tumor, either of the blood vessels or of the supporting cells. The treatment for that condition might be surgical removal of the tumor followed by radiation or chemotherapy rather than the supportive measures required for a stroke. Had the patient's problem been widespread

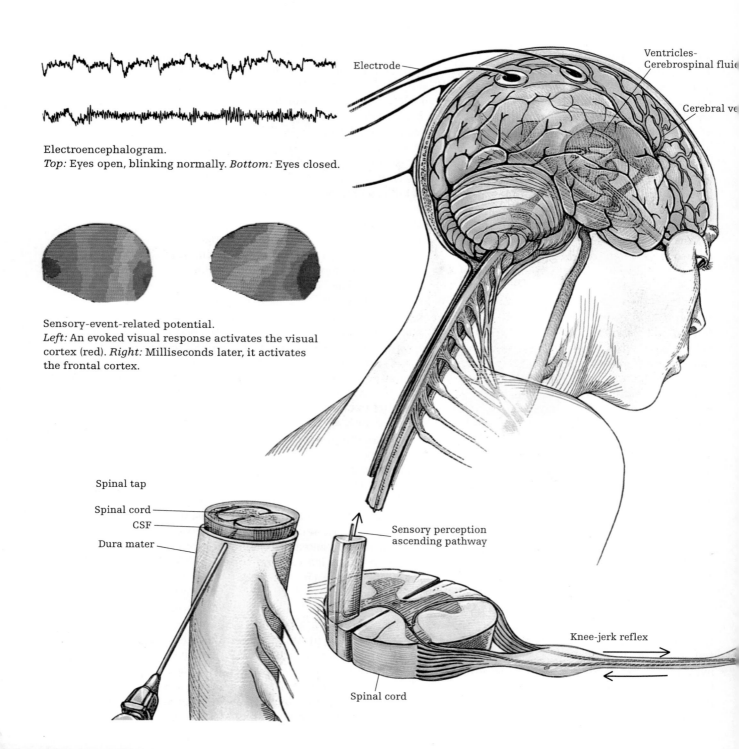

Electroencephalogram.
Top: Eyes open, blinking normally. *Bottom:* Eyes closed.

Sensory-event-related potential.
Left: An evoked visual response activates the visual cortex (red). *Right:* Milliseconds later, it activates the frontal cortex.

Electrode

Ventricles-
Cerebrospinal fluid

Cerebral ve

Spinal tap

Spinal cord

CSF

Dura mater

Sensory perception
ascending pathway

Knee-jerk reflex

Spinal cord

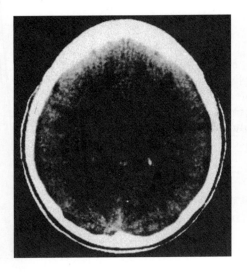

X ray of a normal brain.

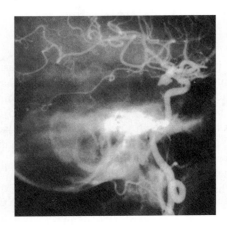

Angiogram.

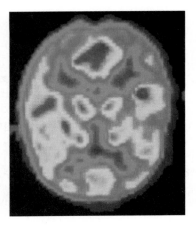

PET scan, showing activation of the auditory cortices as the subject listens to a Sherlock Holmes mystery.

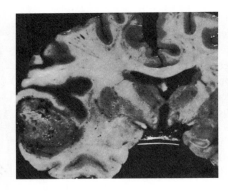

Postmortem photograph of an astrocytoma in the cerebral cortex.

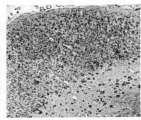

Postmortem slide of the cerebral cortex of an Alzheimer's patient. The cortex is loaded with plaques, which show here as black spots.

Figure 12.1 In addition to an interview with the patient to determine the history of the illness and after performing a physical examination to test nerve function, the neurologist may request additional tests. These tests could include analysis of the electrical signs of the brain's activity, such as an electroencephalogram (EEG) or a sensory-event-related potential (*both, upper far left*). Such tests detect evidence of a local or generalized dysfunction in the brain's activity. Additional tests could then include examination of the brain's shape and size by conventional x ray or by one of the more sophisticated imaging instruments. The x ray of a normal brain shows mainly the skull, because the brain itself does not have any density that will block the passage of the x rays, unless special "soft tissue" imaging is done. These other imaging devices can produce pictures of the brain's structure in relation to its specific patterns of blood flow, termed an angiogram, or in relation to its patterns of glucose utilization, termed a positron emission tomogram (PET scan). Such studies help to distinguish between various disorders that can affect the same parts of the brain.

In some cases, chemical and microscopic analysis of the cerebrospinal fluid (CSF) (*lower far left*) may provide helpful information regarding the presence or absence of infection or the nature of an injury.

Ultimately, when no diagnosis can be reached, an eventual postmortem examination may be the only way to verify the actual disease process.

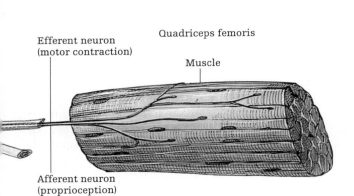

Efferent neuron (motor contraction)

Quadriceps femoris

Muscle

Afferent neuron (proprioception)

tumors with invasion of the central nervous system, surgical removal would not be feasible. If the diagnosis were a degenerative disorder such as Alzheimer's disease, a disease process in which neurons are destroyed, no treatment would be currently possible. Here the hope for future generations is at present focused on determining those genes that render people at high risk for Alzheimer's and on the development of very early treatments, such as vaccines, that might be able to reduce the progression of the disease.

Examination of the nervous system after death, the "postmortem examination," provides direct physical evidence of the nature and extent of a disease. The postmortem examination helps establish the relative importance of particular diagnostic signs and

tests after the fact. This is especially instructive in cases where diagnosis was difficult or impossible while the patient was alive. The information gained from a postmortem examination helps in the evaluation of future patients who present similar problems.

Normal Versus Abnormal Variations in Mood and Thought

Virtually all of us have occasional strange thoughts or impulses. Usually, however, we maintain our normal behavioral patterns by resisting the impulses that we recognize in ourselves as abnormal. Most of us also have peculiarities, which we call eccentricities when we observe them in someone else—moods, fixations, suspicions, odd habits, giggling, nervous tics. Such eccentricities are, in a sense, learned behaviors. In most cases, these behaviors have a reinforcing, or self-strengthening, value—even though the reward is not always easy to recognize. No matter how strange or annoying the behavior may be, it has a positive value for the performer. It attracts attention or reduces stress or it achieves some other end that the person craves, and, in this context, the behavior makes sense.

Everyone also has fluctuations in mood. We are occasionally elated by some unexpected good fortune and occasionally saddened by loss or disappointment. Our general state of health, our work habits, and our degree of exposure to stress or fatigue can all influence our responses to such events. Likewise, seasonal transitions, the anniversaries of tragic losses, and even "jet lag," can trigger fluctuations in normal moods and affect our behavior—increasing or decreasing appetite, self-perceived vigor, sleep satisfaction, and sexual awareness.

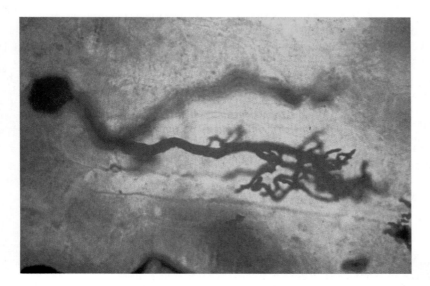

Postmortem examination of the brain allows neuroscientists to see the changes effected by disease. This Purkinje cell of an aged rat looks very different from the normal cell shown on page 310, but, in this case, the difference is due to age, not to disease. This type of change is a normal effect of age in rats, as was discovered by doing many such examinations.

These occasional intrusions of "strange thoughts" and normal fluctuations in mood differ substantially in quality and quantity from the severe problems that occur in those patients whose behavior requires psychiatric attention in a clinical setting. (Table 12.1 on the following page lists the categories of psychiatric disorders currently accepted by American psychiatrists.) Many patients are highly disturbed over their inability to control their fears, delusions, mood fluctuations, or frank losses of contact with reality. The inability to control their own thought content threatens to destroy the very qualities of high-order brain function that are considered the distinguishing characteristics of human beings. The doctor whom such a disturbed patient may eventually consult must decide whether the emotional or intellectual fluctuation is different enough from the normal range of fluctuations to require some special intervention. To do so, the doctor must analyze the behavioral problem in a more specific manner.

We now come to an important fork in the path taken by scientists toward understanding the different forms of disease that can affect mental capacities. In light of the historical evidence available, we can draw the following—admittedly oversimplified—conclusion about how people have interpreted brain diseases. Disturbances characterized by a progressive loss of sensory, motor, and mental function and known from postmortem studies to cause significant and reproducible changes in the structure of the brain became the province of the neurologist, and such "neurodegenerative" conditions were accepted as diseases. On the other hand, when pathologists were unable to find consistent changes in the brain, despite the continued emotional or intellectual problems of the patient before death, the diagnostic categories constructed from those findings became the province of the psychia-

The artist Vincent van Gogh (1853–1890) did this drawing, *Wooded Landscape with Houses,* in the village of Auvers shortly before his suicide. Art historians interpret the atypical presentation of natural forms, trees, and cottages as a manifestation of his progressive mental disturbance.

trist. Although there are many exceptions to this generalization, it serves to illustrate an important attitudinal difference that historically has colored the interpretation of abnormal behavior. When abnormal behavior was accompanied by physical evidence of something wrong with the brain, then the disease was regarded as real. However, in the absence of such objective changes to account for the behavioral symptoms, the problems were generally regarded as less real, perhaps even an act on the part of the patient to gain attention.

We next examine in some detail three of the most serious neurodegenerative diseases. Understanding their causes and consequences provides an instructive contrast

I. Disorders of Infancy, Childhood, or Adolescence
These diseases include inheritable disorders leading to mental retardation such as trisomy 21 (formerly called Down's syndrome or mongolism); phenylketonuria and related diseases, in which essential enzymes are missing; and the Lesch-Nyhan syndrome, one of several untreatable, severe behavioral problems that include self-mutilation, bizarre movements, and mental retardation. In these cases, a single, particular genetic error has been found, but in no case is it clear how the specific metabolic abnormalities lead to the highly abnormal behavior and retarded mental development.

II. Organic Brain Syndromes
These diseases exhibit a progressive and irreversible loss of mental capacity as the brain is being destroyed by infection, vascular insufficiency, or toxicity. Some of the most common organic brain syndromes are repeated cerebrovascular accidents, or "strokes," in which brain tissue dies from inadequate arterial blood supply; Alzheimer's disease, a progressive and untreatable degenerative disorder of adults, affecting primarily the neocortex and hippocampal brain regions; acute or chronic toxicity (literally, poisoning) caused by exposure to alcohol or other toxic chemicals, such as insecticides and poisonous metals (arsenic, bismuth, or lead, for example). Pellagra, porphyria, and general paresis, produced by definable organic causes, belong to this general category.

III. Disorders of Drug Dependence
The severe behavioral problems produced by the disorders of drug dependency stem from the direct toxic effects of using the drugs, ranging from poisonous additives to the use of nonsterile needles; the variable degrees of potency that lead to inadvertent overdosing; and the criminality associated with acquiring the money to buy drugs and with the penalties for drug possession.

The most common chemical dependency disorder is alcoholism. Aside from its direct toxic effects on the brain, liver, and heart, excessive use of alcohol is also a major cause of fatal automobile accidents, aggressive assaults, homicides, and many suicides. Specific chemical dependencies have been described for several classes of drugs: opiates (heroin, morphine, methadone, codeine, demerol); barbiturates; marijuana and related products of the *Cannabis* plant; cocaine; amphetamines; hallucinogenic drugs (LSD, psilocin, phencyclidine [PCP, or angel dust]); and volatile chemicals (glue solvents and amyl nitrate).

IV. Psychosomatic (Psychophysiological) Disorders
These disorders involve medical illnesses, the precipitating causes of which can be directly related to behavioral or social factors in the patient's environment. A combination of biological, behavioral, and social factors triggers the onset of recurrent episodes of a particular complex of medical symptoms: dysfunction of the gastrointestinal tract, some forms of arthritis, some chronic skin irritations, some forms of asthma, and some forms of high blood pressure. In these problems, one sees an exaggerated response of the body mediated largely by signals within the autonomic nervous system.

V. Situational Disorders
These disorders are the extreme individual reactions to conditions of severe environmental stress, such as battlefield shock, termed "combat fatigue," or the depression that may accompany grieving over the death of a close friend or relative. The transient nature of the disorder and the striking relation in time to the stressful life event distinguish it from more severe behavioral problems that require treatment.

VI. Character and Personality Disorders
These behavioral problems of varying severity range from mild forms of antisocial behaviors to obsessions, compulsions, and overt antisocial acts including aggressiveness, kleptomania (compulsive stealing), pyromania (compulsive setting of fires), and more serious criminality. In general, the onset of such behaviors occurs in late adolescence, after which the behaviors generally fall into a lifelong pattern; the abnormal behaviors are rarely noticed by the subject as being any sort of problem.

VII. Neuroses
The neuroses are behavioral disorders characterized either by anxiety (unrealistic apprehension and nervousness) and fears (phobias) or by overpowering drives to perform apparently irrational activities (obsessive-compulsive acts, such as repeated handwashing). These disorders are estimated to affect perhaps 5 percent of the population, so they are not uncommon. With some exceptions, they are rarely incapacitating, and they may respond well to treatment with tranquilizing drugs or psychotherapy directed at uncovering the unrecognized conflicts that create the problem.

In general, the neurotic patient finds the symptoms of the neurosis—the panic attacks, for example, or the fears or irrational repeated behaviors—very distressing and seeks treatment to eliminate them. This quality distinguishes a neurotic disorder from the same sorts of behavioral problems found in patients with so-called character or personality disorders. In the latter case, subjects believe that their behaviors, which others find odd or objectionable, are

TABLE 12.1 (cont.)

totally justified. Such eccentric behaviors may, in fact, be learned adaptations to conditions of expected stress—perhaps an extreme form is the rituals that professional athletes perform when peak ability is required.

In general, patients with neuroses do not show disturbances in reality testing or thought processes or in the perception of sensory events. This category of mental disorder also includes dissociative disorders in which sufferers disassociate themselves from conflicts in their present situations, real or perceived. The major forms of dissociation are those in which the patient's concept of self undergoes severe alterations: forgetting about large periods of one's life (psychogenic amnesia); ignoring the existence of one's own personality (depersonalization); and exhibiting more than one personality, each of which predominates at different times, totally altering the subject's behavior patterns and social relations (multiple personality disorder).

VIII. Psychoses

The term "disease" is most convincingly applied to these severe mental disorders. There are two forms of psychosis: the affective disorders and schizophrenia. Each major form includes several patterns and subclasses of behavioral abnormality. Both of these sets of diseases are severely incapacitating and often chronic, and they virtually always demand therapy. In each case, an accurate diagnosis based on structured interviews and behavioral observations, supplemented by chemical, functional, and structural tests, is the best guide to an informed selection of the best therapy. The partial success of selective drug treatments for the schizophrenias and the affective disorders has helped investigators to deduce possible mechanisms of the underlying physiological malfunction.

SOURCE: Based on American Psychiatric Association, *Diagnostic and Statistical Manual,* 4th ed., Washington DC, 1994.

with the psychiatric diseases discussed later. Importantly, each of these neurological diseases has serious behavioral and emotional components, offering implications for psychiatric diseases in which the objective signs of chemical or structural pathology are still minimal.

Degenerative Diseases of the Brain

As people live longer, owing partly to improved treatments for the infectious and cardiovascular diseases that were once unavoidably fatal, the incidence of degenerative disorders of the brain has increased. A *degenerative disorder* is one in which the disease process is progressive (that is, once the disease starts, it grows unremittingly more severe). Three of the most frequent and devastating degenerative disorders, each named

for the physician who first described it, are Parkinson's disease, Huntington's disease, and Alzheimer's disease. Each is marked by the destruction of specific sets of neurons in rather distinctive ways, including very specific changes in emotion and thinking. Modern textbooks of neurology are adapting the terminology of dropping the possessive form of the discoverer's name for the simpler terminology, Parkinson, Huntington, or Alzheimer disease, but, for now, we will stay with the traditional forms.

Parkinson's Disease

In the early nineteenth century, Dr. James Parkinson, a London physician, noticed a common set of symptoms in several of his patients. They displayed a rhythmic trembling of the hands and arms while otherwise inactive. When he himself tried to move their arms and legs, he noted an underlying stiffness to the muscle tone that would yield intermittently to continued pulling, producing a feeling of gears moving across a cogwheel—move-stop-move-stop-move. These patients had trouble starting movements (such as walking or writing) and, when they got started, they had trouble stopping. After Dr. Parkinson's description of these findings, other doctors soon reported that they had patients with very similar problems. For the next 150 years, the degenerative disease that Dr. Parkinson had identified continued to be diagnosed, yet physicians had no clues to what the cause might be and no way to treat it. One of the few signs of the disease in postmortem examinations of the brain was a loss of the pigmented neurons that give the substantia nigra and locus coeruleus their "colorful" names.

Not until the late 1950s and early 1960s, after the discovery of the neurotransmitters norepinephrine and dopamine and the establishment of their presence in normal human and animal brains, were the first steps made in understanding Parkinson's disease. An Austrian neuropathologist, Dr. Oleh Hornykiewicz, was able to correlate the loss of these black- and blue-pigmented neurons in Parkinson's disease patients with a dramatic loss of the transmitter dopamine from the brain regions in the basal ganglia. (As discussed in Chapter 4, the basal ganglia initiate programs of movement and monitor them for accuracy of performance while they are going on.) Hornykiewicz also detected losses of norepinephrine and of serotonin. Having found the substantially decreased dopamine and knowing the chemical pathways by which substantia nigra neurons can synthesize dopamine, Hornykiewicz and his colleagues conceived of a treatment. Might it be possible to force the synthesis of the missing dopamine by treating the Parkinson's patients with large doses of its immediate

chemical precursor, the amino acid dihydroxyphenylalanine (known by its initials DOPA)? Fortunately, DOPA is able to cross the blood–brain barrier. After many trials and errors in search of effective and tolerated doses, the treatment worked. Now available in oral form, DOPA treatment is able to greatly diminish the signs and symptoms of the missing dopamine. (Sometimes DOPA is referred to as L-DOPA; the L has chemical significance to amino acid chemists, because mammals use only the L forms of amino acids, and bacteria use the D forms. Early treatment of Parkinson's disease with DOPA used mixtures of the L and D forms, but, as soon as chemists learned how to isolate the L form, its purification made the drug twice as effective.)

Despite its initial effectiveness in most patients, L-DOPA treatment does not halt or even slow the underlying degeneration. Moreover, after variable periods, from months to years, the patient stops responding to the treatment. The reasons for the loss of response to DOPA are not known, but it may be that other systems of degenerating neurons, such as those that produce norepinephrine and serotonin, eventually become more prominently affected. A second complication is the recognition that as many as 50 percent of patients with Parkinson's disease also manifest significant depression, as discussed in a later section of this chapter, and that treatment with antidepressant medications may improve the effectiveness of the movement-dysfunction treatment. (One other fact is worth noting, in light of material presented in a later section of this chapter: when they are trying to find the right dose of DOPA for a patient, physicians sometimes set the dosage too high. As a result, the patient's symptoms change to mania, confusion, and other behaviors associated with acute schizophrenia.)

In North America, nearly 1 million people are diagnosed with Parkinson's disease. Its causes and the reason that dopamine neurons seem especially vulnerable to the underlying age-related degenerative process are not precisely known. At one time, the cause was held to be a virus infection that affected the brain. Viruses such as the poliovirus, the rhabdovirus (which causes rabies), and the human immunodeficiency virus (HIV) are all known to kill neurons but are not implicated in Parkinson's disease. Recent research has traced the cause in young people who were drug abusers to a contaminant of the underground synthesis of heroin-like drugs, which produces a toxin that selectively destroys the neurons of the substantia nigra. This toxin is closely related in chemical structure to certain herbicides, and, interestingly, the incidences of Parkinson's disease in different locations throughout the world are related to the degree of industrialization in each area. For these reasons, some epidemiologists (scientists who map the distribution of diseases geographically and demographically, looking for correlative evidence) have suggested that such environmental toxins may be a more frequent cause of Parkinson's disease than has been recognized.

Recently, new insight into the origins of Parkinson's disease has come from the discovery of the mutated gene that is responsible for a relatively rare inheritable form of the disease in a large Italian family. (In this family, the disease develops at unusually young adult ages, and all of the affected members of the family have the same gene change in common.) The normal product of the mutated gene proved to belong to a group of proteins called "synucleins," of uncertain function but located in presynaptic nerve terminals in the brain. The mutated version has been reported to be unable to bind to the synaptic vesicles that would otherwise carry the protein out of the neuronal cytoplasm and down the axon. Interestingly, at postmortem examination, neurons in the substantia nigra and basal ganglia of the affected people in this family often show cytoplasmic depositions of a fibrillary nature (revealed with certain dyes that bind to acidic proteins). These deposits, termed *Lewy bodies,* do indeed contain the mutated α-synuclein, suggesting its role in causing Parkinson's disease. How this protein leads to the early inheritable form of the disease remains to be determined, as does its possible intersection with the environmental "toxins" hypothesis. Scientists have produced transgenic mice that express the abnormal gene and hope to learn more by studying them.

Although there is as yet no way to reverse the disease process once it has begun, scientists continue to look for new ways to restore the missing dopamine's role in brain functioning. One highly innovative method that has cured experimental Parkinson's disease in laboratory animals has recently found some success in human beings. Bits of the center of the adrenal gland (where cells normally make and secrete norepinephrine and epinephrine) have been transplanted into the brains of patients with Parkinson's disease. Once transplanted, the adrenal medullary cells seem to function in part like the lost substantia nigra neurons. Perhaps someday in the future it will be possible to harvest embryonic stem cells and feed them with combinations of growth factors that can direct them to form new dopamine neurons.

Huntington's Disease

The basal ganglia are also implicated in another serious neurologic disease with emotional and cognitive symptomatology, described in the late nineteenth century by the American physician George Huntington on the basis of cases that he, his father, and his grandfather had observed in their practices. This disease generally began in the patients' late 30s and early 40s with mild mental problems, especially forgetfulness and outbursts of temperamental behavior, along with depression. Awkward movements, sudden collapses, and uncontrollable flailing movements of the arms and upper body sooner or later appeared as well. Some patients showed rigidity and trembling somewhat like that seen in Parkinson's patients. The movement problems, as well as slurred speech and worsening mental faculties, became progressive, leading to total disability and finally death.

The most striking feature of this disease, however, was not the dramatic movement disorder and rapid progression of symptoms. The Huntingtons observed that the disease occurred in clusters within families and followed a certain pattern of inheritance, the pattern termed *autosomal dominant*. To understand this term, recall that every physical trait—hair color, skin color, height, body build—that is inheritable is represented by specific chemical sequences of nucleic acids in DNA called genes; genes encode this information in an individual's chromosomes. Hair color and eye color may be related to just one or at most a few genes, whereas traits such as body build require the interactions of many genes. Human beings have 23 pairs of chromosomes; 22 of these pairs are referred to as autosomes, and one pair, the X and the Y, are called the sex chromosomes. In some inheritable diseases, a change in one gene is sufficient to produce the entire disease. When a disease-causing gene is located on a sex chromosome, as in color blindness and hemophilia, the disease is termed *sex linked*. Diseases that are inherited from genes on one of the other 22 pairs of chro-

mosomes are called autosomal disorders. When the disease-producing gene is dominant, it needs to be present in only one parent to produce the disease (if the child lives long enough).

By following generation after generation of families with Huntington's disease and carefully tabulating the results of their offspring's marriages, the Huntingtons established that the children of any parent whose mother or father had the disease had a 50 percent chance of having the disease too. If a third-generation child was free of the disease, none of that person's children or anyone in subsequent generations would show it, unless a descendant happened to marry a person who carried the disease. Because most Americans in the nineteenth and early twentieth centuries had their children in their late teens and early 20s, the disease frequently did not show up in the people until two generations of their descendents had already come into the world. As a result, even the best-intentioned parent had no way of controlling the disease. Postmortem examinations revealed only a modest degree of pathology, mainly a loss of neurons in the basal ganglia and cerebral cortex. About 30,000 people in North America have this diagnosis today; the relatives who still have a 50:50 chance of developing the disease number about five times that many.

Although no treatment exists for victims of Huntington's disease, some progress has been made in detecting its inheritance. By studying the patterns of the disease in a remote South American village where there was extensive inbreeding and a very high incidence of the disease, scientists have determined that the gene is carried on a specific part of chromosome 4. The mutant gene and its normal counterpart were eventually identified (and the normal gene product named "huntingtin"). Huntingtin is a large protein previously unknown (its normal functions are still unknown), expressed widely in the brain and in other tissues as well. Uniquely (at the time), the mutation that was found in the gene of those who had inherited the disease was an increase in the number of repetitions of the nucleotide sequence cytosine-adenine-guanine (CAG). The CAG triplet encodes the amino acid glutamine. Whereas the normal gene contains several CAG sequences, the mutant form has many, many more. In fact, it appears that the more CAGs, the earlier the onset and the more severe the illness. (Several other inheritable diseases are now also known to have similar trinucleotide expansions.)

Now that the mutant protein has been identified, aggregates of the material have been found in the nuclei of the kinds of neurons that die in Huntington's disease. Huntingtin (the protein produced by the gene) has been found to bind to other specific large proteins, currently known as "huntingtin-associated proteins"; the mutated form binds much more tightly to them than to the normal gene product. Because mice in which the huntingtin gene is "knocked out" (mutated so that it cannot be expressed at all) show no signs of neurodegeneration, researchers reckon that the additional glutamines cause the protein to perform its binding function too well. A genetic test based on these differences in the huntingtin gene has enabled investigators to identify which children of a Huntington parent have not inherited the gene. Perhaps the further characterization of the functions of the normal and abnormal huntingtin will reveal the source of the neurodegeneration and why it occurs only in a very small proportion of the neurons that express huntingtin.

Residents of the village in northern Venezuela with the high incidence of Huntington's disease.

Alzheimer's Disease

The German physician Alois Alzheimer was the first to describe (in 1907) a case of progressive forgetfulness leading within a few years to loss of all mental faculties in a previously healthy woman in her late 40s. Studying the patient's brain at postmortem, Alzheimer observed major wasting of the cerebral cortex. He then stained the brain with compounds that deposited silver salts in the nerve cells and, by examining thin slices under the microscope, discovered that the brain was filled with large collections of tangled fibrils within the nerve cell bodies of the cortex. The progressive loss of mental abilities seen in this patient, and later in other relatively young patients whose brains at autopsy revealed the same dramatic degenerative process, became known as Alzheimer's dementia or, because it was first described in relatively young adults, as presenile dementia.

After many cases were studied, scientists decided that age of onset was less important as a distinguishing characteristic than was the progressive loss of mental abilities. The disease does not generally appear until a person's late 60s, and the early symptoms of forgetfulness may be very subtle, so a solid diagnosis prior to the appearance of advanced signs and symptoms is very difficult.

Alzheimer's disease has some of the general features of both Parkinson's disease and Huntington's disease. As in Parkinson's disease, specific changes occur in the brain chemistry. Several neurotransmitters are lost, especially within the cerebral cortex. A number of treatments have been attempted; however, no drug that replenishes those missing transmitters has been more than transiently helpful. In any case, the underlying progressive nature of the disease is not affected by this sort of treatment.

As with Huntington's disease, some signs have indicated that inheritability of Alzheimer's disease is higher in certain families, especially for the form of the disease that has an early onset, as in the original patient. Until recently, Alzheimer's families were too rare to study in detail, but international research began in the late 1980s to document inheritable Alzheimer's disease in families. Subsequent studies of both familial and non-familial Alzheimer's patients have found that mutations of at least four genes can enhance a person's risk for developing the disease. The most thoroughly studied are small mutations in a gene on chromosome 21 that encodes a large protein called the *amyloid precursor protein* (APP). In the brains of Alzheimer's patients, abnormal fragments of APP, ranging from 40 to 43 amino acids in length are produced, which aggregate into tangles in the cytoplasm of the neurons that will die. Three or four other genes have been identified that can modify the rate of abnormal APP fragment aggregation. Two called *Pre-Senilin 1*

and *2* (on chromosomes 14 and 1, respectively) increase the expression of the abnormal fragments. Very recent research suggests that the presenilins are proteins that may cleave the amyloid protein into the forms that aggregate within neurons. Genes for two other plasma proteins not specific to the brain, apolipoprotein E and α2 macroglobulin, also may contribute to a person's vulnerability to the still-unclear disease-causing process. In this case, there are multiple normal alternative genetic forms, termed *alleles,* rather than frank mutations; inheritance of certain alleles of these plasma proteins increases risk through unknown interactions with the other proteins. The location of the amyloid precursor protein gene on chromosome 21 is interesting because there is an extra copy of that entire chromosome and hence of that gene in Down's syndrome (see Chapter 3), the only other neuropathological state known to produce intraneuronal protein tangles.

An estimated 10 percent of all Americans over age 65 show mild to moderate dementia, of which Alzheimer's is by far the most frequent cause. Alzheimer's disease increases with age through age 80, and, as our population lives longer and longer, its incidence is expected to grow substantially. With more and more people surviving into their 70s, the expectation is that in 2000 more than 20 percent of the population may be suffering from Alzheimer's disease. Because Alzheimer's patients often survive 10 or more years, with progressive loss of mental function, the high demand that their care places on hospital and nursing resources may mean catastrophic costs for our health-care system unless some solution to the problem can be found.

A newer cause of neuropsychological impairment, often extending to a frank dementia, is HIV infection. Unlike the viruses responsible for polio and rabies, however, the HIV does not directly infect neurons. Scientists trying to understand the reasons that neurons die and synaptic connections are lost in this condition (affecting millions of people worldwide) are focusing on the same kinds of causes as are being investigated in Alzheimer's, Parkinson's, and Huntington's diseases—toxins, free radicals, inflammation, and other unknowns.

Imagine living at the time when Dr. Alzheimer described his first case of progressive forgetfulness followed by bizarre outbursts of wild behavior and then degeneration in a few short years to the point of total unresponsiveness. When he presented this case to the German Psychiatric Society, he was almost booed from the room; physicians in that era were not prepared to believe that a physical abnormality in the brain could be the cause of this sort of behavior. Imagine further that he had not serendipitously used a stain capable of revealing the loss of neurons and the accumulation of fibril tangles and therefore was unable to find any obviously physical abnormality in the brains that he was studying. What sort of theories might have been proposed to explain the disease? In the next section, we examine serious diseases of behavior in which the physical findings remain almost, but not completely, invisible.

Diagnosis by Analysis of Behavior

Medical understanding of functional brain disorders whose known symptoms are primarily behavioral lags far behind that of most organic brain disorders. A major reason is the current lack of "objective" tests that can successfully detect a source for the disorder. Often patients with cognitive or emotional problems show no abnormality in general medical, sensory, or motor function, in EEGs, brain x rays, or tests of the cerebrospinal fluid. Even postmortem examination may fail to reveal a reason for the problem. Nevertheless, it is standard practice in evaluating a patient with behavior disorder of unknown cause to apply all these diagnostic tests (except, of course, the postmortem) to eliminate possible organic causes before starting clinical psychiatric treatment.

In earlier days, it was not unusual for psychiatrists who evaluated the same patient to disagree strenuously about the diagnosis. However, many psychiatrists in the 1950s and 1960s, notably those of the St. Louis school under Eli Robins, came to believe that the diagnosis of a psychiatric condition should be based on more than simply the apparent absence of organic illness. Standard diagnostic tools were clearly needed. Psychiatrists have therefore begun to adopt generally accepted criteria for diagnosing psychiatric "disease states." Through a process of comparing groups of patients with different symptoms and behaviors of specified duration and intensity, doctors have established sets of criteria that must exist in order for specific psychiatric diagnoses to be reached. With these criteria, which are constantly being tested and revised, more and more doctors now use consistent objective diagnostic categories to identify psychiatric diseases rather than relying on intuitive impressions of what the problem might be.

Some of these criteria focus on relatively obvious features. How old was the patient when the problems first arose? How long have the problems persisted? Does the patient have associated problems in appetite, sleep, or movement? Are there problems in interacting with other family members or with a peer group? Is there a family history of similar problems? Has the patient suffered any particular stress lately?

Using such criteria, the most recent diagnostic manual recognizes more than a dozen distinct categories of psychiatric disease, of which six categories are most frequently diagnosed:

1. Disorders of infancy, childhood, and adolescence (such as mental retardation, dyslexia, autism, attention-deficit disorder, and severe-conduct disorder)

2. Delirium, dementia and other cognitive disorders (such as Alzheimer's, Parkinson's, and Huntington's disease, and those cases of HIV in which a cognitive disturbance is the first symptom to appear)

3. Substance-related disorders (the addictive diseases)

4. Schizophrenia and other psychoses

5. Mood disorders (such as depression and mania)

6. Anxiety disorders

The present-day psychiatric interview begins with a brief, standardized set of questions constituting a uniform doctor–patient exchange called the Mental Status Examination. Generally, the clinician probes the patient's mental and emotional condition within a carefully structured format. Similar questions are asked of all patients and initial answers are compared with later results as the patient's treatment proceeds. This practice allows clinicians to track the patient's progress, gain knowledge about the natural or treated course of the disease itself, and compare results across different patient populations.

The interview probes seven major areas of mental and emotional functioning:

1. *Consciousness.* Is the patient alert and responsive to the interviewer? Is the patient aware of where, when, and why the interview is taking place?

2. *Affect and emotional tone.* Is the patient's emotional state appropriate to circumstances? Does the patient exhibit or describe signs that could be interpreted as depression, euphoria, anxiety, fear, aggression, or rage? If so, additional series of questions may be used to rate the patient's emotional status such as the Hamilton Rating Scale shown on page 383.

3. *Motor behavior.* Is the patient dressed appropriately and able to remain at ease while being interviewed? Does the patient exhibit prolonged posturing or repeat purposeless motor acts (twirling the hair or rubbing the ears or nose, for example)? Does the patient make unusual, abrupt, or purposeless spontaneous movements?

4. *Thinking.* Does the patient express any specific inappropriate ideas or preoccupations about himself or herself ("I am Adolf Hitler!" "Aliens have chosen me to destroy the world.")? Are answers to questions delivered at a normal speed? Does the patient express exaggerated fears of real or imagined conditions?

5. *Perception.* Does the patient describe an inappropriate awareness of sensations? Does the patient describe nonexistent events (hearing voices or feeling attacks of pain)?

6. *Memory.* Can the patient describe recent and more distant current events correctly? Can the patient perform mental acts requiring memory and concentration?

7. *Intelligence.* Can the patient express a logical flow of ideas or associations in response to a thought problem ("What does the statement 'A rolling stone gathers no moss' mean?") and arrive at a logical conclusion? Is ability appropriate to educational achievements and occupational history?

HAMILTON RATING SCALE

PATIENT _____   DATE _____ TIME _____

RATER _____   SCORE _____

1 DEPRESSED MOOD
(Sad, hopeless,
helpless, worthless)

0 Absent
1 These feeling states indicated only on questioning
2 These feeling states spontaneously reported verbally
3 Communicates feeling states non-verbally—i.e., through facial expression, posture, voice, and tendency to weep
4 Patient reports VIRTUALLY ONLY these feeling states in his spontaneous verbal and non-verbal communication

2 FEELINGS OF GUILT

0 Absent
1 Self-reproach, feels he has let people down
2 Ideas of guilt or rumination over past errors or sinful deeds
3 Present illness is a punishment. Delusions of guilt
4 Hears accusatory or denunciatory voices and/or experiences threatening visual hallucinations

3 SUICIDE

0 Absent
1 Feels life is not worth living
2 Wishes he were dead or any thoughts of possible death to self
3 Suicide ideas or gesture
4 Attempts at suicide (any serious attempt rates 4)

4 INSOMNIA (EARLY)

0 No difficulty falling asleep
1 Complaints of occasional difficulty falling asleep—i.e., more than 1/2 hour
2 Complaints of nightly difficulty falling asleep

5 INSOMNIA (MIDDLE)

0 No difficulty
1 Patient complaints of being restless and disturbed during the night
2 Waking during the night—any getting out of bed rates 2 (except for purposes of voiding)

6 INSOMNIA (LATE)

0 No difficulty
1 Waking in early hours of the morning but goes back to sleep
2 Unable to fall asleep again if gets out of bed

7 WORK AND ACTIVITIES

0 No difficulty
1 Thoughts and feelings of incapacity, fatigue or weakness related to activities, work or hobbies
2 Loss of interest in activity, hobbies or work—either directly reported by patient, or indirect in listlessness, indecision, and vacillation (feels he has to push self to work or join activities)
3 Decrease in actual time spent in activities or decrease in productivity. In hospital, rate 3 if patient does not spend at least three hours a day in activities (hospital job or hobbies) exclusive of ward chores
4 Stopped working because of present illness. In hospital, rate 4 if patient engages in no activities except ward chores, or if patient fails to perform ward chores unassisted

8 RETARDATION
(Slowness of thought and
speech; impaired ability to
concentrate; decreased
motor activity)

0 Normal speech and thought
1 Slight retardation at interview
2 Obvious retardation at interview
3 Interview difficult
4 Complete stupor

9 AGITATION

0 None
1 Fidgetiness
2 "Playing with" hands, hair, etc.
3 Moving about, can't sit still
4 Hand-wringing, nail-biting, hair-pulling, biting of lips

The first page of the Hamilton Rating Scale.

Other interview formats have evolved in recent years and are used by both psychiatrists and psychologists to try to get at the same qualities of underlying causes. Some structured formats evaluate a patient's mental function and the stability, fluctuation, or progression of symptoms. Others collect descriptions from family and friends of events leading up to the patient's problems. Others focus on precise details of symptoms and signs as described by the patient and provide results roughly equivalent to those obtained by physical examination in a patient with a neurological problem. In some cases, the data gathered through such interviews lead to a specific diagnosis; in other cases, they do not. In cases where the interview produces no specific diagnosis, clues that need follow-up are pursued in more definitive verbal tests of intellectual function (so-called intelligence testing) and emotional status ("personality profiles" and affect—that is, mood—or self-rating scales) and in tests of language, logic, mathematical, and abstract "cognitive" abilities.

Along with the use of uniform interviews to identify specific, reproducible forms of behavior problems and to analyze a particular patient's behavior, an additional purpose has evolved. Psychological findings acquired from interviews can be combined with objective tests of the brain's chemistry, structure, and function to help medical scientists refine the bases for psychiatric diagnosis and select the most appropriate form of treatment.

 ## The Biological Basis of Psychosis

Evidence in support of a biological basis for the major psychiatric diseases comes largely from two sources. Clinical studies of blood relations (parents, siblings, and first cousins) point to the likelihood of genetic factors in susceptibility. In addition, human and animal studies on the effects of drugs that mimic or antagonize brain transmitters strongly suggest that a biological "explanation" exists for many major behavioral diseases.

Clinical Studies

Family-pedigree studies show that an unusually high incidence of depression or schizophrenia in a family can sometimes be traced through several generations. Scientists look for a very high "penetrance" of inheritable factors—that is, they look to see how many members of a family have the disease. A number that exceeds the incidence in the general population is an indication that the factor may be inherited, although local environmental or even cultural factors also could explain the concordance. Such patterns exist in some forms of acute intermittent porphyria and in Huntington's, Parkinson's, and Alzheimer's diseases, as we have just seen.

Relative risk studies may be used, for example, to survey the blood-related family members of a psychotic patient for incidence of psychosis. Scientists then determine whether this incidence rate exceeds the rate for members of a comparable "control" population—people in the same geographic, economic, educational, and age groups as those to which the relatives of the patient belong: In both affective psychosis (serious mood disorders) and schizophrenia, such studies show that a person's risk of exhibiting one of these diseases increases directly with the closeness of his or her genetic relationship to someone with that disease. Evidence that strongly supports the hypothesis of inheritable factors emerges from studies of the incidence of psychosis among half siblings, who have only one biologic parent in common. The increased incidence of depression or schizophrenia among such siblings over that of the general population indicates the importance of genetic information in these psychiatric diseases.

Twin and adopted-twin studies put the link between genetic relatedness and mental disease to an even stricter test. If a genetic link exists, twins should have similar outcomes because they have similar genetic backgrounds. Identical twins, who develop from the same fertilized egg and who have totally identical genetic information, should show the most concordance (that is, if one has the disease based only on genes, the other twin would also eventually have it). Fraternal twins, who result from the impregnation of two different ova by different sperm and who have less genetic background in common, should be less concordant than identical twins but more concordant than half brothers or half sisters. In fact, in schizophrenia, in affective psychosis, and in alcoholism, twin studies do document the very high degree of inheritability predicted by such logic (see Figure 12.2). Even if a twin does not exhibit the disease, the healthy twin's children are just as likely as the children of the psychotic twin to express the susceptibility.

In adopted-twin studies, investigators examine the outcome for twins when one or both are reared by adoptive parents. Such a situation is a form of "natural" experiment: the genetic backgrounds of the twins are identical or at least highly similar, but their living environments and life experiences will differ. The question is, In what proportion of the twin pairs will both twins show the psychiatric disorder? Adopted-twin studies undertaken in countries such as Denmark and Sweden, where medical records are complete, show that, in some 50 percent of such twin pairs, both twins develop the same psy-

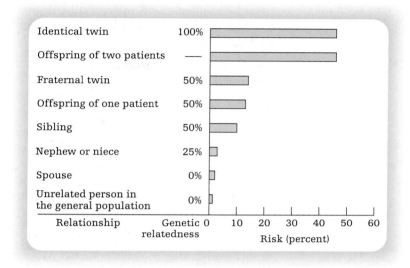

Figure 12.2 The risk of developing schizophrenia in one's lifetime is largely a function of genetic relatedness to a schizophrenic rather than of environmental or experiential factors.

chiatric disease. This rate is almost as high as it is when the children grow up with their biological parents, and it strongly suggests that child-rearing practices themselves have very little to do with the manifestation of the inheritable trait that makes these children susceptible to the psychiatric disease. However, in high-risk families, the parents may well suffer from other serious mental illnesses even if they themselves are not schizophrenic.

It is no simple matter to separate genetic and environmental factors. Although twin and adoption findings document the existence of an inheritable factor, the rate of concordance is never 100 percent in any twin study, even though identical twins have 100 percent of their genes in common. This discrepancy both reveals the difficulty of isolating the genetic factor responsible for psychiatric disease and indicates the degree to which environmental influences can affect its expression.

Chemical Studies

Biochemical and physiological tests that precisely measure specific aspects of brain function have already led some researchers to formulate theories about the cellular abnormalities that underlie mental disorders. Perfected to a high degree of accuracy, tests that detect the presence of these abnormalities could eventually be employed in "screening." Such tests, if applied objectively to large numbers of people, would make diagnosis possible long before a potential patient developed clear behavioral symptoms.

Psychopharmacology, the study of the effects of drugs on behavior, has led to drug treatments for both schizophrenia and affective psychoses. The success of these treatments strongly suggests that some preexisting chemical abnormality is "treated" by the drugs, and the drugs often do reestablish normal mental function. But the fact that they are not consistently successful in all cases of schizophrenia or affective psychosis suggests that the same symptoms may arise from different biological causes. If the same clusters of signs and symptoms do arise from more than one pathological change, that would help to explain the incomplete patterns of inheritance as well as the failures of drug therapies.

Animal responses to drugs provide another biological model for what may be abnormal in mental diseases. Although the effects of drugs on the behavior of animals do not exactly match those of humans, the fact that an animal's nervous system can be "depressed" by certain drugs and "excited" by others suggests that "behavior" can be manipulated by chemical alterations in the brain. When these drugs are found to operate on the same neurotransmitter systems in animals and humans and when depression and excitement are found to have opposing effects on that same transmitter system, the assumption of a link between brain chemistry, cell function, and abnormal behavior becomes even more reasonable.

None of these methods alone can establish with certainty that any mental disease of unknown cause can actually be laid to a specific biological factor. But when many lines of evidence lead to the same general conclusion, the theory becomes very compelling. Because the evidence that major depression and schizophrenia have real, although incompletely defined, biological causes is stronger than that for any other mental diseases at this time, let us now turn to an examination of those two common categories of psychosis.

Major Depressive Disorder

Everyone is occasionally low spirited, but usually the low emotional state can be attributed to some logical cause—perhaps a tragedy (the death of a mate, a child, or a parent) or a disappointment (getting a low grade or losing a championship game). The effects of such an event may last a few days to a few weeks. A person with depression as a disease (which the most recent diagnostic manual perversely describes as a "disorder"), however, has the same unhappy feelings, but they are far more intense and far longer lasting, and the cause is not usually apparent. Consider the following interview with a depressed patient.

DOCTOR: *I know that you have been feeling depressed, and I think that all of us have ups and downs and the blues sometimes.*

Is the depression you've been having different from the "ordinary blues"?

KATIE: *Yes, definitely.*

DOCTOR: *What seems so different about it to you?*

KATIE: *Well, you are just so down that you can't manipulate.*

DOCTOR: *So, when you're depressed, you have a lot of trouble functioning?*

KATIE: *Right, uh huh.*

DOCTOR: *Is the type of depression you're feeling a kind of sadness or more than that?*

KATIE: *It's more the hopelessness. . . . I can't talk about this.*

DOCTOR: *You're really having a hard time talking about these topics?*

KATIE: *Uh huh.*

DOCTOR: *When you are depressed do you think it's hard even to think about being depressed?*

KATIE: *Uh huh, and that gets me more upset.*

DOCTOR: *Do you think your sleep is affected when you are depressed in this way?*

KATIE: *For several months I don't think I've slept at all.*

DOCTOR: *How do you deal with these feelings—being sad and uncomfortable with people?*

KATIE: *To be honest with you, lately, I've just given up. I'm not coping with it very well at all.*

DOCTOR: *Does that make you feel that sometimes life is not worth living?*

KATIE: *Yes.*

DOCTOR: *Does it help to realize that the guilt and the sadness are really symp-toms of an illness and not necessarily the way you have to feel?*

KATIE: *Well, I guess if I could believe that.*

DOCTOR: *But you are tending not to believe that?*

KATIE: *I'm having some trouble with my spiritual beliefs right now.*

The Symptoms of Emotional Diseases

"Affect" is a term that scientists use for an overall emotional state, or mood. Thus, "affective psychosis," or *mood disorder,* refers to a psychiatric disease whose central symptom is abnormally extreme, long-lasting emotions. *Depressive psychosis,* then, is a severe mood disturbance in which prolonged periods of inappropriate depression alternate either with periods of normal mood or with periods of excessive, inappropriate euphoria and mania.

Depressive psychosis takes three major forms. In *unipolar depression,* the patient suffers from recurrent episodes but exhibits normal moods in between. In *mania,* the patient has episodes of inappropriate elation, lack of concern about important problems, overconfidence, and hyperactivity—alternating with episodes of depression. Bursting with apparently endless energy, thoughts jumping quickly from one subject to another, the manic patient has little need for sleep. The third form contains elements of depression alternating with mania and is sometimes referred to as "bipolar" depression. The biblical description of King Saul's behavior bears a strong resemblance to present-day manic-depressive disease. Briefly, Saul's emotional balance was restored by the music therapy of his successor-to-be; eventually, however, Saul commited suicide by falling on his sword.

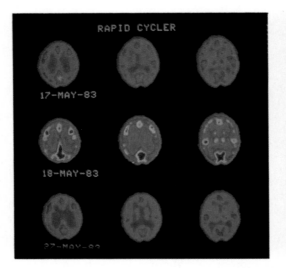
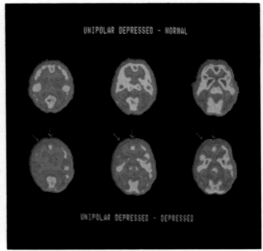

Left: The metabolic alterations of a rapid-cycling bipolar patient moving from depression to mania. Each row of the PET scans displays three different sections of the brain. The center row illustrates a hypomanic phase, whereas the top and bottom rows illustrate two different states of depression. *Right:* Metabolic alteration in a unipolar depressed patient. In the top row, the patient is in a normal good mood. In the bottom row, the patient is depressed. During the depression, metabolic activity is reduced most prominently in the frontal cortex and anterior cingulate cortex, a narrow band of cortex near the midline that plays an important role in the regulation of emotion.

In depressive disorders, the sadness, grief, and hopelessness or the elation and euphoria are so intense that these emotions persist well beyond the event that may have triggered them. In fact, many times these intense feelings seem to arise with no specific triggering event. However, when the English psychiatrist George Brown had his patients keep track of their life events in detailed diaries, he observed that very stressful events in family or work relations had often been present at the time of the first significant episode of depression. Along with the changes in normal mood, patients often describe many other physical and mental problems: an extreme lack of self-confidence, poor ability to concentrate on anything other than their sadness, intense feelings of hopelessness, despair for the future, and, often, recurrent thoughts of death and suicide. Problems with sleeping and eating are prominent. Some depressed patients have difficulty falling asleep, awaken early, and lose substantial amounts of weight from lack of appetite. Others sleep and eat excessively. In the discussion that follows, we consider affective disease as one general phenomenon because many psychiatrists view the different expressions of the disease as variations on the same underlying, but unknown, thematic biological problem.

The Incidence of Depression

Many people with severe depressions never report their problems to a doctor or a hospital, so figures describing how many people have diagnosable depression must be im-

TABLE 12.2 Diagnostic distinctions between forms of depression

Feature	Psychotic	Neurotic
Precipitating events	Absent, rare	Frequent
Thought and motor problems	Frequent	Rare
Daily pattern	Worse in A.M.	Worse in P.M.
Sleep problems	Early awakening	Onset problems
Weight loss	Often	Rare
Self-regard	Self-reproach, guilt	Self-pity
Course	More acute	More chronic
Former personality	Normal	Usually normal
Dexamethasone suppression test	Frequently abnormal	Usually normal
REM latency	Short	Normal

precise. Estimates from many countries, however, show that depression is clearly the most prevalent of psychiatric diseases. Affective psychosis may account for as much as 70 percent of the psychiatric diagnoses in a general medical practice. Statistics based on U.S. population figures indicate that about 1 of 4 adults will experience some form of severe mood disturbance at some time in their lives. Twelve of every 100 adult men and 18 of every 100 adult women will see a psychiatrist, a clinical psychologist, or a general physician and be diagnosed as having affective psychosis. In the United States, 3 to 4 percent of adults may be receiving treatment for their depression at any given time. Suicide, which many psychiatrists and psychologists attribute directly to affective psychosis, may account for more than 25,000 deaths per year, making it a leading cause of death.

A direct relation exists between a person's age and risk of experiencing different kinds of depression. Bipolar disorder is more likely to begin in one's 20s and 30s, whereas major recurring depressions are most frequent later in life, from the 40s to the 60s. Women predominate among depressed patients from puberty on.

The Diagnosis of Depression

When a doctor receives a patient complaining of problems with affect, the first interview questions may focus on how long the symptoms have been present, whether the person has ever had such problems before, and whether there are associated sleep and appetite disturbances or other physical symptoms. Next, the doctor determines whether the patient has any of the diseases found in other organs that sometimes produce severe emotional problems: for example, certain infections; disorders of the thyroid or adrenal glands; and the so-called autoimmune diseases (such as systemic lupus erythematosis) that lead to inflammation of connective tissues and joints. Certain degenerative disorders of the nervous system, such as Alzheimer's disease and Parkinson's disease, as noted earlier, can have accompanying depression. If the doctor rules out all of these diseases and if the affective symptoms have been present for more than 2 weeks, a diagnosis of affective psychosis can be strongly considered (see Table 12.2).

In addition to considering the patient's complaints and their duration, frequency, and variations, the clinician might administer

Chemical Tests of Psychosis

In considering the neurodegenerative disorders, we saw how useful it is for understanding the nature of the diseases to have an objective physical test that reveals something of the abnormality—loss of pigmented cells in Parkinson's disease; loss of neurons in Huntington's; and the accumulation of neuronal tangles, loss of cerebral cortex mass, and loss of neurotransmitters in Alzheimer's disease. Furthermore, the establishment of the precise patterns of inheritance in Huntington's disease and in at least some forms of Alzheimer's disease led to the identification of chromosomal abnormalities, which may soon shed light on exactly what is missing or extra in these chromosomes and which brain cells have the broken gene.

However, as we have also seen, despite the application of a lot of effort, little similar objective evidence of pathology has turned up thus far in schizophrenia or in depression. One test that has received some attention in this regard emerged from studies on abnormalities in the sleep cycles of depressed patients and attempts to understand the endocrine system's role in the abnormal sleep.

Evaluating the regulatory effectiveness of the endocrine system in depressed patients depends on an experimental procedure known as the *dexamethasone suppression test* (DST). The drug dexamethasone suppresses the signals coming from the brain and pituitary that drive the adrenal cortex to secrete natural cortisone. Normally, when the adrenal glands release cortisone into the bloodstream, the brain and the pituitary recognize the presence of the adrenal steroid and stop activating further secretion (see Chapter 6). Dexamethasone, a powerful synthetic version of natural cortisone used to treat allergic and inflammatory diseases, overrides a normal person's own cortisone secretions. In the presence of the drug, the responses of the brain and pituitary to the feedback signal can be tested.

Chronic abnormal hyperactivity of the adrenal cortex, such as that caused by tumors of the adrenal gland, is manifested in a loss of this feedback. In the presence of continuous hyperactivity, dexamethasone cannot suppress the brain and pituitary signals that cause the adrenal glands to secrete steroids. (A number of other medical conditions, such as diabetes mellitus, also cause failure to suppress steroid secretion.) Psychotically depressed patients do fail to suppress their steroid secretion, although they have no detectable problems with either the adrenal or the pituitary glands. In the neurotic forms of depression, steroid secretion is suppressed more effectively by dexamethasone.

Despite initial enthusiastic reception, the success of the dexamethasone test as a diagnostic procedure to discriminate chemically between psychotically depressed patients and neurotically depressed patients still has a long way to go. This does not mean that the idea of such a test is silly. More likely it means that scientists have not yet recognized all the variables that need to be evaluated in the interpretation of suppression and nonsuppression.

A potential diagnostic procedure that is receiving more limited attention is the use of *positron emission tomography* (see Figure 12.1). Positrons are emitted from certain unstable isotopes of oxygen and fluorine; scientists make use of these isotopes to label molecules such as glucose, and they employ

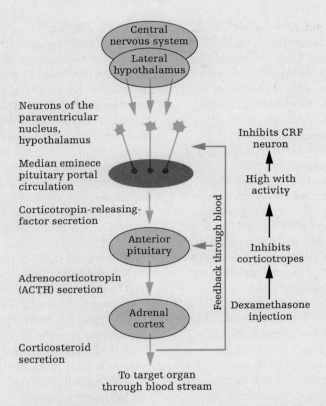

The dexamethasone suppression test provides a means to assess the relative status of the brain's control over the pituitary–adrenal axis. In a typical program, the patient receives a small oral dose of dexamethasone, a powerful synthetic version of the cortisone normally made and secreted by the cells of the adrenal cortex. Under usual conditions, this small dose of the powerful steroid would signal the brain to suppress further secretion of the hypothalamic corticotropin-releasing factor (CRF) and of the pituitary adrenocorticotropin hormone (ACTH). In response, urinary excretion of natural adrenal steroids would greatly diminish for the next 12 to 18 hours. In patients with adrenal tumors and in other patients undergoing extreme stress, such as that which occurs in some forms of affective psychosis, dexamethasone fails to suppress the brain and pituitary hormone signals, and adrenal steroids continue to be excreted in the urine in normal or excess amounts. This failure to suppress adrenal steroid production has been employed as a research tool to discover the presence of some forms of depression. A new strategy in the development of antidepressant medications is to seek drugs that can block the initial action of corticotropin-releasing factor and stop the cascade at its inception.

continued

positron detectors around the patient's head, connected to powerful computers that determine the source of the positron-emitting compounds within the brain. Normally, the results of this test are expressed as colors across a spectrum, the most heavily labeled brain areas being white-red, and the least heavily labeled being blue. In individual patients examined while depressed and during recovery, selective decreases in brain metabolism, especially over the frontal lobe areas, have been observed. However, the test is still only a research tool; it is quite expensive to use and has not yet been repeated in a large enough series of subjects to determine whether the brain's decreased use of glucose causes the depression or is a result of the depression and whether metabolic conditions besides depression might show similar changes.

While such endocrine work continues, very recent studies have suggested another avenue, which could eventually provide a means of chemical diagnosis. That avenue is the search for genetic markers. The new tests come from attempts to identify the nature of the transmission of depression across generations within communities that:

(1) are geographically well defined; (2) keep excellent family records; (3) permit limited access to the outside world; and (4) are treated by psychiatrists who use diagnostic criteria that are comparable to those in common scientific use. Recent studies suggest that there may be multiple genetic markers capable of predicting which offspring of a family may inherit factors that increase their risk of developing depression. In a study of manic-depressive illness in the Amish population of southeastern Pennsylvania, a linked genetic marker on chromosome 11 showed a high degree of correlation across three generations over four different families. In an unrelated study of depression among the non-Ashkenazi Jews in Israel, the genetic marker seemed to be linked to the X chromosome. Nevertheless, these genetic findings have not been reproducible in other populations by other investigators, making it likely that multiple genetic factors will eventually have to be identified.

Although all these studies will require validation through replication by other groups of researchers, biological underpinnings for the psychoses are beginning to emerge.

certain tests before reaching a diagnosis. Two tests have recently been shown to provide objective information that helps distinguish many subjects with affective psychosis from the temporary, less-serious forms of depression. One test focuses on sleep problems, whereas the other (see box beginning on page 390) isolates disturbances in the way in which the brain regulates the endocrine system. Neither test is infallible, however, or specific.

Sleep disturbances are a frequent complaint of the depressed patient. Some researchers have made EEG recordings of the brain's activity during sleep and then used computers to examine recordings of large numbers of patients and measure more precisely the duration of the several different stages of sleep (see Chapter 7). Recently, such research has focused on how long it takes the patient to fall asleep and reach the stage of rapid-eye-movement (REM) sleep. The studies appear to show that psychotically depressed patients take less time—about 55 minutes on the average after falling asleep—to enter the first REM-sleep episode. This amount of time is slightly less than half that required by normal subjects or by people with only mild depression. Depressed patients who enter REM quickly often have very favorable responses to antidepressant drugs.

Is sleep abnormality a cause or a side effect of an underlying brain disease that leads to depression? Are altered sleep-stage durations an expression of this brain problem? No one as yet has a biological explanation of how psychotic depression influences the neuronal circuits that regulate sleep.

The Possible Biological Basis of Depression

What little is known about the biological causes of depression stems from chance observations of the behavioral effects of certain drugs that were being used on humans and animals for other purposes. Observation of these changes in behavior led to biochemical studies of what those drugs did to neurotransmitters in the brains of animals. A few examples illustrate this roundabout way of developing drugs and the role that drugs play in the search for the bases of mental illnesses.

In the early 1950s, an extract from the root of an East Indian shrub was developed in the United States as a sedative to treat schizophrenia and, in lesser doses, high blood pressure. However, human subjects given the drug, known commonly as *reserpine,* for high blood pressure became depressed and frequently suicidal. When reserpine was later shown to deplete the brain's contents of the neurotransmitters norepinephrine, serotonin, and dopamine, scientists wondered whether the loss of any or all of these transmitters might be "the"

cause of human depression. This was not unlike the reasoning that loss of dopamine neurons could be the cause of the movement dysfunctions of Parkinson's disease.

At about this time, a new drug thought to help the effectiveness of certain antibiotics was being tested on tuberculosis patients who became hyperactive, exhibiting mania-like symptoms in response. This effect was found to be associated with the ability of the drug to block a brain and liver enzyme, *monoamine oxidase* (MAO), that normally breaks down the same three monoamine transmitters depleted by reserpine. Researchers interpreted this evidence, combined with their knowledge of reserpine effects, to mean that the inhibition of MAO might produce mania by prolonging the actions of these neurotransmitters. Another important finding, at about the same time, was that *amphetamine,* a stimulant drug, activates neurons to release the catecholamines dopamine and norepinephrine. These discoveries and others led American psychiatrists Joseph Schildkraut and Seymour Kety to propose a catecholamine hypothesis of depression, in which they conceived of depression as being caused by a loss of transmission at the catecholamine synapses in the brain.

Later, antidepressant drugs also were found to produce their effects specifically on these transmitters. Normally, the catecholamines, serotonin, and certain other neurotransmitters are recaptured by the nerve terminals that secrete them. The molecular pumps, or *transporters,* that do this recapturing are similar but distinct protein molecules selectively expressed by the neurons that make and release these neurotransmitters. The early antidepressant drugs of this sort were found to block this reuptake process at norepinephrine, dopamine, and serotonin terminals, apparently prolonging the presence of the amines on the synapses of the receiving cells. Thus, the hypothesis went, the drugs worked because they helped counteract an underlying deficiency in the process of catecholamine transmission. Unfortunately, some of these drugs caused abnormal heart rhythms, because they also prolong the effects of norepinephrine released from sympathetic nerves, so pharmacologists focused on developing antidepressants that blocked the reuptake of serotonin alone. Such "serotonin selective reuptake inhibitors" (sometimes referred to as "SSRIs") have been very effective in the treatment of depression and, surprisingly, of other diseases for which effective medications had not been available, such as obsessive-compulsive disorder. The pervasive innervation of the emotion-regulating regions of the brain are illustrated in Figure 12.3.

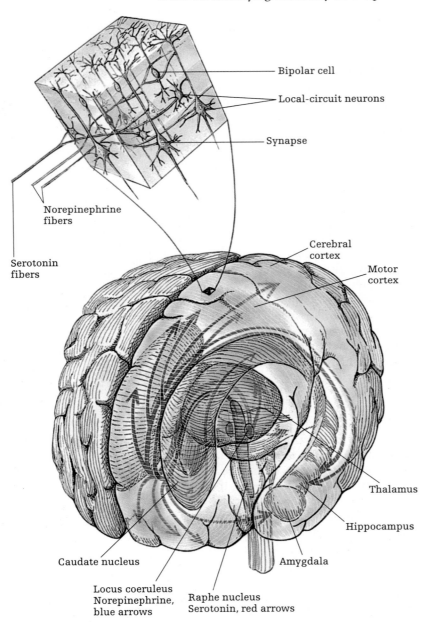

Bipolar cell

Local-circuit neurons

Synapse

Norepinephrine fibers

Serotonin fibers

Cerebral cortex

Motor cortex

Thalamus

Hippocampus

Caudate nucleus

Amygdala

Locus coeruleus
Norepinephrine, blue arrows

Raphe nucleus
Serotonin, red arrows

Figure 12.3 A schematic representation, based on experimental work with animal brains, of the possible circuitry in the human brain of two monoamine neurotransmitters that may be implicated in affective disorder.

Serotonin (red arrows): The raphe nuclei of the pons and brainstem extend their divergent axons toward selected target neurons throughout the central nervous system. These thin axons act to modify the activity of neurons in many brain regions, and, in some cases of affective psychosis, these neurons may be underactive. Antidepressants can supplement the amount of synaptically released serotonin by decreasing active reuptake of the serotonin being released from synaptic locations.

Norepinephrine (blue arrows): The locus coeruleus extends a highly divergent branched circuitry toward selected target neurons in almost all areas of the forebrain, midbrain, and cerebellum. According to some hypotheses, norepinephrine-mediated transmission may be overactive in mania and underactive in depression. Thus, antidepressant drugs act to supplement this underactive transmission. Although serotonin and norepinephrine fibers take similar general routes, their circuits appear to include different target neurons.

When a testable statement of this clarity is put forward, researchers can perform experiments whose results either support or refute the initial hypothesis. Some of these tests have yielded results that are difficult to reconcile with the original idea. For example, fewer than 10 percent of people treated with reserpine actually get depressed, yet all of them show catecholamine and serotonin depletion. In addition, many other effective antidepressants have no obvious effects on monoamine reuptake. Furthermore, the drugs must be taken for several days before an improvement is observed in the patient's affect, even though the effects on reuptake are observed immediately. Lastly, mania and the manic phase of manic-depressive psychosis respond very well to long-term treatment with small doses of the salts of lithium, even though this treatment has no specific effect on the catecholamine systems. These extended tests, therefore, have not in general confirmed the catecholamine hypothesis.

In the past quarter century, scientists have turned their attention to the longer-term effects of antidepressant drug treatments and particularly to explaining the lag between treatment and improvement. Many of the studies have focused on measuring the effectiveness of synaptic transmission by norepinephrine or serotonin. Cellular responsiveness to these transmitters was found to shift in concert with changing intensities of synaptic transmission, increasing when amine supplies are depleted and decreasing when amine supplies are augmented (see Figure 12.4). The change in responsiveness takes place over a period of 3 to 7 days. Some scientists believe that this delay explains the delay in clinical response and that the regulation of synaptic responsiveness is the primary event being treated. If transmitter chemistry at the level of synaptic responsiveness is the most pertinent correlate of emotion, then the

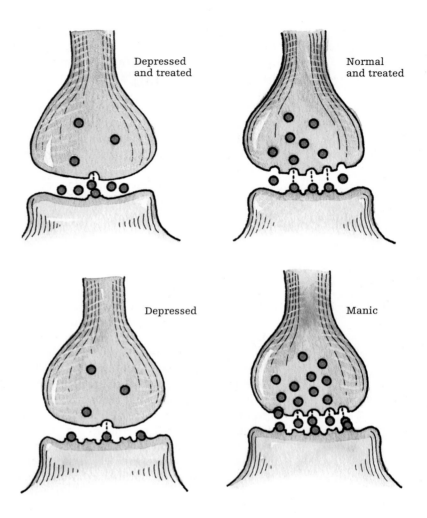

Figure 12.4 Schematic diagram of the relation between transmitter synthesis, storage, release, and response in a normal monoaminergic synapse (*upper right*) and the possible differences in the brain of a depressed subject (*lower left*), where, despite normal numbers of receptors, transmission is reduced. This relation is opposite that conjectured for the brain of a manic patient (*lower right*), where transmitter release and response may be excessive. Treatment with antidepressant drugs may improve function (*upper left*) by eliciting an increase in the number of receptors and thereby restore a semblance of normal levels of responsiveness.

catecholamine hypothesis could well require further revision.

In any case, much more work is required to sort out differences between individual patients and their responses to specific drugs. For example, some measurements of transmitter metabolism made on spinal fluid have detected two separate subgroups of psychotically depressed patients. Those with lower levels of the metabolic by-products, or *metabolites,* of norepinephrine have better responses to norepinephrine-directed antidepressant drugs than to other antidepressants. Those with very low levels of serotonin metabolites form a group with a much higher incidence of suicide. However, much has been learned about neurotransmitters since these simple theories were generated some 40 years ago. Today, few researchers would conclude that such diseases are built on one single, specific chemical-transmitter system. Indeed, the most consistent and long-lasting remissions from depression are found when patients are given both antidepressant medications and behavioral therapy, such as group or individual counseling. The most recent area of novel treatments for depression has focused on drugs that antagonize responses to the neuropeptide substance P or to the neuropeptide corticotropin-releasing factor (CRF).

Other Forms of Treatment

Aside from drug treatments, two other forms of biological therapy for depression are in use. A 4- to 8-day series of electroconvulsive (shock) treatments can be very helpful. In these treatments, the patient is given a short-acting general anesthetic and a muscle relaxant, and then a generalized convulsion is induced by applying electrical stimulation to the brain through electrodes on the scalp. These treatments are always given in the hospital under vigilant medical care.

Although an objective description of this therapy may sound a bit barbaric, ECT often produces a dramatic and rapid improvement in mood. Indeed, after ECT, nearly two-thirds of patients experience a permanent remission of the depressive episode (the remission occurs gradually, over the next several days). Except for short-term amnesia, which may in fact be a part of ECT's therapeutic effect, no other serious side effects are found. Therefore, the use of ECT has much to recommend it, in spite of the fact that the reasons for its therapeutic action are unknown and that continued treatment with other forms of antidepressant medication also may be necessary. More selective activation of the brain by magnetic stimulation, particularly of the frontal cortex, has been reported to produce comparable therapeutic responses without the general seizures produced by ECT.

Another form of treatment, still experimental, is directed toward altering patients' sleep patterns. Cyclically depressed patients have insomnia the night before their moods switch from depression to mania. Extending this observation, researchers have found that depressed patients with severe sleep disturbances show brief (2- to 5-day) improvements when kept awake and active all night. They theorize that the one night of enforced wakefulness may help resynchronize the patient's circadian rhythms and lead to more balanced affect. Support for this therapeutic procedure, still to come, might be a source of insight into the workings of the rhythm-regulating brain centers (described in Chapter 7). Some patients who have "winter depression" have benefited from exposure to full-spectrum indoor lighting that simulates the sun's light during the long winter (see Chapter 7). One basis for this effect could be that seasonal variations superimpose their ultradian rhythms on the patient's daily rhythms. At present, however, the most effective and lasting treatments for depression combine antidepressant drug treatment with some form of interpersonal psychotherapy.

Schizophrenia

The psychiatric disorders known collectively as *schizophrenia* are perhaps the most devastating, puzzling, and frustrating of all mental diseases, defined medically as a group of severe and generally chronic disturbances of mental function characterized by disturbed thinking, feeling, and behaving. Schizophrenia is referred to as a group of diseases and has been ever since the Swiss psychiatrist Eugen Bleuler coined the term "schizophrenia" in 1908.

The Symptoms of Schizophrenia

A simplified summary of the basic symptoms of schizophrenia might include:

1. Disorders of perception (hearing nonexistent voices or smelling nonexistent "poison" gas)

2. Disorders of thinking, especially very loose associations (the appearance of a car may lead to thoughts of a face, which may then suggest the faces of those the patient believes to be controlling his or her brain)

3. Disorders of emotion (laughing or crying at inappropriate times, often with rapid shifts from one extreme response to the other)

Many of Gerry Smith's peculiar-sounding statements quoted at the beginning of the chapter fit these general categories of schizophrenia symptoms.

Gerry Smith is diagnosed as schizophrenic. His family allowed him to be interviewed on television and offered some photographs of his childhood. About allowing a camera crew to film his schizophrenic son, the father of Gerry Smith said: "It's awful bad when you only got one kid too because . . . we loved the boy and we done everything we could for him. I just hope the people and the public can understand what . . . we're doing. I hope it helps the public. It may not help us, it may not help Gerald. I certainly hope it helps somebody. It certainly won't do them no harm, would it? That's the way we feel about it."

His mother looked through the family album. "When this one here was made, we had moved to a different location and at that point his allergies had started real bad. And this one was made on a Sunday, we might have been getting ready to go to church, I don't remember, and they decided they'd make the picture. He always had to clown with his face."

"Then he decided that he'd gained too much weight, so he'd go on a crash diet. And he did. And he went from looking like that to looking like this. Which wasn't to me a healthy look. And that was when he started going downhill or what you would say, but that's when his sickness probably started coming to a head."

When Gerry talks about himself, he displays the disordered thinking characteristic of the schizophrenic. "I'm a very sensitive person and I pick up . . . I pick up a lot of . . . I pick up very sensitive things. The least little bit of aggression of a person's face freaks me out. . . . I'm afraid I will be killed . . . by a Martin Luther King . . . type of thing."

The overall behavior of schizophrenic patients is primarily characterized by abnormally distorted perceptions of what is real and what is not. Some patients hear voices or sense extreme threat from everyday sights—the faces of their mothers or their husbands, for instance. They are unable to separate fact from fantasy and believe that their ideas of the world are imposed on their minds by outside forces. The specific course in individual patients can be highly varied, however. Sometimes a stressful life event seems to precipitate the onset of thought and behavioral problems. More often, no causal event can be identified. Some patients improve quickly, whereas others remain disturbed, with episodes of extremely aberrant behavior persisting for years.

Many patients lose the ability to concentrate and to relate one idea or observation to another in a logical way. Others retain highly logical or effective thinking in some parts of their lives but lose it with minimal provocation. It is also typical for schizophrenic patients to be unable to generalize. They would not be able to identify the common features of a table and a chair or an apple and an orange. This inability to make general abstractions is said to arise from an extremely "concrete" (overly literal) way of looking at the world.

Some patients giggle incessantly, even in solemn or grave situations. Others sit mute and motionless for hours. Still others have periods of extremely disruptive aggressive behavior and require restraint to prevent hurting themselves or others. These presentations are only a few of the wide variation that caused Bleuler to call them "the schizophrenias."

It seems clear that the thinking process is disturbed in all of these patients. But it is not at all clear that the same, unknown cause is the source of the cognitive problem in all cases or that the other extremely varied clinical symptoms can have the same fundamental biological basis. Another perplexing aspect of this group of thinking abnormalities is their episodic nature. Some schizophrenic patients can behave and function quite normally for long periods of time, with only occasional lapses into severe states of disorientation and delusions.

The Incidence of Schizophrenia

Schizophrenia is a major health problem, accounting for a very high proportion, perhaps more than 50 percent, of admissions to psychiatric hospitals. Looked at in another way, this group of diseases represents more than one-fourth of all the patients in any hospital at any given time. In the United States, more than 300,000 new cases of schizophrenia are diagnosed every year.

The incidence of schizophrenia can be estimated in very personal terms. If you live to be 55, you have a 1 in 100 chance of being diagnosed as a schizophrenic. More than half of those diagnosed are under 30, and the peak period for showing the signs of the disease falls between ages 20 and 30. Men tend to express their disease at younger ages than women do. Because schizophrenia can be a lifelong illness and often begins early in adult life, it accounts for a substantial loss of potential productivity. Obviously, it is a major human tragedy when it strikes.

Basic Types of Schizophrenia

Clinical studies of patients with schizophrenia in the past several decades have suggested that there are two basic forms of the disease. Each has a characteristic course and by and large responds in a characteristic way to the major forms of treatment.

In one form of schizophrenia, patients exhibit more of the "positive symptoms" of the disease (bizarre additions to their behavior): hallucinations, thought disorders, and delusions. In the other form, patients display more of the "negative symptoms" (behavioral deficiencies): loss of emotional responses, inanimate postures, loss of spontaneous speech, and general lack of motivation. Both categories of symptoms were described in the early 1900s by Bleuler and by his contemporary, German psychiatrist Emil Kraepelin. In the early 1980s, English psychiatrist Tim Crow suggested that each set of symptoms might, in fact, represent a different disease process. He began the practice of referring to patients with positive symptoms as type I and patients with negative symptoms as type II.

Other psychiatrists take issue with this split because sometimes the same patient can show positive and negative symptoms at different times or even simultaneously. The distinction, however, seems to have some value in predicting responsiveness to antipsychotic medications. Most drugs have been found to be more effective against the positive symptoms and least useful against the negative symptoms, although new classes of medications can benefit the latter category. Furthermore, brain scans of patients with predominantly positive symptoms show little or no anatomical brain abnormality, whereas patients with mainly negative symptoms often show loss of brain size, with shrinkage of the cerebellum and enlargement of the cerebral ventricles (see Figure 12.5 on the following page).

The two basic subtypes also have substantial differences in the long-term course of their disease. In a study of several hundred schizophrenics studied in Germany, patients who presented with complaints of acute onset of hallucinations (almost always

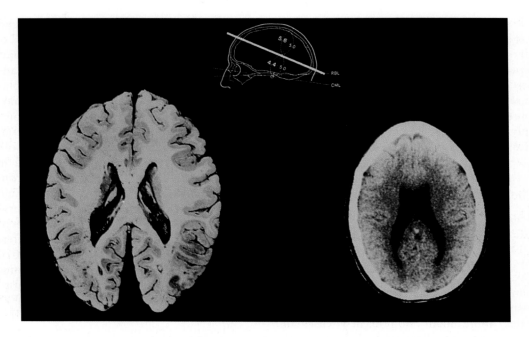

Figure 12.5 A computerized axial tomogram (CAT) scan allows the psychiatrist to see the surface of the brain and the outlines of the ventricles. In comparison with the normal brain (*left*), the brain of the schizophrenic (*right*) has greatly enlarged ventricles, indicating a wasting process in the cerebral cortex.

the delusion of voices speaking to them) had the best outcomes. Most of these patients also had delusions and paranoia—that is, they based their behavior on an unreal but organized series of conclusions. Such patients, for example, may believe that they are famous people, such as Jesus Christ or Napoleon, or that there is a plot to assassinate them. An optimistic outcome was especially likely if the abnormalities in thinking and behaving developed suddenly (in less than 6 months) in patients who had previously shown a fairly normal life pattern, including normal interactions with other people. The most pessimistic outcomes were found in subjects who had long histories of personality or behavior problems, who did not do well in school or in social situations,

and in whom the onset of serious symptoms was more gradual. Except for patients who first expressed their abnormal thought patterns immediately after delivering a child, precipitating events had no obvious value in predicting outcome.

When well-studied groups of schizophrenic patients are followed for long periods of time, some interesting findings emerge. About one-fourth of all the patients may be expected to have a complete recovery and to have no obvious residual signs of having had the disease. More than half of the remainder also substantially improve but nevertheless show some residual signs, such as occasional memory or sleep problems or not feeling exactly "right" or just not being able to tolerate tension and stress very well.

This group of schizophrenic patients does especially poorly when they return to disruptive family situations. Some psychiatrists view this outcome as an indication that the disruptive family life actually led to the disease.

About three-fourths of those who improve do so within the first 3 years after the diagnosis is made. Those given antipsychotic drugs show greater improvement, faster. Those who do not respond in the first 3 years after diagnosis, however, do not actually show the progressive decline in function that was once the expected outcome. In fact, many cases of complete recovery 20 or 30 years after the initial appearance of the disease have been documented.

Biological Clues to the Nature of Schizophrenia

Converging lines of research have led to the modern view that the schizophrenic diseases have a biological basis.

1. A strong genetic factor would seem to account for the fact that there is a higher incidence of schizophrenia in people who are related to a known schizophrenic than there is in the general population.

2. Psychosis-inducing (psychotogenic) drugs, whose mechanisms of action can be related to specific brain transmitter systems, can produce signs and symptoms that resemble certain kinds of symptoms in schizophrenic subjects.

3. Antipsychotic drugs help many schizophrenic patients to achieve a positive therapeutic response, which is seen to be directly related to the drug's ability to interfere with certain specific chemical-transmitter systems.

These observations suggest that specific brain parts and specific chemical systems may be disturbed by the underlying disease process. Other evidence is beginning to show how schizophrenia develops. However, before we examine this evidence in detail, we should note that no specific causes of schizophrenia have yet been identified directly. Some investigators of schizophrenia have concluded that people with schizophrenia often have a history of birth injury or an otherwise complicated delivery, sometimes including a serious virus infection in the mother or a mother–infant blood incompatibility. Application of modern histochemical markers to identify neurons on the basis of their neurotransmitter or unique metabolic enzymes has revealed discrete abnormalities in the numbers and locations of neurons in the cerebral cortex and thalamus, perhaps suggesting abnormalities in the development of critical circuits. Given the well-known pattern of cortical development as an inside-out process (see Chapter 3), the abnormal cortical features are most compatible with a developmental insult in the second trimester of pregnancy, leading to the development of abnormal circuits, which much later in life renders these persons susceptible to schizophrenia.

The Genetics of Schizophrenia As noted earlier in this chapter, the chances of having schizophrenia increase with the degree to which a person is directly related to someone already known to have schizophrenia. In some parts of the world—certain remote parts of Sweden, for example—the incidence of schizophrenia within certain family pedigrees is very high (see Figure 12.6 on the following page).

As stated earlier, the chances of being diagnosed as a schizophrenic by the age of 55 are about 1 in 100. However, for those who are identical twins of a schizophrenic, the chances increase to nearly 1 in 2. The reasons

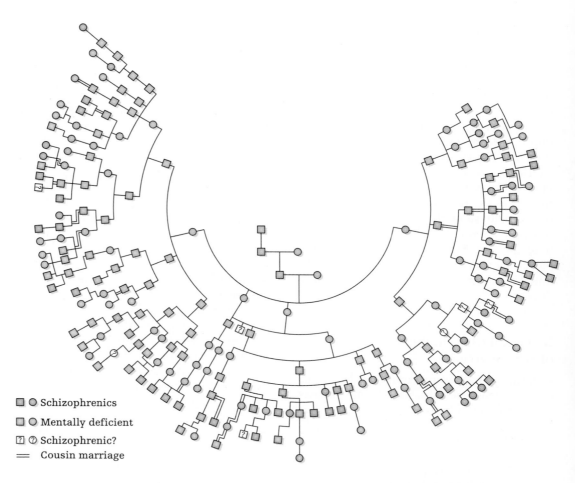

Figure 12.6 The diagrams here and on the facing page illustrate the incidence of schizophrenia and of mental retardation within two very large families living in an isolated community in far northern Sweden. Excellent medical records were available to the investigators. Marriage partnerships among the earliest ancestors are linked by horizontal lines, and the offspring of a marriage are indicated by vertical lines. For the four most recent generations, the four outermost rings in each family, colors encode the most probable diagnosis as schizophrenia (in green), mental retardation (in blue), or presumed normal (in yellow). Although there has been some inbreeding, as shown by double lines indicating marriages between cousins, there is an extraordinarily high propagation of severe disease in almost all children, indicating that the end result cannot be attributed solely to "inbreeding."

- ☐ ○ Schizophrenics
- ☐ ○ Mentally deficient
- ☐ ○ Schizophrenic?
- ═ Cousin marriage

for this difference are the same as those for the familial patterns in affective psychosis. A fraternal twin of a schizophrenic has about one-third the chance of developing schizo-phrenia as an identical twin does, but that is still 14 times more likely than that for a person who is unrelated to a schizophrenic. Children born to two schizophrenic parents

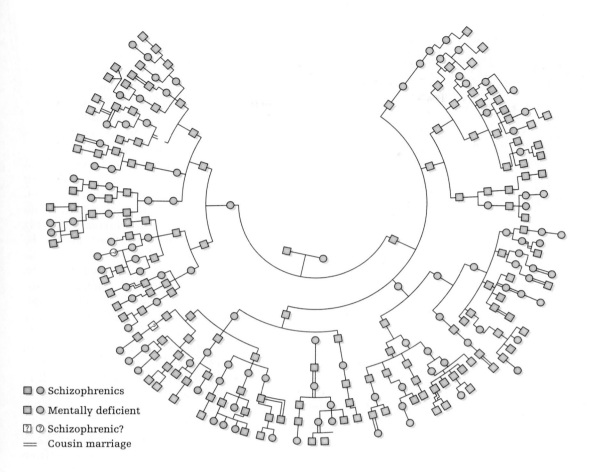

■ ○ Schizophrenics
■ ○ Mentally deficient
⧄ ⊘ Schizophrenic?
═ Cousin marriage

have almost as great a chance of becoming schizophrenic as identical twins do—about 1 in 2. Other close relatives of schizophrenics—first cousins, brothers, sisters, or even half brothers and half sisters—also show, on average, an increased incidence of schizophrenia over the general public.

Given these genetic tendencies, it is tempting to conclude that the brain conditions that cause schizophrenia must have some biological basis. This conclusion might misinterpret the facts, however, and the arguments are quite similar to those considered in the genetics of affective psychosis. After all, if identical twins are truly identical

in all their inherited biological properties, why is the incidence of schizophrenia not 100 percent in both twins? This incomplete expression strongly suggests that environmental factors—perhaps the support of family or friends and the stresses of growing up—also must have a lot to do with "becoming schizophrenic." Some clinicians, in fact, take the position that an abnormal parent behaves in a way that transmits the behavioral disorder to the children and that twins or other close relatives might simply have a similar environment.

Adopted-twin studies again provide a partial answer to such views. Identical

Given the relative rarity of multiple births, the variable penetrance of the genetic susceptibility to schizophrenia, and the general population incidence of the disease, the chances of four identical quadruplets being diagnosed as schizophrenic are 1 in 2 billion. The Genain sisters, shown here at their 51st birthday party, are that case. Problems for Nora, Iris, Myra, and Hester began in high school, and the women have been in and out of hospitals since then. Inasmuch as they share identical genetic material, doctors at the National Institute of Mental Health believe that the variations in the degree of their illnesses stem from differential family treatment.

twins born of schizophrenic parents and brought up in different family settings still have as great a chance—about 1 in 2—of becoming schizophrenic as they would if their own parents reared them. Even related children born of schizophrenics but who are not twins and are reared by adopted families that are not schizophrenic show the expected high incidences. The adopted-out children of nonschizophrenic parents raised in those families show no increase in incidence. One other interesting possibility raised early on by critics of the twin studies was that perhaps just being a twin was enough to increase the incidence of schizophrenia. This suggestion is relatively easy

to dispense with, however: twins as a group do not show any higher incidence of schizophrenia than that of the population at large. The genetics of schizophrenia is relatively complicated, but the message is nonetheless clear: some inheritable predisposing "factor" can lead to the development of schizophrenia.

Scientists already have some ideas about the environmental factors that might lead to schizophrenia in a predisposed person. Perhaps the culprit is a *schizogenic* bacterium or virus that is, a schizophrenia-producing microbe. Such an infection might be "caught" in early childhood from a close sibling or parent and remain latent in the brain until later in life. Brain-infecting viruses with such long latencies are now recognized, and an inheritable factor might make some people more susceptible than others. In fact, some studies of the spinal fluid of chronic, or type-II, schizophrenics have found signs of infection by viruses, such as cytomegalovirus, that can be harbored in cells and destroy them slowly over many years. The structural atrophy seen in the brains of type-II patients (see Figure 12.7) could be viewed as loss of brain tissue from a progressive viral infection. Behavioral changes, then, might not be unlike the dementia that accompanies long-term (untreated) syphilis.

Environmental factors could also conceivably include contamination of food or water supplies in a particular geographical region. For example, the west coast of Ireland, the northwestern coast of Yugoslavia, and the northern part of Sweden have much higher incidences of schizophrenia than other parts of the world, perhaps because of environmental factors of this type. Similarly, there are about two-and-a-half times as many admissions per person for schizophrenia in the New England states as in the Middle West. A possible alternative explanation for the higher incidences in some of these places might be their relative social isolation, which could lead to greater frequency of inbreeding, thus enlarging the susceptible population. The fact is, however, that the explanations for such high-incidence pockets of schizophrenia have yet to be discovered.

Biochemical Hypotheses of Schizophrenia

Many investigations of the underlying causes of schizophrenia have focused on biochemical models. One resulting proposal is that enzymes in the brain of the schizophrenic may produce some abnormal chemical that causes the signs and symptoms. The ability of the drug LSD to produce vivid visual hallucinations (colorful, but amorphous) supports this idea, but research on LSD has produced no significant understanding of the nature of actual hallucinations in schizophrenia, in which auditory hallucinations, especially voices, are most common and visual hallucinations are extremely rare. Theorists have suggested several chemicals whose presence in the brain might produce psychosis, but so far no such chemicals have been reliably identified.

Defective functioning of endorphin transmitters also has been considered. An abnormal version of such a transmitter might directly cause the signs and symptoms of schizophrenia. Or failure to produce enough of the right endorphin, in combination with genetic and environmental influences, might be a destabilizing factor. But attempts to measure abnormalities of specific transmitter systems in the brains of schizophrenics have not as yet been very illuminating.

Another approach to deciphering the puzzle of schizophrenia has been to focus on a transmitter system discussed earlier in

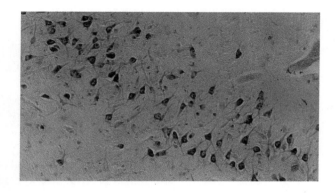

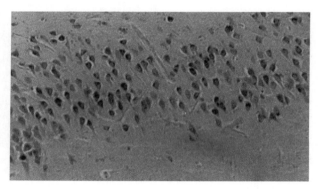

Figure 12.7 Some cases of schizophrenia reveal abnormal cellular structure in postmortem examination. In this illustration, the hippocampal neurons stained purple brown (*above*) show abnormal shape and position, as well as reduced frequency, compared with those from a normal subject of the same age who died from a nonneurological cause (*below*).

connection with the regulation of movement and with the movement deficits of Parkinson's disease. That neurotransmitter is dopamine.

Dopamine and Schizophrenia

Two lines of research and chance observation have led to an increased interest in the hypothesis that abnormalities in dopamine transmission in the brain may play an important part in the expression of schizophrenia.

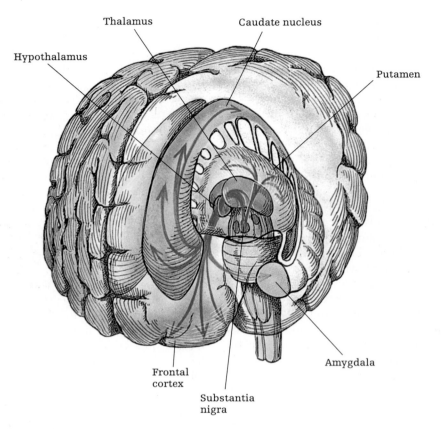

Hypothalamus — Thalamus — Caudate nucleus — Putamen — Amygdala — Frontal cortex — Substantia nigra

Figure 12.8 A schematic representation of the possible circuitry in the human brain of dopamine, a neurotransmitter possibly implicated in schizophrenia. The source of the dopamine fibers in the forebrain and midbrain are two single-source nuclei, one in the substantia nigra and the other in the nearby midbrain. Dopamine fibers arising in these two nuclei innervate extrapyramidal targets in the basal ganglia, and they innervate limbic-system targets in the amygdala, septum, thalamus, and frontal cortex. In schizophrenia, this system may be overactive, and this overactivity may be regulated by antipsychotic drugs that antagonize the actions of dopamine.

In Parkinson's disease, this system is destroyed by the disease process, and dopamine transmission is achieved by treating the patient with L-DOPA, which surviving neurons can convert into dopamine.

One line of evidence comes from the abuse of amphetamines, a group of drugs whose chemical structure is very similar to that of dopamine. Investigations have suggested that the dopamine system is critical to the excitatory hyperactivity that the amphetamine produces. Human beings who dose themselves with large amounts of amphetamine are craving the ecstatic, excited feeling that the drug produces. Continued use leads to tolerance, requiring the drug abuser to take ever increasing doses. Those who continue to take high doses for many days can go through a series of behavioral changes very much like some aspects of the acute paranoid hallucinations exhibited by some type-I schizophrenics. Animals, too, when given large doses of amphetamine, first show extreme hyperactivity and then bizarre repetitive movements that, in a very general way, resemble some of the bizarre postures and motor behaviors seen in the schizophrenic patient. Interestingly, some victims of Parkinson's disease who receive too much L-DOPA (see page 376) may undergo a similar acute psychotic episode, with hallucinations, delusions, and paranoias that pass when the L-DOPA dosage is reduced or stopped. These observations have suggested that schizophrenia may arise from excessive dopamine transmission.

Evidence making this hypothesis even more compelling is that those drugs capable of treating the acute paranoid hallucinatory states of the schizophrenic—drugs called "antipsychotic" or "neuroleptic" (*neuro*, "nerve"; *lepsis*, "to take hold of," or "seize")—also relieve paranoia in the amphetamine abuser, normalize the hyperactivity in the amphetamine-overdosed animal, and help clear the confused thinking of the L-DOPA-overmedicated Parkinson patient. Indeed, prolonged treatment with anti-psychotic drugs leads to drug-induced Parkinsonism. These drugs—the phenothiazines and haloperidol are two examples—appear to produce their main antipsychotic effect by antagonizing dopamine transmission.

The other line of evidence for the dopamine hypothesis is obtained through postmortem analysis, and it, too, supports the idea that some kind of problem in the dopamine-transmitting sites results in excessive dopamine transmission. Post-

mortem examination shows that schizophrenic patients have slightly elevated amounts of dopamine in some of the dopamine-rich areas of their brains such as the striatum in the basal ganglia (see Figure 12.8). These areas also show changes indicating that their responsiveness to dopamine had inappropriately increased along with the increase in dopamine content. Chronic use of antipsychotic drugs may have caused some of these changes (that is, taking drugs that block dopamine receptors may have led to an adaptive increase in the number of receptors). But, even taking that possibility into account, the increases that have been observed are still noteworthy and greater than chronic use is likely to have caused. Furthermore, these differences are much more marked in schizophrenics who died at younger ages. As noted earlier, in general, antidopamine antipsychotic drugs also produce their most effective actions in younger schizophrenics with mainly positive symptoms.

Like so many hypotheses, however, this one has holes. Dopamine changes, though reproducible in some studies, have not been seen in all such studies. Furthermore, dopamine transmits information in many parts of the brain, and theorists have yet to explain how dopamine-system malfunctions that result in perceptual, cognitive, or emotional problems would not result in more obvious sensory or motor problems as well. And, even though most antipsychotic drugs cause patients to improve in direct correlation with the drug's ability to antagonize dopamine, there are other, "atypical" antipsychotic drugs that have no observable interaction with dopamine at all (which is why they were dubbed atypical). Yet these drugs do produce tangible beneficial actions in schizophrenics, including those who were unresponsive to the typical antipsychotic drugs. There is also the disturbing fact that many schizophrenics with mainly negative symptoms do not readily improve with any of the existing medications. Apparently, many systems in the brain influence the behavioral problems of schizophrenia, and whether the dopamine-transmitter system itself is the key culprit remains to be seen.

Recent studies have raised an interesting alternative chemical explanation. Attempts to develop drugs that can antagonize the prevalent excitatory neurotransmitter glutamate (see Chapter 2) revealed an interesting side effect—namely, hallucinations. In fact, members of this class of experimental drugs were found to bear many chemical similarities to the well-known hallucinogen phencyclidine, or "PCP," raising the possibility that a "hypoglutamatergic" transmission could occur in schizophrenia.

Substance-Abuse Disorders

By this point in our coverage of mental diseases, you are probably willing to accept the fact that some diseases of behavior are truly as biologically based as the neurological diseases covered at the beginning of the chapter. We turn lastly to a very common group of behavioral problems in Western society that, until recently, were regarded as maladaptive, freely chosen, "bad" behaviors that either did not merit or were impervious to therapy. They are the chemical-dependency syndromes, often termed "addictions," in which a person becomes obsessed with acquiring and using one or more of a host of chemical substances. The most common problematic addictions are to the legal active substances in alcoholic beverages and in tobacco products. Rarer but also problematic are addictions to illegal drugs such as amphetamines, heroin, and marijuana. Each of these substances produces dependency such that, when the drug is unavailable, the drug user becomes mentally distressed and often physically ill, until more drug is obtained. Even caffeine-containing products can meet the definition of dependence producing, although, for cultural reasons, most people are unwilling to consider this legal drug a social or health problem. When the maladaptive pattern of behavior is sufficiently severe to interfere with family or occupational activities or to lead an otherwise law-abiding citizen into crime, medical intervention is clearly warranted, and many physicians would consider the patient to have a disease.

Recent biological research seems to support that conclusion. For example, alcoholism offers a very strong case for genetically inheritable vulnerability. Although the incidence of heavy alcohol consumption is about 12 percent of the U.S. adult population, in some families and some ethnic cultures, the incidence is much higher. Furthermore, alcoholism is much higher in fathers and brothers of alcoholics than in the general population. In addition, in some family studies, especially with adolescent behavioral problems, the incidence of alcoholism in the children of adopted-away male offspring is maintained at a high rate, suggesting that upbringing and cultural factors are not the key issues. The children of alcoholics demonstrate consistent, but not universal, abnormalities in their responses to alcohol, as seen in tests of cerebellar function (such as body sway when standing with eyes shut and arms extended in front), in the patterns of their electroencephalograms, and in responses evoked from the brain by simple visual or auditory stimuli. On all these tests, young adult males from families with a history of serious alcoholism appear to be more tolerant of alcohol than are adults with no such history and comparable amounts of prior alcohol experience. In short, though the practice of consuming alcoholic beverages is almost universal in all cultures and populations, alcohol addiction seems to run in families.

The argument for genetic factors is strengthened by two other observations. People of Japanese ancestry carry about a 50 percent chance of not having the liver and muscle enzyme necessary to metabolize alcohol. When such people ingest alcohol, they experience a severe toxic reaction that includes a marked facial flush and often sweating, rapid heart beat, and trembling. These symptoms are similar to those experienced by alcoholics who attempt to strengthen their resolve not to drink by taking the drug Antabuse, which in fact acts by inhibiting the very enzyme missing in so many people of Japanese descent. Surveys of Japanese with severe alcohol drinking problems show that very few of them come from the group lacking the enzyme; the latter are blessed with a genetic mechanism that encourages them to shun alcohol.

Animal research also makes a strong case for a genetic theory of drug addiction over the theory that peer pressure and personality problems are the major contributing factors. Experimental animals allowed an opportunity to administer to themselves the drugs that human beings have defined as "reinforcing" (as described in Chapter 9) will work very hard to get these drugs. Virtually every drug that humans have shown a desire to take, experimental animals will also self-administer, although for various logistical reasons this result was much harder to document for tobacco; PCP and LSD are not, however, readily self-administered by experimental animals.

Rats, for example, will work very hard to gain access to alcohol-containing solutions, and, if offered a choice, they will demonstrate that they prefer alcohol-containing solutions to other sweet or intensely flavored drinks. Moreover, rats and mice can be bred to produce offspring who are inherently more alcohol preferring than their parental strains—a major experimental result repeated in Finland, the United States, and Sardinia. The brains of the alcohol-preferring rats raised in the United States and Sardinia show deficits of dopamine and serotonin circuits. Often their alcohol consumption is reduced when they are given serotonin-selective-reuptake inhibitors.

These findings have spurred renewed efforts to find medications that work along different principles than that of the aversive-reinforcement strategy of Antabuse. Two medications appear promising. *Naltrexone,* an orally active form of a morphine-antagonizing drug, has effectively reduced recidivism (a return to drug taking) in those recovering alcoholics who are most compliant in taking their medication. A completely different drug, *Acamprosate,* seems to have a similar effect but may work by modifying actions of the excitatory transmitter glutamate. In both cases, alcoholics who are taking the treatments report less enjoyment from drinking episodes and less desire to continue to drink.

The effectiveness of medications in treating other substance-abuse problems has been less clear-cut. Whereas naltrexone is of limited value in alcohol abuse (that is, it is effective only in alcoholics who willingly take their medications daily), it has never been effective in reducing heroin abuse. On the other hand, *methadone,* a weak opiate agonist with some intrinsic antagonistic features, is effective in reducing the opiate-withdrawal response and the drug taking that it stimulates. Long-acting forms of the medicine convert an addict's decision to comply from a daily decision into one that must be addressed at longer intervals. However, none of the effective drugs for amphetamine or cocaine abuse have been accepted by people addicted to these drugs. Reports on reductions of tobacco use is somewhat more encouraging. Generally, this form of treatment relies on alternative forms of nicotine delivery that mitigate the withdrawal effects without resembling—and therefore without reinforcing—smoking. Skin patches that exude nicotine and chewing gums or sprays that release high quantities of nicotine into the blood until the patient has overcome an urge to smoke are two examples.

Undoubtedly, identifying the genes that underlie the increased desire to consume alcohol will help foster recognition that the real problem is not the tendency to abuse alcoholic beverages at all, but rather that this drug-use problem arises from some other form of aversive stress, anxiety, or emotional response to social events. Then prevention efforts will focus on identifying families carrying such genes and trying to find alternative means to relieve any alcoholism-promoting problems that they may have.

Brain, Mind, and Behavioral Disorders: Future Directions

Our journey through the history and the vagaries of humanity's approach to mental illness pauses here. We have seen that serious mental diseases are beginning to be characterized by specific hypotheses that can be tested and even modeled in experimental animals. Even though verification of these hypotheses has yet to be concluded, treatment procedures and diagnostic tests based on the suggested causative mechanisms hold great promise for more sharply focused future research. Perhaps small subsets of the major psychoses will submit to definition by these hypotheses, adding to the ranks of those behavioral diseases found to have organic causes.

The behavior disorders that lie beyond our present knowledge represent as much our failure to understand the biology of the cognitive and emotional operations of the brain as they do our inability to characterize the mechanisms underlying its disorders. It is quite clear from current research activity that the brain makes thousands of molecules exclusively important for the vitality of the brain. These molecules, whose identities are yet to be established, will undoubtedly cast new light on the specific properties of neurons and glia and suggest new methods of communication between brain cells, as well as new modes of synapse and circuit modifiability. Behavioral events will become far better understood through the new, noninvasive research methods; these methods are capable of resolving which particular brain structures participate in phenomena that remain vague, such as attention, calculation, and abstract analysis. Eventually, we will have enough data in hand to determine how far we can carry the view that everything that the normal as well as the disordered brain does, no matter how complex, can be explained in relation to the interactions between its operational units.

Summary

1. Everything that the brain does, both when it is healthy and when it is ill, can ultimately be described in terms of the cells and chemicals of the brain.

2. The study of neurological and psychiatric diseases adds to our understanding of how these states of ill health can be produced and how they are analyzed so that others can be protected from them in the future.

3. Historically, people suffering from diseases that affected their behavior, especially thinking and moving behaviors, were regarded as either evil or possessed by spirits. Humane treatments for the mentally ill were rare until well into the nineteenth century.

4. Scientific analysis and understanding of two once-major causes for institutionalization of patients with abnormal behavior resulted from the discovery of the brain's dependence on vitamin B (niacin) and of a crude but effective fever therapy for neurosyphilis.

5. Neurological diseases are characterized in general by consistent clusters of objective pathologic findings in brain structure, function, and chemistry. Each symptom and pathologic cluster establishes the nature of the disease and separates that disease from others, even though there may be no solid understanding of the nature of the problem or a treatment for it.

6. Three of the better-understood degenerative neurologic diseases are Parkinson's disease, a temporarily treatable movement disorder in which dopamine-containing circuits die; Huntington's disease, an untreatable, inheritable movement disorder with different chemical and structural deficits; and Alzheimer's disease, an untreatable progressive loss of intellectual function with still different chemical and structural deficits.

7. Psychiatric disorders are characterized by abnormal behavior in emotion, thought, and social interactions, but they have few objective signs based on structural, chemical, or functional tests of the brain. Clusters of these emotional and thought problems allow discrimination of different forms of psychiatric disease, each with different natural histories, treatment outcomes, and future expectations and each with different hypothetical explanations on which the treatments are in part based.

8. The two forms of mental illness for which scientists have acquired the most biological evidence are: (a) affective disorder, a generally treatable disorder of extreme highs and lows of emotion that has been related to underutilization of signals mediated by norepinephrine and serotonin circuits, and (b) schizophrenia, a potentially treatable but serious disorder of thought and analytical abilities that has been related to overactivity within some of the brain's dopamine circuits.

9. Some neurologic and psychiatric diseases have a strong genetic component and have been linked to specific gene areas on specific chromosomes. Environmental factors, from toxins to nutrition to emotion, can build on the inherited genetic susceptibilities to produce or resist expression of the disease. In the future, the diagnosis, treatment, and prevention of these diseases may be based on a true molecular understanding of the cause of the pathology.

10. Substance abuse by humans also is becoming understood through genetic, neuroscientific, and animal-model research, revealing the neurotransmitter systems that underlie the reinforcing effects of these drugs and providing opportunities for new insights into possible means to treat the addictions.

Key Terms

diseases
disorders
diagnostic tests
treatments
animal models
neurodegenerative
  diseases

major depression
mania
schizophrenia
addiction
genetic tests
electroconvulsive
  therapy

Further Reading

Andreasen, N. C., Ed. 1986. *Can Schizophrenia Be Localized in the Brain?* American Psychiatric Press, Washington, DC. A thoroughly readable and up-to-date coverage of the information by which psychiatrists and neuroscientists may be able to link up their respective points of view.

Breakefield, X. O., and Cambi, F. 1987. Molecular genetic insights into neurologic diseases. *Annual Review of Neuroscience* 10:535–594. An excellent and up-to-date summary of the basis for the recent insights into the inheritable and possibly inheritable neurological disorders of humans and other animals.

Diagnostic and Statistical Manual III-R. 1987. American Psychiatric Association Press, Washington, DC. A small book that details the diagnostic criteria that are to be considered the standards of reference.

Gottesman, I. I., and Shields, J. 1982. *Schizophrenia: The Epigenetic Disorder.* Cambridge University Press, Cambridge, UK. A monograph that covers the historical and recent findings on the schizophrenias as diseases that may be genetically transmitted in part.

Kendler, K. S., and Prescott C. A. 1999. A population-based twin study of lifetime major depression in men and women. *Archives of General Psychiatry* 56:39–44. A comprehensive analysis of sex-specific prevalence of depression in the United States by one of the leading epidemiologists.

Sacks, O. 1985. *The Man Who Mistook His Wife for a Hat and Other Clinical Tales.* Summit, New York. A famous neurologist recounts some of the cases that he has seen—people whose neurological diseases or injuries produced extraordinary effects.

Weinberger, D. R. 1999. Schizophrenia: new phenes, new genes. *Biological Psychiatry* 46:3–7. A brief review of recent genetic studies and the varying phenotypic ("phenes") presentations of schizophrenia by one of the major protagonists of the developmental-etiology hypothesis.

Interactive Resources

To continue your study online, visit our Web site at www.worthpublishers.com/bloom. Click on "Chapter 12" for resources including practice quizzes, flash cards, simulations, links to related Web sites, and updates on new research.

GLOSSARY

accommodation   In visual processing, the adjustments of the pupil and lens in focusing.

acetylcholine   A prevalent neurotransmitter in both the brain, where it may help regulate memory, and in the peripheral nervous system, where it controls the actions of skeletal and smooth muscle.

action potential   A nerve impulse; temporary reversal of the interior membrane's electrical state from negative to positive. An action potential results from a brief change in the neuron membrane's permeability to sodium and potassium ions. Also referred to as depolarization.

activational effects   Effects of hormones on brain cells that, during prenatal development, were subject to the organizational effects of those hormones; the early hormones, in effect, "prime" the cells to be activated at a later time. See also **organizational effects**.

acupuncture   A method developed in Chinese medicine for pain suppression through stimulation of skin and muscle by means of insertion of needles at specified points of the body.

adaptation   Diminishing responsiveness of a sensory receptor to prolonged presentation of a stimulus.

addiction   The compulsive desire to take drugs, such as opiates, cocaine, amphetamine, alcohol, and nicotine.

adipocyte   A single fat cell.

adiposity   Stored fat; now believed to be the primary regulator of feeding and digestion.

adrenal cortex   Endocrine organ that secretes corticosteroids for metabolic functions, aldosterone for sodium retention in the kidneys, androgens for male sexual development, and estrogens for female sexual development.

adrenal medulla   Endocrine organ that secretes epinephrine and norepinephrine for the activation of the sympathetic nervous system.

affective psychosis   Psychiatric disease in which prolonged periods of deep depression, unrelated to events in the life of the patient, alternate either with periods of normal mood or with periods of excessive, inappropriate euphoria, and mania.

aggregation   See Table 3.1, Processes of Neural Development.

alpha rhythms   Patterns of brain wave activity with rhythms of 8 to 12 waves per second; associated with a state of calm while awake.

Alzheimer's disease   A degenerative, and eventually fatal, brain disorder with symptoms including deterioration of mental capacities, memory loss, disorientation, and motor deficits; may be familial in some cases.

amacrine cells   Local-circuit neurons that regulate the spread of the visual signal within the retina.

amino acid transmitters   The most prevalent transmitters within the brain. These neurotransmitters include glutamate and aspartate, which are excitatory, and glycine and gamma-amino butyric acid (GABA), which are inhibitory.

amphetamine   A stimulant drug that activates the release of the catecholamines dopamine and norepinephrine.

amygdala   A forebrain structure and important component of the limbic system. Sometimes called the amygdaloid complex because it is composed of a number of nuclei.

amyotrophic lateral sclerosis   A fatal neurological disorder of unknown etiology; symptoms include gradual paralysis due to loss of motor neurons in the spinal cord and loss of input to the spinal cord form the brain; also known as Lou Gehrig's disease.

androgens   Group of sex steroid hormones, including testosterone, found more abundantly in males than females; responsible for male sexual maturation.

angiography   X-ray examination of the brain by means of dyes injected into the carotid artery, and then dispersed through other brain vessels; used for the detection of irregularities in the vascular system, such as blocked arteries.

angiotensin II A protein fragment produced by the actions of renin and other enzymes on angiotensinogen; causes arterial muscles to constrict, inducing a prompt, large rise in blood pressure.

angiotensinogen Small protein made by the liver and converted into angiotensin II, through the actions of renal and plasma enzymes, to increase blood pressure.

anorexia nervosa Disorder in which severe loss of appetite is presumably caused by psychological factors; most frequently affects young females and can lead to starvation. Anorectics are obsessed with food, have a severely distorted body image, and often suffer from depression and social isolation.

anoxia Severe deficit of oxygen reaching the body tissues.

anxiety Unrealistic apprehension and nervousness.

aphasia Disturbance in language comprehension or production.

arcuate fasciculus A collection of intracortical nerve fibers connecting Wernicke's area and Broca's area; critical for speech and speech perception.

association cortex The large areas of the cerebral cortex thought to receive and integrate information from more specialized areas—sensory, motor, and limbic areas and memory stores—allowing humans to think, decide, and plan.

astigmatism An irregularity on the surface of the cornea causing the images entering the eye from certain angles to be distorted.

astrocyte The most common type of glial cell. Thought to scavenge excess neurotransmitter and ions from the spaces between neurons. May also contribute metabolic fuel to very active neurons and redirect blood flow to especially active regions.

atherosclerosis Disease caused by deposition of fatty substances on the inside of artery walls and hardening of the arteries, so that blood flow is diminished or blocked. Obstruction in the brain's blood vessels can result in tissue damage (stroke); if damage is extensive, dementia can result.

audition The sense of hearing.

auditory nerve A bundle of nerve fibers extending from the cochlea to the brain and containing two branches: the cochlear nerve for the transmission of auditory information and the vestibular nerve for the relaying of information related to balance.

autonomic nervous system The division of the peripheral nervous system responsible for regulating the activity of the internal organs; includes the sympathetic and parasympathetic nervous systems.

autoreceptor Presynaptic receptor that monitors the amount of a neuron's own neurotransmitter and so helps regulate the production and release of the chemical.

autosomal dominant disorders Diseases that are inherited from a dominant gene on one of the twenty-two pairs of non-sex chromosomes.

axon The fiberlike extension of a neuron through which the cell sends information to target cells.

axonal transport An energy-requiring intracellular transport system by which the neuron maintains the viability of its dendritic branchings and its synaptic terminals.

basal ganglia A cluster of ganglia located at the base of the cortex composed of the caudate nucleus, globus pallidus, and the putamen; play an important part in the motor system and possibly in some forms of procedural memory.

basilar membrane In the inner ear, this membrane separates the cochlear canal and the tympanic canal. Its movement in relation to the tectorial membrane forces the cilia of the receptor cells to bend, producing the sensation of sound.

Betz cells Cortical neurons that communicate directly with the motor neurons of the spinal cord.

bipolar depression See **manic-depressive psychosis.**

bipolar neurons In the retina, a neuron that transmits information from the rods and cones to the ganglion cells within the eye.

blastocyst Embryo about the fifth day after fertilization, being a hollow sphere of cells with a small mass of cells adhering to one point on its inner surface.

blood/brain barrier Diffusional barrier created by astrocytes and cells in the walls of the blood vessels within the brain; prevents some blood-borne substances, like neurotransmitters, from entering the brain from the bloodstream.

BOLD Blood Oxygenation Level Dependent contrast is based on the fact that the magnetic properties of hemoglobin depend on its oxygenation state. Thus, when tissues are depleted of oxygen (e.g., deoxygenated), they become paramagnetic; when they contain abundant oxygen, they become diamagnetic. The local magnetic field surrounding blood-containing vessels is altered when the hemoglobin paramagnetic, leading to a decrease in magnetic resonance (MR) signal.

brainstem The vital core components of the brain controlling functions essential for survival, including respiration, heart rhythm, blood pressure, eating, drinking, and sleep.

Broca's area Brain region located in the frontal lobe of the left hemisphere and responsible for the production of the sounds of speech. Damage to this area results in Broca's aphasia, a disorder that is characterized by impaired speech production, although comprehension of language is unimpaired.

bulimia Eating disorder in which the person eats excessive amounts of food and then induces vomiting or takes laxatives to force the food out of the body before calories can be absorbed; often associated with anorexia nervosa.

Cannon-Bard theory Theory of emotion formulated by Walter Cannon and modified by Phillip Bard, postulating that the psychological experience of emotion and the associated physiological reactions are simultaneous.

cataract A visual disturbance, often a result of aging, in which the lens of the eye becomes clouded.

catecholamines The neurotransmitters dopamine, epinephrine, and norepinephrine; these function both in the brain and in the sympathetic nervous system.

catecholamine hypothesis of depression Proposal that depression is caused by a loss of transmission at the catecholamine synapses in the brain.

CAT scan See **computerized axial tomography**.

central nervous system The brain and spinal cord.

cerebellum A relatively large structure attached to the roof of the hindbrain. Its intricate, regular cellular architecture helps control movement by connections to the pons, medulla, spinal cord, and thalamus. Also may serve to store some responses learned through classical conditioning.

cerebral cortex The outermost layer of the cerebral hemispheres of the brain; responsible for all forms of conscious activity.

cerebrospinal fluid Liquid found within the ventricles of the brain and the central canal of the spinal cord; acts in conjunction with the meninges as a shock absorber for the brain and spinal cord.

cholecystokinin Hormone released from the lining of the stomach during the early stages of digestion; acts as a powerful suppressant of normal eating. Also found in the brain in small amounts.

chorda tympani A branch of the facial nerve innervating taste receptors of the tongue; relays information from the front portion of the tongue to the brain.

choroid plexus A group of specialized blood vessels, located in the ventricles, that produce the cerebrospinal fluid.

cingulate gyrus A component of the limbic system, encircling the hippocampus and other limbic structures.

circadian rhythm A cycle of behavior or physiological change lasting approximately 24 hours.

classical conditioning Learning in which a stimulus that naturally produces a specific response (unconditioned stimulus) is repeatedly paired with a neutral stimulus (conditioned stimulus), with the result that the conditioned stimulus eventually comes to evoke the same response as the unconditioned stimulus; also known as Pavlovian conditioning.

cochlea Snail-shaped, fluid-filled organ of the inner ear responsible for transducing mechanical energy to neural energy to produce auditory sensation.

cochlear canal One of three sections of the cochlea.

cochlear nerve A branch of the auditory nerve responsible for transmitting auditory information from the cochlea to the brain.

cognition The process or processes by which an organism gains knowledge of or becomes aware of events or objects in its environment, especially as regards the organism's relationship to that environment.

cognitive dissonance   Leon Festinger's theory that people are motivated to avoid disharmony and achieve consistency between their actions and their beliefs.

computerized axial tomography (CAT) scan   An imaging method using a computer and X-rays to produce a sequence of two-dimensional "slices" through the brain; allows neurologists to diagnose and localize lesions within the brain.

conditioned response   In classical conditioning, the learned response to a previously neutral stimulus.

conditioned stimulus   In classical conditioning, a previously neutral stimulus that has come to evoke the same response as an unconditioned stimulus with which it has repeatedly been paired.

cone   A primary receptor neuron for vision located in the retina and most densely in the fovea; sensitive to light of color and used primarily for daytime vision.

consciousness   Awareness of one's own mental and/or physical actions.

convergent circuit   Neural-connection pattern in which a target cell receives simultaneous incoming messages from a number of transmitting cells.

cornea   A thin, curved, transparent membrane on the surface of the front of the eye; begins the focusing process for vision.

corpus callosum   The large bundle of nerve fibers linking the left and right cerebral hemispheres.

corpus luteum   The follicular tissue remaining after the release of the ovum during ovulation; under the influence of luteinizing hormone, it secretes large quantities of progesterone.

cortisol   Hormone manufactured by the adrenal cortex; secreted in its greatest quantity before dawn in human beings, readying the body for the activities of the coming day.

cross cuing   In split-brain patients, the use by one hemisphere of cues available to it to detect information supposedly only accessible to the other hemisphere. Use of sounds, for example, to identify an object that cannot be seen.

cytoplasm   All material enclosed by the plasma membrane of a cell.

cytoplasmic organelles   See **organelles.**

declarative knowledge   Memory of facts and experiences; tends to be knowledge that can be verbally communicated. See also **procedural knowledge.**

delta waves   Brain wave activity, at approximately four cycles per second, associated with relatively deep sleep (stage 4).

delirium   A condition of extreme mental confusion, often accompanied by excess activity; generally due to metabolic problems; usually reversible.

dementia   A sustained, multidimensional loss of cognitive ability due to brain damage; generally irreversible.

dendrite   Treelike protrusion from the soma of a neuron; along with the soma, constitutes the receiving zone for messages from other cells.

depolarization   See **action potential.**

desynchronization   The uncoupling of two or more physiological rhythms that ordinarily work together.

dexamethasone suppression test   A diagnostic procedure used to evaluate the regulatory effectiveness of the endocrine system in depressed patients.

diencephalon   The portion of the forebrain composed of the thalamus and hypothalamus.

differentiation   See Table 3.1, Processes of Neural Development.

diffuse enteric nervous system   A subdivision of the peripheral nervous system; regulates the digestive tract.

dimorphism   Male-female anatomical difference.

divergent circuit   Neural-connection pattern in which an individual neuron sends simultaneous messages to a number of other neurons.

dopamine   Neurotransmitter; a catecholamine. Known to function in the control of complex movements, since dopamine-transmitting neurons are destroyed in victims of Parkinson's disease. Also thought to function in regulating emotional responses and to play a role in the expression of schizophrenia.

dorsal horn   Area of the spinal cord where many nerve fibers from peripheral pain receptors synapse with other ascending nerve fibers.

dorsal raphe nucleus Group of serotonin-containing neurons in the pons that play a role in the regulation of sleep and waking.

Down syndrome A disorder in human beings caused by nondisjunction, which in turn leads to the presence of an extra copy of chromosome 21; characterized by severe mental retardation and various physical abnormalities. Formerly known as mongolism.

dyslexia Disturbance in the ability to read not caused by mental retardation or physical injury.

ectoderm One of three distinct layers of cells differentiating from the embryonic disc very early in embryonic development; develops into the nervous system, as well as the skin, hair, and fingernails.

electroencephalogram (EEG) Recording of the electrical activity of the brain, achieved by placing electrodes on the surface of the skull.

embryonic disc The flat plate of cells that forms across the inside of the blastocyst during the eighth day of prenatal development; from it the embryo will develop.

endocrine organ Organ that secretes a substance (hormone) directly into the bloodstream to regulate the cellular activity of certain other organs; also known as a gland.

endoplasmic reticulum The network of intracellular membrane channels by which substances are distributed to different parts of the cell. In neurons, rough endoplasmic reticulum is studded with ribosomes and is very active in the production of products for outside secretion, namely neurotransmitters; smooth endoplasmic reticulum, also known as the Golgi apparatus, forms the membrane packages for these cellular products.

endorphins Neurotransmitters in the brain that can produce cellular and behavioral effects like those of morphine.

epinephrine Hormone released by the adrenal medulla; acts with norepinephrine to activate the sympathetic division of the autonomic nervous system; also has limited functions within the pons and medulla. Sometimes called adrenalin.

estrogen A group of sex steroid hormones found more abundantly in females than males; responsible for female sexual maturation.

evoked potentials A measure of the brain's electrical activity in response to sensory stimuli; achieved by placing electrodes on the surface of the skull, repeatedly presenting a given stimulus, then using a computer to average the results.

excitation Synaptic message in which one cell commands another to activity.

exocrine gland Gland whose hormones do not enter the bloodstream but reach their target cells through ducts.

external auditory canal A part of the outer ear responsible, along with the pinna, for focusing and funneling auditory stimuli to the structures of the middle ear.

filopodia Fingerlike extensions of the growth cone; a temporary structure at the growing ends of developing axons.

follicle Hollow ball of tissue containing the ovum.

follicle-stimulating hormone (FSH) Hormone released by the anterior pituitary gland; its release is triggered by the hypothalamus. It stimulates the production of sperm in the male and growth of the follicle in females.

forebrain Largest major division of the brain; its subdivisions are the diencephalon and telencephalon. The forebrain is credited with the highest intellectual functions.

fornix The two-way fiber system of axons connecting the hypothalamus and the hippocampus.

fovea A small area of the retina that contains only cones and where visual acuity is highest.

frontal lobe One of the four subdivisions of each hemisphere of the cerebral cortex. The frontal lobe has a role in controlling motor functions and associating the functions of other cortical areas.

functional MRI (fMRI) The process of imaging brain function using magnetic resonance imaging. Brain function is detected either as a change in the BOLD contrast secondary to the hemodynamic response, or as an increase in cerebral blood flow.

gamma-amino butyric acid (GABA) Amino acid transmitter in the brain whose primary function is to inhibit the firing of neurons.

ganglia Small encapsulated clusters of neural cells that direct internal muscles and glands;

located entirely outside the central nervous system.

ganglion cells   A layer of retinal neurons whose axons form the optic nerve.

general adaptation syndrome   Theory by Hans Selye explaining animals' physiological reaction to stress; consists of three phases: (1) alarm, (2) resistance, and (3) exhaustion.

gland   See **endocrine organ.**

glaucoma   A disease of the eye marked by high pressure within the eyeball, which compresses the retina and destroys the ability of the rods and cones to function.

glia   Specialized cells that serve a supporting role in the nervous system. See also **astrocyte: oliogodendrocyte.**

glossopharyngeal nerve   Cranial nerve that conveys taste information from the posterior portion of the tongue to the brain.

Golgi method   An early and successful staining method to reveal the complete form of a nerve cell for microscopic analysis.

gonad   Primary sex gland: testis in males and ovary in females.

gonadotropin-releasing hormone (GnRH)   Hormone secreted by the hypothalamus initiating the female reproductive cycle; stimulates the pituitary gland to produce and secrete follicle-stimulating hormone and luteinizing hormone.

granule cell neurons   Nerve cells within the cerebellum that form a thick layer beneath the Purkinje cells; believed to play a role in motor coordination and balance.

growth cone   A distinctive structure at the growing end of most axons; site where most new material is added to the axon.

gustation   The sense of taste.

habituation   Simple learning in which a stimulus that an organism originally responded to is presented so often that the organism stops responding to it.

hair cells   Auditory receptor cells, having cilia that project from their tops. The cilia bend from the relative actions of the basilar membrane, in which the cells are anchored, and the tectorial membrane, producing the nerve impulses that start on their path to the brain.

hemispherectomy   Surgical removal of the cortical covering of an entire hemisphere.

hierarchical circuit   Neural-connection pattern in which cells are linked as in a chain, with information ascending or descending from one level of the circuit to the next. Pattern common to the sensory systems.

hindbrain   Region of the brain responsible for controlling internal body states and motor coordination, and also serving as a relay region between the spinal cord and other areas of the brain; composed of the pons, medulla oblongata, and cerebellum.

hippocampus   Seahorse-shaped structure located within the telencephalon and considered an important part of the limbic system; functions in learning, memory, and emotion.

homeostasis   The process by which the body maintains a uniform internal environment.

horizontal cells   Inhibitory local-circuit neurons that restrict the spread of the visual signal within the retina.

hormones   Chemical messengers secreted by endocrine and exocrine glands to regulate the cellular activity of target cells.

Huntington's disease   A hereditary neurologic disease characterized by motor movement disorders, slurred speech, and progresively worsening mental capacities. Symptoms do not begin to appear until patient is about 40 years of age.

hyperopia   Also known as far-sightedness; inability to focus well on close objects. This common vision problem arises from the retina being too close to the lens so that the image of nearby objects fails to fall sharply on the retina.

hypophysiotropic hormones   Hormones secreted by the hypothalamus via the pituitary-portal circulatory system for the regulation of the pituitary gland.

hypothalamus   A complex brain structure composed of many nuclei with various functions; functions include regulating visceral integrative functions, monitoring information from the autonomic nervous system, and controlling the functions of the pituitary gland. Located under the thalamus in the diencephalon.

idiopathic hypogonadotropic hypogonadism Rare genetic deficiency in which there is no production of testosterone at puberty, even though the male has the normal XY genotype.

imprinting A species-specific learning behavior in certain birds whereby the young become attached to and follow the first moving object they encounter after hatching.

incus A component of the ossicles, the incus receives auditory vibrations from the malleus and, in turn, passes on these vibrations to the stapes; commonly called the anvil.

induction See Table 3.1, Processes of Neural Development.

infarct Damage to brain tissue produced by circulatory obstruction of the brain's blood vessels and resultant lack of circulation.

inferior colliculi Collections of neurons and their connections, protruding from the upper surface of the midbrain, that relay auditory information to the brain.

infradian rhythm Cycle of behavioral or physiological change occurring over a period longer than 24 hours (e.g., hibernation of some animals).

inhibition In reference to neurons, a synaptic message that prevents the recipient cell from firing.

intercellular Referring to activity between two or more cells.

intermediate zone Layer of cells formed between the ventricular and marginal zones of the neural tube during the proliferative phase of neural development.

intracellular Referring to activity within a given cell.

ions Electrically charged atoms.

iris A circular muscle that alters the amount of light entering the eye by dilating or constricting the pupil, the opening in its center.

islet cells of the pancreas Endocrine organ that secretes insulin to increase glucose uptake, glucagon to increase glucose levels, and somatostatin for the regulation of insulin and glucagon secretion.

James-Lange theory William James's theory of emotion, based on the ideas of Carl Lange, proposing that the experience of emotion results from an individual's perception of his or her own physiological changes, such as increased heart rate.

juxtaglomerular cell Specialized kidney cell that, when blood pressure drops, secretes the enzyme renin into the bloodstream; renin converts angiotensinogen to angiotensin II in a process to elevate blood pressure to normal levels.

Klinefelter's syndrome Chromosomal abnormality in which the individual has an XXY genotype instead of the normal male XY. These males show some feminization as adolescents and adults, having little beard growth, small penis and testis, and unusually high voices; many show some breast development during puberty.

Korsakoff's syndrome A disease associated with chronic alcoholism, resulting from a deficiency of vitamin B_1. Patients sustain damage to the left dorsomedial nucleus of the thalamus and loss of neurons in the cerebellum and frontal cortex. Consequently, they suffer severe cognitive deficits.

lateral geniculate nucleus Thalamic nucleus specialized for the processing and relaying of visual information.

lens An adjustable structure of the eye that completes the focusing process initiated by the cornea.

leucocyte pyrogen An uncharacterized substance released by the white blood cells of a person with an infection; activates heat-gain mechanisms and drives body temperature up.

limbic system A group of brain structures, including the amygdala, hippocampus, septum, and basal ganglia, that work in alliance to help regulate emotion, memory, and certain aspects of movement.

lipofuscin A fatty pigment deposited in the cells of many organs during the aging process; known as "age spots" when the pigment appears in the skin.

lipoprotein lipase (LPL)   Enzyme responsible for the removal of fats from the blood and for the ability to store them in adipocytes: LPL levels may be part of the signaling and control system for the regulation of body fat.

local circuit   Simple neural-connection pattern with limited range of influence; operates as a filter within one or more levels of a hierarchical circuit to broaden or narrow the flow of information as it moves through the hierarchy. May be excitatory or inhibitory.

locus coeruleus   Within the pons, a concentrated set of neural cell bodies whose axons secrete the neurotransmitter norepinephrine.

long-term memory   The final phase of memory in which information storage may last from hours to a lifetime.

lordosis   Receptive sexual posture of some female mammals, facilitating intercourse and necessary for fertilization to occur.

luteinizing hormone   Hormone secreted by the pituitary gland; during the human female reproductive cycle, causes the wall of the follicle within the ovary to break and release the mature ovum and stimulates the production of progesterone by the corpus lutem. In males, stimulates the production of testosterone.

Magnetic resonance imaging (MRI)   The process (most often used with human subjects) that produces images using signals that arise from nuclear magnetic resonance. Spatial discrimination of the signals is achieved by the application of magnetic field gradients. The contrast of the images can be tuned to certain parameters that are specific to certain tissues (e.g., those containing white matter fibers) or to certain functions (e.g., memory, emotion, etc.).

malleus   A component of the ossicles, the malleus receives the vibrations of the tympanic membrane and passes them on to the incus; commonly called the hammer.

mania   An affective psychosis in which the patient displays inappropriate elation, unconcern for important problems, overconfidence, and hyperactivity in both motor and speech patterns.

manic-depressive psychosis   A severe affective disorder characterized by alternating episodes of mania and depression; also known as bipolar depression.

marginal zone   The outer surface of the embryonic neutral tube.

medulla oblongata   The brain region between the pons and spinal cord that operates as a control center for respiration, blood pressure, and heart rhythm.

meiosis   The process of "chromosome reduction" by which one member of each pair of chromosomes is separated and compartmentalized in the germ cells, egg, and sperm, and whose genomes correspond to half those of somatic cells.

melatonin   A hormone, converted from serotonin in the pineal gland and released by it into the bloodstream; in many animals, melatonin effects physiological changes related to time and lighting cycles.

memory consolidation   The changes, physical and psychological, that take place as the brain organizes and restructures information that may become a permanent part of memory.

meninges   The membranes that encase the central nervous system.

mesoderm   Layer of cells that develops between the ectoderm and endoderm in embryonic development.

method of loci   A mnemonic device in which a person visualizes a familiar place and then imagines placing things to be remembered at prominent points along the route. When recall is performed, the person mentally revisits the place, retracing the path and finding the items placed at each location.

microtubule   Organelle that acts as a fine "strut" to help maintain a cell's structure and, in neurons, guides the transport of substances to the axon or dendrites from the soma and back to the soma from these protrusions.

midbrain   Smallest major region of the brain, between the pons and diencephalon; it has few distinctive features, among them being the inferior and superior colliculi.

migration   See Table 3.1, Processes of Neural Development.

minicolumn   Basic organizational unit of the cortex consisting of vertically connected neurons that span the layers of the cortex.

mitochondria Organelles that provide energy for the cell by converting sugar and oxygen into special energy molecules.

mitosis Cell division and duplication resulting in two daughter cells.

monoamine oxidase (MAO) The brain and liver enzyme that normally breaks down the monoamines norepinephrine, serotonin, and dopamine.

motivation In psychology, a hypothetical state inferred from an organism's goal-directed behavior.

motor neuron Neuron that carries information from the central nervous system to the muscle.

mnemonic devices Techniques to aid in storing and recalling memories.

multiple sclerosis Neurological disorder in which the myelin covering of some neurons is destroyed; patient suffers various neural and muscular dysfunctions, depending on the nerves involved.

myasthenia gravis Disease in which the acetylcholine receptors on the muscle cells are destroyed, so that muscles can no longer receive the signal to contract.

myelin Compact wrapping material that surrounds and insulates axons of some neurons; produced by oligodendrocytes in the central nervous system and Schwann cells in the peripheral nervous system.

myopia Also known as near-sightedness; inability to focus well on far objects. This common vision problem is caused by the eyeball being too deep, so that the retina is too far from the lens and the image of distant objects fails to fall sharply on the retina.

N-acetyltransferase (5-hydroxy-*N*-acetyltransferase) Enzyme produced within the pineal gland of some animals and functioning in the conversion of serotonin to melatonin; determines the amount of melatonin released by the pineal gland into the bloodstream.

neglect syndrome Condition found in some patients with extensive damage to the posterior area of the right cerebral hemisphere; patient acts as if the left side of his or her perceived space has ceased to exist.

neocortex The cerebral cortex.

neostriatum The caudate nucleus, a structure within the basal ganglia that receives information from all areas of the cerebral cortex, including all forms of sensory information and information regarding the motor system.

nerve-growth factor (NGF) Substance whose role is to guide neuronal growth during embryonic development, especially in the peripheral nervous system.

neural crest Cluster of young neurons remaining outside the neural tube after its formation; develops into the peripheral autonomic nervous system.

neural plate Embryonic structure that develops from the ectoderm and from which the neural tube develops.

neural tube Hollow tube formed early in embryonic development, from the fusing of parallel ridges that form across the neural plate; the top of the tube becomes the brain, and the remainder becomes the spinal cord.

neuroblast In embryonic development, a cell destined to develop into a neuron.

neurofibrillary tangles Skeins of microtubules that have proliferated inside a brain neuron and eventually replace the neuron, making the cell nonfunctional. Diagnostic criterion for Alzheimer's disease.

neuroglia See **astrocyte; oligodendrocyte.**

neurology The branch of medicine concerned with the study of the diseases of the brain.

neuron Nerve cell; specialized for the transmission of information.

neurosis Behavioral disorder in which patient suffers anxiety or phobia or performs obsessive-compulsive acts.

neurotransmitter Chemical released by nerve cells at a synapse for the purpose of relaying information.

nociceptors In animals, nerve endings that signal the sensation of pain; in human beings called "pain receptors."

norepinephrine Neurotransmitter, a catecholamine, produced both in the brain (notably, in the locus coeruleus) and in the peripheral nervous system (the sympathetic division of the autonomic nervous system). Has diverse behavioral effects.

nucleus In the brain, an aggregation of neurons

that is anatomically distinct from surrounding matter; cells making up a nucleus usually function as a unit.

nucleus locus coeruleus   See **locus coeruleus.**

nucleus of the solitary tract   Synaptic relay station in the medulla; receives information regarding taste from the chorda tympani, glossopharyngeal nerve, and the vagus nerve and passes it on to the thalamic arcuate nucleus.

obsessive-compulsive behavior   Overpowering drive to perform apparently irrational activities; symptom of neurosis.

occipital lobe   One of the four subdivisions of each hemisphere of the cerebral cortex; specialized for visual perception.

ocular dominance columns   In layer 4 of the primary visual cortex, the columns of cells that alternately receive input from the left and right eye.

oddity problem   A learning procedure in which animals are shown two identical objects and one odd one and are rewarded for picking the odd object. After a number of successful trials with the same three objects, the objects are changed. The goal is to have the subjects form a concept of oddness.

olfaction   The sense of smell.

oligodendrocyte   Specialized glial cell found in the central nervous system; responsible for myelination of neurons.

operant conditioning   Learning theory stating that behavior is shaped by its consequences: a behavior that brings reward will be learned and repeated; one that brings punishment is unlikely to be repeated.

opponent-process theory   The theory proposing that color vision is possible by the nature of the "opposing" characteristics of certain color pairs and the nature of the receptive fields of the retina's ganglion cells interacting with the horizontal cells.

ophthalmologist   Medical doctor specializing in visual problems and whose duties may include prescribing glasses or contact lenses.

optic chiasm   Area where the optic nerves from each eye come together and some fibers cross over to the opposite hemisphere of the brain; at the base of the front of the hypothalamus.

optic nerve   Bundle of nerve fibers (the collected axons of the retina's ganglion cells) that carries visual information from the retina of each eye to the optic chiasm, where it becomes the optic tract.

optic tract   The continuation of the axon bundles after the cross-over at the optic chiasm; axons of the optic tract run to one of four second-level receiving centers.

organelles   Small structures within a cell that maintain the cells and do their work: for example, mitochondria, microtubules, and endoplasmic reticulum.

organizational effects   Prenatal effects of hormones on cells of the brain to sensitize the cells so that they will later respond to the presence of the hormone; the hormones probably change a cell's anatomical development by altering its genetic messages.

organ of Corti   The auditory receptor organ found within the cochlea; composed of the hair cells, basilar membrane, and tectorial membrane.

ossicles   The three tiny bones that compose the middle ear; includes the malleus, incus, and stapes.

oval window   A membrane-covered opening in the bone surrounding the cochlea; it receives auditory vibrations from the stapes and transmits them into the fluid-filled cochlea.

ovulation   The process by which an ovum matures and is released from the ovary.

ovum   The female egg cell.

oxytocin   A peptide hormone released by the axons that comprise the posterior pituitary; causes contraction of the uterus during the final stages of labor. Its function in males, where it is equally abundant, is unknown.

Papez circuit   A set of interconnected brain structures that James W. Papez proposed functions in the experience of emotion. This set of structures constitutes much of what is now known as the limbic system.

papillae   The small bumps on the surface of the tongue around which the taste buds lie.

parasympathetic nervous system   A branch of the autonomic nervous system concerned with the conservation of the body's energy and resources during relaxed states.

parathyroid Endocrine organ that secretes calcitonin and functions in maintaining normal calcium balance in the body.

parietal lobe One of the four subdivisions of each hemisphere of the cerebral cortex; plays a role in sensory processes and in the perception of spatial location.

Parkinson's disease A neurological disease whose symptoms include fine tremor, rigidity of movement, and difficulty in initiating movements and in terminating movements once started; caused by deficient amounts of the neurotransmitter dopamine due to destruction of dopamine-producing neurons in the substantia nigra and the ventral tegmentum.

pathology The branch of medicine concerned with study of the cellular dysfunctions that cause disease.

Pavlovian conditioning See classical conditioning.

pellagra A disease caused by dietary insufficiency of niacin, resulting in delirium, confusion, and general disorientation often accompanied by periods of mania.

peptides Chains of amino acids that function as neurotransmitters, neuromodulators, or hormones.

perception Awareness of objects and events in the environment attained through the brain's interpretation of sensory data.

periaqueductal gray area A cluster of neurons lying in the thalamus and pons; contains endorphin-producing neurons and opiate receptor sites and thus can modulate the sensation of pain.

peripheral nervous system A division of the nervous system consisting of all the nerves not part of the brain or spinal cord.

peristalsis Contractions of the circular and longitudinal muscles of stomach and intestines that propel food through the digestive system; innervated by the diffuse enteric system.

phase-advance The adjustment of a biological clock after it gains time relative to the 24-hour day; occurs after eastbound air travel.

phase-delay The adjustment of a biological clock after it loses time relative to the 24-hour day; occurs after westbound air travel.

phase shift A change in the timing of one's biological clock with respect to clock time. See **phase-advance; phase-delay.**

phenylketonuria (PKU) A hereditary abnormality caused by absence of an enzyme needed to metabolize the amino acid phenylalanine, which is present in many common foods. If untreated (treatment is a diet low in phenylalin), phenylalanine accumulates, and severe retardation results.

phobia Unrealistic and persistent fear of particular things or events; a symptom of neurosis.

phosphorylation The attachment of phosphate molecules to another substance, often altering the character of the substance involved. In the cell membrane of neurons, the substances believed to become phosphorylated are proteins—specifically, the proteins composing the ion channels. Such chemical change could alter a channel's specificity (e.g., from sodium to potassium).

pineal gland An endocrine organ found in the brain; in some animals, it seems to serve as a light-influenced biological clock.

pinna The external part of the ear, serving, along with the external auditory canal, to focus and funnel auditory stimuli to the structures of the middle ear.

pitch Auditory sensation determined by the number of cycles per second of the sound wave; many cycles per second corresponds with sounds of high pitch, and fewer cycles per second corresponds with sounds of low pitch.

pituitary gland Endocrine organ closely linked with the hypothalamus; composed of two lobes, the anterior and posterior. It secretes a number of hormones that regulate the activity of other endocrine organs in the body.

pituitary-portal circulation A restricted network of blood vessels that carry blood only between the base of the hypothalamus and the anterior lobe of the pituitary gland.

planum temporale The upper surface of the temporal lobe; enlarged on the side of the dominant hemisphere.

plaque An amorphous collection of amyloid protein in the cortical gray matter of patients with Alzheimer's disease.

plasma membrane Cell membrane; the thin layer of tissue that surrounds a cell and forms a boundary between the cell's interior and its environment.

plasticity Capacity for adjusting to change; characteristic of early neural development, although not limited to early development.

pons A component of the hindbrain that works in conjunction with the medulla and diencephalon to control respiration and heart rhythms. The pons is a major route by which the forebrain sends information to and receives information from the spinal cord and peripheral nervous system.

porphyria Inherited metabolic disease in which the body is unable properly to construct the hemoglobin molecules that allow red blood cells to transport oxygen; results in an organic mental disorder characterized by periods of normalcy fluctuating with episodes of agitation, depression, and disturbance of memory.

positron emission transaxial tomography (PET) scan A diagnostic imaging procedure enabling scientists to map activity (e.g., glucose utilization) within the living brain by recording the emission of positrons from injected molecules (e.g., glucose) labeled with positron-emitting compounds.

postganglionic fibers Within the autonomic nervous system, the axons that emerge from the neurons of the autonomic ganglia and connect directly with target organs.

postsynaptic neuron Neuron receiving information across the synapse from a presynaptic neuron.

preganglionic fibers Within the autonomic nervous system, the axons that connect spinal nerves with autonomic ganglia.

presbyopia The progressive loss of near vision associated with increasing age.

presynaptic neuron Neuron sending information across the synapse to a postsynpatic neuron.

primary visual cortex Major structural component of the visual system, responsible for processing of visual information received from the thalamic nuclei. Information from the primary visual cortex, also known as area 17 or the striate cortex, is then distributed throughout a hierarchy of other vision-related regions of the cerebral cortex.

proactive inhibition A process in which previously learned information interferes with the learning of new information because the contents of both sets of information are similar.

procedural knowledge In contrast to declarative knowledge, knowledge of how to do something—skills. Generally, procedural knowledge is difficult to express verbally.

process A tentaclelike extension of a cell.

progesterone During the female reproductive cycle, hormone secreted by the corpus luteum that increases the blood supply to the uterine wall, preparing it for the egg's implantation should fertilization occur.

programmed cell death/synapse refinement See Table 3.1, Processes of Neural Development.

proliferation See Table 3.1, Processes of Neural Development.

proprioception The ability to sense limb position and muscle tension; monitored by sensory receptors in muscles and tendons.

psychopharmacology The study of the effects of drugs on behavior.

psychoses Severe mental disorders including the affective disorders and schizophrenia; often chronic and severely incapacitating.

pupil The opening in the iris; responsible for regulating the amount of light entering the eye.

pulvinar A large nucleus in the thalamus receiving visual input from the superior colliculus and, ultimately, from the retina.

Purkinje cells The primary output cells of the cerebellar cortex, they integrate information from the cerebral cortex, thalamus, medulla, and spinal cord regarding location and position of the head, limbs, and trunk.

pyramidal tract The large nerve-fiber bundle composed of the axons of Betz cells and other cells of the motor cortex. One tract originates in each hemisphere, and they cross over from the side of origin to the other side of the spinal cord; thus, damage to one side of the motor cortex produces motor disabilities on the opposite side of the body.

rapid eye movement (REM) sleep The fifth and deepest stage of sleep; although there is rapid movement of the eye muscles, there is total relaxation of the skeletal muscles. Most vivid dreams occur during REM sleep.

receptive field A receptor cell's region of sensitivity.

Reissner's membrane Membrane within the cochlea separating the vestibular canal and the cochlear canal.

renin Enzyme secreted by juxtaglomerular cells of the kidneys when blood pressure drops; converts angiotensinogen into angiotensin II in a process to restore blood pressure levels to normal.

resting potential The electrical potential across the membrane of an unstimulated neuron, with the inside of the cell negative relative to the outside.

reticular formation A zone of extended nonnuclear structures within the midbrain, pons, and medulla that plays an important role in arousal (sleep and wakefulness) and attention; its nonspecific neurons receive sensory information from various neural sources and act as a filter, passing on only information that is novel or persistent.

retina The light-sensitive, image-recording part of the eye; has a highly organized, layered structure composed of primary receptor neurons (rods and cones), bipolar neurons, amacrine cells, and ganglion cells.

retinotopic organization The correspondence between points in space and comparable points in each retina; despite the crossing over of some nerve fibers of each optic nerve at the optic chiasm. This organization is maintained throughout the organization of the nervous system.

reuptake The process by which some presynaptic neurons draw back excessive neurotransmitter into its vesicles.

ribosomes Organelles for protein synthesis, both for products to be secreted outside the cell (attached to rough endoplasmic reticulum) and for products (enzymes, structural proteins) used within the cell ("free" ribosomes).

rod A sensory neuron located in the periphery of the retina; sensitive to light of low intensity and specialized for nighttime vision.

rough endoplasmic reticulum See **endoplasmic reticulum.**

round window A membrane-covered opening in the cochlea which allows the fluid within the cochlea to move back and forth upon stimulation from the stapes.

sacral segments Lower area of the spinal cord;

along with the brainstem, receives preganglionic information for the parasympathetic nervous system.

satiety factors Digestive hormones secreted into the gut during a meal, influencing when a meal should end.

schizophrenia A group of severe and generally chronic disorders of mental functioning characterized by disturbed thinking, feelings, and behaviors.

Schwann cell Specialized glial cell found in the peripheral nervous system; responsible for the production of myelin.

sensitization A behavior in which an organism learns to respond vigorously to a previously neutral stimulus.

septum A structure of the telencephalon and part of the limbic system; forms the wall between the fluid-filled lateral ventricles.

serotonin A monoamine neurotransmitter believed to function in temperature regulation, sensory perception, and the onset of sleep. Neurons using serotonin as a transmitter are found in the brain and in the gut.

short-term memory A phase of memory in which a limited amount of information may be held for several minutes.

sleep spindles Bursts of brain wave activity synchronized at about 12 to 15 cycles per second but lasting less than one second at a time; interrupts low-voltage, slow activity during stage-3 sleep.

smooth endoplasmic reticulum See **endoplasmic reticulum.**

soma The cell body of a neuron.

somatic sensation Relating to the sense of touch.

somatostatin A ubiquitous peptide hormone produced by the pancreatic islets (acting to regulate insulin and glucagon secretion), by cells in the lining of the gut (acting to slow peristalsis during nutrient transport), and by neurons in the brain and autonomic nervous system.

stapes A component of the ossicles, the stapes has a footplate that transmits auditory vibrations to the inner ear via the oval window; commonly known as the stirrup.

stimulus An environmental event capable of being detected by sensory receptors.

stimulus detector unit Component of the nervous system consisting of specialized sensory receptor neurons.

striatum See **neostriatum**.

substance P Neuropeptide that, among other possible functions, appears to be a specialized transmitter of pain-related information from peripheral nerves to the central system.

substantia nigra Within the midbrain, a concentrated set of neural cell bodies that secrete the neurotransmitter dopamine.

subventricular zone Layer of cells forming between the ventricular and intermediate zones of the neural tube; region where many neurons and glial cells form and migrate to form the forebrain.

sulci The deep grooves in the cerebral hemispheres of primates and certain other mammals (singular **sulcus**).

summation The aggregation of neurotransmitter and its subsequent action potential on a single nerve cell due either to (1) a presynaptic neuron firing a number of times in rapid succession or (2) numerous presynaptic neurons firing simultaneously.

superior colliculi Nuclei protruding from the top of the midbrain; functions as a relay station in the visual system, along with the integration of information used in spatial orientation.

suprachiasmatic nuclei Hypothalamic structures considered the chief pacemaker of the brain, synchronizing many of the circadian rhythms of the body.

sylvian fissure The large groove in the cortex dividing the temporal lobe from the rest of the cortex; longer and straighter in the left hemisphere.

sympathetic nervous system A branch of the autonomic nervous system responsible for mobilizing the body's energy and resources during times of stress and arousal.

synapse The area of contact between the axon of a presynaptic neuron and the dendrite or soma of a postsynaptic neuron; site of information transfer between nerve cells.

synaptic transmission The process of information transfer at the synapse.

synaptic gap The small space separating the presynaptic and postsynaptic cells.

synaptic vesicles The tiny storage organelles ("bladders") within an axon where a neuron's neurotransmitter is stored; each vesicle contains thousands of copies of the transmitter molecules.

tachistoscope An instrument that flashes visual stimuli for short, regular intervals onto the visual field, used for the testing of hemispheric dominance.

tectorial membrane Component of the organ of Corti, this rigid flap of tissue extends over the hair cells and works in conjunction with the basilar membrane in the sensation of auditory stimuli.

telencephalon Portion of the forebrain containing the cerebral cortex.

temporal lobe One of the four major subdivisions of each hemisphere of the cerebral cortex; functions in auditory perception, speech, and complex visual perceptions.

thalamus Portion of the diencephalon, serving as a relay station for almost all sensory information coming into and out of the forebrian.

thyroid An endocrine organ that secretes thyroxin and acts in the regulation of body growth and rate of metabolism.

timbre Auditory sensation that is rich mixture of frequencies and allows for discriminations between similar sound sources.

trophic factors Chemical substances thought to be transferred from the mesoderm to the ectoderm to influence embryonic development.

Turner's syndrome Chromosomal abnormality in which individuals have only one X chromosome and no X or Y to make a pair. These females, designated as XO, are characterized as being sterile, short, and immature looking, along with having poor visual-spatial abilities.

tympanic canal One of the three sections of the cochlea through which fluid passes during the sensation of auditory stimuli.

tympanic membrane Commonly known as the eardrum, this thin, fibrous membrane vibrates in proportion to the intensity of sound waves, passing on the vibrations to the structures of the middle ear.

unconditioned response In classical conditioning, a response that naturally follows the presentation of an unconditioned stimulus.

unconditioned stimulus In classical conditioning, a stimulus that naturally evokes a specific response without training.

ultradian rhythm Cycle of behavioral and physiological change that is repeated more than once a day (e.g., human sleep cycle).

unipolar depression An affective disorder typified by episodic depressive problems alternating with an otherwise normal mood level.

vagus nerve The largest of the cranial nerves, the vagus nerve has numerous branches that supply all the parasympathetic innervation of the heart, lungs, and intestinal tract; also carries sensory information coming in from these regions back to the preganglionic level and relays information from the receptors located in the palate and throat to the brain.

valium Benzodiazepine thought to work by promoting the effectiveness of the inhibitory functions of GABA; tranquilizer commonly used to alleviate stress and anxiety.

vasopressin A peptide hormone released by the nerve fibers comprising the posterior pituitary gland; acts in the body to increase blood pressure during extreme emergencies when fluid or blood are lost; acts to decrease urinary excretion of water, for which it has also been called the antidiuretic hormone. In the brain, other neurons use the peptide for synaptic regulation.

ventricular zone The inner surface of the embryonic neural tube.

vestibular apparatus A complex of organs located at the sides of the skull and beneath the ear; provides the sense of balance and is used in monitoring head and posture movements, along with spatial orientation.

vestibular canal One of the three sections of the cochlea through which fluid passes during sensation of auditory stimuli.

Wada test A diagnostic test used for the localization of hemispheric functioning; involves the injection of sodium amytal, an anesthetic, into the carotid artery supplying blood to one hemisphere of the brain.

Wernicke's area Brain region located in the temporal lobe and responsible for the comprehension of language and the production of meaningful speech. Damage to this area results in Wernicke's aphasia, a disorder characterized by fluent but meaningless speech.

Zeitgeber German term that refers to the environmental cues affecting biological rhythms.

Z lens Device that projects a visual image directly onto one half of the retina of one eye, ensuring that only one hemisphere receives visual information; used in the testing of hemispheric dominance.

REFERENCES

Adams, R. A. 1980. The morphological aspects of aging in the human nervous system. In J. E. Birren and K. Bergmann (eds.), *Handbook of Mental Health and Aging*. Englewood Cliffs, N.J.: Prentice-Hall.

Alajouanine, T. 1948. Aphasia and artistic realization. *Brain*, 71:229–241.

Alexander, D., A. A. Ehrhardt, and J. Money. 1966. Defective figure drawing, geometric and human, in Turner's syndrome. *Journal of Nervous and Mental Diseases*, 142:161–167.

Alkon, D. L. 1983. Learning in a marine snail. *Scientific American*, 249:70–84.

Allerberger, F. 1997. Julius Wagner-Jauregg (1857–1940). *J. Neurol. Neurosurg. Psychiatry* 62:221.

Alzheimer, A., R. A. Stelzmann, H. N. Schnitzlein, and F. R. Murtagh. 1995. An English translation of Alzheimer's 1907 paper, "Uber eine eigenartige Erkankung der Hirnrinde." *Clin. Anat. 8(6):* 429–431.

Amiel-Tyson, C. 1982. Neurological signs, etiology, and implications. In P. Straton (ed.) *Psychobiology of the Human Newborn*. New York: Wiley.

Anand, B. K., and J. R. Brobeck. 1951. Hypothalamic control of food intake in rats and cats. *Yale Journal of Biological Medicine*, 24:123–133.

Annett, M. 1964. A model of the inheritance of handedness and cerebral dominance. *Nature*, 204:59–60.

Annett, M. 1974. Handedness in the children of two left-handed parents. *Quarterly Journal of Psychology*, 65:129–131.

Annett, M. 1981. The genetics of handedness. *Trends in Neurosciences*, 3:256–258.

Arendt, A. 1972. Altern des "Zentral nerven Systems." In *Handbuch der Allgemeiner Pathologie*. Berlin: Springer-Verlag.

Aschoff, J. 1981. Circadian rhythms: Interference with and dependence on work-rest schedules. In L. C. Johnson et al. (eds.), *Biological Rhythms, Sleep and Shift Work*. New York: SP Medical and Scientific Books.

Aschoff, J., ed. 1980. *Biological Rhythms*, vol. 4, *Handbook of Behavioral Neurobiology*. New York: Plenum.

Aschoff, J., M. Fatranska, H. Giedke, P. Doerr, D. Stamm, and H. Wisser. 1971. Human circadian rhythms in continuous darkness: Entrainment by social cues. *Science* 171:213–215.

Aschoff, J., U. Gerecke, A. Kureck, H. Pohl, P. Rieger, U. von Saint-Paul, and R. Wever. 1971. Interdependent parameters of circadian activity rhythms in birds and man. In M. Menaker (ed.), *Biochronometry*, vol. 3. Washington, D.C.: National Academy of Sciences.

Aschoff, J., and R. Wever. 1962. *Naturwissenschaften* 49:337.

Aschoff, J., and R. Wever. 1965. Circadian rhythms of finches in light-dark circles with interposed twilights. *Comparative Biochemistry and Physiology*, 16:507–514.

Bahrick, H. P., P. O. Bahrick, & R. P. Wittlinger. 1974. Those unforgettable high-school days. *Psychology Today*, December:50–56.

Bakan, P. 1978. Why left-handedness? *Behavioral and Brain Sciences*, 2:279–280.

Bakan, P., G. Dibb, and P. Reed. 1973. Handedness and birth stress. *Neuropsychologia*, 11:363–366.

Bard, P. 1934. On emotional expression after decortication with some remarks of certain theoretical views. Part I, *Psychological Review*, 4:309–329; Part II, 4:424–449.

Barnes, D. M. 1986. Nervous and immune systems linked in a variety of diseases. *Science*, 232:160–161.

Bauman, M. L., and T. L. Kemper. 1982. Morphologic and histoanatomic observations of the brain in the untreated human phenylketonuria. *Acta Neuropathologica (Berlin)*, 58:55–63.

Beecher, H. K. 1959. *Measurement of Subjective Responses: Quantitative Effects of Drugs*. New York: Oxford University Press.

Bell, A. P., M. S. Weinberg, and S. E. Hammersmith. 1981. *Sexual Preference: Its Development in Men and Women*. Bloomington: Indiana University Press.

Berger, T. W., B. Alger, and R. F. Thompson. 1976. Neuronal substrate of classical conditioning in the hippocampus. *Science* 192:483–485.

Bernard, C. 1855. *Leçons de Physiologie Experimentale Appliqué à la Médecine*. Paris: J. B. Ballière.

Berry, H. K. 1969. Phenylketonuria: diagnosis, treatment, and long-term management. In G. Farrell (ed.), *Congenital Mental Retardation*. Austin: University of Texas Press.

Binkley, S. 1979. A timekeeping enzyme in the pineal gland. *Scientific American*, 240:66–71.

Birren, J. E., and R. B. Sloane (eds.). 1980. *Handbook of Mental Health and Aging.* Englewood Cliffs, N.J.: Prentice-Hall.

Bishop, M. P., S. T. Elder, and R. G. Heath. 1963. Intracranial self-stimulation in man. *Science,* 140:393–396.

Bisiach, E., and C. Luzzatti. 1978. Unilateral neglect of representational space. *Cortex,* 14:129–133.

Bleuler, Eugen. 1964, c1950. *Dementia praecox; or The group of schizophrenias.* Translated by Joseph Zinkin; foreword by Nolan D. C. Lewis. New York: International Universities Press.

Body, H. 1976. An examination of cerebral cortex and brainstem aging. In R. D. Terry and S. Gershon (eds.), *Neurobiology of Aging.* New York: Raven.

Bondareff, W. 1980. Neurobiology of aging. In J. E. Birren and K. Bergmann (eds.), *Handbook of Mental Health and Aging.* Englewood Cliffs, N.J.: Prentice-Hall.

Botwinick, J. 1977. Intellectual abilities. In J. E. Birren and K. W. Schaie (eds.), *Handbook of the Psychology of Aging.* New York: Van Nostrand Reinhold.

Bower, G. 1981. Mood and memory. *American Psychologist,* 36:128–148.

Bowlby, J. 1969/1982. *Attachment and loss: Attachment.* New York: Basic Books.

Brain, P. F. 1979. *Hormones, Drugs, and Aggression,* vol. 3. Annual research reviews. Montreal: Eden Press.

Brain, P. F. 1980. Diverse action of hormones on "aggression" in animals and man. In L. Valzelli and L. Morgese (eds.), *Aggression and Violence: A Psychobiological and Clinical Approach.* Milan: Edizioni Saint Vincent.

Brazier, M. A. 1988. *History of Neurophysiology in the 19th Century.* New York: Raven Press.

Brewton, C. B., K. C. Liang, and J. L. McGaugh. 1981. Adrenal demedullation alters the effect of amygdala stimulation on retention of avoidance tasks. *Neuroscience Abstracts,* 7:870.

Broca, P. 1861. Remarques sur la siège de la faculté du langage articulé, suivés d'une observation d'aphemie (perte de la parole). *Bullétins de la Société Anatomique de Paris.* Tome VI, 36, 330–357.

Brody, H. 1955. Organization of the cerebral cortex. III. A study of aging in the human cerebral cortex. *Journal of Comparative Neurology,* 102:511–556.

Bronshtein, A. I., and E. P. Petrova. 1967. The auditory analyzer in young infants. In Y. Brackbill and G. Thompson (eds.), *Behavior in Infancy and Early Childhood.* New York: Free Press.

Broughton, R. 1975. Biorhythmic variations in consciousness and psychological functions. *Canadian Psychological Review,* 16:217–239.

Brown, G. W. 1998. Genetic and population perspectives on life events and depression. *Soc. Psychiatry Psychiatric Epidemiol. 33:*363–372.

Bruner, J. S. 1969. Foreword to *The Mind of a Mnemonist,* by A. R. Luria. New York: Avon Books.

Brust, J. C. M. 1980. Music and language: Musical alexia and agraphia. *Brain,* 103:367–392.

Buckingham, H. W., Jr., and A. Kertesz. 1974. A linguistic analysis of fluent aphasics. *Brain and Language,* 1:29–42.

Bünning, E. 1973. *The Physiological Clock: Circadian Rhythms and Biological Chronometry.* New York: Springer-Verlag.

y Cajal, S. Ramón. 1909/1911. *Histologie du système nerveux de l'homme et des vertébrés.* (Transl. by L. Azoulay). Paris: Maloine (2 Vols.), pp. 862–890.

Cannon, W. B. 1927. The James-Lange theory of emotion: A critical examination and an alternative theory. *American Journal of Psychology,* 39:106–124.

Cannon, W. B. 1929. *Bodily Changes in Pain, Hunger, Fear, and Rage.* New York: Appleton-Century-Crofts.

Caplan, D., and J. C. Marshall. 1972. Generative grammar and aphasic disorders: A theory of language representation in the human brain. *Foundations of Language,* 12:583–596.

Champion, R. A. 1950. Studies of experimentally induced disturbance. *Australian Journal of Psychology,* 2:90–99.

Chase, M. H. 1973. Somatic reflex activity during sleep and wakefulness. In O. Petre-Quadens and J. Schlag (eds.), *Basic Sleep Mechanisms.* New York: Academic Press.

Cohen, J. 1967. *Psychological Time in Health and Disease.* Springfield, Ill.: Charles C. Thomas.

Cohen, N. J. 1981. Neuropsychological evidence for a distinction between procedural and declarative knowledge in human memory and amnesia. Ph.D. thesis, University of California, San Diego.

Cohen, N. J., and L. R. Squire. 1980. Preserved learning and retention of pattern analyzing skill in amnesia: Dissociation of knowing how and knowing that. *Science,* 210:207–209.

Cohen, N. J., and L. R. Squire. 1981. Retrograde amnesia and remote memory impairment. *Neuropsychologia,* 19:337–356.

Coleman, D. L., and K. P. Hummel. 1969. Effects of parabiosis of normal with genetically diabetic mice. *American Journal of Physiology,* 217:1298–1304.

Conel, J. L. 1939–1963. *The Postnatal Development of the Human Cerebral Cortex* (7 vols.). Cambridge, Mass.: Harvard University Press.

Corballis, M. C. 1983. *Human Laterality.* New York: Academic.

Coren, S., and C. Porac. 1977. Fifty centuries of righthandedness: The historical record. *Science, 198*:631–632.

Corso, J. F. 1975. Sensory processes in man during maturity and senescence. In J. M. Ordy and K. R. Brizzee (eds.), *Neurobiology of Aging*. New York: Plenum.

Costa, E., and A. Guidotti. 1979. Molecular mechanisms in the receptor action of benzodiazepines. *American Review of Pharmacology and Toxicology, 19*:531–545.

Cotman, C. W., and J. McGaugh. 1980. *Behavioral Neuroscience: An Introduction*. New York: Academic Press.

Cowan, W. M. 1981. *Studies in Developmental Neurobiology*. New York: Oxford University Press.

Cragg, B. G. 1975. The development of synapses in the visual system of the cat. *Journal of Comparative Neurology, 160*:147–166.

Crisp, A. H. 1983. Treatment of anorexia nervosa: What can be the role of psychopharmacological agents? In K. M. Pirke and D. Ploog (eds.), *The Psychobiology of Anorexia Nervosa*. New York: Springer-Verlag.

Crow, T. J. 1998. From Kraepelin to Kretschmer leavened by Schneider: The transition from categories of psychosis to dimensions of variation intrinsic to homosapiens. *Arch. Gen. Psychiatry 55*:502–504.

Curtiss, S. 1977. *Genie: A Psycholinguistic Study of a Modern-Day "Wild Child."* New York: Academic Press.

Czeisler, C., G. S. Richardson, R. M. Coleman, J. C. Zimmerman, M. C. Moore-Ede, W. C. Dement, and E. D. Weitzman. 1981. Chronotherapy: Resetting the circadian clocks of patients with delayed sleep phase insomnia. *Sleep, 4*:1–21.

Czeisler, C. A., E. D. Weitzman, M. C. Moore-Ede, J. C. Zimmerman, and R. S. Knauer. 1980. Human sleep: Its duration and organization depend on its circadian phase. *Science, 210*:1264–1267.

Damasio, H., T. Grabowski, R. Frank, A. M. Galaburda, and A. R. Damasio. 1994. The return of Phineas Gage: Clues about the brain from the skull of a famous patient. *Science* May 20, 264(5162):1102–1105.

Darwin, C. 1965. *The Expression of the Emotions in Man and Animals*. Originally published in 1872. Chicago: The University of Chicago Press.

Davidson, R. J., and W. Irwin. 1999. The functional neuroanatomy of emotion and affective style. *Trends in Cognitive Science* Jan. 3(1):11–21.

Davis, J. D., and D. J. Brief. 1981. Chronic intraventricular insulin infusions reduce food intake and body weight in rats, *Soc. Neurosci. Abstr. 7*:655.

Davis, J. D., R. J. Gallagher, R. F. Ladove, and A. J. Turansky. 1969. Inhibition of food intake by a humoral factor. *Journal of Comparative Physiological Psychology, 67*:407–417.

Dax, M. 1836. Lésion de la moitié gauche de l'enchephale coincidant avec l'oubli des signes de la pensée. *Gaz. Hebd. Med., 2.*

Decety, J., D. Perani, M. Jeannerod, V. Bettinardi, B. Tadary, R. Woods, J. C. Mazziotta, and F. Fazio. 1994. Mapping motor representations with positron emission tomography. *Nature 371*:600–602.

Delgado, J. M. R. 1969. *Physical Control of the Mind: Toward a Psychocivilized Society*. New York: Harper & Row.

Dement, W. C. 1972. *Some Must Watch While Some Must Sleep*. New York: W. H. Freeman.

Dennis, M., and H. Whitaker. 1976. Language acquisition following hemi-decortication: Linguistic superiority of the left over the right hemisphere. *Brain and Language, 3*:404–433.

Dennis, W. 1960. Causes of retardation among institutional children: Iran. *Journal of Genetic Psychology, 96*:46–60.

Deutsch, J. A. 1973. The cholinergic synapse and the site of memory. In J. A. Deutsch (ed.), *The Physiological Basis of Memory*. New York: Academic Press.

Diagnostic and Statistical Manual IV. 1995. Washington, D.C.: American Psychiatric Association Press, Inc.

Dickerson, J. W. T., and H. McGurk (eds.). 1982. *Brain and Behavioural Development; Interdisciplinary Perspectives on Structure and Function*. London: Surrey University Press.

Dorner, G. 1976. *Hormones and Brain Differentiation*. New York: Elsevier.

Drillien, C. M. 1964. *The Growth and Development of the Prematurely Born Infant*. Edinburgh, Scotland: Livingstone.

Drucker-Colin, R. R., and C. W. Spanis. 1976. Is there a sleep transmitter? *Progress in Neurobiology, 6*:1–22.

Dubois, A., H. A. Gross, and M. H. Ebert. 1984. Gastric function in primary anorexia nervosa. In K. M. Pirke and D. Ploog (eds.), *The Psychobiology of Anorexia Nervosa*. New York: Springer-Verlag.

Durden-Smith, J., and D. deSimone. 1983. *Sex and the Brain*. New York: Arbor House.

Dyer, R. G., N. K. MacLeod, and F. Ellendorf. 1976. Electrophysiological evidence for sexual dimorphism and synaptic convergence in the preoptic and anterior hypothalamic areas of the rat. *Proceedings of the Royal Society, London. B 193*:421–440.

Ebbinghaus, H. 1885/1964. *Memory contribution to experimental psychology.* New York: Dover.

Ebert, P. D. 1983. Selection for aggression in a natural population. In E. C. Simmel et al. (eds.), *Aggressive Behavior: Genetic and Neural Approaches.* Hillsdale, N.J.: Lawrence Erlbaum.

Edelman, G. M. 1976. Surface modulation in cell recognition and cell growth. *Science, 192:*218–226.

Edelman, G. M., and V. B. Mountcastle. 1978. *The Mindful Brain.* Cambridge, Mass.: Massachusetts Institute of Technology Press.

Eisdorfer, C., and F. Wilkie. 1973. Intellectual changes with advancing age. In L. F. Jarvik, C. Eisdorfer, and J. E. Blum (eds.) *Intellectual Functioning in Adults,* pp. 21–29. New York: Springer-Verlag.

Elliott, J. 1979. Finally: Some details on *in vitro* fertilization. *Journal of the American Medical Association, 241:*868–869.

Emde, R. W., J. J. Gaensbauer, and R. J. Harmon. 1976. *Emotional Expression in Infancy.* New York: International Universities Press.

Epstein, C. J. 1986. *The Neurobiology of Down Syndrome.* New York: Raven.

Faust, I. M., P. R. Johnson, J. S. Stern, and J. Hirsch. 1978. Diet-induced adipocyte number increase in adult rats: a new model of obesity. *American Journal of Physiology, 235:*E279–E286.

Festinger, L. 1957. *A Theory of Cognitive Dissonance.* Stanford, Cal.: Stanford University Press.

Finch, C. 1973. Catecholamine metabolism in the brains of aging male mice. *Brain Research, 52:*261–276.

Finger, S. 1994. *Origins of Neuroscience: A History of Exploration into Brain Function.* New York: Oxford University Press.

Frankenhaeuser, M. 1971. Behavior and circulating catecholamines. *Brain Research, 31:*241–262.

Frankenhaeuser, M. 1975. Experimental approaches to the study of catecholamines and emotion. In L. Levi (ed.), *Emotions: Their Parameters and Measurement,* New York: Raven Press.

Freeman, R. D., and L. N. Thibos. 1973. Electrophysiological evidence that abnormal early visual experience can modify the human brain. *Science, 180:*876–878.

Fuller, C., F. Sulzman, and M. Moore-Ede. 1981. Shift work and the jet lag syndrome: Conflicts between environmental and body time. In L. C. Johnson et al. (eds.), *Biological Rhythms, Sleep, and Shift Work.* New York: SP Medical and Scientific Books.

Fulton, J. F., and P. Bailey. 1929. Tumors in the region of the third ventricle: Their diagnosis and relation to pathological sleep. *Journal of Nervous and Mental Disorders, 69:*1–25.

Funkenstein, H. H., P. G. Nelson, P. Winter, Z. Wollberg, and J. D. Newman. 1971. Unit responses in the auditory cortex of awake squirrel monkeys to vocal stimulation. In M. B. Sachs (ed.), *Physiology of the Auditory System.* Baltimore: National Educational Consultants.

Galaburda, A. M., and T. M. Kemper. 1979. Cytoarchitectonic abnormalities in developmental dyslexia: A case study. *Annals of Neurology 6:*94–100.

Galaburda, A. M., M. Le May, T. L. Kemper, and N. Geschwind. 1978. Right-left asymmetries in the brain. *Science, 199:*852–856.

Garber, B. B., and A. A. Moscona. 1972. Reconstruction of brain tissue from cell suspensions. I. Aggregation patterns of cells dissociated from different regions of the developing brain. *Developmental Biology, 27:*217–234.

Gates, A., and J. Bradshaw. 1977. The role of the cerebral hemispheres in music. *Brain and Language, 4:*403–431.

Gazzaniga, M. S. 1970. *The Bisected Brain.* New York: Appleton-Century-Crofts.

Gazzaniga, M. S., and J. E. Le Doux. 1978. *The Integrated Mind.* New York: Plenum.

Geer, J. H., G. C. Davison, and R. I. Gatchel. 1970. Reduction of stress in humans through nonveridical perceived control of aversive stimulation. *Journal of Personality and Social Psychology, 16:*731–738.

Geinisman, Y., and W. Bondareff. 1976. Decrease in the number of synapses in the senescent brain: A quantitative electron microscopic analysis of the dentate gyrus molecular layer in the rat. *Mechanisms of Aging and Development, 5:*11–23.

Geschwind, N. 1979. Specializations of the human brain. *Scientific American, 241:*158–168.

Geschwind, N., and P. Behan. 1982. Left-handedness: Association with immune disease, migraine, and developmental learning disorder. *Proceedings of the National Academy of Science USA, 79:*5097–5100.

Geschwind, N., and W. Levitsky. 1968. Human brain: Left-right asymmetries in temporal speech region. *Science, 161:*186–187.

Gimpl, M. P., I. Gormezano, and J. A. Harvey. 1979. Effects of LSD on learning as measured by classical conditioning of the rabbit–nictitating membrane response. *J. Pharmacol. Exp. Ther. 208:*330–334.

Gispen, W. H., and J. Traber (eds.). 1983. *Aging of the Brain,* Developments in Neurology, vol. 7. New York: Elsevier.

Gladue, B. A., R. Green, and R. E. Hellman. 1984. Neuroendocrine response to estrogen and sexual orientation. *Science, 225:*1496–1499.

Globus, A., M. R. Rosenzweig, E. Bennett, and M. C. Diamond. 1973. Effects of differential experience on dendritic spine counts in rat cerebral cortex. *Journal of Comparative Physiology and Psychology, 82*:175–181.

Gold, P., and J. L. McGaugh. 1975. *Short-Term Memory*. New York: Academic Press.

Goldschneider, I., and A. A. Moscona. 1972. Tissue-specific cell-surface antigens in embryonic cells. *Journal of Cell Biology, 53*:435–449.

Golgi, C. 1884. Recherches sur l'histologie des centres nerveux. *Arch. Ital. Biol. 3*:285–317.

Goodglass, H., and N. Geschwind. 1976. Language disorders (aphasia). In *Handbook of Perception*, vol. 7, *Language and Speech*. New York: Academic Press.

Goodsit, A. 1985. Self psychology and the treatment of anorexia nervosa. In D. M. Garner and P. E. Garfinkel (eds.), *Handbook of Psychotherapy for Anorexia Nervosa and Bulimia*. New York: Guilford Press.

Gordon, H. W., and A. Galatzer. 1980. Cerebral organization in patients with gonadal dysgenesis. *Psychoneuroendocrinology, 5*:235–244.

Gorski, R. A., J. H. Gordon, J. E. Shryne, and A. M. Southam. 1978. Evidence for a morphological sex difference within the medial preoptic area of the rat brain. *Brain Research, 148*:333–346.

Gottlieb, D. I., and Glaser, L. 1981. Cellular recognition during neural development. In D. I. Gottlieb and L. Glaser, *Studies in Developmental Neurobiology*. New York: Oxford University Press.

Gould, S. J. 1977. *Ontogeny and Phylogeny*. Cambridge, Mass.: Harvard University Press.

Gould, S. J. 1980. *The Panda's Thumb: More Reflections in Natural History*. New York: Norton.

Goy, R. W., and B. S. McEwen. 1980. *Sexual Differentiation of the Brain*. Cambridge, Mass.: Massachusetts Institute of Technology Press.

Goy, R. W. 1968. Organizing effects of androgen on the behavior of rhesus monkeys. In R. P. Michael (ed.), *Endocrinology and Human Behavior*, New York: Oxford University Press.

Gray, J. A. 1977. Drug effects on fear and frustration: Possible limbic site of action of minor tranquilizers. In L. L. Iversen et al. (eds.), *Handbook of Psychopharmacology*, vol. 8, pp. 433–529. New York: Plenum.

Greenough, W. T., C. S. Carter, C. Steerman, and T. J. DeVoogd. 1977. Sex differences in dendritic patterns in hamster preoptic area. *Brain Research, 126*:63–72.

Greenough, W. T., and F. F. Chang. 1984. Anatomically detectable correlates of information storage in the nervous system of animals. In C. W. Cotman (ed.) *Neuronal Plasticity*, 2d ed. New York: Raven.

Greenough, W. T., R. W. West, and T. J. DeVoogd. 1978. Subsynaptic plate perforations: Changes with age and experience in the rat. *Science, 202*:1096–1098.

Greenwood, P., D. H. Wilson, and M. S. Gazzaniga: 1977. Dream report following commissurotomy. *Cortex, 13*:311–316.

Griffin, D. R. 1976. *The Question of Animal Awareness*. New York: Rockefeller University Press.

Griffin, D. R. 1984. *Animal Thinking*. Cambridge, Mass.: Harvard University Press.

Griffiths, J. D., and P. R. Payne. 1976. Energy expenditure in small children of obese and non-obese mothers. *Nature, 260*:698–700.

Grossman, S. 1967. *A Textbook of Physiological Psychology*. New York: Wiley.

Guillery, R. W., V. A. Casagrande, and M. D. Uberdorfer. 1974. Congenitally abnormal vision in Siamese cats. *Nature* (London), *252*:195–199.

Gwinner, E. 1968. Circannuale Periodik als Grundlage des Jahreszeitlichen Funktionswandels bei Zugvögeln. *Journal für Ornithologie, 109*:70–95.

Halberg, F., E. A. Johnson, B. W. Brown, and J. J. Bittner. 1960. Susceptibility rhythm to *E. Coli* endotoxin and bioassay. *Proceedings of the Society for Experimental Biology and Medicine, 103*:142–144.

Halmi, K. A. 1985. Behavioral management for anorexia nervosa. In D. M. Garner and P. E. Garfinkel (eds.), *Handbook of Psychotherapy for Anorexia Nervosa and Bulimia*. New York: Guilford Press.

Hamburger, V., and R. Levi-Montalcini. 1949. Proliferation, differentiation, and degeneration in the spinal ganglia of the chick embryo under normal and experimental conditions. *Journal of Experimental Zoology, 111*:457–501.

Harlow, H. F. 1949. The formation of learning sets. *Psychological Review, 56*:51–56.

Harlow, J. M. 1868. Passage of an iron rod through the head. *Boston Medical and Surgical Journal, 39*:389–393.

Harris, L. J. 1980. Which hand is the "eye" of the blind? A new look at an old question. In J. Herron (ed.), *Neuropsychology of Left Handedness*. New York: Academic Press.

Hart, B. 1967. Sexual reflexes and mating behavior in the male dog. *Journal of Comparative and Physiological Psychology, 66*:388–399.

Hebb, D. O. 1949. *The Organization of Behavior*. New York: Wiley.

Hebb, D. O., and W. R. Thompson. 1968. The social significance of animal studies. In G. Lindzey (ed.), *Handbook of Social Psychology*, Cambridge, Mass.: Addison-Wesley.

Hemingway, Ernest. 1899–1961. "The Short Happy Life of Francis Macomber," in Finca Vigaia (Ed.), *The complete short stories of Ernest Hemingway*. New York: Simon & Schuster, 5–28.

Hering, E. 1964. *Outline of a Theory of the Light Sense*. (Translated by I. M. Hurvich and D. Jameson) Cambridge, Mass.: Harvard University Press.

Hess, W. R. 1957. *The Functional Organization of the Diencephalon*. New York: Grune & Stratton.

Hetherington, A. W., and S. W. Ranson. 1939. Experimental hypothalamicohypophyseal obesity in the rat. *Proceedings of the Society for Experimental Biology and Medicine, 41*:465–466.

Hier, D., and W. Crowley. 1982. Spatial ability in androgen-deficient men. *New England Journal of Medicine*, May 20, 1982.

Hoffman, S., and G. M. Edelman. 1983. Kinetics of homophilic binding by embryonic and adult forms of the neural cell. *Proceedings of the National Academy of Sciences, 80*:5762–5766.

Hohmann, G. W. 1966. Some effects of spinal cord lesions on experienced emotional feelings. *Psychophysiology, 3*:143–156.

Hollyday, M., and V. Hamburger. 1975. Reduction of normally occurring motor neuron depletion following supernumerary limb transplantation in chick embryo. *Neuroscience Abstracts, 1*:779.

Holmes, T. H., and M. Masuda. 1972. Psychosomatic syndrome: When mothers-in-law or other disasters visit, a person can develop a bad, bad cold. Or worse. *Psychology Today*, April.

Hornykiewicz, O. 1963. Die topische Lokalisation und das Verhalten von Noradrenalin und Dopamin (3–hydroxytyramine) in der Substantia Nigra des Normalen und Parkinsonkranken Menschen. *Wiener Klinische Wochenschrift 75*:309–312.

Hornykiewicz, O. 1966. Dopamine (3-hydroxytyramine) and brain function. *Pharmacol. Rev. 18*:925–964.

Hubel, D. H., and T. N. Wiesel. 1962. Receptive fields, binocular interaction, and functional architecture in the cat's visual cortex. *Journal of Physiology, 160*:106–154.

Hubel, D. H., and T. N. Wiesel. 1965. Binocular interaction in striate cortex of kittens reared with artificial squint. *J. Neurophysiol. 28*:1041–1059.

Hubel, D. H., and T. N. Wiesel. 1969. Anatomical demonstration of columns in the monkey striate cortex. *Nature 221*:747–750.

Hubel, D. H., and T. N. Wiesel. 1979. Brain mechanisms of vision. *Scientific American, 241*:150–162.

Hubel, D. H., and T. N. Wiesel. 1998. Early exploration of the visual cortex. *Neuron 20*:401–412.

Hughes, M. 1982. Sex differences in brain development: Process and effects. In J. W. T. Dickerson and H. McGurk (eds.), *Brain and Behavioural Development*. London: Surrey University Press.

Hunt, R. K., and M. Jacobson. 1972. Development and stability of positional information in Xenopus retinal ganglion cells. *Proceedings of the National Academy of Sciences, 69*:780–783.

Huntington, G. 1872. On Chorea. *Medical and Surgical Reporter 26*:317–321.

Hutt, S. J., C. Hutt, H. G. Lehard, H. von Bernuth, and W. J. Muntjewerff. 1968. Auditory responsivity in the human neonate. *Nature, 218*:888–890.

Ibuka, N., S. T. Inouye, and H. Kawamura. 1977. Analysis of sleep-wakefulness rhythms in male rats after suprachiasmatic nucleus lesions and ocular enucleation. *Brain Research, 122*:33–47.

Inouye, S. T., and H. Kawamura. 1979. Persistence of circadian rhythmicity in mammalian hypothalamic "island" containing the suprachiasmatic nucleus. *Proceedings of the National Academy of Science USA, 76*:5961–5966.

Jackson, J. H. (1835–1911) 1931–. Selected works of John Hughlings Jackson, edited for the guarantors of *Brain*. London: Hodder and Stoughton Limited.

Jacobson, M. 1978. *Developmental Neurobiology*. New York: Holt.

James, W. 1884. What is emotion? *Mind, 9*:188–204.

James, W. 1890. *The Principles of Psychology*, vol. 2. New York: Holt.

Jarvik, J. F. 1983. Age is in—is the wit out? In D. Samuel et al. (eds.), *Aging of the Brain*. New York: Raven.

Jaynes, J. 1976. *The Origin of Consciousness in the Breakdown of the Bicameral Mind*. Boston: Houghton-Mifflin.

Jaynes, J. 1977. Reflections on the dawn of consciousness. *Psychology Today, 11*:58.

Jencks, C., M. Smith, H. Acland, M. J. Bane, D. Cohen, H. Gintis, B. Heyns, and S. Michelson. 1972. *Inequality: A Reassessment of the Effect of Family and Schooling in America*. New York: Basic Books.

Johnson, L. C., W. P. Colquhoun, D. I. Tepas, and M. J. Colligan (eds.). 1981. *Biological Rhythms, Sleep, and Shift Work*. New York: SP Medical and Scientific Books.

Jolly, A. 1972. *The Evolution of Primate Behavior*. New York: Macmillan.

Jonec, V., and C. Finch. 1975. Aging and dopamine uptake by subcellular fractions of the C57 B1/6J male mouse brain. *Brain Research, 91*:197–215.

Jones, R. K. 1966. Observations on stammering after localized cerebral injury. *Journal of Neurology, Neurosurgery, and Psychiatry, 29*:192–195.

Jost, A. D. 1979. Basic sexual trends in the development of vertebrates. In *Human Reproduction*. London: Paladin.

Jouvet, M. 1977. Neuropharmacology of the sleepwaking cycle. In L. L. Iversen et al. (eds.), *Handbook of Psychopharmacology*, vol. 8, pp. 233–293. New York: Plenum.

Kandel, E. R. 1976. *Cellular Basis of Behavior: An Introduction to Behavioral Neurobiology*. New York: W. H. Freeman.

Kandel, E. R. 1979. Small systems of neurons. *Scientific American, 241*:61–70.

Kandel, E. R., and J. H. Schwartz. 1982. Molecular biology of learning: Modulation of transmitter release. *Science, 218*:433–442.

Kaplan, J. R., S. B. Manuck, T. B. Clarkson, F. M. Lusso, D. M. Taub, and E. W. Miller. 1983. Social stress and atherosclerosis in normocholesterolemic monkeys. *Science, 200*:733–735.

Katchadourian, H. A., and D. T. Lunde. 1980. *Fundamentals of Human Sexuality,* 3d ed. New York: Holt.

Kay, D. W. K., and K. Bergmann. 1980. Epidemiology of mental disorders among the aged in the community. In J. E. Birren and K. Bergmann (eds.), *Handbook of Mental Health and Aging*. Englewood Cliffs, N.J.: Prentice-Hall.

Kimura, D. 1973. Manual activity during speaking. II. Left-handers. *Neuropsychologia, 11*:45–50.

Kimura, D. 1979. Neuromotor mechanisms in the evolution of human communication. In H. D. Steklis and M. J. Raleigh (eds.), *Neurobiology of Social Communication in Primates*. New York: Academic Press.

Kimura, D., and Y. Archibald. 1974. Motor functions of the left hemisphere. *Brain, 97*:337–350.

Klein, K. E., and H. M. Wegmann. 1974. The resynchronization of human circadian rhythms after transmeridian flights as a result of flight direction and mode of activity. In L. E. Scheving et al. (eds.), *Chronobiology*. Tokyo: Igaku.

Klintsova, A. Y., and W. T. Greenough. 1999. Synaptic plasticity in cortical systems. *Curr. Opin. Neurobiol. 9*:203–208.

Koestler, A. 1969. The urge to self-destruction. In *The Place of Value in a World of Facts*. Proceedings of the 14th Nobel Symposium, Stockholm.

Kolers, P. A. 1976. Pattern-analyzing memory. *Science, 191*:1280–1281.

Kolers, P. A. 1979. A pattern-analyzing basis of recognition. In L. S. Cermak and F. I. M. Craik (eds.), *Level of Processing in Human Memory*. pp. 363–384. Hillsdale, N.J.: Lawrence Erlbaum.

Kosslyn, S. M. 1994. *Image and brain: The resolution of the imagery debate*. Cambridge, Mass.: Massachusetts Institute of Technology Press.

Kraepelin, Emil. 1971. *Dementia praecox and paraphrenia*. George M. Robertson, ed. Huntington, N.Y.: Krieger.

Kuffler, S. W. 1953. Discharge patterns and functional organization of mammalian retina. *J. Neurophysiol. 16*:37–68.

Kuhl, P. K., and J. D. Miller. 1975. Speech perception by the chinchilla: voiced-voiceless distinction in alveolar plosive consonants. *Science, 190*:69–72.

Lacoste-Utamsing, C. de, and R. Holloway. 1982. Sexual dimorphism in the human corpus callosum. *Science, 216*:1431–1432.

Lacoste-Utamsing, C. de, and D. J. Woodward. 1982. Sexual dimorphism in human fetal corpora callosa. Abstracts of the 1982 meeting of the Society for Neuroscience.

Landfield, P. W. 1983. Mechanisms of altered neural function during aging. In W. H. Gispen and J. Traber (eds.), *Aging of the Brain*. New York: Elsevier.

Landfield, P. W., J. L. McGaugh, and G. Lynch. 1978. Impaired synaptic potentiation processes in the hippocampus of aged, memory-deficient rats. *Brain Research, 150*:85–101.

Landmesser, L. 1981. Pathway selection by embryonic neurons. In W. M. Cowan (ed.), *Studies in Developmental Neurobiology*. New York: Oxford University Press.

Lange, C. G., and W. James. 1922. *The Emotions*. Baltimore: Williams & Wilkins.

Lansdell, H. 1962. A sex difference in effect of temporal lobe neurosurgery on design preference. *Nature, 194*:852–854.

Lashley, K. S. 1950. *In Search of the Engram*. Society of Experimental Biology Symposium. No. 4: Physiological Mechanisms in Animal Behavior. Cambridge: Cambridge University Press.

Lassen, N. A., D. H. Ingvar, and E. Skinhoj. 1978. Brain function and blood flow. *Scientific American, 239*:62–71.

Lavie, P., and D. F. Kripke. 1975. Ultradian rhythms: The 90-minute clock inside us. *Psychology Today, 8*:54–65.

Ledbetter, D. H., J. T. Mascarello, V. M. Riccard, et al. 1982. Chromosome 15 abnormalities and the Prader-

Willi syndrome: A follow-up report of 40 cases. *American Journal of Human Genetics, 34*:278–285.

LeDouarin, N. M., D. Renaud, M. A. Teillet, and G. H. LeDouarin. 1975. Cholinergic differentiation of presumptive adrenergic neuroblasts in interspecific chimeras after heterotopic transplantations. *Proceedings of the National Academy of Science, 72*:728–732.

LeDoux, J. E. 1985. Brain, mind, and language. In D. A. Oakley (ed.), *Brain and Mind*. New York: Methuen.

LeDoux, J. E., D. H. Wilson, and M. S. Gazzaniga. 1977. A divided mind: Observations on the conscious properties of the separated hemispheres. *Annals of Neurology, 2*:417–421.

LeMay, M. 1977. Assymetries of the skull and handedness: Phrenology revisited. *Journal of Neurological Sciences 32*:243–253.

Leibowitz, S. F. 1983. Noradrenergic function in the medial hypothalamus: Potential relation to anorexia nervosa and bulimia. In K. M. Pirke and D. Ploog (eds.), *The Psychobiology of Anorexia Nervosa*. New York: Springer-Verlag.

Levi-Montalcini, R. 1952. Effects of mouse tumor transplantation of the nervous system. *Annals of the New York Academy of Science, 55*:330–343.

Levi-Montalcini, R. 1966. The nerve growth factor: Its mode of action on sensory and sympathetic nerve cells. *Harvey Lectures, 60*:217–259.

Levi-Montalcini, R., and V. Hamburger. 1953. A diffusable agent of mouse sarcoma producing hyperplasia of sympathetic ganglia and hyperneurotization of the chick embryo. *Journal of Experimental Zoology, 123*:233–288.

Levine, S. 1960. Stimulation in infancy. *Scientific American, 202*:80–86.

Levy, J. 1978. Lateral differences in the human brain in cognition and behavioral control. In P. Buser (ed.) *Cerebral Correlates of Human Experience*. New York: North Holland.

Levy, J., and T. Nagylaki. 1972. A model for the genetics of handedness. *Genetics, 72*:117–128.

Lim, R., D. E. Turriff, S. S. Troy, B. W. Moore, and L. F. Eng. 1977. Glial maturation factor: Effect on chemical differentiation of glioblasts in culture. *Science, 195*:195–196.

Lindsay, P. H., and D. A. Norman. 1977. *Human Information Processing*, 2d ed. New York: Academic Press.

Linnoila, M., C. W. Erwin, D. Ramm, and W. P. Cleveland. 1980. Effects of age and alcohol on psychomotor performance of men. *Journal of Studies in Alcohol, 41*:488–495.

Loewi, O., and E. Navratil. 1926. Über humorale Übertragbarkeit der herzenwirkung. X. Mittei lung Über das Schicksal des Vagusstoff. *Pfluger's Arch. Gesamte Physiol. 214*:678–688.

Loo, Y. H., T. Fulton, K. Miller, and H. Wisniewski. 1980. Phenylacetate and brain dysfunction in experimental phenylketonuria: Synaptic development. *Life Sciences 27*:1283–1290.

Lorente de No, R. 1884. On the sensorial localizations in the cortex cerebri. *Brain 7*:145–160.

Lorenz, K. Z. 1971. *Studies in Animal and Human Behaviors* (Robert Martin, translator). Cambridge, Mass.: Harvard University Press.

Lucas, A. R. 1981. Towards the understanding of anorexia nervosa as a disease entity. *Mayo Clinic Proceedings, 56*:254–264.

Luce, G. G. 1971. *Biological Rhythms in Human and Animal Physiology*. New York: Dover.

Lund, R. D. 1978. *Development and Plasticity of the Brain: An Introduction*. New York: Oxford University Press.

Maccoby, E., and C. Jacklin. 1974. *The Psychology of Sex Differences*. Palo Alto, Cal.: Stanford University Press.

MacLean, P. D. 1980. Sensory and perceptive factors in emotional functions of the brain. In A. O. Porty (ed.), *Explaining Emotions*. Berkeley: University of California Press.

Mandler, G. 1975. *Mind and Emotion*. New York: Wiley.

Marañon, G. 1924. Contribution à l'étude de l'action émotive de l'adrenaline. *Revue Française d'Endocrinologie, 2*:301–325.

Margules, D. L., B. Moiset, M. J. Lewis, H. Shibuya, and C. B. Pert. 1978. β-Endorphin is associated with overeating in genetically obese mice (*ob/ob*) and rats (*fa/fa*). *Science 202*:988–991.

Marx, J. L. 1982. Autoimmunity in left-handers. *Science, 217*:141–144.

Mayer, D. J. 1979. Endogenous analgesia systems: Neural and behavioral mechanisms. In J. J. Bonica et al. (eds.), *Advances in Pain Research and Therapy*, vol. 3. New York: Raven.

Mayer, J. 1955. Regulation of energy intake and the body weight: the glucostatic theory and the lipostatic hypothesis. *Annals of the New York Academy of Science, 63*:15–42.

McCormick, D. A., G. A. Clark, D. G. Lavord, and R. F. Thompson. 1982. Initial localization of the memory trace for a basic form of learning. *Proceedings of the National Academy of Science USA, 79*:2731–2735.

McGaugh, J. J. 1982. *Memory Consolidation*. Hillsdale, N.J.: Lawrence Erlbaum.

McGaugh, J. L. 1983. Hormonal influences on memory storage. *American Psychologist, 38*:161–174.

McGeer, E. G., N. B. Boyce, J. O'Kosky, J. Suzuki, and P. L. McGeer. 1985. Acetylcholine and aromatic amine systems in postmortem brain of an infant with Down syndrome. *Experimental Neurology, 87*:557–570.

McGeer, P. L., and E. G. McGeer. 1981. Amino acid transmitters. In G. J. Siegel et al. (eds.), *Basic Neurochemistry,* 3d ed., pp. 233–254. Boston: Little, Brown.

McGlone, J. 1978. Sex difference in functional brain asymmetry. *Cortex, 14*:122–128.

McGlone, J. 1980. Sex differences in human brain asymmetry: A critical survey. *Behavior and Brain Science, 3*:215–263.

McGlone, J., and A. Kertesz. 1973. Sex differences in cerebral processing of visuo-spatial tasks. *Cortex, 9*:313–320.

McRae, D. L., C. L. Branch, and B. Milner. 1968. The occipital horns and cerebral dominance. *Neurology 18*:95–98.

Melzak, R., and P. D. Wall. 1965. Pain mechanisms: A new theory. *Science, 150*:971–979.

Meyer, D. R. 1958. Some psychological determinants of sparing and loss following damage to the brain. In H. F. Harlow and C. N. Woolsey (eds.), *Biological and Biochemical Bases of Behavior.* Madison: University of Wisconsin Press.

Michael, R. P. 1980. Hormones and sexual behavior in the female. In D. T. Krieger and J. C. Hughes (eds.), *Neuroendocrinology.* Sunderland, Mass.: Sinauer Associates.

Milner, B. 1972. Disorders of learning and memory after temporal lobe lesions in man. *Clinical Neurosurgery, 19*:421–446.

Mintz, G., and L. Glaser. 1978. Specific glycoprotein changes during development of the chick neural retina. *Journal of Cell Biology, 79*:132–137.

Mirsky, A. F., and O. W. Quinn. 1988. The Genain quadruplets. *Schizophr. Bull. 14*:595–612.

Mishkin, M. 1978. Memory in monkeys severely impaired by combined but not by separate removal of amygdala and hippocampus. *Nature, 273*:297–298.

Molfese, D. L., R. B. Freeman, Jr., and D. S. Palermo. 1975. The ontogeny of brain lateralization for speech and nonspeech stimuli. *Brain and Language, 2*:356–368.

Møllgaard, K., M. C. Diamond, E. L. Bennett, M. R. Rosenzweig, and B. Lindner. 1971. Quantitative synaptic changes with differential experience in rat brain. *International Journal of Neuroscience, 2*:113–128.

Money, J. 1961. Sex hormones and other variables in human eroticism. In W. C. Young (ed.), *Sex Internal Secretions,* vol. 2. Baltimore: Williams & Wilkins.

Money, J., and A. A. Ehrhardt. 1972. *Man & Woman, Boy & Girl.* Baltimore: Johns Hopkins University Press.

Moore-Ede, M. C., F. M. Sulzman, and C. A. Fuller, 1982. *The Clocks that Time Us.* Cambridge, Mass.: Harvard University Press.

Moruzzi, G., and H. W. Magoun. 1949. Brain stem reticular formation and activation of the EEG. *EEG. Clin. Neurophysiol. 1*:455–476.

Moscona, A. A., and R. E. Hausman. 1977. Biological and biochemical studies on embryonic cell recognition. In J. W. Lash and M. M. Burger (eds.), *Cell and Tissue Interactions.* New York: Raven.

Moscovitch, M. 1981. Multiple dissociations of function in the amnesic syndrome. In L. S. Cermak (ed.), *Human Memory and Amnesia.* Hillsdale, N.J.: Lawrence Erlbaum.

Mountcastle, V. B. 1975. The view from within: Pathways to the study of perception. *Johns Hopkins Medical Journal, 136*:109–131.

Mountcastle, V. B. 1978. An organizing principle for cerebral function: The unit module and the distributed system. In G. M. Edelman and V. B. Mountcastle, *The Mindful Brain.* Cambridge, Mass.: Massachusetts Institute of Technology Press.

Moyer, K. E. 1976. *The Psychobiology of Aggression.* New York: Harper and Row.

Murphy, M. R., P. D. MacLean, and S. C. Hamilton. 1981. Species-typical behavior of hamsters deprived from birth of the neocortex. *Science, 213*:459–461.

Nachtigall, L. B., P. A. Boepple, F. P. Pralong, and W. F. Crowley, Jr. 1997. Adult-onset idiopathic hypogonadotropic hypogonadism—a treatable form of male infertility. *N. Engl. J. Med. 336*:410–415.

Nauta, W. J. H. 1972. Neural associations of the frontal cortex. *Acta Neurobiologiae Experimentalis, 32*:125–140.

Nauta, W. J. H., and V. B. Domesick. 1980. Neural associations of the limbic system. In A. Beckman (ed.), *Neural Substrates of Behavior.* New York: Spectrum.

Nauta, W. J. H., and M. Feirtag. 1979. The organization of the brain. *Scientific American, 41*:78–105.

Nebes, R. 1972. Dominance of the minor hemisphere in commissurotomized man in a test of figural unification. *Brain, 95*:633–638.

Nisbett, R. E. 1972. Hunger, obesity, and the ventromedial hypothalamus. *Psychological Review, 79*:433–453.

Norman, D. A. 1982. *Learning and Memory.* New York: W. H. Freeman.

Nottebohm, F. 1980. Brain pathways for vocal learning in birds: A review of the first 10 years. In J. M. Sprague and A. N. Epstein (eds.), *Progress in Psychobiology and Physiological Psychology,* vol. 9. New York: Academic.

Nottebohm, F., and A. P. Arnold. 1976. Sexual dimorphism in vocal control areas of the songbird brain. *Science, 194:*211–213.

Ojemann, G. A., and C. Mateer. 1979. Human language cortex: Localization of memory, syntax, and sequential motorphoneme identification systems. *Science, 205:*1401–1403.

Ojemann, G. A., and H. A. Whitaker. 1978. The bilingual brain. *Archives of Neurology, 35:*409–412.

Oke, A., R. Keller, I. Mefford, and R. N. Adams. 1978. Lateralization of norepinephrine in the human thalamus. *Science, 200:*1411–1413.

O'Keefe, J., and L. Nadel. 1978. *The Hippocampus as a Cognitive Map.* London: Oxford University Press.

Olds, J. 1955. Physiological mechanism of reward. In M. R. Jones (ed.), *Nebraska Symposium on Motivation,* pp. 73–138. Lincoln: University of Nebraska Press.

Olds, J. 1958a. Self-stimulation of the brain. *Science, 127:*315–323.

Olds, J. 1958b. Satiation effects in self-stimulation of the brain. *J. Comp. and Physiol. Psych.* 51:675–678.

Olds, J. 1958c. "Self-stimulation experiments and differentiated reward systems," in H. H. Jasper, L. D. Proctor, R. S. Knighton, W. C. Noshay, and R. T. Costello (eds.), *Reticular formation of the brain.* Boston, Mass.: Little, Brown, 671–687.

Olds, J. 1962. Hypothalamic substrates of reward. *Psychological Review* 42:554–604.

Olds, J. 1965. A preliminary mapping of electrical reinforcing effects in the rat brain. *J. Comp. and Physiol. Psych.* 49:281–285.

Olds, J. 1977. *Drives and Reinforcements: Behavioral Studies of Hypothalamic Functions.* New York: Raven.

Olds, J., and P. M. Milner. 1954. Positive reinforcement produced by electrical stimulation of septal area and other regions of the brain. *J. Comp. and Physiol. Psychol.* 47:419–427.

Olpe, H. R., and M. W. Steinmann. 1982. Age-related decline in the activity of noradrenergic neurons of the rat locus coeruleus. *Brain Research, 251:*174–176.

Olton, D. S. 1977. Spatial memory. *Scientific American, 236:*82–98.

Olton, D. S., J. T. Becker, and G. E. Handelmann. 1980. Hippocampal function: Working memory or cognitive mapping. *Physiological Psychology, 8:*239–246.

Olton, D. S., and R. J. Samuelson, 1976. Remembrance of places passed: Spatial memory in rats. *Journal of Experimental Psychology: Animal Behavior Processes, 2:*97–116.

Oppenheim, R. W. 1981. Neuronal cell death and some related regressive phenomena during neurogenesis: A selective historical review and progress report. In W. M. Cowan (ed.), *Studies in Developmental Neurobiology.* New York: Oxford University Press.

Ordy, J. M., and K. R. Brizzee (eds.). 1975. *Neurobiology of Aging: An Interdisciplinary Life-Span Approach.* New York: Plenum.

Ordy, J. M., and B. Kaack. 1975. Neurochemical changes in composition, metabolism, and neurotransmitters in the human brain with age. In J. M. Ordy and K. R. Brizzee (eds.), *Neurobiology of Aging.* New York: Plenum.

Ornstein, R. 1978. The split and whole brain. *Human Nature, 1:*76–83.

Ornstein, R. 1977. *The Psychology of Consciousness.* New York: Harcourt.

Orton, S. T. 1937. *Reading, Writing, and Speech Problems in Children.* New York: Norton.

Overmeir, J. B., and M. E. P. Seligman. 1967. Effects of inescapable shock upon subsequent escape and avoidance responding. *Journal of Comparative and Physiological Psychology, 63:*28–33.

Palmer, J. D. 1975. Biological clocks of the tidal zone, *Scientific American, 232:*70–79.

Papez, J. W. 1937. A proposed mechanism of emotion. *Archives of Neurology and Psychiatry, 38:*725–744.

Pavlov, I. P. 1927. *Conditioned Reflexes.* London: Oxford University Press.

Penfield, W. 1954. *Epilepsy and the functional anatomy of the human brain.* Boston, Mass.: Little, Brown.

Penfield, W. 1975. *The Mystery of the Mind.* Princeton: Princeton University Press.

Penfield, W. 1975. The physiology of epilepsy. *Advances in Neurology,* vol. 8, 1–9.

Pengelley, E. T., and S. J. Asmundson. 1971. Annual biological clocks. *Scientific American, 224:*72–79.

Pert, C. B., G. Pasternak, and S. H. Snyder. 1973. Opiate agonists and antagonists discriminated by receptor binding in the brain. *Science* Dec. 28, 182(119):1359–1361.

Petersen, A. C. 1979. Hormones and cognitive functioning in normal development. In M. A. Wittig and A. C. Petersen (eds.), *Sex Related Differences in Cognitive Functioning—Developmental Issues.* New York: Academic.

Pfaff, D. W. 1980. *Estrogens and Brain Function.* New York: Springer.

Piaget, Jean. 1963. *The Origins of Intelligence in Children.* New York: Norton.

Pick, J. 1970. *The Autonomic Nervous System*. Philadelphia: Lippincott.

Platt, C. B., and B. MacWhinney. 1983. Error assimilation as a mechanism in language learning. *Journal of Child Language*, 10:401–414.

Ploog, D. 1981. Neurobiology of primate audiovocal behavior, *Brain Research Review*, 3:35–61.

Popper, K. R., and J. C. Eccles, 1977. *The Self and Its Brain*. New York: Springer-Verlag.

Pratt, O. E. 1980. A new approach to the treatment of phenylketonuria. *Journal of Mental Deficiency Research*, 24:203–217.

Quinn, W. G., W. A. Harris, and S. Benzer. 1974. Conditioned behavior in Drosophila melanogaster. *Proc. Natl. Acad. Sci. USA* 71:708–712.

Raisman, G., and P. M. Field. 1973. Sexual dimorphism in the neuropil of the preoptic area of the rat and its dependence on neonatal androgen. *Brain Research*, 54:1–29.

Rakic, P. 1974. Neurons in rhesus monkey visual cortex: Systematic relation between time of origin and eventual disposition. *Science: 183*:425–427.

Rakic, P., J.-P. Bourgeois, M. F. Eckenhoff, N. Zecevic, and P. S. Goldman-Rakic. 1986. Concurrent overproduction of synapses in diverse regions of the primate cerebral cortex. *Science, 232*:232–234.

Rakic, P., and R. L. Sidman. 1973. Sequence of developmental abnormalities leading to granule cell deficit in cerebellar cortex of weaver mutant mice. *Journal of Comparative Neurology. 152*:133–162.

Ratcliffe, S. G., J. Bancroft, D. Axworthy, and W. Mclaren. 1982. Klinefelter's syndrome in adolescence. *Archives of Disease in Childhood, 57*:6–12.

Reinberg, A., P. Andlauer, and N. Vieux. 1981. Circadian temperature rhythm amplitude and long-term tolerance of shiftworking. In L. C. Johnson et al. (eds.), *Biological Rhythms, Sleep and Shift Work*. New York: SP Medical and Scientific Books.

Reinberg, A., N. Vieux, P. Andlauer, and M. Smolensky. 1983. Tolerance to shift work: A chronobiological approach. In J. Mendlewicz and H. M. van Praag (eds.), *Biological Rhythms and Behavior Advances in Biological Psychiatry*, vol. 2, pp. 20–34. Basel: S. Karger.

Reinis, S., and J. M. Goldman. 1980. *The Development of the Brain*. Springfield, Ill.: Charles C. Thomas.

Richter, C. 1965. *Biological Clocks in Medicine and Psychiatry*. Springfield, Ill.: Charles C. Thomas.

Rife, D. C. 1950. Application of gene frequency analysis to the interpretation of data from twins. *Human Biology*, 22:136–145.

Risse, G. L., and M. S. Gazzaniga. 1978. Well-kept secrets of the right hemisphere: A sodium amytal study. *Neurology 28*:950–993.

Roffwarg, H. P., J. N. Muzio, and W. C. Dement. 1968. Ontogenetic development of the human sleep-dream cycle. In W. B. Webb (ed.), *Sleep: An Experimental Approach*. New York: Macmillan.

Rogers, J., G. R. Siggins, J. A. Schulman, and F. E. Bloom. 1980. Physiological correlates of ethanol intoxication, tolerance, and dependence in rat cerebellar Purkinje cells. *Brain Research, 196*:183–198.

Rogers, J., S. F. Zornetzer, W. J. Shoemaker, and F. E. Bloom. 1981. Electrophysiology of aging brain: senescent pathology of cerebellum. In S. J. Enna et al. (eds.), *Brain Neurotransmitters and Receptors in Aging and Age-Related Disorders. (Aging*, vol. 17). New York: Raven.

Rolls, E. T., and G. J. Morgenson. 1977. Brain self-stimulation behavior. In G. J. Morgenson, *The Neurobiology of Behavior: An Introduction*. Hillsdale, N.J.: Lawrence Erlbaum.

Romberch, J. (1520) 1966. "Method of loci," in F. Yates, *The Art of Memory*. Chicago, Ill.: University of Chicago Press.

Rose, G. A., and R. T. Williams. 1961. Metabolic studies of large and small eaters. *British Journal of Nutrition, 15*:1–9.

Rose, S. P. R., P. P. G. Bateson, and G. Horn. 1973. Experience and plasticity in the nervous system. *Science, 181*:506–514.

Rosenzweig, M. R. 1970. *Biology of Memory*. New York: Academic Press.

Rosenzweig, M. R. 1979. *Development and Evolution of Brain Size: Behavioral Implications*. New York: Academic Press.

Rosenzweig, M. R. 1984. Experience, memory, and the brain. *American Psychologist, 39*:365–376.

Rosenzweig, M. R., E. L. Bennett, and M. C. Diamond. 1972. Brain changes in response to experience. *Scientific American, 226*:22–29.

Rosvold, H. E., A. F. Mirsh, and K. H. Pribram. 1954. Influence in amygdalectomy on social behavior in monkeys. *Journal of Comparative and Physiological Psychology, 47*:173–178.

Routtenberg, A. 1978. The reward system of the brain. *Scientific American, 239*:122–131.

Rutishauser, V., R. Brackenburg, J. P. Thiery, and G. M. Edelman. 1976. Mechanisms of adhesion among cells from neural tissues of the chick embryo. *Journal of Cell Biology, 70*:A220.

Safanuma, S., and O. Fujimura. 1970. Selective impairment of phonetic and nonphonetic transcription of words in Japanese aphasic patients: Kana vs. kanji in visual recognition and writing. *Cortex*, 6:1–18.

Sagan, C. 1977. *The Dragons of Eden: Speculations on the Evolution of Human Intelligence.* New York: Random House.

Samuel, D., S. Algeri, S. Gershon, V. E. Grimm, and G. Toffano (eds.). 1983. *Aging of the Brain.* New York: Raven.

Schacter, S. 1959. *The psychology of affiliation.* Stanford, Cal.: Stanford University Press.

Schachter, S. 1971. Some extraordinary facts about obese humans and rats. *American Psychologist,* 26:129–144.

Schachter, S., and J. E. Singer. 1962. Cognitive, social, and physiological determinants of emotional state. *Psychological Review,* 69:379–399.

Schaie, K. W. 1980. Intelligence and problem solving. In J. E. Birren and R. B. Sloane (eds.), *Handbook of Mental Health and Aging.* Englewood Cliffs, N.J.: Prentice-Hall.

Schemmel, R., O. Mickelson, and J. L. Gill. 1970. Dietary obesity in rats: Influence of diet, weight, fat accretion in seven strains of rats. *Journal of Nutrition,* 100:1041–1048.

Schildkraut, J. J., and S. S. Kety. 1967. Biogenic amines and emotion. *Science* 156:21–28.

Seligman, M. E. P. 1973. Fall into helplessness. *Psychology Today,* 7:43–48.

Seligman, M. E. P. 1975. *Helplessness.* New York: W. H. Freeman.

Seligman, M. E. P., and S. F. Maier. 1967. Failure to escape traumatic shock. *Journal of Experimental Psychology,* 74:1–9.

Selye, H. 1956. *The Stress of Life.* New York: McGraw-Hill.

Shaffer, J. W. 1962. A cognitive deficit observed in gonadal aplasia (Turner's syndrome). *Journal of Clinical Psychology,* 18:403–406.

Sheard, M. H. 1983. Aggressive behavior: Effects of neural modulation by serotonin. In E. C. Simmel et al. (eds.), *Aggressive Behavior: Genetic and Neural Approaches.* Hillsdale, N.J.: Lawrence Erlbaum.

Siffre, M. 1963. *Hors du temps.* Paris: Julliard.

Simon, E. J., J. M. Hiller, and I. Edelman. 1973. Stereospecific binding of the potent narcotic analgesic (3H) Etorphine to rat-brain homogenate. *Proc. Natl. Acad. Sci. USA* 70:1947–1949.

Skinner, B. F. 1938. *The Behavior of Organisms.* New York: Appleton-Century-Crofts.

Slobin, D. I. 1979. *Psycholinguistics,* 2d ed. Glenview, Ill.: Scott-Foresman.

Sodersten, P., and K. Larsson. 1974. Lordosis behavior in castrated male rats treated with estradiol benzoate or testosterone propionate in combination with an estrogen antagonist MER-25, and in intact male rats. *Hormones and Behavior,* 5:13–18.

Sperry, R. W. 1945. Restoration of vision after crossing of optic nerves and after contralateral transplantation of eye. *Journal of Neurophysiology,* 8:15–28.

Sperry, R. W. 1951. Mechanisms of neural maturation. In S. S. Stevens (ed.), *Handbook of Experimental Psychology.* New York: Wiley.

Sperry, R. W. 1966. Brain bisection and consciousness. In J. Eccles (ed.), *Brain and Conscious Experience.* New York: Springer-Verlag.

Sperry, R. W. 1974. Lateral specialization in the surgically separated hemispheres. In F. O. Schmitt and F. G. Worden (eds.), *The Neurosciences: Third Study Program.* Cambridge, Mass.: Massachusetts Institute of Technology Press.

Sperry, R. W. 1982. Some effects of disconnecting the cerebral hemispheres. *Science,* 217:1223–1226.

Spinelli, D. H., and F. E. Jensen. 1979. Plasticity: The mirror of experience. *Science,* 203:75–78.

Spinelli, D. H., F. E. Jensen, and G. V. DiPrisco. 1980. Early experience effect on dendritic branching in normally reared kittens. *Experimental Neurology,* 62:1–11.

Spooner, J. W., S. M. Sakala, and R. W. Balch. 1980. Effect of aging on eye tracking. *Archives of Neurology* 37:575.

Springer, S. P., and G. Deutsch. 1985. *Left Brain, Right Brain,* revised edition. New York: W. H. Freeman.

Squire, L. R. 1981. Two forms of human amnesia: An analysis of forgetting. *Journal of Neuroscience,* 1:635–640.

Squire, L. R. 1984. Memory and the brain. In S. Friedman et al. (eds.), *Brain, Cognition, and Education.* New York: Academic Press.

Staudt, J., and G. Dorner. 1976. Structural changes in the medial and central amygdala of the male rat following castration and androgen treatment. *Endokrinologie,* 67:296–300.

Stein, J., and S. Fowler. Visual dyslexia. *Trends in Neurosciences,* 4:77–80.

Steinberg, M. S. 1963. Reconstruction of tissues by dissociated cells. *Science,* 141:401–408.

Sternberg, D. B., and P. E. Gold. 1981. Retrograde amnesia produced by electrical stimulation of the amygdala: Attenuation with adrenergic antagonists. *Brain Research,* 211:59–65.

Strumwasser, F., J. W. Jacklet, and R. B. Alvarez. 1969. A seasonal rhythm in the neural extract induction of behavioral egg-laying in *Aplysia. Comparative Biochemistry and Physiology,* 29:197–206.

Strumwasser, F., F. R. Schlechte, and S. Bower. 1972. Distributed circadian oscillators in the nervous system of *Aplysia. Federation Proceedings,* 31:405.

Swanson, L. W., T. J. Teyler, and R. F. Thompson (eds.). 1982. *Hippocampal Long-term Potentiation: Mechanisms and Implications for Memory.* Neurosciences Research Program Bulletin, vol. 20, No. 5. Cambridge, Mass.: Massachusetts Institute of Technology Press.

Takahashi, J. S., and M. Zatz. 1982. Regulation of circadian rhythmicity. *Science, 217:*1104–1111.

Tatlor, A. M., and J. E. Turnure. 1979. Imagery and verbal elaboration with retarded children: Effects on learning and memory. In N. R. Ellis (ed.), *Handbook of Mental Deficiency, Psychological Theory, and Research,* 2d ed. Hillsdale, N.J.: Lawrence Erlbaum.

Taylor, J. (ed.). 1958. *Selected Writings of John Hughlings Jackson,* vol. 2: London: Staples.

Teuber, H. L., B. Milner, and H. G. Vaughan. 1968. Persistent anterograde amnesia after stab wound of the basal brain. *Neuropsychologia,* 6:267–282.

Thompson, R. F., T. Berger, and J. Madden. 1983. Cellular processes of learning and memory in the mammalian CNS. *Annual Review of Neuroscience,* 6:447–491.

Thompson, R. F., L. H. Hicks, and V. B. Shryrkov. 1980. *Neural Mechanisms of Goal-Directed Behavior and Learning.* New York: Academic Press.

Thurstone, L. L., and T. G. Thurstone. 1941. Factorial studies of intelligence. *Psychometric Monographs.* No. 2. Chicago: University of Chicago Press.

Tinbergen, N. 1963. The evolution of animal communication—a critical examination of the methods. *Symposium Zoological Society London 8:*1–6.

Toivonen, S., and S. Saxen. 1968. Morphogenetic interaction of presumptive neural and mesodermal cells mixed in different ratios. *Science,* 159:539–540.

Tomlinson, B. E., G. Blessed, and M. Roth. 1968. Observations in the brains of nondemented old people. *Journal of Neurological Science,* 7:331–356.

Tomlinson, B. E., G. Blessed, and M. Roth. 1970. Observations in the brains of demented old people. *Journal of Neurological Science,* 11:205–242.

Tordoff, M. G., J. Hoffenbeck, and D. Novin. 1982. Hepatic vagotomy (partial hepatic denervation) does not alter ingestive responses to metabolic challenges. *Physiology and Behavior,* 28:417–424.

Toyoshima, Y., and H. Sakai. 1982. Exact cortical extent of the origin of the corticospinal tract (CST) and the quantitative contribution to the CST of different cytochritectonic areas. *J. Hirnforsch.* 23:257–269.

Trankell, A. 1955. Aspects of genetics in psychology. *American Journal of Human Genetics,* 7:264–276.

Trayhurn, P., P. L. Thurlby, C. J. H. Woodward, and W. P. T. James. 1979. Thermoregulation in genetically obese rodents: The relationship to metabolic efficiency. In M. F. W. Festing (ed.), *Genetic Models of Obesity in Laboratory Animals.* London: Macmillan.

Valzelli, L. 1981. *Psychobiology of Aggression and Violence.* New York: Raven.

Varon, Silvio. 1985. *Factors Promoting the Growth of the Nervous System.* Discussions in Neurosciences, Foundation for the Study of the Nervous System, vol. II, no. 3.

Vergnes, M. 1975. Déclenchement de réactions d'agression interspécific après lésion amygdalienne chez le rat. *Physiology and Behavior,* 14:271–276.

Volpe, B. T., J. E. LeDoux, and M. S. Gazzaniga. 1979. Information processing of visual stimuli in an extinguished field. *Nature, 282:*722.

von Bekesy, G. 1968. Problems relating psychological and electrophysiological observations in sensory perception. *Perspect. Biol. Med.* 11:179–194.

von Euler, U. S., and J. H. Gaddum. 1933. An unidentified depressor substance in certain tissue extracts. *J. Physiol.* 72:74–87.

von Helmholtz, H. 1962. *Handbuch der physiologischen optik.* Hamburg: Voss (3 vols.), 1856, 1860, and 1866. [Vol. 3 translated by J. P. C. Southall as *Handbook of Physiological Optics.*] New York: Dover Publications.

Wada, J. A., R. Clarke, and A. Hamm. 1975. Cerebral hemispheric asymmetry in humans. *Archives of Neurology, 32:*239–246.

Wagner-Jauregg, J. 1931. Verhütung und Behandlung der progressiven Paralyse durch Impfmalaria [Prevention and treatment of progressive paralysis by malaria inoculation]. *Handbuch der experimentellen Therapie.*

Watkins, L. R., and D. J. Mayer, 1982. Organization of endogenous opiate and nonopiate pain control systems. *Science, 216:*1183–1192.

Wehr, T. A., A. Wirz-Justice, F. K. Goodwin, W. Duncan, and J. C. Gillin. 1979. Phase advance of the circadian sleep-wake cycle as an anti-depressant. *Science,* 206:710–713.

Weiss, J. M. 1971. Effects of coping behavior in different warning-signal conditions on stress pathology in rats. *Journal of Comparative and Physiological Psychology,* 77:1–13.

Weiss, J. M. 1971. Somatic effects of predictable and unpredictable shock. *Psychosomatic Medicine,* 6:1–39.

Weiss, J. M. 1972. Psychological factors in stress and disease. *Scientific American, 226*:104–113.

Werner, E. E., J. M. Bierman, and F. E. French. 1971. *The Children of Kauai.* Honolulu: University of Hawaii Press.

Wernicke, C. 1874. *Der aphasissche symptomenkomplex* [The aphasic symptom complex]. Breslau: Cohn & Weigart.

Wernicke, C. 1894. Grundriss der psychiatrie [Fundamentals of Psychiatry]. *Psychophysiolgische einleitung* [Psychophysiological Introduction].

West, D. B., J. Diaz, and S. C. Woods. 1982. Infant gastrostomy and chronic formula infusion as a technique to overfeed and accelerate weight gain in neonatal rats. *Journal of Nutrition, 112*:1339–1343.

West, D. B., R. H. Williams, D. J. Braget, and S. C. Woods. 1982. Bombesin reduces food intake of normal and hypothalamically obese rats and lowers body weight when given chronically. *Peptides, 3*:61–67.

White, C. T. 1974. The visual-evoked response and pattern stimuli. In G. Newton and A. H. Riesen (eds.), *Advances in Psychobiology,* vol. 2. New York: Wiley.

Whiting, B. B., and J. W. M. Whiting. 1975. *Children of Six Cultures: A Psychocultural Analysis.* Cambridge, Mass.: Harvard University Press.

Wickelgren, I. 1998. Obesity: How Big a Problem? *Science 280*:1364–1367.

Wiesel, T. N. 1982. Postnatal development of the visual cortex and the influence of environment. *Nature, 299*:583–592.

Willen, J. C., H. Dehan, and J. Cambier. 1981. Stress-induced analgesia in humans: Endogenous opioids and naloxone-reversible depression of pain reflexes. *Science, 212*:689–691.

Wilson, S. A. K. 1925. The old motor system and the new. *Arch. Neurol. Psychiatry 11*:385–404.

Winick, M., and R. E. Greenberg. 1965. Appearance and localization of a nerve growth-promoting protein during development. *Pediatrics, 35*:221–228.

Wisniewski, K. E., M. Laure-Kamionowska, F. Connell, and G. Y. Yen. 1986. Neuronal density and synaptogenesis in the postnatal stage of brain maturation in Down syndrome. In C. J. Epstein (ed.), *The Neurobiology of Down Syndrome.* New York: Raven.

Witelson, S. F. 1976. Sex and the single hemisphere: Specialization of the right hemisphere for spatial processing. *Science, 193*:425–427.

Witelson, S., and W. Pallie. 1973. Left hemisphere specialisation for language in the newborn: Neuroanatomical evidence of asymmetry. *Brain: 96*:641–646.

Wood, F., D. Stump, A. Mckeehan, S. Sheldon, and J. Proctor. 1980. Patterns of regional cerebral blood flow during attempted reading aloud by stutterers both on and off haloperidol medication: Evidence for inadequate left frontal activation during stuttering. *Brain and Language, 9*:141–144.

Woods, S. C., E. Decke, and J. R. Vasselli. 1974. Metabolic hormones and regulation of body weight. *Psychological Review, 81*:26–43.

Woods, S. C., E. C. Lotter, L. D. McKay, and D. Porte. 1979. Chronic intracerebroventricular infusion reduces food intake and body weight of baboons. *Nature London 282*:503–505.

Woods, S. C., G. J. Taborsky, Jr., and D. Porte, Jr. 1986. Central nervous system control of nutrient homeostasis. In F. E. Bloom (ed.), *Handbook of Physiology—The Nervous System IV.* Bethesda, Md.: American Physiological Society.

Woolridge, P. E. 1963. *The Machinery of the Brain.* Toronto: McGraw-Hill.

Woolsey, T. A., and J. R. Wann. 1976. Areal changes in mouse cortical barrels following vibrissal damage at different postnatal ages. *Journal of Comparative Neurology 170*:53–66.

Yates, C. M., J. Simpson, A. F. J. Maloney, A. Gordon, and A. H. Reid. 1980. Alzheimer-like cholinergic deficiency in Down syndrome. *Lancet: 2*:979.

Zaidel, E. 1975. A technique for presenting lateralized visual input with prolonged exposure. *Vision Research, 15*:283–289.

Zaidel, E. 1976. Auditory vocabulary of the right hemisphere following brain bisection or hemidecortication. *Cortex, 190*:191–211.

Zajonc, R. B. 1980. Feeling and thinking. *American Psychologist, 35*:151–175.

Zuckerman, M. 1979. *Sensation-seeking: Beyond the Optimum Level of Arousal.* Hillsdale, N.J.: Lawrence Erlbaum.

CREDITS

CHAPTER 1

page 2
top, The Granger Collection
bottom, From "Human Amnesia and the Medical Temporal Region," Stuart Zola-Morgan and David Amaral, *The Journal of Neuroscience,* October, 1986. Photograph by Kris Trulock and Marcia Lee Earnshaw

page 9
The Granger Collection

page 12
Zentralbibliothek Zurich

page 13
The New York Public Library

page 14
Courtesy of Burndy Library

page 16
bottom, Frank McCoy/Scripps Clinic and Research Foundation

page 22
bottom, New York Academy of Medicine

Chapter 2

page 28
Manfred Kage/Peter Arnold

page 31
Frank McCoy/Scripps Clinic and Research Foundation

page 33
The Granger Collection

page 53
Frank McCoy/Scripps Clinic and Research Foundation

page 54
Michael E. Phelps, Lewis Baxter, and John Mazziota, UCLA School of Medicine

Chapter 3

page 60
Photo by Lennart Nilsson. From *Behold Man,* Little, Brown and Company, Boston.

page 71
From "The Development of the Brain," by W. Maxwell Cowan, *Scientific American,* September, 1979. Photograph by J. Michael Cochran and Mary Bartlett Bunge.

page 76
Travis Amos

page 78
Mia Tegner

page 87
Torsten Wiesel

page 89
top, Nick Dolding/Stone
bottom, Courtesy of Charles Nelson

Chapter 4

page 104
The British Museum (Natural History)

page 115
Frank McCoy/Scripps Clinic and Research Foundation

page 132
From *Tissues and Organs,* by Richard Kessel and Randy Kardon, W. H. Freeman and Company

Chapter 5

page 145
From the WNET series, *The Brain*

page 149
top, Dr. Don Fawcett/J. Heuser/T. Reese/Photo Researchers
bottom, Ed Reschke/Peter Arnold, Inc.

page 157
Courtesy of Dr. Jean Decety, INSERM U280, Lyon, France.

Chapter 6

page 169
NASA

page 195
Schiffman/Gamma Liason

page 202
From the WNET series, *The Brain*

Chapter 7

page 210
The Granger Collection

page 213
Travis Amos

page 214
Charles Arneson/Scripps Institute of Oceanography, University of California, San Diego

page 216
Frank J. Miller/Photo Researchers

page 226
From the WNET series, *The Brain*

INDEX

Note: Page numbers in *italics* indicate illustrations; those followed by t indicate tables.

ambient, biological rhythms and, 213
body. *See* Body temperature
Temporal lobe, 21, *22, 24*
  in emotion, 247
  in memory, 282–284, 286, 288–289, 292,
    320–321, 345
Temporal lobe epilepsy, 279–280
Tension proprioceptors, 155
Testis-determining factor, 78
Testosterone, 181t, *182*, 201
  aggression and, 250–251
  brain development and, 79, *79*, 84–85
Thalamus, 19, *19*, 19t, *24, 25*
  in dyslexia, 331–332
  in emotion, 242, *242*, 245, *245*, 247
  in memory, 292, 293, 294–295
Theta rhythms, in sleep, 228, *228*
Thiamine deficiency, Korsakoff's syndrome
  and, 293–294
Thinking. *See under* Cognition; Cognitive
Thompson, Richard, 306
Thyroid hormones, 181, 181t, *182, 183*
Thyroid-stimulating hormone, *183*
Thyrotropin, 181t
Thyrotropin-releasing hormone, 181, *183*
Thyroxin, 181t, *182*
TIM, 220–221
Timbre, 129, *129*
Time-giving cues, 214, 222–223, 225–226
Tinbergen, Niko, 271
Tongue, taste detection by, *136*, 136–137
Tonotopic system, 132
Touch. *See* Tactile system
Tranquilizers, for anxiety, 268–269
Trephination, *363*, 363–364
Triads, *147*, 148
Trophic factors, 66
Tropomyosin, 148
Tryptophan, 216
T tubes, *147*, 148
T-tubular system, *147*, 148
Turner's syndrome, 84–85
Twin studies
  of depression, 385
  of schizophrenia, 403–404
Tympanic canal, *130*, 131
Tympanic membrane, *130*, 131

Ultradian rhythms, 210. *See also* Biological
  rhythms
  in humans, 228, 228–232

Umami, 136
Unconditioned response, 304
Unipolar depression, 387
Urine flow, circadian fluctuations in,
  221–222

Vagus nerve, 137, *138, 171, 172*
Valium, 268
Vascularization, cerebral, 52–53, *53*
Vascular-volume receptors, 187
Vasoactive intestinal polypeptide, 181t
Vasopressin, 45–46, 177, 181t, 186
  circadian fluctuations in, 222
  as neurotransmitter, 180
Veins, cerebral, 52–53, *53*
Ventral cochlear nucleus, *128, 133*
Verbal abilities. *See* Language processing
Veridicality, of memory, 278
Vestibular apparatus, 5, *6*
Vestibular canal, *130*, 131
Viral infections, schizophrenia and, 403,
  404
Vision
  accommodation in, 107
  binocular, 119–121
  central disturbances of, 112–113
  color, 109, 112, 121–122, *122*
  cortical representation of, 115–121
  development of, 125
  feature detection and recognition in,
    123–124
  object, 122–124
  peripheral disturbances of, 112–113
  spatial, 122–124
Vision problems, 112–113
Visual cortex
  amblyopia and, *87*, 87–88, *88*
  columns in, 87, *87*, 115–116, 119–120
  development of, 86–88, *87, 88*
  layers of, 115
  in mental imaging, 344
  primary, 115
  structure and function of, *114*, 115–121
Visual fields and pathways, *324*
  development of, 76–77
Visual pathways, development of, 76–77
Visual-spatial processing
  in language processing, 332, 333
  in right hemisphere, *341*, 341–342, *342*
Visual system, 104–126
  development of, 124–125

information channeling in, 101–103, 103t
information processing in, *114*, 115–121
ocular dominance columns in, 87, *87*,
  119–120
parallel processing in, 120–121, 125–126
properties of, 101t
retinotopic organization of, 111, *114*,
  118, 119
structure of, *106*, 106–115, *108, 110*
Vital-fluid theory, 13–14
Vitamin B$_1$ deficiency, Korsakoff's syndrome
  and, 293–294
Voluntary movement, 5, *7*, 146, *146*,
  151–152
Von Bekesy, Georg, 132
Von Euler, Ulf, 46
Von Helmholtz, Hermann, 104
Von Wagner-Jauregg, Julius, 367

Wada test, 327–328
Wagner-Jauregg, Julius von, 367
Wall, Patrick, 258
Waller, Augustus von, 15
Water-volume regulation, 186–187
Weiss, Jay, 265–267
Wernicke's aphasia, 328, 329t, 342
Wernicke's area, 328, *328*, 329–330
White muscle, 148
Wiesel, Torsten, 87, 118, 352
Willis, Thomas, 12
Wilson's disease, 158–159
Winter depression, 234, 236, 396
Wisconsin Card Sort, 293
Wolffian ducts, 78
Women. *See also* Gender
  reproductive cycle of, 232–234, *233*
Word deafness, 329t
Working memory, 94, 278
  spatial, 280–282, *282, 283*

X chromosomes, 78
X-rays, of brain, *371*

Y chromosomes, 78

Zaidel, Eran, 340
Z bands, *147*, 148, 150
Zeitgebers, 214, 222–223, 225–226
Z lens, *340*, 340–341
Zygote, 60, *61*